Stopped at Stalingrad

Stopped at Stalingrad
The Luftwaffe and Hitler's Defeat in the East, 1942–1943

Joel S. A. Hayward

University Press of Kansas

Published by the University Press of Kansas (Lawrence, Kansas 66049), which was
organized by the Kansas Board of Regents and is operated and funded by Emporia
State University, Fort Hays State University, Kansas State University, Pittsburg State
University, the University of Kansas, and Wichita State University

Library of Congress Cataloging-in-Publication Data

Hayward, Joel S. A.
    Stopped at Stalingrad : the Luftwaffe and Hitler's defeat in the
east, 1942–1943 / Joel S. A. Hayward.
        p.   cm. — (Modern war studies)
    Based on the author's thesis (doctoral)—University of Canterbury.
    Includes bibliographical references and index.
    ISBN 0-7006-0876-1 (alk. paper)
    1. World War, 1939–1945—Campaigns—Eastern Front.   2. Stalingrad,
Battle of, 1942–1943.   3. Germany. Luftwaffe—History—World War,
1939–1945.   4. Hitler, Adolf, 1889–1945.   5. Strategy.   I. Title.
II. Series.
D764.H374   1998
940.54′21747—dc21   97–22541

British Library Cataloguing in Publication Data is available.

Printed in the United States of America

10 9 8 7 6 5 4 3 2 1

The paper used in this publication meets the minimum requirements of the American
National Standard for Permanence of Paper for Printed Library Materials Z39.48-1984.

Contents

Illustrations

All photographs are from the USAFHRA, except nos. 1, 2, 29, and 35, which are reproduced with permission from the collection of James S. Corum, and nos. 3, 4, 8, 10, 11, 13, 22, 23, and 30, which come from the author's own collection.

MAPS

Abbreviations

AMWIS	[British] *Air Ministry Weekly Intelligence Summary*
BA/MA	*Bundesarchiv-Militärarchiv* (Federal Military Archives), Freiburg im Breisgau, Germany
FHO	*Fremde Heere Ost* (Foreign Armies East). The *OKH* department responsible for the evaluation of all military intelligence about the Soviet Union, including the analysis of Soviet intentions and strategy
KTB	*Kriegstagebuch* (war diary)
NARS	National Archives and Records Service, Washington, D.C.
Ob.d.H	*Oberbefehlshaber des Heeres* (commander in chief of the army). Walther von Brauchitsch until 19 December 1941, then Adolf Hitler
Ob.d.L	*Oberbefehlshaber der Luftwaffe* (commander in chief of the Luftwaffe). *Reichsmarschall* Hermann Göring
OKH	*Oberkommando des Heeres* (High Command of the Army)
OKL	*Oberkommando der Luftwaffe* (High Command of the Air Force)
OKM	*Oberkommando der Marine* (High Command of the Navy)
OKW	*Oberkommando der Wehrmacht* (High Command of the Armed Forces)
TB	*Tagebuch* (diary)

USAFHRA   United States Air Force Historical Research Agency, Maxwell Air Force Base, Montgomery, Alabama

VVS   *Voyenno-vozdushnyye sily* (Soviet Air Force)

WiRüAmt   *Wehrwirtschafts und Rüstungsamt* (War Economy and Armaments Office)

Designation and Structure of Operational Units and Commands

Luftflotte. By the time the war in Europe finished in May 1945, the Luftwaffe had organized all its operational aircraft into seven *Luftflotten* (air fleets), three more than it had when hostilities broke out six years earlier. They were designated *Luftflotten 1, 2, 3, 4* (the original four), *5, 6, 7,* and *Reich* (created during the war, the latter being responsible for home air defense). Each *Luftflotte* was similar to an individual "Air Force" within the United States Army Air Forces; that is, it was a self-contained air command, comprising all types of combat units (bomber, dive-bomber, ground-attack, fighter, and reconnaissance), as well as transport, flak, and signals units. Senior operational commanders—usually of *Generaloberst* or *Generalfeldmarschall* rank—headed the command staff of each air fleet, exercising full authority over subordinate *Luftgaue* and *Fliegerkorps.*

Luftgau. Each *Luftflotte* possessed one or more *Luftgaue* (air districts), the administrative commands designed to take care of the fleet's principal signals, supply, maintenance, and training matters, thereby permitting operational commands to concentrate solely on the "task at hand": the enemy's destruction. Forward *Luftgaue,* which constructed, maintained, and supplied airfields near the front, were frequently named after the main centers within combat zones. Richthofen's forward *Luftgau* during the 1942 campaign, for example, bore the designation *Luftgau Rostov,* named after the city on the Don River that served as the gateway to the Caucasus.

Fliegerkorps. The largest operational commands within air fleets were the *Fliegerkorps* (air corps). These commands, always designated by roman numerals (*Fliegerkorps I, II, III, IV,* and so on), normally functioned under the authority of the air fleet in the region. On numerous occasions throughout the war, however, the Luftwaffe High Command directed certain *Fliegerkorps* to operate independently and under the direction of their own commanders, who were usually of *Generalleutnant* or *General der Flieger* rank. Air fleets seldom controlled more than one *Fliegerkorps* at a time, although in critical theaters or during major offensives—such as the one analyzed throughout this work—a fleet might assume control of two (and sometimes even elements of a third). *Fliegerkorps* differed markedly in size and composition, depending on the importance of theaters and the nature of operations each air corps was called upon to perform, but "typical" corps during the first two years of war in the east possessed between 350 and 600 aircraft of different types (bombers, fighters, and so on).

Geschwader. Within *Fliegerkorps,* the largest homogeneous air formations were the *Geschwader,* usually translated as "wings" (a convention followed here, despite their differing from both American and British "wings"). All aircraft in a *Geschwader* were of the same basic type. That is, although the aircraft could be of different models and variants, a *Kampfgeschwader* (*K.G.,* bomber wing) comprised only bombers, a *Stukageschwader* (*St.G.,* dive-bomber wing) comprised only dive-bombers, and a *Jagdgeschwader* (*J.G.,* fighter wing) comprised only fighters. Initially a "standard" *Geschwader* comprised a small headquarters staff (usually commanded by an *Oberstleutnant* or an *Oberst*) and three *Gruppen* (groups) with ninety aircraft, although later in the war a fourth *Gruppe* was added to each in order to provide operational training for inexperienced crews before they undertook combat missions. Receiving daily operational orders from their parent *Fliegerkorps,* the command staffs of each *Geschwader* implemented those instructions with little autonomy or freedom of action, but they carried primary responsibility for the morale, discipline, efficiency, and operational performance of their *Gruppen.*

Gruppe. A *Gruppe* (group) usually comprised three *Staffeln* (squadrons) of nine aircraft, plus a headquarters staff with three more aircraft, bringing its total strength to thirty. During critical periods on the eastern front, however, many hard-pressed *Gruppen* functioned at only half strength or less. *Gruppen* were usually numbered in roman numerals, their designation appearing before that of their parent *Geschwader.* For example, *III./J.G. 52* refers to the 3rd Group of the 52nd Fighter Wing.

Note: Following common translation practices, *Geschwader, Gruppen,* and *Staffeln* have been translated throughout this book as "wings," "groups," and "squadrons," but readers should note that these formations did not correspond in size or purpose to either USAAF or RAF formations with those designations.

Equivalent Officer Ranks

Luftwaffe	USAAF	RAF
Generalfeldmarschall	General (five star)	Marshal of the Royal Air Force
Generaloberst	General (four star)	Air Chief Marshal
General der Flieger	Lieutenant General	Air Marshal
Generalleutnant	Major General	Air Vice-Marshal
Generalmajor	Brigadier General	Air Commodore
Oberst	Colonel	Group Captain
Oberstleutnant	Lieutenant Colonel	Wing Commander
Major	Major	Squadron Leader
Hauptmann	Captain	Flight Lieutenant
Oberleutnant	First Lieutenant	Flying Officer
Leutnant	Lieutenant	Pilot Officer

Preface

After February 1943, the shadow of Stalingrad ever lengthened ahead of Adolf Hitler. The battle for that city had ended in disastrous defeat, shattering the myth of his military "Midas touch," ending his chances of defeating the Red Army, permanently damaging relations with Italy, Rumania, Hungary, and other allied nations,[1] and, of course, inflicting heavy losses on his eastern armies. More than 150,000 Axis soldiers, most of them German, had been killed or wounded in the city's approaches or ruins; 108,000 others stumbled into Soviet captivity, 91,000 in the battle's last three days alone. (Although Hitler never learned of their fate, only 6,000 ever returned to Germany.)

The battle has attracted considerable scholarly and journalistic attention. Literally scores of books and articles on Stalingrad have appeared during the fifty years since Stalin's armies bulldozed into Berlin, bringing the war in Europe to a close. Most have been published in Germany and, to a lesser degree, Russia, where the name Stalingrad still evokes powerful and emotional imagery.[2] Comparatively few have been published in the English-speaking world. This is understandable; because no British, Commonwealth, or American forces took part in the battle, they can number none of their own among its many heroes, martyrs, prisoners, and victims. Moreover, although the German defeat at Stalingrad was immediately seen in the West as a turning point, its effects were not directly felt by the Anglo-American nations.

The main focus of Stalingrad historiography, including the dozen books published in 1992 and 1993 to commemorate the battle's fiftieth anniversary, has been the fighting, encirclement, suffering, and destruction of Paulus's Sixth Army. Few books and articles have devoted adequate attention to the activities of the Luftwaffe, although it made substantial contributions to all battles throughout the 1942 summer campaign—of which Stalingrad was the climax—

and was alone responsible for the maintenance of the Sixth Army after Zhukov's forces severed it from all but radio contact with other German army formations.

This book provides a detailed history of the Luftwaffe's operations during the entire summer campaign, as well as during its essential preliminary operations in the Crimea and the ill-fated airlift that grew out of its failure. A paucity of previous works on the subject—most of little worth and focusing only on the airlift[3]—allowed me to interpret documentary evidence according to my own understanding, without having soaked up the biases and views of others and with no compulsion to make my views conform to received opinion. Nonetheless, I owe a debt to the late *Generalleutnant* Hermann Plocher, whose work on German air operations in Russia provided me with a basic chronological outline of planning and operations, as well as a helpful starting point for archival exploration.

During the 1950s, the United States Air Force Historical Division sponsored a German Air Force Historical Project, commonly referred to as the "GAF Monograph Project." Under this project's auspices, former Luftwaffe officers wrote a series of monographs on their air force's organization, planning, and operations before and during the Second World War. Several studies focused on the war against the Soviet Union, notably Plocher's three-volume operational history, *The German Air Force versus Russia.*[4] He wrote these volumes before his recall to duty in the new German Air Force in 1957. They were subsequently translated into English, heavily edited by Harry Fletcher of the USAF Historical Division, and published in the mid-1960s.

Plocher organized his narrative by year, then by geographical region. Thus, his volume on Luftwaffe operations in 1942 devotes three chapters to events in southern Russia, including the Crimean campaigns, the drive to Stalingrad, and the airlift and its aftermath. Although his treatment of these events is generally sensible and reliable, he wrote in the same journalistic and melodramatic manner as Hans-Detlef Herhudt von Rohden, who had written an earlier study of the Stalingrad airlift, and Franz Kurowski, who later covered the events of 1942 in two books on the Luftwaffe (particularly its fighter units) in Russia.[5] Both Rohden and Kurowski wrote in an emotive style, preferring anecdotal narrative to thorough, dispassionate analysis. Rohden's account is especially weak. His biases and prejudices are evident throughout, often manifest in the purported words of key participants, and it would appear that he even concocted several conversations and conferences. His work is of limited value to historians. Plocher's scholarship is much better, and certainly reveals no evidence of deliberate falsification. Still, hyperbole abounds in his narrative. Moreover, it *describes* without *explaining,* and it is slender (because each volume also had to include operations in the central and northern combat zones), poorly organized, repetitive, and inaccurate in places. It is also uneven in its treatment of topics, doubtless owing to time and space constraints.

My study attempts to do far more than merely locating and adding the many pieces missing from my predecessors' depictions and touching up their flaws. I have painted a new picture, having reconsidered the campaign in the light of a far wider body of documentary sources, reexamined the known data—including the sources they used—from a different vantage point, and employed a different methodology. As a result, my work places emphasis on different factors, analyzes many previously ignored actions and events, and provides what I believe to be the first scholarly treatment of the Luftwaffe's deployment in southern Russia during 1942 and the first months of 1943.

It is a campaign history, following an analytical pattern common to the genre, comprising a consecutive consideration of four different but intertwined aspects of the campaign: genesis, purposes, operational execution, and consequences. Accordingly, I endeavor to show that Operation *Blau,* the 1942 campaign, grew out of the failure of Operation *Barbarossa,* the 1941 campaign, to destroy the Red Army and Air Force in a rapid blitz campaign. By January 1942, the Wehrmacht's eastern armies and air fleets had suffered five months of constant offensive fighting followed by two months of intense defensive fighting. This had weakened them to such an extent that they were no longer capable of carrying out large-scale offensive operations along the entire eastern front. Consequently, Hitler and the Wehrmacht High Command planned a much less grandiose campaign for summer.

To create a broad context for that campaign, I analyze Hitler's strategic ambitions during the last months of 1941 and the first of 1942, when economic considerations were as important to the formulation of a new strategy as the depleted state of the eastern armies and air fleets. Fearful of heavy attacks on Rumanian oil fields, his main source of oil, and aware that *Barbarossa* had virtually exhausted the Reich's reserves, Hitler considered the protection of the Rumanian oil fields and the acquisition of new sources essential if he were to wage a prolonged war against the growing list of nations he now opposed. He therefore formulated a major campaign for summer, aiming first, through preliminary offensive operations in the Crimea, to protect Rumanian oil centers from Soviet air attacks, and second, through a powerful thrust to the Don River and then into the Caucasus, to deliver that oil-rich region into German hands.

In April 1942, the Führer outlined his strategy in War Directive No. 41, containing operational orders for all three branches of the Wehrmacht. Throughout *Barbarossa,* and especially during the difficult winter battles that followed, the Luftwaffe had served as a "fire-fighting" force, hastily concentrated at critical points to compensate for the army's lack of firepower. Now, with his armies understrength and deficient in armor and artillery, Hitler once more deployed the Luftwaffe in support of ground forces. During the preliminary operations in the Crimea and the main campaign itself, the Luftwaffe would provide direct support, involving operations against targets on the battlefield, as well as indirect support, involving interdiction operations against march routes, supply lines, mobilization points, and other targets in the enemy's rear. It is outside the scope of my book to analyze the soundness of the Wehrmacht High Command's emphasis on tactical air warfare at the expense of a strong strategic bombing capability; suffice to say that during the campaign under study, as in the one preceding it, the eastern air fleets were almost exclusively committed to army support.

Because all air operations during the 1942 campaign were closely connected to army operations, I describe and explain the latter in some depth, as I do the working relationship between the two service branches. Interservice cooperation during the campaign was generally effective, thanks in large part to the efforts of General Wolfram von Richthofen, the senior air commander involved in most operations and the Luftwaffe's foremost expert on close support tactics. Richthofen, who often felt frustrated by the responsibilities and restrictions associated with this close-support orientation (and who once described the Luftwaffe as "the army's whore"),[6] displayed generalship of the highest order as he implemented effective army support. Despite his faults, which I try not to gloss over, he was a superb tactical air commander, possibly the best of the Second World War. His centrality in my account stems from neither antipathy nor admiration but from a clear recognition that, from the very moment he arrived in southern Russia in April 1942, it was *his* air campaign. First as an air corps commander and then as head of the entire air fleet, he proved himself a courageous, resolute leader and a stern, rigid disciplinarian and administrator. He earned the respect and, in most cases, affection of his men. In spite of his arrogant, brusque manner, he was an excellent leader and, no less important, an energetic and reliable subordinate. At all times he skillfully exploited his forces' limited capabilities to the fullest, producing satisfactory results under the worst of circumstances and superb results under the best. Even the British Air Ministry recognized his outstanding abilities, noting in 1943 that he was resolute and tough and that, "with his good name and appearance, brutal energy and great personal courage, he is the German ideal of an Air Force General."[7]

Naturally, people who wage war—including Richthofen and many other prominent soldiers and airmen described throughout this work—do not lose their humanity when they pull on their boots and fasten the buttons of their tunics each day. Even the most senior commanders, well versed in the science of warfare, remain motivated by subjective factors of great complexity and are prone, like us all, to ambition, jealousy, anger, fear, and depression. These factors often influence decision-making and leadership effectiveness. Therefore, as well as providing what I believe to be ample strategic and operational context and detail, I have attempted to draw from the diaries of key commanders and, where possible, regular airmen their personal perspectives of decisions, actions, and events. While those perspectives were often perceptibly distorted by the authors' values, biases, and vantage points—Richthofen's detailed but colorful diary entries are a prime example—they have neither been accepted at face value nor disregarded because of these "flaws." Rather, I have criticized these records according to accepted methodological principles, explaining internal inconsistencies, errors, and examples of bias but not avoiding the use of certain passages because of their subjectivity. Although I have tried to avoid all unnecessary anecdotes, however fascinating they are, I have quoted extensively from the diaries and personal papers of key airmen in the hope of bringing alive human aspects of both significant and mundane incidents, as well as revealing the strengths and weaknesses of the commanders and troops who battled so hard to satisfy their leaders' strategic ambitions.

Acknowledgments

My first thanks go to my dear wife, Kathy, who has always supported me as I pursued my academic goals yet never complained during my student years about our poor income or my long hours of daily study or months of absence. I have a loving partner, and my children have a loving mother. I am a fortunate man.

This book began life as my doctoral dissertation, and I owe my greatest intellectual debt to my dissertation supervisor, Vincent Orange of the University of Canterbury. Vincent is an inspiring mentor, skilled guide, rigorous critic, and good friend. He proved such an excellent supervisor of my master's thesis that I happily chose to work under him again for my doctorate. Not once in the three years I devoted to the project did I regret that choice. Thank you for everything, Vincent.

James S. Corum, Professor of Comparative Military Studies at the School of Advanced Airpower Studies, Air University, cast his expert gaze over drafts of most chapters and made numerous suggestions to improve the text. As well as offering encouragement, Jim provided copies of photographs and documents from his personal collection. He also frequently interrupted his work to answer questions and offer his opinion on matters large and small. This book is very much better as a result of his efforts.

Thanks are due to Melrose Bryant and the other circulation librarians of the Fairchild Memorial Library, Air University, for their cheerful and never-failing assistance. Access to the extensive microfilm collection of *OKL* records was a great help, as was free and unrestricted use of the library's photocopier.

Colonel Richard S. Rauschkolb and the staff of the United States Air Force Historical Research Agency (USAFHRA) at Maxwell Air Force Base, Alabama, awarded me a scholarship to carry out primary research in its splendid archive and showed me courtesy and kindness at all times during my stay. I am grateful to all the USAFHRA staff for making my stay pleasant and rewarding. I especially wish to thank Barbara Anne Lee and Marvin Fisher, whose warmth and friendship helped me cope with separation from my wife and children while in America. I have fond memories of the many lunches that Marvin and I spent together on the base, and of the evenings I enjoyed with him and his lovely wife, Dorris, at their home. Without Marvin's constant direction and advice, my exploration of the USAFHRA's rich document collections would not have been as fruitful.

I am also grateful to the *Deutscher Akademischer Austauschdienst* (German Academic Exchange Service) in Bonn for awarding me a generous scholarship, which enabled me to conduct extensive archival research in the *Bundesarchiv-Militärarchiv* (*BA/MA,* Federal Military Archives), in Freiburg im Breisgau, Germany. The *BA/MA*'s archivists gave me a cordial reception and helped make my months of research in their copious records very rewarding.

My stay in Freiburg also allowed me to pick the brain of Horst Boog, recently retired Scientific Director of the Bundeswehr's *Militärgeschichtliches Forschungsamt* (Military History Research Office). Dr. Boog's marvelous knowledge of all matters relating to the Luftwaffe, and of the archival sources upon which its recorded history is based, is matched by his willingness to share that knowledge with a young, unknown scholar from New Zealand. I have gained many valuable insights into German military history from Dr. Boog, not only during our discussions in Germany and New Zealand but also during long hours spent reading his many books and articles. I hope my work reflects those insights, but if it does not, the fault lies with the student, not the teacher.

I studied several of Dr. Boog's publications, and many other German-language works relating to my topic, at the library of the *Albert-Ludwigs-Universität Freiburg.* The staff of that fine library kindly permitted me to use their resources—and even take books away on short-term loan—despite the fact that I was not a student of the university. I must thank Herr Hans-Joachim Stübig, of the university's *Akademisches Auslandsamt,* for making this possible and assisting me in many other ways.

The New Zealand Embassy of the Federal Republic of Germany, especially its cultural attachés Annett Günther and Günter Haselier, liaised effectively with German agencies to ensure that my stay in Freiburg was as stress-free and costless as possible. My accommodation in the beautiful village of Staufen, provided by the local *Goethe-Institut,* was very satisfactory, for which I thank Judith Geare of the New Zealand branch of the *Institut.*

Last, but not least, the University of Canterbury also provided excellent assistance. In particular, I extend my gratitude to W. David McIntyre, former head of the history department, and John Cookson and Ian Campbell, the department's successive bursars, for financial assistance far exceeding the amount ordinarily granted to postgraduate students. I appreciate their generosity and feel favored to have been a student in that department, with its supportive and encouraging environment. I am also grateful to Michelle Rogan, the geography department's talented cartographer, for creating the excellent maps that illustrate my text.

Of course, although these people all contributed to my book, they carry no responsibility for any errors or misinterpretations of which I may be guilty.

Joel S. A. Hayward

1

Hitler's Utopian Strategy

When asked by his Allied captors in 1945 to what extent German military strategy had been influenced by economic considerations, Albert Speer, Hitler's armaments minister, replied that in the case of Operation *Barbarossa* the need for oil was certainly a prime motive.[1] Indeed, even during initial discussions of his plan to invade the Soviet Union, Hitler had stressed the absolute necessity of seizing key oil fields, particularly those in the Caucasus region, which accounted for 90 percent of all oil produced in the Soviet Union. For example, during a war conference at the Berghof on 31 July 1940, Hitler revealed to senior commanders his intention to shatter Russia "to its roots with one blow."[2] After achieving the "destruction of Russian manpower," he explained, the German army would strike to the Baku oil field, the richest in the Caucasus and one of the most productive in the world.

Despite Hitler's optimism, the 1941 campaign—which opened along a 2,000-kilometer front and involved 148 combat divisions—failed to shatter Russia "to its roots with one blow." Consequently, it failed to bring the Caucasus under German control. After reverses during the winter of 1941–1942, the Wehrmacht no longer had the means to undertake wide-ranging offensives along the entire front, by then over 2,500 kilometers long. The summer campaign of 1942, although still immense, was necessarily less ambitious. It opened along a front of 725 kilometers and involved 68 German and 25 Allied divisions. Soviet oil remained a major attraction for Hitler. The offensive aimed to destroy the main Russian forces between the Donets and Don Rivers, capture the crossings into the mountainous Caucasus region, and then seize the rich oil fields. The fields' perceived importance to the German economy, and hence the war effort, cannot be overstated. On 1 June 1942, four weeks before the summer campaign began, Hitler told the assembled senior officers of Army Group South: "If I do not get the oil of Maikop and Grozny then I must end this war."[3]

OIL: THE "ACHILLES' HEEL" OF THE WEHRMACHT

The immense Caucasus region is bounded by the Black Sea on the west and the Caspian on the east, and is traversed by the Caucasus Mountains. The region north of the mountains produced grain, cotton, and heavy farm machinery. Its two main oil fields—Maikop, near the Black Sea, and Grozny, near the Caspian— produced about 10 percent of all Soviet oil.[4] South of the mountains lies the densely populated region of Transcaucasia, today comprising the nations of Georgia, Azerbaijan, and Armenia. In 1942, this heavily industrialized region had a population density greater than the state of New York.[5] Baku, capital of Azerbaijan and situated on one of the world's richest oil fields, alone produced 80 percent of all Soviet oil (24,000,000 million tons in 1942).

The Caucasus was also rich in coal, peat, and nonferrous and rare metals. For example, the manganese deposits at Chiaturi in Transcaucasia formed the richest single source in the world, yielding 1.5 million tons of manganese ore in 1940 (over half the Soviet Union's total). Additionally, the Caucasus, especially the Kuban region, was one of the nation's wealthiest agricultural areas, producing large harvests of wheat, corn, sunflower seeds, and sugar beets.

In order to make sense of Hitler's insistence on the capture of this region, it is necessary to outline briefly the origin and significance of the Wehrmacht's "Achilles' heel": its lack of oil. German economists realized in the first year of Nazi rule that the nation's heavy dependence on overseas imports of crude oil would be a serious problem in the event of war. It imported around 85 percent of the 3 million tons it consumed per year, most of it coming from the United States, Venezuela, and Iran. The remainder came from domestic crude production and from a synthetic oil industry still in its infancy.[6] Therefore, the government took urgent steps toward self-sufficiency in fuels and lubricants by sinking new wells and encouraging the rapid expansion of the synthetic fuel industry. It paid companies subsidies to encourage exploratory drilling within Germany, which resulted in domestic crude oil production increasing fourfold from 238,000 tons in 1933 to 1 million tons in 1940.[7] Methods of producing synthetic oil had been perfected only in the late 1920s, and when the National Socialists came to power in 1933 only three small plants existed. Despite the high cost of producing synthetic fuel (four times as much as crude), the government continuously enlarged this industry throughout the 1930s, so that the annual production of oil products from coal rose from less than 200,000 tons in 1933 to 2,300,000 tons at the outbreak of war in 1939.[8]

In August 1936, Hitler addressed a lengthy memorandum to Hermann Göring, commissioner of foreign exchange and raw materials, noting what he considered Germany's urgent economic and military requirements and outlining future steps to correct perceived deficiencies.[9] The ultimate solution to Germany's problems, insisted Hitler in terms echoing those used in *Mein Kampf*, "lies in expanding the living space of our people; that is, in extending the sources of its raw materials and foodstuffs." (In Hitler's worldview, "living space" did not primarily mean space for settlement as much as land and resources for economic exploitation.) The short-term goal, he continued, must be an immediate "economic mobilization" resulting in Germany quickly reaching "a position of political and economic self-sufficiency." The production of all raw materials essential for modern warfare must be intensified. German fuel production, he emphasized, must be increased "at the fastest pace" because "the future conduct of war will depend on the completion of this task rather than the stockpiling of gasoline." Hitler concluded by setting Göring two clear-cut tasks: "(1) The German army must be ready for war within four years, and (2) the German economy must be fit for war within four years."

Göring responded to the memorandum by having his economists formulate a detailed "Four-Year Plan" for the Reich's economic development. Göring's plan provided for an increase in oil production from less than 2 million tons in 1936 to 4,700,000 tons in 1940, over half of which would be produced synthetically.[10] However, in July 1938, the Karinhall Plan superseded the Four-Year Plan, placing far greater emphasis on economic preparations for an increasingly likely war. Realizing that Germany's present consumption of oil had risen to about 7,500,000 tons—and this was in peacetime—Göring's economists resolved to overcome the glaring inadequacy of previous programs by planning an increase in the annual output of finished oil products to 11 million tons by the beginning of 1944.[11] Even these production targets proved increasingly unrealistic, prompting Göring's staff to drew up several new oil plans, beginning in September 1939 with a revision of the Karinhall Plan and ending in January 1944 with the Mineralöl Plan.[12]

Despite intense efforts to improve Germany's oil situation, in 1938—the last full year of peace—only about a third of the 7,500,000 tons of oil Germany consumed was produced domestically by oil refineries and the new synthetic plants being built. The bulk of the other 5 million tons still came from the United States, Venezuela, and Iran. A smaller, but nonetheless significant amount (451,000 tons), came from Rumania.[13] Accordingly, Germany's oil situation received a severe blow in September 1939 when its overseas imports ceased with the imposition of the Anglo-French naval blockade.

The cessation of oil imports caused grave concern among German economists, although its effects were not immediately felt. During the prewar months of 1939, oil imports from overseas reached an all-time peak, so that despite the blockade from September onward imports for the year as a whole amounted to 5,165,000 tons, up 200,000 tons from the previous year.[14] However, during the following year imports dropped dramatically; only 2,075,000 tons managed to enter the Reich in 1940, and this was only from other countries within the Continent. Just over 1 million tons of this came from Rumania and another 619,600 tons from the Soviet Union, in accordance with the German-Soviet trade agreements of 1939 and 1940.[15] Naturally, oil imports from the Soviet Union ceased immediately when the Germans invaded in June 1941, although 256,300 tons of oil had already been imported in the first half of that year.[16]

Easily the largest oil producer in non-Soviet Europe, Rumania was the only nation capable of replacing a significant portion of the lost overseas imports. In March 1939, it signed an economic treaty with Germany, and in May 1940 the two nations signed an oil pact.[17] Germany certainly benefited, gaining over 1 million tons that year.[18] During 1939 and 1940 Rumania continued to export oil to non-Axis nations, but as it drew closer to the Axis powers after Germany's victories in the west during 1940 these exports dropped off considerably. In August 1940, Rumania participated in the second of the Vienna Awards, then acceded in November to both the Tripartite Pact and the Anti-Comintern Pact. In 1941, Rumania became Germany's strongest economic and military ally when it joined wholeheartedly in the invasion of the Soviet Union. In addition to supplying its own troops at the front, it exported 2,086,000 tons of oil to the Reich that year, much of it going directly to the Wehrmacht in Russia.

Germany's increasing reliance on Rumanian oil during the first two years of war gave Hitler much anxiety. He frequently expressed concern that the Ploesti oil fields in Rumania lay within striking distance of Soviet long-range bombers. "Now, in the era of air power," he told his generals on 20 January 1941, "Russia can turn the Rumanian oil fields into an expanse of smoking debris . . . and the very life of the Axis depends on those fields."[19] We shall see how Hitler's fear of air attacks by Soviet bombers stationed on the Crimean Peninsula led him to conduct a lengthy campaign in 1942 to "clear up" the Crimea.

The destruction of Rumania's oil industry would indeed have dealt a catastrophic blow to the German war effort. Oil was the most critical item in Germany's war economy, yet by 1940 almost all its oil imports came from Rumania.[20] Nonetheless, even without the benefit of hindsight it is clear that Hitler's concerns were unfounded, as his own military intelligence should have told him at the time. During the entire war, the Soviet Union had only a rudimentary long-range bombing capability.[21] The Soviet long-range bomber command had relatively few aircraft, and none with precision bombing capabilities until late 1943. It certainly could not assemble a bomber force of sufficient strength to deliver *massed* air strikes against the Ploesti oil installations, which were, in any event, protected by formidable antiaircraft defenses.[22] Soviet medium bombers attempted numerous raids throughout the war, but these proved ineffectual and cost many aircraft.

Hitler and his military economists also worried about the small size of Germany's oil reserves. All prewar oil planning called for the accumulation of substantial reserve stocks, particularly of aviation fuel for the Luftwaffe and diesel fuels for the *Kriegsmarine*. Yet when war began in September 1939, reserve stocks sat at half the planned levels. In fact, they equaled only a quarter of the Reich's annual *peacetime* consumption. Reserves decreased dramatically during the first few months of war and subsequently never rose to an adequate level.

Germany's rapid conquests of Norway, Denmark, the Low Countries, and France actually resulted in slight increases in its meager oil reserves. During these campaigns the Wehrmacht consumed relatively little oil, mainly because of the small number of protracted battles and a heavy reliance on horse-drawn supply columns. German forces actually "managed to win their victories [in 1940] using a mere 12 million barrels of oil products, or about the same as the United States produced every three days."[23] Additionally, stocks of oil products captured during the short campaigns, especially against France, were larger than the amounts consumed. For instance, 250,000 tons of aviation fuel alone (the equivalent of five months' production) were captured during the French campaign.[24]

Nonetheless, a new, long-term liability quickly eroded the benefit of these gains. The conquests made Germany responsible for meeting the oil needs of all its occupied nations, stretching from Norway to the Spanish border, which could no longer obtain supplies from outside Europe.[25] When Mussolini declared war on France and Britain on 10 June 1940, Germany's oil situation suffered another reverse. Italy had no significant domestic production of oil and, with the implementation of the Allied blockade that followed its declaration of war, could obtain only negligible amounts from Albania (which it had annexed in April 1939). Thus, from June 1940 onward, Italy was almost totally dependent on Germany for oil and, as a result, became a serious drain on the latter's production and stocks.[26]

BARBAROSSA

Unlike the rapid German campaigns of 1939 and 1940, Operation *Barbarossa,* the massive offensive launched in June 1941 to conquer the Soviet Union, seriously depleted the Reich's oil reserves. Germany simply could not satisfy the oil requirements of the 3,600,000 German and allied soldiers, 600,000 vehicles, 3,600 tanks, and over 2,700 aircraft participating in the offensive. Although Germany's war economy could sustain short blitzkrieg campaigns it could not support the drawn-out war of economic attrition that developed when the Soviet Union did not collapse within a few weeks, as both friends and enemies expected.

Even before *Barbarossa* started, German economists had been predicting oil supply problems and issuing warnings to military planners. In March 1941, for example, *General der Infanterie* Georg Thomas, head of the War Economy and Armaments Office, warned both Göring and Keitel in a detailed report that reserve stocks would be exhausted by late October.[27] From that time onward, he argued, it would no longer be possible to offset the significant shortage of oil. The only possibility of alleviating desperate oil shortages in the event of a protracted war was for Germany to exploit Soviet oil production. Thomas insisted:

It is crucial to seize quickly and exploit the Caucasus oil fields, at least the areas around Maikop and Grozny. In oil fields that have not been completely destroyed, it will take about a month to resume production, and another month for its transport. We will have to seize those areas by no later than the end of the operation's second month. . . . If this proves unsuccessful, we must expect the most serious repercussions, with unpredictable consequences for military operations after 1.9.[1941] and for the survival of the economy.

As a result of Thomas's repeated warnings to Hitler that Germany would soon run dry, in May 1941 the dictator ordered substantial cuts in all areas not directly affecting frontline military operations. This affected the civilian economy, home requirements of the armed forces, and deliveries to Italy and all other European countries dependent on Germany. Only a month later, Walther Funk, the economics minister, expressed to Jodl, head of the High Command of the Armed Forces (OKW) operations staff, deep concern that the economy was now receiving "even less than 18 percent of peacetime consumption" and that the requirements of the economy had been "threshed to the limit."[28] However, despite conveying to Jodl his "gravest misgivings about any further curbs," Funk could not prevent subsequent cuts in the oil quota for the civilian sector. These cuts were so extensive that British Air Ministry observers secretly referred to them early in 1942 as "the severest form of rationing."[29]

Despite these domestic consumption cuts, the prolonged campaign in the east quickly began to inflict severe economic burdens on the Wehrmacht. The production and supply of vital war materials, including oil products, could not keep pace with demand. Moreover, during the eastern campaign German units were unable to utilize captured fuel, as they had during the campaigns of 1939 and 1940. The octane content of Soviet petrol was simply too low for German vehicles. It could be used only after the addition of benzol in complex installations constructed specifically for that task.

Within months of the campaign's start in June, the Wehrmacht's oil situation became desperate. For example, on 11 September 1941, Generaloberst Franz Halder, the army chief of staff, recorded in his diary that the eastern forces would need twenty-nine trainloads of fuel per day throughout October and twenty per day throughout November if they were to carry out the new offensive.[30] However, the OKW insisted that it could not supply more than 75 percent of the amount required throughout October and only 15 percent of that required throughout November. (As it turned out, the OKW failed to supply even those quantities.)

Although the German army had yet to lose a single major battle on the eastern front, by October 1941 German military planners grimly realized that their blitzkrieg against the Soviet Union had failed. Moreover, they now knew that both German and Rumanian oil reserves were exhausted and that current production in both nations was insufficient to satisfy the requirements of the Wehrmacht and industry (as well, of course, as civilian consumption). Rumania's oil supplies to the Reich had increased from 150,800 tons in June 1941 to 361,600 tons in August, but this increase was possible only because Rumania reluctantly supplied Germany with a large portion of the oil earmarked for its own domestic consumption, which was exhausted by late September.[31] Accordingly, deliveries to the Reich decreased after that point, dropping to 222,800 tons in October, to 213,000 in November, and, after a short-lived quarrel between Germany and Rumania over payment, to a mere 104,000 in December. In January 1942, they rose slightly to 111,000 tons but fell sharply again in February, when only 73,000 tons were delivered to the Reich.[32] Although deliveries gradually rose again, the dramatic drop in the last months of 1941 proved almost disastrous for the German war effort.

Although many members of the German High Command had believed in July that the Soviet armed forces were close to total collapse, by late August they realized that the eastern campaign was still far from over. On 26 August, Thomas, whose earlier predictions were now proving correct, submitted to the *OKW* a new report on the oil situation. He argued that the small and rapidly diminishing reserve stocks of oil still available to Germany would be exhausted in the following months (a correct assessment, as noted earlier) and that current production levels were insufficient to satisfy demands. Moreover, he stated, even if production was "pushed to its limits it would be impossible to supply all the required oil. Accordingly, our only option is to cut consumption in accordance with the availability of supplies."[33] Further cuts would be made in all areas not directly affecting front-line military operations, warned Thomas, which would result in considerable "political, military and economic disadvantages."[34]

Four days after Thomas submitted this report to the *OKW,* he attended a meeting with *Generalmajor* Eduard Wagner, the army's quartermaster general. Wagner explained that Army Groups South and Center on the eastern front were experiencing critical fuel shortages, a situation exacerbated by major rail transportation problems.[35] He added that oil requirements for the following months might still be met if additional reductions were made in the consumption of civilian and nonoperational military sectors, as well as of the occupied territories. Yet his conclusion was bleak: by the beginning of 1942, oil supplies would be exhausted and "new oil fields would have to be captured."[36]

On 7 October 1941, even as *Generalfeldmarschall* von Bock's panzer spearheads sealed off massed Soviet forces in the Vyazma and Bryansk pockets (one of the most devastating double envelopments in military history), Thomas submitted another lengthy report on the deteriorating oil situation. It was possible, the report stated, to satisfy requirements of urgently needed aviation fuel and lubricants until the end of the year. Nonetheless, this would leave only 31,000 tons of these products to start off the new year, a dangerously low level and a huge drop from 1 October, when there had been 181,000 tons.[37] Although there were still 289,000 tons of motor and carburetor fuel available, current production levels were insufficient to prevent this stock from being completely exhausted by mid-November. In fact, by the end of that month there would be a shortfall of 32,000 tons, which would increase to as much as 97,000 tons by the end of December. These were not the only critical fuel shortages. On 1 October, less than 250,000 tons of diesel fuel were available, and, at current rates of consumption, shortages of this fuel would be around 25,000 tons at the end of November, rising to 50,000 tons at the end of December. Similarly, while the heating oil situation was not yet desperate, production levels remained low and stocks were rapidly decreasing. It was clearly no longer possible to supply anything close to the 100,000 tons of heating oil the Italians emphatically stated they needed each month. Thomas predicted that only 60,000 tons could be delivered to Italy in October, and 55,000 tons per month in November and December.[38]

To complicate matters, the oil situation of the *Kriegsmarine* also grew steadily worse through 1941 (matching its fortunes against the Royal Navy). On 13 November, *Großadmiral* Erich Raeder provided Hitler with a detailed analysis of the navy's "very difficult oil situation."[39] The navy's total stock of diesel oil and imports from Rumania was still sufficient to satisfy its current requirements. However, its total stock of fuel oil had dropped considerably, and almost a third could not be used without additional chemical alteration. On 12 December, Raeder, who was painfully aware that the navy's oil needs were considered by Hitler and his closest military advisers to be far less important than those of the massive armies on the eastern front, informed the Führer that the navy's oil situation had now become "very critical."[40] Its requirements, he pointed out, "have been cut by fifty per cent." This, he added sharply, was causing "an intolerable restriction on the mobility of our vessels."

Thus, it was clear to Hitler and his planners during the closing months of 1941 that the unexpectedly prolonged campaign on the eastern front had severely weakened Germany's oil situation. Moreover, they were acutely aware that oil shortages were now even affecting the operational capability of the troops in the east still struggling to deliver the final knockout blow to the Soviet armed forces. A meeting between Wagner and the War Economy and Armaments Office on 22 October, for example, revealed that forces on the eastern front, still slogging forward with dogged tenacity in clothing unable to keep out the wind and rain, were consuming far more fuel than previously calculated.[41] This greater consumption resulted from worn-out engines, difficult terrain, and bad weather. The army could now cover only thirty-five to forty kilometers on the amount of fuel considered sufficient for one hundred kilometers, which meant that far more fuel had to be supplied. No less than twenty trainloads were now needed per day by troops in the east, despite their heavy reliance on horse-drawn supply columns. However, even if this quantity of fuel was available, increases in deliveries could not be made because of transportation problems on the railways. Dozens of loaded trains were backed up, waiting for railway troops and battalions of the Reich Labor Service and Organization Todt to regauge rail lines, sidings, and marshaling areas to the German width and to organize truck columns connecting railheads with the advancing troops. This problem was exacerbated by the activities of Russian partisans, who did considerable damage to railways used by the Germans. Because the required increases in fuel deliveries could not be attained, troop mobility (particularly in Army Group Center) began to suffer. As it happened, this logistics problem actually proved to be a blessing in disguise: when German fuel supplies came close to total exhaustion in mid-November, the backlog of trains (around 120 by then) served as an unexpected reserve and managed to keep the eastern armies operational.

On 3 November, while Bock's Army Group Center was preparing for its final drive on Moscow, *Generalfeldmarschall* von Brauchitsch, the beleaguered and soon-to-be-relieved commander in chief of the army, paid a visit to the headquarters of Army Group South. This mighty force, commanded by *Generalfeldmarschall* von Rundstedt, occupied much of central and eastern Ukraine and most of the Crimea. It was still advancing slowly eastward toward strategic objectives considered by Hitler to be more important than Moscow (which he had characterized back in July as "merely a geographical concept").[42] To the dismay and frustration of many of Hitler's military advisers, these objectives (economic rather than military) included Kharkov, the fourth-largest industrial center in the Soviet Union; the Donets Basin, famous for its coal and iron industries; and the oil-rich Caucasus region. For instance, in his supplement to War Directive No. 34, dated 21 August 1941, Hitler had stated: "The most important aim to be achieved before the onset of winter is not the capture of Moscow but, rather, the occupation of the Crimea, of the industrial and coal-mining area of the Donets Basin, the cutting of the Russian supply routes from the Caucasus oil fields, and, in the north, the investment of Leningrad and the establishment of contact with the Finns."[43] Attacks on the Rumanian oil fields and refineries were clearly still preying on Hitler's mind, because he emphasized in this supplement that "the capture of the Crimean Peninsula is of extreme importance for safeguarding our oil supplies from Rumania." The very next day he returned to this theme in a different document:

> Apart from the fact that it is important to capture or destroy Russia's iron, coal and oil reserves, it is of decisive importance for Germany that the Russian air bases on the Black Sea be eliminated, above all in the region of Odessa and the Crimea.
>
> This measure can be said to be absolutely essential for Germany. Under present circumstances no one can guarantee that our only important oil-producing region is safe from air attack. Such attacks could have incalculable results for the future conduct of the war.[44]

Similarly, two days later he explained to *Generaloberst* Heinz Guderian the absolute need to neutralize the Crimea, "that Soviet aircraft carrier for attacking the

Rumanian oil fields."[45] The significance of Hitler's constant fear of Soviet air attacks on his main source of oil by Crimea-based bombers would soon become apparent.

When Kharkov fell to von Reichenau's Sixth Army on 24 October, Hitler was delighted. However, when von Stülpnagel's Seventeenth Army (on Sixth Army's right flank) moved into the Donets Basin, it discovered that much of the industrial machinery was gone. Many plants had been sabotaged, while hundreds of other industrial enterprises had been taken apart by Soviet engineers and technicians to be reconstructed at locations in the distant region of the Urals. This outstanding achievement has received little scholarly attention, yet it must rate as one of the Soviet Union's greatest wartime achievements.

Cheated of his anticipated spoils, Hitler insisted that Army Group South push on toward his other objectives in southern Russia. During his visit to this army group on 3 November, Brauchitsch informed its stunned leaders that the Supreme Command and the High Command of the Army *(OKH)* still wanted the areas around Maikop (the northernmost Caucasus oil field) and Stalingrad to be "captured at all costs this winter." Accordingly, he continued, "ways and means of attaining these objectives would have to be found. In the case of Maikop oil is naturally the incentive; in the case of Stalingrad [it is] the urgent necessity of destroying the Russian command's last 'major' north-south link."[46]

Army Group South continued to claw its way eastward. Almost three weeks later, on 21 November, units of *General der Kavallerie* von Mackensen's *III. Armeekorps* (from von Kleist's First Panzer Army) occupied Rostov, at the mouth of the Don River. Despite intense resistance, they even managed to capture intact the main Don bridge leading into the Caucasus. Not knowing that these numerically weak units would soon be driven from the city (it was retaken only eight days later) and that his corps would be savagely mauled by the powerful Soviet Southern Front, Mackensen believed he had cut the Russian supply routes from the Caucasus and, accordingly, saw his victory at Rostov as a major blow against the Soviet war machine.

Hitler was equally optimistic. The Caucasus oil fields, the nearest of which was now tantalizingly close (a mere 300 kilometers away), were still at the forefront of his plans for Army Group South. On the day it took Rostov, he gave this already overstretched force, together with First Panzer Army and Eleventh Army, the unachievable task of cutting off "even the British and Soviet links over the Caucasus," beginning with the oil fields around Maikop. Seventeenth Army received an equally unreasonable task: the capture of Stalingrad and its surrounding industrial areas, in order to "cut off the enemy's north-south link on the Volga."[47]

Army Group South's capture of Rostov scared Soviet military strategists, who recognized the threat to their oil fields. "If Germany succeeds in taking Moscow," warned Marshal Timoshenko in a secret speech to the Supreme Defense Council in Moscow, that is obviously a grave disappointment for us, but it by no means disrupts our grand strategy. . . . Germany would gain accommodation [that is, shelter from the cruel Russian winter], but that alone will not win the war. The only thing that matters is oil. As we remember, Germany kept harping on her own urgent oil problems in her economic bargaining with us from 1939 to 1941. So we have to do all we can (a) to make Germany increase her oil consumption, and (b) to keep the German armies out of the Caucasus.[48]

The Red Army's immediate task, he continued, was to throw the Germans back just far enough to destroy the matériel they had assembled for their intended offensive into the Caucasus.

The Soviet offensive in the south, when it finally came, liberated Rostov and threatened to inflict enormous damage on the units of Army Group South as it drove them back westward. The recapture of Rostov (the first major defeat suffered by the German army in any theater up to that time) shattered Hitler's hopes of capturing and exploiting the Caucasus oil fields—or even damaging the Soviet Union's ability to transport oil from the Caucasus to its armies and factories—before the end of 1941. On 29 November, even as German troops were hastily evacuating Rostov in the face of overwhelming Soviet forces, Army Group South reported that, while its winter line will "more or less remain the same" (aside from some inevitable local changes), "the plan to clear out the Donets bend or reach Maikop will not now be carried out."[49] The following day, Rundstedt informed the Führer that because of heavy losses of men and equipment, the vastly superior strength of the enemy's forces, and the appalling weather, Army Group South was suspending all "operational movements" and going over to the defense "on a tactically acceptable line."

According to Halder, Hitler became "extremely agitated" and angrily forbade this withdrawal.[50] Rundstedt, whose greatest concern was the safety of his already suffering troops, replied via Brauchitsch that he could not comply with Hitler's order; he asked that the order be changed or that he be relieved of his post. Hitler saw this as a direct challenge to his authority and, on 1 December, stripped Rundstedt of the command of the army group and replaced him with Reichenau (formerly in command of Sixth Army). As it turned out, Reichenau also realized the hopelessness of the situation and pleaded with Hitler to withdraw his men to the line of the Mius River. This time the Führer relented, and the hard-pressed forces around Rostov moved back to more defensible positions.

This withdrawal back to the Mius was a bitter pill for Hitler to swallow. He now realized that the Caucasus oil fields had slipped from his grasp, at least until the following year. He had actually feared this outcome for some time, despite his renewed optimism in the period immediately following the German capture of Rostov. On 7 November, when he still believed *Barbarossa* could be brought to a successful conclusion in 1941, he complained to the rapidly failing Brauchitsch (who suffered a heart attack the following day) that the seizure of the oil fields would have to be delayed until the following year. Similarly, on 19 November he informed his closest advisers that the first objective for 1942 would be the Caucasus oil fields, and that the campaign launched for this purpose in March or April would aim to take German forces right to the "Russian southern frontier" (the Soviet-Iranian border).[51]

In the first week of December, the Rostov defeat paled into insignificance against events unfolding along the rest of the eastern front. In the far north, the vanguard of von Leeb's Army Group North was in danger of encirclement at Tikhvin, east of Leningrad, forcing an angry Hitler to permit a minor retreat. Things were even worse for Army Group Center. In mid-November, the first solid frosts had permitted a renewal of the offensive against Moscow, and by the end of the month the fall of the city appeared certain. However, the exhausted Germans were halted within sight of the Kremlin's towers by a devastating combination of, on the one hand, diminishing troop strengths, major supply difficulties, savage frosts (of around $-35°C$), and paralyzing blizzards; on the other, the courage and tenacity of warmly clothed and steadily reinforced Soviet troops desperately fighting to save their capital.

On 6 December, the Soviets launched their massive counteroffensive, which lasted until the middle of April 1942 when it petered out and the Germans were themselves able to prepare a renewed offensive. Stunned by events but trying to maintain a confident air in front of his generals, Hitler discussed with Halder the need to rehabilitate troops but argued that, while this was indeed necessary, he still had objectives to be attained during the winter. Caucasus oil continued to feature prominently in his plans; as well as eliminating the Ladoga Front near Leningrad and linking up with the Finns, he said, the Donets bend in the south had to be secured, "as a jump-off base for Maikop." The following day, 7 December, Hitler was still talking inanely about renewing the drive to the south. "We must take the Maikop oil region," he stated. "Rostov should not be written off for this winter. . . . With decent weather we can launch counterattacks."[52]

On 8 December, Hitler, apparently resigned at last to the failure of his blitz campaign, issued War Directive No. 39 to the three services.[53] In this directive he acknowledged that the merciless winter and the consequent difficulties in bringing up supplies compelled his forces "to abandon immediately all major offensive operations and to go over to the defensive." Although Hitler outlined steps to be taken toward the rehabilitation of troops, he did not intend there to be any major withdrawals. Indeed, only two days earlier he had remarked that "the Russians have not voluntarily abandoned any ground; we cannot do it either. In principle, there can be no reduction in the line."[54] War Directive No. 39 firmly stated that there could be no withdrawals unless rear areas had been prepared that offered troops "better living conditions and defense possibilities." Given the difficulty of preparing such rear areas in the snow-covered Soviet wastelands, where the earth was frozen solid, very few of the tortured units at the front were able to move back.

Hitler's anger at senior commanders who appeared to disobey his order culminated in his so-called *Haltebefehl* (stand fast order) of 16 December, in which he ordered the "front to be defended down to the last man."[55] He even sacked those commanders—including Guderian, his ablest panzer commander—who ignored repeated demands to stand fast. As it turned out, however, many of Hitler's senior commanders were later to admit that his rigid *Haltebefehl*—which they considered insane at the time—was the right decision.

War Directive No. 39 also sheds light on the topic at hand: Hitler's pursuit of Soviet oil. It reveals that, despite the heavy battering his worn-out forces were receiving in the east, he still held fast to his goal of taking the Caucasus oil fields during 1942. In order to free up the bulk of Manstein's Eleventh Army for this vital mission, Sevastopol, the Soviet Union's main naval base and shipyard on the Black Sea, was to be captured as soon as possible.

PREPARATIONS FOR THE NEW YEAR

It became clear toward the end of the 1941–1942 winter that Soviet counteroffensives, despite the severe destruction they inflicted, were not going to dislodge the bulk of the strained and exhausted German forces still stretched out along the eastern front. Accordingly, military planners and intelligence officers on both sides began making preparations for the coming spring and summer.

Many officers of the Soviet general staff—including Marshal Shaposhnikov, chief of the general staff, and Vasilevskii, his deputy—were acutely aware of the Red Army's lack of trained reserves and matériel. Accordingly, they became (in Vasilevskii's words) "firmly convinced" that the Red Army should adopt a "temporary strategic defensive" posture for the spring and early summer of 1942.[56] In a meeting at the end of March 1942, they stressed to Stalin the need to engage in defensive fighting within well-prepared positions, and, "in the process of this defensive action, to launch powerful counterblows against the assault groupings of the enemy." The aim of this defensive strategy was not only to frustrate the inevitable German summer offensive but also to create a situation where Soviet forces could themselves launch a "decisive offensive with minimal losses." Principal attention during the transition to this strategic defense, they argued, should be focused on the Moscow sector, where the German offensive would probably occur. Therefore, their principal task should be "the creation of mighty, trained reserves and the stockpiling of weapons, ammunition, tanks, planes, and other combat equipment as well as the necessary matériel with which to supply troops in the subsequent offensive."[57]

Stalin agreed with his general staff that the inevitable German summer offensive would be a resumption of the campaign against Moscow. This view was apparently reinforced by effective German deception operations[58] and the desperation with which *Generaloberst* Model's Ninth Army had successfully held on to Rzhev, a place with no visible importance to the Germans except in connection with a new offensive toward Moscow.[59] Vasilevskii (who shared this view) later wrote that "the preconceived, erroneous idea that in the summer the main enemy strike would be launched in the central sector dominated the Supreme Commander in Chief all the way up to July."[60] Even the Soviet general staff study of the Battle of Stalingrad, written in the middle of *1943*, still argued that the main German target in 1942 had been Moscow and that the actual attack in the southern sector, toward Stalingrad and the Caucasus, aimed "not so much [at] the seizure of the oil fields as it did the drawing away of our main reserves to the south and the weakening of the Moscow front, in order in this way to increase the chances of success in the attack against Moscow."[61] In the first months of 1942, Soviet planners were not alone in holding this view. It was also widely expressed in contemporary British and American intelligence reports. For example, a confidential report of the Military Intelligence Division of the U.S. War Department, dated 26 March 1942, argued at length that "the German strategical plan will aim at the encirclement and destruction of the Russian central army group around Moscow."[62]

Stalin normally favored constant attack, a predisposition that had already resulted in both strategic and tactical blunders (and would again in the future). Nonetheless, during this period he appeared to be in general agreement with the sound strategic appreciation of his general staff, who continued to argue that the Red Army should first wear out the enemy in defensive battles and then, when their own forces were suitably strengthened and supplied, and the enemy's were sufficiently depleted, launch powerful counteroffensives. This was not, however, the only plan presented to him in March 1942. Timoshenko submitted a proposal for conducting a major offensive operation in May with the combined forces of three fronts (Bryansk, Southwestern, and Southern). He aimed to destroy Army Group South and regain much occupied territory. Shaposhnikov begged Stalin not to be enticed by Timoshenko's ambitious plan, pointing out that the lack of men and matériel ruled out such a massive undertaking, which would, in any event, have required a major reinforcement of the Southwestern Front.[63]

Stalin ignored the logic of Shaposhnikov's argument. He remained skeptical of plans for an "active" defensive that did not include any significant offensives, and challenged what he perceived to be the foolishness of remaining idle and allowing the enemy to seize the initiative. "We cannot remain on the defensive and sit on our hands until the Germans strike first!" he lectured Shaposhnikov during a joint meeting of the State Defense Committee and the *Stavka* at the end of March.[64] While the Red Army should adhere to a basic strategic defensive, it was imperative also to conduct individual offensives over a wide front. He was particularly impressed with Timoshenko's revised and downscaled version of his plan to seize Kharkov. Marshal Zhukov, Stalin's most gifted operational commander, tried to persuade him not to carry out this plan but, instead, to adopt Shaposhnikov's policy of strategic defense and let his own Western Front make one significant but localized strike at the dangerous German forces in the central sector (still only 150 kilometers from Moscow). Zhukov, like Shaposhnikov, was brushed aside by the dogmatic Stalin, who scornfully referred to the former's plan as just a "half-measure."[65]

To Shaposhnikov's bitter disappointment, Stalin embraced Timoshenko's plan. He ordered individual preemptive offensives near Leningrad, in the region of Demyansk, in the Smolensk and Lgov-Kursk sectors, in the Kharkov area, and in the Crimea. Vasilevskii later described the "negative consequences" of Stalin's contradictory decision "to defend and attack simultaneously." This decision, he argued,

> resulted in an intolerable expenditure of forces. The events which unfolded in the summer of 1942 clearly showed that, had there been only the reversion to temporary strategic defense along the entire Soviet-German front and had the conduct of offensive operations (e.g., the Khar'kov operation) been rejected, the country and its armed forces would have been spared serious defeats, and we could have resumed active offensive operations much sooner and could have again taken the initiative into our hands.[66]

Indeed, Stalin's counteroffensives proved outright failures (as shown below), resulting not only in the strategic initiative being regained by the Germans but in the loss of hundreds of thousands of Soviet troops.

As for German planning during the end of the 1941–1942 winter, one notes that even at his bleakest moments Hitler's thoughts were with the coming spring offensive. On 3 January 1942, for instance, he confided his plans to Ōshima Hiroshi, the Japanese ambassador to Berlin. For the time being, he told Ōshima, he would not conduct another offensive in the center of the front but would "take up again the offensive in the direction of the Caucasus as soon as the weather is favorable."[67] Two weeks later, on 18 January, Hitler also disclosed these intentions to Bock before the latter flew to Poltava to take command of Army Group South following the untimely death of Reichenau. Bock, whose rebuilt army group would carry out the coming offensive, received two missions: "to hold for the present and attack in the spring."[68]

Despite these optimistic statements, throughout December 1941 and the first few weeks of 1942 Hitler seriously doubted whether his eastern armies could still be saved. Although months later he admitted to courtiers and confidants that during the height of the winter crisis he sometimes doubted he could stave off a catastrophe,[69] he was careful to keep these doubts hidden from his generals and, of course, the public. In a rousing speech delivered in the *Berliner Sportpalast* on 30 January 1942, the ninth anniversary of his election to power, he spoke of his "unbounded confidence, confidence in my own person, so that nothing, whatever it may be, can throw me out of the saddle, so that nothing can shake me."[70]

By the middle of February, even though Soviet offensives continued to inflict heavy damage on German forces, Hitler had shaken off the depression that gripped him in December and January and was regaining his confidence. He felt encouraged by Rommel's brilliant counterattack at El Agheila in Libya on 21 January, which caught the British Eighth Army off guard and, within ten days, forced it to abandon all recent gains in the Benghazi bulge. On 12 February, he was thrilled by the escape of the *Gneisenau, Scharnhorst,* and *Prinz Eugen,* which dashed from Brest through the English Channel in broad daylight to safer waters in Norway. He could take personal pride in the success of this daring operation; the idea of these capital ships dashing through the Channel under the nose of the British had been his own. He was also heartened on 15 February by the news that Great Britain had suffered the worst military defeat in its history: the fall of Singapore to the Japanese army. During that same period the Japanese inflicted similar humiliations on the Americans in the Philippines.

German fortunes on the eastern front also began looking promising. Repeatedly situations that appeared extremely perilous were, by means of superior tactics and tremendous endurance, stabilized and brought under control. Some were even transformed into minor successes. Hitler felt especially proud of Army Group Center's ability to close many gaps in its line and form a new front. Although he knew that German and Soviet forces would remain locked in bloody battle for some time yet, and that in places his men were barely holding on, he felt that the worst was over and that he had accomplished his first objective; he had arrested the panic among his generals and prevented a rout similar to Napoleon's in 1812. Moreover, he regarded his armies' successful resistance to the Soviet winter offensive as further proof that his "stand fast" order was the right decision and that the generals he dismissed were incompetent, cowardly, and defeatist. His iron will had mastered the winter crisis, he believed. Now it would drive the summer offensive.

The plan for a major offensive into the Caucasus to seize the oil fields was, to a much greater extent than the previous year's attack on the Soviet capital, Hitler's own strategic conception.[71] During the height of the winter crisis, he had unfairly but repeatedly cursed the general staff for having imposed its Moscow campaign on him. Now that he had pulled Germany back from the brink of disaster, he was determined to trust his instincts and order a campaign to attain his own strategic objectives (based on his awareness of the Reich's economic problems). Moreover, he would no longer limit himself to issuing general instructions but would, in his new capacity as commander in chief of the army (since Brauchitsch's resignation on 19 December), take complete and immediate charge of the direction of operations.[72]

Operation *Barbarossa* had been conceived in basic accordance with Carl von Clausewitz's fundamental rule of warfare that the proper objective of a campaign is the defeat of the enemy's military forces in the field and that the seizure of economic and political objectives must follow, not precede, this. However, Hitler's decision in the winter of 1941–1942 to seize the Caucasus oil fields, rather than force a decisive battle on the Soviet armed forces, violated Clausewitz's advice. He was certainly aware of Clausewitz's teachings. Indeed, he was well versed in military theory and had studied most key works in this field, including Clausewitz's. On occasions he would pompously point this out to generals who challenged him on matters of strategy. "There's no need for you to try to teach me," he lectured Guderian during one particular disagreement. "I've studied Clausewitz and Moltke and read all the Schlieffen papers. I'm more in the picture than you are!"[73] His decision to avoid a confrontation with the bulk of the Soviet forces, and aim instead at the conquest of the Caucasus in order to exploit its economic resources, was based not on ignorance of military theory but on a deep concern over his struggling economy and the perceived lack of feasible alternative strategies.

Heavy losses during winter left the Wehrmacht unable to undertake wide-ranging offensives along the entire eastern front. By 31 January 1942, the eastern armies had suffered 917,985 casualties, including 28,935 officers, and the eastern Luftwaffe forces had suffered 18,089.[74] Although substantial replacements arrived during the following months, they proved incapable of offsetting losses inflicted during the winter crisis, let alone rebuilding adequate reserves. Loss of matériel also caused grave concern; 424 tanks were destroyed in the first three weeks of December alone, a rate of destruction that continued until well into January. Various efforts to replace these tanks brought little immediate improvement. On 30 March, the High Command of the Army *(OKH)* reported that the sixteen panzer divisions deployed in the east had only 140 operational tanks between them—less than the standard complement of a single division.[75] Moreover, the mobility of the eastern armies was restricted by huge losses of horses and motor vehicles. By the end of January, well over 100,000 vehicles had been destroyed, including 42,851 motorcycles, 28,942 cars, and 41,135 lorries. Again, despite increases in production, these losses simply could not be offset. Indeed, once the objectives of the summer campaign were established during early spring, the units of Army Groups North and Center were deprived of most of their motor vehicles in order to ensure that Army Group South regained at least 85 percent of its former mobility in time for the offensive. The removal of so many motor vehicles naturally led to a significant reduction in the combat effectiveness of Army Groups North and Center, a situation exacerbated by the shortage of horses and fodder. Supply stocks were almost exhausted, and transportation difficulties held up the delivery of weapons and equipment already loaded on trains.

As a result of these problems and his realization that the German economy now had to cope with a prolonged war of economic attrition, on 10 January 1942 Hitler began reorganizing the armaments industry.[76] His long-term objective was still "the buildup of the Luftwaffe and *Kriegsmarine* for the purpose of fighting the Anglo-Saxon powers," but the "strategic demands of 1942 make it impossible, for the time being, to attain this objective through a reduction of armaments destined for the army." Therefore, the army would have to be given a disproportionately large share of manpower and armaments so that it could accomplish its approaching offensive commitments. It would be made ready for these commitments by 1 May 1942. As well as assuring that the army would have supplies sufficient "for about four months' continuous operations," it would be necessary to build up a "backlog of ammunition for the main weapons, amounting (excluding the original allotment) to six times the average monthly consumption of the eastern campaign."

Despite the long-term benefits of this reorganization, which gave the highest priority to the acquisition of coal and oil, it could not, of course, immediately change the condition of the German army. At the end of March 1942, only 8 of the 162 divisions deployed on the eastern front were fully operational. Three more could be brought up to full offensive capability after a short rehabilitation period, and 47 could perform limited offensive tasks. The other 104 divisions could be deployed only for defensive duties.[77] Accordingly, during late winter and spring 1942, Hitler and his military planners realized that they could not possibly conduct a wide-ranging offensive that would force a decisive battle on the Soviet armed forces. Therefore, if an eastern offensive were to be conducted at all in 1942—and there exists no evidence that the German High Command ever seriously considered the eastern forces adopting an essentially defensive posture—the one choice left to be made was in which sector to strike. Only Hitler's proposed drive to the Caucasus offered a solution to the glaring problems of the war economy, which were growing worse with every passing month. If the oil fields could be captured, their output would certainly relieve the severe oil shortages currently experienced by both Germany and Italy, and would also allow their armed forces to continue the prolonged struggle against the growing list of nations now at war against them.

By early 1942, existing sources clearly could not provide Germany with enough oil to resume offensive operations against the Soviets on the scale of the 1941 campaign, let alone to wage war on the western powers on a scale sufficient to bring about their defeat. Since the outbreak of war, only slight gains had been made in domestic crude oil extraction, which never accounted for over 20 percent of the Reich's total supply. Synthetic production, on the other hand, had risen to 4,116,000 tons in 1941 (from 2,200,000 in 1939) and would continue rising steadily for another two years, until Allied bombers began pounding synthetic fuel plants.[78] However, these gains in synthetic production failed to offset the declining output of Rumanian oil fields. For various reasons, including the wells' gradually decreasing productivity, their yield had dropped from 8,701,000 tons in 1937 to 5,577,000 in 1941.[79] Much of this amount was needed by Rumania itself, whose own economy was straining to cope with the demands of war. Also, as noted previously, Rumanian deliveries to Germany had dropped off sharply in the last months of 1941. At the beginning of December 1941, Marshal Antonescu had personally warned Hitler by telegram that, while he would do everything he could to increase deliveries, "in the last five months we exported to Germany and

Italy amounts greater than the monthly output of 125,000 tons of fuel oil, which exhausted our available reserves."[80] Despite his repeated assurances that Rumania "would do everything possible to increase her deliveries to Germany,"[81] it appeared unlikely in the first months of 1942 that supplies of Rumanian oil would ever return to the levels of mid-1941. Indeed, on 12 February 1942 Antonescu informed Ribbentrop that, "as for crude oil, Rumania has contributed the maximum which it is in her power to contribute. She can give no more." Alluding to the much-discussed drive on the Caucasus, Antonescu added that "the only way out of the situation would be to seize territories rich in oil."[82]

This was certainly a compelling argument to use with the navy. As noted earlier, Raeder had complained as early as October 1941 to Hitler about the navy's oil situation and had warned him in December that it was now "very critical." By early 1942, the situation had deteriorated considerably, leaving the navy barely operational. The dash of the Brest group through the English Channel and on to Norway had consumed 20,000 tons of fuel oil alone, and by 1 April the navy's oil reserves had dropped to 150,000 tons.[83] Fortunately for Raeder, the shortage of fuel oil did not greatly hamper the operations of Dönitz's U-boats—which were still coming far nearer than any other Axis force to strangling the Allied war effort—because they operated on diesel oil, which was still in adequate supply.

The oil shortage virtually immobilized not only the German surface fleet but also that of the Italians. In December 1941 the Italian navy had received 29,600 tons of fuel oil, instead of the 40,000 promised, and it received only 13,500 in January 1942. "There is only one dark spot—the lack of oil," Ciano jotted in his diary on 8 February 1942. "Just now we have barely a hundred thousand tons, and only a negligible quantity gets through to us from abroad. This immobilizes the navy, particularly the large ships, which otherwise would enjoy total supremacy in the Mediterranean."[84]

The Luftwaffe also suffered oil shortages and in 1941 had been forced to draw upon its reserves for more than 25 percent of its consumption. As a result, its reserves at the end of 1941 fell to 254,000 tons, a great drop from the 613,000 tons it had a year earlier.[85] This alarmed Luftwaffe economists, who insisted that much more aviation fuel was urgently needed. Göring demanded a rapid increase in the output of existing synthetic fuel facilities—still the principal source of aviation fuel—and the immediate construction of additional plants. Despite these efforts, production increases could not be achieved overnight, and by the spring of 1942 the shortage of refined aviation fuel began significantly restricting the Luftwaffe's training program and preventing the renewal of an air offensive on anywhere near the scale of the Battle of Britain.

Considering that these oil shortages seriously threatened Germany's continued war effort, Hitler's plan to seize the Caucasus oil fields made perfect sense. As he argued to his generals early in 1942, their seizure would relieve Germany's critical oil shortages and enable it, if necessary, to continue fighting in a drawn-out war of attrition. Their seizure would also greatly offset the constant danger of Allied air attacks against the Ploesti plants in Rumania and its own synthetic fuel plants within the Reich itself. Additionally, Germany's armaments industry would benefit considerably from the seizure of extensive Caucasian manganese deposits. More important, the severance of the various railways between the oil and industrial regions and Moscow, the capture of the oil fields themselves, and the blocking of the vital Volga River system would be a massive, and probably mortal, blow to the Soviet economy and war effort.[86]

Surviving documentation reveals that very few *OKW* and *OKH* officers openly expressed doubts about Hitler's proposed campaign, and that none actually challenged its feasibility. It may be, of course, that after the dismissal of Brauchitsch and Rundstedt, none were brave enough to risk the Führer's wrath. It appears more likely, however, that Hitler's military advisers were in general agreement that, within the limited range of options available, his plan contained the most merit. Even Halder, who personally thought (but never made a strong case to the High Command) that the eastern armies should maintain an essentially defensive posture for the time being, apparently embraced the general plan. For example, he emphatically stated to a colleague that the conquest of the Caucasus was "absolutely vital" for Germany's continued war effort, adding that "the Reich will not survive for long" without Caucasus oil.[87] Having doubtless studied detailed briefings from the War Economy and Armaments Office, he knew that Germany's oil situation was critical. On 16 February 1942, for instance, this office had grimly concluded, in a lengthy report on Germany's fuel situation: "One thing is now clear: without Russian oil we simply cannot utilize fully the regions of Russia we now occupy. But above all, without Russian oil the German war machine must from now on become increasingly more impotent."[88]

Indeed, as the year progressed, senior German planners felt more persuaded that Hitler's emphasis on the capture of oil resources was well founded. For example, on 6 June (three weeks before the start of the campaign), the *OKW* glumly reported that oil supplies throughout the rest of 1942 would be "one of the weakest points in our defensive capabilities." The significance of this comment is obvious; *defensive* actions require far less oil than offensive actions, so the situation must certainly have looked grim. Because oil shortages were so critical, the report continued, "the operational freedom of all three services will be restricted, and the armaments industry will also suffer. Reserves have been reduced almost to nothing, so we are now forced to rely on production."[89]

It appears that during this period there was little discussion between Hitler and his military advisers over the important question of how Caucasus oil was to be transported to the Reich. The overworked Führer may not even have realized the importance of this matter, considering it best simply to cross that bridge when he came to it. Apparently, he supposed Axis convoys would carry much of the oil across the Black Sea to Rumanian ports, while the remainder would be carried across that sea, through the Bosporus and Dardanelles, and into the Aegean Sea. From there it would travel to Italian and occupied Greek ports. He had almost certainly not read the March 1941 report by the War Economy and Armaments Office, appended to a letter sent by Keitel to the *OKH*. This report warned that, even if the Caucasus oil fields could be captured intact, very little oil (only 10,000 tons per month) could be carried overland to Germany.[90] Moreover, even if the Black Sea could be made safe for shipping, there would be no ships available for the transport of Caucasus oil up the Danube because river tankers on the Danube were already working to capacity transporting Rumanian oil.[91] The only remaining route was across the Black Sea, through the Dardanelles, and on to Mediterranean ports. Accordingly, the report concluded, "The opening of the sea routes and the security of the tankers in the Black Sea is the prerequisite for the use of Russian supply sources in sufficient quantity to support the further continuation of the war." Clearly, to attain this prerequisite was virtually impossible by early 1942; the Germans would have had to wipe out the Soviet Black Sea Fleet (which still had, according to Raeder, "naval supremacy . . . [allowing] great freedom of movement")[92] and eliminate British air and sea power from the eastern Mediterranean.

Despite not considering how best to solve this logistical nightmare, Hitler was well aware of the need to make the Black Sea safe for German shipping. However, he and Raeder appear to have worried more about supplying German armies via the Black Sea than about shipping Caucasus oil back to the Reich or Rumanian refineries.[93]

When planning the forthcoming campaign, both Hitler and the German High Command placed considerable emphasis on the need to advance on the Caucasus oil fields so rapidly that the Soviets would not have time to destroy permanently the oil wells and refineries. If the latter were destroyed, the bulk of the Caucasus oil would have to be refined elsewhere until new refineries could be constructed. Only Rumanian refineries, which still had a considerable surplus refinement capacity,[94] could handle large quantities of additional crude, but (for the reasons mentioned earlier) it would be extremely difficult to ship significant amounts of oil from the Caucasus to Rumania.

During the planning stage of the Caucasus campaign, Hitler and the German High Command felt encouraged by typically optimistic (and typically inaccurate, as it turned out) intelligence reports on the status of the Soviet armed forces issued by the *Fremde Heere Ost* (Foreign Armies East), the department of the *OKH* responsible for the evaluation of all military intelligence about the Soviet Union. On 23 March 1942, for example, the *FHO* issued a detailed estimate of Soviet reserve strengths, which argued at length that the Soviet manpower potential was "by no means inexhaustible," but, rather, was almost completely drained. Similarly, in the first week of April the *FHO* issued another report, which concluded that "the enemy can no longer withstand losses such as he took in the battles from Bialystok to Vyazma-Bryansk [June to October 1941]. He also cannot for a second time throw reserves into the scales the way he did in the winter of 1941/42."[95]

WAR DIRECTIVE NO. 41

On 28 March, after a lengthy period of discussion, the *OKH* presented Hitler with a plan for the Caucasus offensive—to be code-named *Fall Blau,* or Case Blue—which closely paralleled his wishes. Hitler gave his endorsement to the basic concepts of the plan and turned it over to the *OKW* operations staff to write an implementing directive. After he drastically amended the draft Jodl submitted to him, he finally issued War Directive No. 41 on 5 April.

"The winter battle in Russia," Hitler proudly stated in the preamble to this directive, "is approaching its end. Through the unequaled courage and self-sacrificing devotion of our soldiers on the eastern front, a defensive success of the greatest scale has been achieved for German arms."[96] While this was certainly a fair and accurate appraisal, the following passage shows that he either misunderstood or deliberately misrepresented the fighting capability of the Soviet armed forces. "The enemy," he wrote, "has suffered the severest losses in men and matériel. In an effort to exploit apparent initial successes, he has expended during the winter the bulk of his reserves earmarked for later operations."

Spelling out the aim of the new offensive, he declared that "as soon as the weather and the state of the terrain provide the necessary prerequisites," it was important once again to seize the strategic initiative and, through German military superiority, "force our will upon the enemy." The objective this time was not only to destroy the remaining Soviet military potential, but also to "deprive them of their most important military-economic sources of strength." It was necessary, therefore, to deploy "all available forces of the German armed forces and our allies," although the occupied territories in western and northern Europe, especially the coasts, had to remain secure under all circumstances.

The general plan involved Army Group Center holding fast, while an effort would be made to "bring about the fall of Leningrad and link up with the Finns north of the city"; in the region of Army Group South, a major campaign would be launched into the Caucasus. Nothing was said about Moscow. Clearly, it could wait. However, because of the damage inflicted upon the eastern army in the winter months, these objectives (Leningrad and the Caucasus) would "have to be achieved only one at a time." Initially, therefore, "all available forces are to be assembled for *the main operation in the southern sector,* with the objective of destroying the enemy forward of the Don, in order to secure the oil regions of the Caucasus and the passes through the Caucasus [range] itself."

Before the major offensive into the Caucasus could commence, the directive stated, it would be necessary "to clear the Kerch Peninsula in the Crimea and to bring about the fall of Sevastopol." In preparation for this campaign, the Luftwaffe, and later the *Kriegsmarine,* would have the task of "energetically hindering enemy supply traffic in the Black Sea and the Kerch Straits." Along with these preliminary operations in the Crimea, army units would have to "cut off and destroy" the Soviet forces within the Izyum bulge.

Because of the general manpower shortage and difficulties involved in bringing up available units, the main operation "to seize the Caucasus front by decisively smashing and destroying Russian forces located in the Voronezh area to the south, west or north of the Don . . . will have to be carried out in a series of consecutive, but interconnected and supplementary, attacks." During these attacks, the directive stated, it was essential to conduct small, tight encirclements, because the sweeping maneuvers of the previous year had given too many Soviet troops "the possibility of escaping destruction."

The first phase of the offensive would commence with "an enveloping attack or breakthrough from the area south of Orel in the direction of Voronezh. Of the two panzer and motorized formations forming the pincers, the northern one will be stronger than the southern." The objective of this breakthrough was "the capture of Voronezh itself." Then, while certain infantry units were to establish a strong defensive front between Orel, the starting point of the attack, and Voronezh, panzer and motorized formations were to "continue the attack south from Voronezh along the Don with their left wing to support a second breakthrough toward the east, which was to be made from the general area of Kharkov." The primary objective of this second phase of the offensive was "not to crush the Russian front as such, but, in conjunction with the motorized formations advancing down the Don, to destroy the Russian forces." The third phase of the offensive was to be carried out so that the forces advancing down the Don could link up in the Stalingrad area with forces advancing from the Taganrog-Artemovska area between the lower course of the Don and Voroshilovgrad across the Donets to the east. These forces, as well as attempting to "establish bridgeheads east or south of the Don," were to "link up finally with the panzer army advancing on Stalingrad."

Ironically, in light of the fact that the campaign has come to be associated with the name of that city, the capture of Stalingrad was actually not a major objective. Hitler certainly considered it far less important than the Caucasus. The directive only stated that an attempt should be made "to reach" Stalingrad "or at least to subject this city to the bombardment of our heavy weapons to such an extent that it is eliminated as an armament and transportation center in the future." As the historian Gerhard Weinberg points out, it is ironic that "the place whose name will always be associated with one of the great battles of World War II was largely ignored by the Germans beforehand and renamed Volgograd by the Soviet Union afterwards."[97]

Hitler knew that his offensive had a significant weakness; it would leave a long and exposed flank along the Don. Accordingly, his directive stated, during the offensive it would be necessary to ensure not only "the strong protection of the northeast flank of the attack operation, but also . . . the immediate strengthening of the defensive positions along the Don." In a decision he would later curse himself for making, Hitler allotted this vital task to Italian, Hungarian, and Rumanian divisions.

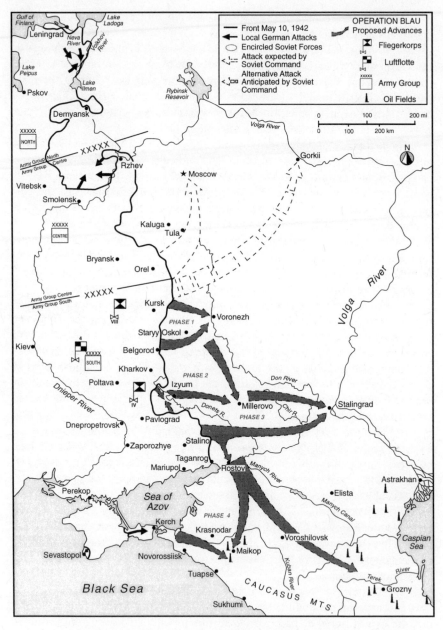

1. The summer campaign projected in Hitler's war directive of 5 April 1942

Because the Hungarians and Rumanians did not get on well, Hitler considered it best to keep their forces apart. He had long realized, however, that it was essential to use these forces in the 1942 offensive to bolster his own depleted armies.[98] In the weeks preceding the issue of War Directive No. 41, Keitel had visited the various capitals on Hitler's behalf and had succeeded in persuading the Italians and Hungarians to provide a full-strength army each and the Rumanians to provide two further armies in addition to their formations already on the eastern front.[99]

The Führer was also aware of the frightful death toll caused during the previous winter by a lack of prepared defensive positions. Although he firmly believed his new campaign would bring victory (at least in the southern sector) before the onset of another winter, he was not prepared to risk leaving his men exposed, without strong defensive positions, to the danger of both the winter and Soviet counterattacks. Particular emphasis, therefore, was "to be laid on very strong anti-tank defenses. From the beginning these positions are to be prepared with a view to them being possibly used in winter, and are to be equipped for such in every possible way."

Hitler insisted on a strong concentration of Luftwaffe forces for the offensive and ordered that, as in previous campaigns, their first task would be the destruction of "the enemy air force and its ground organization within the combat zone . . . with the concentration of all available forces." Then, aside from directly supporting the army, they must "cover the deployment of forces in the area of Army Group South by intensifying air defenses." If a concentration of Soviet forces is perceived, their "principal roads and the railways leading to the battle area are to be brought under constant attack well into the rear area." Emphasizing that major fighting (either offensive or defensive) could commence on other sectors of the eastern front immediately after, or even during, the Caucasus offensive, Hitler's directive also stated that "the possibility of a rapid transfer of Air Force units to the central and northern battle zones must be ensured, and the ground organization necessary for this must be maintained as far as possible."

Finally, Hitler's directive outlined briefly the main task allotted to the meager *Kriegsmarine* forces operating in the Black Sea. The German Black Sea Fleet—part of *Admiral* Marschall's *Marine-Gruppenkommando Süd,* which also controlled the German naval forces in the Aegean Sea—was, "insofar as our combat and escort forces and our tonnage permit, to assist in supplying the Army and Air Force by sea." Recognizing that the combat power of the Russian Black Sea Fleet remained "unbroken," Hitler ordered that "light naval forces" be transferred there and made ready for operations as soon as possible.

According to Paul Carell, author of several books on the eastern front, Hitler's directive for the summer campaign of 1942 was, next to the original directive for *Barbarossa,* "the most fateful paper of the Second World War."[100] Indeed, it committed German armed forces on the eastern front to a major campaign with economic objectives taking precedence over strictly military objectives, yet the attainment of these economic objectives had the potential to deliver a heavy, possibly mortal, blow to the Soviet Union. That the campaign ultimately failed, and led to the greatest defeat in German military history, does not mean that it could not have ended in triumph. As in 1941, German armed forces very nearly brought their eastern offensive to a successful conclusion. The following pages will show just how close Hitler actually came in 1942 to attaining his principal objectives in the east. With a particular emphasis on the Luftwaffe, this work shall closely examine the nature and scope of the vital role that airpower played in the campaign.

2

The Need to "Clear Up" the Crimea:
November 1941 to May 1942

Hitler's directive for the 1942 summer campaign in the east clearly reflects the unfinished nature of the previous year's campaign. Although the Führer claimed to Mussolini on 30 April 1942 that, with the exception of just a few "blemishes which will shortly be eradicated, . . . the Crimea finds itself in our hands," the reality was very different.[1] In April 1942 the Crimea was neither firmly nor entirely in German hands, as Hitler well knew. It was certainly not the "bastion in the Black Sea" that he described to his Italian counterpart. On the contrary, powerful Soviet forces still held both Sevastopol, the main Soviet naval base and shipyard on the Black Sea, and the strategically important Kerch Peninsula, which Hitler planned to use as a springboard to the Caucasus. Therefore, as he stated in his directive for the 1942 summer campaign, before the major offensive into the Caucasus could commence it would be necessary "to clear the Kerch Peninsula in the Crimea and to bring about the fall of Sevastopol."

A number of historians have criticized the reasoning behind the Crimean campaign. They insist that, because most of the Crimea was already in German hands in early 1942 and there was no major threat from those regions still occupied by Soviet forces, the campaign was a waste of valuable time, manpower, and matériel. For example, Gerhard Weinberg declares that Hitler should have drawn "the obvious conclusion" that there was "no need for a preliminary campaign to clear the Crimea." "Once the Germans took over the Soviet Black Sea coast," he argues, "*any* Soviet forces left on the Crimea would be doomed anyway."[2] In order to understand Hitler's and the German High Command's strategic reasoning behind this time-consuming "prerequisite," and to judge the merits of its critics' arguments, we need to focus briefly on the events that unfolded in the Crimea during the last months of 1941 and the first months of 1942.

THE FIRST CRIMEAN CAMPAIGN

As early as 22 July 1941, exactly one month after *Barbarossa* commenced, Hitler had ordered the eventual capture of the Crimea,[3] principally because of what he continued to perceive as the danger to Rumanian oil fields of Crimea-based Soviet bombers.[4] He apparently also saw the capture of the Crimea as a prerequisite for the planned offensive into the Caucasus. Once it had taken Sevastopol, von Manstein's powerful Eleventh Army—or at least its mountain troops[5]—would cross the Kerch Straits into the northern Caucasus in order to intercept enemy forces falling back from the lower Don.[6]

The Crimean campaign commenced in early October 1941. By 16 November, Manstein's Eleventh Army, supported by *Generaloberst* Alexander Löhr's *Luftflotte 4,* had forced its way across the strongly defended Perekop Isthmus into the Crimea and had managed, despite Soviet numerical superiority (both in the air and on the ground), to seize almost the entire peninsula. Enemy air attacks were extremely heavy, Manstein later complained: "The Soviet Air Force dominated our airspace! Its fighters and fighter-bombers incessantly attacked any discernible targets."[7] The situation was clearly grim:

> Not only did the frontline infantry and batteries have to dig in, but it was also necessary to dig pits for every vehicle and horse behind the battle zone as protection against the enemy aircraft. It got so bad that flak batteries no longer dared to fire in case they were immediately destroyed from the air. It wasn't until the last days of the offensive, after [fighter ace Werner] Mölders and his fighter group had been called in to assist the army, that the sky could be kept clear during the day. And at night not even Mölders could prevent the enemy air attacks.

The Red Air Force *(Voyenno-vozdushnyye sily,* or *VVS)* did not have things entirely its own way. Luftwaffe units (and not, of course, merely Mölder's own) provided German ground troops with effective support, both "indirect" and "direct." The powerful bomber and dive-bomber forces of *Fliegerkorps IV* struck first at all enemy airfields in the Crimea,[8] then attacked "troop concentrations, vehicular columns, tanks, field fortifications [and] bunkers," providing Manstein's troops with excellent support.[9] Meanwhile, units of both this air corps and *Fliegerkorps V* attacked the Soviet supply system, inflicting heavy damage on Soviet merchant shipping in the Black Sea and Sea of Azov, as well as on harbor installations at Jeisk, Novorossiisk, Primorsko-Akhtarskaya, Rostov, and Kerch.[10]

Despite this pounding, by early December—when strong Soviet counterattacks began to drive German troops back from the gates of Moscow—Manstein's own exhausted army had failed to capture the fortress-city of Sevastopol. The fall of this fortress would have been, to quote a secret British Air Ministry report, "a serious blow to the Soviet fleet, as it would mean that Russian warships would be compelled to use the greatly inferior ports of Novorossiisk, Batumi and possibly

Poti."[11] The main naval ports on the northern coast, Odessa and Nikolayev, had already been captured by Axis forces.

In December, Hitler still believed that the Crimea would have to be "neutralized" entirely in order to protect permanently Rumanian oil fields from Soviet bombers. This view, it should be noted, was shared not only by Manstein,[12] whose battered Eleventh Army would have to do the fighting in the Crimea, but also by Löhr, whose air fleet would have to support Manstein's ground assault.[13] Perhaps more important, it was also shared by Marshal Antonescu. His oil fields and refineries had been attacked (as had key bridges and harbor installations) as many as ninety-five times since *Barbarossa* began by twin-engined bombers of the Soviet Black Sea Fleet's naval air arm based at Odessa and on the Crimea itself.[14] These air attacks were generally weak and ineffectual, thanks to substantial German air defenses around the oil fields and refineries. When *Barbarossa* commenced, there were no less than twenty-four heavy and numerous light flak batteries around Ploesti alone.[15] The presence and quantity of these forces, which included strong fighter units, reflect Hitler's deep concern over the safety of his main source of oil.

Although one scholar has recently stated that Rumanian oil production was "unaffected" by these Soviet air attacks,[16] on several occasions they caused significant damage and heightened fears for the fields' safety. On 13 July 1941, for example, a raid left seventeen oil tanks ablaze at Ploesti's *Orion* refinery. Although the fires were extinguished within twenty-four hours and around 12,000 tons of oil were saved, this attack caused considerable damage and losses and claimed the lives of seven firemen. In total, 9,000 tons of oil and seventeen railway tanker wagons were destroyed in various raids against the *Orion* refinery alone.[17] Ploesti's *Vega* refinery was another frequent target, and on one occasion, the night of 18 July 1941, an attack resulted in the loss of around 2,000 tons of much-needed auto fuel.[18] These attacks would have greatly reinforced Hitler's belief that the Rumanian oil fields were highly vulnerable to air attack and that the Crimea, the only feasible base for Soviet long-range bomber fleets after the loss of the Ukraine, would have to be "neutralized" entirely in order to protect those oil fields from possible destruction.

Hitler also believed that the capture of the Sevastopol naval base and shipyards would significantly diminish the operational capability of the troublesome Soviet Black Sea Fleet. "The fall of Sevastopol," he told Count Ciano late in November, "should not be far distant. With it, any serious possibility of Russian naval interference in the Black Sea will collapse."[19] It was essential, he reasoned, to remove immediately the threat posed by that fleet to Axis shipping, especially to the supply convoys he planned to use in support of his armies as they advanced into the Caucasus. Much to his chagrin, the Soviet fleet (commanded by Vice Admiral Filipp Sergeevich Oktyabrskii) had suffered only negligible damage from air attacks by units of *Luftflotte 4* and continued to dominate totally the vast Black Sea, an expanse of water larger than the Baltic Sea. Far stronger than its

German and Rumanian counterparts, it then consisted of no less than a battle-ship, five cruisers, two flotilla leaders, fifteen destroyers, and forty-one submarines, as well as numerous torpedo boats, minelayers, minesweepers, patrol boats, fast gunboats, and auxiliary vessels. It also commanded the many light naval vessels of Rear Admiral Sergei Gorshkov's Azov Flotilla and an air arm with over 300 aircraft, half of which were fighters.[20]

In the first months of *Barbarossa,* vessels and aircraft from this powerful naval force had attacked Constanza, the Rumanian naval port serving as the main base to the small Rumanian fleet and, later, the even smaller German fleet. A defensive minefield claimed the flotilla leader *Moskva,* prompting the Soviet command to keep its surface vessels away for several months. The fleet's Crimea-based aircraft continued to strike at Constanza, however, conducting as many as thirty-four day and twenty-five night attacks on that city and its surroundings by the end of 1941.[21] They also attacked the Rumanian naval bases of Galatz (inland, on the Danube) and Sulina, as well as strategic targets such as the great railway bridge across the Danube at Chernovod (the most vulnerable point of the oil pipeline—which they badly damaged on 9 October) and the Ploesti installations. Results were generally poor and losses always high. In the first four months alone, the Luftwaffe mission in Rumania claimed 143 enemy aircraft destroyed, 69 by antiaircraft guns and the rest by fighters.

The Soviet fleet had also greatly hindered Axis efforts to seize Odessa, the commercial port and naval base on the northwestern coast of the Black Sea. The German High Command had been hoping to capture this port quickly and to use it and nearby Kherson to supply troops operating on the southern flank. In August, they even had a number of small transport vessels anchored at Burgas and Varna (Bulgaria's main ports on the Black Sea), loaded with ammunition and equipment, waiting for a signal to set sail for Odessa.[22] However, the Soviet fleet ensured that German troops would have to wait for those supplies. Its cruisers and destroyers (and occasionally its aircraft) pounded the Rumanian units that first tried to take Odessa in August. It then landed fresh reinforcements and equipment in time to slow down the advance in September of a large German-Rumanian combined force, which suffered a very high casualty rate. The fleet also began evacuating civilians, wounded soldiers, and equipment.

Finally, when it became clear to Oktyabrskii in mid-October that Odessa could not be held and that the troops there could be used more effectively in the defense of the Crimea, the Soviet naval and merchant fleets conducted an impressive Dunkirk-like evacuation. Despite unremitting attacks from aircraft of *Fliegerkorps IV,* perhaps as many as 350,000 soldiers and civilians and 200,000 tons of matériel were ferried to Sevastopol.[23] Several ships were sunk and many others damaged by German dive-bombers, but losses were surprisingly low for such a large undertaking. Operating from the well-equipped Sevastopol base, vessels from the Soviet naval fleet continued to upset German attempts to supply its eastern army by sea. Submarines struck at German, Rumanian, and Bulgarian

traffic along the west coast of the Black Sea, sinking 29,000 gross registered tonnage (GRT) before year's end. Soviet warships (including those anchored in the
harbor itself) unleashed their full firepower on German positions in the southwestern Crimea. The capture of Sevastopol, Hitler fumed, could wait no longer.

Just as important, the Führer believed that the total clearing of the Crimea
would have a favorable effect on the attitude of neutral Turkey, which he constantly feared would succumb to what Gerhard Weinberg recently described as
"endless efforts, projects, schemes, and hopes on the part of the British" for it to
join the side of the Allies.[24] The Turks had a largely obsolete but still sizable fleet
in the Black Sea and numerous well-equipped divisions stationed along their
borders with Russia, Bulgaria, and Greece. Their intervention alongside the Russians or western Allies would be a major setback for the Germans. Moreover, Turkey was the Reich's major source of chromium, a metal essential for the manu-
facture of almost all armaments. Since the imposition of an Anglo-French naval
blockade, Germany had become reliant on Turkey for this precious substance. It
was therefore essential, the Führer reasoned, to convince the Turkish government
that *his* forces, not Stalin's, were dominant in the regions immediately to the
north and that no alliance with the Allies should be made.

Accordingly, in War Directive No. 39, issued on 8 December, Hitler insisted
again upon Sevastopol's immediate capture.[25] Resigned to the temporary break-
down of his blitz campaign in the east, he admitted in the directive that, because
of the early and severe onset of winter and consequent logistical problems, his
forces were compelled "to abandon immediately all major offensive operations
and to go over to the defensive." However, even despite the pounding his eastern
forces were receiving, he insisted that Army Group South continue to push on
toward its objectives in the Crimea and then, if possible, toward those in the Caucasus.

The assault on Sevastopol (first planned for 27 November) was now scheduled to commence on 10 December, but bad weather severely disrupted Eleventh
Army's preparations and caused a further seven-day delay. Manstein believed
that he could take the city before the end of the year. Even if he could not, he
reasoned, he could drive a deep wedge through the northeastern perimeter to a
point allowing his heavy artillery to sweep Severnaya Bay, thereby cutting the
vital Soviet naval lifeline to the historic fortress-city.[26] Aware that the fortress
would be a difficult nut to crack, he committed six of his seven divisions to the
attack, leaving only one German division and two Rumanian brigades to protect
the rest of the Crimea, including the vulnerable Kerch Peninsula. In other words,
he left fewer than 20,000 men to guard an area the size of Belgium.

On 17 December, Eleventh Army, supported by units of *Luftflotte 4,*
launched its attack on Sevastopol (quickly placed by the Transcaucasian Front
under Oktyabrskii's direct command).[27] Advancing under cover of a heavy air
and artillery barrage, Manstein's troops initially made encouraging progress.
They broke the fortress's outer ring of fortifications on the first day and made

significant but steadily smaller gains for several more days. By 22 December, the 22nd Infantry Division had pushed its way through the second defensive line and, in spite of stiffening resistance, was bearing down on the third and final line, within sight of Severnaya Bay. The previous day, however, Oktyabrskii managed to bring in by ship (despite the fact that the harbor had been repeatedly mined from the air by aircraft of *Fliegerkorps IV*)[28] a rifle division, a naval infantry brigade, and 3,000 replacements. These fresh troops, coupled with supporting fire from cruisers and destroyers from the Soviet fleet, soon slowed the German attack to little more than a snail's pace.[29]

Things got considerably worse for Manstein in the last week of 1941. Commencing the day after Christmas, Gorshkov's Azov Flotilla and vessels from Oktyabrskii's main fleet, supported by the latter's air arm, landed troops on the Crimean side of the narrow Kerch Straits (less than four kilometers wide in places). These landings were hastily organized and executed in a primitive manner—without proper landing craft or equipment barges—and, as a result, most were unsuccessful. Troops landed at no fewer than ten locations on the Kerch Peninsula but were able to make good their foothold at only four. However, they quickly established strong bridgeheads at those four sites: on either side of Kerch (26 December), Feodosiya (three days later), and Eupatoria (5 January 1942).[30]

Oktyabrskii was an extremely cautious man with little tactical flair. He was apparently shaken by the loss of the flotilla leader *Moskva* in June 1941 and the cruiser *Chervona Ukraina* in August (sunk by Stukas during an attack on Sevastopol harbor). These were acceptable losses, given the size of his fleet and the seriousness of the situation, but he now adopted an almost completely defensive strategy. It was only in response to direct orders from his superiors that he took great risks to ensure the success of the daring Kerch landings that they had ordered, such as using his largest warships to carry troops in heavy fog through mined stretches of partly icebound water easily within reach of German bombers. The first wave at Feodosiya, for instance, consisted of 23,000 men, carried by two cruisers, seven destroyers, six minesweepers, fifteen subchasers, and fourteen transport ships. German air attacks were sporadic and light and caused only minor damage; the only vessels from this initial convoy put out of action were a minesweeper and a guard boat.[31]

The success of the main landings made it patently clear to the command staff of *Fliegerkorps IV* that its air-mining efforts around the coastline of the Kerch Peninsula, conducted in conjunction (but not close cooperation) with *Admiral Schwarzes Meer,* the Germans' own Black Sea Fleet, had been an outright failure. "The results of the air-mining operations bear no relationship to the effort expended," the air corps staff bitterly complained in a radio message to both the admiral of that so-called fleet (in reality only a flotilla of light naval vessels) and the naval liaison officer with Manstein's army.[32] Because the mining missions bore no fruit and only resulted in "a useless wasting of *Fliegerkorps IV*'s stretched-out forces," the radio message continued, the German fleet should stop insisting on these missions. "The aircraft thus freed up can better help the army in its struggle on the ground and against the ships it needs to target." As it was, thick fog, low cloud, and snowstorms in this period prevented all but a few of *Fliegerkorps IV*'s aircraft from attacking the first waves of Soviet troops. *General* Otto Hoffman von Waldau, head of the Luftwaffe's operations staff, was clearly frustrated that his airmen were powerless to counter the initial landings. "I only hope," he noted in his personal diary on 29 December, "this weather will clear!"[33] His hope *was* realized, but not for several days. By then it was too late; the enemy had firmly dug in.

General Halder had actually feared these landings since early December, when he first learned of "unusual [Soviet] movements on the east shore of the Sea of Azov."[34] The Soviet troop buildup had been detected and monitored by reconnaissance units of *Luftflotte 4*, which passed this information on to the High Command, as well as to local army and navy commanders. Its warnings to *Admiral Schwarzes Meer*, for instance, can be found in the fleet's extensive war diaries.[35] Nonetheless, the meager and quickly outnumbered German and Rumanian forces protecting the Crimea were unable to prevent the landings or dislodge the more than 40,000 troops dug in at Kerch and Feodosiya by 29 December.

Fearing that his soldiers would be cut off and destroyed by the rapidly reinforced troops landed at Feodosiya, *Generalleutnant* Hans Graf von Sponeck, commander of the German troops defending the Kerch Peninsula, ordered his men to withdraw to the Crimean mainland. Manstein, who still thought it possible to contain the bridgeheads, tried in vain to countermand Sponeck's order and direct his men to throw back the Soviets before they could consolidate their positions. Because of alleged radio communication difficulties, however, his instructions were apparently never received and the withdrawal continued.[36] As Halder jotted unhappily in his diary, 29 December was "a *very* heavy day!" "In the Crimea," he continued, "Count von Sponeck withdraws the 46th Division from the Kerch Peninsula at the first impression of an enemy landing at Feodosiya. He has immediately been removed from his post, but the damage done can hardly be made good." Two days later ("another heavy day!"), Halder noted that Manstein had suspended the assault on Sevastopol in order "to free up forces for Feodosiya. There the enemy has reinforced and expanded [his beachhead]." Oktyabrskii, relieved that his risks had paid off handsomely, was as delighted as Halder was dejected. "The troops of the Transcaucasian Front and the ships of the Black Sea Fleet," he informed Sevastopol's defenders on 30 December, "have taken the towns of Kerch and Feodosiya. The fighting continues . . . [but now] our units are moving into the rear of the enemy troops besieging Sevastopol."[37]

In close but not always effective cooperation with Soviet ground and air forces, Oktyabrskii's fleet worked tirelessly and courageously in this otherwise chaotic period. On 5 January 1942, it landed a battalion of naval infantry at Eupatoria, a Black Sea port on the western side of the Crimean Peninsula, while its destroyers covered them from the sea with their gunfire. Although the 150th Infantry Regiment (hastily diverted by Manstein from Sevastopol) was able to destroy these forces in just over two days, the Soviet fleet continued reinforcing by sea the troops already on the Kerch Peninsula.[38] "The situation in the Crimea remains serious for the Axis forces," reported British Air Ministry intelligence officers, who had cracked the Luftwaffe's "Enigma" codes and were reading its secret radio communications.[39] Encouraged by the continuing Soviet landings, they optimistically stated that the threat to Sevastopol appeared to be "neutralised" for some time.

The Kerch Straits froze over twice during the winter, allowing Soviet engineers to build an ice road. During the twenty-seven days this ice road was open— 28 December to 1 January, and 20 January to 11 February—they sent across to the Kerch Peninsula an impressive amount of men and matériel, including 96,618 well-equipped troops, 23,903 horses, 6,513 motor vehicles, and hundreds of artillery pieces.[40] If Manstein hoped to recapture this region with his exhausted army (many companies were without commissioned officers and had only 40 or 50 men out of a normal complement of 150 to 200), he clearly had a fight on his hands.

THE SHORT-LIVED SONDERSTAB KRIM

Painfully aware that the situation in the south was now as critical as in the other sectors of the eastern front, Göring hastily organized a new tactical operations staff to provide maximum air support to ground forces engaged in severe defensive battles in the southern zone.[41] The man he chose to head this new operations staff was a much respected commander: General der Flieger Robert Ritter von Greim, head of Fliegerkorps V, whose impressive career included distinguished service in the First World War and, in an organizational capacity, with Chiang Kai-shek's Chinese air force in the 1920s.

Göring, who invited Greim to Karinhall on 7 January 1942 for a personal briefing, instructed the latter to organize this operations staff quickly from members of his Fliegerkorps headquarters, which had recently been transferred from near Rostov to Brussels. With his staff he was to proceed urgently to Poltava (450 kilometers due north of the Crimea) and report to Löhr's Luftflotte 4, the overworked air fleet he was to assist.[42] Greim's air corps had actually belonged to Luftflotte 4 from the onset of Barbarossa until 30 November 1941, when half its staff and various units were transferred to Brussels in order to be used for minelaying operations against the British.[43] At that time Göring, Jeschonnek, and the Luftwaffe High Command actually believed the war in the east was almost over. Therefore (although it seems foolish in hindsight), they even began sending air units back to Germany for rehabilitation or further transfer to the west and south.[44] On 29 October, Hitler himself promised Mussolini (after telling him that the war in the east was already won) that he would send a significant part of Kesselring's Luftflotte 2—then supporting Amy Group Center—to assist Axis activities in the Mediterranean. Much to the horror and disgust of Generalfeld-

marschall von Bock, still battling forward toward Moscow, the first units of *Luftflotte 2* were withdrawn on 5 November.[45] In December, when he was forced to admit that the struggle in the east was far from over, Hitler had to order many air units back to the eastern front, especially to reinforce the understrength and overworked *Fliegerkorps VIII,* commanded by *General der Flieger* von Richthofen.[46] After the transfer to the Mediterranean of *Luftflotte 2* and *Fliegerkorps II* (minus *Nahkampfführer II,* a close air support unit that remained behind), Richthofen's air corps was operating virtually alone in the critical central zone before Moscow.[47]

In the absence of Greim's air corps, the vast regions of the German-controlled Soviet south were also proving far too difficult for *Luftflotte 4*'s single corps headquarters *(General der Flieger* Kurt Pflugbeil's *Fliegerkorps IV)*[48] to manage by itself. *Fliegerkorps IV*'s massive zone of operations, *excluding* the Crimea, was an area almost the size of prewar Germany. This air corps helped First Panzer Army and Sixth and Seventeenth Armies stem Soviet advances farther to the north in the regions around Taganrog, the Donets Basin, and Izyum. It also committed numerous squadrons to attacking the Soviet Black Sea Fleet and Azov Flotilla and supporting the small German fleet and Manstein's troops in the Crimea.[49]

That is not to say that Pflugbeil's *Fliegerkorps IV* provided Manstein's troops with little support in their desperate efforts to hold the Crimea. On the contrary, units of Pflugbeil's overworked corps, flying from Kherson and Nikolayev in appalling weather conditions, continued to fly reconnaissance missions and hammer away at the Soviet beachheads, harbors, and supply ships.[50] The Soviet buildup at Feodosiya in the days following the successful initial landings, by way of illustration, was severely hampered by air attacks. "In a troop supply and support sense," a Red Army general staff report of 1943 states:

> The fact that from the moment of the occupation of Feodosiia enemy aviation, using the proximity of airfields, attacked the port, the town, and approaching transports was of great significance. Four large transports, including the "Tashkent" (one of the powerful ships most adaptable for the transport of a large number of horses), had sunk very quickly and sat on the bottom in port. Much ammunition and food had sunk with the transports.
>
> Enemy aviation operated with impunity, since our fighters, operating from inadequate and distant airfields on the Taman Peninsula [which forms the eastern bank of the Kerch Straits], rarely appeared for 10–15 minutes. When our fighters arrived, the enemy was leaving; he bided his time until the departure of our planes, then he fiercely attacked Feodosiia again. It was a great mistake that the transport of sufficient anti-aircraft artillery was not planned in the first supply trains.[51]

This report greatly disparages the important role played in the landings by the *VVS.* Soviet aircraft were not, as claimed, only flying from bases on the other side of the Kerch Straits; fighter units flew from Sevastopol and, once airfields on the Kerch Peninsula were recaptured, from Feodosiya, Semikolodsy, Beregovo, Kerch, and (across the straits) Tamanskaya. Bombers flew from airfields near Krasnodar (in the northwestern Caucasus).[52] These units were "very active" in support of the advancing Soviet ground forces, according to one writer, and "although a much smaller number of German planes eased the situation to some extent, [they] could not change it."[53] Indeed, numerically inferior Luftwaffe units battled valiantly in the Crimea against both the Red Air Force and Army, but while their attacks inflicted considerable damage on the Soviets (particularly on the ground), they were unable to do more than slow down the Soviet advance. Nonetheless, in light of the prevailing conditions, this was still a significant achievement. Even Halder, who ordinarily paid little attention to Luftwaffe activities, noted in his diary on 2 January 1942—"a day of wild fighting"—that "in the Crimea a temporary check has been imposed on the enemy by the Luftwaffe."

Owing to the inability of existing forces to drive the Soviets from the Crimea, Löhr diverted Greim's new operations staff, then en route to Poltava, south to the Crimean town of Sarabus, where Manstein had his headquarters.[54] It arrived on 15 January, the very day Manstein's troops launched their attack on Feodosiya and other Soviet-held positions in the eastern Crimea. The attack's initial progress was very good, prompting a relieved Waldau to jot in his diary that it had "taken the Russians by surprise" and that hopefully the possibility now existed "to resolve the situation" at Feodosiya.[55]

When Greim arrived in Poltava, a conference was hastily arranged to discuss military objectives, the intended role of the Luftwaffe, and methods of coordinating air and ground activities. *Luftflotte 4* created a new tactical air command for Greim, named *Sonderstab Krim* (Special Staff Crimea), which would support Manstein's Eleventh Army as it attempted to drive the Soviets from the Crimea. *Sonderstab Krim* initially received the 4th Squadron of the 122nd Long-Range Reconnaissance Group, the Headquarters Staff and the 3rd Group of the 77th Fighter Wing, the 2nd and 3rd Groups of the 77th Dive Bomber Wing, the 3rd Group of the 27th Bomber Wing, the 3rd Group of the 51st "Edelweiss" Bomber Wing, and the 1st Group of the 100th Bomber Wing.[56] Most of these units, which arrived at various times throughout January, were based at Sarabus in the Crimea, although a few had to operate from more remote airfields at Nikolayev and Kherson. *Oberst* Wolfgang von Wild's recently formed *Fliegerführer Süd* (Air Command South) was also subordinated to *Sonderstab Krim,* because its specialized sea bomber and mining squadron (Blohm und Voß BV 38s) and naval reconnaissance units (Arado Ar 196s), which were to be transferred to airfields at Saki in the Crimea, would be invaluable in surveillance and antiamphibious operations.[57]

The operational strength of units assigned to *Sonderstab Krim* was low, as a result of difficulties experienced by the hastily assembled ground organization and, more important, to supply and maintenance problems caused by the unusually severe winter. Snow and mud frequently prevented spare parts and other supplies from reaching their destinations. Runways had to be constantly cleared of snow and warming equipment, of which there was far too little, employed to get engines starting. In most cases, this equipment consisted of tin ovens (often made from gasoline cans) connected to long, flexible tubes directing the heat onto engines and control surfaces. To ensure that aircraft on standby-alert duty had engines warm enough to start at short notice, "alert boxes" were frequently used. These were heated wooden shacks with large holes cut in one side, into which the noses of aircraft were inserted. Low-viscosity lubricants and special hydraulic fluids that did not freeze in extreme temperatures were essential. On many occasions even the tools used by maintenance personnel had to be heated to prevent their causing frost burns to the users.[58]

The morale of airmen and ground crews—who generally lived in poor accommodations, often with little or no heating—dropped in keeping with the temperature. Very few had received leave, or even a day off, since the eastern campaign first began. Constant snow and biting blizzards made life for many seem unbearable. Medical officers reported an increase of men suffering not only from frostbite and other physical effects of the cold but also from nervous exhaustion.

Although weather conditions were not quite as harsh in this zone as in the far north, or even before Moscow, barely a third of *Sonderstab Krim*'s aircraft were operational in mid-January 1942.[59] Operational levels this low were not limited to air units operating in the southern zone. Indeed, they were extremely low along the entire eastern front. On 10 January 1942, the *Luftflotten* in the east had a combined actual strength of 1,591 aircraft (excluding transport and army service planes), of which only 633 (40 percent) were operational.[60] When one considers that the eastern *Luftflotten* had deployed 2,703 aircraft on the eve of *Barbarossa* (with the same exclusions), and 2,080 (77 percent) were then operational, it is easy to imagine the poor state those *Luftflotten* were in by January 1942.[61]

Sonderstab Krim began operating just in time to participate in the recapture of Feodosiya, which Manstein accomplished on 18 January after several days of bitter fighting. Its fighters chased off their Soviet counterparts, still flying from Sevastopol, Semikolodsy, Beregov, Kerch, and Tamanskaya. Its dive-bomber units provided Manstein's men with effective support as they pounded enemy troop concentrations, artillery batteries, and airstrips. The bomber units now assigned to this staff had already done considerable damage to the harbor installations in Feodosiya, and they continued to target this and other ports in the Black Sea and Sea of Azov, as well as Soviet supply ships en route to the Kerch Peninsula.[62] Manstein had previously doubted whether he could expect any Luftwaffe assistance at all, because bad weather over the last few days had kept most aircraft grounded. However, he later wrote, when Feodosiya was recaptured "it now turned out that, despite the dreadful weather conditions, the Luftwaffe had actually done a fine job, having sunk several transport vessels."[63]

Manstein's troops quickly reached the heavily defended Parpach Line, the narrow, eighteen-kilometer-wide isthmus joining the Kerch Peninsula to the rest of the Crimea. Despite this good start, Manstein's intention to destroy the Soviet forces huddled behind the Parpach Line suffered a major setback. On the very day he retook Feodosiya, a crisis developed 400 kilometers to the north, forcing both Army Group South and *Luftflotte 4* to shift quickly their operational focuses. Troops of Marshal Timoshenko's Southwestern Front had poured across the Donets River on either side of the town of Izyum, 116 kilometers southeast of Kharkov, and torn a large and constantly expanding hole in the thin line of the overstretched German Seventeenth Army.[64] "We shall go through difficult days before this crisis is resolved," Halder noted unhappily in his diary on 19 January. Indeed, the Soviets rapidly expanded this breach to more than eighty kilometers wide and nearly as deep, thereby seriously endangering Seventeenth and Sixth Armies, their railway supply and communications routes, and those of First Panzer Army. "The worst thing is that we have nothing that can meet the enemy tanks on anything approaching equal terms," Halder complained the following day.

Löhr immediately perceived the danger and directed *Fliegerkorps IV* to concentrate all available aircraft against the Soviet breakthrough, particularly in the region of Seventeenth Army.[65] He also directed *Sonderstab Krim* to release key units for commitment in the Izyum area, thereby effectively breaking up Greim's new command before it could attempt with the mass of its forces the task for which it was recently formed: the destruction of Soviet forces still in the Crimea. Greim had to send north some of his best units, including a fighter group, a dive-bomber group, and two bomber groups.[66]

Although necessary, the transfer of *Fliegerkorps IV* and *Sonderstab Krim* units to the Izyum area was also a case of "robbing Peter to pay Paul." It left ground forces in the vast areas to the south with barely adequate air support. Special missions involving concentrated airpower were out of the question. *General* Waldau, for instance, noted in his diary on 24 January that, because of severe frosts in the Caspian Sea region, large-scale Soviet oil shipments were now having to travel overland by rail (instead of by sea). They thus became a superb target for the Luftwaffe. "Unfortunately," he lamented, "we are stuck with the mass of our forces at Izyum."[67]

As it happened, bad weather conditions seriously impeded the performance of air units supporting *Armee-Gruppe von Kleist* (the army command hastily formed by Bock and placed under Kleist's operational command) as it struggled to stem the Soviet tide surging forward past Izyum toward Dnepropetrovsk. Nonetheless, when conditions allowed, they still managed to make their presence felt. Their interdiction attacks on Red Army railheads and mobilization points, supply systems, and march routes made it difficult for the Soviets to advance or regroup effectively (and, on rare occasions, even to move large bodies of troops in the open). They airlifted supplies to isolated German troops, assisted the penetration of defenses, and, in close cooperation with ground forces, destroyed enemy positions, pockets of resistance, and spearheads.

The Soviet attack lost momentum as it cut deeper into German-held territory in the last days of January. It was hampered both by stiffening German defenses and by the difficulty of maintaining supply lines during unremitting snowstorms and temperatures as low as −35°C. The Soviet thrust was also handicapped by its isolated nature, which allowed Bock to shore up steadily both shoulders of the bulge and, by 11 February, to seal off the breakthrough.

Meanwhile, the transfer to the Izyum region of much-needed air units, and several valuable army units (including a tank battalion), had been the last straw for Manstein, who realized that he now lacked the forces to exploit immediately his success at Feodosiya. These ill-timed transfers coincided with a renewed Soviet attack on Sudak, a town on the south Crimean coast halfway between Yalta and Feodosiya. A small naval infantry force, supported by three destroyers and several smaller vessels, landed at Sudak and struck at Manstein's southern flank until beaten back (and evacuated by sea) several days later. The frustrated general was forced to postpone his attack on the Parpach Line until after he had dealt with this threat to his flank and built up again the supplies and forces necessary to complete the main task. He was bitterly aware that this postponement worked to the Soviets' advantage; air reconnaissance missions revealed that, despite the valiant interdiction efforts of Greim's remaining air units, thousands of Soviet reinforcements were pouring across the Kerch Straits and digging themselves in behind the Parpach Line. As he later recorded in his memoirs:

> We soon discovered that the enemy was pushing reinforcements across to the Kerch Peninsula. Now having his "Kerch ice road," he could put up with the loss of Feodosiya harbor. Air reconnaissance continually showed the enemy to be concentrated in strength in his Black Sea harbors and the airfields in the area north of the Caucasus. As early as 29 January an assessment of the enemy showed his forces on the Parpach front to be more than nine divisions, two rifle brigades and two tank brigades [with new T-34s]. What's more, the Sevastopol front, especially the artillery, was also becoming active again.[68]

Indeed, under the cover of darkness or foggy conditions vessels from Oktyabrskii's fleet continued to carry reinforcements, heavy weapons, and supplies into Sevastopol. They also evacuated the wounded and fired at German positions with their heavy guns.[69]

Manstein was gravely aware that his depleted and worn-out forces, committed to containing possible Soviet breakouts from both ends of the Crimea (from Sevastopol on the west and the Kerch Peninsula on the east), had to keep the Soviet troops bottled up until he could gain enough reinforcements to plan further offensive actions of his own. This, he knew, could take months. In the meantime, he could not allow the Soviets to exploit their recent achievements in the Crimea, "where their control of the sea offered them especially good prospects." "Success here," he later explained, "could have had significant repercussions on the entire situation in the east—politically with regard to the attitude of Turkey and economically through the recovery of the peninsula for air attacks against the Rumanian oil regions."[70]

THE DISSOLUTION OF *SONDERSTAB KRIM*

Meanwhile, Greim was struggling to forge the remains of his command into a cohesive and effective fighting force. This proved to be an extremely difficult task; *Sonderstab Krim,* still only a few weeks old, had been hastily formed to support the army in a region without a developed ground organization or supply system. Fuel, ammunition, spare parts, and other essential supplies arrived slowly and in insufficient quantities. This resulted in lower operational levels than was caused by bad weather alone. Control of operations was continually hampered by poor communications, in part caused by the weather but mainly the result of woefully insufficient signals personnel and equipment. Also, existing airfields on the Crimean Peninsula itself, of which there were few, were unsatisfactory for large-scale operations. Unfortunately, no materials or equipment were available for the construction of even makeshift runways. As a result, bombers could not operate from these fields but had to fly from distant fields at Kherson and Nikolayev. This increased flying distances to the targets and reduced the bomb loads that could be carried. Moreover, for much of January and February 1942, the entire region was covered by low cloud or extensive ground fog, or whipped by strong winds or snowstorms. As already noted, these weather conditions adversely influenced air operations over the Crimea.

Despite these difficulties, Greim was determined to contain the Soviets. Fearing further landings at any moment, he directed his reconnaissance units to conduct unremitting surveillance missions over Crimean coastlines and, in coordination with light German naval forces, over the vast expanses of the Black Sea. He ordered other units to interdict traffic on the "ice road" across the Kerch Straits and to attack vessels still supplying Soviet forces at both ends of the Crimea. Ground attack units were to strike at those forces, especially the divisions dug in behind the Parpach Line, while fighters were to keep the sky clear of their Soviet counterparts and attack their airfields.[71]

Many of Greim's units were not suitably trained or equipped for these tasks.[72] For example, the 1st Group, 100th Bomber Wing *(I./K.G. 100)*, was a mine-laying unit with no specialized training in antishipping attacks, the difficult task assigned to it. The 3rd Group, 27th Bomber Wing *(III./K.G. 27)*, was given this same assignment but, because of supply problems, received no suitable bombs or detonators. These supply problems also curtailed the operations of the 3rd Group, 51st Bomber Wing *(III./K.G. 51)*, recently returned from the Izyum area. This unit *was* trained for antishipping operations, but it received too few bombs and had to operate from the unprepared Saki airfield on the western Crimea. As a result, it was able to undertake only a small number of missions. A lack of specialized equipment and suitably equipped airfields (with navigational beacons, boundary lights, "visual lorenz" systems, and flare paths) also thwarted plans for concentrated night attacks against supply movements to Sevastopol by all bomber groups. Superb antiaircraft defenses within the fortress inflicted prohibitive losses on aircraft attempting daylight raids. Accordingly, such missions were cancelled, except for times when weather conditions provided aircraft with adequate cover. On those occasions, of course, the aircrafts' own gun-and bomb-aiming accuracy was greatly diminished.

Because of the many problems resulting from its hasty formation, *Sonderstab Krim* never had the ability to make a significant impact on the conduct of operations in the Crimea and Black Sea. Nor was it given time to overcome its unavoidable "teething problems" and prove its real worth. On 11 February 1942, Göring ordered its dissolution. Units originally drawn from *Fliegerkorps V* reverted to their original corps headquarters. Two months later (as described later), that corps headquarters, still under Greim's leadership, became the nucleus of *Luftwaffenkommando Ost* (Air Force Command East). This new command was formed on 10 April to provide air support for Army Group Center in the absence of Richthofen's powerful *Fliegerkorps VIII*, which had, ironically, been sent westward for brief rehabilitation in preparation for its participation in the siege of Sevastopol.[73]

Despite its many problems and its dissolution after just one month of service, *Sonderstab Krim* had not been a failure. On the contrary, in its short life it provided local air, naval, and ground forces with the best reconnaissance information weather conditions permitted. It claimed to have destroyed sixty-seven enemy aircraft, of which twenty-three were shot down in the air. It sunk or put out of action 25,000 tons of Soviet shipping and badly damaged a pilot boat and lightly damaged an E-boat. It also wrecked various harbor installations at Kerch and Kamysh-Burun. Its claimed destruction of ground targets included 335 motor and horse-drawn vehicles, fourteen artillery batteries (of which three were antiaircraft), fourteen railway trains, seven locomotives, ten fuel tank trucks, one fuel depot, one cantonment camp, and one supply depot. Additionally, its attacks on troop and matériel concentrations, headquarters, and defense installations often produced pleasing results.[74]

Göring replaced Greim with *Oberst* Wolfgang von Wild, whose *Fliegerführer Süd* (Air Command South) assumed command of the remaining air units in the Crimea on 18 February. Wild proved an excellent choice of commander. During the First World War he had served as a cadet in the Imperial German Navy, and he was commissioned into the Weimar Republic's small fleet in 1923. In the mid-1930s he transferred to the newly formed Luftwaffe and by the outbreak of hostilities in 1939 had risen to the rank of major. With his naval background, it was appropriate that he saw action during the Polish campaign in one of the coastal air units. From April to October 1941, he commanded *Fliegerführer Ostsee* (Air

Command Baltic), which distinguished itself in the far north by its excellent reconnaissance and antishipping work, conducted in close cooperation with the local naval command.[75] When Göring disbanded Air Command Baltic in October, he sent Wild, his staff, and various elements (notably *Aufkl. Gr. 125*—the 125th Reconnaissance Group), after rehabilitation in Germany, to the south of Russia. There they resurfaced as *Fliegerführer Süd*. Thus, as well as having already briefly commanded sea-mining and bombing squadrons and long-range naval reconnaissance units over the Black Sea, Wild brought solid experience in naval support and antishipping operations to his new post as commander of all air units in the Crimea.

Like his predecessor, the new Crimean air commander was very worried about further Soviet landings on the Crimea or the southern coast of the Black Sea. Accordingly, the principal mission he assigned to his units was the surveillance of enemy activities. His reconnaissance units were to conduct constant surveillance missions over Crimean and Sea of Azov coastlines and, in coordination with light German naval forces in some regions, over the expanses of the Black Sea. The other main mission was the interdiction of enemy supply movements. Although Wild had fewer bomber and destroyer units at his disposal than Greim previously had, he directed them to attack enemy supply vessels in the Kerch Straits and en route to Soviet forces on the other end of the Crimea. These missions involved increasingly closer cooperation with the small but steadily expanding German Black Sea Fleet. Consequently, it may be appropriate at this point to shift briefly the spotlight away from the main players in the drama—the Luftwaffe units in southern Russia—and onto the supporting cast: the naval forces operating in the Black Sea, which to date have received little scholarly attention.

THE GERMAN BLACK SEA FLEET

While the invasion of the Soviet Union was still in its early planning stage, Hitler and his military advisers had been well aware of the Soviet Black Sea Fleet's impressive size[76] and the need to destroy it in order to ensure the safety of both Axis shipping and the southern flank of the German advance. *Großadmiral* Raeder, for instance, informed the Führer on 4 February 1941 that oil shipments to Greece and Italy would have to travel across that expanse of water, through the Bosporus and Dardanelles, and into the Aegean Sea.[77] It was also important, he said, to reinforce strongly the Rumanian coastal defenses—but probably not those of Bulgaria to the same degree—in order to safeguard the southern flank of the army. In fact, the transfer of two coastal batteries to Constanza was already in progress. It would be necessary to appoint a German admiral to coordinate the deployment of German and Rumanian forces along the Rumanian coast. That admiral would need authority to direct the Rumanian units of the coastal defenses, comprising its small Black Sea Fleet, Danube flotillas, coastal batteries, mining vessels, and naval reconnaissance units. The task of destroying the Soviet Black Sea Fleet (and its Baltic counterpart), he continued, would be given to the Luftwaffe, which would undertake "surprise attacks" on bases and ships. Support for these operations would be given by Rumania and Bulgaria, which were to provide mines and coastal guns.

Six weeks later, on 18 March, Raeder reported to Hitler that the Naval Mission to Rumania (under *Vizeadmiral* Fleischer) had taken up its duties alongside its army and air force counterparts, which had been in Rumania since October 1940.[78] They had entered ostensibly at the invitation of Antonescu, who claimed they were there merely to "train" his own forces, but in reality they had two tasks: to protect the oil fields and prepare for deployment against Soviet forces in southwestern Ukraine. Raeder further reported that the naval liaison staff in Bulgaria, far smaller than *Vizeadmiral* Fleischer's in Rumania, had also taken up its duties (attached to the Bulgarian Naval High Command in Sofia). Whereas the former naval command was created in preparation for the coming attack on the Soviet Union, the latter was intended principally to coordinate German-Bulgarian operations during the planned invasion of Greece. In return for Bulgaria's assistance—it was to allow German forces to build up and attack from within its borders—Hitler promised that it could take from Greece the Aegean coastal province of Thrace (except for a narrow strip along the Turkish border). The German naval staff in Bulgaria, which followed the establishment of an air force mission almost three months earlier, was supposedly necessary to coordinate that nation's defenses against possible Turkish aggression should it choose to intervene in the Balkans. It was also needed because Britain's naval position in the eastern Mediterranean had purportedly been improved by its exploitation of bases in Crete, the Peloponnese, and Lemnos.

It is worth noting that Hitler ordered this campaign against Greece not because of any territorial designs on Greece or the other Balkan States but because Italy's own impetuous offensive against Greece late in October 1940, which stalled almost immediately, had brought British forces into the region. Honoring an earlier commitment to Greece, Britain landed air and ground units on the islands of Crete and Lemnos a few days after Mussolini's troops had crossed the border. Hitler was furious about Il Duce's "regrettable blunder." British aircraft were now within striking distance of Rumanian oil fields, he fumed, and if Allied armies attempted a full-scale landing on the Greek mainland, Germany's entire position in the Balkans would be jeopardized.[79] The British War Cabinet, as it happened, was aware of the Reich's dependence on Rumanian oil. During the weeks following the Italian invasion of Greece, cabinet members trying to determine what type of military response to make almost unanimously accepted the decision eventually to launch air attacks against the oil fields.[80]

Despite the reinforcement of some sections of the Rumanian and Bulgarian coastlines and the establishment of a full naval mission in Rumania and a small naval liaison staff in Bulgaria, Hitler and his military advisers actually placed

little importance on the need for strong naval forces in the Black Sea. The bulk
of the Soviet fleet would be destroyed by sudden blows from the air, they reasoned, and the remaining vessels would be bottled up in their harbors by minefields and light naval forces until all the Soviet ports had been captured by land
forces. "In this theater," one Soviet admiral later wrote, "such a plan was comparatively reasonable since the enemy had but limited naval forces at his disposal
and could not challenge the Soviet Black Sea Fleet in action."[81] Indeed, when
Barbarossa commenced on 22 June 1941, Germany had no naval forces in the
Black Sea region except for some river gunboats and minesweepers of the
Danube Flotilla.[82] Back in March, the German naval staff had dropped its idea of
transporting small submarines overland to Rumania because, it concluded, they
were sorely needed elsewhere (especially in home waters and the English Channel) and would take at least four months to arrive.[83] The Rumanian navy, with its
main base at Constanza, was certainly no match for the Soviet fleet. When the
war in the east began, it comprised just four destroyers (two dating from the First
World War), one modern submarine of 700 tons, two more not yet ready for service, three heavy torpedo ships (launched *before* the First World War), three modern motor torpedo boats, three obsolete gunboats (also launched during the First
World War), and some minelayers, patrol boats, tugs, and auxiliaries.[84] The Bulgarian fleet was even smaller. With only six antiquated patrol boats, two minesweepers, two motor torpedo boats (Bulgaria's only vessels constructed after
1918), three training ships, and a few light gunboats, it posed no threat to the Soviet fleet. As the German naval staff complained in February 1942: "The material
worth of the Bulgarian naval forces . . . is very insignificant."[85]

The Soviet Black Sea Fleet began the war with few experienced senior officers. Most, including Admiral I. K. Koshchenov, its commander (and the seven
other Soviet admirals), had disappeared during Stalin's purges of 1937 and
1938. After Koshchenov, who had commanded the Black Sea Fleet for six years
(1931–1937), came P. I. Smirnov (1937), I. S. Iumashev (1938–1939), and finally
Oktyabrskii (from mid-1939). The latter, a member of the Communist Party
since 1919, certainly benefited from the purges. Although he had been in the navy
since 1917 and had trained at the Petrograd Communist University in 1922 and
the Frunze Naval College in 1928, Oktyabrskii only rose to high command when
Stalin decided to "retire" whole echelons of purportedly disloyal officers. When
he assumed command of the powerful Black Sea Fleet in mid-1939, Oktyabrskii
had no previous command experience with large warships. Throughout the 1920s
and 1930s he had served on and eventually commanded torpedo boats, and before he took over the Black Sea Fleet he was in charge of the insignificant Amur
Military Flotilla.

The main consequence of Stalin's purges was a mass promotion of junior
officers to take the place of those removed. Sergei Gorshkov, for example, became
captain, first class, at the age of twenty-eight and rose to rear admiral only three
years later when he took over command of the Azov Flotilla in 1941. Unlike this

commander, during the first months of war few of the prematurely promoted officers possessed sufficient natural acumen to compensate for their dearth of experience. Nonetheless, what the Black Sea Fleet lacked in command experience, it made up for in crew training, discipline, and morale, which were all excellent as a result of new training schools and programs. Having benefited from recent building programs, the fleet was also very powerful. When war commenced, it comprised numerous heavy warships, including the *Pariskaya Kommuna,* a 23,000-ton battleship. Although this ship had been launched in 1911, it was significantly reconstructed and modernized in 1937 and now, with its twelve 305-mm guns, packed a strong punch. The fleet also contained five cruisers, two of them new and another fully modernized. Among its other modern vessels were three flotilla leaders, ten fast destroyers with powerful modern guns, and almost four dozen submarines. As well as scores of light vessels, most deployed in squadrons at individual naval bases, the Black Sea Fleet also possessed a naval air arm with no less than 626 aircraft (about half of them fighters).[86] Although many were inferior to those of the Germans and their Axis partners in the region, these naval aircraft initially outnumbered their enemy counterparts. They conducted reconnaissance missions, mined enemy waters, protected naval bases, and escorted merchant and naval vessels at sea.

Moreover, operating in the shallows of the Sea of Azov were light vessels of the Azov Flotilla, commanded by the adroit and courageous Gorshkov. This flotilla originated in 1941 as an ancillary but subordinate section of Oktyabrskii's main Black Sea Fleet. Determining its total complement at the outbreak of hostilities is difficult, but even in mid-1942, after losing numerous vessels to German mines and air attacks, it still comprised four gunboats, a monitor, three river gunboats, three patrol ships, four armored launches, seven torpedo boats, twelve minesweeping launches, and fifty-six light patrol boats.[87]

When Axis forces carved their way into the Soviet Union in June 1941, the Luftwaffe immediately commenced attacks against the Soviet Black Sea Fleet. Löhr's *Luftflotte 4* had recently been withdrawn from the Balkans and given a new operational sector, which stretched eastward from Rumania up toward Kiev and across toward the Crimea, Rostov, and the Black Sea. *Fliegerkorps IV,* the air corps on the southern wing of this huge sector, was primarily engaged in destroying enemy air forces and supporting the advance of the German Eleventh Army and the Rumanian Third and Fourth Armies into the Ukraine. It also had to perform a variety of other tasks in the far south, including the defense of Rumanian oil fields and German, Rumanian, and Bulgarian shipping along the west coast of the Black Sea and through the Bosporus (carried out in cooperation with Rumanian air units), as well as long-range reconnaissance, antinaval, and interdiction operations over the Black Sea and Sea of Azov.[88]

Fliegerkorps IV initially operated from Rumanian soil, but as the front steadily moved eastward the bulk of its units were transferred to captured bases and airfields in the southern Ukraine. Consequently, flying distances to targets on the farthest coasts of the Black Sea decreased, allowing more sorties per day, and penetration ranges increased, allowing raids on previously unreachable targets. Its primary targets in the Black Sea during the first months of the conflict were the major naval bases and commercial ports of Odessa and Nikolayev (where there were large shipyards), the commercial port of Kherson, the naval base at Novorossiisk, and the mighty fortress-city of Sevastopol, with its naval base (the most important in the Black Sea), commercial port, and shipyards.[89] The railhead at the Novorossiisk end of the main railway from the Caucasus and the oil pipelines in Tuapse and Batumi (the latter at the very limit of *Fliegerkorps IV*'s operational range) were also singled out for attack. All these targets were repeatedly bombed and, in special missions, the ports of Odessa, Nikolayev, and Sevastopol were mined from the air.[90]

The Soviet naval and merchant fleets were located, kept under constant surveillance, and subjected to harassing attacks by units of *Fliegerkorps IV*, which only rarely coordinated its operations with the few Axis naval forces in the Black Sea. Because those forces had little offensive capability and kept to the sea's western reaches—and possibly because of interservice rivalry—they were apparently considered by local air commanders to be of little consequence. These airmen were acutely aware that they had been delegated the task of destroying the enemy fleet only because of the weakness of the paltry Axis naval forces in the Black Sea.

At the outbreak of hostilities, many of the larger Soviet warships sat anchored in Sevastopol harbor. Sizable freighter fleets sat docked in Odessa. Antinaval air attacks (especially against heavily defended warships) were always difficult, but when vessels were caught by surprise riding at anchor or while evacuating troops from cities under siege, they presented aircrew with excellent targets. On 18 August—to give a noteworthy example of how destructive such attacks on stationary shipping could be in good weather—the Luftwaffe sank or permanently put out of action over 30,000 tons of shipping (both warships and merchant vessels) during a single raid on Odessa.[91] Landing troops behind enemy lines was also dangerous for Soviet vessels. For instance, on 21 September, a small but powerful convoy comprising two cruisers, four destroyers, and various smaller craft left the relative safety of Sevastopol to undertake a landing behind Rumanian lines near Grigorevka, west of Odessa. Although it successfully accomplished the landing, the convoy lost a destroyer, a gunboat, and a tug, and had two other destroyers damaged during fierce attacks by Stukas of *St.G. 77*.[92] In general, however, it was possible for Oktyabrskii's large warships, bristling with antiaircraft guns and aided by the powerful Soviet air forces stationed on the Crimea, to protect Soviet shipping lanes around the Black Sea coasts and ferry reinforcements to Red Army positions.

Luftflotte 4's commanders quickly realized that possession of the Crimea was the key to success in the Black Sea. This would not only deny Oktyabrskii's fleet its well-equipped main base and other important harbors but also significantly alter the balance of power in the air, which still favored the Soviets. Moreover, if they could capture the Crimea's many airfields, their own aircraft would command the Black Sea and be capable of striking heavily not only the distant Caucasian bases of the Soviet fleet, including Batumi, but also cities and industrial centers deep in the heart of Transcaucasia. Unfortunately, Manstein's assault on the Crimea late in 1941 made slow progress, and it was not until the return of units from the Moscow front to provide air support that the Germans succeeded in taking the peninsula (except, as already noted, for Sevastopol). This check was to prove an important factor in delaying the establishment of the Luftwaffe on operational bases in the Crimea, from which further activity in the Black Sea area could be carried out. To assist *Fliegerkorps IV* in its antishipping work in the Black Sea and the Sea of Azov, Wild's *Fliegerführer Süd* arrived in the region shortly after the German breakthrough into the Crimea.

By Christmas 1941, German ground forces had captured the key naval bases of Odessa, Nikolayev, Feodosiya, and Kerch, in addition to the commercial ports of Kherson, Eupatoria, Balaclava, Yalta, Dvuyakornaya Bay, and Kamysh-Burun. Several of these ports had only recently been refitted to serve the Soviet navy. Three cruisers and three destroyers remained in Sevastopol to provide naval gunfire support for the besieged ground forces. The rest of Oktyabrskii's main fleet was now forced to operate from inadequate bases on the Caucasian coast. Similarly, his Azov Flotilla's main bases were Mariupol and Rostov, but when these ports fell to the Germans late in 1941, urgent measures had to be taken to transform the commercial and fishing ports of Jeisk, Primorsko-Akhtarskaya, and Temryuk into makeshift naval bases.

The loss of proper naval bases caused Oktyabrskii considerable maintenance and supply problems. Many merchant vessels and troopships and several warships had been sunk or badly damaged during the evacuation of Odessa and Kerch and the supply of Sevastopol. By the end of 1941, the fleet had lost a cruiser, a flotilla leader, seven destroyers, and numerous submarines. The Luftwaffe destroyed the cruiser, a destroyer (and another under construction), and three submarines; minefields claimed the rest.[93] Ships were difficult to replace now that the great shipyards at Odessa and Nikolayev had fallen into German hands. Construction and repair facilities existed at Sevastopol, Novorossiisk, and Tuapse, but they were vulnerable to air attack and incapable of building and repairing vessels quickly enough to prevent a slow but steady decrease in the fleet. Submarines fared slightly better than surface vessels. As a result of the construction of eight new submarines at Sevastopol, at the end of 1941 the Soviet fleet still had forty-three in commission, almost as many as it had when hostilities commenced.[94] The Soviet admiral had other logistical problems. Novorossiisk and Poti were each well equipped to service the needs of a dozen or so naval vessels but lacked sufficient docks, cranes, and storage facilities to cope with more traffic. They were incapable of docking, refueling, and loading large numbers of both merchant and naval vessels at the same time. Many warships, therefore, had to use the smaller Caucasian ports of Tuapse and Batumi, which were not equipped as naval bases. Before the war they had served only for loading oil and manganese ore. However, despite being handicapped by mounting losses and these logistical difficulties, Oktyabrskii's fleet managed to retain a high operational capability. The successful landings on the Kerch Peninsula in December 1941 and January 1942 demonstrate that it was still able to undertake large-scale operations.

Thus, German air units in and around the Crimea during the winter of 1941–1942 proved incapable of significantly restricting the operations of the Soviet fleet. More importantly, while Luftwaffe units identified and attempted to interdict unusually large troop movements around the Sea of Azov and the Caucasus coast near the Kerch Straits, they failed to prevent those troops from embarking on Gorshkov's and Oktyabrskii's vessels and making major landings on the Kerch Peninsula and other key points on the Crimea.

The strategic importance of those amphibious landings must be emphasized. They compelled Manstein to break off the siege of Sevastopol, allowing the Soviets time to reinforce it by sea with men and matériel. "In this way," writes one German naval historian, "the siege was prolonged by six months, a delay which had not been allowed for in the calculations of the German General Staff."[95] Accordingly, by February 1942 it became clear to German military planners that they had *under*estimated the strength of the Soviet Black Sea Fleet, which had embarrassed them in a series of successful naval operations, and *over*estimated the Luftwaffe's ability to secure the Black Sea for Axis shipping. Because most aircraft were not designed or equipped for antinaval missions, and few pilots and aircrew were trained for them, the Luftwaffe had not destroyed the bulk of the fleet by "sudden blows from the air," as the High Command had originally planned. Nor had its bombing and air-mining efforts succeeded even in preventing vessels from slipping in and out of their ports, let alone conducting major operations.

Raeder and the naval staff were naturally concerned that the Soviet fleet still posed a major threat to Axis shipping, especially to vessels supplying the army by sea. "Russian naval forces in the Black Sea must be attacked and destroyed," Raeder told the Führer on 13 February 1942.[96] "The degree of success obtained will determine the outcome of the war in the Black Sea area." It is important, he said, to occupy all enemy bases and ports there. "Measures," he added, "are being taken to improve our position in the Black Sea. E-boats, Italian anti-submarine vessels, small submarines, landing craft (MFPs), etc., are being added to our forces; minefields are being laid."

The decision to increase substantially Germany's maritime presence in the Black Sea had actually been reached as early as November 1941, when Hitler still thought it possible in the coming weeks to "continue to advance toward the southeast in the direction of the Caucasus and to destroy the Russian Black Sea Fleet."[97] The supply of his eastern armies by sea was clearly still at the forefront of the Führer's mind. Because his overland logistical network was continuously upset by primitive roads, a lack of rolling stock, and guerrilla attacks, he urgently needed a less vulnerable supply route into the Ukraine. In War Directive No. 39, issued on 8 December, he insisted: "The number of small ships being constructed in Germany, allied and occupied countries for supply purposes (particularly for use across the Black Sea and in the Aegean) must be increased still further, even if it means abandoning all claims and security measures which are not absolutely essential." German shipbuilders had already been working for several weeks at shipyards in Rumania and Bulgaria, especially at Burgas and Varna, building new light vessels and repairing ships captured at Odessa, Rostov, and Nikolayev.[98] These ships, destined to join the German Black Sea Fleet, could not have been repaired in situ because most of the shipyards and repair facilities, and a number of warships under construction, had been blown up by the Soviets as they fled.

After the fall of Odessa in mid-October 1941, the Germans had opened their new sea transport route between Constanza and Ochakov (on the mouth of the Dnieper River) and had sent through three supply convoys by the end of the year. The convoys were protected by defensive minefields, units of the Rumanian Air Force, and motor torpedo boats and other small escort vessels. Realizing the potential significance of these convoys to German logistics, Vice Admiral Oktyabrskii immediately dispatched warships to the Black Sea's western reaches. Offensive minefields were laid, and submarines and motor torpedo boats were sent in to attack the vessels. These actions (especially the minefields) caused frustrating, if not severe, losses to the German-led convoys. On the first convoy run, for instance, three tugs sank after hitting mines. On the following run, the convoy lost its flagship and two Rumanian motor torpedo boats.[99] Oktyabrskii could have achieved more spectacular results if he had sent in heavier warships, but he was apparently reluctant to expose them to heavy air and coastal attack (except in dire need or when directly ordered); more important, they were needed for the coming landings on the Kerch Peninsula. In any event, the convoys soon came to a halt as the icy winter closed in. Operating conditions became impossible after mid-December, forcing the German ships to return to the Danube for the winter.

Realizing after the Soviet landings on the Kerch Peninsula that the enemy fleet was far from defeated and still upsetting all German plans in the region, the German naval staff undertook measures to enhance its own offensive capabilities. First it worked to increase the effectiveness of forces already in the Black Sea. In previous months, the German and Rumanian flotillas had generally operated independently of each other. On the command level, the German Naval Mission to Rumania worked in close collaboration with that nation's naval authorities. However, communication difficulties between German and Rumanian naval squadrons, and between those and air squadrons, prevented effective cooperation on an operational level. The mission was smaller than its army and air force counterparts, and accordingly received far fewer liaison officers fluent in Rumanian. As a result, the liaison staffs attached to Rumanian naval squadrons were small and often poorly equipped to overcome differences in radio communications and procedures. Also, liaison efforts were hindered at times by a shortage of Rumanian officers fluent in German, which led to a dependence on inexperienced *Volksdeutsch* (ethnic German) Rumanians, many unacquainted with military processes or terminology.[100] The reluctance of German seamen (of all ranks, including officers) to work as equals alongside their Rumanian "allies," and the Rumanian sailors' unhappiness at finding themselves practically (although not at first officially) under German command, doubtless further hampered the liaison process.

This state of affairs, the German naval staff insisted, simply had to change. Only when these flotillas were forged into an organized, cohesive, German-led "fleet" that coordinated its efforts with those of the Luftwaffe and the small Rumanian air force would it be possible to alter, even slightly, the balance of naval power in the Black Sea. Accordingly, in the last weeks of 1941, the German naval missions worked hard in conjunction with the Rumanian and Bulgarian naval staffs to improve communications (as did the army and air force missions with their corresponding staffs). Efforts to standardize radio, telephone, and Teletype equipment and procedures were intensified, but, despite supplying their Axis partners with new equipment and training teams, the Germans were not entirely successful in persuading them to adapt their communication methods to German systems, to use prepared ciphers, and to translate and distribute the German radio regulations. In order to overcome the shortage of interpreters, liaison personnel, and members of the officer corps who were familiar with German military concepts, practices, and terminology, the German missions increased the number and quality of training programs for both interpreters and officers. These training programs (also conducted by the other two service branches) were generally well received by the Bulgarian armed forces, which had not yet been tested in battle and were keen to learn the principles behind Germany's string of recent military successes. They were not, on the other hand, well received by the Rumanian armed forces, which had been trained along French lines, had suffered high losses so far in the war, and now had an aversion to anything German. Even the Rumanian army, in combat alongside the Wehrmacht since the eastern campaign started, disliked these training programs. "Resistance to German influence in training went so far," a German general noted after the war, "that many Rumanian commanders of field units 're-schooled' officers and soldiers returning from German training courses."[101]

Despite Bulgaria's willingness to receive German military training, Hitler's naval staff realized that they could not yet use that nation's naval forces openly in offensive missions against the Soviet fleet. Unlike Rumania, Bulgaria had not declared war on the Soviet empire and would not, therefore, use her small fleet in a combat role. Many Bulgarians felt culturally and ethnically akin to the Russian people and fondly remembered that Russia had once helped them throw off the shackles of Ottoman rule. As a result, although Bulgaria had publicly demonstrated its loyalty to the Axis cause by signing the Tripartite Pact in March 1941,

by allowing the invasion of Greece and Yugoslavia to be launched from its territory the following month and by declaring war on Britain and the United States
that December, it never severed diplomatic relations with the Soviet Union.
Nonetheless, to the dismay and disgust of the Soviet government (which strongly
protested),[102] Bulgaria openly allowed German warships to make extensive use of
naval bases at Burgas and Varna, German shipbuilders to use shipyards and repair facilities at those ports, and Axis merchant vessels to use port facilities in
order to supply German armies in southern Russia.

Despite all these problems and difficulties, the German, Rumanian, and Bulgarian naval staffs did manage to create a proper German-led command structure directing and overseeing all naval activities. To coordinate and supervise
effectively Axis maritime operations in the Black Sea, *Admiral Schwarzes Meer,*
the small German flotilla, assumed direct control of all shipping outside (and
influenced most inside) Rumanian and Bulgarian territorial waters. *Admiral
Schwarzes Meer* was really only a redesignated version of the German Naval Mission to Rumania, although its new name (effective from 2 January 1942) was
clearly intended to indicate the small command's new responsibilities.[103]

Although *Admiral Schwarzes Meer* was led by *Vizeadmiral* Götting and
exercised local autonomy, it formed part of *Admiral* Marschall's *Marine-Gruppenkommando Süd* (Naval Group Command South), the naval staff commanding
all German shipping in the Aegean and Black Seas.[104] This naval staff had been
formed after the rapid conquest of Greece in April 1941 in order to protect the
coasts against Allied invasion, prevent the establishment of air bases in the
Aegean (for raids on Rumanian oil fields), and secure Axis shipping routes
through the Dardanelles, Aegean Sea, and eastern Mediterranean. It had its
headquarters in Sofia, the capital of Bulgaria, and its major bases at Piraeus, Sa-
lonika, Crete (all in Greece), Varna (Bulgaria), and Constanza (Rumania).

The expansion of *Admiral Schwarzes Meer* was a slow process. In the closing
days of 1941, Raeder ordered the transfer of easily transportable warships (initially a squadron of six MTBs and various small patrol boats) from the North
Sea and the Baltic, but they did not arrive at their destination for several months.
First they had to travel down the Elbe to Dresden. Then, as much weight as possible (including the engines) was removed before they were lifted by cranes onto
special oversized trucks that carried them along the autobahn to the Danube below Regensburg. Finally, they traveled down the Danube to wharves in Constanza, where they joined the German fleet.[105] The largest vessels to enter the
Black Sea by this route were six submarines of 250 tons, which were shipped
down the Danube in pieces and then assembled in Rumanian ports.

Although it had already provided numerous vessels for Marschall's Aegean
flotilla, the Royal Italian Navy *(Regia Marina)* agreed to supply the Black Sea
Fleet with submarines, torpedo boats, patrol boats, and minesweepers, as well as
small transports, tankers, and other supply ships. The initial consignment consisted of four MTBs, four small motorboats, each armed with a torpedo, and four

small submarines.[106] These vessels could not travel through the Dardanelles for fear of British warships in the eastern Mediterranean and Soviet warships in the entrance to the Black Sea. Instead, they had to travel across the Alps on massive trucks, like modern-day Hannibal's elephants, then float down the Danube on barges to the Rumanian port of Galați.

Additional vessels were produced in the Black Sea region itself. German technicians had struggled since August 1941 to repair the great shipyards at Nikolayev, which the Soviets left heavily damaged and littered with wrecks. By early 1942 they were able to make limited use of the facilities. They began constructi ng "naval ferry barges" *(Marine-Fährprähme)*, flat-bottomed, self-propelled barges of around 200 tons. They armed many of these (which they then designated "artillery carriers," or *Artillerieträger*) with antiaircraft weapons, including their superb 88-mm guns. They also built large, 700-ton "war transporters" *(Kriegstransporter)*, some of which they converted into submarine chasers.[107]

These actions resulted in the slow but steady growth of Axis naval strength in the Black Sea during the early months of 1942. In 1941, Axis vessels had conducted very limited escort and transport operations. By the middle of 1942, they would be capable of performing those tasks more effectively, following in the wake of advancing armies to assume the duties of coastal and harbor defenses in occupied territories, and even carrying out minor offensive operations against the enemy fleet.

Realizing that *Admiral Schwarzes Meer* would soon be able to play a greater combat role in the Black Sea, on 2 February 1942 *Luftflotte 4* requested the small fleet to supply it with a naval liaison officer. The air fleet explained that it was "strengthening its operations against the Russian Black Sea Fleet" and, therefore, needed an experienced naval officer at its headquarters "in order to guarantee close cooperation between the air fleet, *[Marine] Gruppe Süd* and *Admiral Schwarzes Meer.*"[108] Admiral Marschall complained in *Marine-Gruppenkommando Süd*'s war diary that, while he would provide *Luftflotte 4* with a suitable officer, it would be extremely difficult for the new appointee to have much influence on joint-service planning because of his "limited resources, unfamiliarity with other service branches, and lack of tactical and operational knowledge."[109]

Despite his grumbling, Marschall was clearly keen to increase cooperation between his small but steadily growing fleet and the three air commands then within *Luftflotte 4*'s operational zone: *Deutsche Luftwaffe Mission in Rümanien, Fliegerkorps IV,* and *Sonderstab Krim.* Accordingly, on 9 February he radioed the naval staff a request for a suitable officer.[110] "Success against the Russian Fleet will depend," he insisted, "on close cooperation between *S-Flottille* [the planned MTB squadron], submarines and *Luftwaffe* units." The air force's marked intensification of operations against shipping and the transfer of small Axis warships and submarines to the Black Sea means that "still closer operational and tactical cooperation with *Luftflotte 4,* especially *Fliegerkorps IV,* is crucial." He requested, therefore, the appointment of a "suitable officer with fleet experience." The last thing he wanted was a glorified desk clerk. The new liaison officer, he stated, should be a "seagoing reserve officer with naval combat experience." To ensure that the new appointee gained a working knowledge of air command matters and tactics, Marschall continued, he should first be sent away for specialized training. In the meantime, he recommended, the naval staff should give the job to *Korvettenkapitän* von Bothmer, chief of staff to *See Kommandant Ukraine* (naval commander, Ukraine). An experienced and capable officer, he had been largely responsible for the repair and successful exploitation of various Ukrainian ports and the laying of defensive minefields (carried out mainly by Rumanian destroyers and minelayers) along sections of the Ukrainian coastline. He could serve as naval liaison officer to *Luftflotte 4* while fulfilling his regular duties. The naval staff agreed and gave Bothmer the job.

Admiral Schwarzes Meer's war diaries reveal that both Bothmer and his eventual successor, *Konteradmiral* von Eyssen (appointed in May), worked vigorously in their positions as liaison officers to break down interservice rivalry and ensure that no operational or tactical dissension existed between their fleet and local German air units. Their task was made easier by recent improvements to the radio communication system in the region, resulting in a steady transfer of up-to-the-minute intelligence information between the various naval and air commands. This information—on weather conditions and the activities and position of enemy vessels—was gathered mainly by sea and air reconnaissance and a sophisticated radio intercept service. Communication between *Admiral Schwarzes Meer* and local Rumanian and Bulgarian air units remained poor, however, mainly because of language problems.

By late February—even before most of the expected warships had arrived and undergone sea trials—the naval staff was able to formulate a strategy for *Admiral Schwarzes Meer,* which now had the potential to make a significant contribution to the coming eastern campaign. On 23 February, Raeder issued *Marine-Gruppenkommando Süd* a detailed directive for "Operations in the Black Sea."[111] Oktyabrskii's fleet, he complained, still possesses naval supremacy in the Black Sea. This allows the Soviets to act almost as they wish, and threatens the security of the army's southern flank, as well as Axis supply convoys in support of the planned Army offensive. As soon as the ice situation permits, Raeder stressed, those seaborne supply transports must commence again because: "it must not be forgotten that any transport of supplies by sea, even though only a small part of the army's requirements, relieves the difficult land transport situation to a perceptible degree, and that any increase in sea transports, even if it is only small, will be considered essential by the army." Soviet forces, with their "well-known toughness and ruthlessness," will attempt not only to thwart any Axis offensive actions but also to strengthen their own position in the Crimea. To achieve this, the Soviets will continue to rely on their naval forces. The strength of those forces, observed Raeder, "together with the lack of any sort of defense on our part," allows strong Soviet landings behind German lines. These landings must be prevented at all costs.

The army's first objective in the coming months, he continued, is to seize as soon as possible Sevastopol and the sections of the Crimea recently recaptured by the Soviets. When this is accomplished, it is important to hold the Crimea with as few army forces as possible so that divisions are freed up to participate in the major campaign to the east and southeast. This is only possible if German forces block the Kerch Straits and prevent further Soviet amphibious landings on the Crimean and Sea of Azov coasts. Accordingly, there are now several key tasks for the German naval forces in the Black Sea. First, as soon as the ice situation permits, it is necessary to start sending army supplies by sea to the south Ukrainian, western Crimean, and western Sea of Azov ports. Later, when the army pushes into the Caucasus, supply transports must be sent to ports on the eastern coast of the Black Sea. Second, all measures must be taken to secure this supply traffic. Third, the army must receive maximum naval support when it launches its offensives against Sevastopol and the Kerch Peninsula and later, during its occupation of the Crimea. Fourth, Soviet landings behind German lines must be prevented at all costs. "In order to carry out these tasks, ... we must stop Russian naval forces operating undisturbed on the supply routes and along the occupied coasts, or we must at least make it difficult for them to do so."

"The most effective way to do this would be to destroy the Russian means of combat," wrote Raeder, stating the obvious. Acknowledging that German air forces had performed the lion's share of offensive operations in the Black Sea, he noted that so far "only the Luftwaffe has been able to combat the Russian naval forces, which form the backbone of their operations." It was hoped that Luftwaffe units would maintain, if not increase, their level of antinaval operations, but, he cautioned, this air support should not be counted on once the main summer campaign commences:

> The air forces on the Crimea have been reinforced, to be sure, for the necessary task of fighting Russian naval forces and transports, and *Reichsmarschall* Göring has especially recognized the necessity of using them for that task. Nevertheless, when the army offensive begins they will be used mainly to support the army, and will be available for attacking the Black Sea Fleet only occasionally.

The German navy would clearly have to do more itself. Raeder knew that Oktyabrskii lacked aggression and operational imagination. Rather than using his fleet's numerical superiority to great advantage (possibly by launching full-scale attacks on Rumanian- or German-occupied Ukrainian cities, ports, and naval bases on the western coasts of the Black Sea), he had been frightened by early losses and subsequently dissipated his superiority on missions supporting the army and protecting supply traffic in the eastern reaches. Experience thus shows,

Raeder claimed, that the Soviet fleet is unwilling to engage in high-risk activities and might surrender its initiative if hard-pressed by opposing naval forces. Despite the ongoing transfer of Axis vessels to the Black Sea, he admitted that *Marine-Gruppenkommando Süd* still had "very inadequate means" for carrying out aggressive measures. "The naval staff believes," he nonetheless added,

> ... that there are still possibilities for preventing the enemy from keeping the initiative everywhere entirely undisturbed, if the few means available are utilized to the very fullest and numerous improvisations are resorted to. Certain losses must be reckoned with. If our countermeasures succeed in paralyzing the activity of the Russian naval forces against the occupied coasts, harbors, and supply routes, then these losses are absolutely justified in the face of the advantage won.

Raeder concluded his directive with a brief discussion of mining operations in Soviet ports. These operations had not produced significant results in the first six months of the conflict (as the present study has already demonstrated), prompting *Marine-Gruppenkommando Süd* to place them low on its list of priorities. The *Großadmiral,* on the other hand, argued that they should continue. They were essential for securing transport routes to the Dnieper and the northwestern Crimean ports and, later, to harbors on the southern coast of the Crimea and in the Kerch Straits. "Group South," he stated, "calls these operations defensive and hardly important, but they can certainly be considered effective with a view to securing the main operations later."

Thus, by February 1942 the strength of *Admiral Schwarzes Meer* had grown, and it would continue to grow at an increasingly accelerated pace for several more months. The range of missions it received for the coming campaign had also greatly expanded. The High Command clearly expected the fleet to begin playing a far greater part than it previously had. As well as conducting escort and transport operations—still its main mission—it would lay defensive minefields in its own coastal waters and offensive minefields in those of the enemy. It would provide coastal and harbor defenses in the occupied territories, especially the Crimea, and engage, where possible, in offensive operations against the Soviet fleet. Although in February the Luftwaffe still performed the vast majority of these tasks, the increasing participation of the navy in coming months would (as we shall see) result in greater joint-service cooperation and noticeable changes in the tactical deployment of air units assigned to antishipping duties.

FLIEGERFÜHRER SÜD

Both Wild and Manstein—to return to the events of mid-February—were gravely concerned by the constant threat of a major breakout, either from the Kerch Peninsula or Sevastopol, or further landings elsewhere on the Crimea. Manstein, acutely aware of the huge Soviet buildup of men, matériel, and fortifications in the Parpach region, urgently requested fresh reinforcements and directed his existing forces to regroup and consolidate their positions in preparation for the inevitable breakout attempts.

Wild, who was determined to provide his colleague with maximum support, ordered his air units to strike Soviet batteries, bunkers, field fortifications, and defense lines, as well as railheads, marshaling yards, and mobilization points behind the front. However, his antinaval work, including the prevention of further enemy landings, remained his highest priority. He ordered his reconnaissance units to conduct constant surveillance missions over Crimean coastlines and, in coordination with *Admiral Schwarzes Meer,* over the vast expanses of the Black Sea. They covered a massive area stretching from the northern reaches of the Sea of Azov to the coasts of Turkey. Wild also ordered the interdiction of enemy supply movements, especially in Sevastopol, Kerch, and Kamysh-Burun, and the presumed Soviet supply and embarkation ports of Anapa, Novorossiisk, and Tuapse. Although he lacked sufficient bomber and destroyer units, he directed the ones he did have to attack enemy supply vessels in the Kerch Straits and en route to Soviet forces at the other end of the Crimea.

February 24, for example, was a "typical" day for *Fliegerführer Süd.* A total of 97 aircraft (47 fighters, 26 dive-bombers, 23 bombers, and 1 reconnaissance plane) took to the air.[112] Throughout the daylight hours—from 0600 to 1710 hours—Bf 109 fighters of *III./J.G. 77* struggled for air superiority. They also conducted surveillance and protection missions over the German-occupied Saki airfield, naval reconnaissance over Sevastopol, surveillance of the enemy front, weather reconnaissance, and escort duties for the vulnerable Ju 87 Stukas and Ju 88 medium bombers. Two dozen Stukas of *III./St.G. 77* bombed battery installations near Semisotka and Ak Monai, behind the Parpach Line, recording direct hits on many of them.

At 0910, eight Ju 88s from the 3rd Group of the *Edelweiss* bomber wing were dispatched to attack the Soviet battleship *Pariskaya Kommuna,* which had been pounding German positions with its massive guns and was recently seen in Sevastopol harbor. When they arrived over the target area, they came under fire from both medium and heavy flak and the guns of a single Soviet fighter. They suffered no losses on that occasion but were unable to locate the battleship. Instead, they bombed a heavy cruiser near the headland of Yushnaja Bay, near Sevastopol, which they apparently failed to sink despite scoring a hit on the stern with a heavy 1,000-kg bomb that set the ship on fire.

Five He 111 medium bombers from *I./K.G. 100* were sent out on various missions during the day. Two were directed to locate the battleship, which they failed to do. Therefore, one attacked enemy railheads and embarkation points, while the other attacked enemy aircraft. The latter hit a flying boat with cannons and machine guns, and watched it disappear, leaving a thick trail of smoke. Both He 111s came under fire from heavy flak and the guns of a tanker. A third He 111 unsuccessfully searched for an enemy convoy but despite engine trouble still attacked the city of Sevastopol. The other two He 111s of *I./K.G. 100* to fly on 24 February conducted night bombing raids on the center of Sevastopol with their massive 1,800-kg bombs and returned safely to base despite the best attempts of the city's searchlight operators and antiaircraft gunners to bring them down. A Soviet night fighter almost accomplished the task, filling one plane with holes and knocking out an engine. Nine He 111s of *III./K.G. 27* also bombed the city; another attacked the shipbuilding yards, but this time with incendiary bombs. They caused a major explosion and left the city aflame in several places.

At 1535, a solitary Ju 88 from the *4. (F) 122* long-range reconnaissance group finally located the battleship *Pariskaya Kommuna,* which had eluded Wild's units for most of the day. This aircraft had been sent seven hours earlier on a long-distance mission to reconnoiter the ports of Sevastopol and Kerch on the Crimea and Novorossiisk, Anapa, and Tuapse on the Caucasus coast. Over Sevastopol it reported the presence of a heavy cruiser, which was almost certainly the same vessel that the bombers from *III./K.G. 51* had earlier tried to sink. It also revealed the existence of thirty enemy aircraft on an airfield at Anapa. The *Pariskaya Kommuna,* which had apparently sailed undetected from Sevastopol, was now safely docked in Novorossiisk, along with a flotilla leader, three destroyers, and various smaller vessels. As long as it remained there, protected by its own guns and those of the other vessels and port flak battalions, it was in no serious danger.

Increasing attacks during this period by *Fliegerführer Süd,* and occasionally by elements of *Fliegerkorps IV,* concerned Vice Admiral Oktyabrskii so much that he instructed his captains to exercise extreme caution in regions patrolled by enemy air forces. It was no longer possible for ships to bombard enemy positions in the Crimea as often and openly as before. Destroyers and flotilla leaders, he ordered, could undertake artillery attacks on German positions only at night and while moving (that is, they must not fire while stationary or riding at anchor).[113] They were also to change headings more often and avoid shelling from the same locations. Naturally, this greatly diminished the frequency and accuracy of their bombardments. Use of the older cruisers for fire support was permitted only when poor weather prevented the Luftwaffe from taking to the skies, but the *Pariskaya Kommuna* and the two new cruisers were not to be risked in these missions at all without the vice admiral's permission.

On 21 February, Halder noted in his diary that a major Soviet offensive on the Crimea appeared imminent. He did not have long to wait. As Manstein later recalled: "After weeks of apparent quiet that were really loaded with tension, the enemy finally launched his expected major attack on 27 February."[114] Powerful thrusts were made simultaneously from Sevastopol and Kerch, aided by the Soviet fleet, which shelled German coastal positions.[115] The German commander knew he could probably contain the Sevastopol offensive but realized that his troops were vastly outnumbered by the forces surging across the Parpach Line.

Desperate to prevent a massive enemy breakout into the interior of the Crimean Peninsula, he threw everything he possessed into the fray. The Soviet forces achieved local penetrations, especially in the northern sector of the Parpach Isthmus (held by Rumanian units), but were unable to shatter the defenses of the German army.

During the first two days of the attack, bad weather prevented *Fliegerführer Süd* from assisting Manstein's beleaguered troops. On 27 February, only three aircraft made it into the air, two of which were sent out to search for the crew of a missing bomber. The third was sent to Sevastopol on a torpedo mission, which had to be broken off because of the weather.[116] Two days later, the temperature rose several degrees, creating unexpected thaws that temporarily relieved the situation for the German soldiers by bogging down the enemy advance, particularly in the marshy northern sector. The increase in temperature also allowed Wild's air units to provide direct support of the army on the battlefield. On 1 March, for example, no less than 120 aircraft—including 53 fighters, 40 Stukas, and two dozen bombers—were able to take to the skies.[117] Their *Schwerpunkt* (point of main emphasis) was the sector around Tulumschak, where the enemy had almost broken through the weakening Rumanian lines. The slow but deadly Stukas performed their typical duties as the army's "flying artillery." With sirens screeching, they attacked Soviet tank assembly points near Tulumschak. They claimed thirteen tanks and three motor vehicles destroyed, and damaged at least five other tanks. They bombed the village of Tulumschak itself, destroying houses, storage centers, and supply trucks. They also bombed and machine-gunned troop concentrations in and around the village. These troops suffered not only from Stuka attacks but also from heavy raids by twenty Ju 88 medium bombers, which left much of the village in flames. Other bombers struck at troop concentrations in Ak Monai (leaving the station and a train burning), as well as troops, tanks, artillery batteries, and field fortifications in different sectors of the Parpach Line. Only one aircraft, a Ju 88 from the 3rd Group of the "Edelweiss" wing, failed to make it back to base.

Supporting the hard-pressed Eleventh Army was clearly Wild's highest priority; only four aircraft (He 111s, carrying torpedoes) were used that day for antishipping missions.[118] During their flights over the western coast of the Crimea, two failed to locate any shipping targets. The third made two unsuccessful attempts to torpedo a 5,000-ton merchant vessel. As no bubble paths could be seen, the pilot reported, the torpedoes apparently failed to activate upon hitting the water. The final He 111 conducted a detailed search for enemy shipping off the southern coast of the Crimea but failed to sight a single vessel.

For the next two days, *Fliegerführer Süd* continued to pound enemy forces at both ends of the Crimea, with several notable successes. Bombers attacked troop concentrations and armored columns on the roads between Kerch and Ak Monai, for instance, inflicting considerable damage on tanks and trucks, while a He 111 on a joint reconnaissance-torpedo mission over the enemy harbors along the Caucasus coast hit and sunk a 6,000-ton supply ship with two torpedoes.[119] Losses continued to be low; only a single Bf 109 failed to return from a mission during these two days.

During this period, Manstein's headquarters—fearful of enemy landings on the south Crimean coastline—instructed both *Admiral Schwarzes Meer* and the sea-mining units of *Luftflotte 4* (mainly belonging to Wild's force) to mine the waters in the Kerch Straits and around the Crimea. However, on 6 March *Luftflotte 4*'s command staff informed *Vizeadmiral* Götting that it simply could not undertake any mining missions at present.[120] If it were to carry out its "also-requested long-range reconnaissance and defensive missions," the air fleet explained, it would be "unable to spare even a single aircraft for other duties in the Crimea and the greater part of Army Group South's combat zone during the entire period of the mining operations." That would clearly be unacceptable. If Manstein's command really wanted the mining operations to go ahead, the air fleet continued, then "*Luftflotte 4*'s operations against ground targets at the front must be cut back." Needless to say, no Luftwaffe units were withdrawn from combat duties in order to drop mines around the coasts. Instead, defensive minefields in front of Feodosiya, Yalta, and Eupatoria harbors were laid by a motley collection of Rumanian vessels commanded by *Admiral Schwarzes Meer*.[121]

Meanwhile, the first Soviet breakout attempt had gradually lost momentum, and by the evening of 3 March, German troops felt they had come through the worst of the storm. At Sevastopol the Soviets were pushed back into their previous positions. Their attack, the British Air Ministry noted in its secret intelligence summary for that week, "does not appear to have effected any material change in this area."[122] At the other end of the Crimea, the German defensive line had been battered but not broken, although it now receded twelve kilometers farther west in the northern sector. "A period of exhaustion on both sides then ensued," Manstein later recalled.

That period of inaction was short-lived. On 13 March, the Soviets (under Lieutenant General D. T. Kozlov, commander of the Crimean Front) began another mass attack from the Parpach Line, this time with eight rifle divisions and two tank brigades. It was a bloody battle. "We were able to knock out 136 tanks in the first three days of the attack," Manstein wrote,

> but as it progressed a number of heavy crises developed. The harshness of the fighting is illustrated by the fact that the regiments of the 46th Division, against which the heaviest blows fell, each had to fend off between 10 and 22 attacks during the first three days alone. On 18 March the 42nd Corps was forced to report that it was now incapable of withstanding further heavy attacks.

The defenders surrendered a few kilometers in certain sectors but managed to contain the enemy breakout, even though at great cost in men and matériel. To stave off defeat, the German commander had to throw the newly constituted

22nd Panzer Division into the fray, despite the fact that it had just arrived at the front and had not yet been put through its paces in exercises. A heavy rainstorm deprived this "green" division of air support during an attempted Soviet counter-attack on 20 March. Although it bungled its part in the operation and suffered high losses (thirty-two tanks were knocked out in only a few short hours), its very presence at the front added significant weight to the defense and helped bring the main Soviet attack to a gradual standstill.

Kozlov was as tenacious in attack as Manstein was in defense. "In waves that rose and receded every several days," wrote historians Ziemke and Bauer, the Soviet general "stayed on the attack into the second week of April, coming close at times but never succeeding in breaking out of the isthmus."[123] Indeed, by 11 April, his armies had suffered such high losses that their offensive capacity was spent. It would soon be their turn to bear the brunt of a powerful attack.

The situation had often been so critical during March and the first days of April that dive-bombers, fighter-bombers, and other tactical aircraft of *Flieger-korps IV* were frequently diverted from the Izyum area to support the smaller *Fliegerführer Süd* in the Crimea. This diversion of forces was only possible be-cause the situation in the region around Izyum had improved in recent weeks. German troops there had sealed off and destroyed the large Soviet penetration that threatened to rip apart the front in January and February, and were now suc-cessfully beating off a series of renewed attacks, each slightly weaker and more disorganized than its predecessor. *Fliegerkorps IV* provided these troops with the maximum support permitted by the slowly improving but still hostile weather conditions. In April, as the immediate threat of a Red Army breakthrough dis-solved, units of *Fliegerkorps IV* also conducted interdiction missions against So-viet rail traffic east of the Donets River and difficult counterpartisan operations in the vast forests south of Bryansk.[124] They also undertook three heavy night raids on "strategic" targets: an explosives factory in Tanbov, an aircraft factory in Voronezh, and a tractor works and gun factory in distant Stalingrad.[125]

Meanwhile, the reinforcements hastily diverted south from the Izyum area in March and early April joined with units of *Fliegerführer Süd* to attack the well-supplied and well-organized Soviet force of over 200,000 men on the Kerch Pen-insula, as well as ports and naval bases on the Crimea and the Caucasian coast.[126]

Despite urgently needing the assistance of these other air units to provide Eleventh Army with adequate air support, cut off enemy supply routes, and pre-vent further amphibious landings, *Fliegerführer Süd* proved its worth as a fighting force in a way its short-lived predecessor *(Sonderstab Krim)* had been unable to do. Its ground organization and logistical network had improved, as had the num-ber and condition of suitable airfields. This improvement, coupled with a gradual rise in temperature—which turned everything into a mud lake for a short time—resulted in higher operational rates and an increase in daily missions. As the situ-ation on the ground gradually improved, various units were even sent westward for long-overdue leave or refresher training, which, along with these other improvements, doubtless led to an increase in morale. Throughout this period, *Fliegerführer Süd,* operating alongside units of *Fliegerkorps IV,* conducted effective battlefield support and interdiction missions in support of Eleventh Army's efforts to contain the Soviets on the Kerch Peninsula. The bulk of the "direct support" burden still rested with the slow but deadly Stukas (usually protected from enemy fighter attacks by Bf 109 escorts). Acting on some days as an on-call "fire brigade" to patch up frontline difficulties, Wild's Stuka groups knocked out dozens of enemy tanks, assault guns, and trucks, and wrecked scores of dug-in tanks, bunkers, artillery batteries, and field installations.

Destroying tanks and other armored vehicles from the air was no mean feat. At that stage Stukas had no guns capable of penetrating thick armor; their only weapons capable of damaging a tank were their bombs, but scoring a direct hit on a moving tank on the battlefield was extremely difficult and placed the aircraft in grave danger from flak and even small-arms fire. In the confined spaces of the Parpach Isthmus, however, the massed Soviet armor thrust into the attack had no cover or room to maneuver. Moreover, although some of the tanks deployed were the fast and heavily armored T-34s, most were old and incapable of surviving much punishment. As Halder noted in his diary on 18 March: "At Kerch, the number of tanks committed is extraordinary, but the majority are worthless, obsolete types from training units and so on." As a result, the remarkable tank kill rates alleged by Stuka pilots may not be as exaggerated as they first appear. Having said that, it is worth noting that most of *Fliegerführer Süd*'s army support missions during this period were not directly over the battlefield but were of the "indirect" type. Stukas, Ju 88s, and He 111s repeatedly struck (and did considerable damage to) targets in the Soviet rear areas, including harbors, airfields, mobilization points, railheads, and supply and maintenance systems.

Wild committed almost every available aircraft to ground attack during these times of crisis but never neglected his reconnaissance and antishipping duties in favor of army support. On the contrary, as the danger to German ground forces steadily decreased through March and early April, Wild increased *Fliegerführer Süd*'s surveillance, convoy interdiction, and naval attack missions at a corresponding rate. His aircraft attacked shipping en route to the Crimea and flew reconnaissance missions over, and bombing raids against, Sevastopol, Kerch, and other ports in the region.

These missions, and those of the *Fliegerkorps IV* units assigned antishipping work, were conducted according to strict instructions from the *OKL*'s Operations Staff. Realizing that the small number of aircraft in the Crimea was incapable of performing effectively a wide variety of tasks, on 12 March the operations staff issued *Luftflotte 4* a list of instructions.[127] It insisted that "the *Schwerpunkt* of antishipping operations in the Black Sea is to be the ports of Sevastopol, Kerch, and Kamysh-Burun and their sea-lanes. Sevastopol, in particular, is to be the point of maximum effort!" As a result, the *OKL* instructions state, "antishipping missions in the sea's wider expanses are to be curtailed." Even Novorossiisk was to be left alone, at least until all shipping in Crimean waters had been attacked. Routine air reconnaissance missions should only be carried out in regions of the Black Sea where bombers or torpedo planes can intercept ships, and very few aircraft should be used for longer-range missions. For antishipping operations to be successful, the instructions continue, "the local command must keep suitable combat aircraft in a high state of readiness, so that they can respond to vessel sightings by air reconnaissance as soon as the radio message comes in." To add weight to these instructions, especially the section stating that shipping in and around Sevastopol was to be the main target, the *OKL* order concluded: "The Führer himself expects that, from now on, the steady shipping traffic around Sevastopol comes to a halt."

Fliegerführer Süd's daily operational reports for March and April reveal that Wild responded to these instructions by continuing his ground attack missions in support of Manstein's army while focusing his antishipping missions more closely on interdiction of sea routes to each end of the Crimea. Attacks on merchant shipping along Crimean coastlines increased in frequency, while raids on, and reconnaissance missions over, Novorossiisk and other Caucasian ports decreased. To overcome his force's numerical weakness, he ordered raids on enemy vessels to be carried out in rapid successive attacks by small groups of bombers or torpedo aircraft. Strikes against Sevastopol and other Crimean harbors were conducted in the same manner, although fighter escorts were needed to protect the bombers from *VVS* fighters stationed on airfields on the Kerch Peninsula and in the northwestern Caucasus. As it happened, the vast diversity of tasks performed by German air forces did not pass unnoticed by the commanders of those Soviet airfields, who tried to exploit the chaotic conditions in the Crimea by launching bombing raids against key German command centers and military installations. In the first week of March, for example, *VVS* bombers launched raids on Nikolayev, Feodosiya, and Saki and, on 19 March, struck Feodosiya, Simferopol, and other German-held Crimean centers.[128] They encountered almost no opposition in the air. Nonetheless, because of powerful flak defenses and the weakness of participating bomber forces, they proved incapable of inflicting significant damage and suffered heavy losses.

Aware by the middle of March that Manstein was planning a campaign to take Sevastopol and recapture the Kerch Peninsula, Wild initiated a program of regular exchanges and reliefs in order to bring his units back up to strength. Moreover, in anticipation of the coming campaign, he stepped up both the number of raids on enemy ports and shipping and the number of aerial photographic missions undertaken by the *4. (F) 122* long-range reconnaissance group. In order to provide ground commanders with clear and detailed photographs of all relevant locations, he ordered photographic reconnaissance of enemy fortifications, mobilization points, supply depots and routes on the Crimea, the presumed embarkation and supply ports along the Caucasus coastline, and airfields and transportation routes in the northern Caucasus. On 25 March, for instance, Ju 88s of *4.*

(F) 122 photographed enemy ports on the Crimea and in the Kerch Straits (Sevastopol, Kerch, Kamysh-Burun, and Tamanskaya) and those along the Caucasus coast (Novorossiisk and Tuapse), as well as Soviet airfields and train stations in the northwestern Caucasus (Krymskaya, Krasnodar, and Kropotkin).[129]

According to Luftwaffe general Hermann Plocher, *Fliegerführer Süd's* antishipping operations, usually conducted in cooperation with units of *Fliegerkorps IV*, "could scarcely halt the Soviet supply movements by land or sea."[130] Individual missions, he wrote, were "usually highly successful, but the cumulative effect on Russian supply traffic in the entire Black Sea area amounted simply to that of nuisance raids." Plocher is certainly correct about the performance of certain individual missions. Many *were* extremely successful. On 23 March, for example, nine Ju 88s from the 3rd Group of the "Edelweiss" wing attacked enemy shipping in Tuapse harbor, sinking one submarine and damaging two others.[131] On the same day, a 5,000-ton and two 2,000-ton merchant ships were sunk with torpedoes by He 111s of *II./K.G. 26* during a reconnaissance mission over Sevastopol. Plocher is wrong, however, about the "cumulative effect" of these missions. While they resulted in the sinking or damaging of relatively few enemy warships, they were certainly more than a "nuisance" to the Soviet logistical networks and sea supply convoys. The authors of the 1943 Red Army general staff study on the organization of the Crimean Front during this period reported as follows:

> By this time the enemy had activated his aviation and intensified raids on the ports of Kerch', Kamysh-Burun, and Novorossiisk. The Novorossiisk Port was particularly subjected to frequent enemy raids. Thus, on 7 and 8 April the enemy succeeded in burning part of the storage depots in Novorossiisk as a result of a massive air raid; 600 tons of hay, 190 tons of rusks, 700 inner tubes and tires, and 60 tons of tomatoes were destroyed, and 150 meters of station road were damaged. A second raid against the port sunk two transport ships and damaged another.
>
> Torpedo-carrying airplanes were often used. In night raids enemy aviation mined Novorossiisk Bay and especially the Kerch' Strait and Kamysh-Burun Port. In the first ten days of April alone, six ships with an overall displacement of 22,000 tons were sunk by bombing and mining, and much valuable cargo was lost.
>
> Without going into an account of the losses we suffered in April and the necessary measures taken against the particularly intensive actions of enemy aircraft, it should be mentioned that the effectiveness of enemy aviation raids was felt very strongly.[132]

This discussion of German air operations in the vast regions of southern Russia and the Black Sea has reached the point in April 1942 when Hitler issued War Directive No. 41, which (as already noted) called for the "clearing up" of the Crimea before the summer campaign into the Caucasus could commence. Throughout the previous two months, the Führer and his senior military advisers had frequently discussed the absolute necessity of holding back and eventually destroying the powerful Soviet forces at both ends of the Crimea. Because of the peninsula's strategic significance, both as a potential "aircraft carrier," from which the enemy could launch attacks on Rumanian oil fields, and as a spring-board for German advances into the Caucasus, there could be no question of leaving the enemy forces bottled up there. To prevent them from bursting out into the Crimean mainland, and to free up the army presently containing them, they would have to be destroyed. As the weather usually improved first in the south, and because the Crimea was needed as a springboard for German troops into the Caucasus, it was logical to achieve this before the major summer offensive. The only question—assuming that Manstein's battered defenses would not crack, which looked likely several times in February and the first half of March—was whether to start the offensive with Sevastopol or the Kerch Peninsula. Bock, commander of Army Group South, had wanted to start with the mighty fortress, while Manstein, whose Eleventh Army would again have to do the fighting, knew that he faced a far greater threat from the Soviet armies bottled up behind the Parpach Line.[133] Hitler apparently agreed with him that it was better to confront the Soviets where they were strongest than to have them at his back. Early in March, therefore, *Generalfeldmarschall* Keitel signed an order summarizing the various instructions issued by the Führer in recent weeks. Describing the future missions of Army Group South, he insisted that the Kerch Peninsula would have to be captured before the siege of Sevastopol could be started.[134] The following chapter will describe and analyze the decisive role played by the Luftwaffe in the two enormous battles to "clear up" the Crimea: first, Operation *Trappenjagd,* the offensive to destroy the well-equipped armies lying in wait behind the Parpach Line; and then Operation *Störfang,* the second siege of Sevastopol, the strongest fortress in the world.

3

Operation "Bustard Hunt": May 1942

Manstein grimly realized that the destruction of the enemy forces on the Kerch Peninsula and in Sevastopol would be extremely difficult with the forces likely to be at his disposal. Aerial reconnaissance revealed that they substantially outnumbered his own. He recalled after the war that "the ratio of forces in the Crimea provided no grounds for any real optimism regarding the outcome of both massive undertakings."[1] Sevastopol, he continued, was defended by as many as seven Soviet rifle divisions, one rifle brigade, two naval brigades, and one dismounted cavalry division. Once the Kerch campaign commenced, the only Axis forces available on the northern and eastern fronts of Sevastopol to contain them were the 54th Corps and the newly arrived 19th Rumanian Division, which had been sent there to release the German 50th Division for Kerch. The only Axis force left on the southern front would be the 72nd Infantry Division. The entire south coast of the Crimea would have to be protected against surprise enemy landings by the understrength Rumanian Mountain Corps, which then comprised only the 4th Mountain Brigade.

On the Kerch front the Soviets' numerical superiority was even greater than at Sevastopol. "At the end of April," Manstein wrote in his memoirs, "they had seventeen rifle divisions, three rifle brigades, two cavalry divisions and four tank brigades—a total of twenty-six large formations."[2] The field marshal's account, detailed as it is, fails to reveal clearly the awesome strength of the three armies formed by those formations: the 44th, 47th, and 51st. For instance, he scarcely mentioned their defenses, logistics system, and state of combat readiness and totally ignored the participation of the 47th Army (perhaps because only half of it was ever used against his own force), even though as many as 40,000 of its men were deployed on the Kerch Peninsula.[3]

The Soviet command had more troops on that peninsula than it could conveniently deploy in its confines. The front itself, stretching along the line of the

Ak Monai positions, measured only eighteen kilometers in width, yet behind it waited no fewer than 210,000 well-equipped troops. This led in some sectors to what even a Red Army general staff report called "an unacceptable density of forces."[4] The 51st Army, to give an example, crammed nine full divisions in and behind the northern part of the front, which, after recent gains, now protruded westward. This narrow sector measured less than six kilometers across. This means that there were more than seventeen soldiers to every meter of front. On the other hand, the huge amount of available manpower on the peninsula—the same report notes that both the front and army rear areas were "saturated" with reserves—allowed the Soviet command to stage a defense in massive depth. At least theoretically, this defense would increase in strength farther east where the peninsula widened to as much as fifty kilometers, allowing troops to be used far more effectively than in the congested narrows of the isthmus. To reach the ports of Kerch and Kamysh-Burun, situated on the Kerch Straits seventy-five kilometers behind the front, the Germans would have to bulldoze through three carefully prepared defensive lines: the Parpach Line, extending across the isthmus at its narrowest point; the Nasyr Line, running parallel to it eight kilometers to the east; and the Sultanovka Line, stretching across the peninsula at one of its broadest points thirty kilometers in front of Kerch.

Although the Sultanovka Line (the so-called Turkish Wall that followed the remains of ancient fortifications) was formidable, the Parpach Line easily surpassed it in strength. The latter had a ten-meter-wide and five-meter-deep antitank ditch, first built in 1941 but substantially expanded by Soviet engineers after the amphibious landings in midwinter. Behind it lay wide minefields and barriers of barbed wire, and farther back countless "Spanish horsemen" (huge iron hedgehogs of welded-together railway tracks) protected concrete bunkers, artillery positions, and machine-gun posts.

Because the sea on either side of the Parpach Line excluded the possibility of outflanking maneuvers, Manstein accepted that his main attack would have to be frontal. He also knew, however, that the forces at his disposal—five German infantry divisions and the 22nd Panzer Division, augmented by two Rumanian divisions and a brigade—would be outnumbered by almost three to one; therefore, a purely frontal assault along the front was unlikely to achieve anything. He racked his brain for an alternative plan—one that would allow his troops not only to break through the strong Parpach defenses but also to destroy the main bulk, or at least a substantial part, of the Soviet formations in the process of the first breakthrough.

There was, Manstein concluded, only one possibility. During recent attacks, the enemy had managed to extend his front in the northern sector of the narrow front by around seven kilometers. The Soviet command was gravely aware that this protruding section was highly vulnerable, especially after the failed attempt of the 22nd Panzer Division to stab into the base of the small salient and destroy the cutoff forces. As a result of these heightened fears, the Soviet command significantly reinforced the bulge. This explains why the 51st Army was so densely packed there. The German general learned from ground and air reconnaissance that "the Soviets had massed two-thirds of their troops (both frontline and reserve) in and behind this northern sector alone. In the southern sector they deployed only three divisions in the line and two or three in reserve."[5] Accordingly, he devised a plan that would see his troops, strongly supported by the Luftwaffe, burst through the Parpach Line "not in the protruding enemy sector, but down in the southern sector along the coast of the Black Sea; that is, where they least expected it." After four or five kilometers these forces—two infantry divisions and the 22nd Panzer Division—would be through the main line. They would then wheel north and drive into the rear of the enemy divisions concentrated in and behind the bulge, cutting off and eventually destroying them. While this took place, other Axis forces would advance rapidly toward Kerch, thereby protecting the eastern flank of those encircling the "pocket" and preventing the enemy in the rear from organizing any counteroffensive operations.

On 31 March, Manstein issued a preliminary directive for the operation, to be code-named *Trappenjagd* ("bustard hunt"). War diaries of German officers in the Crimea reveal the humor in this strange choice of name; they describe how Manstein and other senior officers (including Richthofen, after he arrived)[6] occasionally liked to go on hunting expeditions. Their game was not the wolf or bear, or any other dangerous predator in the region, but the harmless great bustard, the largest land bird in Europe. Vast numbers of these prized game birds, well known for their timidity and remarkable running speed, lived around the Black Sea. According to several diarists, they tasted delicious when slowly roasted. Despite the humorous imagery, Manstein was acutely aware of the great risks involved in his forthcoming "bustard hunt," and two days later told both the *OKH* and Bock, commander of Army Group South, that he still considered the discrepancy in forces too great.[7] Bock replied that, while the *OKH* might make another division or two available late in May, the operation should commence as soon as possible to prevent the Soviets themselves from seizing the initiative in the meantime. On 16 April, Manstein took his *Trappenjagd* plan to Hitler, who approved everything except for the Luftwaffe dispositions. He would see to them himself.[8]

The Führer was by experience and inclination an "army man" who, despite his superb grasp of technical details, lacked experience in air tactics and strategy. During the successful first years of the war, he had rarely meddled in air force affairs. He was content to leave most decisions to Göring, the Luftwaffe's pompous commander in chief, and Milch, the latter's capable and dedicated deputy. Over the winter of 1941–1942, however, the Führer came to appreciate the key role played by air support. In numerous places along the eastern front, he had seen the Luftwaffe patch up frontline difficulties, sometimes even significantly affecting the outcome of battles. Clearly impressed, he began to interfere in air matters—often without consulting Göring. Late in February, to illustrate this point, *Generaloberst* Georg von Küchler, commander of Army Group North, had

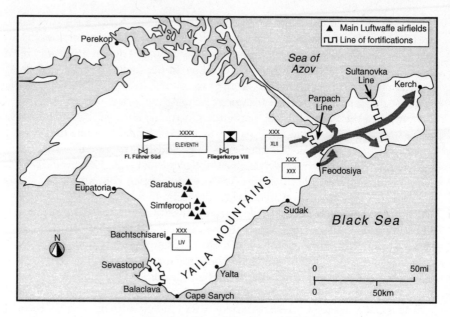

2. The Crimean campaign, May–July 1942

laid plans for a counterattack near Volkhov in the far north. On 2 March, Hitler personally ordered a "thorough air preparation of several days" before the opening of the attack.[9] The weather was so unfavorable, however, that few aircraft could take to the air. Consequently, the Führer expressly ordered Küchler, who was anxious to get under way, to postpone the offensive "until weather conditions permit the full deployment of the Air Force."[10] A month later he lectured him on the importance of close air support. Back in January, he said, Toropets would not have been lost, and with it key German fuel dumps and supply depots, if the group commander had fully understood the potential of this support.[11] Perhaps with this "failure" in mind, Hitler decided to organize the deployment of air units for the important Kerch offensive himself.

That offensive, he had stated late in February, demanded "massed airpower."[12] On 17 April he held a lengthy conference with his air staff to work out the nature and level of this "massed airpower."[13] Until he could discuss the situation with *Generaloberst* Richthofen, whose powerful *Fliegerkorps VIII* he planned to use in the Crimea alongside Löhr's *Luftflotte 4,* Hitler initially dealt only with the dispositions of Löhr's fleet. Heavy siege guns were being sent to the Crimea for the assault on Sevastopol, he said, including the 800-mm railway cannon "Dora," the heaviest gun in the world. Because these siege guns were difficult to move and impossible to camouflage, their defense from air attack was absolutely crucial. *Luftflotte 4,* he pointed out, was solely responsible for their safety. Its lone antiaircraft unit was incapable of protecting them, so a second would be sent from the Rumanian or Bulgarian area. Both were to be equipped with light and heavy searchlights. The transportation of the guns and equipment was to be protected by light flak guns on the trains themselves and by the deployment of fighter aircraft. *Luftflotte 4,* said Hitler, was to ensure that the guns and equipment arrived safely and (just as important) on time. The air fleet was also "to test whether or not the possibility exists, shortly before the arrival of those trains, to destroy on the ground the enemy aircraft situated at the airfields of Sevastopol by an attack with strong forces." Moreover, it must report immediately on the current availability of flak units before Sevastopol and the Kerch Front, and whether these units were being strengthened before each attack commenced. Acutely aware that Rumanian troops had, as Manstein later complained, "limited usefulness in an offensive role," Hitler also ordered *Luftflotte 4* to pay special attention to the 18th Rumanian Division's sector and to "rebut with strong air support" any attacks made against it from Sevastopol.

If the Kerch campaign were to succeed, Hitler emphasized, it was absolutely necessary to cut off Soviet forces from their supplies. *Luftflotte 4,* therefore, must note the following:

> During the period until the attack itself begins, the supply of the Kerch Peninsula must be interrupted in the strongest manner. Because of the short travel time of the ships between Novorossiisk and Kerch, it will often be impossible to attack them at sea. The point of main effort *[Schwerpunkt]* of the fight against supplies will therefore be the harbors of Kerch and Kamysh-Burun as well as Novorossiisk and Tuapse.

Despite this energetic fight against supplies to the Kerch Peninsula, he added, the operational readiness of the units of *Luftflotte 4* must be further increased. To enhance the fleet's offensive capabilities, it would be given temporary authority over the 55th Bomber Wing. Also, Göring, as commander in chief of the Luftwaffe, would supply enough new aircraft to bring the fleet up to full strength. To boost the number of experienced airmen for the operation (and especially for the He 111 units), *Luftflotte 4* was to draw personnel from the fourth (training) *Gruppe* of each wing. When selecting aircrew from these groups, it was important to note that even pilots unable to fly by instruments alone would be used during periods of good weather. They would be placed under the command of older and more experienced flight leaders.

New airfields on the Crimea must immediately be created and supplied, Hitler added, so that the approach flights—not only of fighters and Stukas but also of most bombers—could be kept as short as possible and the number of operations increased. If the supply of those airfields by road and rail could not be achieved in time for the attack, then air transport must be used. Should this situation arise, *Luftflotte 4* must request assistance from the quartermaster general of the air force. The air fleet itself and not the army, Hitler stressed, was responsible for the protection of its airfields.

The Führer placed great emphasis on the employment of the deadly and effective SD2 fragmentation bombs, developed during the previous year specifically for use in the east. These small 2-kg bombs—christened "Devil's eggs" by aircrew—fragmented into between 50 and 250 pieces of shrapnel, which sprayed out in a five-meter radius. Large numbers could be dropped at once and detonated on impact or just above the ground with devastating effects on troop concentrations. SD2s, Hitler explained, "are best used against living targets. A satisfactory result can only be achieved when the bombs are used against crowds." The equipping of *Luftflotte 4* bomber units with these bombs was to be speeded up. Regardless of whether the production goal was reached, he added, it was essential that the special canisters they needed (of which around 6,000 were supposed to be available by the end of April) would be delivered immediately to that air fleet. The supply of the bombs themselves must be regulated so that no shortages could possibly occur. To determine how many were needed, planners were to base their calculations on the assumption that the campaign against the Kerch Peninsula would take fourteen days.

Hitler knew that the Parpach Line would be extremely hard to break through. Soviet artillery batteries and other installations, he therefore insisted, were "to be hit with the heaviest available bombs. The air fleet must also ascertain whether it is possible, by using the heaviest bombs, to create a safe path for German tanks across the massive enemy antitank ditches." Göring must fully strengthen *Luftflotte 4* in time for the attack against the Kerch Peninsula. While the air fleet in general was to be strengthened, the heaviest possible concentration of airpower for the capture of Kerch was to be obtained. So important was this operation, he stressed, that once it got under way the other sectors of the front in the southern zone would have to go without air support. The only exception permitted, Hitler concluded, would be the defense of troops attacked from Sevastopol.

THE ADVENT OF VON RICHTHOFEN

One historian claims that shortly after this conference "the potential for concentrating German air power in the Crimea increased dramatically. Richthofen, who interceded personally with Hitler, convinced the Führer of the need to employ *Fliegerkorps VIII* in the operation."[14] *Generaloberst* Wolfram Freiherr von Richthofen certainly did meet Hitler at this time, and his powerful close air support force *was* subsequently sent to the Crimea to support *Luftflotte 4*'s attacks on Kerch and Sevastopol. But even a cursory reading of Richthofen's personal diary for April reveals that the decision to send him to the Crimea was made in his absence and without his prior knowledge by Hitler and Jeschonnek, the Luftwaffe chief of staff. "Arrived in Lüneburg on 12 April for a four-week holiday," Richthofen penned on 18 April. "At last! But on 18 April, while entertaining guests, received a phone call from Jeschonnek: By order of the Führer, I must immediately leave again, to work at Kerch. Get there quickly, get everything started! Then I can again take a few days off. Formal orders still to come. No use complaining."[15] The following day he flew to Berlin in a Fieseler Fi 156 Storch and, in Jeschonnek's company, rang Hitler from the Air Ministry. "The Führer," he wrote that night, "insisted in a very respectful manner that I should take part at Kerch, because I'm the only person who can do the job." The risk of failure, Hitler emphasized, "must be minimized, because the first blow struck this year must be successful."

Hitler clearly thought that the transfer to the Crimea of Richthofen's *Fliegerkorps VIII*, a specialized close-support force with an unparalleled combat record, would guarantee that his "first blow" against the Soviets in 1942 would be a success. Richthofen was an arrogant and aggressive man (whose diary entries are full of harsh and often unfair criticisms of both superiors and subordinates), but he was an extraordinarily successful and influential tactical air commander. He was, as another historian wrote, "certainly one of the best tacticians in the history of air warfare."[16]

Richthofen was born into an aristocratic family in Barzdorf, Silesia, on 10 October 1895.[17] As a young ensign, he served in the 4th Hussars Regiment from March 1913 until September 1917. He then transferred to the Imperial Air Service, eventually joining the famous Richthofen Squadron, whose first commander had been his cousin Manfred, the legendary "Red Baron." After the war he studied engineering, eventually gaining a doctorate. He resumed his military career in November 1923, and throughout the 1920s his *Reichswehr* service included time in the cavalry, infantry, and artillery. From April 1929 to October 1932, he served as air attaché in the German embassy in Rome, where he befriended Italo Balbo, the Fascist hero and Italian minister of aviation.

In October 1933, Richthofen joined the fledgling Reich Air Ministry, which evolved into the Luftwaffe two years later. In 1936 he served as chief of staff to both *Generalmajor* Hugo Sperrle and his successor, *Generalmajor* Helmuth Volkmann, commanders of the "Condor Legion," which earned fame (and infamy, after the bombing of Guernica) during the Spanish civil war. In November 1938, promoted to *Generalmajor* himself, he became the final commander of that unit. During the Spanish war he experimented with close air support tactics and aircraft (including a few early Ju 87 Stukas) and, no doubt influenced by his experiences as both a soldier and pilot during the Great War, developed tactics and a ground-air liaison system improving air support effectiveness. Also, his experiences in Spain removed his earlier doubts about the dive-bomber. Realizing that it was far more accurate than current horizontal bombers—and, therefore, more useful for tactical purposes—he returned to Germany as one of its advocates.

Because of his outstanding successes in Spain and his competence in the use of the dive-bomber and new methods of tactical air employment, which had a significant effect on German air planners, Richthofen was quickly hailed as the

Luftwaffe's expert in this field. In July 1939, he formed a special close-support force *(Fliegerführer z.b.V.)*, which quickly expanded into the powerful *Fliegerkorps VIII*. Under his command, this specialized ground attack corps distinguished itself in Poland and France by its excellent support of advancing panzer spearheads (for which he won the Knight's Cross and promotion to *General der Flieger*).

His sluggish Stukas, on the other hand, proved so vulnerable to enemy fighters in regions where air superiority had not been attained that he was compelled to provide fighter escorts. Even so, they were severely mauled by British fighters during the Battle of Britain, forcing the air fleet commanders hastily to withdraw them. However, Richthofen's corps provided exemplary close support in the absence of enemy fighters during the Balkans campaign and the airborne invasion of Crete. Enjoying the luxury of almost total air superiority, his Stukas inflicted heavy losses on Allied troops, transports, and shipping. For his dynamic leadership he was awarded Oak Leaves to the Knight's Cross.

Richthofen's air corps won further laurels in the eastern campaign, especially during the height of the winter crisis when, operating by itself after the transfer of Kesselring's units, its support of the army in the critical central zone before Moscow was outstanding. In recognition of these achievements, he was promoted to *Generaloberst* on 1 February 1942. This was a unique honor for an air corps commander; he now had the same rank as the air fleet commanders and the most senior Luftwaffe staff officers, such as Jeschonnek and the late Udet.

In preparation for the major summer campaign, the various units of *Fliegerkorps VIII* had been sent in early April back to their home bases in the Reich for rehabilitation. The rebuilding of the badly battered units was still in progress when Richthofen flew to *Luftflotte 4*'s headquarters in Nikolayev on 21 April, accompanied by his good friend, Jeschonnek. The latter explained that Richthofen's refitted corps, when it finally arrived in the region, was to work in close cooperation with *Luftflotte 4*. However, contrary to the previous custom of placing all corps under the control of the fleet in the region, Richthofen's was not going to be placed under *Luftflotte 4*'s authority. *Fliegerkorps VIII,* under Richthofen's command at all times, would actually take charge of air operations during the offensive and answer only to Göring.[18] It would also provide the lion's share of the army's close support.

This greatly offended the honor of *Luftflotte 4*'s senior officers, especially Günther Korten, the air fleet's chief of staff. Korten, an intuitive and talented officer who later succeeded Jeschonnek as Luftwaffe chief of staff, demanded that he lead the air units himself.[19] This demand fell on deaf ears, to the indignation of his colleagues. They were, Richthofen recorded in his diary, "deeply peeved and viewed my arrival with considerable mistrust." His criticisms of their "not very convincing preparations" for the offensive only made things worse. Eating in the officers' mess, he sarcastically wrote, "was like sitting in a house with a corpse. . . . in the evening the fleet drowned its grief in alcohol."

The following day he flew to the Crimea in order to talk with local air commanders. He was not impressed by how apathetic they appeared and, to their distaste ("they pull stupid faces"), angrily informed them that they "must be woken from their winter sleep."[20] He also had a lengthy meeting with Manstein. This conference went surprisingly well, despite the potential for a major ego clash between these two brilliant but conceited personalities. "Manstein was surprisingly mellow and accommodating," the air commander jotted that evening. "He understood everything. It was extremely uplifting." On many other occasions he described his army counterpart in similarly glowing terms. The respect was clearly mutual. "Baron von Richthofen," the army general later recalled, "was certainly the most outstanding air force leader we had in World War II."[21] "He made great demands on his units," the general continued,

> but always went up [in an aircraft] himself to oversee important attacks. Moreover, one was always meeting him at the front, where he would visit even the most advanced units to get a clear picture of the possibilities of providing air support for army operations. Our cooperation, both at Eleventh Army and later at Army Groups South and Don, was always excellent.

The partnership of these men, two of the most talented operational commanders of the Second World War, was probably unrivaled during that great conflict. The specter of petty rivalry revealed itself extremely rarely, and even then it appeared only in the pages of their private diaries. There were no public squabbles or instances of major dissension. This cannot be said for the professional relationships of many top Allied field commanders, whose ego clashes and strategical differences often caused significant problems (the case of Montgomery and Patton in the Mediterranean and in northwestern Europe springs to mind). One has to search hard for evidence that the two Germans operated in anything but total unison. On 28 April, to show how insignificant the exceptions are, Richthofen recorded in his diary that he felt snubbed that day by his partner: "Waited for *Generalfeldmarschall* Bock [commander of Army Group South]. Said '*Guten Tag*' to him, after which Manstein apparently tried to prevent me meeting further with him." Despite feeling annoyed, he said and did nothing to inflame the situation, but a few days later took great delight in beating Manstein in a debate over tactical differences in front of the 30th Army Corps' command. "Victory!" he jubilantly penned that night. "It's pathetic to say, but I'm 'top general'!"[22]

In close consultation, they meticulously coordinated their operations and created joint *Schwerpunkte* (points of main effort). Manstein knew that his own forces were numerically weak and would, therefore, require the best possible air support. Poor communications could prove disastrous, so he stressed the need for effective liaison between ground and air forces. Orders from the 30th Army Corps, for example, which doubtless originated from him, instructed its staff to deal directly with *Fliegerkorps VIII* rather than proceed through normal air fleet channels as in past campaigns.[23]

Richthofen's main task in this period was to ensure that all air preparations for the attack were going to plan. When he arrived back in Nikolayev on 27 April, the day before his command staff arrived in the Crimea and three days before he assumed formal command, he was very disappointed by *Luftflotte 4*'s preparations for the offensive, due to commence on 5 May. While having coffee with Alexander Löhr, the Austrian-born air fleet commander, he lectured his own senior officers about their poor preparation efforts. "They were," he recorded that evening, "extremely inferior." This was apparently not a popular message, as revealed by his next comment: "Some friction and difficulties."

During this time Richthofen traveled constantly from base to base in his light Storch aircraft, which often came under enemy fire and occasionally had to make forced landings. He took these risks in order personally to brief his wing and group commanders and flak battalion leaders, and to exhort them to speed up their preparations. Believing that commanders are only as good as the men they command, on many occasions he addressed not only officers but also large groups of assembled troops.

His concerns about the operational readiness of local air units were exacerbated by the slow arrival of others returning from rehabilitation in the west. "Two fighter groups and a ground-attack wing," he complained in his diary on 2 May, "are stranded in Silesia because of bad weather. They were supposed to have arrived today in *Luftflotte 4*'s sector." He was clearly unhappy and asked Jeschonnek whether the campaign should be postponed until they arrived. He also discussed the situation with Manstein, who agreed to postpone it for two days (that is, until 7 May).[24] The army leader was well aware that the success of *Trappenjagd* depended on the strongest possible air support. It is a ground operation, he explained to his corps and division commanders that day, but its main effort is in the air. Aircraft would have to "pull the infantry forward."[25] Only the day before, he had enthusiastically stated that the operation would have "concentrated air support the like of which has never existed."[26] On 4 May, however, Richthofen was forced to postpone the operation a further day because enemy air attacks on forward airfields prevented him from positioning his fighters close to the front.[27] When the missing ground-attack wing turned up in Nikolayev the following day, without the two fighter groups, which were then in Rumania and Bulgaria, he wanted to postpone it again. However, after consulting weather reports, which predicted good weather on the scheduled start date, and learning that the groups were on their way (they actually arrived the following day), he decided against delaying the attack. It would go ahead, as arranged, on 8 May.

Richthofen realized that he had a remarkably strong force at his disposal, comprising no fewer than eleven bomber, three dive-bomber, and seven fighter *Gruppen*. Despite his unhappiness at the general state of preparations, he never doubted that *Trappenjagd* would be successful and that his air units would play a decisive role. "I actually have the impression," he wrote in his diary after inspecting the front on 28 April, "that, compared to the middle front, the battle here will be very light and easily accomplished at no great cost." Repeating himself, he closed his entry that night with the words: "I believe the battle *will* be very easy." That evening, Bock recorded in his own diary his feelings about the offensive. He was far less optimistic. While he was impressed by the army's "careful preparations" for the attack, he still worried about the "extraordinary risk" it entailed.[28] His anxiety grew as the launch date approached. He was especially concerned about the enemy's defensive depth and, on 5 May, even proposed giving up the wheel to the north.[29] Manstein insisted that this crucial northward turn was the only way of destroying the bulk of enemy forces in the first breakthrough. The army group commander relented and allowed the operation to go ahead as planned.

In recent days, Manstein had done everything possible to convince the Soviets that he was going to attack in the northern sector and that they should continue to mass troops there. Radio messages meant for the enemy's listening posts were sent, deceptive reconnaissance missions and troop movements were undertaken, and false artillery positions were constructed. He also recruited Richthofen's units, which pounded the enemy in the northern sector. The air commander was keen to help out, seeing the deception operations as excellent opportunities to test his units' combat capabilities. He was clearly pleased with the result. "Giant fire-magic!" he wrote after witnessing a bombardment on the eve of the attack. "The infantry should see what we have to offer. It would increase their courage." He had actually tried a week earlier to deploy his aircraft in a diversionary attack, believing it would deceive the enemy, put his units through their paces, and raise morale.[30] On that occasion, however, he was unable to persuade Manstein, who quickly squashed the idea, arguing that it would divide available air assets and, with more than a week to go until the start date, forfeit the advantage of surprise.[31]

THE LUFTWAFFE'S RECENT OPERATIONS

Before we analyze the course of the battle itself, which commenced in the early hours of 8 May, it is necessary to describe and briefly explain the Luftwaffe's recent activities in the region. After all, during the operation's planning stages in the first weeks of April and before Richthofen's units finally arrived in and around the Crimea later that month, local air units continued to perform their various tasks. Pflugbeil's *Fliegerkorps IV* performed the vast majority of all air operations in the massive southern sector of the eastern front. Most of Pflugbeil's units were deployed in support of German armies in the Ukraine but, as already noted, several operated alongside *Fliegerführer Süd* in support of Manstein's troops in the Crimea. In April, the latter units were called upon to perform a wide range of antishipping tasks, including sea mining. To prevent dug-in enemy forces on the Kerch Peninsula from gaining reinforcements by sea from the

Kuban, and to ensure that no full-scale, Odessa-style evacuations occurred, Manstein requested that *Fliegerkorps IV* mine the Kerch Straits.[32]

On 2 April, units commenced mining operations in the straits, which continued sporadically for several weeks.[33] Reluctant to "waste" its already overtaxed resources on what it perceived to be a low-priority task, the air corps committed only a small number of aircraft (He 111s and Ju 88s) to the mining missions. As no more than three magnetic mines could be carried in each, they proved incapable of laying dense minefields. The mines they dropped were never more than a nuisance to enemy ships plying the sea-lanes. *Admiral Schwarzes Meer*, aware from air reconnaissance that Soviet minesweepers still patrolled the straits, actually anticipated this poor result: "Because of Russian minesweepers reportedly in the Kerch Straits, one must accept that the contamination of these waters from the air will not be effective until Kerch itself is once again in our hands."[34]

Wild's *Fliegerführer Süd*, still operating alongside *Luftflotte 4* units, ceaselessly bombed and strafed enemy field installations, artillery batteries, troop concentrations, and army rear areas in the Kerch Peninsula, and struck at Sevastopol's defensive strong points and supply centers. His small force was also determined to interdict sea supply routes and prevent enemy landings or evacuations during the coming offensives. As a result, it kept all Soviet forces, supply lines, and possible reinforcement routes in the region under close and constant surveillance. Even Soviet naval historians acknowledged after the war that *Fliegerführer Süd*'s reconnaissance work was of the first order. "In February 1942," wrote Achkasov and Pavlovich, "previous high-sea convoy routes were replaced by new routes, since enemy aerial reconnaissance had increased on the former. However, in April we had to stop using the new routes, because they too were discovered by enemy reconnaissance."[35]

Fliegerführer Süd also hammered enemy ports and potential embarkation points on the Crimean and Caucasian coasts. "In the southern sector of *Luftflotte 4*'s combat zone," Luftwaffe historians noted in 1944, "the heaviest weight of the fighting fell on the harbors in question, which supplied Sevastopol and the enemy forces dug in on the Kerch Peninsula."[36] Wild's force lacked the resources necessary to immobilize totally the Soviets' shipping operations. In particular, it proved incapable of preventing Soviet vessels laying both offensive minefields in sea-lanes now starting to be used by German supply ships and defensive minefields around Sevastopol and the south Crimean coastline.[37] Nonetheless, through careful deployment and constant attacks, *Fliegerführer Süd* was able to destroy many harbor installations and disrupt a substantial amount of enemy supply shipments.

German air units did not have the skies over the Crimea and the Black Sea entirely to themselves. During the winter, the Soviet aviation industry, now safely relocated beyond the Urals, had slowly regained and then increased its prewar productive capacity. Accordingly, *VVS* forces, including those in the south, slowly recovered their strength. The Luftwaffe estimated at the beginning of March that the *VVS* had no fewer than 722 aircraft based on forty separate airfields through-out *Luftflotte 4*'s huge combat zone.[38] Although this estimate is more than 15 per-cent too high, the *VVS* certainly had at least as many aircraft in the region as the Germans. Desperate to regain the Crimea, the Soviets operated fighters, fighter-bombers, and bombers from four airfields on the Kerch Peninsula and ten in the northwestern Caucasus. Few of the fighters, however, were the excellent new mod-els (such as the Yakovlev Yak-7B and the Lavotchkin La-5) now being produced in the Urals. The majority of those went straight to the central zone in anticipa-tion of a new German campaign to take the capital, as did most of the lend-lease British and American aircraft already reaching the Soviet Union. While the *VVS* units in the south did receive some of the latest aircraft, by March the vast bulk of their fighters and bombers were still antiquated and inferior types posing no real threat to the Luftwaffe's latest Bf 109Gs. Their fighters included the Polikar-pov I-153 *Chaika* (Gull), the I-15 *Chato* (Snub-nose), and the truncated I-16 *Rata* (Rat), all dating from the Spanish Civil War period. The first two, both biplanes, were no match for their vastly superior German counterparts, and even the latter, a monoplane of better design, usually came off worst in aerial combat. As a result, these fighters "fell like flies."[39]

Determined to keep the airspace over Manstein's troops free of enemy air-craft, *Fliegerführer Süd* devoted a great deal of effort to the surveillance, bomb-ing, and strafing of enemy airfields, both on the Kerch Peninsula and in the north-western Caucasus. Powerful enemy flak defenses made this a dangerous task, but Wild's units still managed to damage significantly many airfields and occasion-ally destroy aircraft caught on the ground. Of course, they also had to protect their own airfields from air attacks, which were constantly attempted but rarely accomplished by the courageous though outclassed Soviet fliers. In April alone, Wild's units claimed ninety-two enemy aircraft destroyed in the air and a further fourteen on the ground, suffering only seven recorded losses.[40] The most success-ful single day was 30 April, when Bf 109s of *II./J.G. 77* and *III./J.G. 52* shot down twenty-four Soviet fighters and bombers attacking their airfields (almost all of Spanish Civil War vintage), for no losses.[41] These figures, it should be pointed out, relate only to *Fliegerführer Süd.* Units belonging to Pflugbeil's *Fliegerkorps IV* and, after their arrival late in April, Richthofen's *Fliegerkorps VIII,* racked up their own impressive tallies. On 2 May, for example, Richthofen's fliers engaged Soviet aircraft during a bombing raid on their airfields. "32 verified kills," the air commander proudly jotted in his diary, "with no losses." The *VVS* proved unable, therefore, to hamper significantly German preparations for their Crimean cam-paigns. By the time *Trappenjagd* commenced, local Soviet air forces had been se-verely weakened and German air superiority won.

When Richthofen's illustrious air corps arrived in the Crimea, it immedi-ately assumed operational command (informally at first, officially during the as-sault on Sevastopol) of Wild's far smaller force. As a result, even the *Luftwaffe's* own historians, when looking back on the 1942 Crimean campaigns, focused closely on *Fliegerkorps VIII*'s sensational support of Manstein's army but failed to mention specifically the role played before and during the campaigns by the less glamorous *Fliegerführer Süd*. The daily operational reports of Wild's command, however, reveal that its contribution to German successes was significant. From 18 February, when it replaced *Sonderstab Krim* as the principal air force in the Crimea and Black Sea regions, until the opening of *Trappenjagd* on 8 May, *Fliegerführer Süd* did an effective job with the limited forces at its disposal. During that period, it conducted extensive reconnaissance and dropped no fewer than 350,000 propaganda leaflets over enemy lines. It rained bombs down on Sevastopol and the ports in the Kerch Straits, sinking 68,450 tons of enemy shipping (a third by torpedoes) and two submarines.[42] It critically damaged another submarine, which probably also sank, and less seriously damaged a large number of ships, including 42,000 tons of merchant shipping, one heavy cruiser, one light cruiser, four submarines, and a tug. Its list of "probably damaged vessels" includes 21,500 additional tons of merchant shipping, a further submarine, and a patrol boat.

Fliegerführer Süd also reported that it shot down as many as 204 enemy fighters and bombers and smashed another 30 on the ground. On the battlefield (mainly at Kerch) it blew up three flak batteries and five artillery installations and heavily damaged twenty-five others. It knocked out no fewer than 64 tanks, damaged another 29, put 98 trucks off the road for good, and left a further 36 damaged. Its attacks on army rear areas were equally effective, resulting in the destruction or incapacitation of seventeen locomotives and trains, and the total destruction of five petrol dumps, various railway and industrial installations, and numerous bridges. Heavy blows against ammunition dumps, infantry installations, and troop concentrations "also produced good results." It is clear, therefore, that Wild's force contributed significantly to German achievements in the critical period leading up to the opening of *Trappenjagd*. Its ability to contribute substantially to all forthcoming campaigns in the region, including both *Trappenjagd* and *Störfang*, was by no means diminished by the arrival of Richthofen's powerful corps.

TRAPPENJAGD: THE BUSTARD QUICKLY CAUGHT

On 7 May, Richthofen held his final briefings with *Oberst* von Grodeck, whose motorized "Grodeck Brigade" had been set up as Manstein's reserve force, and later with Löhr and Korten, *Luftflotte 4*'s commander and chief of staff. With less than twenty-four hours until the campaign commenced, they still had matters to discuss, including interservice cooperation, the latest situation reports, and their intentions for the following day's offensive. *General* Schulz, Manstein's new chief of staff, paid Richthofen a visit later that evening. He did so, the latter scathingly wrote, "in order to get some backbone."[43]

Even as they talked, the preliminary operations for the attack got under way. Four companies of combat engineers and infantrymen climbed into thirty small assault boats and pushed off from Feodosiya harbor into the darkness of the Black Sea. This secret fleet's mission was to land just behind the Parpach anti-tank ditch at the same time as the main frontal offensive reached it early the next morning. This was only possible because the Soviet Black Sea Fleet was relatively inactive around Crimean coastlines at that time. Increasing air attacks on his ships by *Fliegerführer Süd* and elements of *Fliegerkorps IV* had, as mentioned previously, concerned Vice Admiral Oktyabrskii so much back in February that he had ordered his captains to take great care in regions patrolled by enemy air forces. In particular, they were to conduct coastal bombardment missions only under cover of darkness and were to risk none of their larger vessels except during periods when poor weather grounded the Luftwaffe. At that time, of course, the long hours of winter darkness provided Oktyabrskii's vessels with excellent protection from air attack. Now, with far shorter nights and better weather conditions, plus much stronger Luftwaffe forces in the Crimea, far fewer naval missions were undertaken. Armed merchantmen, usually escorted by cruisers or destroyers, were still supplying Sevastopol most nights, and a few destroyers continued occasionally bombarding German positions on the southeast coast of the Crimea, but the Black Sea Fleet was only lightly and sporadically patrolling the Kerch Peninsula's southern coast.[44]

Also during the night of 7 and 8 May, Manstein's divisions carried out last-minute preparations and moved into position for the attack. To hold the northern section of the front, Manstein had committed *General* von Matenklott's 42nd Army Corps, comprising one German and three Rumanian divisions. Three infantry divisions of the 30th Army Corps were to rip a hole in the southern part of the front. The corps' 22nd Panzer and 170th Infantry Divisions were then to race through and drive deep into the Soviet rear, before wheeling north in the planned enveloping move.

At 0315, the German artillery erupted in a deafening barrage, accompanied by heavy howitzers, rockets, and guns from Richthofen's antiaircraft units used in direct fire against ground targets. The infantry surged forward ten minutes later, followed shortly after by waves of *Fliegerkorps VIII*'s bombers and Stukas, which pounded the formidable enemy defensive lines and shattered bunkers and gun implacements. Ground-attack planes struck enemy airfields, logistics systems, and almost anything moving in the Soviet rear. These initial air operations, which created havoc in both forward and rear areas, were conducted in accordance with detailed and specific requests from the two army corps.

Many bomber units operated from airfields in Nikolayev and Kherson in Ukraine and therefore flew 330 and 270 kilometers, respectively, to reach the Kerch front. Others operated from fields in the central Crimea (many centered around Saki, Simferopol, and Sarabus) and were able, as a result, to fly far more missions and carry heavier bombloads. Most Stukas and other ground-attack aircraft, including the brand-new Henschel Hs 129 (which "made a good impression" on Richthofen),[45] flew from these and newly prepared fields even closer to the front. The Grammatikovo base, for example, was only forty kilometers west of Ak Monai.

German fighters ceaselessly patrolled the skies above the Kerch Straits, preventing most enemy aircraft based on airfields on the Taman Peninsula from breaching their screen. The *VVS* desperately tried to stop Luftwaffe operations by putting up every available fighter, but their counterattacks were poorly organized, and their vastly outclassed and outnumbered fighters proved little more than sitting ducks. No fewer than eighty-two were shot down on the first day alone by German fighters combing the skies for enemy planes as they sought, and gained, air superiority over the battlefield.[46] After the war, the official Soviet history placed blame for the *VVS*'s poor showing squarely on the shoulders of Lieutenant General D. T. Kozlov, the Crimean Front commander, and Commissar First Rank L. Z. Mekhlis, the *Stavka*'s front representative. "The Command of the Front," states the official history, "absolutely failed to effect coordination of ground and air forces. Our aviation operated outside the general plan of the defensive operation and despite existing opportunities was not able to damage the enemy's air forces."[47] German losses were indeed low. The first day was by far the worst: ten aircraft lost with their crews, and a further ten damaged.

Richthofen arrived that first morning at his forward command post "just as the first bombs were falling."[48] Remarkably, in light of his previous optimism, he suffered butterflies in his stomach: "Usual attack tensions," he complained that evening, "combined with morning chill. Always the same strange atmosphere, which only gradually loses its tension with its frequency." He was soon delighted, however, by the performance of his air units, which conducted an impressive 2,100 missions and provided "giant fire-magic the entire day."

An hour after the artillery barrage first began, the assault boats shot toward the section of coast where the antitank ditch ended in the sea. Under cover of Bf 109s strafing the bunkers and gun nests on the rim of the ditch, the boats sailed right into the ditch itself, allowing the troops to leap ashore and begin spraying machine-gun fire at the startled Soviets. Meanwhile, the infantry divisions of Fretter-Pico's corps, assisted by artillery and covered by a constant stream of fighters and dive-bombers, had struggled through barbed wire entanglements and minefields and, under a hail of enemy machine-gun fire, succeeded in crossing the ditch itself. Aided by the troops from the assault boats, they were able to penetrate the enemy's forward positions. "Nevertheless," recalled Manstein,

the battle was certainly not easy. The ground won on the far side of the tank ditch was not yet sufficient for the [22nd] Panzer Division to be moved over. Additionally, the following attack by the 42nd Army Corps could only move forward with great difficulty. All the same, we had already encountered ten enemy divisions in the front and shattered its southern wing. Furthermore, the enemy's reserves appeared to remain behind his northern wing.[49]

During the night of 8 and 9 May, the 22nd Panzer Division was unable to advance across the antitank ditch. Although engineers had blasted the ditch's steep walls with explosives in order to create several crossings, they were not yet wide or firm enough to take the division's tanks. Fretter-Pico therefore decided instead to send first the lighter "Grodeck Brigade," comprising a Rumanian motorized regiment and two German truck-mounted infantry battalions. At noon, *Oberst* Grodeck's brigade surged across the ditch and past the 132nd Infantry Division, with orders to head toward Kerch with all possible speed. Stunned by the speed of the brigade's advance, Soviet divisions in its path "fled back and disintegrated."[50] As it happened, Richthofen glumly wrote that evening, the brigade "advanced so fast that, when it reached the eastern Tartar Ditch [the Sultanovka Line], it ran straight into our bombs. There were several losses."

Eleventh Army units had previously been instructed to mark their positions clearly in order to prevent "friendly fire" incidents like this.[51] As in earlier campaigns, they were supposed to lay out white identification panels and, if necessary, use flares and smoke pots.[52] Ground troops were not yet able to establish direct radio contact with aircraft overhead. Interservice communication was facilitated instead by *Fliegerverbindungsoffizier* (air liaison officers, or *Flivos*), specially trained air force officers attached to forward ground units. In constant radio communication with their air corps, *Flivos* appraised the corps of the situation and the intentions of the ground units, advised army commanders on the most practical use of airpower, and passed on their requests for air assistance.[53] This system worked well when Luftwaffe units were attacking clearly defined enemy positions during static or slow-moving operations, but not satisfactorily during operations like *Trappenjagd*, when the situation on the ground was far more fluid.

The fluid nature of the battle created another problem for Richthofen. He liked to direct his forces from command posts as close to the front as possible. Because the front itself moved forward many kilometers each day, he constantly moved his command posts to keep pace. This created enormous problems for his signals teams, who struggled to relocate radio equipment and lay telephone wires (connecting his new posts to airfields and army posts) fast enough. On 12 May, for example, Richthofen furiously wrote in his diary that a certain signals expert who disagreed with him "is and remains worthless and a pompous ass!" Similarly, two days later he complained that his signals teams took so long to wire up a new command post that he had to wait several hours for vital reports to arrive. "The signals personnel here are pathetic and fail constantly," he seethed. Despite his constant hounding, his signals teams proved incapable of satisfying his often-unfair demands. Right up until the day Kerch fell, he complained about their performance.

Late in the afternoon of 9 May—to return to the battle—the 22nd Panzer Division finally crossed the Parpach ditch and, accompanied by infantry, rolled eastward several kilometers. It beat off an attack by a Soviet tank brigade, then swung, as planned, to the north. Yet everything was going far too slowly for the army commander. "Back to the command post," Richthofen recorded, "where Manstein was. In my opinion, he was worried. I calmed him down and pointed to our decisive actions planned for the next few hours. He remained skeptical." Despite Manstein's concerns about the rate of progress, things were actually going according to plan. If the 22nd Panzer Division kept pushing northward, it would reach the sea before dark, trapping the greater part of the two Soviet armies still fighting in the northern sector of the front. However, an hour before dusk, all operations ground to a halt when a heavy spring rain poured down, quickly turning the ground into a muddy morass. Richthofen, whose air units had flown more than 1,700 sorties and shot down forty-two enemy aircraft that day, with only two losses, felt frustrated by the weather but confident of ultimate success. "Unless the weather itself stops us," he bluntly wrote, "no Russian will leave the Crimea alive."

The 22nd Panzer Division struggled forward through the mud until several hours after dark. A thick fog covered the saturated ground the next morning, preventing the early resumption of both air and ground operations. Throwing up mud and carving deep track marks in the loamy soil, the tanks, still supported by infantrymen, finally began churning forward again in the early afternoon. A powerful Soviet artillery barrage hit the division with punishing blows until Richthofen, watching from his Storch high above the battlefield (which almost cost him his life when enemy flak filled his plane with shrapnel), threw every available aircraft into the fray. The Soviet guns were quickly silenced. Grodeck was still pushing forward toward Kerch but wanted air support to take some of the heat off his brigade. However, Richthofen's planes were of little use to him, because pilots and gunners were unable to distinguish German from Russian troops in the chaotic conditions on the ground.[54] The air commander's jubilant diary entry for that evening reveals that, all things considered, the operation was progressing well: "By sunset we have isolated ten Red divisions, except for a narrow gap. The pocket is almost closed. In the morning the extermination can begin."

During the night of 10 and 11 May, poor visibility curtailed the Luftwaffe's operations against the narrow gap in the pocket centered around Ak Monai. Dense ground fog in the morning hampered operations until 1100, but once the fog lifted, Richthofen's units attacked in mass the enemy units still holding open the gap. "Only after plenty of air support," he claimed, "were they [the 22nd Panzer and 132nd Infantry Divisions] able to break through to the Sea of Azov and close the pocket, out of which the enemy has been streaming since last night." No fewer than ten panic-stricken divisions were trapped, but those who had managed to escape and flee eastward were hardly better off. They made splendid targets for Richthofen's ground-attack aircraft, which rained down bombs of all calibers, including "devil's eggs" and other antipersonnel projectiles. The air leader was initially delighted by the "wonderful scene."[55] "We are inflicting the highest losses of blood and matériel," he wrote. However, after overseeing air operations on other sectors of the Kerch Peninsula—where, he alleged, the army "still had winter fear in their bones" and were not attacking the enemy aggressively enough—he flew again over the area where the gap in the pocket had been. This time he was amazed by the level of destruction. "Terrible! Corpse-strewn fields from earlier attacks. . . . I have seen nothing like it so far in this war." He was so shocked, in fact, that the following day he took *General* Martini, the Luftwaffe's chief signals officer, to see the grisly sight.

On 12 May, the 50th Infantry and 28th Light Divisions remained around the pocket, which steadily disintegrated throughout the day, while all other available German forces raced eastward along essentially the same path that Grodeck's brigade had taken. By dusk, the 132nd and 170th Infantry Divisions were within sight of the Sultanovka Line, with the 22nd Panzer Division, which had turned east immediately after closing the pocket, steadily advancing behind them. Grodeck's brigade was now in a vulnerable position on the eastern side of the Sultanovka Line but was able to fight off heavy attacks with the aid of urgently requested fighter aircraft.

Things were going poorly indeed for the Soviets. Two days earlier, the *Stavka* had ordered Kozlov to pull his armies back to the Sultanovka Line. They were to hold this line at all costs. However, the commander vacillated and delayed executing the order for almost forty-eight hours. He then failed to organize the withdrawal properly.[56] Thus, when German troops appeared on 12 May at the Sultanovka Line, far behind Kozlov's headquarters, the Soviet command structure collapsed. Numerous divisions, broken and disoriented, began retreating eastward in various states of disorder. Kozlov's command was no longer capable of effecting decisive actions. The few remaining *VVS* units in the region, for instance, were never ordered to provide retreating columns with air cover. As the official Soviet history states: "Frontal aviation was not employed by the command in a reasonable manner. It did not even attempt to organize mass strikes on the most important enemy groupings and cover the pull-back of its [ground] forces, who were subjected to constant attack by enemy aviation."[57]

Enjoying total air supremacy, Richthofen's units flew over 1,500 sorties that day. They provided the army with excellent support by dropping ammunition to Grodeck's brigade, pounding the enemy columns streaming eastward and dug-in troops behind the Sultanovka Line, and hammering Kerch and the other ports on the peninsula's eastern tip. Manstein's earlier prediction that *Trappenjagd* would have "concentrated air support the like of which has never existed" was apparently being fulfilled. That notwithstanding, 12 May was an unhappy day for Richthofen. To his horror, the Luftwaffe High Command ordered him hastily to send many of his key units 500 kilometers north to Kharkov, where a major Soviet offensive had just struck. (To allow a proper narrative flow, the Luftwaffe's deployment during the Kharkov defensive fighting will be described later after the conclusion of the Crimean campaigns.) His diary entry for that day has a matter-of-fact tone: "Apparently Kharkov is a colossal mess; the Russians broke through with tanks in two places. We must release one fighter, one dive-bomber and two bomber groups!"[58] His entry for the following day reveals more clearly his feelings on the matter: "The matter at Kharkov stinks considerably. I must give up further bomber groups, two fighter groups and two dive-bomber groups. That is, practically everything! By order of the Führer. I report, therefore, that the successful completion of Kerch now looks questionable."

Despite the air commander's angry statement, the likelihood of German success on the Kerch Peninsula was certainly *not* questionable; when the 132nd and 170th Infantry Divisions broke through the Sultanovka Line in the morning of 13 May, followed a few hours later by the 22nd Panzer Division, total success seemed imminent. Nonetheless, between them and Kerch lay columns of fleeing Soviet troops, who hoped to save themselves by crossing the narrow straits to the Caucasian mainland, but also pockets of stiff resistance. The following afternoon, the 132nd Infantry Division brought Kerch under fire from the south, while the 170th Infantry Division pushed right into the city's outskirts. Resistance remained fierce. Richthofen knew that the Soviets hoped to hold back the German advance long enough to allow the troops massed on the beaches to be ferried across the straits by small vessels of the Black Sea naval, merchant, and fishing fleets in a Dunkirk-like evacuation. He was also acutely aware that his air corps no longer possessed sufficient forces to contribute substantially to the battle. "The Russians are sailing across the narrows in small craft," he fumed on 14 May, "and we can do nothing about it. It makes me sick!" The next day, Jeschonnek arrived at his command post ("which is now superfluous because I have nothing left to command"), in order to inspect the front. The highly frustrated air commander took Jeschonnek to Kerch. "One isn't sure whether to cry or curse," he bitterly wrote that night: "The Reds remain massed on the beaches and cross the sea at their leisure. Infantry and tanks can't advance because of the desperately resisting Reds and we [the Luftwaffe] can't do anything because we don't have adequate forces. The whole situation will yet turn out badly."[59]

Kerch fell on 15 May, prompting Halder prematurely to state that "the Kerch offensive may be considered closed. Only the promontory north of the city must still be cleared up."[60] Two days later, however, he had to admit that certain enemy units continued to put up "fanatical resistance." Despite suffering terrible losses, those units clearly still hoped to hold back German troops long enough for a seaborne evacuation to be organized. Although Richthofen's account suggests that the Luftwaffe was powerless to prevent any attempts to evacuate the terrified Soviets, between 13 and 17 May aircraft of *Fliegerführer Süd* made constant attacks against troop concentrations on the beaches and gunboats and other small vessels in the Kerch Straits.[61] Despite their numerical weakness, they destroyed various flak and artillery installations, bombed assembly and embarkation points, sank and damaged a number of small vessels, and forced several others aground. Their efforts, coupled with those of the army, which laid a blistering artillery barrage on 17 May, quickly brought the improvised Odessa-style evacuation to an end. Richthofen, who had constantly fumed in his diary that the army lacked aggression, was relieved to see the result of the army's concentrated gunfire: "Finally the army brings every available gun together and fires with 80 batteries into the narrows. Infantry advances and breaks through. By sunset the battle is all but over. At last!"[62] John Erickson, a British historian, graphically described the same scene:

> Over the remnants of the Crimean Front Manstein now laid a mass artillery barrage, blowing men, guns and tanks to pieces; with more gunfire the Germans drove off the Black Sea Fleet motor gunboats trying desperately to lift the troops off the beach where they were being battered to death. In this "ghastly mess" . . . [the Soviet command] struggled to exercise some control over the situation but this broke down in the great welter of chaos and confusion.[63]

Sporadic fighting on the Kerch Peninsula continued for another week, but on 19 May Manstein felt sufficiently satisfied with the situation to declare *Trappenjagd* completed. It was a stunning success. "According to our reports," he recorded in his memoirs,

> around 170,000 prisoners, 1,133 guns and 258 tanks fell into our hands. Five German infantry divisions and one panzer division, as well as two Rumanian infantry divisions and one cavalry brigade, had destroyed two full armies [and the greater part of a third] comprising 26 major formations. Only insignificant elements of the enemy were able to cross the Straits of Kerch to the Taman Peninsula.[64]

Although he failed to mention it, the Wehrmacht had also smashed Crimean *VVS* forces. They destroyed airfields, hangars, supply systems, and as many as 323 aircraft during the two-week battle.[65] The only *VVS* unit left in the Crimea was the Third Special Air Group of the Sevastopol Defense Region, operating from airfields within the fortress area.[66] It now comprised a meager 60 obsolete aircraft, a substantial drop from its November 1941 strength of more than 300. Vastly outclassed and outnumbered (more than ten to one) by German aircraft, these old machines would prove incapable of contributing to the defense of the fortress during the coming siege.

Not wishing to suggest that his army had won the Battle of Kerch by itself, Manstein praised Richthofen's air corps for its outstanding support. "*Fliegerkorps VIII* contributed decisively to this successful outcome," he added. "A true battle of annihilation was victoriously fought."[67] The air corps—which flew between 1,000 and 2,000 missions per day before the diversion of key units to Kharkov, and between 300 and 800 after—had certainly lived up to expectations. In particular, the crushing blows it dealt the enemy in the first days of the battle, including precision attacks on field headquarters and command posts, enabled Axis ground forces to overcome their numerical inferiority and break through the apparently impregnable defensive lines. After the war, the Soviets blamed themselves for *Fliegerkorps VIII*'s effectiveness in those first days:

> The unconcern of the Army and Front staffs, the insufficiently camouflaged command posts, and the failure to periodically move their locations, facilitated the German aviation, which bombed these posts in the first attacks, destroying wire communications and the control of troops. The staffs were not prepared for the utilization of radio and other means of communication.[68]

Richthofen was naturally delighted by his corps' superb performance over the last two weeks of furious combat but realized, even during the euphoric days after fighting finished, that a much tougher task for his men lay ahead: the siege of Sevastopol, probably the world's strongest fortress at that time. After spending the afternoon of 19 May surveying the carnage on the beaches near Kerch—where "dreadfully many dead horses and Russians lay strewn, and stinking accordingly"—he had a lengthy telephone discussion about the future with Jeschonnek and Martini.[69] "One sees," he noted in his diary, "that the *OKW* are too optimistic regarding future deadlines and the army's combat strength. I have doubts!!"

Before we turn our attention to the assault on Sevastopol, the strategic significance of the Kerch victory should be emphasized. First, it enabled Manstein to concentrate almost all forces in the Crimea for a massive assault on Sevastopol without fear of being struck in the back. Second, with the peninsula now in his hands and the narrow straits under the sweep of his guns, Hitler had his planned "springboard" into the Caucasus. As one historian wrote: "Manstein's victory had kicked open the back door to Stalin's oil paradise."[70]

SEVASTOPOL: A "TOUGH NUT TO CRACK"

On 20 May, Richthofen and the Eleventh Army commander met to discuss the coming campaign. According to the airman's diary, Manstein heartily agreed that the attack on the fortress required at least the level of air support provided in previous weeks. The assault would not be possible if *Fliegerkorps VIII* was (as in the Kerch campaign's latter stages) prematurely diverted elsewhere or its combat strength reduced. Two days later, after flying back to the Reich to brief his superiors, Richthofen had the opportunity to emphasize that the maximum concentration of airpower was needed at all times during the attack. He found Hitler most attentive: "I give a short talk about our experiences at Kerch and the requirements for Sevastopol. The Führer seems to agree. . . . Then we were alone [for dinner]. The Führer is very nice, calling me his specialist, etc."[71] They got on famously, even laughing together about the eccentricities of Göring and the hunting fraternity. Apparently mocking the *Reichsmarschall*'s "quest for trophies," the War Lord jokingly asked why "soldiers don't hang the jawbones of dead Russians in their rooms." Although Göring may never have learned that he had been the butt of Hitler's jokes that night, he was well aware that his own star had fallen in recent months and was clearly annoyed that Richthofen, for whom he had no affection, had dined alone with the Führer. "The *Reichsmarschall* has bawled out Jeschonnek," the bewildered air corps commander noted in his diary four days later, "because I was with the *Führer.*"[72]

Göring was the subject of another of Richthofen's discussions on 21 May, this time with Jeschonnek. The leadership of *Luftflotte 4,* Jeschonnek had said, was going to change as soon as the initial operations of the coming summer campaign got under way. Alexander Löhr, the talented air fleet commander, would be promoted and sent to the Balkans, where he would serve as Commander in Chief, Southeast. Göring wanted to replace him with Bruno Lörzer, his close friend and commander of *Fliegerkorps II.* Fortunately, Hitler and Jeschonnek had other plans. After the siege of Sevastopol, they insisted, Richthofen would himself assume command of *Luftflotte 4.* A "hands-on" commander who liked nothing better than to be in the thick of the action, Richthofen was not thrilled by the news of his pending promotion, feeling that his "level of effectiveness would decrease sharply."[73] However, the Luftwaffe chief of staff, he noted in his diary that night, remained adamant. "Jeschonnek maintains—rightly so—that the higher Luftwaffe command is lousy, so I must move up, where the action is. I must show them how things should be done."

After four days with the Reich's top military leaders, including Jodl, Göring, and Milch, Richthofen climbed aboard a He 111 at Lüneburg at dawn on 25 May for his six-hour flight back to Simferopol in the Crimea. After lunch and attending to the pile of paperwork that had built up in recent days, it was back to business as usual. To catch up on recent events in the area and to brief his senior officers on the coming campaign, he held a meeting that lasted until late in the evening. The defense of the Kerch Peninsula, where sporadic fighting continued in the stone quarries north of Kerch (a further 3,000 Soviets had been captured only the day before) was high on the agenda. It was essential to prevent a repeat performance of the enemy landings on the peninsula, which had taken place while the army's back was turned during the previous siege of Sevastopol. Moreover, it was important to cut off the supply ships that slipped into Sevastopol each night. Wild's *Fliegerführer Süd,* he said, would assume responsibility for the Kerch Peninsula's security and for naval reconnaissance over the Black Sea.[74]

Wild doubtless received this news with mixed emotions; because the powerful *Fliegerkorps VIII* would again carry out the vast bulk of ground attack missions, his own small force would be able for the first time in months to concentrate solely on the antinaval tasks for which it was formed. It would no longer have to dissipate its strength by undertaking a wide range of missions. However, his command would no longer need, for antinaval missions alone, many of the ground-attack units it possessed late in April, when it carried out a multitude of tasks.[75] Accordingly, he knew that Richthofen, who had already poached some of his units for the Battle of Kerch, would strip his already small force to the bone, leaving it greatly weakened. This did, in fact, occur. When the initial air and artillery assault on Sevastopol began on 2 June, *Fliegerführer Süd* comprised only one fighter, one torpedo bomber, and one long-range reconnaissance group. Its other fighters, dive-bombers, and bombers had been formally absorbed into *Fliegerkorps VIII.*[76]

Although *Fliegerführer Süd* received responsibility for the Kerch Peninsula's security and for naval interdiction and reconnaissance over the Black Sea, it would not be patrolling the southeastern Crimean coastlines alone. Units of both *Fliegerkorps IV* and *VIII*, trying to cut off seaborne supplies to the fortress, would also patrol the sea lanes around Sevastopol. They were not the only other Axis forces trying to cut off these supplies; early in June, small warships of *Admiral Schwarzes Meer* began operating in Crimean waters. Their presence had been requested by Manstein's command staff, which wanted them "to interfere with incoming and outgoing naval traffic at the start of the Battle for Sevastopol."[77] By the time the ground battle commenced on 7 June, this force would comprise a German flotilla of six MTBs and a few light patrol vessels (based in Simferopol) and an Italian flotilla of four MTBs, six midget submarines, and four armed motorboats (based in Yalta).[78] This force would grow even stronger in following weeks.

Marine-Gruppenkommando Süd had originally planned to deploy all these vessels from Yalta, under the joint command of the Italian flotilla commander, *capitano di fregata* Bimbelli, the German flotilla commander, *Leutnant* Birnbacher, and the commander of the local air force, Wild himself.[79] However, *Vizeadmiral* Götting persuaded his superiors to keep the forces separate, arguing that "the massing of all forces in the small harbor at Yalta constitutes an unwarranted risk, as such a concentration of boats would not escape the enemy's notice and would lead to heavy air attacks."[80] Realizing that his forces could only contribute to the battle if deployed in close cooperation with the Luftwaffe, Götting considered the idea of a joint command far more reasonable. Accordingly, he ordered Birnbacher "to proceed to [Wild's headquarters at] Saki to confer with Air Commander South and Commander Mimbelli and set up a common operational H.Q. there for the period of operations in the sea area off Sevastopol."[81]

As instructed, a naval-air command was established in Saki under Birnbacher's, Mimbelli's, and Wild's joint command. To improve interservice communication, naval signals teams constructed powerful new radio transmitters in the Crimea.[82] These greatly accelerated the dissemination of important information—especially vessel sightings by reconnaissance aircraft—among the various air and naval commands and bases. To increase interservice cooperation, *Marine-Gruppenkommando Süd* also sent *Konteradmiral* Eyssen, the naval liaison officer to *Luftflotte 4,* to work at Wild's headquarters.[83] Relations soon became extremely good; Wild even informed his naval colleagues that they could request air reconnaissance missions as they saw fit. His willingness to work closely with them did not pass unnoticed. The naval command in Sofia, for example, was clearly impressed. Wild "has himself been a naval officer," it reported, "and possesses an extraordinary understanding of naval combat leadership." As a result, "cooperation between naval and air forces in the operational zone exists, and without friction."[84]

Events during the assault on Sevastopol show that even the best attempts at interservice cooperation can be hampered by simple misunderstandings. For example, shortly after the initial air and artillery assault began on 2 June, the Italian and German MTBs, midget submarines, and armed motorboats began antishipping missions in the sea-lanes around Sevastopol. Despite Wild's own desire for close cooperation between his aircraft and these naval forces, Richthofen, his boss, felt frustrated by their presence. Although *Admiral Schwarzes Meer* had ordered its vessels to display larger and more prominent identification markers,[85] Richthofen feared they were still at risk from attack by German aircraft mistaking them for Soviet ships. Accordingly, on 10 June Eyssen sent Götting, commander of *Admiral Schwarzes Meer,* the following radio message: "As it is impossible always to be informed if and when submarines and light forces of the German and Italian navies are in Crimean waters, Commanding General, 8th Air Corps [Richthofen], has given orders prohibiting his planes from making any attacks whatsoever on any submarines or light forces—including Russian vessels in the entire Black Sea."[86]

Götting was stunned. "There is no valid reason," he insisted, "why these air attacks on submarines and light forces should be prohibited in the whole Black Sea area, as at present the German and Italian E-boats and submarines are only operating in the Crimean area."[87] He ordered Eyssen to get this ridiculous prohibition modified so that aircraft could resume all operations over the vast expanses of the Black Sea. The only areas in which antishipping attacks should be avoided were the sea-lanes around the Crimea. On 12 June, Eyssen discussed the prohibition with a disbelieving Wild, who commanded the only aircraft operating outside the requested small restriction zone. Agreeing that Richthofen's prohibition was counterproductive, the air commander immediately modified it according to Götting's request. Accordingly, antishipping missions over all sea regions outside the Crimean restriction zone quickly resumed.

PREPARATIONS FOR THE ATTACK

We left Richthofen in the last week of May, making preparations for the coming assault on Sevastopol. Both he and Manstein knew that Sevastopol would be (as American intelligence officers graphically wrote a few months later) a remarkably "tough nut to crack."[88] "Its main defenses," wrote Hermann Plocher, were directed seaward, with powerful defensive positions extending along the coastal area from Mamashni through Cape Kherson to Balaclava. Its land defenses consisted of two converging belts of fortifications, the outer perimeter of which encircled the city at a distance of 9 to 12 miles, running from Balaclava to Belbek. The inner belt of forts circled the inner city and the port south of Severnaya Bay at a distance of 3 miles. Innumerable defense installations of all sorts were distributed throughout the entire fortress area, and virtually no part of the terrain was without its fortifications.

To the north of Severnaya Bay were 11 strongpoints, some of which were of modern construction. . . . Since November of 1941, almost the entire local population of the area had participated in the intensive work on Sevastopol's fortifications. Russian civilians blasted hundreds of bunkers and gun and mortar positions out of the rugged, rocky and vegetation-covered terrain, and laid numerous mine-fields throughout the area. To increase the strength of these defenses still more, they constructed additional field fortifications such as anti-tank ditches and barbed-wire entanglements.[89]

The defenders themselves constituted a substantial force. General I. E. Petrov's Independent Maritime Army comprised seven rifle divisions, four brigades, two regiments of marines, two tank battalions, and various other units. In total, aside from civilians, who had fiercely resisted previous German siege attempts and could be counted on to repeat their valiant efforts, there were no fewer than 106,000 frontline troops in the fortress.[90] They were well armed, having around 600 artillery pieces of various calibers and more than 2,000 mortars, and were steadily supplied and reinforced by vessels of Oktyabrskii's Black Sea Fleet.

Manstein assembled his own strong force of seven and a half German and one and a half Rumanian divisions (and each German division was around 20 percent larger than its Soviet counterpart), excluding four other divisions assigned the task of guarding the Kerch Peninsula and south Crimean coastlines.[91] Determined to shatter the city's formidable defenses, the German commander amassed an impressive number of artillery pieces (1,300 guns and 720 mortars in total), which formed 121 individual batteries. His heavy siege artillery included huge 19-cm cannons and 30.5-, 35- and 42-cm howitzers, as well as two 61.5-cm howitzers ("Thor" and "Odin"). These massive guns, which fired 2,200-kg shells, were specially designed for use against concrete installations. Even so, they were not the heaviest guns in Manstein's arsenal. That honor went to the mighty "Dora," which, with its 80-cm caliber and 32-meter-long barrel, was easily the heaviest cannon of the Second World War. Originally designed to bombard the Maginot Line but not completed in time, "Dora" was a monster. The transportation of its components to the Crimea required sixty railway cars. At Bachtschisarei, thirty kilometers northeast of Sevastopol, it sat on two double railway tracks and (as per Hitler's instructions to *Luftflotte 4*) required the constant protection of two flak battalions. It could hurl high-explosive shells weighing almost five metric tons a distance of forty-seven kilometers, or seven-ton armor-piercing shells (the height of a two-story house) a distance of thirty-eight kilometers.

The great strength of Manstein's firepower was substantially enhanced by the presence of an unprecedented concentration of combat aircraft. Richthofen's *Fliegerkorps VIII*, which had proved its worth as "airborne artillery" during recent massive bombardments of fortifications and strongpoints on the Kerch Peninsula, would again join forces with Eleventh Army. Richthofen planned to deploy his 400 or so combat aircraft alongside Wild's *Fliegerführer Süd* and elements of Pflugbeil's *Fliegerkorps IV*, which would put a total of almost 600 aircraft under his operational command. If the High Command granted him the units he wanted, he would have three long-range reconnaissance squadrons and five fighter, two ground-attack, three dive-bomber, and six bomber *Gruppen*.[92] Late in May, however, he was gravely concerned that the High Command would deny him this strength by not returning to him the key air units recently sent to other sections of the eastern front. Hitler had apparently decided that those units should be retained and used for planned counteroffensives in the Kharkov and Izyum regions.[93] "Jodl, an old artillerist, keeps telling the Führer that artillery is enough for here," Richthofen glumly wrote in his diary on 30 May. "Manstein passes my pleas against this view on to Bock and Halder. Jeschonnek won't take a stand." To his great relief, his pleas had the desired effect. "In the evening," he continued, "arrived the decision that two further bomber groups are being sent here, so that we [*Fliegerkorps VIII* alone] now possess three dive-bomber, six bomber and three fighter *Gruppen*." He was still not entirely happy, complaining that even these forces are "few enough." As it happened, by the time the assault on the fortress commenced, he commanded no fewer than 600 aircraft, comprising three reconnaissance squadrons (one being long-range) and four fighter, three dive-bomber, and seven bomber groups.[94]

This powerful force was slightly stronger in bomber aircraft than Richthofen originally planned but lighter in ground-attack and fighter aircraft. Although he doubtless lamented the loss of ground-attack aircraft, he was not unduly concerned by his fighter strength. After all, the pathetic Soviet air force in the Crimea, with only sixty old planes, was outnumbered ten to one. His air corps, therefore, could begin air operations immediately, without having first to wage a time-consuming battle for air superiority. Moreover, because his bombers would encounter little enemy air opposition, far fewer fighter escorts than normal were needed.

Because the *VVS* posed no threat to German forces in the Crimea, Richthofen felt able to commit the majority of his flak units (which formed the 18th and 27th Flak Regiments) to ground combat missions. He did, of course, comply with the Führer's instruction that "Dora" and the other massive siege guns receive strong antiaircraft protection, but he committed most other flak units to service alongside Manstein's regular field artillery. Powerful leaders often find delegation difficult, and Richthofen, who liked to involve himself in all aspects of combat operations, was no exception. He simply refused to place his flak units even temporarily under the operational command of Eleventh Army's artillery officers, insisting instead on directing their use himself. Additionally, rather than dispersing his flak units among army divisions, as the artillery officers requested, he insisted they remain together so that their gunfire could be concentrated at crucial points as the need arose.[95] This decision would, as we shall shortly see, cause interservice friction during the middle stages of the assault on the fortress.

Aside from this disagreement over the employment of flak batteries, relations between Richthofen and his army counterpart, Manstein, remained excellent. As with the previous Kerch campaign, they held a number of interservice conferences to iron out minor conceptual differences, coordinate operations, and create joint *Schwerpunkte*. Manstein divided Eleventh Army into three attack forces, positioning them north, east, and south of the fortress. From the north, 54th Army Corps (comprising the 22nd, 24th, 50th, and 132nd Infantry Divisions and the reinforced 213th Infantry Regiment) would strike suddenly and with great force, with the aim of shattering the formidable enemy defensive lines and securing the northern shore of Severnaya Bay and the heights around Gaitany.[96] From the south, 30th Army Corps (with the 72nd and 170th Infantry Divisions and the 28th Light Infantry Division) would conduct an assault, three days later, in order to occupy the Sapun Heights south and southeast of the city. Sandwiched between these two large attack forces was the far smaller 6th Rumanian Mountain Corps (the 18th Rumanian and 1st Rumanian Mountain Divisions), assigned the task of containing enemy forces east of the city while protecting the other two corps' flanks as they carried out the main operations in the north and south.

The campaign would commence on 2 June with a five-day "artillery preparation"—starting first with a particularly strong "fire strike" *(Feuerschlag)*—designed "to shatter the defenders' morale, destroy strong and important enemy combat installations, and pin down elements of the enemy's artillery in advance of the [German] infantry's attack."[97] Because *Fliegerkorps VIII* would provide much of the firepower during this five-day artillery barrage, lengthy interservice meetings occurred late in May to coordinate closely the operation. Manstein's command proposed the following program:

> First, the initial "fire strike" is to be delivered mainly by the Luftwaffe, which is to repeat its massive attacks each following day. Aircraft are to target enemy reserves beyond the range of German artillery and within the fortified regions of Sevastopol.
>
> Second, continuous destructive air raids are to be made, during both day and night, against the city and harbor, supply installations in rear areas within the fortress region, airfields and shipping traffic.

Third, systematic attacks to neutralize enemy artillery and mortar batteries are to be undertaken in coordination with German artillery. These batteries are to be located by spotter planes. Air units are also to destroy particularly troublesome targets, such as coastal batteries, which are beyond the
reach and accurate observation of ground forces.

Finally, when the infantry launches its attack, it is to receive the maximum
support available as it pushes through the enemy's defensive lines. On the
first day of the ground assault, the main emphasis will be in the 54th Army
Corps' sector. Then, as the operation unfolds, emphasis can be shifted to the
30th Army Corps' and 6th Rumanian Mountain Corps' sector.[98]

Richthofen was in general agreement with this program, although he
stressed that his air force would not, of course, be able to perform all these "direct" and "indirect" support tasks simultaneously. Some tasks would clearly have
to take precedence over others, depending on the way the operation unfolded. He
personally believed that his force's greatest contribution would be the "shattering of the fighting morale of those inside the fortress."[99] Accordingly, he stated to
his units on 2 June, throughout the five-day artillery preparation the enemy was
to be kept under constant pressure so that "without any pause for psychological
recovery, their morale collapses wherever they are attacked, and, furthermore,
they suffer the highest losses.[100]

Determined to crush the enemy's fighting spirit, the air commander deployed the vast bulk of his units against the fortress, leaving antishipping missions almost entirely to Wild's small *Fliegerführer Süd* and the German and Italian naval flotillas patrolling Crimean coastlines. The fact that he committed few
other units to these sea reconnaissance and interdiction missions, and left only
numerically weak air and naval forces to carry them out, reveals how low they
came on his list of priorities. This point is reinforced by Richthofen's disdain for
Fliegerführer Süd. On 27 May, for example, he bitterly (and unfairly) complained
in his diary that its state of readiness (including the establishment of observation
posts and air warning networks) was appalling. "Nothing has been done in the
last months," he wrote, "and, despite orders to *Fliegerführer Süd*, still nothing has
been done in the last weeks." The following day, he described in equally harsh
terms an air attack on an enemy convoy, which included a heavy cruiser and several destroyers. "*Fliegerführer Süd* attempted [to sink it] with the *II./K.G. 26*, the
old group from Lüneburg. Absolutely pathetic. They fired off 29 torpedoes without any success!!" His scathing remarks were certainly unwarranted and reveal
his poor knowledge of naval combat matters; aiming torpedoes accurately was
hard enough for slow-moving U-boats but remarkably difficult for aircraft attacking ten times faster and usually without the benefit of surprise. Additionally, German torpedoes were so unreliable in this period that, even when aircraft (and
U-boats, for that matter) managed to hit enemy vessels, their torpedoes often

failed to detonate. *Großadmiral* Dönitz complained in his memoirs, for instance, that more than a third of all torpedoes fired during the first half of the war failed to detonate and that, "until the introduction of the new magnetic detonator in December 1942, the effectiveness of our torpedoes was no greater than it had been in the First World War."[101]

4

Operation "Sturgeon Catch": June–July 1942

On the morning of 2 June 1942, Richthofen awoke at 0330 and pulled on his uniform and boots. By 0545, after eating breakfast, conferring with his chief of staff, and taking care of a few last-minute matters, he was flying in the cloudless sky above the combat zone in his Fieseler Storch. Within minutes, the stillness of early dawn was broken by the thunder of 1,300 German guns and the incessant scream of Stukas and rumble of bombers as the most intense artillery and aerial barrage to date in the eastern campaign commenced. Most of *Fliegerkorps VIII*'s aircraft operated from airfields around Saki, Sarabus, and Simferopol, all within seventy kilometers of the city, so they scarcely had time to climb to attack altitude before they reached their target areas.[1]

Their first massive strike, from 0600 to 0630, was against barracks northeast of the city and reserve concentrations and mobilization points in the villages of Schablykina and Balossowa, to the southeast.[2] It was followed at 0700 by twelve hours of "rolling attacks" on the city itself by almost all units, with the notable exception of *III./L.G. 1*, which attacked flak and artillery installations. Scores of Stukas attacked key installations, including the city's harbor facilities, submarine bases, water pumps, reservoirs, and electricity stations. Dozens of fires broke out, especially in the oil depots on the south shore of Severnaya Bay. Richthofen, now watching the "impressive picture" from a tall, specially constructed observation tower near the front, was amused by the havoc caused by his aircraft. "During the first attack an oil tank begins to burn," he wrote. "The Russians are apparently trying to extinguish it. The fire begins to die out after half an hour or so. Then comes a new wave, the Russians duck for cover, and the fire begins to grow again. After lunch they finally give up and just let it burn!"[3] While combat units rained bombs down on the city, which was well aflame by evening, reconnaissance aircraft of *3. (H.) 13* directed the fire of the army's artillery batteries.[4] For the Luftwaffe, it was an impressive first day; 723 missions were flown, 525 tons of high-explosive bombs dropped (including one massive 1,700-kg and seven 1,400-kg bombs, designed to shatter concrete fortifications), and six enemy aircraft had been shot down. Two of these were destroyed over Sevastopol, the other four over the Kerch Straits while trying to reach the Crimea from airfields in the Caucasus. Despite heavy flak, German losses were remarkably low: only one Ju 87 failed to return to base.[5]

Throughout the next four days, artillery and aircraft incessantly pounded the fortress, now continuously aflame. The *Schwerpunkt* on 3 June was the defensive line facing the 30th Army Corps south of the city, on 4 June the line facing the Rumanians in the east, and on 5 June that facing the 54th Army Corps in the north. On 6 June, the day before the infantry began its assault, it was again the line facing the 30th Army Corps.[6] Richthofen usually watched the bombardment from his observation tower but, as the tower was situated south of Sevastopol, he had to watch attacks on the northern and central sectors from his Storch. He was especially pleased by his air units' performance. Between 3 and 6 June, they conducted a further 2,355 missions, showering down almost 1,800 tons of high-explosive bombs and, to keep the city burning, 23,800 small, 1.1-kg incendiary bombs.[7] In order to weaken further the fighting spirit of the city's defenders, German air units also dropped an enormous number of propaganda leaflets exhorting troops to throw down their arms and surrender, thereby preventing an inevitable bloodbath. In the two weeks from 24 May to 6 June, they dropped no fewer than 638,000 such leaflets, or an average of almost 50,000 per day.[8]

The Luftwaffe had scattered countless leaflets over Soviet troops since *Barbarossa* began almost a year earlier, but there is no way of gauging how effective they were in persuading troops to desert or surrender. They were probably no more influential than leaflets dropped by the Royal Air Force over Germany, the value of which "Bomber" Harris, head of Bomber Command, summed up nicely: "I always said that the only thing leaflet raids would achieve would be to supply Germany with toilet paper for the rest of the war!"[9] While the Wehrmacht occasionally attributed increases in Soviet desertion rates to the impact of leaflet drops,[10] it certainly received little reward for the amount of time and energy devoted to this work. Leaflets were relatively cheap to produce but, because of their bulk, took up valuable space on trucks, trains, and transport planes. They also occupied a lot of space in aircraft bomb bays, greatly reducing the number of bombs that could be carried simultaneously.

Despite the steady rain of propaganda material, the defenders' fighting spirit remained unbroken. Their courage and fortitude were remarkable, considering the blistering intensity of the artillery and air bombardment. For the soldiers and citizens huddled in their bunkers, it was like a scene from Dante's *Inferno*. As Lieutenant General Laskin recalled:

> About 2,000 guns and mortars kept firing at our positions without a moment's interval. Shells whined overhead and exploded on all sides. The thun-

der of guns merged into a deafening roar, splitting our eardrums. Bombers in groups of twenty to thirty attacked us without caring for their targets but coming in wave after wave and literally ploughing up the earth throughout our defense area.

German aircraft were in the air above our positions all day long. We could not hear their engines in the continuous thunder of guns and shell explosions. Groups of bombers following in rapid succession looked like countless flocks of fantastic black birds. A whirlwind of fire was raging at all our positions. The sky was clouded by smoke from explosions of thousands of bombs and shells. Yet planes kept coming in wave after wave and showered us with a hail of bombs. . . . An enormous dark grey cloud of smoke and dust rose higher and higher and finally eclipsed the sun.[11]

This hellish blitz was far more ferocious than those inflicted thus far in the war on Warsaw, Rotterdam, London, or Malta. Because it made survival above ground almost impossible (except for troops protected by meters of solid concrete in larger forts and defensive installations), most soldiers and citizens retreated to numerous bunkers, cellars, tunnels, and caves honeycombing Sevastopol and surrounding ravines and valleys. In one of these underground refuges, carefully prepared in recent months but still inhospitable, the Soviet command did what it could to plan and direct the city's defense. It was a miserable existence, described graphically by Boris Voyetekhov, a Soviet journalist living in this subterranean world deep beneath the rubble of broken buildings. In the military headquarters, he wrote,

dim electric lamps, supplied by local storage batteries, helped one to grope one's way. . . . In the gloom, people jostled or bumped into one another. Many doors opened off the corridors into small rooms where tense, energetic people worked, and from them you heard snatches of telephone conversations, radio voices, signals, and the rattle of typewriters, insistent voices of switchboard operators, the uproarious laughter of writers of anti-Fascist leaflets, the slow, studied words of the decipherers, the occasional screams of the wounded, the abrupt answers of officers on duty, and the clanking of a sentry's tread. . . . When the municipal supply of electricity failed [after heavy blows by Richthofen's Stukas] and one diesel [generator] broke down and the fans stopped, the crowds of people working below the ground rapidly consumed the air and it became difficult to breathe. It was a tragic sight to see the women workers, who were unsparing in their toil. Their pale sallow eyes were inflamed day in and day out, they gasped for breath at telephones or typewriters, in canteens and in barber shops.[12]

Throughout this period, to provide a contrast, Richthofen directed his forces from the security and comfort of a spacious Tartar castle in Bachtschisarei. In rooms adorned by paintings and tapestries, he held frequent briefings and conferences with senior commanders, including his own flak and the army's artillery officers. These meetings were not always cordial. His flak leaders, for instance, resented the fact that their army counterparts were still trying to control their guns. Richthofen was furious and, during a heated argument on 3 June, informed the army that it must stop interfering with Luftwaffe operations. Flak units were his to direct, not the army's. The next day, he discussed the situation with Manstein, but, despite their bond of mutual friendship and respect, they failed to reach a solution agreeable to both services. Arguments over the control of flak guns continued sporadically until the city fell to Axis forces early in July. For example, Richthofen noted unhappily in his diary on 13 June that there had been a "great squabble with army commands (division, corps, and army) over flak operations." "I keep all flak guns subordinate," he explained,

> and deploy them together in great concentration at *Schwerpunkte* against ground targets. The army wants formally to control them and spread them throughout divisions and, therefore—as always, like last time at Kerch—fritter them away. The most basic reason: the competitive jealousy of the army's artillery [officers], to whom I cannot give my flak guns because they are senile and want to deploy them according to the tactical viewpoints of Wallenstein [leader of the Habsburg forces in the Thirty Years' War of the seventeenth century]. I remain stubborn and let the army commands continue to rage.

THE INFANTRY'S TURN

When the massive "preparatory" bombardment finished after five days and nights, Manstein's infantry began its own assault on the fortress. In the predawn hours of 7 June, the 54th Army Corps moved forward under cover of an earth-shaking air and artillery barrage. On the morning of 7 June, Manstein recalled, "even as the first reds of morning turned gold, and the shadows of dawn faded in the valleys, our artillery opened up with all its force as a prelude to the infantry's assault on the enemy, while squadrons of the Luftwaffe plunged down on their designated targets."[13] Richthofen and Jeschonnek—who had flown to the Crimea especially to watch the infantry advance—viewed the "excellent fire magic" from high above the battlefield in the former's Storch. To their dismay and disgust, ground troops appeared to be afraid of their own artillery fire and failed to advance closely behind the curtain of falling shells and bombs stretched out across the enemy's defensive positions.[14] Moreover, they made almost no headway against enemy forces that were clearly neither broken nor demoralized. "The infantry," Richthofen cursed that evening, "suffered heavy losses as it struggled to gain a single kilometer of this difficult terrain. The anticipated large and fast breakthrough simply failed to materialize. Apparently even our heaviest artillery failed to achieve anything at all." Indeed, Soviet defenders had been lying low, waiting for the appearance of German infantry before they unleashed their own savage artillery attack from guns positioned in solid rock strongpoints or steel and concrete bunkers. "The Russian artillery and armored fortifications spring to life everywhere," the air commander continued. "The whole horizon is one tremendous gun-flash." To counter this unexpected opposition, he threw every available aircraft into the battle, forcing many aircrew to fly up to eight sorties daily. It was a remarkable achievement for both fliers and ground personnel; his units conducted an impressive 1,368 sorties that day, dropping as many as 1,300 tons of bombs.[15] However, despite ceaselessly pounding Soviet positions until midnight, Richthofen's aircraft were unable to silence the enemy's guns. "The entire day," he complained, "was a real disappointment."

The following few days were not much better, with the infantry gaining little ground and suffering heavy losses. Its advance was blunted by the fire of Soviet artillery pieces, which pounded out a ground-shaking percussive beat, accompanied by the steady cadence of scores of lighter but no less deadly flak guns. "We hope gradually to beat down the enemy by mass-bombing," the frustrated Richthofen explained on 8 June, during which his aircraft conducted a further 1,200 sorties "and dropped as many tons of bombs."[16] His ground organization, he added with relief, was beginning to run smoothly, although conducting that many missions—almost nonstop between 0300 and 2400 hours—was "extremely strenuous." Werner Baumbach, who ended the war as commander of bomber forces, recalled:

> Our work at Sevastopol made the highest demands on men and material. Twelve, fourteen and even up to eighteen sorties were made daily by individual crews. A Ju 88 with fuel tanks full made three or four sorties without the crew stretching their legs. It meant tremendous wear and tear for the aircraft and the ground staff, those unknown soldiers who could not sleep a wink in those days and nights and were responsible for the safe condition of their machines.[17]

Fortunately for the exhausted Luftwaffe service and maintenance personnel, working in sweltering heat (up to 105° F), the army's operations decreased slightly in intensity over the next two days as commanders met and discussed new tactics. As a result, demands on *Fliegerkorps VIII* were not as great. On 9 June, 1,044 sorties were flown and 954 tons of bombs dropped; the next day, 688 sorties and 634 tons.[18] However, even these slightly lower quantities, coming as they did after a week of constant bombing missions, placed enormous demands on Richthofen's logistical network. On 11 June—another heavy day of fighting, during which his aircraft flew 1,070 sorties and dropped around 1,000 tons of bombs[19]—he noted unhappily that he no longer had sufficient bombs and fuel to keep up mass-bombing raids and that, at the present rate of consumption, he had "only enough left for 1.5 more days of bombing!" He was clearly worried, adding that "the specter of failure now seriously looms."

As it was no longer possible to "carpet bomb" the fortress—that is, by dropping large tonnages of bombs across wide areas in order to destroy all obstacles and defensive positions—Richthofen immediately ordered a change in bombing procedures. From now on, fewer positions would be attacked simultaneously, and aircraft would strike at designated targets in long and narrow lines. This "column bombing," he explained in his diary on 12 June, would keep enemy strongpoints under constant pressure without wasting bombs on low-priority targets and allow the replenishment of both his fuel and bomb stocks. As it happened, even these new tactics failed to solve *Fliegerkorps VIII*'s logistical problems. On 14 June, for instance, Richthofen complained that he still experienced a "bomb calamity," and, three days later, his units were able to drop only 800 tons of bombs, instead of the planned 1,000 tons, because of an acute shortage of aircraft fuel.[20]

Almost every night during this period, *VVS* units on the Caucasus mainland launched raids against German positions in the Crimea, including Simferopol, Theodosiya, Eupatoria, and, in particular, Yalta.[21] Having radar stations able to track bombers' flight paths but lacking specialized equipment for night air interception, *Fliegerkorps VIII* was almost powerless to stop them.[22] All it could do was illuminate them with spotlights and pound away at them with their flak guns, hitting very few. These *VVS* bombing missions, however, were hampered by a lack of precision navigation and bomb-aiming equipment and were poorly directed, perhaps because the Luftwaffe's massive strength in the region had prevented thorough and detailed air reconnaissance in previous weeks. Accordingly, they seldom inflicted significant damage on the most important targets: German airfields and army logistics routes and centers. The few *VVS* aircraft present in the Sevastopol Defense Region managed to conduct a small number of nuisance attacks against German positions. Yet after their airfields were identified and brought under the sweep of the Luftwaffe's horizontally fired flak guns, their ability to undertake daylight missions fell off sharply. During the day, Richthofen could see the enemy's airfields from his observation tower and noticed that, when enemy pilots started their engines before takeoff, large clouds of dust were blown up. Each time he saw these telltale dust clouds, he immediately radioed the information through to his flak batteries, which opened fire on the airfields at the very moment the aircraft prepared for takeoff, and to his fighter units, which dispatched aircraft to catch and shoot down any Soviet planes managing to get airborne. "Destroyed 18 Russian [planes] in this manner today," he chuckled on 13 June, "four by bombing. It is great fun!"

Despite this brief expression of pleasure, Richthofen was far from happy. He gravely feared that, because progress at Sevastopol was slow and army losses disturbingly high—10,300 casualties in the first five days[23]—the High Command would convert the operation into a regular siege and redeploy the bulk of his units farther north in preparation for the beginning of Operation *Blau*. Hitler had threatened this on the first day of the ground assault, when reports of the infantry's slow progress first reached him. However, after cooling down (and doubtless learning of Eleventh Army's emphatic requests for *Fliegerkorps VIII* to remain)[24] the Führer decided to give Manstein three more regiments and Richthofen a little more time. That time, the latter worried, was fast running out. Things appeared to go better on 13 June, when Fort Stalin, with one of its massive turrets cracked open by fire from "Thor," "Odin," or "Dora," fell to the 22nd Infantry Division and other local gains were made north of the city. Although Bock was still impatient, and counted on having the greater part of *Fliegerkorps VIII* near Kharkov in time to start *Blau* on 20 June, Richthofen received a short breathing space. His units would remain in the Crimea for the time being. "Therefore, I feel reassured," he noted, "and can continue fighting in peace until we achieve final victory!"[25]

Axis forces would certainly soon gain "final victory" at Sevastopol but not, as Richthofen expected (and most historians still believe),[26] with himself in direct operational command of air forces. On 15 June, Göring informed him by telephone that he would soon be transferred 750 kilometers north to Kursk, where he was to prepare new headquarters for *Fliegerkorps VIII* so that it could move north and commence operations as soon as Sevastopol fell. Naturally, he would retain formal command of the air corps, at least until given leadership of *Luftflotte 4,* but *Oberst* Wild would take over direct control of air operations against Sevastopol. The latter would be guided and assisted by *Oberstleutnant* Torsten Christ, *Fliegerkorps VIII's* chief of staff, who would remain behind in the Crimea.[27]

Richthofen was clearly disgusted by Göring's decision, calling it "dreadful and, from a combat and troop perspective, weird." He accused the *Reichsmarschall* of doing nothing for the Luftwaffe's interests, "let alone those of his people and units."[28] He was also bitterly disappointed that he would not be present when the fortress fell, lamenting on 22 June that "I am ordered to go immediately to the north. I have only three days to get there, instead of the previously mentioned seven!" "It is a pity," he continued, "that one can never finish what one starts here in the east. After a while, it takes away all the pleasure."

Wanting a smooth transfer of power to Wild, the air commander invited his successor to his quarters for a chat on 16 June.[29] He was well aware that he had disparaged *Fliegerführer Süd's* efforts on several recent occasions, and had at one time even placed *Oberst* Köster, commander of *K.G. 51,* in charge of one or two major antishipping missions. That left Wild, an expert on air-naval matters, feeling that his own substantial achievements in recent months were not valued. Accordingly, Richthofen acted toward him in a friendly and conciliatory manner. His previous criticisms, he explained, sprang from neither personal nor professional enmity but from an awareness that Wild simply "lacked experience in every respect." To overcome this handicap, he must share power with *Oberstleutnant* Christ, who, although his junior, was more experienced in the day-to-day running of an air corps. Far from placating Wild, these insensitive instructions left him feeling deeply insulted. Not only was Christ of lower rank, but in recent weeks he had made no secret of his own disdain for his superior. Still, as a professional soldier, Wild accepted that he had to concern himself more with winning battles than gaining promotions. He agreed to work with Christ as equals. The next day, 17 June, the two met to iron out their differences.

CUTTING THE ENEMY'S LIFELINE

Wild took over the daily running of *Fliegerkorps VIII* on 23 June, a day before Richthofen flew to his new headquarters in Kursk. Not only have scholars failed to describe and explain Wild's role in the battle after receiving this "promotion," but they have scarcely mentioned his activities during the previous weeks of bloody fighting. Throughout that period, Wild planned and directed *Fliegerführer Süd's* daily reconnaissance and antishipping operations, carefully coordinating them with missions of the local Axis naval forces. Although these air and naval forces caused little material damage to enemy vessels (which doubtless explains their lack of interest to most historians of the eastern front), they still made a noteworthy contribution to the Axis offensive. In particular, their operations forced the Soviet command to curtail its naval fire support missions and to reduce, and finally stop, its supply convoys to the besieged city.

It has already been noted that in recent months Soviet warships had repeatedly shelled Axis positions along Crimean coastlines and often supported Sevastopol's heroic defense by firing on elements of Manstein's army as they regrouped for their new assault. Even more important, cruisers, destroyers, and submarines risked air attack on most nights to keep the city supplied with food, medicines, ammunition, and reinforcements, and to evacuate women, children, and wounded soldiers. By the middle of May, the Luftwaffe's large presence in the Crimea had forced Vice Admiral Oktyabrskii to reduce the number of coastal bombardment missions carried out, but warships and submarines continued supplying Sevastopol. After the new assault began on 2 June, responsibility for cutting the city's naval lifeline fell on *Fliegerführer Süd* and the light naval forces about to begin operations from Yalta and Simferopol.

Fliegerführer Süd, almost impotent after Richthofen poached most of its combat units for attacks on the fortress, was unable to do more than keep enemy vessels under constant surveillance and, if any were seen, send out small attack forces. On the first day of the massive air and artillery bombardment, for instance, Richthofen's corps conducted as many as 723 sorties. Only 56 of these were by *Fliegerführer Süd's* aircraft; 33 by fighters, the rest by torpedo bombers and reconnaissance planes.[30] The fighters flew escort missions and patrolled the skies over the Kerch Peninsula, searching for enemy aircraft operating from Caucasian airfields. A few bombers participated in raids on Sevastopol, but most reconnoitered Caucasian ports and the Black Sea's vast expanses between the Crimea and the Turkish coast. These long-range missions were important; they revealed that Oktyabrskii's powerful fleet rode at anchor in various Caucasian ports and, therefore, posed no immediate threat to Axis forces in the Crimea. Manstein, who still feared enemy amphibious landings, was doubtless relieved to learn this. *Fliegerführer Süd*'s offensive missions were also valuable; Bf 109s shot down four of the six enemy aircraft destroyed that day, and He 111s, after spotting a small convoy headed for Sevastopol, sank by torpedo a 4,000-ton tanker.[31]

Throughout the rest of the initial five-day artillery and air bombardment, *Fliegerführer Süd* followed this operation pattern. Fighters patrolled the skies above the Kerch Straits, preventing most enemy aircraft based on airfields on the Taman Peninsula and north Caucasus from breaching their fighter "screen" during daylight hours. A few bombers attacked Sevastopol. The rest, armed with machine guns and torpedoes, flew long-range reconnaissance and naval interdiction missions. Offensive operations, however, bore less fruit than on the first day; between 3 and 7 June *Fliegerführer Süd* made a small number of bombing raids on Sevastopol, destroyed only three aircraft over Kerch, and, despite attacking a few convoys and lone warships, neither sank nor badly damaged any of them.[32]

Because enemy supply convoys sailed mainly at night, they were extremely difficult to detect from the air. Wild's airmen dropped flares to illuminate Sevastopol's harbor installations and sections of the Crimean and Caucasian sea-lanes where convoys were believed to be. Nonetheless, as this location method was based mainly on guesswork and random checking, it proved woefully inadequate. *Admiral Schwarzes Meer*'s signals teams in Constanza and the Crimea intercepted Soviet naval radio communications, and were thus often able to plot sailing courses, but many intercepted messages proved to be decoy signals sent by small torpedo boats and minesweepers in order to disguise the genuine location of large warships and merchantmen. Even when *Fliegerführer Süd* managed to locate vessels, by either reconnaissance or signal interception, they usually slipped away under cover of artificial smoke screens or the protection of fighters urgently dispatched from north Caucasian airfields.[33] As a result, Wild's airmen failed to prevent warships, merchantmen, and submarines from slipping into Sevastopol each night.

Around 7 June, German and Italian midget submarines, MTBs, and armed motorboats commenced operations from Yalta and Simferopol, enhancing the ability of Axis forces to block the sea-lanes leading into Sevastopol. Friedrich Ruge, a German naval historian and former admiral, noted that these light forces inflicted little material damage on enemy vessels, but "their presence made the situation still more difficult for the Soviet Navy."[34] Indeed, as soon as Vice Admiral Oktyabrskii learned of their presence—during the night of 8 and 9 June, Soviet destroyers unsuccessfully attacked midget submarines with depth charges after spotting them on their radar screens[35]—he ordered his captains to reduce further the number of gunfire support missions carried out in Crimean waters.

They also had to switch to area fire (as opposed to individual target bombardment) while under way and without stopping or slowing to check and correct the accuracy of their gunfire.[36] Even more important, Oktyabrskii cut back the number of supply missions undertaken by surface vessels, ordering instead a substantial increase in the number carried out by his less vulnerable submarines.

The transport of vital supplies aboard submarines began early in May. Yet even with all spare fuel, torpedoes, and ammunition removed, their cargo capacity (only eighty to ninety tons) remained far lower than that of merchantmen or destroyers.[37] Consequently, until the light Axis naval forces began patrolling Crimean waters early in June, Oktyabrskii used few submarines for supply purposes. By the middle of the month, however, he perceived the risk to his surface vessels to be so great that he ordered half his forty-strong submarine fleet to carry out the vast bulk of supply missions. He could not deploy the entire fleet on these vital missions because he also needed them to attack German shipping elsewhere in the Black Sea, especially the increasing number of convoys plying the sea-lanes between Rumania and Ukraine. The official Soviet history states:

> With every day it became more difficult to bring troops, ammunition, armaments, and foodstuffs into Sevastopol; and to evacuate wounded and sick from the besieged city. Only battle ships and fast-moving transports of the Black Sea Fleet could operate on the sea communications lines. In June, because of the pressure of the situation, submarines began to be used for transport.[38]

As it happened, submarines were almost as vulnerable as surface ships; because they carried far less fuel and more cargo than usual, their operational range dropped significantly. As a result, they had to sail to Sevastopol by the shortest route and on the surface, submerging only when detected by Axis aircraft, MTBs, and submarines.[39] Despite this, submarines distinguished themselves as blockade breakers. During the monthlong assault on the fortress, they completed seventy-eight supply missions, delivering almost 4,000 tons of food, medicine, ammunition, and gasoline (carried in their ballast tanks). On their return voyages, they evacuated more than 1,300 civilians and wounded troops.[40]

Fliegerführer Süd always operated in close cooperation with the German and Italian MTB, armed motorboat, and midget submarine flotillas. Their respective strengths and weaknesses complemented each other. As already noted, *Fliegerführer Süd* was unable to contribute substantially to night combat operations, but it did provide Axis naval forces with up-to-the-minute reconnaissance information. During the long summer days, it flew constantly over Soviet ports and sea-lanes and was able, as a result, to inform its naval partners which enemy vessels were in port, which were at sea, on which courses they sailed, and where they were likely to be when they reached Crimean waters after nightfall. Because Axis naval forces were vulnerable during daylight hours to attack by Soviet aircraft and vessels but were hard to detect at night, they operated only during the hours of darkness. Using radio intercepts and the detailed reconnaissance information provided by *Fliegerführer Süd,* they patrolled the sea-lanes in the vicinity of Cape Sarych and the approaches to Sevastopol Bay. They stalked Soviet warships and transports hoping to sneak into the besieged city, with the cover of darkness protecting them from air attacks. Their patrols were even assisted on occasion by Wild's aircraft, which dropped illuminating flares and attacked Soviet warships pursuing them.

Despite the disdain for Italian military efforts commonly expressed by both Allied opponents and German "friends" (not to mention most postwar military historians), the Italian flotilla in the Crimea proved very successful, far more so, in fact, than its less aggressive German counterpart. Equipped with better torpedoes, the Italian flotilla was responsible for almost all enemy ships damaged or destroyed by Axis naval forces. After several recent unsuccessful torpedo attacks on convoys, its first offensive success came during the night of 10 and 11 June. MTBs and armed motorboats attacked a small Soviet convoy near Cape Khersones (ten kilometers from Sevastopol) and succeeded in "probably" sinking a 5,000-ton Soviet motorboat.[41] Although the Italian crews were unable to observe the vessel sinking after being torpedoed, reconnaissance planes from *Fliegerführer Süd* later found an empty rescue dinghy and a large oil patch.[42] Two nights later, Italian MTBs and armed motorboats scored their first confirmed "kill," although credit had to be shared with the Luftwaffe. Attacking another convoy near Cape Khersones, the Italian vessels hit and badly damaged a 10,000-ton freighter with two torpedoes. The Soviets attempted to tow the listing and burning ship into Sevastopol Bay, but a lone Ju 88 on a reconnaissance mission swooped down and finished it off with two 500-kg bombs.[43] On 19 June, an Italian MTB patrolling the sea-lanes around Sevastopol scored a "kill" which it did not have to share; it attacked and sank a 3,000-ton troop transport evacuating wounded troops from Sevastopol. Apparently there were no survivors.[44]

Each night, Axis warships and submarines attacked not only surface vessels but also enemy submarines en route to Sevastopol. On 15 June, a midget submarine torpedoed and sank a surfaced Soviet submarine sailing off Cape Sarych.[45] Three nights later, a different midget submarine destroyed a second Soviet submarine in the same stretch of water.[46] The following night, 19 June, two Italian MTBs left their base in Yalta to chase a submarine sighted by reconnaissance aircraft off Cape Ay-Todor (five kilometers west of Yalta). They caught and sank it near Cape Sarych.[47] By that time, the panic-stricken Oktyabrskii had already ordered a sharp reduction in the number of supply missions undertaken by warships and merchantmen, prompting the observation "Enemy naval activity has greatly decreased" to be typed into *Admiral Schwarzes Meer*'s war diary on 19 June.[48]

After sinking numerous surface vessels during the previous two weeks, including two destroyers, several large freighters, and a few MTBs,[49] *Fliegerführer Süd* scored its first submarine kill on 26 June. He 111s struck a convoy sailing along the southeast Crimean coastline, sinking not only a submarine but also a destroyer.[50] After that, Oktyabrskii stopped all supply missions by surface vessels; only submarines, MTBs, and fast patrol boats would now attempt the perilous voyage to Sevastopol. A few days later, at dawn on 1 July, Stukas attacked a small flotilla of patrol boats near Cape Khersones, sinking one. Later that day, He 111s destroyed four more.[51] During the following two days and nights, He 111s managed to sink several others.[52] Yet for Wild's aircrews, the pleasure of destroying these vessels was far surpassed by the joy felt on 2 July when the flotilla leader *Tashkent* was sunk (and the cruiser *Komintern,* a destroyer, and several large freighters were badly damaged) by bombers and Stukas during a raid on Novorossiisk harbor.[53] To the constant frustration of these aircrew, *Tashkent* had made more than forty supply trips between Novorossiisk and Sevastopol during the previous month, sometimes shelling German positions as it steamed along Crimean coasts.[54] During those trips it survived no fewer than ninety-six air attacks, dodging 400 bombs and ten torpedoes. On 27 June, *Tashkent* had actually been the last Soviet surface warship to enter Sevastopol. It carried 944 troops into the fortress and evacuated 2,300 civilians and wounded soldiers.[55] It is ironic that this seemingly unsinkable warship was destroyed on 2 July, the day *after* the fortress fell to Manstein's army.

Axis naval successes, it should be pointed out, were not achieved without cost. When Oktyabrskii first learned on 9 June that German and Italian naval forces operated in Crimean waters, he immediately ordered their destruction. When told that Italian midget submarines, MTBs, and armed motorboats operated from Yalta, he felt both dismayed and disgusted. Yalta had been bombed repeatedly in previous weeks by Soviet aircraft flying from bases in the northwestern Caucasus. That the Italians were able to establish a naval base there during that period showed how ineffectual those raids were. Oktyabrskii not only demanded that bomber units strike Yalta with everything available but also directed his own light warships to attack the port.

Soviet air units straightaway made Yalta their main target, bombing it every night in increasingly heavy raids. After several attacks left MTBs and motorboats with minor damage, *Konteradmiral* Schweinitz, naval commander, Crimea, urgently asked *Admiral Schwarzes Meer* on 12 June for permission to disperse the Italian vessels among several Crimean harbors.[56] Even before Schweinitz received a reply, the Soviets dealt Yalta a punishing blow. Before dawn on 13 June, bombers struck harbor installations and docks. Even as antiaircraft guns burst into life and naval personnel rushed to their air-raid shelters, a lone Soviet MTB slipped into the harbor and fired several torpedoes at the berthed vessels before speeding off under the cover of a dense smoke screen.[57] These torpedoes did considerable damage, sinking a midget submarine and spraying several other craft with shrapnel.

Stunned by this audacious attack, Schweinitz immediately requested *Fliegerkorps VIII* to establish in Yalta an additional flak battery and *Admiral Schwarzes*

Meer to send strong antitorpedo nets to both Yalta and Simferopol.[58] These requests were approved, but the guns and nets did not arrive for over two weeks. In the meantime, Soviet air and naval attacks on Yalta and other German-held Crimean ports continued. Although many of these attacks caused minor damage to harbor installations, few inflicted substantial damage to vessels. The worst came on 19 June, when *VVS* bombers severely damaged two midget submarines and crippled an MTB.[59] Overall, however, these attacks achieved little; Axis naval losses remained low and combat successes high.

The Axis flotillas' nightly patrols, which perfectly complemented *Fliegerführer Süd*'s sea reconnaissance and interdiction missions, had an impact on the Battle of Sevastopol far outweighing the material damage they inflicted on enemy vessels; these naval and air operations compelled Oktyabrskii to curtail his fleet's fire support missions and to reduce, and finally stop, its vital supply convoys to the besieged city. The gradual cutting of the city's lifeline had a major affect on its defenders' ability to resist Manstein's assault. Not only did the blockade disrupt and finally prevent troop reinforcements, but it gradually starved defenders not only of food and medicine but also of ammunition. Late in June, for example, they became so desperate for the latter that they sent down naval divers to retrieve shells (and anything else of value) from the wrecks of ships lying on the bottom of Sevastopol harbor.[60] Even the tons of shells they brought up were incapable of satisfying the demands of artillery and flak gunners. Their guns became increasingly quiet, to the delight of *Admiral Schwarzes Meer,* which rightly claimed in its war diary on 28 June that their gunfire decreased "as a result of the disruption of their supplies by our naval forces and planes."[61]

THE FALL OF THE FORTRESS

Despite Richthofen's impatient criticisms during mid-June, the army actually made steady progress. After taking Fort Stalin on 13 June, 54th Army Corps pressed forward relentlessly and with heavy losses toward the northern shore of Severnaya Bay, gradually beating back courageous and tenacious Soviet forces. Over the next four days, it succeeded in taking several other major defensive installations, including Forts Cheka, GPU, Siberia, Volga, and Maxim Gorki I.

Taking Maxim Gorki I was certainly 54th Army Corps' most difficult task. On 17 June, *Oberleutnant* Maué, a Stuka pilot from *St.G. 77,* earned his place in airpower history by scoring a direct hit on the seemingly impregnable fort's eastern turret, knocking out its massive 30.5-cm naval guns.[62] The other guns were put out of action by repeated hits from Manstein's heavy siege howitzers and the explosives of engineers who finally reached the fort later that day after several previous attempts. Even then, however, the 1,000 men inside the three-level fort fanatically defended every room and passageway. Suffering appalling losses but determined to fight to the last cartridge, they held on for over three days. Their

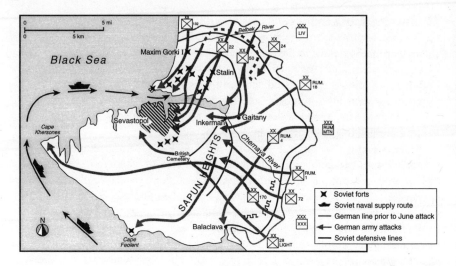

3. The assault on Sevastopol, June–July 1942

last radio message to the Soviet command in Sevastopol reveals the horror of the situation: "There are twenty-two of us left! We are preparing to blow ourselves up. We are signing off now. Farewell!"[63] When German sappers finally forced their way through corpses and rubble into the fort's innermost parts, they were relieved, but probably also shocked, to find only forty badly wounded men still alive.

In the south, meanwhile, the 30th Army Corps had also made substantial progress, having fought through dense bush and craggy ravines to drive a deep wedge into the defensive lines in front of the Sapun Heights. Also suffering heavy losses, it captured the fortified strongpoints of Chapel Mountain, North Nose, Ruin Hill, and Kamary, while the 1st Rumanian Mountain Division succeeded in taking Sugar Loaf.

Fliegerkorps VIII played a key role in these successful but costly operations. Its units ceaselessly pounded not only the forts and major defensive installations but also secondary defenses, artillery and flak batteries, and army rear areas. "During the night," Richthofen penned in his diary on 17 June, "the 54th Army Corps positioned itself, then [during the day] overran the Red front lines and took the majority of the forts north of Severnaya Bay. We [air units] pin down the artillery east of Sevastopol and at the front and destroy much. We [strike] the forts again and again." Between 13 June, when Fort Stalin fell, and 17 June, when the other major forts in the north were taken, his corps flew a total of 3,899 sorties and dropped 3,086 tons of bombs.[64] Despite persisting fuel and bomb shortages, this average of 780 sorties per day is only a slight drop from the average of 835 during the offensive's first eleven days.

By 19 June, the sector north of Severnaya Bay was entirely in German hands, except for Fort North and other fortifications on "Battery Headland," the peninsula dominating the bay's entrance. On the evening of 17 June, Richthofen's units had delivered massive blows to these forts, prompting him to write with pleasure that "our giant fire-magic fell on Battery Headland. The infantry were very enthusiastic!" His units continued pounding the forts—inflicting on them, so he claimed, far more damage than the artillery—until 54th Army Corps finally succeeded in capturing them on 21 June.[65]

Throughout this period, *Fliegerkorps VIII* also battered the city of Sevastopol itself. To its terrified inhabitants, for instance, 19 June was like a nightmare. From first light until noon, bombers conducted immense "rolling attacks" with high-explosive bombs against supply depots, barracks, hangars, and other key buildings in the city. They also hit flak and artillery batteries to the east and southeast. From noon until dusk, they repeated their attacks with incendiary bombs.[66] That evening, Richthofen noted with delight that the entire city was "a sea of flames" with smoke clouds reaching 1,500 meters and stretching from Sevastopol to Feodosiya, 150 kilometers away. These clouds of smoke were so dense that at times they hampered air operations the following day.

The 54th Army Corps found it extremely difficult to drive Soviet troops from their last fortified defenses north of Severnaya Bay. After capturing the forts, they still had to destroy forces fighting defiantly from the scores of caves and tunnels honeycombing the rocky cliffs and ravines. Civilians and troops had previously prepared many of these strongholds for defense, storing ammunition and supplies and even giving some protective steel gates. When German sappers attempted to break into the first of these keeps, its fanatical occupants blew it up, killing themselves and many sappers. By 21 June, however, German troops had captured most of the other strongholds intact and gained control of the entire sector north of Severnaya Bay. They quickly brought the still-smoldering city and its naval base under the sweep of their guns. The only obstacle separating them from the city, with its buildings in ruins and people in hiding, was the 1,000-meter-wide bay itself.

30th Army Corps also drove slowly but relentlessly forward, taking the Eagle's Perch strongpoint and the Fedyukiny Heights. These gains set up the corps nicely for an assault on the strategically important Sapun Heights, along which the Soviets had their strongest fortifications south of the city. The Rumanian Mountain Corps also made slow but steady gains, so that Axis troops possessed almost all of Sevastopol's outer defensive positions by the morning of 26 June. They would now be able to pull tight the noose around Sevastopol.

During the previous week, *Fliegerkorps VIII* had flown 4,700 sorties and dropped 3,894 tons of bombs in support of the army's efforts.[67] This daily average of 671 sorties and 556 tons of bombs, while still substantial, was a 15 percent drop from that of the previous week, which was itself 10 percent lower than that of the week before. Considering that the air corps' rate of operational readiness had increased significantly in the last month (from 49.8 to 64.5 percent),[68] this mission decrease reveals the severity of the chronic fuel and bomb shortages.

The least active days in this period, however, apparently were caused not by these shortages but by the change of operational command. During the four days following Richthofen's departure for Kursk on 23 June, the daily mission average fell dramatically to only 400.[69] This infuriated Wild, who refused to let the units now under his command slacken their efforts. By flying from base to base, admonishing local commanders for their flagging performance, he managed quickly to pull it back up again. In fact, for the last five days of the Sevastopol campaign the daily mission average rose to 961, the highest it had been in over three weeks.[70] Ironically, this excellent performance rate could not have been achieved without the fuel and bomb reserves built up during the corps' most slothful days.

In the week or so up to 26 June, *Fliegerkorps VIII* had devoted around half its efforts to "direct" army support missions. In order to help 54th Army Corps break through the strong defenses north of Severnaya Bay, the air corps bombed and strafed caves, tunnels, bunkers, trenches, and pockets of resistance. It also attacked enemy artillery and flak batteries still inflicting heavy losses on Manstein's infantry. The corps devoted the rest of its efforts to "indirect" army support missions. It struck barracks, reserve centers, communication systems, dockyards, fuel dumps, supply depots, transport columns, and roads. Both types of missions were successful. The corps destroyed not only numerous strongpoints, bunkers, and gun batteries but also several key logistics centers and supply columns. Stukas, far more accurate than conventional horizontal bombers, again proved their worth against such targets. For example, one account of the operations noted:

> On 21 June . . . *I./St.G. 77* flew three missions against anti-tank batteries and two days later they caught and destroyed a whole horse transport column accompanied by a few tanks in ravines at Inkerman. . . . Unable to winkle out Russian defenders in the natural caves and caverns of this region, *St.G. 77* sealed them in, blocking the exit tunnels to one such system at map reference G9B with some precision bombing. Another horse transport column along with tanks and troops was decimated in ravine N2C.[71]

The constant scream of Stukas, rumble of medium bombers, and pounding of artillery tormented the burning city's defenders. Still, the tenacious inhabitants refused to give in, even when Manstein's divisions had captured virtually all their outer defensive positions by 26 June and Wild's aircraft and the light naval forces had cut their naval lifeline by about the same date. They were also not swayed by the 2,776,000 propaganda leaflets rained down on them since the campaign began (1,152,000 in the last week alone).[72] They would defend their ruined city to the bitter end.

Despite the Soviets' extraordinary tenacity, Manstein's troops had managed (albeit at great cost in men and matériel) to push them back into the fortress's inner defense zone. The fjordlike cliffs on Severnaya Bay's southern shore formed this zone's northern front, while the heights of Inkerman (site of the old but strong Inkerman fort), the precipitous Sapun Heights, and the cliffs around Balaclava formed its eastern and southern fronts. These natural geographical obstructions, dotted with numerous fortifications, gun positions, and bunkers, presented Manstein with a major tactical dilemma. "The [Eleventh] Army Command," he later wrote, "now had to decide how this inner fortification belt would be prised open."[73] Attacking the city from the north would require elements of 54th Army Corps to cross the exposed, 1,000-meter-wide Severnaya Bay, which was protected by dozens of guns positioned along the southern shore. On the other hand, attacking the city from the south or east would require regiments of 30th Army Corps to assault the well-defended and seemingly impassable Sapun Heights.

Against the advice of his senior commanders, Manstein decided upon the former course of action. Under the cover of darkness, dense smoke screens, and heavy artillery and air attacks, an infantry regiment and an engineer battalion of 54th Army Corps would launch a powerful amphibious attack across Severnaya Bay.[74] In the meantime, 30th Army Corps would assail the Sapun Heights from the southeast. Its assault would doubtless divert the enemy's attention before, and dissipate his forces during, the attack across the bay. Once the assault troops reached the southern shore, they would join the battle by storming the heights from the other side. The amphibious operation would take place on the night of 28 and 29 June.

On 28 June, as the assault teams prepared their boats and equipment for that night's perilous operation, 54th Army Corps sent one of its divisions, the 50th, across the Chernaya River east of the bay to attack the old Inkerman fort. This division succeeded in taking the fort, but not without witnessing one of the most tragic moments in the dying city's last days. Enormous caverns, used by the Soviets as ammunition dumps and refuge centers for thousands of civilians and wounded troops, existed inside the cliffs above the old fort. As German troops entered Inkerman, the ground beneath their feet shuddered from the impact of a tremendous detonation deep inside the caverns. "A few fanatical commissars," to quote Manstein, blew up the cavern to prevent Germans from seizing their ammunition.[75] The blast killed thousands of refugees and wounded troops. It was, he concluded, "a clear sign of the contempt for human life which has become a principle of this Asiatic power!"

At 0100 hours on 29 June, Manstein's assault teams shot across Severnaya Bay under cover of dense smoke screens. Praying that they would cross without detection, the army commander had directed his artillery batteries not to open fire until the enemy did. To his great relief, the first wave was not spotted until the boats had reached the south shore and their crews spilled out, firing their automatic weapons at stunned Soviets. From then on, German guns and Stukas blasted every enemy artillery position revealed by its muzzle flash, allowing other assault teams to cross the bay with acceptable losses. Even as this attack took place, 30th Army Corps' artillery roared into life, smashing enemy defenses on the Sapun Heights, followed half an hour later by its infantry, which slowly but steadily forced its way forward. By early afternoon, 54th Army Corps' assault teams had established a solid beachhead on Severnaya Bay's southern shore, and advance regiments of the other German corps had gained a foothold on the heights.

Cooperation between the three service branches (ground, air, and naval forces) was excellent. Under Wild's capable direction, *Fliegerkorps VIII* had "kept up an incessant raid on the city . . . in order to muffle all noise from the northern shore."[76] Indeed, the air corps had begun pounding enemy positions on the cliff tops of the bay's southern shore and, in particular, on the Sapun Heights before the assault boats left the bay's northern shore.[77] *Fliegerkorps VIII* operated at a furious pace all day, pinning down and destroying enemy positions in both combat areas. "German aircraft were literally raging over the battlefield," wrote Vladimir Karpov, "bombing and strafing machine-gun nests and wiping out the last pockets of resistance."[78] Conducting a staggering 1,329 missions and dropping 1,218 tons of bombs, the air corps performed far better than it had since the opening days of the battle more than three weeks earlier.[79] Because most Soviet flak batteries had already been destroyed, and those surviving were short of ammunition, the corps' losses were extremely low; only two Ju 87s failed to return to base, and even their crews survived.

Admiral Schwarzes Meer's light forces had also supported the amphibious operation. The previous night, its Italian MTBs had escorted numerous army assault boats as they carried out a feint landing operation near Cape Feolent.[80] The Soviets fell for the ruse, believing the deceptive maneuver to be a genuine operation and diverting forces from other stretches of coastline to protect that particular stretch. The deception fooled even the authors of the postwar official Soviet war history, who complacently claimed that "the Hitlerites had unsuccessfully attempted to execute a night amphibious landing at Cape Feolent."[81] Also on the night before the real amphibious operation, the 17th Defense Flotilla's naval ferry barges had cleared a route for the assault boats through suspected enemy minefields in Severnaya Bay. Additionally, when Manstein's troops finally shot across the bay in their seventy combined operations assault boats and twelve rubber ferries (apparently all provided by *Admiral Schwarzes Meer*),[82] MTBs from the 1st E-Boat Flotilla protected them on the seaward side from Soviet naval attacks. Their assault and flak guns, ammunition, and provisions immediately followed in four of the German fleet's naval ferry barges.[83]

By the evening of 29 June, German commanders realized they would not wait long for the city to fall. Manstein recalled: "After the successful crossing of the bay, the fall of the Heights of Inkerman and the 30th Army Corps' breakthrough of the Sapun positions, the fate of the Sevastopol fortress was sealed."[84] The following day, 54th Army Corps took Fort Malakoff, scene of bitter fighting in the Crimean War, eighty-seven years earlier, and broke into the city's outer ring of fortifications.

At the same time, 30th Army Corps breached the Sapun Line. The 28th Light Infantry Division took the British Cemetery, which the desperate defenders had turned into a strongpoint. The battle was bloody. Manstein recalled that, among the shattered marble monuments once erected for the British dead in the Crimean War, corpses of Soviet troops lay strewn over graves torn open by shelling. Rolling up the Sapun positions in a southward direction, the 72nd Infantry Division made faster progress, taking "Windmill Hill" and with it the main road into Sevastopol.

Manstein was deeply impressed by the courage and fanatical fighting spirit of the ruined city's defenders. Even now, he knew, with their city reduced to rubble and their once-powerful formations broken into motley groups of poorly equipped and starving soldiers, they would not surrender.[85] His own men would have to take the city street by street, building by building. In terms of losses, he had already paid a terrible price for the city. Unwilling to pay more, but well aware that house-to-house fighting would be extremely costly, he directed his artillery to mount a massive, daylong bombardment of the city. He also requested Wild (not Richthofen, as some authors assert)[86] to smash the city with everything available.

Although his ground and air crews were physically and mentally drained by the previous day's ceaseless operations, and his bomb and fuel reserves were almost exhausted, Wild agreed to the army commander's request. On 30 June, his flak guns joined the artillery bombardment, his fighters attacked any visible troops, vehicles, and vessels, and his bombers and dive-bombers again pulverized the city. These units performed as well as the day before, conducting 1,218 sorties and releasing 1,192 tons of bombs.[87] After Sevastopol was "ruthlessly bombarded" this time, wrote Vladimir Karpov, it was again left "in flames and veiled in black smoke rising from its ruins."[88] As the bombardment reached its dreadful crescendo, terrified citizens and many troops—now without the barest means of survival, let alone resistance—fled through streets covered with bricks, twisted girders, and broken pipes to the beaches west of the city. There they huddled in caves, waiting in vain for small boats to take them off the cursed Crimea.

Oktyabrskii was now incapable of planning and directing even small-scale defensive operations in the city. Late on 30 June, the grieved vice admiral assembled what remained of the military soviet in his subterranean headquarters deep beneath the flaming ruins.[89] The *Stavka,* he announced, had decided to evacuate Sevastopol in view of the futility of its further defense. Stalin himself had ordered that senior commanders and Party and administrative officials were to leave the city aboard submarines. Except for rearguard units, troops were to withdraw to the Khersones Peninsula and its neighboring bays at the very western tip of the Crimea, where they would continue fighting until they could be evacuated at night as vessels became available.

That night, Oktyabrskii, Petrov (the garrison commander), and other senior officers and officials fled the city. They left Major General Novikov, commander of an infantry division (that no longer existed except for a few scattered remnants), in charge of all rearguard actions. After setting up his command post in the 35th Coastal Battery, Novikov hurriedly formed new units from the remains of muddled and broken regiments. In order to protect tens of thousands of civilians and shell-shocked and wounded soldiers now fleeing to the beaches, he also tried to erect a defensive line across the Khersones Peninsula west of the city. His efforts proved inadequate.

Manstein's artillery and Wild's air units began their assault at dawn on 1 July. They pounded not only the coastal batteries in which the defenders sought refuge and the hastily prepared defensive field positions, which offered no shelter from these vicious bombardments, but also the vehicle-littered beaches where panic-stricken civilians and soldiers alike threw themselves against the sides of cliffs, desperately praying for evacuation. *Fliegerkorps VIII*'s attacks were especially devastating, as Victor Gurin recalled: "At dawn . . . the first German aircraft attacked our positions. Coming from the side of the sea, wave after wave, they bombed and strafed the shore defenses and the cliffs where our men were entrenched and dropped leaflets demanding our surrender. Our casualties were severe."[90] These nightmarish attacks, which caused swirling, choking black smoke to envelop the beaches, snapped the nerves of many defenders. Boris Voyetekhov described their terror:

> They ran with maddened eyes, with tunics torn and flopping; panic-stricken, bewildered, miserable, frightened people. They seized feverishly any kind of craft they could find—rafts, rubber floats, automobile tyres—and flung themselves into the sea. Nobody harmed them. "Let them go their way," the men of the rear guard muttered as they chose positions for their last battle.[91]

Despite this frightful state of affairs, the Soviet Black Sea Fleet made no attempt to evacuate the civilians and troops trapped on Cape Khersones, although insignificant numbers were taken off under cover of darkness by fishing boats and light coastal vessels. The fleet had been savagely mauled in recent weeks, with numerous submarines, destroyers, MTBs, patrol boats, and transport vessels being damaged or destroyed. Realizing that they still had a long war to fight, its commanders concluded that they simply could not afford the high losses likely to be inflicted during an evacuation attempt, which the enemy no doubt expected.

Not only were Axis light naval forces patrolling the waters off Cape Khersones, these commanders reasoned, but those waters were now under the sweep of German heavy guns. Even more important, the numerous powerful Luftwaffe forces in the Crimea were able, now that they had concluded their missions against Sevastopol, to turn their attention to the fleet. Indeed, just to make sure that the fleet did stay away, Wild kept Cape Khersones under steady air attack for several days and, on 2 July, dispatched seventy-eight bombers, forty dive-bombers, and forty fighters to attack the fleet's Caucasian bases.[92] In Anapa, Taman, Novorossiisk, and a few smaller ports, they badly damaged numerous large warships (including, as already mentioned, the *Tashkent* and *Komintern*), freighters, and harbor facilities. After this blow, an evacuation attempt was out of the question.

Although Novikov's troops on the peninsula held out for several more days, fighting courageously until they exhausted their rations and ammunition (and often, at that point, blowing themselves up to prevent their batteries or bunkers from falling into enemy hands), Eleventh Army occupied Sevastopol in the afternoon of 1 July. Manstein felt worn out but greatly relieved to take the fortress at long last; no fewer than 196 days had passed since 17 December, when his troops first broke through its outer ring of fortifications.

Back at the Wolf's Lair in East Prussia, the Führer was ecstatic. Despite his generals' pessimism, 1942 was turning out to be a splendid year. A month earlier, his eastern armies had thrown back a major Soviet offensive at Kharkov and, in a superb counterattack, humiliated Stalin by destroying the attacking forces. Only ten days earlier, Rommel had stung British pride by storming Tobruk and taking 33,000 prisoners. Now Manstein had captured the city that Stalin repeatedly swore would never fall: Sevastopol, the world's strongest fortress and the gateway to the Caucasus. Hitler immediately sent the exhausted army commander the following radio message:

> In grateful appreciation of your outstanding services in the victorious battles of the Crimea, culminating in the annihilation battle of Kerch and the conquest of the fortress of Sevastopol, mighty in both its natural and constructed fortifications, I hereby appoint you field marshal. By your promotion and the creation of a commemorative shield for all [your] Crimean soldiers, I pay tribute before the entire German people to the heroic achievements of the troops fighting under your command.[93]

Despite the fact that *Fliegerkorps VIII* had contributed substantially to the battle's successful conclusion, its commander did not receive a similar promotion from the Führer. Hitler intended no snub. Back in May, he had informed Richthofen that he would be given command of *Luftflotte 4* once Operation *Blau* got under way. That promotion was now due to take effect in a few weeks. Raising him to field marshal before then, or even shortly afterward, would certainly not be appropriate; he was still an air corps commander and had only recently been made *Generaloberst*, the same rank as air fleet commanders. Also, in the last week or so Hitler had promoted to field marshal a number of distinguished generals long overdue for the honor, including Rommel, Küchler, and now Manstein; despite his superb record to date, Richthofen would have to prove himself as an air fleet commander before he joined these eminent warriors in the highest of ranks.

After learning on 1 July that the fortress had been captured, Richthofen, busy directing air operations north of Kharkov, felt disappointed that his role in the battle had been downplayed (which it had not) by other participants. Disguising his feelings, however, he noted curtly in his diary that "Sevastopol has reportedly fallen." The following day, he received a special report on the matter, apparently from Alexander Löhr (whom he affectionately referred to in his journal as "the little Japanese Emperor" because of his high cheekbones, small and narrow eyes, and diminutive stature).[94] He also received a telegraph from Manstein. Considering Fliegerkorps VIII's outstanding support of Eleventh Army, this telegraph was surprisingly short and lacking in the respectful expressions common to this type of message. "On the day of Sevastopol's fall," it simply said, "the commander and troops of 11th Army think of you with special gratitude. Manstein, Generalfeldmarschall."[95] The air commander was clearly annoyed by the telegraph's brevity, and by his army counterpart's promotion. Unable to disguise his feelings this time, he jealously wrote that "Manstein is now a field marshal. I'm so glad; once again someone has won [Hitler's] special favor."[96] Mocking Manstein's background, he added spitefully that "after all, the Prussian aristocracy are the best at playing soldier."

Meanwhile, Oberst Wild, who had demonstrated sound tactical judgment and boundless energy in recent weeks but received only a simple note of thanks from his absent superior, remained busy in the Crimea. Shortly before Sevastopol fell, he began transferring various elements of Fliegerkorps VIII north to the Kursk area, where they again came under Richthofen's direct control. After he had finished the main "mopping-up" missions around Sevastopol, he sent the rest northward. Fliegerführer Süd, comprising several more units than it had even before the Battle of Kerch, would stay in the Crimea under his command. It would have three main tasks in the coming months: to protect German positions in the Crimea from persistent attacks by enemy aircraft based in the northern Caucasus; to keep the enemy fleet under constant surveillance and attack, ensuring that it undertook no amphibious operations in the region; and, when the time came, to support the German army's advance toward the Caucasus oilfields.

Although a few isolated pockets of resistance remained for several more weeks, Axis forces concluded their main "mopping-up" operations around Sevastopol on 4 July. Only then were their commanders finally able to reflect on the previous month of ferocious fighting. It had been a bloody campaign; the city's stubborn defense by both soldiers and civilians—which has appropriately gone down in history as a paragon of heroism and self-sacrifice—cost Manstein dearly in matériel. His units exhausted the contents of 103 trains, including 46,750 tons of general munitions and 20,000 tons of bombs.[97] However, the battle cost him far more dearly in men. According to official German statistics published at the time, 4,337 German officers and men were killed, 1,591 missing, and 18,183 wounded.

Rumanian sources stated that their own casualties came to around 2,500 killed, missing, and wounded.[98] The Soviets, on the other hand, claimed that Axis casualties amounted to "approximately 150,000."[99] Based on the battle's rate of progress, the number of German reinforcements required, and the time needed afterward to bring Eleventh Army back to full strength, it is clear that German figures are too low and Soviet figures too high. Those factors indicate that the total number of Axis casualties (killed, missing, and wounded) was probably around 75,000.[100] This was an extremely high price to pay.

Despite their heavy losses, Manstein's commanders considered the campaign to have been successful. Their forces took the city, smashed the armies defending it, killed many tens of thousands of troops and citizens, and took over 90,000 prisoners (30,000 at Cape Khersones on 4 July alone). They also captured an impressive amount of booty, including 467 guns, 758 mortars, 155 antitank and flak guns, and two dozen tanks.

Even more important, Axis forces had severely weakened the enemy's position in the region and greatly strengthened their own. They had destroyed or damaged many vessels from the Soviet Black Sea Fleet and deprived it of its main base. Weak and forced to operate from greatly inferior bases along the Caucasus coast, the fleet no longer posed a major threat to German plans for the coming months. Additionally, Axis forces had shown Turkey that they, and not Stalin's forces, controlled the Black Sea region and that the Turks should not consider entering a partnership with the Allies. They had also removed the threat of enemy air attacks on Rumanian oilfields from bombers based in the Crimea. Finally, they were now able to move troops across the Kerch Straits into the oil-rich Caucasus, without having to worry about guarding their rear from attacks by powerful Soviet forces in Sevastopol.

Fliegerkorps VIII's contribution to the victory was substantial. In the corps' after-action report to Göring's command staff, dated 3 July, it claimed without exaggeration that its "unremitting fire on the city, port and airfields inflicted on the enemy the heaviest losses in men and matériel."[101] Since 2 June, the air corps, including Wild's subordinate *Fliegerführer Süd,* had conducted no fewer than 23,751 sorties and dropped 20,528 tons of bombs. Despite working ceaselessly every day, mainly in bombing missions against Soviet positions in front of the advancing infantry, but also in a wide variety of other tasks, it lost only thirty-one aircraft to flak and none to enemy fighters.

Bombers and dive-bombers had markedly aided the infantry by attacking almost everything that moved on the ground, both on the battlefield and in rear areas. They were frequently directed to their targets by tactical reconnaissance aircraft, which also directed the army's artillery fire. They were protected by strong fighter forces, which, the report stated, also "maintained constant surveillance of the battlefield, using bombs and other weapons to attack field positions and batteries, motor and horse-drawn traffic, as well as sea traffic in the port itself."

The corps' after-action report clearly reveals that its impressive mission rate was matched by its "kill" rate. Its aircraft destroyed a huge amount of enemy equipment, including 611 motor vehicles, 123 aircraft (18 on the ground), 38 artillery pieces, 10 tanks, a locomotive, and a large barge mounted with flak guns.[102] They damaged hundreds more motor vehicles and 7 other artillery guns. Their attacks on enemy defensive installations and logistics systems also produced impressive results. They silenced 48 artillery batteries, demolished 28 barracks and industrial buildings, 20 bunkers, 11 ammunition depots, 10 fuel depots, an observation post, and a bridge, and damaged another 43 batteries, 2 barracks, and a bridge.

Few of the corps' 600-odd aircraft had operated routinely against enemy shipping, which shows how unimportant Richthofen considered these missions. Those that were deployed against shipping, however, performed well and contributed substantially to the success of the sea blockade. Directed by *Fliegerführer Süd,* Wild's specialized antinaval unit, these bombers and dive-bombers scoured the sea-lanes around the Crimea and the Caucasus coast in search of enemy warships and supply convoys. Excluding the Axis naval forces' own "kills," they succeeded in sinking 4 destroyers, a submarine, 3 MTBs, 6 coastal vessels, and 4 freighters with a combined weight estimated at 10,800 tons.[103] They also managed to damage another 2 destroyers, 10 coastal vessels, and 2 freighters together reckoned to weigh 12,000 tons.

Air units were not the only Luftwaffe forces to make a large impact during the monthlong assault on Sevastopol. Flak units, most belonging to *Flak-Regiment 18,* also distinguished themselves. The regiment's superb high-velocity "eighty-eights" were deadly not only when blazing at flying enemy aircraft but also when shooting directly at tanks, bunkers, and artillery positions. These alone fired 181,787 rounds, while lighter guns fired another 231,146.[104]

Usually employed alongside the artillery but remaining, as noted, under the Luftwaffe's command, *Flak-Regiment 18*'s guns proved invaluable to Eleventh Army's attack. As well as destroying 24 aircraft (2 on the ground), they blew up 105 vehicles and silenced 44 artillery batteries, another 20 guns, and 93 machine-gun nests.[105] They knocked out 355 bunkers, field fortifications, fortified houses, and other strongpoints. Their remarkable firepower also contributed significantly to the destruction of several major forts, including Forts Stalin, Molotov, Volga, Balaclava, and GPU.

Flak-Regiment 18 struck not only these obvious battlefield targets but also key objects in rear areas. It destroyed or left burning numerous ammunition and fuel depots, and demolished an electric power station and various barracks and aircraft hangars. It also played an important part in the maintenance of the sea blockade, sinking eight small freighters and several other light vessels.

It is clear, then, that Richthofen's units performed superbly and that their outstanding achievements played an essential part in the city's fall. Functioning mainly as "flying artillery," they provided the army with an unprecedented level of tactical air support. However, this level of support was accomplished only because of a unique combination of circumstances. First, because most of the eastern front was relatively quiet in April, May (except for the short-lived Soviet offensive at Kharkov), and most of June, Richthofen had been given a strong air force at a high level of operational readiness. Second, this powerful force faced weak aerial opposition in the Crimea. As a result, both air and flak units could commence army support operations without having first to wage a time-consuming and costly battle for air superiority and then spend a considerable number of sorties on escort and protection operations. Third, almost the entire force was deployed against a single target (although it was, of course, extremely strong). Finally, it operated against that target from well-prepared airstrips in the immediate vicinity, which allowed a very high number of missions to be conducted each day.

This remarkably favorable set of circumstances existed nowhere during Operation *Blau,* the coming summer campaign. In contrast, *Luftwaffe* forces would soon be dissipated along the eastern front and even within the southern campaign zone itself. They encountered increasingly powerful *VVS* forces, which cost them time, effort, and high losses. They also often had to operate from poorly prepared airfields, sometimes far from their targets, which were widely scattered over a vast area. The Luftwaffe's close air support level reached a peak at Sevastopol, and it would not be equaled in the coming push toward the Caucasus oilfields.

5

Stampede to the Don: June–July 1942

Long before Sevastopol fell on 1 July, the Luftwaffe had played a key part in smashing a major Soviet offensive around Kharkov, over 500 kilometers to the north. *Fliegerkorps IV* and elements of *Fliegerkorps VIII* distinguished themselves in a series of nonstop defensive missions, then greatly aided the army as it threw back and destroyed the Soviet forces. *Fridericus* (Frederick), the brilliant German counteroffensive, grew into 1942's first large-scale battle of encirclement and annihilation. It also placed important areas of the Donets Basin in German hands, thereby giving Axis forces an excellent staging area for the coming summer campaign. Accordingly, before turning to the Luftwaffe's central role in that ill-fated campaign, I will discuss its successful operations at Kharkov.

In March, as noted previously, Stalin had rejected the sound advice of his army chief of staff, who argued that the Red Army should adopt a temporary strategic defensive posture for the spring and early summer of 1942. Instead, the Soviet leader, still claiming that constant attack was the best strategy, supported Marshal Timoshenko's plan to launch individual preemptive offensives near Leningrad, in the Demyansk region, in the Smolensk and Lgov-Kursk sectors, in the Kharkov area, and in the Crimea. The Crimean campaign—really only a series of attempts by armies trapped on the Kerch Peninsula to break into the Crimean mainland—ended miserably. As will now be shown, the Kharkov campaign, the only other offensive in the combat zone under study, ended not only in outright failure but also in a disaster of staggering proportions.

Timoshenko, in overall command of both the Southwestern and the Southern Front, had 640,000 men, 1,200 tanks, 13,000 guns and mortars, and 926 combat aircraft at his disposal.[1] His plan called for the Southwestern Front to launch two convergent attacks. The main force, comprising Lieutenant General Gorodnyanskii's Sixth Army and Major General Bobkin's "Army Group," would strike from the Barvenkovo area, south of Kharkov.[2] The slightly weaker force, comprising

120

Twenty-eighth Army and formations drawn from Twenty-first and Thirty-eighth Armies, would drive out of the Volchansk area, north of the Ukrainian capital. The two pincers would strike westward and meet behind Kharkov, thereby recovering the city and trapping the bulk of *General der Panzertruppe* Paulus's Sixth Army.

The Southwestern Front's powerful force of twenty-three rifle divisions, two cavalry, and two tank corps easily outnumbered the German formations they directly opposed: fourteen infantry and two tank divisions of Paulus's Sixth Army and an infantry division of *Armee-Gruppe von Kleist*.[3] The rest of this *Gruppe*—actually formed from Seventeenth Army and First Panzer Army—faced the exhausted Southern Front. Because this front had not yet recovered from recent batterings, Timoshenko planned to use it during his offensive only to protect the vulnerable south face of the Izyum salient.

German forces in the Kharkov region were themselves preparing to launch an offensive, code-named *Fridericus,* in the middle of May. Bock intended it to eliminate the dangerous Izyum salient, destroy the Soviet forces trapped within, and establish secure positions on the left bank of the northern Donets River. These positions would serve as the staging area for the main summer campaign. The plan was relatively simple: Sixth Army would thrust into the bulge from the north, while *Armee-Gruppe von Kleist* would do so from the south. They would meet in front of Izyum, having cut off a large part of an enemy front. However, before Bock could implement *Fridericus,* the Soviets struck first.

At dawn on 12 May—as Manstein's tanks and Richthofen's aircraft were closing the Ak Monai pocket on the Kerch Peninsula, far to the south—Timoshenko launched his mighty offensive. Striking with stunning speed and ferocity, and greatly outnumbering their opposition, his formations smashed through Sixth Army's defenses both north and south of Kharkov.[4] By midday, forward units had advanced to within twenty kilometers of the city. Within a day or two at the most, Timoshenko claimed, it would again be in Soviet hands.

Paulus, whose army bore the brunt of the savage attack, immediately appealed to Bock for reinforcements. The latter, who now felt that *Fridericus* could not proceed as planned, gave him the 23rd Panzer Division, which was to have been used as one of the offensive's spearhead units. This angered Halder, the German army's chief of staff. During a heated telephone conversation that afternoon, he told Bock that he must not waste the troops earmarked for *Fridericus* on repairing minor "blemishes." This comment stung the army group commander, appalled by his superior's ignorance of the situation at the front. "It's not a question of patching up local blemishes," he angrily replied. "It's neck or nothing!"[5]

Despite their disagreement, it appears that Bock finally managed to convince the army chief of staff that the situation at Kharkov was extremely critical. The latter stressed this to the Führer, who immediately ordered Richthofen to dispatch to the Kharkov region most of his bomber and dive-bomber units, which were still fighting furiously at Kerch.[6] After learning that these aircraft were on their way, and having seen the Luftwaffe's decisive contribution to numerous defensive battles, the reassured Bock told his worried Sixth Army commander "not to be in too great a hurry and not, in any circumstances, to attack without air support."[7]

Hitler certainly needed to transfer aircraft urgently from the Crimea. When Soviet divisions first smashed through German lines near Kharkov, Löhr's *Luftflotte 4* had very few aircraft to throw against them. Most of its units—half of *Fliegerkorps IV* and all of *Fliegerkorps VIII* and *Fliegerführer Süd*—were concentrated in the Crimea. Half of *General der Flieger* Pflugbeil's *Fliegerkorps IV* remained in the Ukraine, but (to quote its after-action report of 12 June) it had "only weak fighter forces at its disposal, because the mass of fighters, as well as almost all its bomber and dive-bomber units, had been relinquished for the execution of the Kerch operation."[8]

Pflugbeil's fighters attacked Soviet forces with their machine guns, cannons, and small bombs from the opening moments of the offensive,[9] but they were unable to do more than occasionally disrupt supply columns and pin down infantry formations. They did manage quickly to wrestle air superiority over the battlefield from their *VVS* counterparts, who greatly outnumbered them but were poorly trained and deployed.[10] However, without bombers, dive-bombers, and ground-attack aircraft, Pflugbeil's fighters were powerless to blunt the devastating enemy attack.

By the evening of 14 May, Timoshenko had opened broad gaps both north and south of Kharkov and had created the right conditions for introducing the bulk of his armor and mobile formations. During the previous two days he had deployed his armored formations, for the first time in the war, according to Heinz Guderian's maxim: "Not in dribbles, but in mass!"[11] His use of tanks in the German manner had doubtless contributed to his recent successes. Even so, the Soviet marshal had not yet deployed more than 20 percent of his available armor. He had been holding back his powerful Twenty-first Tank Corps in order to use it, when he saw the right moment, to maximum effect. Now, after two days of unchecked progress, Timoshenko had the opportunity to throw the corps effectively into the battle in order to complete the encirclement of German forces around Kharkov. However, he failed to seize the moment. According to the official postwar Soviet history, he was misled by false intelligence reports stating that Bock was concentrating a large panzer force near Zmiev (twenty-five kilometers south of Kharkov) and, as a result, he delayed introducing his mobile formations. The marshal's failure to deploy his armor on 14 or 15 May, the official history continues, "negatively affected the development of the operation. The advancing troops exhausted their strength and the pace of the advance dropped sharply. By this time the enemy had succeeded in pulling up reserves and in organizing the rear area defenses."[12]

Not only had Bock regrouped his ground forces by 15 May, but by then most of the air units diverted from the Crimea had arrived. These included three groups of the 77th Dive-Bomber Wing, which had distinguished itself in almost every major operation since the war started. One group arrived at Kharkov on 13 May, the others two days later.[13] They were joined by two groups of the 27th Bomber Wing, which also reached Kharkov on 13 May, three groups of the 51st "Edelweiss" Bomber Wing, which came between 13 and 15 May, and three groups of the 55th Bomber Wing, which came on 14 May. The last unit to make its way north, a group of the 76th Bomber Wing, arrived late on 15 May. Pflugbeil borrowed units not only from Richthofen, but also from Greim, whose recently formed *Luftwaffenkommando Ost* operated in the central army zone before Moscow. Greim sent him a Stuka group, which flew south on 14 May, and a bomber group, which made the journey five days later. These transfers taxed the energy and resources of Pflugbeil's service and maintenance personnel, who worked ceaselessly to organize and equip airfields and prepare arriving aircraft for their new missions. They also gave beleaguered German ground forces what historians Ziemke and Bauer later called "an extraordinarily powerful concentration of air support."[14]

Including these additions, *Fliegerkorps IV* now commanded no fewer than ten bomber, six fighter, and four Stuka groups, as well as a close-support group and a tactical reconnaissance *Staffel*.[15] This gave Pflugbeil far more units than Richthofen later had at Sevastopol, although, because of differences in operational readiness—54.5 percent of Pflugbeil's aircraft were combat-ready on 20 May, whereas 64.5 percent of Richthofen's were on 20 June[16]—the strike forces were of almost identical size.

The reinforced *Fliegerkorps IV* immediately made its presence felt. Although the enemy continued advancing south of Kharkov, taking Krasnograd and Taranovka on 15 May, German forces managed to slow its progress and contain the Soviet advance north of the city. The air corps was largely responsible for these achievements. Operating from airfields dangerously close to the front, it provided German ground forces with effective support by launching unremitting and devastating attacks on Soviet troops, vehicles, and armor, as well as pounding mobilization points and logistics systems in army rear areas. It attacked the Soviets not only with aircraft but also with its 88-mm flak guns. Used as direct-fire antitank guns, these high-velocity weapons destroyed scores of Timoshenko's T-34s as they rolled westward. The corps' outstanding work was recognized by all observers. Even Halder (who, as already noted, rarely paid attention to air activities) wrote in his diary on 15 May that "the force of the attack appears to have been broken by the efforts of our Luftwaffe."[17]

Bock was greatly relieved that the Soviet attack was losing speed and strength, but he also felt unsure of what to do next. Although *Fridericus* was due to start in a few days, powerful enemy forces still pinned down and threatened to destroy the bulk of Paulus's Sixth Army, his northern pincer. By 14 May, it had already lost sixteenth battalions. With one pincer missing, the field marshal realized that *Fridericus* could no longer be carried out as originally planned. Should he cancel the offensive, therefore, and merely carry out a *local* counterattack in order to stabilize the front, or should he attempt to conduct the offensive with only one pincer? He preferred the former option; Hitler, who promised to send additional aircraft from other combat zones, ordered the latter.[18] Early on 17 May, *Armee-Gruppe von Kleist* would strike at the weak and unsuspecting Soviet Ninth Army, which was supposedly defending the southern shoulder of the Izyum salient. The *Gruppe* would also drive from Barvenkovo to Balakleya, thereby pinching off the entire salient and trapping Timoshenko's forces.

With five Rumanian divisions protecting their left flank, Kleist's strike force of eight infantry divisions, two panzer divisions, and a motorized infantry division attacked as planned on 17 May. They were supported by several fighter groups, which swept the skies of their Soviet counterparts and strafed exposed troops and supply and reinforcement convoys. Because these convoys possessed few antiaircraft guns and had to travel unprotected more than 100 kilometers from their railheads to their forward units, they were little more than sitting ducks.

Hundreds of bombers and Stukas joined the battle, unloading streams of bombs on tank and supply columns, troops, field fortifications, strongpoints, bunkers, and logistics networks. They also scattered loads of propaganda leaflets over enemy positions, calling on Soviet troops to throw down their arms in order to save themselves from inevitable destruction. In fact, during May they rained down an impressive 8,349,300 leaflets (two-thirds released by *K.G. 55* alone).[19] Additionally, bombers dropped 383 canisters of ammunition and rations to encircled German troops. *K.G. 55* conducted the bulk of these missions, dropping supplies on several occasions, for example, to German pockets of resistance in the small Ternovaya forest and repeatedly bombing enemy forces attempting to eradicate them.[20]

Tactical reconnaissance planes also played their part, monitoring enemy movements, directing attack aircraft to their targets, and checking and correcting the army's artillery fire. Kleist actually considered the role of these observation planes (whose work is still ignored by most historians) to be so important to his operation that he later singled them out for special praise. "The underlying reason for the command's actions," he wrote in a letter of thanks to *Fliegerkorps IV,* "was the provision of tactical reconnaissance fliers. Their tireless missions, which demonstrated their outstanding personal bravery, gave the Command a clear picture of the enemy at all times."[21]

Many aircrew flew more than ten missions per day in this critical period, leaving them and their ground teams exhausted. Their efforts, however, brought great rewards; they shot down numerous enemy aircraft, knocked out scores of tanks and motor vehicles, killed hundreds of horses, destroyed countless artillery pieces, and even wrecked several trains. After the war, *Generalmajor* Hans Doerr, Fifty-second Army Corps' chief of staff, recalled *Fliegerkorps IV*'s outstanding work in the first days of Kleist's offensive:

A decisive share of the success achieved during the first stages of the offensive was contributed by the *IV. Fliegerkorps*, whose units supported the infantry's struggle in such an exemplary manner that, for example, the strongly defended heights south of Bogorodichnoye [on the Donets River, southeast of Izyum] came under annihilating air attacks only 20 minutes after requests arrived from infantry regiments.[22]

According to First Panzer Army's war diary, the new offensive was supported "most effectively by the Luftwaffe."[23] Strong air attacks in front of their advances helped Third Panzer Corps push forward twenty-four kilometers to Barvenkovo and Seventeenth Army twenty-eight kilometers, nearly to Izyum, on the first day alone. *Fliegerkorps IV* also assisted Paulus's army in the region southwest of Kharkov, where fighting intensified on 17 May. Strong Soviet armored forces attempted to break through to Merefa but were stopped in their tracks by a powerful combination of antitank guns and Stukas. Their attacks left burned-out tanks strewn across the battlefield. "The divisions of the Eighth Army Corps," Hans Doerr wrote, "effectively supported by *IV. Fliegerkorps*, prevented the breakthrough and, with that, the envelopment of Kharkov."[24]

Taken by surprise, General Kharitonov's Ninth Army collapsed under the weight of Kleist's attack. Its left wing began a fighting retreat toward the northern Donets, while its right wing fell back toward Barvenkovo and farther to the southwest. This retreat, and the rapid German advance along the northern Donets, placed Soviet forces in great danger of being cut off. Realizing this, and that Timoshenko's northern pincer had been stopped and his southern now swung into empty air, Marshal Vasilevskii, the Red Army's acting chief of the general staff, urgently requested Stalin twice on 18 May to cancel the offensive and redeploy all forces in defensive operations.[25] Stalin refused, pointing out that Timoshenko himself still believed the offensive should continue. Late on 19 May, however, he finally permitted the Southwestern Front to switch to the defensive after Timoshenko, apparently realizing his enormous error, now insisted that a disaster appeared imminent. This decision came far too late.

On 20 June, Kleist's spearheads took Protopopovka, which reduced the mouth of the pocket to only twenty kilometers. "Continuation of this advance," concerned American intelligence officers noted in their brief to the Combined Chiefs of Staff, "would threaten encirclement of all Russian forces west of the Donets." The battle, they added, "has assumed large proportions and much depends on its outcome."[26] No one realized this more than the encircled Soviets themselves. "Like fiery wasps trapped in a bottle," John Erickson wrote, "the trapped armies turned inwards and stabbed at the German pincers."[27] It did no good; after three more days of bitter fighting, German troops succeeded in closing the mouth of the pocket.

Fliegerkorps IV worked vigorously in that period to ensure that few Soviet troops escaped. To strengthen his already powerful bomber fleet for these operations, Pflugbeil briefly borrowed an extra bomber group from *Luftwaffenkommando Ost*.[28] His bombers struck Soviet forces still fighting inside the rapidly closing ring, as well as those trying to smash the ring open from the outside. They annihilated large numbers of men, tanks, armored vehicles, trucks, and guns. In order to prevent enemy formations fleeing through the narrowing gap, they also struck the main bridges across the Donets.[29] They were poorly suited to this work and succeeded only in destroying one bridge and damaging five others. Stukas raced in to do the job properly, destroying seven bridges and damaging four more and a landing stage.[30] Fighters, with complete air superiority and no major concerns about enemy flak—because most flak guns had been destroyed or left on the battlefield by retreating troops—attacked unprotected formations and soft-skinned vehicles both inside and outside the pocket. As a result, few Soviet troops made it through the gap; those that did suffered fearful losses, running headlong into a hailstorm of antipersonnel and high-explosive bombs.

When the ring closed completely, Soviet troops fought like cornered cats. With extraordinary determination and ferocity, they launched themselves against the walls of the ever-tightening ring. Low on food, ammunition, and fuel but driven by the combination of courage and blind fanaticism that the Germans had come to expect, they made desperate and hopeless attacks. On many occasions, they stormed forward with arms linked, shouting, "Urray!" German machine gunners hardly needed to aim; they just sprayed the lines with bullets, killing hundreds at a time. Only one breakout attempt came close to success. On 25 May, two divisions, supported by a number of T-34s, managed to bulldoze their way toward Petrovskoye before they were caught by Pflugbeil's Stukas. "In heavy individual actions," Hans Doerr recalled, describing these events, "*Fliegerkorps IV*'s superb work caused the annihilation of the forces attempting to break out near Petrovskoye."[31]

By 28 May, Soviet resistance finally petered out. The Battle of Kharkov—in which the Soviets tried to encircle the Germans but were themselves surrounded—was over. For Stalin, it was an appalling defeat: 75,000 of his best troops had been killed and another 239,000 staggered into captivity. Over 1,200 tanks, 2,000 artillery pieces, and 542 aircraft were destroyed or captured. Many thousands of horses (vital for transport and towage) also fell into German hands, as did large stockpiles of ammunition and other equipment.[32] For Hitler, it was a grand victory. He had humiliated Stalin only a week earlier, when his forces crushed three armies, captured Kerch, and took 170,000 prisoners. Now, by smashing another three armies, throwing back a major offensive, and bringing the prisoner total for both campaigns to more than 400,000, he inflicted further humiliation. Referring to his coming campaign for the Caucasus, he triumphantly exclaimed to Goebbels that he was now ready "to strangle the Soviet system at its Adam's apple."[33]

It was a classic battle of encirclement and annihilation, and, as Hitler fully realized, one of strategic importance. At a bearable cost, his troops had hacked off the Izyum salient, which had been a constant threat to Kharkov and an extra length of front for them to guard. By gaining important areas in the Donets Basin, they had created an excellent staging area for Operation *Blau,* the planned summer campaign. They had also significantly weakened opposition in the region and regained the strategic advantage. If they could get *Blau* rolling in the near future, they should make splendid progress.

Pflugbeil's *Fliegerkorps IV* had certainly contributed to the German victory. In less than three weeks of furious fighting, it had flown 15,648 sorties and dropped 7,700 tons of bombs, 8,359,300 leaflets, and 383 canisters of supplies.[34] The Ju 52s of its transport squadrons worked hard to keep airfields and army units supplied, flying in 1,545 tons of matériel. For the loss of only 49 aircraft (and 12 men killed and 98 missing), the air corps' reported kill total was astounding. If its claims can be trusted, and Soviet sources do admit very heavy losses to the Luftwaffe, the corps destroyed no fewer than 615 aircraft, 19 of them on the ground. It claimed an impressive 227 tanks destroyed and 140 others damaged. Horizontal bombers, flying at low altitude over armored columns caught in the open without flak protection, actually destroyed as many tanks as the Stukas. All units—bombers, dive-bombers, and fighters—performed equally well against supply convoys. According to their reports, they together wrecked 3,038 motor vehicles and 1,686 horse-drawn wagons and damaged another 462 and 272, respectively. Railway convoys fared no better: Pflugbeil's airmen knocked out 22 locomotives and 6 complete trains, and damaged another 22 trains. They demolished 24 artillery and 2 flak batteries, 49 separate artillery pieces, 14 munitions camps, 10 supply camps, and various other installations, and partially destroyed many more of each. They also killed large numbers of men and horses.

Flak units also distinguished themselves during the Battle of Kharkov. The *I. Flak-Korps* (First Anti-Aircraft Corps) claimed that between 12 and 28 May it shot down 33 enemy aircraft and wrecked 124 tanks, including T-34s and the huge KV-1s and KV-2s.[35] Again, Soviet sources attest to the general reliability of these figures. Although most batteries performed well, some proved remarkably effective. For instance, one battery, commanded by *Leutnant* Reichwald, managed to shoot down six aircraft within the space of a few minutes on 18 May, bringing its total for the eastern campaign to twenty-seven. Reichwald's achievements did not pass unnoticed; in August he received the Knight's Cross.

The air corps played a crucial role in the battle, as army commanders gratefully acknowledged. "Our special thanks go to the air corps and its close-combat aircraft," Kleist wrote to Pflugbeil, "which, in tireless operations, contributed decisively to our victory."[36] Paulus also sent his thanks:

From the onset of the battle, fighters controlled the airspace and shot down numerous enemy aircraft. Assisting the struggle on the ground, dive-bombers and bombers attacked with bombs and other weapons, smashing enemy assembly points, attacking tanks, batteries and columns. The *IV. Fliegerkorps* thereby made an essential contribution to the successful defense, encirclement and destruction of the enemy.

I proclaim to the corps and the elements it controlled my special gratitude for its frictionless cooperation and never-failing support.[37]

Generaloberst Löhr, head of *Luftflotte 4* and Pflugbeil's immediate superior, proudly passed on to the air corps a message from the delighted Bock, whose armies had turned looming defeat into stunning victory.[38] Bock, said the air fleet commander, "proclaims his special gratitude to *Luftflotte 4* for its decisive support of the army group." To this Löhr added his own expression of thanks for the corps' "outstanding performance and its again-demonstrated operational capabilities."

PREPARATIONS FOR *BLAU*

As the intense battles around Kharkov drew to a close, Löhr hoped that his air fleet's next challenge, the assault on Sevastopol, would not be as demanding on ground and air crews. He wanted them fresh and ready for *Blau,* due to start in another month. His hopes were not entirely realized; even before fighting around Kharkov finished, and before he could think of rehabilitating many of his key units, he had to transfer them back to the Crimea. Richthofen, who had been pleading to the High Command for their urgent return, gave them no time to catch their breath. As soon as they arrived back at their Crimean airfields, he threw them into the battle. During the next month, he, and later Wild, aggressively drove them to perform to the absolute limit of their capabilities. Then, when Sevastopol's fall became imminent in the final days of June, Wild began sending them north again, this time to join Richthofen's new headquarters in Kursk or to rejoin Pflugbeil's corps near Kharkov.

While *Fliegerkorps VIII* pounded Sevastopol into rubble, Löhr's other corps, *Fliegerkorps IV*—minus the units Richthofen borrowed and temporarily incorporated into his own corps—supported the army's two minor preliminary offensives in the Kharkov region. Operation *Wilhelm* was a small, two-pronged attack by Sixth Army, designed to trap elements of the Soviet Twenty-eighth Army in what was left of the Volchansk salient (slightly east of Kharkov) and to provide cover on the south for Sixth Army's main thrust during *Blau*'s initial stages. Paulus brought *Wilhelm* to a successful conclusion only six days after its launch on 10 June. Although the bulk of Twenty-eighth Army withdrew eastward, German forces took over 22,000 prisoners and secured excellent jumping-off points east of the Donets River.[39]

Operation *Fridericus II* was another small attack in this region. Its architects intended Kleist's First Panzer Army to encircle the bulk of the enemy's Ninth and Thirty-eighth Armies north and east of Izyum and to move itself forward fifty kilometers into its starting position for *Blau*. After several postponements due to heavy rain, *Fridericus II* began on 22 June. Again, Soviet formations fell back eastward. As a result, Kleist attained his territorial goals by 25 June, capturing 18,500 more prisoners—a haul considered disappointing in these favorable days for the Wehrmacht.[40]

During both *Wilhelm* and *Fridericus II,* Pflugbeil's air corps possessed relatively few ground-attack units. Most were still engaged in the Crimea. Accordingly, he concentrated the few he did have at the army's *Schwerpunkte* and deployed his other units on interdiction and reconnaissance missions. They made strong attacks on road and rail traffic in enemy rear areas and constantly carried out surveillance missions over field positions and supply and reinforcement routes.[41] On the first day of *Fridericus II,* a He 111 of the 55th Bomber Wing even managed to destroy the main Kupyansk bridge over the Oskol River with a 1,000-kg bomb, thereby severing the Soviets' main supply line. Despite temporarily losing his best close-support units, Pflugbeil strove to provide local armies with the maximum support available. He therefore exhorted his men to work at an intense pace, to which they responded with great gusto. For instance, one group of the 51st Bomber Wing alone carried out 300 missions between 10 and 13 June.[42]

Throughout June, while *Fliegerkorps IV* participated in *Wilhelm* and *Fridericus II* and *Fliegerkorps VIII* took part in *Störfang,* Löhr devoted his energies to preparing the entire air fleet for its contribution to the coming summer offensive. In recent months, Luftwaffe construction teams had built a large number of airfields in the Ukraine. The *OKL* ordered their creation so that Löhr's units could support *Blau*'s opening operations from well-equipped airfields right behind the front. As well as these new frontline airfields, engineers built a series stretching back throughout the Ukraine. Air supply units would need these to cope with their increasing workload as the front moved steadily eastward and combat units operated from new airfields, including hastily built or captured ones away from rail or road supply routes.[43]

To ensure that his combat units would always be able to provide the army with the support it needed, Löhr built up large stocks of bombs, fuel, spare parts, and other equipment. He also initiated a program of regular exchanges and reliefs in order to bring his units back up to strength before the campaign commenced. Although interrupted by the battles in the Ukraine and the Crimea, this program proved successful, and by the time *Blau* started, his fleet enjoyed a high state of operational readiness.

For the summer offensive, the *OKL* sent fresh air reinforcements to the southern front, many of them transferred from the central and northern fronts. Several groups even arrived from the Mediterranean, following the abandonment of the assault on Malta.[44] Thus, by 20 June, the eastern air fleets possessed 2,644 aircraft, over 20 percent more than they had only a month earlier and approximately the same number as during the previous summer.[45] Whereas in 1941 most fought on the central front, the majority (1,610 aircraft, or 61 percent) now operated under Löhr on the southern front. The *OKL* left a relatively small holding force of nearly 600 aircraft on the central front, around 375 on the Leningrad front, and the rest in northern Norway and Finland.[46] For Löhr, controlling 61 percent of all aircraft on the eastern front was a substantial improvement from only a month earlier, when he commanded only 46 percent.[47] His fleet was ready for the battle. It was a pity, he thought, that he was leaving for the Balkans.

The army staff also worked hard to rehabilitate and strengthen its forces in time for *Blau*. It could no longer satisfy the manpower requirements of all three eastern army groups, which, despite having received 1,100,000 fresh troops up to 1 May 1942, were still 625,000 men short of establishment.[48] Realizing this, it began sending increasingly more of these replacements to Army Group South in order to ensure that it was capable of carrying out Hitler's bold offensive. For example, 25 percent went to Army Group South in February, 34 percent in March, and 39 percent in April.[49] Even they were not enough. On 1 May, according to a detailed report prepared by the *OKW* operations staff, Army Group South's infantry strength still stood at only 50 percent of its 1941 level (while that of the other two groups stood at a mere 35 percent).[50] Although additional replacements arrived in May and June, the southern army group never reached more than three-quarters of its 1941 level.

Despite the *OKW*'s efforts to send enough new matériel to make good Army Group South's losses in recent months, it achieved this goal only by stripping equipment from the other two army groups. It has already been noted, for example, how the *OKW* deprived them of most of their motor vehicles in order to ensure that Bock's forces regained at least 85 percent of their former mobility. The removal of so many vehicles and the lack of reinforcements of men and matériel naturally led to a significant reduction of the other army groups' combat effectiveness, a situation exacerbated by a drastic shortage of horses and fodder.[51]

Army Group South also received the lion's share of all tanks and assault guns shipped to the east, including new models with guns capable of stopping the formidable T-34s. These tanks, coupled with some transferred from elsewhere on the eastern front, refurbished Bock's tired armored divisions. Many divisions were even given an extra tank battalion (that is, three instead of the usual two). Most of those in Army Groups Center and North, on the other hand, were left with only one battalion each.[52]

By the middle of June, Army Group South was as ready for battle as its supporting air fleet. Reinforcements from the Reich and other sections of the eastern front had raised its strength substantially to 68 well-equipped German combat divisions. They comprised 46 infantry, 9 Panzer, 4 light infantry, 5 motorized infantry, 2 mountain, and 2 elite SS divisions.[53] The army group also included 25 allied divisions. Most were Rumanian, the rest Italian and Hungarian.

Although Bock had previously estimated that he would need eight divisions less than this combined total of ninety-three, his own divisions were slightly understrength (but were far stronger than those elsewhere along the eastern front, which had now dropped from nine battalions each to six),[54] and his allied divisions were even weaker. The latter also tended to be inferior in equipment, training, and, if past experience was any indication, fighting spirit. Still, Bock realized that the million Germans and 300,000 allies under his command formed an extremely potent strike force. Supported by Löhr's powerful air fleet, it was certainly capable of carrying out Hitler's planned offensive.

Blau was divided into three phases. In the opening phase *(Blau I)*, a powerful force would make a direct thrust from the Kursk region while another made an enveloping thrust from around Belgorod, slightly north of Kharkov. They aimed to take Voronezh, an important rail junction and armaments and industrial center, and destroy all Soviet forces west of the city in a pocket between the Oskol and Don Rivers.

After the successful completion of these operations, Army Group South would divide into two new groups: A, under *Generalfeldmarschall* Wilhelm List, and B, under Bock. Then the offensive's second phase *(Blau II)* would commence. While some of the infantry divisions established a strong defensive line from Orel to Voronezh, motorized and armored divisions would continue their southeastward drive along the Don, conducting another double envelopment in conjunction with forces thrusting directly eastward from the Kharkov area.

During the third phase *(Blau III)*, the forces following the course of the Don were to link up near Stalingrad with those advancing from the Taganrog area, thus completing a massive roundup of all Soviet formations in the bend of the Don River. After the successful completion of these operations, specific orders for the Caucasus campaign proper would be given, according to which Axis forces would strike into the Caucasus and seize valuable oil regions, including Baku and the shores of the Caspian Sea.

Löhr planned to deploy both *Fliegerkorps IV* and *VIII* in support of Bock's armies when they rolled eastward and to keep his smaller, specialist antishipping force (Wild's *Fliegerführer Süd*) in the Crimea, protecting the peninsula from enemy ground, sea, and air attacks.[55] To safeguard his airfields and the army's logistics networks, march routes, field installations, and strongpoints from enemy air attacks, the *OKL* again assigned Löhr the *I. Flak-Korps*. Under *General der Flakartillerie* Otto Dessloch's operational command, this recently reinforced flak corps, comprising the strongly armed 9th and 10th Flak Divisions, packed a mighty punch.

Löhr would oversee his fleet's operations during *Blau*'s opening days before departing for the Balkans, where he would take charge of all German forces. Richthofen would replace him as fleet commander, after first transferring command of his beloved *Fliegerkorps VIII* to *Generalleutnant* Martin Fiebig, a close air support specialist to whom he had taught his "trade." Before then, however, Richthofen had to organize the corps' transfer from the Crimea to the Kursk region (which would be carried out immediately after Sevastopol fell). From there it would support the advance of *Generaloberst* von Weich's Second Army and

Fourth Panzer Army, beginning first with their attack toward Voronezh. *Flieger-korps IV* would operate in the region south of Kharkov and, during the drive to Voronezh, support Sixth Army's thrust from Belgorod.[56]

Richthofen arrived at Kursk on the morning of 24 June. He spent the early afternoon setting up his headquarters in a former commissar school, which he described as a "kind of castle-cum-hospital," and the rest of the day flying his Storch along the front.[57] German positions, he noted in his diary, appeared to have been carefully prepared, although there were surprisingly few signs of the enemy, who were "quite weak in the air as well as on the ground." The Soviets, he thought, were well aware of German intentions, having been tipped off by "German battle plans found on a general staff officer whose plane was shot down." They were probably now regrouping and preparing to defend themselves in their present rear areas.

Richthofen was clearly referring to the so-called Reichel affair. On 19 June, *Major* Joachim Reichel, operations officer of the 23rd Panzer Division, crash-landed in a Storch four kilometers behind the Soviet lines. Contrary to the Führer's explicit orders in War Directive No. 41 about the need for absolute secrecy, Reichel carried in his briefcase the operational orders for *General der Panzertruppe* Georg Stumme's Fortieth Panzer Corps and the outlines of the entire first phase of Operation *Blau*.[58] A German patrol found the plane several hours later, intact except for a bullet hole in the fuel tank. It did not, however, find any trace of Reichel, the pilot, or the documents. Two days later, another patrol located what were presumed to be their bodies in shallow graves. Both Stumme's headquarters and the High Command were horrified, and bitterly disappointed, to learn that the patrol found neither the briefcase nor the documents.

Bock wanted to launch *Blau* immediately, before the Soviets could exploit the information. He feared it might be too late; they were already moving troops north from the Rostov sector and assembling a large armored force opposite Sixth Army.[59] On 21 June he asked Halder to pass on his views to the Führer, who was then at his mountain home in Berchtesgaden and had yet to be told of the Reichel incident. When finally informed, Hitler was furious about the officer's stupidity. After returning to his headquarters and reading a detailed report on the matter, he raged against his staff officers and sacked Stumme, *Oberstleutnant* Franz, his chief of staff, and *General* von Boineburg-Lengsfeld, commander of the 23rd Panzer Division.[60]

Stumme was an outstanding officer with an impressive record. He was well liked by his troops, who affectionately called him "lightning ball" because of his boundless energy and constantly red face (caused by high blood pressure). Nonetheless, someone had to pay for Reichel's blunder. Stumme and Franz were promptly court-martialed, convicted of "issuing too-far-reaching orders," and sentenced to five and two years in prison, respectively. Göring, who had presided over their trial, apparently admired their honest and courageous defense and promised to "report this to the Führer." He kept his word and, after Bock also intervened on their behalf, Hitler struck down their sentences in view of their distinguished records. The *OKW* transferred Stumme to the western desert, where he served as Rommel's deputy. Franz followed as the *Afrika Korps'* chief of staff. Tragically, the desert heat proved too much for the "lightning ball"; he died of a heart attack on 25 October 1942, early in the El Alamein offensive.

Hitler now had a major decision to make. Should he cancel *Blau* on the assumption that the enemy knew all about its first phase and had probably redeployed their forces to counter it, or should he still go through with it on the off chance that they had not? Believing after recent substantial victories in the Crimea and the Kharkov region that Soviet resistance was weaker than in the previous year, Hitler decided to trust his intuition and let *Blau* proceed as planned.

As it happened, Hitler made the right choice. Soviet infantrymen had indeed found Reichel's aircraft and seized the papers. Sensing their importance, they sent them up through the channels to Timoshenko himself. The marshal immediately transmitted their contents to the headquarters of the neighboring Bryansk Front, which, along with his own Southwestern Front, looked set to bear the brunt of the German attack. Timoshenko then sent the actual documents on to the general staff in Moscow.[61]

Colonel General Golikov, commander of the Bryansk Front, took the documents seriously and began strengthening his left flank in order to withstand the German onslaught, likely to commence (according to his understanding of Reichel's papers) on 22 June.[62] Timoshenko, on the other hand, had apparently been convinced by Stalin that the papers were probably "fed to us deliberately in order to throw a veil over the true intentions of the German command." As a result, he did nothing to strengthen his own front.[63] This prompted Golikov to request a special commander for the "Voronezh Zone."[64] Stalin, who still believed that the Germans intended to attack Moscow from the south and that they had planted phoney papers in order to lure his capital's defenders out of position, turned him down flat. Then, when the offensive failed to materialize by 25 June (it had actually been postponed several days because of bad weather), Stalin summoned Golikov to Moscow. There he lectured him on the foolishness of believing such a "big trumped-up piece of work." Instead, he must prepare an operation to recapture Orel in cooperation with the Western Front. Verbally battered into submission, Golikov agreed to draw up plans for the attack. He finished them in the early hours of 28 June, at almost the same time as Axis forces struck the first massive blows of the major offensive that Stalin said would never come.

BLAU I: THE VORONEZH OFFENSIVE

After only three hours sleep, Richthofen climbed out of bed at 0145 hours on 28 June, nervous but determined, as always, to watch his planes' first operations in a new campaign. He had spent the last few days hurriedly setting up *Fliegerkorps*

VIII's new command staff—which "is willing but still has a great deal to learn"[65]—and directing the overhauling and reequipping of exhausted units arriving daily from the Crimea, where many of his groups, under Wild's command, were still pounding Sevastopol. He was actually relieved, therefore, that he was able that morning to throw a substantial number of aircraft into the battle. At 0300 he arrived in his Storch over the front, just in time to watch his Stukas and ground-attack aircraft make their first strikes. He was delighted by their performance and, uncharacteristically, by that of the army, which made good progress all that day.

He was remarkably lucky to make this flight. While inspecting Axis positions three days earlier, troops of the German 387th Infantry Division had mistakenly opened fire on his little aircraft, wounding his copilot, puncturing the fuel tank, and filling his plane with holes. After making an emergency landing, he sent the commander of the division involved a letter "thanking" his men for their efforts.[66] "While it is a delight to see the fighting spirit of the German ground troops against aircraft," he sarcastically wrote, "may I request that these troops direct their fighting spirit against the *Red* Air Force." After pointing out that visibility was excellent and his aircraft was clearly marked, he added that "perhaps their gunfire was intended to be an ovation of greeting, in which case permit the commander of the *VIII. Fliegerkorps* to express his gratitude for it and, at the same time, encourage them that similar greetings should in future be carried out with blank cartridges." His diary entry for that day is far more blunt. Well aware that he had escaped death by the closest shave, he angrily scrawled: "Damned dogs! They don't fire at the Russians, but at our Storch!"

Watching his units carry out their initial attacks in front of Weich's advancing armor—to return to the events of 28 June—Richthofen also observed the German spearheads' rapid advance. After a heavy predawn artillery and air bombardment, Forty-eighth Panzer Corps' armored units roared forward, throwing up large clouds of dust into the stifling summer air. Their speed and power stunned Soviet troops, who seemed unable to offer more than token resistance. Followed by motorized infantry, they penetrated enemy defenses at the juncture of Golikov's Thirteenth and Fortieth Armies by midmorning, captured and crossed an undamaged bridge over the Tim River at noon, and reached the Kshen River by late afternoon. Its neighboring formation on the left, Twenty-fourth Panzer Corps, made similar progress, also reaching the Kshen by dusk.[67] Army Group South had previously calculated that Weich's troops would take two days to make these gains. Watching the initial breakthroughs from his Storch, Richthofen felt increasingly optimistic about *Blau*'s outcome. "I have the impression," he recorded that evening, "that things will go smoothly."

In the previous few days, Richthofen and his staff had conducted regular meetings with army group, corps, and division commanders to create joint *Schwerpunkte* and coordinate interservice cooperation. The battle tactics agreed on followed a basic pattern formed during the previous year of war in the east, a pattern Karl Koller, the Luftwaffe's last chief of the general staff, would later describe succinctly as "tanks up front, artillery to the rear and planes above."[68] The "planes above" certainly contributed substantially to the army's achievements during *Blau*, beginning with Weich's successes that first day.

Fighters worked furiously from before dawn to pin down enemy troops in front of advancing armor and to wrestle air superiority from their Soviet counterparts, which they easily outclassed and, for once, outnumbered.[69] Flying "without pause," Bf 109s shot down thirty enemy aircraft that first day alone.[70] However, unable to patrol the airspace above all Axis positions at any given time, they could not always prevent their rivals from strafing German spearheads and Second Hungarian Army, which protected a large section of the line. In response to these attacks and the loss of four He 111s (apparently his only losses that day), Richthofen subjected Soviet airfields to heavy attacks by his bombers, which wrecked one and inflicted substantial damage on several others.

Direct battlefield support of advancing units also proved successful. Striking enemy positions in front of advancing armor, concentrated groups of Stukas and ground-attack aircraft destroyed countless field positions, batteries, bunkers, tanks, and guns. "Overall," the air commander penned that night, probably with only slight exaggeration, "where we are not, [the army's] results are very sparse."[71] General Kazakov, the Bryansk Front's chief of staff, later recalled, "Enemy aviation continuously accompanied his tank and infantry offensive. [It] operated using powerful groups."[72] As many as 100 aircraft at a time were active against single Soviet divisions at the tip of German spearheads. Moreover, Kazakov added, "simultaneous with air strikes against our battlefield combat formations, enemy aviation delivered strikes against concentration regions of army and Front reserves." Indeed, Richthofen wrote in his diary that his bombers, striking into Bryansk Front's rear areas and deeper still, right back to the Don River, had annihilated two armored trains and several supply columns.

As already noted, coordinating air and ground operations was hard at the best of times, but during these battles of fast movement the task became extremely difficult. Because troops of the two opposing forces were almost indistinguishable from the air, Axis spearhead units sometimes fell victim to Luftwaffe "friendly fire," especially when they found themselves occupying positions that air observers and liaison staff still believed to be held by the enemy. One such case occurred that first day, when a company of the elite *Großdeutschland* Division was spotted on a hill two kilometers east of the Tim River by Stukas. Although the soldiers "immediately spread out orange-coloured air identification panels as well as swastika flags and set off smoke signals," the pilots failed to recognize them as German and swooped down and scattered bombs among them.[73] They killed sixteen men, wounded many others, and destroyed numerous weapons and other equipment. Richthofen's diary reveals that he himself ordered the attack, believing the area still to be held by enemy troops. "It was my own fault," he lamented, "because I ordered it, and did not expect such a rapid [German] advance."[74]

During the night of 28 June, Soviet aircraft showered bombs on several Axis positions, including Richthofen's headquarters in Kursk. Poorly equipped for night missions and flying at high altitude to escape German flak, they inflicted little damage. Nature also bombarded the Germans that night, but with water instead of bombs. Torrential rain poured down on the combat zone, transforming airfields, supply roads, and march routes into seas of mud. Troop and supply trucks sank axle-deep and could only be moved by heavy tractors. Tanks and other tracked vehicles moved ahead fitfully, while the gluelike mud sucked at the boots of infantrymen.

Swamped airfields and poor visibility forced Richthofen to cancel a series of predawn attacks he had planned.[75] His units finally got airborne at noon, the same time as armored units began plowing through the mud. The army advanced slowly but steadily that afternoon. Its unbroken progress resulted in large part from the feeble resistance offered by Soviet troops—"The Russians are remarkably soft," the air leader wrote. "Their tanks pull out and their artillery has come to a standstill"—as well as to the excellent support provided by *Fliegerkorps VIII*'s Stukas and ground-attack aircraft. German tactics, General Kazakov recalled, were identical to those of the previous day: "strong artillery preparation and aviation pressure against our combat formations, and tank and infantry attacks with continuous aviation accompaniment in large groups of airplanes."[76]

Late on 29 June, forward units of the 40th Panzer Division closed in on what they believed to be the intact headquarters of Fortieth Army. Receiving this news by radio, Richthofen immediately pounded the village with everything available, hoping to destroy the headquarters before the commander and staff fled.[77] To his bitter disappointment, they managed to escape at the last minute, abandoning their command equipment and wireless vans. Their flight, however, left the entire army leaderless.

The air leader did not mention how long it took the aircraft to strike the headquarters after he ordered the attack, but other comments in that day's diary entry allow us to conclude that the response time was far too long. "My [new] staff," he seethed, "is *not* functioning. I issued an order verbally at 1800, but it was only put into writing at 2330. Impossible!" His communication system was hopeless, he added, and his air liaison officers—the *Flivos* attached to forward ground units—were "terrible." Their failings may partially account for the "friendly fire" attack of the previous day, if in fact Richthofen's comments are accurate.

For the next few days, nightly rainfalls slowed down Weich's attack. "Intermittent thunderstorms made our routes as slippery as soap," wrote *Generalmajor* Wolfgang Pickert, the newly appointed commander of the 9th Flak Division. "These are strenuous, dirty days."[78] Nonetheless, although the hostile weather retarded the Axis advance, it did not stop it. By late afternoon on 1 July, Weich's northern pincer formations had survived a powerful but poorly conceived armored counterattack, occasionally freed its tanks from the quagmire and sent them churning slowly forward, overcome the stiffening resistance of enemy rifle divisions, and thrust several of its own drenched infantry regiments right to the headwaters of the Olym River, only seventy kilometers west of Voronezh.

Fliegerkorps VIII contributed substantially to these gains. Its Stukas and ground-attack aircraft struck the three Soviet armored corps rolling across the steppes, destroying and damaging many tanks and forcing complete brigades to scatter and break off their attack. Its fighters worked at a frenzied pace (as did their ground crews), especially when air opposition stiffened briefly after the Soviet High Command hastily transferred seven additional fighter and ground-attack regiments to the Bryansk Front.[79] These reinforcements proved incapable, however, of regaining control of the skies, although their presence often forced German fighters to reduce their number of bomber escort and infantry attack missions.

Stukas frequently joined the fighters as they roared down on exposed troops, although Richthofen privately questioned the relative value of these missions.[80] His air units would pound and strafe enemy infantry, he pointed out, thereby inflicting heavy losses. Yet, after an area was supposedly "cleared of the enemy," at least according to ground reconnaissance, Soviet troops would pop up again almost as soon as the aircraft left.

The weather was far harsher to the northern pincer formations than to Sixth Army, the southern pincer, which finally launched its own thrust toward Voronezh on 30 June. This powerful army surged forward with remarkable speed, ripping a 35-kilometer-deep gap in the enemy's defenses by nightfall. By late afternoon of the next day, when Fourth Panzer Army's spearheads passed the Olym River, Sixth Army's own forward units (fighting 100 kilometers to the north) had shattered the right wing of Timoshenko's Southwestern Front and established bridgeheads on the east bank of the Oskol River.

Although it possessed significantly fewer Stukas and ground-attack aircraft than Richthofen's corps, and was therefore unable to give the same level of direct battlefield support, Pflugbeil's *Fliegerkorps IV* still provided Sixth Army with effective assistance. It smothered enemy defenses in front of advancing troops with blankets of high-explosive and antipersonnel bombs. It smashed command, communication, and supply systems in rear areas. It also launched heavy bombing raids on more distant targets, including railway lines and junctions at Voronezh (joined by units of Richthofen's corps, which also pounded the city itself, losing a Ju 88 to flak),[81] Michurinsk, Svoboda, and Valuyki.[82]

At midday on 1 July, the northern pincer released the 16th Motorized Infantry Division from its inner flank and sent it south toward Staryy Oskol, while its southern partner released the 100th Light Infantry Division from its own inner flank and sent it north along the Oskol River. Bock planned them to meet behind Staryy Oskol, forming a ring around the bulk of the Soviet Fortieth Army. Second Hungarian Army would then tighten the ring and destroy the trapped formations.

Few operations go exactly to plan, and this one did not. The 16th Motorized Infantry Division crashed headlong into what it believed (according to the interrogation of a captured prisoner) to be a "remarkably strong and well-trained" Soviet motorized brigade. Unwilling to engage this powerful enemy force without reinforcements, the division requested the assistance of ground-attack aircraft. Richthofen, angered by what he called its lack of courage, replied that the only troop concentrations in the region belonged to the division itself and that the supposedly strong enemy brigade "had just departed in three lorries!!"[83] Later that afternoon, the air leader noticed that, while the northern division had finally reached Staryy Oskol, the southern division was still far from closing the pocket. To his disgust, Soviet troops were streaming eastward through the open mouth. He immediately tried to seal the pocket with his Stukas and sent his bombers to pursue the columns streaming out. Although they left the ground strewn with large numbers of corpses, dead horses, and wrecked vehicles, these air units failed to close the pocket or halt the retreat of Soviet formations. Army divisions finally closed the pocket the next day, by which time it was almost empty. The Soviets had even withdrawn most of their heavy weapons.

The air leader blamed the army, claiming that its lack of fighting spirit allowed the enemy time to escape. It seems more likely, however, that Soviet troops escaped because their commanders had learned important lessons from their recent disasters, Kharkov being only one of several, and now employed new tactics—tactics successfully tested during both *Wilhelm* and *Fridericus II*. Rather than defiantly holding ground at all cost, even at the risk of encirclement, as they usually had, they immediately asked for and received permission from the *Stavka* to withdraw eastward the moment their encirclement looked likely.[84] Strong rearguard actions allowed the bulk of their formations to make an orderly withdrawal.

Hitler now realized that he faced a major problem. Although he had previously suspected that Timoshenko's formations would conduct an elastic defense, he had intended to thwart this by moving his armor down the Don fast enough to trap them west of the river. Now, however, enemy formations were putting up no real defense but were flowing back toward the Don with surprising speed. Would they escape across the river while his armored units were still engaged in the battle for Voronezh? If they did, the entire first phase of *Blau*, now renamed *Braunschweig* (Brunswick), would end in failure.

Thinking back to Dunkirk in 1940 and Leningrad the following year, the Führer feared that tying up his precious armor in this damned city could throw his wider plans into jeopardy.[85] Realizing that he had no immediate need to capture Voronezh but could destroy its railways and factories from the air and storm it later, he decided to fly to Bock's headquarters in Poltava and personally order the field marshal to leave the city alone. He made the three-hour journey on the morning of 3 July, but (according to Keitel's description of these events), when confronted by the aloof and aristocratic Prussian field marshal, he lost his nerve. He had always found it hard to discuss thorny matters with his older senior generals, and this time was no different. To Keitel's frustration, the Führer became jovial and friendly.[86] Far from flatly forbidding Bock to take Voronezh, he "beat around the bush" and left the decision ultimately up to Bock. Confused by his commander's vague instructions, the field marshal queried, "Am I right in understanding you as follows: I am to capture Voronezh if it can be done easily or without bloodshed. But I am not to get involved in heavy fighting for the city?" Hitler confirmed this with a silent nod.[87]

Bock vacillated all that day, unsure whether to attack the city or follow Hitler's "suggestion" to leave it alone. Early the next day, 4 July, he learned that a regiment of the 24th Panzer Division had captured a bridge across the Don and had established a bridgehead on the eastern bank. Later that day, forward units of *Großdeutschland*—which had alone destroyed 100 enemy tanks in the last week[88]—established their own bridgehead on the eastern bank. Voronezh was now tantalizingly close and apparently only weakly defended. Therefore, the field marshal decided to ignore his Führer's advice and take the city. After carrying out this coup de main, he argued, he would still have time to send his tanks down the Don to block the flight of Timoshenko's shattered formations.

On 5 July, Hitler heard reports that Soviet troops had flooded into Voronezh. He complained to his cohorts about the army group's recalcitrant and incompetent leadership and finally put his foot down; Bock must halt the advance on the city and send his armor southward. The following day, however, the army group reported that the city had actually been abandoned and that its spearheads had reached the suburbs. Enticed by this news, Hitler relented and let Bock proceed. He did state, though, that an armored corps must be sent down the Don without delay and further panzer units freed up as soon as possible. The field marshal complied, dispatching the Fortieth Panzer Corps (belonging to Sixth Army) southeastward along the Don.

The Führer remained extremely agitated as the unwanted battle for Voronezh took place. His agitation turned to horror when he discovered that Army Group South's intelligence had failed to detect a major Soviet buildup around the city. The Soviet command had assembled no fewer than nine rifle divisions, four rifle brigades, seven tank brigades, and two antitank brigades, and these forces were now pinning down the valuable panzer and motorized divisions of Forty-eighth and Twenty-fourth Panzer Corps. This was clearly Stalin's plan. Aware by now that Reichel's documents were authentic, he was desperate to tie down as many German forces as possible to give Timoshenko a chance to pull the bulk of his formations back from the Oskol and Donets and across the Don. Protected by tenacious rearguards, they had already begun to stream eastward.[89]

Voronezh could not be held for long, as Stalin well knew. On 7 July, Weichs threw more infantry into the battle, which tipped the scales and allowed him to disengage *Großdeutschland* and the 24th Panzer Division and send them along behind the Fortieth Panzer Corps. They finally left at first light on 8 July. Still, the city's defenders fought bravely until they finally succumbed to the superior skill and forces of their assailants later that day.

Blau I was over. Hitler was far from satisfied. While his troops had captured a huge area, they bagged surprisingly few prisoners (around 70,000) and little booty. He was also extremely annoyed at the way his armored units had been swallowed up for the last two days. This might yet have a profound impact on his campaign's next phase. His anger bubbled below the surface for another five days, finally erupting during a situation conference on 13 June.[90] After giving Keitel, Jodl, and Halder a savage verbal lashing, he ordered them to put Bock on the "sick list" and replace him with Weichs.

He could hardly find fault with the Luftwaffe. It had performed extremely well so far, not only during the army's drive eastward toward Voronezh but also during the storming of the city itself and attacks on the Soviet forces massed around it. On 5 July, for example, Richthofen unleashed *Fliegerkorps VIII*'s bomber and dive-bomber forces against the city, leaving its citizens battling numerous fires and choking on the dense clouds of smoke swirling through the broken buildings.[91] The following day, he threw them into battle against the forces opposing the 24th Panzer Division. "The enemy was heavily smashed," he triumphantly wrote, "and fled in disarray toward the northeast." Pflugbeil's corps was apparently doing just as well. "*Fliegerkorps IV* hammers the Don bridges," Richthofen noted, "destroying sections and inflicting terrible damage. Exploding, burning columns line the bridges, while three times as many line the roads."

Richthofen's diary reveals that the Luftwaffe retained control of the skies. For an average loss of four, it claimed forty enemy aircraft destroyed per day. Fighting on 8 July was especially successful: *Fliegerkorps VIII* attacked enemy tanks, ammunition depots, and airfields north and northeast of Voronezh. "Very good against trains," he commented, "and, above all, aircraft. 35 left burning, many others strafe-damaged. . . . 38 also shot down." Two days later, fighters in the Voronezh region practically wiped out a twenty-strong *VVS* formation, allowing only one to limp back to base.[92]

Flak units of various calibers guarded supply lines, railheads, troop concentrations, and airfields. They also advanced with the army's spearheads, protecting both armor and infantry from the steadily decreasing number of enemy ground-attack aircraft in the region. These were mainly the heavily armored Ilyushin Il-2 Shturmoviks. These excellent planes were impervious to small-arms fire but not to the high-velocity fire of light and medium flak batteries. In his diary, *General-major* Pickert describes how he witnessed a low-level attack on German troops near the Oskol River on 3 July. Flak gunners brought down an enemy aircraft as they quickly beat off the attack, immediately receiving Iron Crosses for their efforts. The army certainly appreciated the efforts of the flak teams. A 1955 issue of

Der Luftwaffenring, the Luftwaffe veterans' journal, proudly stated that "in this period, the flak artillery's existing glory received new luster. Every infantry division, every regiment, wanted to have its 'own' flak battery."[93]

Despite these aerial combat and flak successes, *Fliegerkorps IV* and *VIII* proved incapable of preventing increasingly heavy *VVS* bombing raids most nights. "In the night were very dreadful Red bombing raids on Kursk and the Voronezh bridges," Richthofen complained on 6 July. The following night was even worse; raids on the 76th Bomber Wing's airfields caused "continuous aircraft losses."[94] Spread out over a vast area and employed in a wide variety of tasks, mainly as extra artillery, flak batteries were also powerless to stop these raids. They still gave a good account of themselves. The 10th Flak Division alone reported shooting down thirty aircraft between 28 June and 6 July.[95] Its direct battlefield support was just as impressive; in the same period, it claimed fifty tanks and numerous batteries and field fortifications destroyed.

THE OFFENSIVE CONTINUES

Following the capture of Voronezh, the *OKW* promptly disbanded Army Group South, replacing it with two separate commands: Army Groups A and B. *Generalfeldmarschall* Wilhelm List took charge of Army Group A, the smaller of the two commands. It initially comprised First Panzer Army (under Kleist), Rumanian Third Army (Dumitrescu), and Eleventh and Seventeenth Armies (Manstein and Ruoff). This force, operating south of the other, was to strike directly eastward from the Taganrog area to the Don bend, where it was to link up with Army Group B's Fourth Panzer and Sixth Armies, thereby netting a prize catch of fleeing enemy troops. Other formations were to thrust southward, recapture Rostov, and establish bridgeheads south of the Don. After accomplishing those missions, they would plunge into the Caucasus, Eleventh Army joining them by crossing the Kerch Straits.

Following Bock's "retirement" (from his point of view, premature; from Hitler's, long overdue), Weichs assumed command of Army Group B, initially comprising Hungarian Second Army (Jány), Italian Eighth Army (Gariboldi), Fourth Panzer Army (Hoth), and Second and Sixth Armies (von Salmuth and Paulus). This powerful force was to cover Army Group A's northern flank, cut off the Volga shipping traffic, take over defense of the Don bend, hold the front south of Stalingrad, and, if possible, capture the city itself.

The great offensive's second phase commenced on 9 July, two weeks ahead of its projected schedule. Despite the small number of prisoners bagged, the High Command felt optimistic. The enemy was broken, it claimed, and victory likely. Even commanders at the front felt things were going superbly. *Generalmajor* Pickert, for example, wrote in his diary on 11 July that "we are about to inflict an annihilating defeat on the enemy here in the great Don bend. Great success is clearly indicated." However, the offensive's rapid progress (which continued for several more weeks), coupled with partisan attacks on railways, poor roads, and recent rainstorms, threw the army's logistical system into chaos. The 23rd Panzer Division took longer than expected to reach Sixth Army, its progress hampered not by stiff resistance (or "lack of zest," as Richthofen claimed)[96] but by fuel shortages. It had to stop several times and wait for extra fuel to be brought up before it could continue its move south-eastwards toward Millerovo. Likewise, Pickert's diary reveals that fuel shortages often held up the advance of his flak units. "Our fuel supplies scarcely arrive," he complained on 11 July, "which reduces our freedom of movement."[97] Eight days later, his fuel situation was still "uncomfortable." He ordered his batteries forward to the Don to protect army spearheads attempting to cross the river. "The execution of my order looks doubtful," he cursed, "due to a lack of fuel."

Similarly, back on 12 July, while units of First and Fourth Panzer Armies attempted to pinch off Soviet formations around Millerovo—and once again, they locked the door after the horse had bolted; the meeting pincers caught few Soviet troops, the rest having already withdrawn—*Großdeutschland* and the 24th Panzer Division sat stranded halfway between Voronezh and Rossosh, waiting (as they already had for more than two days) to be refueled.[98] Even when supplies arrived, wrote Helmuth Spaeter, *Großdeutschland*'s postwar chronicler, they proved woefully inadequate. The division continued advancing for the next few days, but only after "scraping together all fuel reserves, supplemented by air drops by Ju-52 transports and recovery of fuel from abandoned vehicles, and leaving behind individual tanks and other heavy consumers of fuel—at some cost to the unit's fighting strength."[99]

The Luftwaffe did all it could to alleviate the army's fuel problems, flying in up to 200 tons of gasoline each day during this period. It managed to carry out these vital supply missions even though its own constant transfers from region to region created major logistical problems. "We fly in 200 tons of fuel [for the army]," Richthofen noted on 13 July, "but are ourselves operating on a reduced scale because of breakdowns in our supplies." To keep up with rapidly moving ground forces, air units had to move constantly to new airfields—mainly deserted Soviet air bases—close to the front. Finding new fields often proved difficult. Reconnaissance units sometimes searched all day for bases mentioned by ground troops. Then, before these new fields could be used, signals teams had to lay telephone wires or set up wireless equipment connecting them to the corps command.

These frequent transfers to new airfields created hardships for both ground and air personnel. Their housing was usually primitive, often consisting of "tent cities" (to quote Richthofen's colorful phrase), and their sanitation facilities were rudimentary. At many hastily formed airfields—really only large stretches of flat grass—there was not even running water. Because new airfields were usually far from German railheads and established supply routes, and sometimes even from decent roads, Luftwaffe service and maintenance personnel had to move their equipment—and later all supplies and replacements—forward by air.

Supply units struggled to carry out these missions, but really pushed themselves and their Ju-52 workhorses to the limits of their endurance to satisfy the army's urgent requests for fuel. The Ju-52 had already been in service for ten years, and, although it was strong, reliable, and had excellent short takeoff and landing capabilities, its load capacity was no longer sufficient to satisfy the logistical requirements of both army and air force. Still, the Luftwaffe had nothing to replace it with, even though the Air Ministry had requested a faster and larger transport plane back in 1939, when the Ju-52 was already considered obsolete.

Despite complaining of "having supply difficulties and operating at the limit of our range," and grumbling about what he called the army's lack of fighting spirit ("It makes me sick!" he scrawled two days later), Richthofen remained happy with his air corps' performance. He was also excited about the shattered state of the enemy's defenses. To his 13 July entry he added that "the Russians attempt to escape, broken and leaderless, leaving all their heavy weapons behind." And, only the day before, he had written with unmistakable glee: "the mass of the Russians march to their death."

On 20 July, Richthofen flew to *Luftflotte 4*'s new headquarters at Mariupol (present-day Zhdanov) on the Sea of Azov, 160 kilometers southwest of Rostov. He took charge of the air fleet the following day, a week after blithely noting in his diary: "Read today of my appointment to Chief of *Luftflotte 4*, which took effect back on 3 July! It had been signed by the Führer but stopped by the *Reichsmarschall*."[100] Richthofen briefly retained *Generalmajor* Korten, Löhr's outstanding chief of staff, but the *OKL* promoted him soon afterward to head of his own corps (*Fliegerkorps I*, later renamed Air Command Don). *Oberst* Hans-Detlef Herhudt von Rohden—known to most airpower historians as the last head of the *Luftwaffe's 8. Abteilung* (Military Science Branch)—succeeded him late in August.

The air fleet's staff, used to Löhr's academic, understated, but solid command style, was apparently not thrilled by the arrival of his harsh, arrogant, and brilliant successor. "I must really have a dreadful reputation," Richthofen wrote on 20 July. "Everyone here is scared stiff of me. Mind you, things are so slack here that I will not be able to rein in my temperament for too long." He had been expressing these sentiments in his diary for several weeks. The fleet was slack, he sharply wrote on several occasions, but he would soon see to that. On 7 July, for instance, he had insisted that that he would "command more tightly and from closer to the front" than his predecessor.

Although it would take time to win over several members of his new team, he knew that he had already gained the respect and support of both his air corps commanders. Martin Fiebig, whom he had commanded in the Balkans, arrived "for training" at his *Fliegerkorps VIII* headquarters (by then a mobile command center 200 kilometers west of Kursk) on 6 July.[101] The two old friends and army-support experts got on famously. He was now delighted to pass *Fliegerkorps VIII*'s reins to Fiebig, knowing that his beloved corps remained in good hands and would continue to live up to its reputation as the Luftwaffe's premier close-support force.

He could also rely on Kurt Pflugbeil, *Fliegerkorps IV*'s tall and skeletal commander. He had always liked and trusted Pflugbeil, an outstanding officer with a distinguished service record stretching back to the Great War. When they met on 21 July, Richthofen's first day as fleet commander, he again made a good impression: "Pflugbeil is composed, sensible and good." The new chief discussed his plan to reorganize *Fliegerkorps IV*, transforming it from a general-purpose corps into a well-equipped close-support force with powerful dive-bomber and ground attack groups ("along the lines of *Fliegerkorps VIII*," he had jotted in his diary three days earlier).[102] They talked for so long—"united on everything"—that Richthofen almost missed his appointment with *Generalfeldmarschall* List, the army group commander.

Fliegerkorps IV was not the only force to be reorganized during this period. After Voronezh fell and the Second Army began constructing a solid defensive front along a line from Livny to Voronezh and the Hungarians began building a front immediately to the south, Löhr had taken a few units from each of his air corps and formed a new command, called *Gefechtsverband Nord* (Tactical Air Command North). He intended it to guard those vulnerable regions after Richthofen moved *Fliegerkorps VIII* 200 kilometers south to the Rossosh sector in order to support the advance of Hoth's Fourth Panzer Army. *Gefechtsverband Nord*'s leader, *Oberst* Alfred Bülowius, arrived at Richthofen's headquarters east of Kursk on 10 July. His small command (similar in size to Wild's *Fliegerführer Süd*, still patrolling the Black Sea) operated alone in the Voronezh sector after *Fliegerkorps VIII* flew south the following day.

Gefechtsverband Nord comprised the 76th Bomber Wing, the 10th Reconnaissance Group, and a constantly changing collection of temporarily assigned fighter and dive-bomber groups. Their mission, according to their operational order for 16 July, was simply to "support the fighting of the Second Army."[103] Bombers (and Stukas after a separate order arrived by telephone) were sent that day to "fight in close harmony with the operations officer, Second Army, in the sector north of Voronezh." Fighters were to attack Soviet airfields and, with reconnaissance planes, carry out "continuous surveillance of the combat zone northeast and east of Voronezh." *Gefechtsverband Nord* apparently did a good job in this vulnerable sector, even after fighting intensified in the following weeks. On 26 July, Richthofen noted in his diary: "Around Voronezh, Bülowius is having some good defensive successes."

ROSTOV AND BEYOND

Richthofen took charge of *Luftflotte 4* just in time to oversee the assault on Rostov, gateway to the Caucasus. Aware that his planned encirclements in the central Don region had been only partially successful, Hitler had ordered his powerful armored forces to sweep south to Rostov and prevent Lieutenant General Malinovskii's Southern Front from escaping across the lower Don. These southward-driving forces included Fourth Panzer Army, which he now transferred to Army Group A. In a move strikingly similar to that of the year before—when he sent Guderian's armored forces down to Kiev, a diversion that produced a splendid local victory but probably cost him Moscow—Hitler broke off Fourth Panzer Army's drive toward Stalingrad and turned it south. Deviating further from the original *Blau* plan, he sent Paulus's Sixth Army alone toward Stalingrad, but not necessarily to take the city. Rather, it was to create a solid flank along the Don while its spearheads pushed eastward to prevent the enemy establishing defenses west of the Volga. It would have to accomplish these tasks without the bulk of its armor, which he also sent south toward Rostov as part of First Panzer Army.

By 20 July, the day after the Führer changed his mind and ordered Sixth Army (still alone and without its tanks) to attack Stalingrad,[104] armored spearheads of Fourth Panzer Army had established bridgeheads across the Don near Zymlyanskaya and Konstantinovka (150 and 110 kilometers northeast of Rostov). Meanwhile, First Panzer Army had crossed the Donets 130 kilometers to the north and was plunging down toward Rostov, while southern units of Seventeenth Army, driving due east from the Taganrog area, had wheeled south and reached the Don northeast and southwest of the city.[105] This ripe fruit was ready to be picked.

Richthofen's units played a key role in the battle for Rostov. "The Russians," he wrote, describing the morning of 21 July, "had already evacuated their forward positions. Our troops were therefore able to advance without a struggle." In the afternoon, however, fighting intensified as ground troops encountered pockets of fierce resistance. He immediately threw the bulk of his ground-attack forces, from *both* air corps (not just one, as Plocher suggested), into the battle.[106] He also threw in Stukas from the 1st Group, 77th Dive-Bomber Wing (until recently belonging to Wild's small *Fliegerführer Süd*), which screamed down upon tanks, vehicles, and troops. Hurling both high-explosive and splinter bombs, they inflicted heavy damage. This veteran wing, which had seen action in almost every campaign to date, had only the week before clocked up its 30,000th mission on the eastern front.[107] (If its claims are accurate, it had inflicted far more damage to the enemy on the battlefield than any other wing.)[108] Göring immediately sent the wing his heartiest congratulations on reaching this milestone.[109]

Determined to prevent the enemy from slipping away across the Don, Richthofen deployed his "bombers against the city, bridges and fleeing masses." These included medium bombers not only from his two corps but also from Wild's command. The latter pounded road and rail traffic flowing out of Rostov. These Crimea-based planes had actually been attacking the city and surrounding targets most days for several weeks.[110] Although they packed a relatively weak punch (the entire command released only 23.6 tons of bombs on 21 July),[111] these aircraft still managed to make their presence felt. A He 111 of *II./K.G. 26,* for instance, dropped a huge 1,800-kg bomb on a railway embankment, destroying two freight trains. Other aircraft inflicted various levels of damage on bridges, supply depots, and vehicles.

The following day (a "good day at the front"), the German drive on Rostov progressed well.[112] With Stukas paving their way, army spearheads—including battalions from the SS *Wiking* (Viking) and 13th Panzer Divisions—pushed through the maze of antitank ditches, barbed wire entanglements, and minefields right up to within three kilometers of the city itself. "The Russians flee across the Don," the delighted air leader added, "without their equipment and weapons." Pflugbeil's aircraft pursued them, smashing troops caught in the open and vehicles jammed on the roads. They provided "outstanding support for the attack the entire day," wrote Wilhelm Tieke, author of a "classic" work on the Caucasus campaign.[113] "Scarcely any targets were overlooked. . . . The cooperation between the ground troops and Luftwaffe, guided by the *Flivo* [air liaison officer] . . . was exceptional." While these attacks occurred, Fiebig's aircraft (joined by a small number of Wild's bombers)[114] supported Sixth Army's steady advance in the direction of Stalingrad. Encountering little opposition, the army ambled eastward with no sense of urgency.

The Luftwaffe retained air superiority but did not have things all its own way. The *VVS*—now deploying scores of British lend-lease fighters, including Hurricanes—put up a good fight, destroying several German aircraft each day and constantly harassing ground troops. *VVS* fighters almost killed Fiebig on 23 July, when they sprayed his Storch with bullets and set it on fire. Miraculously, neither he nor his pilot received serious injury.[115] *Oberstleutnant* Ihlefeld, the commander of the 52nd Fighter Wing, had not been as lucky the day before. Caught in his own Storch by enemy fighters, he was very badly wounded. Still, these incidents and the loss of a few aircraft each day pale when contrasted to the *VVS*'s own losses. For example, 26 July was an especially good day for Richthofen's units: they reported destroying 113 enemy aircraft, with *Fliegerkorps VIII* alone claiming 88 of them in Sixth Army's combat zone.[116]

On 23 July—to return to Rostov—*Fliegerkorps IV* unleashed on Rostov around-the-clock raids of blistering intensity. Suffering badly under these streams of bombs and squeezed by powerful German ground formations, which quickly carved their way through the wildly burning suburbs as resistance weakened, the city's courageous defenders could not hold on. With the exception of several isolated groups (including tough secret police troops), finally eliminated in bitter and costly house-to-house fighting, the city's defenders capitulated later that day.

The way to the Caucasus was not yet open. *Generalfeldmarschall* List still had to capture the main bridge across the Don and the subsequent six-kilometer-long bridge embankment across the Don delta between Rostov and Bataisk before his waiting armies could lunge southward into the Caucasus. He ordered forward the 2nd Battalion of the "Brandenburg" Special Purpose Training Regiment, which had been training for this task (and other similar actions in the Caucasus) since April.[117] On 24 July, Stukas of *I./St.G. 77* launched heavy "softening up" raids on the Soviet troops, guns, and flak batteries defending the bridges. Even so, deadly machine-gun fire met the "Brandenburgers" when they tried to storm the bridges, pinning them down and inflicting heavy casualties. After trying unsuccessfully for over twenty-four hours to reinforce the "Brandenburgers," and at one point to withdraw them with bearable losses, the army called back Pflugbeil's Stukas on the morning of 26 July. They arrived "in the nick of time," according to Paul Carell, and repeatedly pounded enemy positions.[118] Their attacks allowed ground troops, including the remnants of the mauled battalion, to finish the job they started.[119] They promptly seized the bridges, across which the first spearheads of Fifty-seventh Panzer Corps rolled the following day.

Aside from small "mopping-up" actions, Hitler's Rostov operation was over. The Führer, now commanding the war from new headquarters (code-named "Werewolf") at Vinnitsa in the Ukraine, was delighted; his courageous troops had smashed open the gateway to the Caucasus, which lay before them bare and, to all appearances, only lightly defended. He could not help noticing, on the other hand, that once again his net contained a surprisingly small catch: only 83,000 more prisoners.

Hitler considered his disappointing prisoner haul to be evidence not that his grand encircling operations had failed but that Soviet resistance had been truly shattered and any panic-stricken forces managing to escape were on their last legs anyway. This mistaken notion may seem absurd in hindsight—although at the time it was shared by American intelligence officers, who noted in their brief to the Combined Chiefs of Staff that the "speed with which Germans seized bridgeheads over the lower Don indicates serious decrease in Russian power of resistance"[120]—but plentiful evidence supported it at the time. After all, Axis troops had delivered heavy blows and gained a fantastic amount of territory in recent weeks. The Soviet command had apparently lost control. Sixth Army, still ambling across the steppes towards Stalingrad, met little opposition. Enemy forces, it said, were in full flight. Kleist's First Panzer Army reported weak resistance and mass enemy desertions. Also, as David Irving points out, even if Hitler personally misread the situation, "there is no evidence whatsoever that General Halder advised him differently until August, and by then it was too late to undo the damage already done."[121]

On 23 July, while his forces stormed Rostov, Hitler's mistaken assessment of his enemy's present state prompted him to issue a war directive deviating substantially from *Blau's* original conception. "The broad objectives I had set for the southern wing of the Eastern front," he trumpeted in War Directive No. 45, "have been largely achieved. Only weak forces from Timoshenko's armies succeeded in avoiding encirclement and reaching the southern bank of the Don."[122] Now, he continued, it was time to finish the task.

No longer deeming it necessary to secure the northern flank and take Stalingrad and *then* head south into the Caucasus, he stipulated that both operations be undertaken at the same time. In Operation *Fischreiher* (heron), Army Group B would construct a solid front along the Don. Then, by thrusting forward to Stalingrad, it would smash the enemy forces concentrated there, occupy the city, and block the land bridge between the Don and the Volga. Meanwhile, fast-moving troops were to advance southeastward along the Volga to Astrakhan, thereby cutting off this valuable waterway. Reflecting his growing infatuation with Stalingrad, formerly not even a main target, he ordered the transfer of a panzer corps composed of two armored divisions from Fourth Panzer to Sixth Army (and thus from the Caucasus to the Stalingrad operation).

In Operation *Edelweiss,* Army Group A was to encircle and destroy the enemy formations that fled across the Don into the northern Caucasus. It was then to carry out its most important task: the occupation of the entire Black Sea coastline, including its naval bases. This would effectively put an end to the Red Fleet. At the same time, mountain and light infantry divisions (including some brought across the Kerch Straits from Eleventh Army) were to take the high ground around Maikop and Armavir and close the passes in the western Caucasus. Finally, a mobile force was to strike south and east to close the military road between Ossetia and Grozny, and strike along the Caspian coast to the great oil metropolis of Baku.

Hitler apparently considered these tasks to be well within his army groups' capabilities. Victory was so close, he maintained, that Army Group South could even afford to shed a number of unnecessary divisions. In the last few days, he had authorized the transfer of two panzer divisions to Army Group Center, where a Soviet attack looked increasingly likely. Now, in his directive, he stated that the elite *Großdeutschland* division was soon going to Western Europe (to allay his growing fears of an Allied invasion—fears based neither on intelligence information nor on specific Allied activities but on his own "intuition"). Further, contrary to his last war directive, issued twelve days earlier,[123] Manstein's powerful Eleventh Army was no longer going to advance across the Kerch Straits into the Caucasus. Rather, a small holding force would remain in the Crimea, while the army's command staff and the bulk of divisions traveled 1,800 kilometers north to do to Leningrad what they had done to Sevastopol. Only Manstein's Rumanian mountain troops would cross the Kerch Straits.

The Luftwaffe, Hitler continued, was to continue providing close and strong support to both army groups. "The early destruction of Stalingrad is especially important," he said. As opportunities present themselves, attacks should be made on Astrakhan and mines laid in the Lower Volga. In view of the Caucasus oil fields' critical importance to the prosecution of the war, he stressed, air raids should immediately be launched against railways and pipelines being used by the enemy. However, attacks on refineries, storage tanks, and ports used for oil shipments should be carried out only if circumstances on the ground make them absolutely necessary.

Hitler's new instructions flew in the face of traditional military doctrine. First, they did not involve a reorganization of the army groups in keeping with their allotted tasks. The specialist Italian Alpine Corps, for example, was not sent to the Caucasus. It remained under the command of Paulus's Sixth Army, still rolling eastward across flat steppes. Frittered away as infantrymen, these excellent alpine troops should have been transferred to List's Army Group A, where they were sorely needed. Hitler assigned List the task of conquering the Caucasus but allocated him only three mountain divisions and several infantry divisions totally unsuited in both training and equipment to the task.

Second, rather than work toward a single *Schwerpunkt*—as espoused by traditional German strategists—Hitler's two groups would diverge at right angles, thus dissipating their strength. Their divergence would open a large and vulnerable gap between them and, even worse, necessitate separate logistics routes. Supply lines were already stretched to the breaking point, with both army groups experiencing fuel and ammunition shortages. Now the War Lord wanted one group to push eastward to Stalingrad, which was possible (but only just) at the present fuel consumption and supply rates. He wanted the other to plunge southward to the distant oil-rich cities of the southern Caucasus, a highly improbable (if not impossible) task at the present rates. Even Maikop, the nearest oil field, was—as the crow flies—335 kilometers away from Rostov, where List's armies stood ready for their drive south. Grozny was almost twice that distance, and Baku, Hitler's ultimate goal, was no less than 1,200 kilometers away. The latter, to illustrate the significance of these distances, was as far from Rostov as that city was from the Polish-Soviet border.

By the time List's troops stormed Rostov, established bridgeheads over the lower Don, and set their gaze to the south, Richthofen was beginning to find his feet as commander of *Luftflotte 4*. On 27 July he flew to Göring's headquarters in Kalinovka, half an hour's drive from Hitler's new command center in Vinnitsa. He spent an hour and a half with his friend Jeschonnek, discussing organizational matters and his forces' future operations. As usual, they agreed on all important matters. Probably intentionally massaging Richthofen's ego, the air force chief of staff mentioned that the former's recent promotion had been well received in higher command circles. "As fleet commander, I am generally held in high esteem," Richthofen joyfully penned in his diary that evening, clearly writing for the memorial of his posterity.

The *Reichsmarschall,* who had apparently forgotten his anger at Richthofen's private tête-à-tête with the Führer two months earlier, certainly acted pleased to see him. Göring was in a "very gracious and understanding" mood and seemed attentive and genuinely interested in events at the front. The bulky demagogue not only approved the fleet commander's plans for the coming campaigns but also further rewarded him for his role in previous ones. "As the first member of the Luftwaffe," Richthofen proudly wrote that night, "he awarded me the East Medal." Actually, he mused, it was only the ribbon; the medal itself had yet to be minted. He was still delighted, aware that the ribbon would sit nicely on his breast next to that of the "Michael," the Rumanian equivalent of the Knight's Cross. Marshal Antonescu had personally pinned it on him after the Kerch campaign. All the German generals considered the "Michael" a true honor, he had written on that occasion.[124] After spending the evening listening to Göring drone on about almost anything that came into his head—followed by a late dinner with him, Jeschonnek and the Luftwaffe's personnel chief, *starting* at ten in the evening—Richthofen was doubtless relieved to be shown to his luxury compartment in Göring's marvelous command train.

He flew back to his headquarters in Mariupol ("home," as he called it) the next morning, 28 July, then spent the afternoon attending to paperwork and talking to Korten, still serving as the fleet's chief of staff. They were both unhappy about Hitler's decision to split the main offensive into two simultaneous campaigns, realizing that the diverging directions of each expanded *Luftflotte 4*'s operational zone to enormous proportions. That zone (already as large as prewar Germany) now tripled in size overnight, stretching northeast to Voronezh, east to the Volga, southeast to the coast of the Caspian Sea, and south to distant Baku. Its eastern front, therefore, measured over 1,600 kilometers. Carrying out the air operations Hitler outlined in his directive seemed impossible, especially as recent fighting and related missions had already taken a heavy toll on the fleet's strength. Its total complement had dropped from 1,610 aircraft to 1,359 in the last month, and its operational readiness had dropped from 71 percent (which, although not as high as that of the air forces in western Europe, was excellent for the eastern front, where logistical, geographical, and climatic problems proved difficult to overcome) to a mediocre 56 percent in the same period.[125]

The air fleet would have to wage three separate campaigns (for the time being, at least). In the far north of his combat zone, *Gefechtsverband Nord* would continue to assist Salmuth's Second Army in its defensive battles in the Voronezh sector. This front had actually become so "hot" in recent weeks, with constant Soviet pressure, that he planned to dissolve Bülowius's small command and replace it with a complete air corps, *Fliegerkorps I.* Korten himself would take charge, the fleet chief noted in his diary on 30 July. He actually wanted the experienced Pflugbeil to command the yet-to-be-formed corps, feeling that Korten was still "too young." This was a silly complaint, considering that the forty-four-year-old Korten was already as old as Richthofen had been when he took over

Fliegerkorps VIII in October 1939. It should not have worried the latter anyway; when the new corps arrived in another month or so, it would not be his responsibility. Back on 18 July, he had asked the *OKL* to let him "get rid of that entire northern sector."[126] It should set up an independent air command, he had argued, with its own *Luftgau* overseeing its supplies and maintenance. The *OKL* had apparently agreed; Richthofen now noted that the new command would not be his concern. It would be under *OKL* direction and, based in Kiev, would have its own organization, command, and logistics systems. He also managed to get rid of the German Air Force Mission in Rumania, which had until now come under *Luftflotte 4*'s command umbrella. Löhr, as commander of all Wehrmacht forces in the Balkans, would take charge of Ploesti's air defense.

Operating south of *Gefechtsverband Nord*, Fiebig's *Fliegerkorps VIII* would assist Sixth Army (and soon Fourth Panzer Army) in its drive toward Stalingrad. This corps was still better suited to army support than Pflugbeil's—although Richthofen noted again on 30 July that he was busily "making *Fliegerkorps IV* the same as *Fliegerkorps VIII*"—and the fleet commander had promised Paulus six days earlier that he would pay careful attention to Sixth Army's air support.[127]

Pflugbeil's *Fliegerkorps IV* would support List's drive to the oil fields, assisted by Wild's small *Fliegerführer Süd*, still operating in the Crimea and over the vast expanses of the Black Sea. Wild was again annoyed to learn that his specialist antishipping and long-range reconnaissance force would be swallowed up by a larger command, as it had been during the assault on Sevastopol. His annoyance turned to anger when he was told that *Fliegerkorps IV* would command its Caucasus operations from Kerch, on "his" territory, and that his force would lose what little autonomy it had left.[128] "He has no grounds [for these feelings]," Richthofen wrote on 9 August, after meeting both Wild and Pflugbeil in Kerch, "because his own performance has hardly been convincing."

Thus, two related but separate major Luftwaffe campaigns—excluding operations in the Voronezh sector, soon to disappear from this study anyway—commenced at the end of July. In order to avoid flitting from one campaign to the other, we will trace the progress of each in turn, beginning with what soon proved to be the least important of the two: *Fliegerkorps IV*'s support of List's drive to the oil fields.

6

Stalemate in the Caucasus: July–December 1942

After taking Rostov, List's forces crossed the lower Don along a 200-kilometer front stretching from the Sea of Azov to Zymlianskaya. *Armeegruppe Ruoff* formed the right wing, crossing at Rostov and establishing a solid bridgehead at Bataisk. This *Gruppe* comprised Ruoff's Seventeenth Army and Dumitrescu's Rumanian Third Army. Kleist's First Panzer Army stood on its left, with more than 400 tanks rolling forward from equally strong bridgeheads farther east. On the left wing, the bulk of Hoth's Fourth Panzer Army advanced steadily (although it would soon disappear from the Caucasus because Hitler transferred it to the Stalingrad sector on 31 July). These Axis forces moved forward rapidly, opposed by remnants of half a dozen Soviet armies already smashed north of the Don. While these shattered formations remained strong in manpower, they lacked competent leadership, cohesion, tanks, most of their heavy guns, and air support.[1]

Stalin feared not only a humiliating rout but also the loss of rich industrial and agricultural regions in the Caucasus. Axis troops already looked set to take the Kuban, one of the Soviet Union's major food-producing areas. The Soviet people, Stalin knew, could ill afford to lose the Kuban's large harvests of wheat, sunflower seeds, and sugar beets. Losing Baku's oil fields, however, would be calamitous. Accordingly, on 28 July he issued his now-famous Order No. 227, which stated, in terms unwittingly echoing Hitler's of December 1941: *"Ni shagu nazad!"* (Not a step back!). This order contained a rousing patriotic appeal to all Soviet soldiers and citizens in the name of the Motherland to increase their resistance to Axis forces and halt their advance. Perhaps to prevent the further disintegration of Stalin's forces before Stalingrad and in the northern Caucasus, it also warned that swift retribution would be meted out to "deserters" and "panic mongers."

Operating from airfields in the Don bend as well as in the Rostov region itself (Stukas were even flying from the city's main airport by 29 July), *Flieger-korps IV* contributed substantially to the disorganization of Soviet forces in the northern Caucasus.[2] When List's troops drove them back across the Don, Pflug-beil's air units continuously bombed and strafed them. As reported by British air intelligence officers, routinely reading the Luftwaffe's secret radio communications, these air attacks severely hampered the Soviets' ability to conduct effective rearguard actions, withdraw in an orderly fashion, and construct defenses in rear areas.[3] Pflugbeil's airmen also achieved pleasing results against logistics systems and road and rail traffic, particularly along the main Baku-Rostov rail line. *Fliegerführer Süd* assisted them by constantly monitoring enemy movements and positions, attacking Black Sea ports, and also carrying out light but relentless raids on enemy traffic in the northern Caucasus.

After Sevastopol fell in the beginning of July, Löhr had stripped *Flieger-führer Süd* of most combat units, transferring them back to *Fliegerkorps IV* and *VIII*. By 15 July, for example, Wild's force retained only three bomber groups (*III./L.G. 1, I./K.G. 100,* and *II./K.G. 26,* the latter mainly used to launch torpe-does), a fighter group *(III./J.G. 77),* two reconnaissance squadrons (one long-range), two flak regiments, and a small sea-rescue team. It had only a handful of Stukas *(E./St.G. 77)* and no ground-attack planes.[4]

Fliegerführer Süd's last major mission had been its strong attack on Novoros-siisk harbor on 2 July, when its bombers and Stukas sank the flotilla leader *Tashkent* and badly damaged the cruiser *Komintern,* a destroyer, and several large freighters. Since then, the force routinely attacked that harbor and others along the Caucasus coastline, as well as Rostov and surrounding towns, but its attacks became increasingly weak as units left for combat elsewhere in the southern sec-tor. With a few exceptions, these raids were of little more than nuisance value, inflicting only minor damage on harbor installations, storage facilities, and supply systems.

Wild simply lacked the means to do more. His remaining units were in a very poor state. On 20 July, for example, his three bomber groups had no more than eighty-nine aircraft between them, only thirty (33 percent) of which were opera-tional.[5] They had worked to the point of exhaustion during the assault on Sevas-topol but, instead of being rehabilitated, now received meager supplies of ammu-nition, fuel, and spare parts and no replacement aircraft. This is understandable: *Fliegerkorps IV* and *VIII* worked furiously to support the army as it drove east-ward in pursuit of Hitler's strategic goals. They had their own substantial fuel and ammunition problems, and their operational capabilities were steadily fall-ing. *Luftflotte 4* had to focus its attention urgently and constantly on their needs; it could hardly worry about Wild's paltry force operating in the Crimea—now a "backwater" of no immediate importance. With this in mind, Richthofen's diary comment that Wild's "own performance has hardly been convincing" seems most unfair.

Dropping a miserable average of forty tons of bombs per day throughout

July, Wild's bombers sank no large warships but only a motley collection of coastal patrol boats and freighters. It was not for lack of trying. On 16 July, twenty-four bombers of *I./K.G. 100* and *II./K.G. 26* launched a joint raid on the bulk of the Soviet Black Sea Fleet, berthed in distant Poti harbor and protected by several strong flak batteries and the ships' own flak guns. They hit several warships, including a heavy cruiser with a massive 1,400-kg bomb, but, despite inflicting a variety of light damage, failed to sink a single vessel.[6] They lost two He 111s in the attempt, however. Throughout July, antishipping missions cost them another four destroyed and three damaged.

Fliegerführer Süd's two dozen operational fighters and two flak regiments proved hopelessly incapable of preventing bombing raids on German positions in the Crimea by *VVS* aircraft based in the Kuban. Early in July, these raids occurred intermittently and only at night. By the end of the month they came daily, and, with *VVS* commanders now realizing that they faced no real danger, often during the day. The heaviest raid took place on 30 July, when twenty-four medium bombers, protected by over a hundred fighters, which attacked with their own cannons and light bombs, rained destruction down on Kerch.[7] Apparently aiming for the train station, they destroyed twenty-two railway wagons full of munitions, blew up a truck, and killed a soldier. German flak teams only succeeded in bring down one Polikarpov I-16 "Rata" fighter and one SB-2 bomber. This Soviet air activity promptly waned in the middle of August after *Fliegerkorps IV* moved many combat units, accompanied by powerful flak batteries, to the Crimea. Until then, Wild's few fighter pilots and flak teams did all they could to protect their region. Between 3 and 31 July, they managed to destroy twenty-four aircraft in aerial combat and another ten with ground fire.[8]

By the beginning of August, Wild's depleted force had little to offer List's troops in the northern Caucasus except for its unequaled knowledge of the terrain, which provided German commanders with a few extra pieces of the widely scattered intelligence jigsaw. In particular, for the last six months its reconnaissance units had conducted daily surveillance missions over the Kuban and northwestern Caucasus. They had taken many thousands of photographs of important ports, cities, towns, roads, railways, rivers, and bridges. German cartographers had already incorporated valuable information from these photographs and crew reports into the new maps now being spread before List and his various corps and division commanders.

Fliegerführer Süd had one other item of apparent value: *experienced* antishipping groups—particularly *II/K.G. 26* and *I/.K.G. 100*—which were then active against both Oktyabrskii's Caucasus ports and those on the east coast of the Sea of Azov (still supplying Soviet troops in the northwestern Caucasus). In the last week of July, Richthofen requested that they operate alongside bombers from *Fliegerkorps VIII* as they attacked Volga River shipping both north and southeast of Stalingrad. They dropped high-explosive bombs as well as magnetic mines, but around 15 percent of these detonated when they hit the water.[9] Wild's groups had a few minor successes. On 27 July, they bombed ships and released thirty-one mines in the Volga on both sides of Stalingrad.[10] They damaged two large transport barges being towed upriver, and learned the next day that their mines had sunk a floating crane and two other towed barges.

According to a report presented to the *OKW* on 29 July by Captain Mössel, the Luftwaffe general staff's naval liaison officer, mines dropped by aircraft proved moderately effective in Caucasian ports, including Poti, where most of Oktyabrskii's fleet lay. Yet they had so far not proved as effective in the Volga, which was generally too shallow.[11] They would be tried in narrower stretches, therefore, where the water was presumably deeper. Wild's units dropped far more bombs than mines anyway, but, although they continued intermittently bombing river traffic, they apparently gave up mining on 4 August. They dropped twenty-eight mines on that last day, six of which exploded prematurely when they hit the water.[12]

Volga shipping was probably far from *Generalfeldmarschall* List's mind as his forces continued rolling southward; he was worried more about his own supplies than his enemy's. Only airlifts of fuel by Pflugbeil's *Fliegerkorps IV* kept his armies moving. By 28 July, Seventeenth Army had crossed the Kagalnik River, 32 kilometers south of Rostov, and was pushing forward on a wide front toward the Kuban. On the other flank, Fourth Panzer Army had captured Proletarskaya and advance units troops had reached the 600-kilometer-long Manych River, which marked the boundary between Europe and Asia. Before the war, Soviet engineers had actually transformed the river into a canal. It now consisted of a chain of dammed lakes, some more than a kilometer wide, with several hydroelectric dams providing electricity for local oil-producing centers.

Crossing this continental divide proved less difficult than Soviet defenders (dug in on the other side) hoped, even after they opened floodgates and flooded the river. While German artillery pinned down those Soviets on 31 July, assault troops of the 3rd Panzer Division shot across the swollen river in nineteen boats, bailing furiously with their mess tins to overcome leaks, and established the first German bridgehead in Asia. They then launched a successful surprise attack on one of the enemy-held dams, allowing panzers to roll across its narrow crown. Pflugbeil's airmen had played a key part in this action, attacking Soviet troops preventing German reinforcements crossing the river. Paul Carell writes: "At about 0600 the German close-support aircraft came roaring in. . . . The bombers silenced the Soviet artillery positions and machine-gun nests. Under cover of the hail of bombs and strafing attacks, the third wave finally succeeded in crossing."[13]

Few of the tanks advancing into Asia under *Fliegerkorps IV*'s protective umbrella belonged to Hoth's Fourth Panzer Army. After that army severed the railway between Stalingrad and the Caucasus, Hitler proclaimed that, while enemy forces south of the Don would continue trying to hold back List's advance, they could now get few reinforcements from the rest of the Soviet Union.[14] Stalingrad, on the other hand, would be defended fanatically and reinforced steadily. On 31

July, he therefore transferred Hoth's Army—minus Fortieth Panzer Corps, which remained in the Caucasus—to Army Group B. It turned around and headed back the way it came, consuming huge amounts of fuel and needing constant airlifts in the process. Its destination: Stalin's city on the Volga.

List's forces continued their southward drive, sweeping the enemy before them. By 3 August, Seventeenth Army's spearheads had covered half the distance to Krasnodar. Vanguard units of the Third and Fortieth Panzer Corps, belonging to First Panzer Army, had made similar progress. They were well on their way to Armavir and Voroshilovsk, respectively. However impressive these advances sound, though, they involved only light mobile forces. Despite the valiant efforts of Pflugbeil's transport groups, which worked around-the-clock to carry fuel for the army, most tanks sat stranded far to the rear, desperately waiting for supplies.[15]

Pflugbeil's transport units were not the only Luftwaffe formations supporting List's swift and seemingly unstoppable advance. Units of the 10th Flak Division—including some with *Flakpanzer,* antiaircraft guns mounted on half-tacks and tank chassis—accompanied all panzer formations to protect the tanks and following infantry from deadly Ilyushin Il-2 Shturmoviks and other enemy ground-attack aircraft. Especially in the few first days after the fall of Rostov, they also had to drive off enemy bombers attempting to destroy bridges across the Don and major north Caucasian rivers. Helmuth Spaeter, *Großdeutschland*'s postwar chronicler, noted several occasions when enemy bombers endeavored to halt that division's advance but "were effectively prevented from doing so by the efforts of the flak artillery."[16] As it was, the *VVS* had far fewer aircraft in the Don bend and northern Caucasus than the Luftwaffe. On 29 July, *Luftflotte 4* reported to the *OKW* that "the Russian air force facing Army Group South's right flank demonstrates its weakness. Stukas even carry out their attacks without fighter escort, and don't get attacked by Russian fighters."[17]

List and Richthofen deployed most flak regiments in support of Seventeenth Army, which had very few tanks and, as a result, needed extra firepower.[18] Flak units again proved devastatingly effective, not in the role for which they were intended, although they notched up pleasing aircraft "kill" totals, but against ground targets, including tanks, field fortifications, and gun positions. They were, of course, equipped for both roles, carrying time-fuse antiaircraft ammunition, as well as armor-piercing and percussion shells.

Pflugbeil's ground-attack and reconnaissance aircraft also supported Axis forces on the battlefield. They provided ground forces with outstanding tactical intelligence information. Wilhelm Tieke remembers how aircraft "released smoke signals showing ground troops the way, reported enemy concentrations and pointed out the best march routes if the ground reconnaissance could not keep pace."[19] Cooperation between ground and air forces remained excellent, he added. In many cases, pilots communicated directly with army units, thus bypassing the usual *Flivo* liaison system. As Tieke noted: "[Pilots] talked with us over

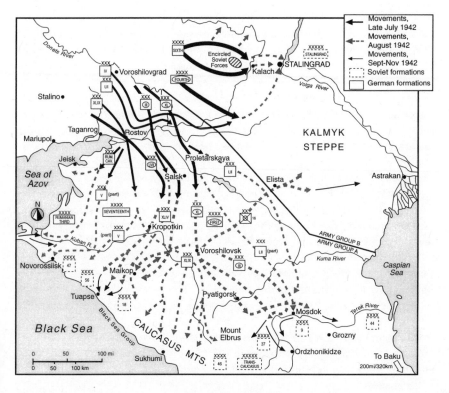

4. Toward the oil fields

the radio or dropped messages and requested that we find them suitable landing areas."[20] After landing, squadron leaders met their army counterparts to coordinate their operations. Naturally, he added, Pflugbeil's airmen not only reported the location of enemy forces but also attacked them aggressively: "With their on-board weapons and fragmentation bombs they joined in the ground battle or suppressed enemy forces. In all, the cooperation was ideal."

Fliegerkorps IV had fewer dive-bomber and ground-attack aircraft than *Fliegerkorps VIII*, so it could not support all German spearhead units at once or even individual units for long. Still, no one on the ground doubted the air force's ability to wreak havoc on the Soviet forces they encountered. For example, when advance detachments of the 3rd Panzer Division reached Voroshilovsk on 3 August, they were delighted to learn that the Luftwaffe had already stamped its imprint on the region: "There were traces of German air attacks everywhere. On the roads overturned vehicles and heavy weapons lay strewn. Freight trains were still burning on open stretches of track. The German *Fliegerkorps IV* had done a good job there."[21]

Escorted by fighters, which also chased away Soviet aircraft, Pflugbeil's bombers worked as energetically as the ground-attack planes. During the last days of July and the first days of August, bomber units mainly directed their efforts against enemy shipping on the lower Volga, ground forces in the Kuban region, and road and rail logistical routes throughout the entire northern Caucasus.[22] When they had time and resources (which was not often), they also mounted raids, joined by Wild's bombers, against Oktyabrskii's ports along the Caucasus coast. The latter's fleet had not yet recovered from the mauling it received during the Axis assault on Sevastopol, and now ventured outside its ports only rarely. *Fliegerführer Süd* closely monitored the ports, looking for—but rarely finding—evidence of imminent naval activity. Small warships of Gorshkov's Azov Flotilla had been supporting their beleaguered army comrades by firing on Ruoff's Seventeenth Army as it advanced along the coast toward the Kuban.[23] Their gunfire had little effect, however, and soon died out when *Fliegerführer Süd* stepped up its torpedo and bombing attacks. Individual warships of Oktyabrskii's main fleet also carried out a few artillery attacks at night on German positions, but they proved ineffective—as did *Fliegerführer Süd*'s attempts to sink the ships[24]—and the fleet attempted no large-scale naval missions. By early August, only merchant vessels, submarines, and small warships regularly plied the waters of the eastern Black Sea. Medium-sized warships still made occasional gunfire attacks on Crimean centers, but only at night and with little effect. The Soviet naval command, which still possessed a substantial force despite its major losses, preferred to keep its large warships in the relative safety of flak-defended ports and prepare its land approaches and harbor defenses for the inevitable attacks by List's armies.[25]

On 2 August, Richthofen noted in his diary that advance units of Kleist's First Panzer Army (and Ruoff's Seventeenth Army, although the air chief mentioned only the former) were now within fifteen kilometers of the Kuban. "Stronger enemy forces remain behind the Kuban River and around Krasnodar," he wrote with concern. His following comments reveal his frustration at not being able to create a single *Schwerpunkt* (point of main emphasis) there for his two corps: "Unfortunately, I have to split up my forces. *Fliegerkorps VIII* must help Sixth Army near Stalingrad, and carry out attacks on railways in that area and shipping on the Volga." That corps, he added with annoyance, also had to carry forward Sixth Army's supplies. Meanwhile, *Fliegerkorps IV* must attack the enemy in the Kuban and railways throughout the northern Caucasus. This, he concluded, must be his *Schwerpunkt* for now, "while later: Stalingrad."

As in previous campaigns, Richthofen and his two corps commanders worked in close cooperation with their army counterparts to coordinate joint *Schwerpunkte*. On 4 August, the fleet chief invited *Generalfeldmarschall* List to his headquarters in Mariupol, where the two commanders discussed fresh air reconnaissance information and planned their operations for the coming days.[26] They were both worried about the fuel situation (so was Halder, who had recently noted in his diary that "the fuel situation in Army Group A remains tight"),[27] but still optimistic about the campaign's chances of success. If fuel supplies held out, they claimed, the oil fields were theirs for the taking. That same day, List submitted to the *OKW* an optimistic situation assessment. The Soviet command apparently intended to make a stand south of the Kuban River to protect Maikop and the main Black Sea naval bases. Yet enemy forces were "dispensing with any sort of unified command," and "a fast thrust to the southwest with sufficient mobile forces will not encounter serious enemy resistance anywhere forward of Baku."[28]

The following days seemed to support his bold claim. By 9 August, vanguard units of Seventeenth Army had reached their first major objective: Krasnodar, the oil refining city on the Kuban River's north bank. Four infantry divisions moved up and took the city, strongly supported by *Fliegerkorps IV*. "Bombers," Richthofen noted on the 8th, "performed extremely well against thick enemy columns there." The infantry footsloggers had made impressive progress. In blazing heat, they had covered thirty miles per day as they marched past seemingly endless fields of sunflowers.[29] On the opposite flank, panzer and mobile units of Fortieth Panzer Corps had swept through Voroshilovsk and on to Pyatigorsk, 425 kilometers southeast of Rostov. They captured the city the following day and rumbled into the Caucasus foothills. Between these two groups, the Third Panzer Corps crossed the Kuban River, took Armavir, and bore down upon Maikop, the first of Hitler's great "oil objectives."[30] On the evening of 9 August, the 13th Panzer Division stormed the city, took around a thousand prisoners, and captured fifty undamaged aircraft.

The Führer's initial joy at Maikop's seizure was shared by many of his cohorts. According to Ciano's diary, Mussolini "attributes a great deal of importance" to its capture. It will have the effect, the Italian foreign minister wrote, "of relieving the Axis, but not immediately, and not altogether, of the pressing oil problem."[31] However, their delight soon turned to bitter disappointment when they learned that Soviet rear guards had already destroyed hundreds of wells, wrecked oil storage facilities, and crippled the refineries by removing vital components.[32] Although this was always a likely result, the damage was far more extensive than the Axis leaders had naïvely hoped. Twelve days after the city fell, the inspector of air defenses reported that only two oil wells were "capable of being developed for use. One well is still burning, although it may soon be possible to extinguish the fire. The other wells have been rendered useless by having cement poured down the bores."[33] The Soviets had also destroyed the large refinery in Krasnodar, he added.

Bringing Maikop back into production would be difficult and time-consuming. At the end of August, Georg Thomas, head of the War Economy and Armaments Office, noted in his monthly situation report that "only insignificant amounts of mineral oil were found" when Maikop fell.[34] The extensive damage inflicted on extraction and processing installations and the sporadic fighting still taking place in the region made it impossible at the moment to conduct a thorough investigation of the oil field. Yet only after specialists conducted such an investigation, Thomas pointed out, could they determine how soon and to what degree the field could be exploited.

On 8 September—that is, a month after German troops first entered the Maikop oil field, choking on thick smoke billowing from burning storage tanks— Dr. Schlicht of the *Mineralöl Brigade* reported to Thomas on progress at Maikop.[35] Difficult terrain—"extremely suitable for partisan warfare"—prevented the transportation of cumbersome drilling equipment, at least until new transportation routes could be created. In the meantime, Schlicht said, German specialists had to determine which wells would be easiest to unblock. This would not be simple; the Soviets had inflicted massive damage, even to pipelines. "Until now," he emphasized, "only 4,000 cubic meters of oil stocks have been uncovered. It will take at least another six months until regular production can resume." Accordingly, "It is essential we give the *Reichsmarschall* [Göring, still plenipotentiary of the Four-Year Plan and, in effect, Germany's economics dictator] a completely accurate picture of Maikop." Göring's understanding of the situation, he added, was grossly overoptimistic: "Questions are already being raised about whether the southern army groups can now be supplied with fuel directly from Maikop."

Schlicht was right: Göring's grasp of matters relating to oil production was extremely weak. For instance, two months later, on 21 November, he presided over an oil conference in Berlin. Maikop, which had yet to produce oil for Axis troops (and never would, except a few dribbles), remained at the forefront of his mind. "I'm fed up!" he exclaimed. "Months have passed since we captured the first oil wells, yet we still aren't getting any benefit."[36] He astounded his audience of technical experts when, referring to the concrete plugs dropped down the bores, he naïvely demanded to know: "Can't you just drill them out with something like a gigantic corkscrew?"

After Krasnodar and Maikop fell, Richthofen believed that Soviet forces in the Caucasus were finished. On 11 August, he noted in his diary: "My impression is still this: the Russian southern army is destroyed. Parts of it are in rout along the Grusinian Army Road [that is, beyond the Caucasus Mountains]." On the other hand, Sixth Army now faced stiff resistance, both in the air and on the ground, as it closed in on Stalingrad. Accordingly, the air commander decided that Stalingrad must now be his fleet's new *Schwerpunkt*.[37] This decision was doubtless influenced by his meeting with Jeschonnek on 10 August, when the Luftwaffe chief of the general staff emphasized Hitler's growing infatuation with Stalin's "own" city.

To create this new point of maximum effort, Fiebig's *Fliegerkorps VIII* would direct all its efforts against Stalingrad and Soviet forces fanatically defending its approaches. Moreover, Pflugbeil's *Fliegerkorps IV* would also send most of its bomber and dive-bomber groups north from the Caucasus, where they were no longer needed. "I'm ordering unusual things," Richthofen stated, "and mixing up all the units! All the main forces of the fleet are going there." He was not exaggerating. As well as transferring many of Pflugbeil's combat units to Fiebig's corps, he ordered the fleet's signals and logistics teams to organize a Stalingrad "transport region," handling a massive 3,000 tons of supplies per day. This tonnage included not only bombs, ammunition, spares, and provisions for the Luftwaffe's own substantial consumption but also the same items for the army's even-greater consumption. To carry this large tonnage, he also stripped Pflugbeil of most of his transport planes. Aircraft alone could not carry these supplies, of course, so he ordered all the fleet's road transport companies, including those in the Caucasus, to the Stalingrad region.

On 15 August, Richthofen held a conference in Rostov, attended by the senior staff of Air District Rostov, which organized his fleet's supply and maintenance matters.[38] He promptly ordered General Vierling to the Stalingrad region to run the new "transport region" and demanded much greater effort by all technicians and transport personnel. That evening he outlined in his diary the main topics discussed during the conference:

[I asked] how things stand with my previous orders for the movement of all transports to the Stalingrad region, in order to ensure that our bomber formations (and, of course, the rest of the fleet) can operate there. Because the railway running east from Stalino [where the last railhead was situated] is no longer usable, we shall have to transport our supplies and equipment a further 350 kilometers ourselves. [It's] a really difficult problem, and a new one, since the rule was always that bomber formations can *only* be supplied by rail. . . . These folk seemed mildly astonished by what I said. I actually felt quite sorry for them, because apparently no one has ever spoken to them like this before.

Richthofen made one other major change to the fleet's command and operational structure at this time. After successfully seeking *OKL* permission, he disbanded *Fliegerführer Süd* on 9 August. It was no longer necessary to have a separate air command in the Crimea, he reasoned, especially now that *Fliegerkorps IV* was moving its headquarters and bomber units there (they arrived at Kerch the same day he dissolved Wild's command). Accordingly, he ordered Pflugbeil simply to take over Wild's units and incorporate them into his corps.

Wild's command had existed for only six months and never had the resources necessary to carry out successfully the wide range of tasks the fleet assigned it. Still, his units had every reason to be proud of their achievements. They had conducted 3,481 air operations, involving 16,626 individual sorties.[39] Their attacks on Soviet shipping achieved good results, considering their limited strength and the difficulty of destroying vessels from the air. They sank—if their kill claims are accurate—68 freighters (together weighing 131,500 tons), a flotilla leader, 2 destroyers, a submarine chaser, 3 submarines, and a variety of smaller warships and merchantmen. They damaged even more vessels than they sank.

Their army support missions were as successful as their antinaval operations. They reported destroying 510 trucks, 280 motor vehicles, 65 tanks, 30 artillery pieces, 11 artillery batteries, 11 fortified gun implacements, 8 trains, 4 locomotives, and a variety of bunkers, installations, buildings, bridges, and railway lines. Perhaps more important, they continuously and systematically reconnoitered the entire Crimea–Caucasus–Black Sea region, clocking up 462 long-range operations alone.

Fliegerführer Süd's impact on local fighting far outweighed the material damage it inflicted on the enemy. It contributed substantially to Axis defensive battles, when Soviet forces attempted to break out of Sevastopol and the Kerch Peninsula, and then to Axis *offensive* battles, when Axis troops attempted to break *into* those areas. First, by bombing and strafing exposed troops, tanks, motor vehicles, and field fortifications, *Fliegerführer Süd* provided the army with reasonable air support on the battlefield. Second, its small-scale but systematic interdiction operations disrupted enemy land and sea supply efforts. Third, by carrying out constant surveillance of Crimean and Black Sea coasts and attacking enemy forces at likely embarkation points, it gathered valuable information on Soviet strengths and movements and prevented further enemy amphibious landings. Finally, its small but frequent and aggressive attacks on enemy warships at sea as well as in port persuaded the Soviet naval command to not attempt major operations.

Wild, prominent in all recent air activities in the Crimea and the Black Sea, leaves our study at this point. Although he had performed extremely well in recent months, he failed to win Richthofen's confidence. His career was far from over, however. The *OKL* soon transferred him to Athens, where he served as Air Transport Commander I (Southeast). He held various other important Luftwaffe posts and, finally promoted to *Generalmajor* on 1 March 1945, ended the war as air attaché in Tokyo. I have no knowledge of Wild's postwar career.

Even before *Fliegerkorps IV* set up its headquarters in Kerch—and before it sent most of its combat groups to the Stalingrad theater—it launched its last ever major air campaign in the Caucasus: a series of heavy bombing raids on Soviet ports along the Caucasus coast, especially those in which Oktyabrskii's fleet lay berthed. These raids commenced on 6 August and continued daily until 19 August, the day British Air Ministry intelligence officers (closely following events from Enigma decrypts) reported the following in their secret *Weekly Intelligence Summary:*

"Air operations have increased somewhat in the North Caucasus, where attacks have been made on shipping, including naval vessels, and on harbor installations at the Black Sea ports, while support has been given to the German army in its thrust towards the ports and to the south along the line Krasnodar-Maikop-Pyatigorsk."[40]

According to the Luftwaffe's historical branch, Pflugbeil's units "carried out attacks in front of our own panzer spearheads, against marching columns as well as transport movements and embarkations along the Black Sea coast."[41] These "transport movements" and "embarkations" were actually large-scale Soviet evacuations from positions along the eastern shore of the Sea of Azov and on the Taman Peninsula. When Dumitrescu's Rumanian Third Army—led by its outstanding 5th Cavalry Division—drove swiftly south along the shore toward the ports of Jeisk and Primorsko-Akhtarskaya, Rear Admiral Gorshkov's Azov Flotilla hastily evacuated 4,000 men and much valuable equipment. Suffering from both German minefields and air attack, small boats carried them through the Kerch Straits to Tuapse and other "safe" ports along the Caucasus coast.[42] Similarly, when the German Fifth Army Corps swung west toward Novorossiisk, warships, transport vessels, and small freighters began evacuating personnel and equipment to ports farther south.[43] Marshal Budenny, Soviet commander in the northern Caucasus, evacuated these ports not only by sea but also by land. Trains, trucks, and wagons carrying troops and equipment jammed all railways and roads leading south. Like the naval convoys, they made perfect targets for German aircraft.

Pflugbeil threw every available bomber into battle against the evacuation fleets and rail and road convoys. Fighters provided protection not only by escorting them in flight but also, joined by Stukas and ground-attack aircraft, by hitting enemy airfields and flak batteries. *VVS* forces in the northwestern Caucasus were outclassed and vastly outnumbered; as a result, they lost many aircraft in the air and on the ground. However, most units still managed to withdraw the majority of their aircraft to airfields in the central and southern Caucasus. From those airfields, they would later gain revenge.

Fliegerkorps IV's bombing attacks—the Luftwaffe's last substantial operations in the Caucasus—produced pleasing results. Every day between 7 and 19 August, air units destroyed several vessels and hundreds of vehicles and killed numerous troops caught in the open. On 9 August, for example, *Fliegerführer Süd* (joined by two further bomber groups on its final day of operations) alone reported destroying 108 trucks, heavily damaging many others, smashing seven trains, wrecking much railway equipment, sinking a 4,000-ton freighter, and badly damaging three others.[44]

Although Pflugbeil's airmen achieved their greatest successes against rail and road targets, which they destroyed in heavy raids, they still performed well against Soviet evacuation convoys at sea. On 10 August, they reported sinking eleven transport vessels, together weighing 12,700 tons, and damaging nine others.[45] The following day, they sank two transport vessels, two coastal traders, and a patrol boat, and damaged another seven vessels. Two days later, they sank more ships and gutted a forty-five-strong Soviet air formation, allowing only ten planes to return to base.

Despite this excellent kill rate, which caused Oktyabrskii intense concern about his fleet's safety, Richthofen could not allow Pflugbeil to continue these antishipping operations for long. He needed urgently to transfer *Fliegerkorps IV*'s bombers and most other aircraft north to the Stalingrad sector. Accordingly, the operations came to a halt on 19 August, after several equally successful days (only the previous day, for instance, Pflugbeil's airmen had sunk a destroyer and four coastal traders and badly damaged six transport vessels and eight other coastal traders).[46] Everything must now be focused on Stalingrad, Richthofen stated in his diary that evening. "The enemy there is increasingly stronger and fights with more determination." In the Caucasus, he added, "the enemy is completely trapped. That's why we [that is, most of *Fliegerkorps IV*'s combat units] are departing from there for a while."

On 20 August, the air fleet chief actually told List that he regretted having to transfer the bulk of Pflugbeil's air corps, "except for very small remnants," to Stalingrad. The decision came from Hitler, he explained, so he had no choice. Trying to reassure the army group commander, he added that he might be able to begin transferring units back to the Caucasus "in six to ten days."[47] Although he made a similar promise to Kleist eleven days later ("we'll be returning as quickly and strongly as possible"),[48] no units would ever permanently return to the Caucasus from Stalingrad. They would be swallowed up by the airlift to support the doomed Sixth Army.

Units began flying northeast to the Stalingrad region as soon as their supply and maintenance staff prepared them for the long flight and the fleet's command staff found bases for them. The 51st Bomber Wing flew north on 16 August, even before attacks on Black Sea ports and shipping ceased, while most others left on 19, 20, and 21 August.[49] Reduced to two bomber and a few Stuka, ground-attack, fighter, and reconnaissance units, *Fliegerkorps IV* no longer possessed the ability to affect decisively the outcome of battles in the Caucasus or even to conduct systematic interdiction in the enemy's rear areas.

THE OIL FIELDS: SO CLOSE BUT YET SO FAR

By the time most of *Fliegerkorps IV*'s combat units departed for Stalingrad, List's twenty-one divisions in the Caucasus were advancing along a front of more than 500 kilometers. The field marshal had shuffled his forces, shifting a panzer corps (the Fifty-seventh) from First Panzer Army to help Seventeenth Army, and then sent them on diverging paths. On the left flank, Kleist's First Panzer Army was proceeding southeast. It aimed to cross the Terek River, seize the Grozny oil fields, breach the mountains, and finally take Baku, Hitler's oil "Mecca." *Armeegruppe Ruoff,* on the right flank, was now advancing in three separate columns, each with its own objective. The Fifth Corps aimed for Novorossiisk, a major naval base situated slightly south of the Taman Peninsula. Mountain troops still in the Crimea were preparing to advance across the Kerch Straits and join the attack. The Fifty-seventh Panzer Corps was on its way past Maikop toward Tuapse, another naval base on the Black Sea. The two divisions of the Forty-ninth Mountain Corps were pushing past Armavir, hoping to cross passes through the main mountain range and descend upon Sukhumi, a naval base south of Tuapse.

By the last week of August, the pace of Army Group A's advances had dropped dramatically. Not only had the terrain become more difficult, but Soviet resistance had stiffened. Even more important, supplies, especially of oil and gasoline, had become alarmingly inadequate. The Wehrmacht's logistical route in southern Russia consisted of a single railway running eastward across the Ukraine to Stalino. From there aircraft and trucks carried supplies to Army Group B in the Stalingrad region, 350 kilometers to the east.[50] However, after Richthofen's recent reorganization of the air fleet, Pflugbeil had no aircraft and very few Luftwaffe trucks available to carry supplies to Army Group A in the Caucasus, which had units dispersed along a front over 750 kilometers away. The cessation of airlifts to those units had a sudden and profound impact on List's advance. The army had its own trucks, but nowhere near enough to transport sufficient fuel, ammunition, and provisions for spearhead units to advance at the speed the Führer demanded. Also, the distance between the last railhead and those vanguards, each with its own supply line, had become so great that the army's truck columns themselves consumed a large portion of the fuel allotted to the forces at the front. Supply personnel attempted to ship supplies forward on Soviet railways but had very little rolling stock. German wagons were in short supply and, in any event, could not be used because of different rail gauges. They also had few undamaged or repaired stretches of line on which to operate. With no aircraft and not enough trucks, they became even more reliant than usual on their horses and mules. Although they had tens of thousands of each, animals were slow and consumed vast quantities of fodder, which was scarce in the desertlike steppes of the northern Caucasus.[51]

By the end of August, Army Group A's spearheads were advancing at a snail's pace: three or four kilometers per day if they were lucky. To Hitler's disgust, List began arguing that, unless his forces received reinforcements, fuel, and air support, they would soon have to take up winter positions.[52] Richthofen felt powerless to help, at least until Stalingrad fell, when he could probably shift his fleet's *Schwerpunkt* back to the Caucasus. Until then, List's forces could expect no airlifts of fuel or supplies. Moreover, their wide dispersion across the width of the Caucasus prevented Pflugbeil's air corps—now weaker than Wild's *Fliegerführer Süd* had been in May—from offering more than token combat assistance. "The armies are so widely stretched out," he penned on the last day of the month, "that we cannot create a single point of maximum effort. . . . Because we now have only extremely weak forces there, we're no longer able to have significant influence."

The only units making satisfactory progress in this period were the 1st and

4th Mountain Divisions, which fought their way through heavy snow and icy winds and seized several 3,000-meter-high passes through the supposedly impregnable Caucasus range. On 21 August, one detachment even scaled majestic, glacier-clad Mount Elbrus, the highest mountain in the Caucasus, and planted the swastika-emblazoned Reich war flag *(Reichskriegsflagge)* on its 5,633-meter-high summit. However, after clambering along almost 200 kilometers of precipitous mountain paths and finally reaching the foothills on the other side of the range, the mountain troops' advance petered out only 20 kilometers from Sukhumi, their coastal objective. They had expected ammunition and provisions to be dropped from aircraft, but Pflugbeil had none to spare. They had also expected units of the Italian Alpine Corps to follow them, bringing supplies by pack animal, but that corps was not behind them; it was 1,000 kilometers away, advancing toward Stalingrad. They had also hoped to encounter little resistance as they descended into the foothills but found instead that strong Soviet forces guarded the exits from the mountains. Thus, worn out by weeks of exhausting marching and climbing at high altitudes, and desperately needing ammunition and provisions, they lacked the strength to descend from the foothills onto the coastal plain.

The activities of these mountain troops were carefully monitored at Hitler's headquarters. The Führer had repeatedly demanded that they strike through the Caucasus to the Black Sea port of Sukhumi as quickly as possible. The seizure of this port—coupled with the capture of Novorossiisk and Tuapse, which Seventeenth Army looked set to take from the north—would cripple Oktyabrskii's fleet, enabling *Admiral Schwarzes Meer* to ferry troops and much-needed supplies across the Kerch Straits.[53] Accordingly, the War Lord exploded when told that his troops had scaled Elbrus (an act with absolutely no military worth and only slight propaganda value) but had failed to reach the coast. As Albert Speer recalled:

> I often saw Hitler furious but seldom did his anger erupt from him as it did when this report came in. For hours he raged as if his entire plan of the campaign had been ruined by this bit of sport. Days later he went on railing to all and sundry about "those crazy mountain climbers" who "belong before a court-martial." They were pursuing their idiotic hobbies in the midst of a war, he exclaimed indignantly, occupying an idiotic peak even though he had commanded that all efforts must be concentrated upon Sukhumi.[54]

Logistical breakdowns, not the time wasted climbing Elbrus, prevented the mountain troops from taking the Black Sea ports, as Hitler probably realized once he cooled down. It made no difference; his troops failed to accomplish the task he set them. His other forces in the Caucasus fared no better. Hampered by acute fuel and ammunition shortages, *Generalleutnant* Leo Geyr von Schweppenburg's Fortieth Panzer Corps (of First Panzer Army) made slow progress as it pushed on toward Grozny, which it was supposed to secure before rolling south to Baku. The swift and deep Terek River, with its high and rocky southern bank, superbly protected Grozny's otherwise-vulnerable oil fields. Determined to keep those fields out of German clutches, local Soviet forces—the Ninth and Forty-fourth Armies of the North Group, Transcaucasian Front—carefully dug themselves in behind the Terek.[55] They also requested and received additional *VVS* air units, which began operating from airfields around Grozny in the last week of August.

Pflugbeil dispatched the 3rd Group of the 52nd Fighter Wing to support the Fortieth Panzer Corps as it attempted to capture Mosdok, cross the Terek, and push southward to Grozny. On 20 August, the group had a total complement of forty-three Bf 109s, of which twenty-eight (65 percent) were serviceable.[56] Considering that Richthofen's fleet as a whole had only 58 percent of its aircraft serviceable—virtually the same amount as the previous month—this fighter group remained in good shape (at least by the standards of the eastern front).[57] However, its operations were severely curtailed most days by fuel and ammunition shortages. Accordingly, it proved incapable of preventing strong Soviet air attacks on Schweppenburg's troops. Enemy air superiority in this region, Wilhelm Tieke recalled, "was crushing."[58]

At the time, Tieke fumed over the Luftwaffe's poor showing. German fighters rarely appeared over the Terek front, and usually only after Soviet aircraft had done their damage and departed. After the war he sought reasons for this and received a letter from *Major* Gordon Gollob, the fighter group's commander, who stated: "It might interest you to know that on the Terek front sector there were no more than four aircraft operational at any one time. . . . We lacked aircraft, we lacked fuel, and ammunition was in short supply. We had to organize ourselves into the smallest groups possible, therefore, in order even to be able to reconnoiter the front." Tieke was apparently pacified: "The German Luftwaffe did all it could," he concluded. Indeed, Gollob's group achieved acceptable results, considering the paltry number of aircraft it managed to get airborne each day. Between 14 and 29 August, during which time army spearheads captured Mosdok and advanced to the Terek, *III./J.G. 52* claimed thirty-two enemy aircraft destroyed.[59]

With bearable losses, Soviet air units continuously attacked pontoon bridges erected across the Terek, sometimes inflicting considerable damage. Despite the *VVS*'s increasingly stiff resistance, matched by that of the Ninth and Forty-fourth Armies—the latter led, incidentally, by General Petrov, the former Sevastopol garrison commander—Schweppenburg's troops succeeded in crossing the river on 2 September and began inching forward toward Grozny. However, their progress throughout the first half of September remained extremely slow and their losses high, largely due to virtually unopposed *VVS* forces. Vladimir Karpov recalled that "convergent Soviet ground and air strikes prevented their breakthrough."[60] Aside from a few aerial victories each day (Gollob, an ace of considerable renown, scored his 150th in this period), *III./J.G. 52* could do little to help them.

On the western flank, meanwhile, Dumitrescu's Rumanian Third Army advanced southwestward along the eastern shore of the Sea of Azov toward the Taman Peninsula. Seventeenth Army pushed southwestward from Krasnodar and Maikop, across the northwestern Caucasus foothills, towards Novorossiisk and Tuapse. Marshal Budenny, commander of the Soviet Northern Caucasus Front, was determined to prevent Dumitrescu from taking the strategically important Taman Peninsula, knowing that without it the Germans would be unable to move reinforcements and supplies across the Kerch Straits. Budenny was also determined to stop Ruoff from seizing the Black Sea naval bases farther south. On 17 August, therefore, he established the Novorossiisk Defense Region, comprising Forty-seventh Army, Gorshkov's Azov Flotilla, the Temryuk, Kerch, and Novorossiisk naval bases, and a composite *VVS* force.[61] These forces, he prayed, would be able to do what no others had so far since *Blau* began: withstand a major Axis offensive *without* abandoning ground.

Budenny's hopes were realized, but not for several weeks. In the meantime, the Rumanian Cavalry Corps humiliated the Soviet Forty-seventh Army in the Taman region.[62] It stormed Slavyanskaya, where the Soviets had attempted to make a stand, repulsed a counteroffensive across the Kuban River, and captured the small port of Temryuk. It then crossed the Kuban and made a rapid thrust to the heights of Nassurovo on the Black Sea coast. There it captured two batteries of Soviet 15-cm heavy guns, which it turned on the port of Anapa, shattering its defenses. To Richthofen's delight, the Cavalry Corps captured Anapa on 31 August. The air leader immediately telephoned Dumitrescu to offer his heartiest congratulations.[63]

Dumitrescu had achieved these tasks without Luftwaffe assistance, his only air support coming from his own very small, inadequately trained, and poorly equipped *Escadrilas* (air squadrons). Although they belonged nominally to Pflugbeil's emaciated *Fliegerkorps IV* and relied on its support services, they operated as an independent group *(Grup Aerian de Lupta),* supporting only Rumanian ground forces. The few *Escadrilas* in the Caucasus employed obsolete aircraft, which could take to the skies only in areas with little or no *VVS* opposition. *Escadrilas 2, 112,* and *114* attempted to meet the Rumanian army's reconnaissance and communication needs with eight early-model German Dornier 17 "Flying Pencil" bombers and twenty-four even older Rumanian-made U.S. Fleet 10G trainer biplanes.[64] *Escadrila 17,* with six underpowered Rumanian *IAR 39* tactical reconnaissance biplanes, supported its divisions on the battlefield by monitoring enemy movements, directing artillery fire, and dropping small bombs.

By capturing the Taman Peninsula (except for one isolated pocket of resistance), the Rumanians had finally closed the Sea of Azov to Soviet shipping and driven out Gorshkov's flotilla. In the last days of August and the first of September, that flotilla mined Azovian ports to prevent their exploitation by Axis forces and broke through the Kerch Straits, evacuating as many weapons and pieces of equipment as possible.[65] It also evacuated army and navy infantry units on the southern coast of the Taman Peninsula to Novorossiisk.

Admiral Schwarzes Meer's small Italian and German flotillas in the Crimea attempted to stop those operations.[66] However, these forces still possessed few serviceable MTBs, the weather was poor, and, most important, Pflugbeil had very few aircraft available to provide cover and conduct supporting raids. Under the circumstances, their attacks on Soviet vessels and embarkation points inflicted satisfactory damage—they sank almost 20,000 tons of shipping between 30 August and 2 September—but they failed to prevent the successful completion of most evacuation operations.[67]

News of the Taman Peninsula's capture was welcomed at Hitler's headquarters. It cleared the way for *Admiral Schwarzes Meer* to begin Operation *Blücher II*, the transportation of the urgently needed Rumanian 3rd Mountain and German 46th Infantry Divisions across the Kerch Straits. For the last week or so, Hitler had constantly complained about delays in transporting them from the Crimea, delays his advisers blamed on rough seas and lack of air support. Sick of what he wrongly called "excuses," on 29 August the Führer ordered the forces to travel by land around the Sea of Azov to the Caucasus.[68] He changed his mind the following day, demanding that they cross the straits immediately, "regardless of the weather and, if necessary, without support by the air force."[69]

Admiral Schwarzes Meer's assault craft and transport barges ferried the divisions across the straits during the night of 1 and 2 September.[70] MTBs, minesweepers, and the small Luftwaffe force Pflugbeil hastily threw together for the task (apparently including aircraft temporarily diverted from the Stalingrad sector)[71] provided protection against enemy attacks. They were hardly needed; Soviet warships and aircraft kept away. For the next few months, Axis naval vessels and a few of Pflugbeil's fighters routinely patrolled the sea-lanes and airspace around the Kerch Straits, protecting *Admiral Schwarzes Meer*'s supply squadrons as they transported fuel, ammunition, and provisions across the straits. In the first two weeks alone (easily the busiest period), they ferried 30,605 men, 13,254 horses, and 6,265 motor vehicles to the Caucasus.[72]

Reinforced and possessing excellent jumping-off positions, *Armeegruppe Ruoff* looked set to take Novorossiisk, then advance down the Black Sea coast, knocking off one naval base after another. However, to Marshal Budenny's relief, Ruoff's Seventeenth Army made much slower progress than the Rumanians recently had. After Pflugbeil's bombers and the bulk of his Stukas and ground-attack aircraft departed for Stalingrad, Ruoff's army received only weak air support. Budenny, who pulled the bulk of Forty-seventh Army back to Novorossiisk, where it dug in and prepared to hold the port at all costs, noticed the absence of strong Luftwaffe forces and called *VVS* units back to the region. Although these units were unable to gain air superiority, at least initially, they made life difficult for Pflugbeil's aircrews, whose operations they frequently interrupted, and for

Ruoff's troops, whose antiaircraft guns and batteries were too dispersed to offer concentrated firepower.

Budenny also brought back tens of thousands of troops previously withdrawn to the south. Oktyabrskii, whose courage steadily waxed as *Fliegerkorps IV*'s strength waned, organized the troop transfers from his headquarters in Poti. His warships, including destroyers, cruisers, and a flotilla leader, carried reinforcements and equipment from Poti to Tuapse and Gelenyik, a small port thirty-five kilometers south of Novorossiisk. Pflugbeil's reconnaissance units, still carefully monitoring all enemy movements and photographing the Caucasian ports each day, immediately detected the troop transfers. His few bombers and dive-bombers carried out nightly attacks on the harbor facilities at Gelenyik, desperately hoping to stop or at least significantly hamper them.[73] Lacking adequate bomber forces, they failed miserably. The Soviet reinforcements from Poti, as well as those evacuated from ports on the Sea of Azov and the Taman Peninsula, arrived safely and immediately dug themselves in behind Novorossiisk. Budenny was determined to hold the coastal road to Tuapse, Sukhumi, and Batumi. Even if Novorossiisk fell, and he hoped it would not, he would stop the Axis advance along the Black Sea coast.

General der Infanterie Wetzel's Fifth Army Corps fought fanatically and suffered terrible losses as it crossed the wooded northwestern Caucasus foothills and reached the outskirts of Novorossiisk, stubbornly defended by its naval garrison and the Soviet Forty-seventh Army. Vanguards broke into the port on 6 September, but it took four days of furious and costly house-to-house fighting before Wetzel could announce the city's capture.[74] This was List's final victory in the Caucasus and, even then, it was not a total victory: strong Soviet forces still held the heights behind the port and the strategically important coastal road. Wetzel's repeated attempts to push out of Novorossiisk's southern suburbs and drive southward failed. They resulted in heavy casualties, especially to the Rumanian 3rd Mountain Division, which was almost wiped out in a Soviet counterattack on 25 and 26 September.[75] Although Axis forces managed to contain that attack, they could do little more than stabilize the front. They clearly lacked the strength to dislodge enemy forces stubbornly holding the coastal plain between Novorossiisk and Tuapse.

Those Soviet forces also thwarted repeated attempts by elements of Fifty-seventh Panzer Corps and Forty-fourth *Jäger* (Light Infantry) Corps to break through the thickly forested hills protecting Tuapse. List wanted to reinforce them with the bulk of Forty-ninth Mountain Corps. Some of that corps' units were still fighting their way through high mountain passes in the main Caucasus range while others were struggling unsuccessfully to descend from the foothills to Sukhumi, their tantalizingly close goal. Believing that these mountain units were too weak to achieve their allotted tasks, the field marshal wanted to withdraw them all, except for enough troops to keep the passes in German hands, and deploy them more usefully against Tuapse.

On 7 September, he requested a visit to his Stalino headquarters by Jodl, the *OKW*'s operations chief, so that he could describe the situation and outline his plans. The latter immediately flew east, talked at length with List, and returned to Hitler's headquarters in the evening. Jodl had often given unpopular advice but seldom stood up to his domineering boss. Explaining this, he once told Halder that he always remembered what his grandmother had told his mother on her wedding day: "In matrimony the husband is always right! And if he says, 'The water's running uphill today,' my answer is, 'Yuh, Yuh, it's up there already!' "[76] Yet Jodl was also an honorable man, unwilling to abandon a colleague to unfair attack. He gathered his courage and informed Hitler that List's assessment was correct: the mountain troops were incapable of completing their assigned missions so they should instead be deployed against Tuapse. He bravely added that List's costly and unsuccessful recent actions had been faithfully carried out according to Hitler's own orders and directives. The field marshal could not, therefore, be blamed for their failure. The Führer exploded. He accused Jodl of disloyalty, dismissed List, and announced to his stunned entourage that he would take personal charge of Army Group A.

Jodl, Hitler's most trusted paladin, clearly hurt the War Lord's feelings by siding with List. For several months, the Führer refused to shake his hand, and he never again ate with his generals. Also, to ensure that no one accused him of issuing orders he never gave, he brought in a team of stenographers to take down every word at military briefings and conferences. Tormented by the heat and a growing realization that his Caucasus campaign was almost over, and filled with disappointment, mistrust, and anger at his general staff, he directed his hostility toward Halder, whom he repeatedly accused of lacking National Socialist ardor and finally sacked two weeks later. He replaced him with Kurt Zeitzler, the forty-seven-year-old chief of staff of a western army group. Zeitzler was not only a fervent Nazi but also a dynamic leader with exceptional organizational abilities, an assertive manner, and boundless energy that earned him the nickname "Thunderball" *(Kugelblitz)*.

Neither Zeitzler's "thunder" nor Hitler's long-distance command of exhausted Army Group South compensated for the group's acute shortages of supplies, reinforcements, and air support. As autumn wind and rain replaced summer sun, the Caucasus campaign steadily petered out, with only very minor changes in the line occurring after the middle of September. By early October, Axis forces were barely moving—and barely surviving, in many cases, due to fierce resistance and shortages of fuel and provisions. Yet, although they almost had Grozny, they were still nowhere near achieving Hitler's major campaign goals. On the left flank, First Panzer Army had managed to push across the Terek River and inch forward toward Grozny before determined Soviet divisions, supported by squadrons of the Fourth Air Army's deadly Shturmoviks, blunted their advance. On the right flank, Seventeenth Army's infantry had held Novorossiisk, despite several small Soviet counterattacks, but failed to break through to Tuapse and the other ports in the south. The army's mountain troops, meanwhile, had abandoned their advance against Sukhumi when snow and rain cut their logistical route through the high mountain passes.

THE LUFTWAFFE IN THE CAUCASUS, MID-AUGUST TO LATE-NOVEMBER

Pflugbeil's stripped-to-the-bones air corps had supported the army as often and strongly as it could, but its efforts after late August made little impact on the ground war. "Field Marshal" Hitler's divisions were too dispersed and Pflugbeil's air units too weak for the latter to create a single *Schwerpunkt*. Instead, he did the only thing he could under the circumstances: split his quarter-strength air "corps" into separate formations, each assigned to a particular army corps or operational group.

The air corps commander deployed a very small air formation in support of the 16th Motorized Infantry Division as it advanced alone across the Kalmuck Steppe toward Astrakhan in order to close the exposed gap between Army Groups A and B and protect First Panzer Army's vulnerable flank. The small Luftwaffe combat force supporting this division, which advanced in fits and spurts because of frequent fuel shortages, seldom participated in combat missions but provided a fair amount of reconnaissance information. It lacked the strength to do more, possessing at the end of September only one Me 110, four Bf 109s, a few FW 189 twin-fuselage surveillance planes, and a few DFS 230 transport gliders.[77] The latter, towed by Hs 126s, supplied both air and army troops.

Fearing a large-scale amphibious operation by Vice Admiral Oktyabrskii's Black Sea Fleet now that he had few forces to throw against one, Pflugbeil deployed most of his long-range reconnaissance aircraft on the same missions they had carried out when part of *Fliegerführer Süd:* constant surveillance of shipping movements and Black Sea ports.[78] These aircraft (mostly Ju 88s) carried out "armed reconnaissance" *(bewaffnete Seeaufklärung),* which means that, where possible, they attacked the objects under surveillance. They frequently hit ports and occasionally vessels, although they rarely inflicted substantial damage on either.[79] When conditions permitted and sufficient aircraft could be gathered together, which was not often, Pflugbeil ordered heavier attacks on the ports and ships.

Fliegerkorps IV's attacks on Oktyabrskii's fleet were far too few and weak to satisfy either *Admiral Schwarzes Meer* or *Marine-Gruppenkommando Süd,* its parent command. They had been constantly nagging *Luftflotte 4* to destroy the enemy fleet in massive bombing raids, a task it no longer had the means to accomplish. On 11 September, for example, they requested *Luftflotte 4* and Army Group A—which would have to do without air support during the proposed raids on the fleet—to "paralyze the enemy by air attacks."[80] Two days later, the German naval command received a disappointing reply: Army Group A was so desperate for air support on and behind the battlefield that it could not spare aircraft for large-scale attacks against the enemy fleet. "The time to concentrate on the Russian fleet," the army's communiqué bluntly stated, "will come only when weather conditions deteriorate."[81] As it happened, that time never came; a month later, in early October, the naval command was still asking for "concentrated air attacks on the principal bases of the Russian Fleet" but already realized that there was "little hope of this until the German Air Force is free of other tasks"—unlikely in the near future.[82] In early November, *Admiral Schwarzes Meer* pointed out to *Luftflotte 4*'s Crimean staff that recent reconnaissance revealed "a heavy concentration of shipping in Poti and Batumi. The entire Russian Fleet is concentrated in those two ports, offering an unusually good target to the Air Force." The navy received the reply it expected: "Air Force Staff, Crimea stated that at present no planes were available for this task."[83] Strangely, even after the Soviets launched their massive Stalingrad counteroffensive later in November, causing Richthofen to transfer *Fliegerkorps IV*'s remaining bombers north to that sector (leaving none in the Crimea and Caucasus), the navy continued asking for air attacks on Black Sea ports.

Before the Stalingrad counteroffensive, Pflugbeil usually committed his two bomber groups, together with his dive-bomber and ground-attack groups, alternately (as need arose) in the combat zone of First Panzer Army in the eastern Caucasus and in that of Seventeenth Army in the western Caucasus. Fighters escorted these bombers and dive-bombers in both sectors. They also operated against *VVS* forces constantly pounding Axis airfields, naval bases, and army installations in the Crimea. Despite the best efforts of the few fighter groups stationed in and around the peninsula, enemy raids sometimes caused substantial damage.[84] These were not the fighters' only security missions; since *Admiral Schwarzes Meer* began transporting men and matériel across the Kerch Straits on 1 September, a small number also patrolled the airspace over those sea-lanes, searching for enemy air units attempting to disrupt this vital logistical route. The naval command pleaded for extra fighters and flak batteries, pointing out its recent losses of transport vessels to air attack. Yet Pflugbeil had no extra fighters or flak guns to give it. In the middle of September, he even took fighters away from those missions to help Ruoff's and Kleist's armies. *Marine-Gruppenkommando Süd* protested, arguing that "fighter protection in the Crimea [was] the minimum requirement" and stressing "the grave consequences for the conduct of the war of further losses of shipping space and escort duties."[85] Its protests achieved little; Pflugbeil returned only a handful of fighters to naval escort duties. He could spare no others. The exhausted and hard-pressed armies needed them far more than the navy.

In the middle of September, Pflugbeil's twin-engined bombers helped First Panzer Army stem a Soviet attack against its eastern flank and launch a small stabilizing attack of its own.[86] Their operations were seldom hampered by enemy aircraft, although the army suffered constant and costly Shturmovik attacks. Soviet air superiority in the Terek bend remained oppressive, despite *III./J.G. 52*'s valiant efforts to keep enemy ground-attack aircraft off Kleist's tanks and troops.[87]

Late in October, Pflugbeil directed all available bomber, dive-bomber, and ground-attack aircraft, which now needed constant fighter protection from enemy air attacks, to support a new offensive by First Panzer Army.[88] On 18 October, Kleist's Fifty-second Corps detected a weak spot in Soviet defenses at the western end of the Terek bend and, in a probing attack, made such good progress that the panzer commander decided to launch an all-out attack in that sector. Richthofen was determined to support the attack and temporarily made available to Pflugbeil several air groups from the Stalingrad area, including the 2nd Group of the 51st Bomber Wing.[89] The attack began on 25 October, with strong air and flak support, and initially made splendid gains.[90] German bombers contributed substantially to the battle on the first day, as the postwar official Soviet history attested: "In the morning of 25 October more than 100 enemy bombers attacked the 37th Army's formations. Simultaneously, German aviation subjected the Army's headquarters to a bombing which severed its communications with the units."[91] Spearheads of Third Panzer Corps quickly breached Soviet defenses and swept forward, to the relief and mounting excitement of Richthofen and Kleist. Joined for a while by Eberhard von Mackensen, the panzer corps' capable commander, they watched the action from what the air leader called a "really primitive" command post near the front.

The three commanders came under heavy Soviet artillery fire at one point and were in considerable danger until Luftwaffe bombers silenced the guns.[92] Then, when Richthofen returned to his sleeping quarters in Baksan, he found that bombers of the Soviet Fourth Air Army had totally gutted it and destroyed several planes sitting on airfields. In coming weeks, Soviet air attacks increased in both regularity and strength, and occasionally caused substantial damage. Wolfgang Dierich, the 51st Bomber Wing's postwar chronicler, described one particularly destructive raid on the Second Group's makeshift base at Armavir. Enemy aircraft, he lamented, scored a direct hit on the fuel dump, causing massive damage:

> There was a flash, and the flames spread to the fuelled and bombed-up aircraft. Since the field had several units on it, and was packed with more than a hundred Ju 88s and He 111s, there was no lack of combustible material. Only one of the *II Gruppe* aircraft survived without damage. The unit was forced to move back to Bagerovo on the Kerch Peninsula, to get a new set of aircraft.[93]

Despite occasional successes like this and "rolling attacks" on German infantry and panzer spearheads, *VVS* units proved incapable of stemming Third Panzer Corps' advance. On 28 October, the 13th Panzer and Rumanian 2nd

Mountain Divisions took the city of Nalchik, smashed several enemy divisions, and added another 7,000 prisoners to the 4,000 captured the previous day.[94] Luftwaffe forces, under Richthofen's personal command, were unable to operate in this sector on 28 and 29 October because of dense ground fog, so they carried out heavy raids on Tuapse instead.[95] They also conducted nightly raids on convoys in the Caspian Sea, sinking between 10,000 and 12,000 tons of merchant shipping each night.[96]

Even with minimal air support, Mackensen's divisions continued pushing forward toward their goal: Ordzhonikidze, the city guarding the entrance to the Grusinian Military Road. That road ran south through the main mountain range to Tbilisi, capital of Georgia. Its capture would make possible a rapid drive through the mountains to the oil-rich Baku region. On 30 October, the 23rd Panzer Division overcame tenacious resistance and captured the town of Chikola. The following day, the 13th and 23rd Panzer Divisions launched a joint attack through Digora toward Alagir, the city guarding the entrance to the Ossetian Military Road. This road ran southwest through the main mountain range to the Black Sea coast. Its capture would enable a rapid drive to the important Poti and Batumi naval bases. On 1 November, Digora fell. The panzer armies swept forward, the 13th Panzer Division toward Ardon, which it captured that night, and on toward Ordzhonikidze; the 23rd toward Alagir, which it took that day, before swinging west to join its sister division.

As these forces approached Ordzhonikidze (and by late on 2 November vanguards were within four kilometers of its western suburbs), Soviet resistance increased significantly. The North Group, Transcaucasian Front bolstered its battered Thirty-seventh Army with fresh reinforcements, including a guards rifle corps, two tank brigades, and five antitank artillery regiments.[97] The weather also took a dramatic turn for the worse, which not only sapped Axis troop morale but also hampered air operations. Pflugbeil's bombers and dive-bombers were able to attack Tuapse on 3 November, sinking around 14,000 tons of merchant shipping (a feat they repeated the following day).[98] Yet the weather in the central Caucasus prevented them from supporting Third Panzer Corps, which suffered high losses in men and equipment as it advanced a single kilometer through torrents of icy rain toward strongly defended Ordzhonikidze. That same day, Kleist, worried about his army's flagging strength and overextended supply lines, asked the *OKH* when he would get reinforcements.[99] He received no immediate answer. He drove his weary troops forward the following day, again without air support. They made small gains for heavy losses, as they did on 5 November and the following morning. If they could only muster their energy for one last push, the city would be theirs.

On 6 November, the weather improved, allowing Richthofen to throw all available air units into the fray. They conducted three massive raids against Ordzhonikidze and its stubborn defenders, but, to the air chief's dismay, German armored units failed to follow up the attack.[100] He quickly learned why: the North

Group, Transcaucasian Front had launched a well-timed and carefully aimed counteroffensive that swept in behind the 13th Panzer Division, trapping it and severing its supply route. Enemy forces also battered the 23rd Panzer Division, inflicting high losses and preventing it from relieving the 13th. Extremely bitter fighting took place over the next few days as Soviet forces attempted to tighten their stranglehold and German troops attempted to break it. Snowed in, the Luftwaffe was unable to help its encircled comrades. On 9 November, Richthofen complained in his diary: "No flying is possible here. . . . We can't even make telephone calls because the wires are iced up. There's not much to do. It's boring. We sleep a lot." That same day, a wide-awake and far from bored Mackensen finally ordered his trapped division to break out.[101] He sent forward strong forces, including the elite SS *Wiking* Division, to relieve the 13th Panzer Division. In the night of 11 and 12 November, the trapped division, including all its wounded but few of its vehicles and heavy guns, managed to break out and withdraw to safer positions behind a line formed by *Wiking* and the 23rd Panzer Division.

Kleist knew that his forces had taken a heavy beating (Third Panzer Corps alone lost 1,275 killed, 273 missing, and 5,008 wounded)[102] and were unable, at least immediately, to attack again. He called for reinforcements, which the *OKH* duly dispatched. In mid-November, however, the reinforcements had not yet arrived when a sudden drop in temperature brought a permanent end to all attempts to revive the operation. The Axis offensive toward Ordzhonikidze—the Führer's last attempt to capture Grozny and a route through the mountains to Baku—had failed dismally. Once again, Soviet forces had snatched a major prize from Hitler's grasping fingers before he could tighten his grip.

Ruoff's Seventeenth Army, meanwhile, had fared no better in its attempt to capture Tuapse and the coastal road to Batumi, despite receiving much better air support than Kleist's troops. Throughout the first three weeks of September, Pflugbeil directed around half his combat units to bomb and strafe Black Sea ports, shipping, and the enemy forces opposing Seventeenth Army, whose attack had stalled after capturing Novorossiisk on 10 September. They conducted these tasks to a satisfactory level, considering their numerical weakness. He sent his other units to Kleist's aid in the Terek bend, where they conducted the operations already described.

Seventeenth Army commenced Operation *Attika* (a new offensive aimed at Tuapse) on 23 September, but only after its commander had successfully demanded improved air support.[103] Pflugbeil concentrated virtually his entire air corps in the Tuapse region, in order to support, both directly and indirectly, attacks by the Fifty-seventh Panzer Corps, which lurched forward on 23 September, and the Thirty-fourth Army Corps, which started two days later. Richthofen temporarily reinforced Pflugbeil's units with a few groups from the Stalingrad sector. This combined force attacked Tuapse (the city and its harbor installations), its road and rail logistical routes, and the enemy troops resisting repeated

Axis attempts to push through the thickly forested hills and mountains east of the port.

The latter operations were by far the hardest. "It's extremely difficult terrain for an attack," Richthofen had noted in his diary after inspecting the combat zone several days before *Attika* began.[104] Indeed, despite detailed radio directions sent by *Flivos* and colored smoke shells lobbed into enemy pockets by mortar and artillery teams, Luftwaffe units found it hard to locate those well-camouflaged troops in the dense oak forests.[105] Even when they did find them, they seldom inflicted substantial damage upon them. They simply lacked the aircraft, fuel, and bombs to conduct large-scale "carpet bombing" of even limited stretches of forest. They also lacked Vietnam-style napalm or wide-coverage incendiary bombs, which are far more effective against forest targets than high explosives. Even if they had possessed these, they could not have used them because of the close proximity of Soviet and Axis troops. As it was, air units had difficulty distinguishing friend from foe. "Only by seeing the colored cloths or light signals that were raised out of the thickets," one Stuka pilot recalled, "could we recognize the friendly lines. We had to change the color of the recognition signals constantly because the Russians would use them to their own benefit."[106]

Despite the Luftwaffe's efforts—sometimes effective, most times not—Seventeenth Army's offensive failed as miserably as First Panzer Army's. The terrain was too difficult and the enemy far too strong for Ruoff's worn-out troops. Against these obstacles, and handicapped by frequent rainstorms, they found momentum remarkably hard to generate and extremely easy to lose. Throughout October and November, they made minor gains for high losses but failed to break through to Tuapse or any other major naval base. Ruoff's troops would never reach those goals; for the rest of the year they maintained their positions in the mountains and foothills around Tuapse, throwing back repeated enemy attacks and waiting for substantial reinforcements that never arrived and major enemy blunders that never occurred. Early in 1943, a powerful Soviet offensive finally forced a dejected Ruoff to withdraw his army from the western Caucasus.

On several occasions—to return to the months of October and November 1942—when fighting at Stalingrad diminished in intensity and Richthofen considered it safe to pull aircraft away, he diverted *Fliegerkorps VIII*'s powerful bomber forces south to join *Fliegerkorps IV*'s weak forces in raids on Tuapse.[107] These raids, often involving a hundred bombers, caused substantial damage to both the city and the port.[108] They were few in number, however, and far less destructive than the cumulative effect of the *VVS*'s constant attacks on key Axis centers, airfields, and naval bases in the Crimea and the Taman Peninsula.[109] By early October, the Luftwaffe was so stretched out by often-unrealistic and constantly taxing demands placed upon it by its commanders that it was powerless to hamper, let alone stop, those raids. Flak batteries on the Crimea were just as restricted as air units. They possessed only light guns, incapable of hitting the high-flying Soviet bombers.[110] The Luftwaffe deployed all its heavy flak guns in the Stalingrad and Caucasus sectors. Accordingly, Crimean flak gunners—including a few Rumanian flak batteries, which belonged to the Rumanian army and therefore functioned independently of the *I. Flakkorps*[111]—seldom managed to bring down enemy planes.[112]

The Luftwaffe also lacked the ability to prevent the ever-stronger enemy air force's mining of Crimean sea-lanes and torpedo attacks on Axis vessels, which now occurred more frequently but with a success rate no better than that of the German groups.[113] These mining and torpedoing missions resulted in the sinking of few Axis vessels, although the former did cause minor interruptions to Axis traffic. When *Admiral Schwarzes Meer* detected mines in certain stretches of water, it suspended all maritime operations in those waters until its minesweepers (or a special Junkers aircraft fitted with minesweeping equipment)[114] cleared them. On 12 October, for instance, the naval command canceled its vital supply missions across the Kerch Straits for twenty-four hours after surveillance teams spotted enemy aircraft dropping mines.[115]

The Luftwaffe—like the Axis flotilla—was unable even to discourage artillery attacks on important Axis installations, bases, and ports by Soviet warships now confidently plying the sea-lanes around the Crimea and the Taman Peninsula. Small warships with light weapons, and sometimes destroyers and cruisers with heavy guns, hit Axis targets on an almost-daily basis. Apparently no longer fearful of destruction by the Luftwaffe, they carried out their attacks both at night and during the day. They usually inflicted only minor damage, as a result of their inaccurate gunfire (seldom corrected during barrages) and the low caliber of most weapons. On occasions, however, they achieved better results. On 2 October, for instance, three destroyers lobbed sixty to eighty shells at Yalta, cutting its communications, inflicting damage on harbor facilities, and killing and wounding several seamen. German coastal batteries returned fire, but their gunners soon broke off fire when they realized they lacked range.[116] Soviet warships sometimes directed their attacks against the coastal batteries, hoping to knock out the only guns capable of thwarting their efforts.[117] With no Luftwaffe forces to worry about, and showing no fear of the German and Italian MTB squadrons, they also attacked Axis shipping in Crimean sea-lanes and in the Kerch Straits. These actions greatly concerned *Admiral Schwarzes Meer,* which complained to Naval Group South as early as 6 October that "the persistent shelling of ports, minelaying operations and attacks on our convoys by the Russian fleet in cooperation with the Russian Air Force is beginning to interfere with vital supplies transported by sea for the Army." The air force, it added, was now too busy with other tasks to mount regular antishipping attacks.

The situation soon deteriorated further. After the Soviets launched their massive counteroffensive in November, *Luftflotte 4* had to send to Stalingrad most of its reconnaissance planes in the Crimea and northwestern Caucasus, leaving *Admiral Schwarzes Meer* and the Crimean air staff with no effective way of monitoring the enemy fleet, let alone attacking it. *Admiral Schwarzes Meer* requested the air fleet to reconsider, pointing out that its vessels were in constant danger from Soviet warships and that only systematic air reconnaissance could provide adequate surveillance of enemy naval movements. The Luftwaffe replied that a few long-range reconnaissance aircraft would keep patrolling the sea-lanes, but "increased reconnaissance during the present critical situation is out of the question."[118] In response to the navy's constant pleading for offensive action against Oktyabrskii's fleet—based on its intense fear that the fleet would launch an amphibious landing on the Crimea, as it had the previous winter—the Luftwaffe repeatedly emphasized throughout November and December that even occasional, small-scale bombing attacks on the enemy fleet could not possibly resume until the terrible situation at Stalingrad improved.

This almost brings the discussion of Luftwaffe operations in the Caucasus during 1942 to a close. However, it is fitting to describe and explain one noteworthy operation: the Luftwaffe's bombing raids on the very oil fields Hitler set out to capture. Early in October, the Führer realized that his forces would probably not reach the main oil fields before rain, ice, and snow forced them to take up winter positions. He therefore ordered the Luftwaffe to damage the oil fields as severely as possible, believing that if *he* couldn't have them (at present, anyway), he should at least deny Stalin's agriculture, industry, and armies their vast output.[119]

On 10 October, Richthofen hurled his entire bomber fleet against the Grozny refineries.[120] That fleet, like those of the other aircraft types, was now in poor shape. He had started Operation *Blau* with an impressive force of 480 bombers, of which 323 (a reasonable 67 percent) were serviceable.[121] Now he had only 232 bombers, of which a mere 129 (55 percent) were serviceable. They could still deliver heavy blows to single targets, however. The damage they inflicted on Grozny reminded the air chief of attacks on Sevastopol; huge flames leapt from shattered fuel tanks and burst pipes, and dense clouds of smoke rose high into the air.[122] He was delighted, joyfully noting in his diary the following evening that smoke clouds were still 5,500 meters high. He repeated the attacks two days later, with equally pleasing results. These raids on oil refineries, though, marked the sum total of *Luftflotte 4*'s "strategic" attacks on enemy industry in the Caucasus. Richthofen simply could not spare aircraft from the Stalingrad sector to carry out further such raids (against the major oil fields at Baku, for instance, which Hitler ordered a month later).[123] It is remarkable that the Wehrmacht High Command did not order the temporary release of all, or at least most, bombers from Stalingrad for these attacks on oil fields. Their extensive damage (particularly Baku's) would have dealt the Soviet Union a far heavier blow than the loss of Stalingrad's remaining suburbs. When Richthofen managed to send squadrons south—not often, because of the intensity of combat in Stalingrad and the perceived importance of continued bombing raids on that already destroyed city—they carried out a small number of interdiction raids on Soviet road, rail, and sea traffic but mainly supported the two German armies by attacking the enemy on the battlefield and in his rear areas.

When Stalin launched his massive offensive on 19 November, Richthofen immediately ordered the withdrawal of all remaining combat units in the Caucasus and their transfer north to the Stalingrad sector, where they were now sorely needed. "I am transferring all *Fliegerkorps IV*'s forces to the penetration region," he jotted in his diary that night, "so that nothing will remain in the Caucasus except for two fighter groups and some reconnaissance units." The transfers would take place, he added, as soon as the dreadful weather eased up. Pflugbeil wasted no time. Despite the weather, which remained bad for several more days, he moved *Fliegerkorps IV*'s headquarters to Salsk, from where he could better assist Axis relief efforts. In accordance with his chief's instructions, he stripped *Admiral Schwarzes Meer*'s forces in the Crimea and First Panzer and Seventeenth Armies in the Caucasus of virtually all their air support. For the protection of Axis support and combat forces and the surveillance of enemy ground, air, and naval formations, he left only two fighter groups (and their staff), a long-range reconnaissance squadron, and a few tactical reconnaissance aircraft in the south.[124] He left no bombers, dive-bombers, or ground-attack aircraft.

The few weak units now remaining in the Caucasus and responsible for that vast region and the eastern reaches of the Black Sea comprised the 3rd Squadron of the 122nd Long-Range Reconnaissance Wing, with only 6 working Ju 88s (out of its total complement of 9); the 1st and 9th Tactical Reconnaissance Squadron, whose operational strength varied from 6 to 12 Bf 110s and Fw 189s each; the Staff and 3rd Group of the 52nd Fighter Wing, with 31 of its 46 Bf 109s operational; and the 13th Squadron of the same fighter wing, with 6 of its 8 Bf 109s operational.[125] Slovakian pilots, flying German machines, composed the latter. With only around 18 surveillance planes and 37 fighters to guard a region the size of Great Britain, these weak units proved incapable of offering protection to army and navy forces from attacks by *VVS* fighters and bombers, which now struck with merciless fury.

Richthofen placed these units under the authority of *General der Flakartillerie* Dessloch's *I. Flak-Korps*, which still possessed strong flak forces in the Caucasus. Redesignating Dessloch's command *Luftwaffengruppe Kaukasus* (Air Force Group, Caucasus), Richthofen instructed the general to direct the operations of all air and flak units supporting Seventeenth and First Panzer Armies. For the rest of 1942, *Luftwaffengruppe Kaukasus* provided those two armies, stuck in a stalemate with their opponents until early 1943, with excellent flak support. However, because of inclement weather and few available aircraft, their air support remained ineffective. The Fw 189s and Bf 110s of the two tactical reconnaissance squadrons constantly monitored enemy movements at and behind the front, but they were too few in number—usually only nine or ten serviceable aircraft supported each entire 200,000-man army—and had very limited offensive capabilities. The long-range reconnaissance squadron continued as it had all year, although on a smaller scale: whereas previously five or more aircraft reconnoitered the eastern Black Sea, the enemy naval bases along the Caucasus coast, and road and rail traffic in the western Caucasus, by mid-December only one or two planes were able to undertake those missions each day. As a result, they had to abandon surveillance of the western Caucasus, and their coverage of the ports and sea-lanes became far less thorough. To *Admiral Schwarzes Meer*'s disappointment, "the increased allocation of reconnaissance planes was still out of the question. The shortage of fuel and lubricating oil had repeatedly forced them to restrict air reconnaissance."[126]

Richthofen soon realized that Dessloch needed air reinforcements if he was to monitor enemy movements and provide even occasional protection from *VVS* attacks. Between mid-December 1942 and mid-January 1943, he steadily increased *Luftwaffengruppe Kaukasus*'s surveillance capabilities by adding the following forces: the staff and 3rd Group of the 125th Sea Reconnaissance Wing (flying from bases in Bulgaria, Rumanian, and the Ukraine, and mainly covering the western Black Sea); the Coastal Squadron, Crimea (operating from Kerch); and the 20th Rumanian Reconnaissance Squadron (Eupatoria).[127] He assigned the command a few sea rescue aircraft and also added the following combat forces: the 43rd Rumanian Fighter Squadron (Kerch); the 3rd Night-Flying Training Squadron; and the "Sattler" Stuka Operational Squadron, Crimea (based in Bagerovo and flying obsolete Stuka models). Because most squadrons had fewer than five operational aircraft—due to lack of fuel and spares and freezing winter weather—these reinforcements made almost no impact on combat in the Crimea, the eastern Black Sea, and the Caucasus.[128] Aside from its strong and effective flak component, *Luftwaffengruppe Kaukasus* remained a motley collection of weak units, capable of nothing more than harassing the enemy. The two armies received a little help from reconnaissance units but hardly ever saw combat aircraft overhead. The group's only noteworthy offensive successes were against enemy aircraft; up to 6 February 1943, it reported shooting down 113 planes and destroying 11 others on the ground, for only six losses.[129]

Luftwaffengruppe Kaukasus possessed no transport groups. Therefore, in periods of crisis, Seventeenth Army occasionally requested *Fliegerkorps VIII* to airlift supplies to isolated groups in the Caucasus. The air corps always obliged, despite the fact that its transport fleets already worked tirelessly to keep Sixth Army alive in Stalingrad. On 7 December, for example, *Fliegerkorps VIII* airlifted 17.5 tons of provisions, 6.5 tons of horse fodder, and 3.5 tons of engineering equipment to cut-off troops of the Forty-fourth Jäger and Forty-ninth Mountain Corps, stuck in the mountains behind Tuapse.[130] The following day, only 8 tons could be dropped because of appalling weather. These tonnages, it should be noted, represent the amount dropped, not the amount received by Axis troops. Usually troops recovered only around two-thirds, the rest either falling into enemy territory, getting lost, or breaking up on impact. As it was, airlifts to Army Group A occurred seldom in December and not at all in January, when biting winter conditions and strong enemy opposition wreaked havoc on the Luft-waffe's attempts to sustain the strangled Sixth Army. The two German armies dispersed throughout the northern Caucasus, some 450,000 men, would survive the rest of winter with almost no more assistance from the air force.

This brings the analysis of German air operations in the Caucasus during 1942 to a close. It is necessary to return at a later point to that vast oil-rich region, to see how Ruoff's and Kleist's armies managed to survive the winter and how the Luftwaffe, in early 1943, helped them make a hasty but successful retreat in the face of imminent destruction. At this point, however, we will shift our focus onto Fiebig's *Fliegerkorps VIII,* which we left back in late July, when Hitler di-rected Sixth Army—and Richthofen sent Fiebig's air corps—to take Stalin's mighty city on the Volga.

7

Toward Destruction:
August–November 1942

August began poorly for the powerful Sixth Army, heading across flat steppes in scorching heat toward Stalingrad. On the first of the month, *Generaloberst* Halder bitterly complained in his diary (as he had several times in the last two weeks): "Our attack can't proceed because of fuel and ammunition shortages." The following day, Richthofen, whose air transport units relieved some of those shortages, noted in his own diary that Sixth Army sat "bogged down" in front of Stalingrad, partly because of stiff opposition but mainly because of acute logistical problems. Unlike the ever-pessimistic army chief, the latter remained confident, adding lightheartedly that "the enemy attempts to fling troops from every point of the compass into the Stalingrad sector. He's hell-bent on holding the city. This means that, when the city falls, Stalin will have to sue for peace. Well, well!" He was not the only senior commander to believe that the fall of the city was the key to German success in the east. Three days earlier, Jodl had trumpeted (with a prophetic resonance that would later haunt him): "The fate of the Caucasus will be decided at Stalingrad."[1]

During the first weeks of August, Sixth Army advanced fitfully, frequently crippled by fuel and ammunition shortages. As noted earlier, Richthofen did everything possible to improve the army's supply situation. He requested the *OKL* to send additional Ju 52 groups, transferred north most of Pflugbeil's (and his road transport companies), created a special Stalingrad "transport region," and ordered immediate increases in transportation levels through intensified effort and improved procedures. The army undertook its own measures to improve its supply situation. The efforts of both service branches bore fruit, particularly those of the Luftwaffe, which continued flying forward large amounts of ammunition and provisions and smaller amounts of fuel (dangerous and difficult to airlift because of its flammability and huge volume). By the third week of August,

Sixth Army began receiving sufficient supplies for it to undertake most of its missions without hardship.

Generalleutnant Fiebig's *Fliegerkorps VIII,* meanwhile, provided the army with effective air support. It struck enemy troops, vehicles, guns, and fortified positions on the battlefield, as well as logistics and mobilization centers and road, rail, and river traffic behind the front. The guns of *Generalmajor* Pickert's 9th Flak Division smashed field fortifications and enemy vehicles and generally kept the airspace above Sixth Army free of the enemy fighters and Shturmoviks that frequently eluded Fiebig's own fighters. The flak division's actions did not pass unnoticed. On 8 August, Pickert personally received Paulus's "praise . . . for the close cooperation between the army and the flak teams."[2]

On 6 August, Hitler ordered Richthofen to support Sixth Army's renewed attack across the Don at Kalach, due to start the following day.[3] The air chief immediately flew to Paulus's command post, where he found the army commander "confident," and then to Army Group B's headquarters, where he found an equally optimistic Weichs furiously raging about the lethargic efforts of his Italian and Hungarian components. They discussed their plans for the coming weeks and carefully coordinated a joint *Schwerpunkt* at Kalach, which, the air leader noted in his diary, "we're going to hit tomorrow with all our forces."

Schwerpunktbildung—the creation of individual points of maximum effort— had not been possible throughout most of July, when widely dispersed army formations advanced at different rates in different directions with different objectives. Moreover, Richthofen lacked sufficient aircraft to concentrate substantial numbers in support of all those formations. Instead, he had to dissipate his forces by deploying smaller numbers alternately in support of various army efforts, sometimes in two or three separate regions at a time. Things were now different. His fleet was still divided (one air corps supported the drive to Stalingrad, the other the drive to the Caucasus oil fields) but at least he could create a single *Schwerpunkt* at the Kalach bridgehead for Fiebig's entire close-support force.

Early on 7 August, Paulus's Fourteenth and Twenty-fourth Panzer Corps sliced into that bridgehead from the north and south, their armored vanguards receiving massive support from Fiebig's air corps and elements of Pflugbeil's. Late in the afternoon, the pincers clamped tight near the west bank of the Don, opposite Kalach, trapping the main body of the Soviet Sixty-second Army. Joined by the Fifty-first Army Corps, the panzer corps began methodically cleaning out the pocket. Hitler was ecstatic; he had envisaged a series of classic double envelopments like this when planning *Blau,* but this was the first encirclement of any significance actually accomplished so far. His booty was impressive, as Richthofen privately noted on 10 August: "*Fliegerkorps VIII* finally clears out the Kalach pocket in conjunction with Sixth Army, capturing 50,000 prisoners and 1,100 tanks."

Throughout this period, Fiebig's dive-bombers and ground-attack units encountered steady, but rarely powerful, *VVS* opposition as they smashed troops, vehicles, and field positions in the pocket. Bombers, escorted by fighters, also encountered little air opposition as they pounded trains and railway installations south of Stalingrad and airfields southwest of the city (claiming the destruction of twenty enemy aircraft on the ground on 10 August alone).[4] General T. T. Khriukin's Eighth Air Army had done all it could in recent weeks to stem the German advance, but its strength had been drastically reduced in savage air combat, and its valiant efforts against Fiebig's technically and numerically superior force achieved nothing.[5] The *Stavka* dispatched a constant stream of reinforcements to Khriukin's force—447 aircraft between 20 July and 17 August[6]—but the vastly outclassed and still-outnumbered Eighth Air Army failed to prevent a steady deterioration of the situation around beleaguered Stalingrad. In fact, the air army's attrition rate ran almost as high as the reinforcement rate, so little improvement in strength occurred.

On 5 August, the *Stavka* substantially bolstered the *VVS*'s local strength when it split the Stalingrad Front into two separate commands: the Southeastern Front, supported by Eighth Air Army, and a new Stalingrad Front, supported by General P. S. Stepanov's hastily formed Sixteenth Air Army. Both air armies received a steady flow of reinforcements, including Yak-1s, Yak 7-bs, Il-2s, Pe-2s, and other newer models. However, most units arrived at the front well below strength. The 228th Shturmovik Air Division, for example, commenced combat operations with only one-third of its prescribed complement.[7] Most units also arrived with inexperienced aircrew—no match for their German counterparts—as well as poor logistical networks and dismal army-air communication and liaison systems. Prematurely assigned to frontline airfields, these units began reconnaissance and combat operations immediately. As a result, they suffered severe losses and failed to rob the Luftwaffe of its overwhelming air supremacy. For instance, if its daily reports are accurate, *Fliegerkorps VIII* suffered no losses as it destroyed 25 of the 26 Soviet aircraft that attacked German airfields on 12 August. It destroyed 35 out of 45 the following day, again for no losses.[8]

With much of the Soviet Sixty-second Army now marching westward into captivity, Paulus struck for Stalingrad. He did not choose the most direct route, due east from Kalach. That route was crisscrossed by deep gullies that would provide the enemy splendid defensive opportunities and frequently force tanks to make lengthy detours. Instead, the army commander decided to send his two panzer corps to the "northeast corner" of the great Don bend, where they would establish bridgeheads for the advance on Stalingrad.

The loss of 50,000 troops and a thousand tanks, coupled with the collapse of the Kalach bulwark, which he prayed would hold back the rising Axis tide, threw Stalin into panic. He cast more reserves into the region and, on 13 August, placed both the Stalingrad and the Southeastern Fronts under the authority of one of his most trusted field commanders, Colonel General Yeremenko.[9] Directing the

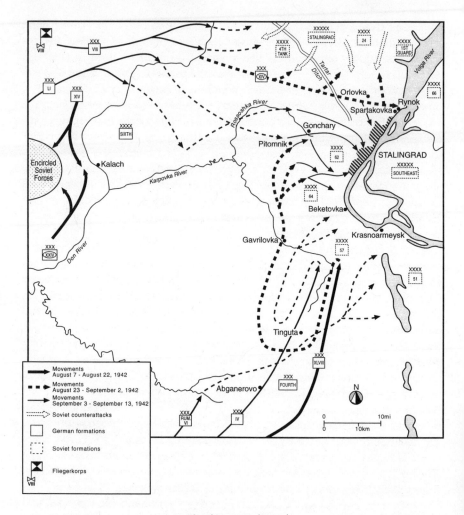

5. The drive to Stalingrad

actions of two fronts was, the latter once remarked, "an extremely heavy burden," especially as it involved conducting operations through two deputies, two chiefs of staff, and two staffs.[10]

Hoth's Fourth Panzer Army, meanwhile, had made excellent progress in the last two weeks. Its drive northward from the Caucasus brought its right-flank vanguards up to Abganerovo Station on the railway seventy kilometers south of Stalingrad. The *VVS* had unsuccessfully tried to blunt its advance by diverting the bulk of its combat forces south, but frantically had to rush it back to the Don bend when Sixth Army began its attack across the Kletskaya-Peskovatka line on 15 August.[11] In two days, Fourteenth and Twenty-fourth Panzer Corps cleared the entire Don bend and Eighth Army Corps captured two small bridgeheads near Trekhostrovskaya, at the bend's easternmost point. Unfortunately for Paulus, the marshy terrain in this sector proved unsuitable for tanks, and Yeremenko threw First Guards Army into the battle. By 18 August, it had pushed divisions westward across the Don and reestablished a thirty-five-kilometer-long bridgehead from Kremenskaya to Sirotinskaya.

Unwilling to waste time and suffer unnecessary losses in a prolonged contest for the Don bend, an uncharacteristically daring Paulus thrust Fifty-first Army Corps across the Don toward Vertyachiy on 21 August. Although this attack left his left flank dangerously exposed, it succeeded brilliantly. Surprised by their enemy's daring, the Soviet defenders fell back helplessly. By the next morning, Fourteenth Panzer Corps' tanks were rolling over two massive bridges thrown across the Don by German engineers.

These were favorable days for Fiebig's *Fliegerkorps VIII*. It deployed most of its bombers against Black Sea ports and shipping and its powerful ground attack and dive-bomber groups against the Soviet formations resisting both Paulus's advance across the Don and Hoth's drive on Stalingrad from the south. The air corps notched up excellent tallies of enemy aircraft: it claimed 139 victims in three days.[12] It also inflicted heavy damage on enemy troops and armor contesting the battlefield. On 21 August, for instance, Richthofen flew over the Don bend north of Kalach and found himself staring down at "extraordinarily many knocked-out tanks and dead [Russians]."[13] Later that day, Ju 88s of *K.G. 76* massacred two reserve divisions caught in the open 150 kilometers east of Stalingrad, prompting the delighted air fleet commander to scrawl excitedly in his diary: "Blood flowed!" (Richthofen's original text says *"Blut gerührt!"* not "beautiful bloodbath!" *[tolles Blutbad]* as both Williamson Murray and Richard Muller assert, basing their statements on the few subjectively edited and frequently inaccurate diary extracts found in the "Karlsruhe Collection.")[14] Two days later—while Hoth's Fourth Panzer Army barely moved in the south because of acute shortages of fuel and ammunition[15]—*General der Panzertruppe* von Wietersheim's Fourteenth Panzer Corps surged across the land bridge between the Don and Volga Rivers, reaching the latter in Stalingrad's northern suburbs at 1600 hours. *Generalleutnant* Hans Hube's 16th Panzer Division, the corps' mailed fist, smashed more than thirty artillery batteries in those suburbs. The enemy gunfire was woefully inaccurate. After the one-armed Hube's men closed in on the wrecked batteries, they learned why: the guns had been "manned" by hastily deployed and totally untrained civilians, mostly women, now lying dead in their bloodstained cotton dresses.

Wietersheim's corps accomplished its remarkable advance (which deeply shocked the Soviet leadership) by moving up closely behind a deluge of shrapnel and high explosives rained down on enemy positions by *Fliegerkorps VIII,* now permanently reinforced by units stripped from *Fliegerkorps IV.* "Since early morning we were constantly over the panzer spearheads, helping them forward with our bombs and machine guns," recalled *Hauptmann* Herbert Pabst, commander of a Stuka squadron. "We landed, refueled, received bombs and ammunition, and immediately took off again. It was 'all go' and splendid advances. As we took off, others landed. And so it went."[16] During 1,600 nonstop sorties, Fiebig's units dropped 1,000 tons of bombs on the enemy troops and defensive positions in the corps' advance path, destroying all opposition (as Richthofen wrote, "totally paralyzing the Russians"). Apparently suffering only three losses the entire day (certainly not ninety, as several postwar Soviet accounts absurdly maintain),[17] they also ravaged *VVS* forces desperately trying to destroy Don crossings and halt Wietersheim's advance. They claimed ninety-one aircraft destroyed in what even the Soviets acknowledged were "fierce battles."[18]

STALINGRAD BLUDGEONED, THEN "SLOWLY STRANGLED"

Richthofen was delighted (as Hitler was, when informed that day), but he did not stop there. Late in the afternoon, Fiebig's corps carried out what the fleet chief called his "second great attack of the day": an immense raid on Stalingrad itself. Bombers smashed buildings to rubble with high explosives and torched various residential areas with incendiaries, leaving houses, schools, and factories wildly burning. In some suburbs, the only structures left standing were the blackened brick chimneys of incinerated wooden houses. "Never before in the entire war had the enemy attacked in such strength from the air," wrote Lieutenant-General Vasili Chuikov with pardonable exaggeration, not having witnessed the even-heavier annihilation raids on Sevastopol.[19] The abrasive but talented commander of the Sixty-second Army was not exaggerating at all, however, when he added that "the huge city, stretching for nearly thirty-five miles along the Volga, was enveloped in flames. Everything was blazing, collapsing. Death and disaster descended on thousands of families."

Estimating fatalities is difficult because of a paucity of reliable statistical data. Yet this hellish attack caused at least as many deaths as similar-sized Allied raids on German cities. For example, it certainly claimed as many victims as the Allied attack on Darmstadt during the night of 11 and 12 September 1944, when the Royal Air Force unloaded almost 900 tons of bombs and killed over 12,300 citizens. The Stalingrad death total may, in fact, have been twice that of Darmstadt, due to the fact that the Russian city was poorly provided with air-raid shelters. Recent popular accounts have advanced a figure of around 40,000,[20] although this seems extravagant when compared with the death tolls in German cities hit by similar bomb tonnages. The postwar official Soviet history merely states: "In one day, scores of thousands of families lost a member, and thousands of children, their mothers and fathers."[21]

Raids continued almost without pause for another two days, although with steadily decreasing intensity.[22] Richthofen flew over Stalingrad on the morning of

25 August, in order to watch that day's "great fire-attack." The city, he later noted in his diary, was "destroyed, and without any further worthwhile targets." He then landed at the forward airfield of one of his bomber units, twenty-five kilometers from the ruined metropolis. The sky was full of "thick, black fire-clouds reaching all the way from the city."[23] After another heavy bombing attack in the afternoon, he added, the dense volcanolike clouds climbed 3,500 meters into the sky. The level of destruction was impressive (except, of course, to the tormented souls who fled the holocaust and now huddled in deep ravines outside the city). Flames leapt from huge oil storage containers and fuel tankers on the Volga, across the surface of which spilled oil burned.[24] That evening, *Generalmajor* Pickert, head of the 9th Flak Division, recorded his own impressions in his diary: "At dusk I went on another 14 kilometers, then spent the night in the open . . . against a backdrop of magnificent smoke and flames, with Stalingrad burning and Russian searchlights blazing. A fantastic picture in the moonlight."[25]

Aside from these massive raids, the Axis advance on Stalingrad stalled for several days. Hube's troops encountered stiff resistance from the Soviet Sixty-second Army and the citizens' militia. Their morale intact despite *Fliegerkorps VIII*'s best efforts, these courageous defenders refused to allow Germans to bulldoze through the rubble-strewn streets of Rynok, Stalingrad's northernmost suburb, into the Spartakovka industrial region. Powerful Soviet attacks inflicted punishing blows on Hube's division. It had raced to the Volga with such speed that it now found itself stranded at the river, separated from other German divisions by over twenty kilometers and surrounded by enraged enemy forces seeking revenge for the destruction of their city. On 26 August, a particularly strong attack sliced a chunk off Fourteenth Panzer Corps' northern flank in the Kremenskaya region. This, and Hube's constant panicky requests for supplies and reinforcements, prompted Wietersheim to request that his corps withdraw from the Volga.[26] Paulus refused but frantically directed Fifty-first and Eighth Army Corps to close the gap between themselves and Wietersheim's corps, bolster the vulnerable northern flank, and push supplies forward to Hube's encircled division, still suffering heavy losses as it clung to the Volga. *Fliegerkorps VIII* effectively supported these endeavors, pinning down enemy troops assailing Hube's division and repelling repeated Soviet attempts to stab into Fourteenth Panzer Corps' exposed northern flank from the Kremenskaya bridgehead. In its brief daily report on air operations, the German naval staff's war diary for 28 August was unusually generous in its praise of Fiebig's units: "The supply road for our forces which reached the Volga River was freed and attacks against it were repulsed, thanks to the splendid support of the Air Force. Tank attacks south of Kremen[skaya] were repulsed with particularly severe losses."[27]

Richthofen, always aggressive and prepared to take risks—unlike Paulus, whom the air chief accurately described two weeks later as "worthy but uninspiring"[28]—insisted that the army could take Stalingrad even now if it launched an all-out assault. Losses would be high, but, in the present circumstances, acceptable. He was disgusted by what he called the army's lack of fighting spirit and its unwillingness to suffer losses to obtain major goals. He had made similar complaints during the assault on Sevastopol. On 22 June, he had grumbled in his diary: "I wish that everyone would just push a little more energetically. The view that advancing cautiously avoids losses is simply *not* correct, because small losses each day soon mount up the longer it takes." History, he now believed, was clearly repeating itself. Therefore, on 27 August, he sent his operations officer, *Oberst* Karl-Heinz Schulz, to express in no uncertain terms to Göring and Jeschonnek his intense frustration "at the army's weakness in nerves and leadership."[29] Schulz returned the next day, informing Richthofen that Göring had responded sympathetically to his views. In fact, both the *Reichsmarschall* and the Führer had expressed anger at the army's slow progress and granted Richthofen permission, as a "morale booster," *expressly* to "request" it to act more aggressively.

The following day, this "morale booster" flew to Hoth's command post to pass on the Führer's sentiments and, hopefully, to spur him on in a friendly manner. Hoth, meanwhile, had heard from the army group that even he had been included in Richthofen's self-righteous accusations to the High Command.[30] The panzer commander was outraged that he, of all people, whose army frequently sat idle for want of fuel, *not* courage, should be accused of lacking fighting spirit. He confronted Richthofen immediately. Shocked by the panzer leader's anger, the airman emphatically denied that he had mentioned him to the High Command. (This should be taken with a large measure of salt, given that the previous month he had privately described Hoth as "aging and doubtless weary" and only a few days earlier had commented harshly that Fourth Panzer Army had "worn-out leadership and feeble troops").[31] Highly embarrassed, he blamed Göring for "twisting" his complaints about army leadership and even unfairly bawled out Jeschonnek on the telephone. Hoth was apparently satisfied; at least Richthofen believed so. This was the first open clash between the arrogant airman and his army colleagues; it would not be the last.

As it happened, Hoth's army surged forward that very day, in an operation that clearly demonstrated his courage and ability. For the last week or so, his army had been stuck halfway between Tinguta and Krasnoarmeysk, unable to advance past a line of heavily fortified hills guarding Stalingrad's southern approaches.[32] His panzers and guns hammered away at those positions and the Soviet Sixty-fourth Army's constantly attacking troops and armor. The loss of thousands of men and scores of tanks for only minor gains proved to Hoth that he could not advance on Stalingrad from his present position. He had to regroup and strike toward the city from a sector held less tightly by the enemy.[33] Under cover of darkness and light but steady attacks by Fiebig's Stukas and ground-attack aircraft, he slowly pulled the bulk of his tanks and other mobile units from the front, replacing them with infantry formations (including numerous elements of the Rumanian Sixth Army Corps) to camouflage his actions. Regrouping his armored units behind Tinguta, almost fifty kilometers behind their earlier positions, he prepared them for their new drive to Stalingrad. Assisted by a strong concentration of aircraft,[34] they raced forward on 29 August, sweeping northwest for twenty kilometers before wheeling northeast toward the city with considerable momentum. Flanking the strongly defended hills that had cost them dear in lives and time, they smashed through the surprised enemy forces vainly trying to block their path. Late that day they reached the Karpovka River. The next day— as Wietersheim finally opened the pocket in which Hube's division lay trapped and pushed forward supplies—they crossed the Karpovka and took a bridgehead at Gavrilovka, less than thirty kilometers southwest of Stalingrad. The Soviet Sixty-second and Sixty-fourth Armies, rightly fearing encirclement, withdrew to the suburbs and hastily erected new positions among surviving buildings and piles of rubble.[35] The former prepared to defend the ruined metropolis from attack against its northern and northwestern suburbs, while the latter guarded its southern precincts.

"Everything's going well," Richthofen excitedly wrote on 30 August, momentarily forgetting his recent bout of bitter frustration. Believing Stalingrad's capture to be imminent, and determined to shatter the enemy's will to resist—an unrealistic goal, as his experiences at Sevastopol should have shown—he ordered fresh terror attacks on the city. Throughout that day and the next, Fiebig's corps struck the city with everything available, diverting aircraft only occasionally to smash enemy airfields east of the Volga.[36]

The army, meanwhile, made pleasing progress. When Fourth Panzer Army pushed forward from the Karpovka River on 31 August, Weichs ordered Hoth to meet Paulus's Sixth Army at Pitomnik (fifteen kilometers east of the city), having crushed the enemy forces currently between them. From Pitomnik, they would together drive into the center of Stalingrad, roughly following the line of the Tsaritsa River. However, Hoth reported on 2 September that virtually no enemy forces lay between his army and Voroponovo Station (only ten kilometers from Stalingrad), prompting Weichs to instruct the panzer commander to swing east into the city without waiting for Paulus. Determined to provide them with maximum support, Richthofen had Fiebig pound enemy positions in and around Stalingrad with his entire corps. The latter responded with characteristic gusto, launching a twenty-four-hour, relentless raid against the already ruined city on 3 September (which Hermann Plocher wrongly claimed was the "first heavy air raid on the city").[37] This crushing attack, similar in scale to that of 23 August, destroyed Sixty-second Army's command center and almost killed Chuikov, its commander. As he vividly recalled:

The enemy's air reconnaissance must have detected our command post and promptly sent in bombers. . . . After sitting like this [in a tiny earth bunker] under bombardment for several hours, we began to grow accustomed to it and took no notice of the roar of engines and the explosion of bombs. Suddenly our dug-out seemed to be thrown into the air. There was a deafening explosion. Abramov [the member of the Military Council] and I found ourselves on the floor, together with the overturned desks and stools. Above us was the sky, choked with dust. Lumps of earth and stone were flying about, and around us people were crying out and groaning. When the dust had settled a little, we saw an enormous crater some six to ten yards from our dugout. Round it lay a number of mutilated bodies, and scattered about were overturned trucks and our radio transmitter, now out of action. Our telephone communications had also been destroyed.[38]

Behind the Luftwaffe's downpour of steel, which pinned the Soviets to the ground and temporarily ended their resistance, Fourth Panzer Army established contact with Sixth Army at Gonchary, near Voroponovo. Paulus and Richthofen—the hatchet apparently buried after recent tension over the latter's accusations to the High Command—studied the burning ruins through field glasses from the relative safety of an infantry command post. Despite the fact that the Soviet Sixty-second and Sixty-fourth Armies had escaped capture and withdrawn into the city (where they would later offer tenacious resistance), both commanders concluded that victory at Stalingrad was only days away. Back in his Ukrainian headquarters, the Führer, whose own concerns about progress evaporated as soon as his troops reached the city's outskirts, also claimed that Stalingrad was as good as won. The entire male population, he informed a disgusted Halder, would have to be "disposed of" as soon as possible because it constituted a dangerous, fanatical Communist element.[39]

Stalin, meanwhile, also believed that the city would fall at any moment, unless he could organize an immediate counteroffensive. On 3 August, during the height of the Stalingrad blitz, he sent an urgent message to General Georgi Zhukov, who had arrived in the burning city only two days earlier to take over its seemingly impossible defense. "The situation at Stalingrad has deteriorated further," he told Zhukov, recently promoted to Soviet deputy supreme commander. "The enemy stands two miles from the city. Stalingrad may fall today or tomorrow if the northern group of forces [First Guards, Twenty-fourth and Sixty-sixth Armies] does not give immediate assistance. . . . No delay can be tolerated. To delay now is tantamount to a crime. Throw all your airpower to the aid of Stalingrad."[40] Zhukov winced when he read his chief's order, knowing that ammunition had not yet reached the armies earmarked for the counteroffensive. He immediately telephoned Stalin, stating that he would indeed attack but could not do so until 5 September, by which time sufficient ammunition should have arrived and effective interservice cooperation would be arranged. In the meantime, he added, he would order his air forces to pound the Axis troops with all their strength. Stalin reluctantly agreed but insisted that "if the enemy begins a general offensive against the city, attack immediately. Do not wait for the troops to be completely ready. Your main job is to keep the Germans from taking Stalingrad and, if possible, to eliminate the German corridor separating the Stalingrad and Southeastern Fronts."[41]

After a day of small gains by Paulus's army, Zhukov's counteroffensive north of Stalingrad started at dawn on 5 September. First Guards, and Twenty-fourth and Sixty-sixth Armies drove forward after a joint air and artillery barrage. The barrage was too weak to damage German forces substantially or even pin them down for long. Zhukov, who watched the action from an observation post at the front, "could tell from the enemy's counterfire that our artillery bombardment had not been effective and that no deep penetration by our forces was to be expected."[42] Indeed, within two hours the already disappointed Soviet commander learned from combat reports that German troops had thrown back their advance and were themselves counterattacking with infantry and armor. Zhukov's only consolation was that he had forced Paulus to cancel a major thrust into the city planned for that day and divert forces north to hold back the Soviet advance. Although still disappointed by his army's poor showing that day, Stalin was also consoled by this news. The diversion of German forces gave his armies time to strengthen the city's inner defensive positions.[43]

Throughout 5 September, *Fliegerkorps VIII*'s bombers and dive-bombers inflicted heavy losses on Soviet troops and armor. That night, *Hauptmann* Pabst described in his diary the operations of his Stuka squadron: "The Russians throw in everything. Always masses of huge tanks. Then we come, circle, search and dive. They camouflage their tanks fabulously, digging them in to protect them from blasts, sparing no effort. But we find and smash most of them."[44] The Luftwaffe certainly contributed significantly to Axis defensive battles that day, as the German Naval Staff's war diary testifies: "Massed enemy attacks from the north, which were launched after an intensive artillery barrage, were dispersed with the assistance of strong air force formations."[45] Similarly, Zhukov informed Stalin that when his troops attacked, "the enemy was able to stop them with his fire and counter-attacks. In addition, enemy planes had superiority in the air and bombed our positions all day." That night, Soviet air units managed partially to restore their pride, bombing Axis positions along the front. Combat groups of the still-understrength Eighth and Sixteenth Air Armies carried out the bulk of these missions. They were joined on many attacks by bombers of Lieutenant General Golovanov's long-range bombing force, divisions of which had been operating in the Stalingrad region since mid-August.[46]

For the next five days or so, intense fighting continued around Stalingrad, with both sides suffering heavy losses for slight Axis gains. Only on 10 September did Hoth's panzers manage to drive a wedge between Sixty-second and Sixty-fourth Armies, tighten the noose around the city, and isolate Sixty-second Army inside the suburbs. Hoth immediately ordered *General der Panzertruppe* Werner Kempf, commander of the Forty-eighth Panzer Corps, to bulldoze into the southern suburbs the following day, taking them "piece by piece."[47] Now disgusted again by the army's failure to exploit recent opportunities or quicken the offensive's tempo, the exasperated Richthofen complained in his diary of the city's "slow strangulation." Even when German troops finally entered the city on 13 September and began clearing it street by street, the air chief remained unhappy. In the last days of August, he claimed (rightly so, in my opinion), Fourth Panzer and Sixth Armies had blown their chance of encircling Soviet Sixty-second and Sixty-fourth Armies in the city's outer defensive zones; instead, they permitted those enemy formations to withdraw into the ruined suburbs, where the former had since fought fanatically for every street (having been isolated from the latter, the remnants of which fought south of the city). To capture Stalingrad was now going to take a great deal of time and cost many lives, and the inevitable close proximity of opposing forces was already making air attacks extremely difficult.

This appalling situation resulted from weak and indecisive army leadership, Richthofen ranted to anyone who would listen. On 13 September, he even phoned Göring to demand that one single army commander take over the Stalingrad sector, and he did not mean the "uninspiring" Paulus.[48] Three days later, by which time only a few small regions of the city had been cleared in bitter fighting for high losses, the fleet chief vented his anger in his diary: "The 'combing' of Stalingrad is progressing very slowly, despite the fact that the enemy is weak and in no shape for hard fighting. This is because our own troops are few in number, lack fighting spirit and their commanders' thoughts are elsewhere."[49] Army leaders simply fail to drive their troops hard enough, even though the capture of a major objective is tantalizingly close. Doubtless comparing Weichs's, Hoth's, and Paulus's bland and cautious leadership styles to his own—aggressive and daring to the point of recklessness—he added harshly: "From the highest levels down, attempts at motivation are only theoretical and, as a result, totally ineffective. The generals merely issue orders, but lead neither by example nor by any rousing actions whatsoever."

Believing that he had to practice what he preached, Richthofen also demanded more aggression from *Fliegerkorps VIII*, telling Fiebig that he had not deployed his corps "actively or flexibly enough" in recent weeks.[50] Not only had operations "lacked focus and zeal," but the corps had yet to overcome several major supply difficulties. The fleet chief then issued what he called "some really sharp orders" and explained to Fiebig the reason for his unhappiness: the army's poor performance at Stalingrad, which naturally influenced the Luftwaffe's ability to make a decisive impact on the battle. "Because the army is a lame duck," he said, "we can do little ourselves." If everyone would only operate more aggressively, Stalingrad would fall in two days.

Fiebig's corps—indeed, the entire fleet—had performed as well as could be expected in recent weeks, given its logistical difficulties, limited resources, mounting attrition rate, vast combat zone, and wide range of tasks. Still, Richthofen was right; the Luftwaffe's performance had dropped. Between 5 and 12 September, for instance, *Luftflotte 4* conducted 7,507 sorties (an average of 938 per day).[51]

When *Blau* had commenced almost three months earlier, the fleet was conducting around 10,750 in the same number of days (a daily average of 1,343). The main reasons for this substantial operational decrease were a quicker-than-expected consumption of reserve stocks of spare parts and equipment, supply difficulties, and high attrition rates. When *Blau* began, the fleet possessed approximately 1,600 aircraft, of which over 1,150 were operational.[52] After eleven weeks of nonstop operations, with insufficient replacement aircraft and spare parts arriving at forward airfields, it now possessed about 950 planes, a mere 550 of them operational. That is, the fleet's total strength had decreased by 40 percent and its operational rate by 14 percent (from 71 to 57). Its bomber fleet had been hardest hit, mainly due to *VVS* fighter attacks and a lack of engine parts (naturally, twin-engined aircraft need more spares than single-engined). Back in June, the air fleet had 480 bombers, 323 of which were operational. On 20 September, it had no more than 232, only 129 of them airworthy.[53]

Despite *Luftflotte 4*'s plummeting strength and Hitler's craving for victory at Stalingrad and in the Caucasus, the *OKL* made no large-scale aircraft transfers from the other, supposedly "quiet" sectors of the eastern front (at least not before the Soviet counteroffensive in November). When *Blau* began, *Luftflotte 4* possessed 60 percent of all German aircraft in the Soviet Union. On 20 September, after eleven weeks of combat, its dramatic drop in strength left it operating in the "decisive" sector with only 38 percent of all aircraft in the east. The *OKL* was unable to transfer units south to adjust the ratio in *Luftflotte 4*'s favor because strong air forces were also sorely needed in the "quiet" central and northern sectors of the front. Constant Soviet probing attacks and attempted offensives in those sectors kept local Luftwaffe forces extremely busy. When critical situations arose, groups—sometimes whole wings—were hastily shifted between the commands in those regions. For example, when a Soviet attack in the far north threatened to hack off the German "bottleneck" south of Leningrad late in August, *Luftwaffenkommando Ost* (operating in Army Group Center's combat zone) dispatched two bomber groups, a Stuka group, and a fighter group to *Luftflotte 1*.[54] Accordingly, although the only major Axis *offensive* operations in the Soviet Union took place at Stalingrad and in the Caucasus, the *OKL* could not draw reinforcements for the rapidly shrinking *Luftflotte 4* from the other two combat sectors, where air commands were hard-pressed to fulfil their *defensive* duties.

Whereas the Luftwaffe's strength in southern Russia was quickly decreasing, the *VVS*'s strength increased at a slow but steady pace. The Soviet improvements resulted from greater numbers of aircraft and crew replacements and diminishing kill levels by German fighters. (On General Rudenko's wise instructions, Soviet fighter pilots avoided dueling with their German counterparts, attacking bombers and reconnaissance planes instead.)[55] According to German records, the *VVS* air armies in *Luftflotte 4*'s immense combat zone carried out only 2,834 sorties between 5 and 12 September, or an average of 354 per day (compared with the German fleet's *poor* total of 7,507 and daily average of 938).[56] Between 16 and 25 September, though, those air armies carried out 4,589 sorties, or 458 per day.[57] This operational increase of 30 percent did not, of course, even remotely challenge the Luftwaffe's air superiority. In the same period, the German fleet carried out twice as many sorties (9,746 in total). Yet it was the start of an operational increase that would continue steadily for several more months until the *VVS* was, in fact, able to challenge the Luftwaffe for its command of the skies over Stalingrad.

THE CITY OF RUBBLE GASPS FOR BREATH

Throughout September, Fiebig's air corps directed most of its attacks against Stalingrad itself, the main targets being the Lazur chemical factory inside the "tennis racket" (a huge rail loop), the *Krasnyi Oktyabr* (Red October) metallurgical works, the *Barrikady* (Barricade) gun factory, and the Dzerzhinski tractor factory. The corps pounded those targets most days, except when aircraft were urgently needed to support an Axis advance or stem a Soviet counterattack in the region north of the city. On 18 September, for example, Lieutenant General Chuikov noticed that the German aircraft crowding the sky above Stalingrad suddenly departed, giving Sixty-second Army a much-needed "breathing space."[58] Fiebig had hastily called them away, he realized, in order to deploy them in the region north of the city, where they were urgently needed to counter a surprise attack by the Stalingrad Front. Six hours later, Chuikov noted with disappointment, "It was clear that the [Soviet] attack was over: hundreds of Junkers had reappeared."

Chuikov quickly noticed that the Luftwaffe carried out surprisingly few raids at night. He could not work out, therefore, why the Stalingrad Front attempted its attacks during the day, "when we had no way of neutralizing or compensating for the enemy's superiority in the air, and not at night (when the Luftwaffe did not operate with any strength)."[59] The city's defenders did not make the same mistake, he added later in his memoirs: "The enemy could not fight at night, but we learned to do so out of bitter necessity; by day the enemy's planes hung over our troops, preventing them from raising their heads. At night we need have no fear of the Luftwaffe." This was certainly true: at Stalingrad, as at Sevastopol, the Luftwaffe conducted almost no night missions to speak of. Its aircraft lacked the specialized night navigation and bomb-aiming equipment necessary for situations like this, when opposing forces battled in close proximity. Also, its airfields, with a few exceptions, were poorly equipped for night operations.

Fiebig's air corps also bombed and strafed any Soviet forces seen among the broken buildings and piles of rubble. Chuikov recalled that "the Luftwaffe literally hammered anything they saw in the streets into the ground."[60] In his detailed memoirs, he also quotes the situation report of a young lieutenant whose com-

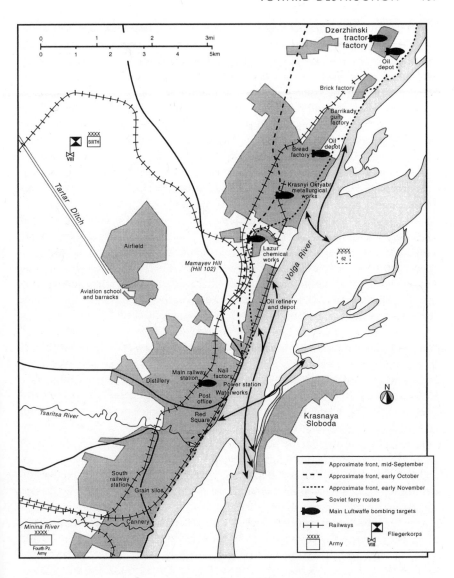

6. Stalingrad: The prize that eluded Hitler

pany came under severe air attacks on 18 September. "From morning till noon," Lieutenant A. Kuzmich Dragan wrote, "clusters of German planes hung in the sky over the city. Some of them would break away from their formations, dive and riddle the streets and ruins of houses with bullets from ground level; others would fly over the city with sirens wailing, in an attempt to sow panic. They dropped high explosives and incendiaries. The city was in flames."[61]

Determined to support German troops now fighting for every house and building by stopping the steady trickle of Soviet reinforcements entering the city from the eastern bank of the kilometer-wide Volga River, Fiebig's corps also directed attacks against the river crossing facilities. Rear Admiral Rogachev's Volga Fleet used numerous crossing points, but mainly "Crossing 62," its moorings at the *Krasnyi Oktyabr* and *Barrikady* factories. The small fleet ferried substantial numbers of men and large quantities of rations and ammunition across the river to the desperate Sixty-second Army. These courageous sailors, Chuikov maintained, "rendered an incalculable service. . . . Every trip across the Volga involved a tremendous risk, but no boat or steamer ever lingered with its cargo on the other bank."[62] Had it not been for them, he concluded, the Sixty-second Army would almost certainly have perished in September.

Alan Clark, British author of a now-outdated popular account of the war in Russia, maintained that if the Luftwaffe "had been employed with single-minded persistence in an 'interdiction' role . . . the Volga ferries might have been knocked out."[63] Clark was clearly unaware of *Luftflotte 4*'s poor state when he wrote these words. Richthofen had no aircraft available for a proper interdiction campaign against the Volga crossings. As noted earlier, by 20 September his air fleet had already lost half its total strength and, because of a drop in serviceability levels, had a mere 516 airworthy planes (when *Blau* began, it had 1,155).[64] Moreover, 120 of those were reconnaissance and sea planes, leaving him with only 396 operational combat aircraft. With this small force, he was already extremely hard-pressed to fulfill his army-support obligations. Having stripped Pflugbeil's *Fliegerkorps IV* to the bones in order to concentrate an acceptable number of aircraft at Stalingrad, he had left the two German armies in the Caucasus with very little air support and could only increase it during times of crisis by returning units temporarily from the Stalingrad region. Thus, he could spare no aircraft for a systematic interdiction campaign against Volga crossings.

Fliegerkorps VIII did not ignore the crossings, of course. Both Fiebig and Richthofen realized that, if Paulus's men were going to destroy the enemy troops fighting fanatically in the ruined city, they had to sever their supply and reinforcement lines. Although they lacked aircraft for a proper interdiction campaign, they continually threw as many bombers and dive-bombers as they could spare each day against the railway lines carrying men and matériel to the eastern bank of the Volga, against the exposed and poorly defended loading and landing platforms and against any barges and steamers seen crossing the river. Fiebig often managed to keep aircraft continuously above the crossing points. As Chuikov remembered: "From dawn till dusk enemy dive-bombers circled over the Volga."[65] Likewise, Lieutenant Colonel Vladimirov noted in 1943: "The enemy bombers, operating in groups of 10 to 50, ceaselessly bombed our troops, the eastern part of the city and the crossings on the Volga. . . . The Germans relied on their aircraft to crush the fire system of our defense [that is, the artillery], paralyze our organization, prevent the arrival of reinforcements, and disrupt the movements of supplies."[66]

German aircraft hunted down each boat and barge, but, as the discussion of air attacks on Black Sea shipping revealed, sinking ships from the air was extremely difficult. The relatively small size of Volga barges and ferries made them difficult targets. As a result, Fiebig's dive-bombers proved far more successful against railheads and ferry landing platforms than they did against the vessels themselves.

German troops penetrated the city to the Volga in the middle of September and brought the central crossings under the sweep of their artillery guns and the weapons of *Generalmajor* Pickert's flak teams. Their gunfire greatly added to the destructive power of Fiebig's Stukas. As a result, the Volga Flotilla had to decrease its daylight crossings substantially. Crossing at night was also risky, Chuikov explained, because "the enemy knew where our ferries crossed and throughout the night lit up the Volga by dropping flares suspended by parachutes."[67] When most ferries began crossing at night, *Fliegerkorps VIII* lost the ability to inflict substantial damage on them. It continued its raids on the loading and landing platforms, however, often wrecking or damaging them or moored boats.

In the first days of October, three 280-meter-long footbridges were constructed near the *Krasnyi Oktyabr* and *Barrikady* factories in order to supplement the overworked ferries.[68] These wooden footbridges, mainly made of barrels and rafts lashed together by rope and linked by iron bars, joined the city with Zaitsevski Island across the Volga's Denezhnaya Volozhka branch. To the amazement of German observers, several thousand men crossed these flimsy bridges. Both the Luftwaffe and the army directed attacks against them, without causing more than minor damage to two. The third bridge lasted only three days. A lucky dive-bomber broke its hawser with a well-placed bomb, allowing the swirling current to drag it away.

Fiebig's units encountered weak opposition as they carried out these attacks on the Volga Flotilla and its loading and landing points. *VVS* fighters increased missions over the river and the road and rail routes from the Russian hinterland to the eastern bank, but they were few in number and generally no match for the German fighters escorting Stukas.[69] Flak protection was especially weak, although it strengthened significantly in October. "The city's anti-aircraft defenses had already been substantially weakened," Chuikov explained, referring to the situation in September.[70] "Part of the anti-aircraft artillery had been destroyed by the enemy, and what remained of it had been moved to the left bank of the Volga." From there, the remaining flak batteries could cover only "the river and a narrow strip along the right bank. From dawn to dusk, therefore, German planes were over the city, over our military units and over the Volga."

German artillery gunners and dive-bomber pilots succeeded in making life difficult for the Volga Flotilla, causing it to switch to night crossings only. However, despite this achievement and the minor damage they inflicted on vessels and landing platforms, they failed to sever the city's vital lifeline. The importance of the Volga Flotilla can be shown by mentioning a few remarkable statistics: between 13 and 16 September, around 10,000 reinforcements from the 13th Guards Division, a crack Soviet unit, crossed the river and entered the battle for the ruined city.[71] They were the forerunners of almost 60,000 others who crossed the river during the next two weeks in a desperate attempt to deny Hitler the prize he now wanted most: the city bearing the name of their leader. The Soviet flotilla carried across not only these troops but also large quantities of small-arms ammunition, mortar bombs, and rations (including thousands of bottles of vodka, considered essential to the maintenance of troop morale). Serving as floating ambulances, the flotilla also evacuated hundreds of wounded soldiers each night. The failure of both the Luftwaffe and the army to stop these magnificent river crossing operations contributed substantially to their failure to capture the city completely before the Soviets launched their massive November counteroffensive.

In the second half of September, Paulus's men made very slow progress as they fought their way street by street through the city from west to east. Noting on 22 September that the army "barely advanced," the self-righteous Richthofen accused it of "constipation."[72] His criticism of the army's vacillation and overcautious deployment back in August may have been justified, but his accusation that German divisions now in Stalingrad fought halfheartedly were certainly not. In bitter and bloody street fighting, usually in smashed houses, rubble-filled factory yards, and even sewers, they attacked constantly and courageously, suffering shocking losses. In his study of the Stalingrad campaign, *Generalmajor* Hans Doerr revealed the character of combat within the ruins:

In the middle of September began the battle for Stalingrad's industrial area, which can be described as "trench" or "fortress" warfare. The time for conducting "operations" was over for good. From the wide expanses of the steppes, fighting had moved into the jagged gullies of the Volga bank, with its copses and ravines, into the city and factory areas of Stalingrad, spread out over uneven, pitted, rugged land, covered with iron, concrete and stone buildings. The kilometer was replaced as a measure of distance by the meter. GHQ's map was the map of the city. A bitter battle for every house, factory, water tower, railway embankment, wall, cellar and every pile of rubble was waged, without equal even in the First World War. . . . The distance between the enemy's forces and ours was as small as it could possibly be. Despite the concentrated activity of aircraft and artillery, it was impossible to break out of the area of close fighting. The Russians surpassed the Germans in their use of the terrain and in camouflage and were more experienced in barricade warfare for individual buildings; they defended firmly.[73]

1. Wolfram Freiherr von Richthofen in 1941 when, as a *Generalleutnant,* he commanded *Fliegerkorps VIII,* the Luftwaffe's premier close-support force. A brain tumor caused his retirement from active service in November 1944, at the rank of *Generalfeldmarschall,* and he died on 12 July 1945.

2. Working closely with Richthofen, *Generaloberst* Erich von Manstein carefully coordinated his army's operations in the Crimea with those of the Luftwaffe. His successful recapture of the Kerch Peninsula and assault on Sevastopol earned him promotion to *Generalfeldmarschall*.

3. Henschel Hs 129s prepare for takeoff, location unknown. Hs 129s were first tested in combat during the Battle of Kerch, making a "good impression" on Richthofen.

4. Ground staff prepare a BF 109 for operations, eastern front 1942.

5. A Luftwaffe photograph of Sevastopol's northwestern defenses. The octagonal *Nordfort* (North Fort) was one of many strong fortifications around the perimeter of this heavily defended city. Constantine Battery (shown in next photograph) was situated on the spit shown in the bottom left-hand corner.

6. Constantine Battery guarded the entrance to Severnaya Bay. Like all fortifications in and around Sevastopol, it was repeatedly attacked by bombers and dive-bombers of Richthofen's air corps.

7. *Fliegerkorps VIII* continuously bombed Sevastopol throughout June, inflicting substantial damage and forcing its terrified inhabitants to flee from the city or hide in tunnels and cellars.

8. *Fliegerführer Süd* and elements of *Fliegerkorps VIII* sank or damaged several Soviet destroyers and other warships attempting to break their "sea blockade." Stukas scored direct hits on the stern of this destroyer as it attempted to unload supplies in Severnaya Bay.

9. The Luftwaffe also attacked merchant vessels, both in ports along the Black Sea's Caucasus coast and en route to Sevastopol. Stukas of the 77th Dive-Bomber Wing sank this merchant ship in Novorossiisk harbor.

10. The powerful 305-mm (12-inch) guns of the Soviet battleship *Pariskaya Kommuna* blast at German positions in the Crimea. By June 1942, Vice Admiral Oktyabrskii, commander of the Soviet Black Sea Fleet, had become so fearful of his capital ships being sunk by the Luftwaffe that he withdrew them to the relative safety of Poti and Batumi, where strong flak defenses afforded them protection. They sheltered there until the Luftwaffe's strength in the eastern Black Sea region dwindled when Richthofen began steadily transferring air units to the Stalingrad sector several months later.

11. In June 1942, *Admiral Schwarzes Meer,* the German Black Sea Fleet, sent several submarine and torpedo boat flotillas to the Crimea. Operating in close cooperation with *Fliegerführer Süd,* the Luftwaffe antishipping command stationed in the Crimea, they proved effective against Soviet warships and merchantmen attempting to carry supplies into Sevastopol. The photograph shows a torpedo being lowered onto a motor torpedo boat of the 1st E-Boat Flotilla.

12. The command staff of *Luftflotte 4* in 1941. Although the air fleet's composition changed considerably during the last months of 1941 and the first of 1942, several senior officers remained to oversee operations during Operation *Blau*, the preceding Crimean offensives, and the following Stalingrad airlift. The fleet commander, Alexander Löhr, is fourth from the right (in a white tunic). Because of his diminutive stature, high cheekbones, and small and narrow eyes, Richthofen privately called Löhr "the little Japanese emperor." The other officer in a white tunic is Günther Korten, who served as Löhr's chief of staff during the first half of 1942 and later succeeded Hans Jeschonnek as chief of the Luftwaffe General Staff. The tall, thin officer second from the right is Kurt Pflugbeil, *Fliegerkorps IV*'s capable commander.

13. Hitler admired Richthofen, a committed National Socialist, aggressive commander, inspiring leader, forthright adviser, and loyal follower. The Führer shakes the air leader's hand at an airfield in southern Russia (date unknown).

14. In July 1942, Richthofen assumed command of *Luftflotte 4*. *Generalleutnant* Martin Fiebig, a close-support expert to whom he had taught his "trade," replaced him as head of *Fliegerkorps VIII*. Fiebig, pictured in conversation with *Oberst* Stahel (with cap), proved an effective air corps commander, displaying energy, courage, and sound judgment even during the worst of circumstances.

15. The Ilyushin Il-2 Shturmovik was probably the most famous Soviet aircraft of the war—and deservedly so. Well armed and armored, it proved an effective ground-attack and close-support machine. Shturmoviks inflicted heavy losses on German army units, particularly in regions where Luftwaffe fighter protection was scarce.

16. *Major* Gordon Gollob, commander of the 3rd Group of the 52nd Fighter Wing (flying Bf 109Gs), shot down this Shturmovik over the central Caucasus in July 1942. It was his 114th verified aerial victory. Within a month, he would reach his 150th, making him the Luftwaffe's top ace of the 1942 eastern campaign.

17. Luftwaffe flak weapons, especially the superb high-velocity 88-mm gun, proved deadly to Soviet tanks, bunkers, and field installations. This photograph shows an "88" in action during the advance to Stalingrad.

18. Except for those guarding airfields, logistics centers, and other key installations from air attack, Luftwaffe flak batteries accompanied army units into combat. The crew of this light gun point to incoming aircraft on the outskirts of Stalingrad.

19. A cautious commander with little tactical imagination, Friedrich Paulus (seated) lacked the strength of character and decisiveness needed to capture Stalingrad or save his army from destruction after its encirclement. Bending over the table is General Rodenburg, commander of the 76th Infantry Division.

20. Whenever possible, Richthofen (with binoculars) carefully coordinated his air units' operations with those of the army, creating joint *Schwerpunkte* (points of maximum effort). Here he watches a Stuka attack with *General der Panzertruppe* Hans Hube (wearing glasses), the highly decorated commander of the Fourteenth Panzer Corps.

21. Ju 87 Stukas were slow and vulnerable to attack, especially when pulling out of dives. When free of enemy air opposition, however, they proved very effective. They could fly all day with little maintenance, carry relatively heavy bomb loads, place their bombs with a high degree of accuracy, and withstand flak hits that would disable or destroy many other aircraft. These Stukas fly over Stalingrad, which they and horizontal bombers turned to ruins between August and November 1942.

22. A Ju 87 Stuka over one of Russia's great rivers, possibly the Volga.

23. Ju 88s at a German airfield in Russia. The large warning sign inside the hangar states "Smoking Forbidden!"

24. The Luftwaffe turned Stalingrad's industrial districts into piles of rubble, buckled steel, and twisted girders.

25. Luftwaffe bombers, dive-bombers, and flak guns, joined by the army's artillery guns, totally destroyed most of Stalingrad, leaving very few buildings standing and none undamaged.

26. This photograph shows the Lazur chemical works' railway siding, a popular target referred to by German aircrews as the "tennis racket."

27. Fiebig directed his bombers to smash Stalingrad's oil installations, including the large oil depot of the Dzerzhinski tractor factory. The photograph shows that oil depot burning wildly, prompting Richthofen to write excitedly in his diary that the "thick, black fire-clouds" climbed 3,500 meters into the sky and stretched for twenty-five kilometers.

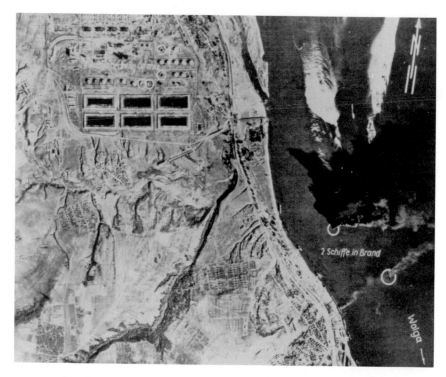

2 Schiffe in Brand

Wolga —

28. Several of *Fliegerkorps VIII*'s Stuka squadrons attacked shipping on the Volga River, both north and south of Stalingrad. They sank numerous tankers and transport barges, including these two ships (circled), which were left burning at Saratov, north of Stalingrad. Yet they failed to sever this major north-south supply artery.

29. Wanting to restore his tattered prestige and unable to stand up to Hitler, *Reichsmarschall* Hermann Göring, the Luftwaffe's commander in chief, promised the Führer that his air force could keep Sixth Army alive and operational at Stalingrad. He made this assurance without having first consulted his airlift experts, studied all available information on the situation at Stalingrad, or sought the opinions of Richthofen and the *Fliegerkorps* commanders involved. Göring did not even bother to oversee the airlift himself. Instead, he disappeared to Paris on a shopping trip and then, on his return, only rarely attempted to involve himself in its progress.

30. Preheating engines—by blowing hot air onto them from tubes connected to special ovens—was not always possible because of a scarcity of heating devices caused by the abandonment of equipment at several airfields that *Fliegerkorps VIII* hastily evacuated in order to prevent them being overrun by the Red Army.

31. Most Luftwaffe airfields involved in the Stalingrad airlift lacked mechanized snowplows like this. Instead, troops armed only with shovels spent long hours each day clearing snow and ice from runways and maintenance areas. Few hangars existed, so most maintenance was carried out in the open.

32. Despite the tremendous effort of cold and exhausted Luftwaffe ground personnel to keep runways free of snow and ice, the combination of poor visibility, caused by constant snow, fog, or low cloud, and uneven runway surfaces, caused by frequent Soviet bombing raids, resulted in numerous crash landings.

33. Heinkel 111s suffered less from the effects of cold than Ju 52s and, because of their defensive machine guns, proved less vulnerable to Soviet fighters. Although very awkward to load and unload, they made fair transport planes, having a similar load capacity to a Ju 52 and a far greater range.

34. *Oberst* Ernst Kühl, commander of all He 111 units involved in the Stalingrad airlift, lived up to his name, which means "cool." An experienced bomber commander with an impressive record of distinguished service, Kühl remained calm, courageous, and decisive even under the most difficult circumstances. Richthofen trusted him completely, calling him "a splendid fellow to have around when the chips are down." This photograph shows Kühl inspecting enemy fighter damage to his He 111.

35. *Generalfeldmarschall* Erhard Milch, deputy supreme commander of the Luftwaffe and air inspector general, was a dynamic leader and outstanding administrator. He displayed excellent managerial skills during the final two weeks of the Stalingrad airlift. Yet he arrived too late to make a substantial difference to its progress and was no more able to overcome adverse weather conditions and considerable enemy air and ground superiority than Richthofen and Fiebig had been.

The tenacity of the city's defenders, many units of which were reduced to one-tenth of strength and had no weapons heavier than tommy guns, won them respect from many German observers still bent on their destruction. *Hauptmann* Pabst, for instance, pounded them every day with his Stuka squadron yet noted in his journal with mild admiration that they "tenaciously defend every pile of rubble."[74] "The Russians," he wrote in another entry, "remain in their burning city and won't budge. There's hardly a house left, just an atrocious chaos of ruins and fire, into which we drop our bombs. . . . But the Russians won't budge."[75]

Despite the Soviets' tenacity, however, the waves of German troops thrown in by Paulus, constantly supported by tanks and aircraft, gradually overpowered them. On 26 September, the German commander was finally able to declare the city center secured, after his men took the central landing area, the last government buildings, and the large bunker that had been Chuikov's headquarters. "Since noon," Paulus reported, winning even Richthofen's grudging approval for once, "the German war flag has been flying over the party buildings."[76] Half the city lay in German hands. Hoth's panzers, now under Sixth's Army's operational control, held the suburbs south of the Tsaritsa River. Sixth Army's own troops occupied the central districts. Yet Paulus had suffered severe losses—7,700 dead and 31,000 wounded in the last six weeks—and still had to capture the strongly defended northern industrial district.

Temporarily buoyed by the penetration of central Stalingrad, Hitler was apparently less concerned (or less well informed) about the high losses and looming difficulties than was his army commander. On 30 September, he opened his drive for the winter relief with a rousing speech to the German people from the Berlin *Sportspalast*.[77] Referring to a string of dismal British failures, including Dunkirk and the hopeless Dieppe fiasco, he ridiculed something he privately admired: the way the British managed to turn humiliating defeats into propaganda victories. "Obviously we cannot even begin to compare our own modest successes with them!" he jeered, boldly adding: "If we advance to the Don, finally reach the Volga, overrun Stalingrad and capture it—and of that they can be certain—in their eyes this is all nothing." Stalingrad would soon fall, he emphasized to his audience, assuring them (in a manner he doubtless later came to regret) that "you can be certain no one will get us away from there."

Fliegerkorps VIII contributed significantly to the army's progress within the city, conducting massive attacks on Soviet pockets of resistance. The air corps' strength fluctuated widely, dropping substantially when Richthofen temporarily (but frequently, throughout September and October) diverted units to assist First Panzer and Seventeenth Armies in the Caucasus or to protect Axis troops in the Voronezh region. Usually, though, the corps operated two or three bomber wings from airfields at Morozovskaya and Tatsinskaya, as well as five or six Stuka groups, three or four fighter groups, and a "destroyer" group from airfields closer to the target area. Despite their low serviceability levels, these units were still sufficient for attacks on Stalingrad, Volga shipping in the vicinity of the city as well as in the stretch between there and Astrakhan, and rail and road logistical routes east of the Volga. In keeping with Richthofen's "proven" army support formula, attacks on the city itself took precedence.

Stuka crews exhausted themselves flying multiple missions against Stalingrad each day. On 15 September, *Hauptmann* Pabst climbed down from his cockpit after seven hours, during which time he had carried out five missions against the city.[78] That was probably a typical day for him. *Major* Paul-Werner Hozzel, commander of the *Immelmann* Stuka Wing *(St.G. 2)* and one of the most successful and acclaimed Stuka pilots of the war, describes how his wing was able to carry out so many missions each day. His units operated from airfields within forty kilometers from the city. "This meant," he explained,

> that we needed for each sortie a chock-to-chock time of not more than 45 minutes, which included taxiing to the start, takeoff, approach flight, the climb to an altitude of 4,000 meters, target pickup, dive bombing attack, low level flight departure, landing, taxiing to the apron. Each turnaround—a new loading, a short technical overhaul, checkout—took us another 15 minutes. We were consistently able to fly with each plane about eight sorties from sunrise to sunset.[79]

Because of the close proximity of opposing forces, air attacks on enemy pockets were always difficult. Detailed aerial photographic maps identified almost every building (those that still stood, anyway), so *Flivos* were able to direct Stuka pilots, who also carried aerial maps, to their targets.[80] Desperate not to hit their own troops, often huddling in buildings or behind walls tens of meters from the targets, pilots were far more careful than usual to place their bombs precisely on their targets and always sought to ascertain the position of German troops.[81] Of course, not even the best Stuka pilots could consistently place their bombs precisely on targets. As a result, "friendly fire" incidents occurred with disappointing (or, from the Soviet viewpoint, pleasing) frequency.

Chuikov's memoirs clearly reveal the considerable impact of *Fliegerkorps VIII*'s "incessant attacks." Following a half-hour artillery barrage, the Soviet commander's worn-out troops launched a localized counterattack before dawn on 14 September. However, although the attack initially made satisfactory progress, "as soon as day broke the enemy brought the Luftwaffe into action; groups of fifty to sixty aircraft flew in, bombing and machine-gunning our counter-attacking units, pinning them to the ground. The counterattack petered out."[82] Events in Stalingrad followed this pattern on numerous occasions. Early on 27 September, for instance, Chuikov's forces launched another small counterattack. "To begin with," he said, "we had some success, but at 8 A.M. hundreds of dive-bombers swooped on our formations. The attacking troops took cover."[83] Two German infantry divisions advanced with strong tank support behind the Luftwaffe's hail of bombs, intent on occupying the *Krasnyi Oktyabr* workers' settlement and Mamayev Kurgan (a hill—actually an ancient burial mound—dividing the city in two). "The Luftwaffe bombed and strafed our units from our forward positions right to the Volga," Chuikov stated. "The strongpoint organized by the troops of Gorishny's division at the Mamayev Kurgan was utterly destroyed by aircraft and artillery. The Army HQ command post was under attack from the air the whole time."

The *VVS* did all it could to defend Chuikov's army and logistical routes from the German air onslaught. It launched nightly bombing raids against German flak positions and airfields, destroying a few aircraft and, just as important, depriving exhausted Luftwaffe personnel of precious sleep.[84] *Hauptmann* Pabst described these attacks in his journal. "In the night," he wrote on 27 September, "the Ivans were very busy. The tremendous noise woke me up. Sand fell from the walls of my sleeping pit [a small dirt bunker]. Again and again, we heard the drone of incoming aircraft and pressed ourselves a little flatter against our straw mattresses, hoping to block out the noise of falling bombs."[85] Pabst's rudimentary (and doubtless uncomfortable) sleeping arrangements may sound strange, but they were common among the Axis forces assailing Stalingrad. Even *Generalmajor* Wolfgang Pickert, commander of the 9th Flak Division, moved out of his trailer and into a tent-covered hollow, hoping it afforded him better protection from bomb blasts.[86]

VVS fighters and ground-attack aircraft conducted defensive operations against German forces in and around Stalingrad, suffering high losses to more experienced and numerically superior Luftwaffe fighter units. A typical mid-September entry in the war diary of the 3rd Group of the Third Fighter Wing states: "During the entire day, the Russians undertook defensive air operations above Stalingrad. [There were also] Shturmovik attacks on the 16th Panzer Division and German forces breaking into the city center."[87] The German group clearly outclassed its opponents, according to that entry: it claimed eleven Soviet aircraft destroyed (five of them Shturmoviks) for no losses.

Soviet fighters also threw themselves wildly at German aircraft, especially the vulnerable Stukas and bombers, bringing down a small but steady number yet losing far more themselves. Pabst described how Soviet fighter pilots aggressively attacked his squadron, occasionally shooting down Stukas or, when their ammunition ran out, trying to ram them. On 25 September, by way of illustration, his squadron was returning from missions against logistical targets east of the Volga when "Russian fighters suddenly turned up. For twenty minutes they attacked us, uninterrupted, from all sides, from above, from below."[88] His aircraft climbed, dove, and weaved as they raced home, pursued by Soviet planes. "One can't express it on paper. It would take too long and lose its immediacy. Yet in practice, it took a high toll on our nerves." He was extremely lucky that day, suffering only seven damaged aircraft and one wounded pilot. Yet, although the *VVS* scored a few aerial victories each day (far fewer than the Luftwaffe, though, which claimed twenty-two destroyed for no reported losses on 27 September alone),[89] it proved incapable of clearing the skies above the city of German aircraft. It still lacked sufficient aircraft and suffered from the same logistical problems that plagued the *Luftwaffe.* On 26 September, Richthofen recorded in his diary: "Over Stalingrad there was not even *a single* Russian aircraft in the sky until late in the day, although around 900 [a huge exaggeration] sat on airfields. No fuel?"

On 27 September, Chuikov urgently appealed to Nikita Khrushchev, the Stalingrad Front's commissar, for increased *VVS* protection. "I make no complaint about our air force, which is fighting heroically," he said, "but the enemy has mastery in the air. His air force is his unbeatable trump card in attack. I therefore ask for increased help in this sphere—to give us cover from the air, if only for a few hours a day."[90] Khrushchev replied that the front was already giving Sixty-second Army all the help it could, but he agreed to pass on Chuikov's request and "press for increased air cover for the city." The "increased" air protection had not arrived, however, before the Luftwaffe launched fresh attacks the next day, keeping up what Chuikov called "a constant, concentrated air attack on our troops, on the ferries and on the Army H.Q. command post." German aircraft, he claimed, "dropped not only bombs, but also pieces of metal, ploughs, tractor wheels, harrows and empty casks, which whistled about the heads of our troops." However fascinating this story is, it is almost certainly apocryphal. Fiebig's units constantly suffered bomb shortages, but at no time in September were they so acute that bomber groups resorted to dropping plows, tractor wheels, and the like.

"FUMBLING AROUND" IN STALINGRAD

October began satisfactorily for the depleted Sixth Army, divisions of which were either throwing back repeated attempts by Don Front to hack open its northern flank or fighting deep inside Stalingrad, battling for individual houses, workshops, and sewers. Only the previous day, divisions holding the northern flank had managed to thwart a powerful attack by Don Front troops, led by 120 tanks. (On 28 September, the *Stavka* had changed Stalingrad Front's name to Don Front, and Southeastern Front's to Stalingrad Front, to reflect their geographical locations more accurately.) If their combat reports are accurate, Paulus's antitank gunners knocked out around sixty tanks, while Pickert's flak troops, firing their "88s" with deadly precision, wrecked almost forty more.[91] On 1 October, while Fiebig's fighters claimed eighteen enemy aircraft destroyed above Stalingrad for no reported losses, the tenacious Don Front pushed forward again in the region north of the city, only to be driven back once more with the loss of sixty tanks.[92] One flak gunner, *Wachmeister* (Technical Sergeant) Gemüd, destroyed twenty-one of those tanks single-handedly, despite being wounded. He became an immediate celebrity. Pickert invited him to his headquarters on the evening of 2 October, and

Richthofen, who called him "extremely courageous," nominated him for the Knight's Cross.[93]

Although Sixth Army's pace of conquest had fallen to single houses or a few workshops per day, operations still seemed to be going relatively well for German air units over Stalingrad. Beginning at nightfall on 30 September, Fiebig's Stukas, Pickert's flak guns, and Paulus's artillery guns savagely attacked barges and ferries attempting to carry Major General Guriev's 39th Guards Infantry Division across the Volga. "Day and night the enemy's artillery and aeroplanes directed withering attacks on our barges and ferries," Chuikov later complained.[94] The Germans proved incapable of halting the transportation of Guriev's men across the river, but they slowed down the rate of reinforcement. "By morning on October 2," Chuikov added, "only two infantry regiments had been landed on the right [or west] bank."

On 2 October—when "nothing special" happened, according to Richthofen, except for "a tiny advance in Stalingrad"—Fiebig's bombers and Stukas launched heavy attacks, again in conjunction with artillery and flak fire, against the *Krasnyi Oktyabr* factory and Chuikov's crude, earthen command post near the Volga. The results were dramatic; near the factory sat huge oil tanks that Chuikov mistakenly took to be empty. Hit by bombs, they exploded with ground-shaking blasts. "Bombs dropped all over the bank," the Soviet commander recalled, "blowing up the oil-tanks full of oil, and a burning mass gushed across our dug-outs towards the Volga. The command post was in the middle of a sea of flames."[95] The situation was horrendous. Chuikov continued:

> The streams of flame burned everything in their path. Reaching the bank of the Volga, the burning oil poured on to the barges standing near the command post. The burning oil floated down with the current. The Volga itself seemed to be bursting into flame. Telephone lines also went up in flames. Communication could be maintained only by radio, which worked with interruptions. We were imprisoned by fire, descending on us from all directions. . . . Surrounded by fire, we stayed where we were and continued administering the Army.

Despite occasional operational successes like this, Sixth Army advanced at a snail's pace through the northern industrial districts. Gains were so small and casualties so great that the army command sank into a mire of pessimism. On 2 October, the chief of staff informed the army group that, "in spite of the most intensive efforts by all forces, the low combat strengths of the infantry will prolong the taking of Stalingrad indefinitely if reinforcements cannot be supplied."[96] Paulus, whose increasingly obvious nervous facial twitch betrayed gnawing doubts about his army's chances of success, had already pulled forward the last of his reserves from back at the Don. Yet, although he now had eleven divisions in and around the shattered city, giving him substantial numerical superiority over Chuikov, he knew his units were all in poor shape and his troops jaded. Next day, he echoed his subordinate's opinion, telling Weichs: "At present even the breaking out of individual blocks of houses can only be accomplished after lengthy regroupings to bring together the few combat-worthy assault elements that can still be found."[97]

Accompanied by Jeschonnek, chief of the Luftwaffe general staff, Richthofen flew to the Fifty-first Army Corps' command post, where they talked at length with Paulus and *Generalmajor* Walter von Seydlitz–Kurzbach, the corps' commander. Surprisingly, the air fleet leader agreed with their assessment: "Success is assured," he told them sympathetically, "but only with an influx of reinforcements."[98] Later that day, he had the opportunity to speak privately to Jeschonnek. "Above all, we lack clarity of purpose and a well-defined *Schwerpunkt*," he asserted. His own depleted air forces lacked the means to continue concentrating forces against Stalingrad, he explained, especially as he often had to dispatch air units south to help Seventeenth and First Panzer Armies, making poor progress in the Caucasus. "We simply can't go on fumbling around everywhere at once with what are, in any event, weak forces. Only when we establish a set of successive goals, and achieve them one at a time, will things go well. Of course," he added, "first of all we have to finish off what we started, especially at Stalingrad and Tuapse."

Axis forces lacked the means to "finish off" Stalingrad in the first weeks of October. On the 6th, Paulus had to suspend offensive operations inside the city for "at least five days" because of what his army's war diary called "the exceptionally low infantry combat strengths."[99] While he hastily regrouped his forces, holding a defensive "line" inside the city, he learned that Hitler had "reaffirmed the total occupation of Stalingrad as Army Group B's most important mission."

Aware that he had virtually no reserves left to send to either Stalingrad or the Caucasus, where the drive to the highly prized oil fields had petered out, the Führer expressed his annoyance at the intolerably low combat strengths of fighting units in relation to their support units.[100] On 8 October, he instructed all his army commanders to account immediately for their subordinate divisions' total ration strength versus combat strength. Nine days later, Sixth Army sent in its strength report. It made disappointing reading. The army had a total ration strength of 334,000 men, but only 66,549 were combat troops (these figures did not include the Fourth Army troops then subordinated to Paulus).[101] Zeitzler, Hitler's recently appointed army chief of the general staff, issued a companion directive to all German army commands, ordering an immediate 10 percent reduction in headquarters personnel, from army group down to divisions.[102] The respective commands were to send the manpower thus freed to the front as combat troops. "Thunderball" Zeitzler also ordered that commands reduce their rear area support personnel in proportion to frontline combat losses and send those freed soldiers forward as replacements. His reasons were sound: support units sharing the hardships of frontline combat and suffering casualties would not only increase reinforcement levels but also eliminate the traditional estrangement between "combat troops" and "rear echelons."

These High Command directives could not, of course, immediately alleviate Paulus's manpower problems. His men needed a rest from offensive action and, between 6 and 14 October, he gave them one. Chuikov's own troops were equally exhausted, so, when German troops settled into temporary defensive positions among the ruins, a weeklong lull occurred. While Chuikov later claimed that "it was not, and could not be, a lull in the proper sense of the word, because our positions were only a grenade-throw from the German positions," the intensity of fighting did drop dramatically.[103] On most days between 6 and 14 October, Richthofen noted in his diary: *Bei Stalingrad absolute Ruhe*—"Absolute quiet at Stalingrad."

This temporary respite not only allowed Paulus to regroup his troops but also permitted Richthofen to concentrate virtually all *Luftflotte 4*'s units, including the bulk of Fiebig's corps, in the Caucasus. Their operations against the Grozny oil refineries and in support of Seventeenth and First Panzer Armies have been analyzed previously, so no description of their activities is needed at this point; suffice to say that Richthofen flew south in order to supervise the air operations personally. As always, he established joint *Schwerpunkte*—albeit small and frequently changing ones—with army commanders during lengthy conferences. These included Mackensen, whom the airman considered "dreadful and boring,"[104] and Ruoff and Kleist, whom he liked, respected, and, on at least one occasion, bravely defended against Göring's angry criticisms.

This situation occurred on 15 October, when Richthofen flew to Hitler's headquarters, armed with photographs of Stalingrad's ravaged suburbs. Hitler, he was amazed to learn, had recently ordered the *Reichsmarschall* to release to the army 200,000 troops from the manpower-swollen Luftwaffe. Göring considered his service branch insulted and pleaded to retain the men under his leadership. He offered to set up twenty Luftwaffe "field divisions" instead. Against the advice of close advisers, the Führer relented, allowing his soft spot for the *Reichsmarschall* to cloud his judgment. Richthofen privately called the decision "most alarming," maintaining that "those troops belong in the depleted army divisions."[105] Hopefully, he added (overoptimistically, as it happened), "the whole thing won't prove a colossal blunder." Extant sources do not reveal whether he openly expressed these views. Although he seldom refrained from speaking his mind, the fact that he mentions no clash with Göring suggests that on this occasion he chose to keep his opinions to himself.

Göring, whose working relationship with Hitler was still intact, although, as he probably knew, his ability to impress him as a military leader had long departed, became excited by Richthofen's claims that the army was performing poorly at Stalingrad and in the Caucasus. He cursed Kleist, Ruoff, and the recently sacked List—to the disgust of Richthofen, who "strongly defended" the first two (but not List, whom he felt deserved what he got).[106] Göring, the fleet commander wrote, "then dragged me off with Jeschonnek to make an unannounced call on the Führer. Once there, he gave a very spirited rendition [of the complaints against the army]."

Hitler was clearly drawn to the charismatic Richthofen, admiring his confidence, drive, and aggression, and wishing that all his operational commanders possessed these qualities. "He was especially affectionate to me," the airman proudly recorded in his diary that night. Indeed, the dictator listened attentively and approvingly to his operational plans and his assessment of "infantry weaknesses, combat leadership and, above all, the terrain." He was clearly angry about the Caucasus campaign's premature death and still upset about his recent clash with List, upon whose head he heaped hot coals. "The Führer vehemently curses List," Richthofen noted, adding: "justifiably." Later that day, Göring told him that Hitler planned to place him in charge of Army Group A in the Caucasus, believing that if anyone could get things going again, he could. (Nothing came of this; upon reflection, Hitler apparently considered Richthofen more valuable as his tactical airpower "troubleshooter.") The *Reichsmarschall* was delighted and, after Richthofen flattered him about a recent speech, promised him a field marshal's baton as soon as Stalingrad fell. The latter laughed it off, replying: "I protest at having to lug a baton around."

During this short lull in fighting at Stalingrad, Richthofen spent most of his time in the Caucasus, close to the bulk of his formations. Naturally, he left sufficient air units in the Stalingrad region to protect Paulus's and Hoth's troops and prevent the *VVS* from temporarily seizing the initiative. Even in the absence of most German fighter groups, which flew south to escort bombers and dive-bombers attacking Tuapse and enemy troops opposing German armies, the *VVS* seemed unable to exploit the situation and press home their attacks with greater safety and consequent success. For example, the 10 October entry in the war diary of the 3rd Group of the Luftwaffe's Third Fighter Wing states: "In the morning hours, weak Russian defensive air activity above Sixth Army's northern flank and Stalingrad. In the afternoon, very weak Russian air activity. . . . We dominate the airspace over Stalingrad."[107]

The German units remaining around Stalingrad did not operate by themselves, as Richthofen's diary reveals. On 6 October, he welcomed to his headquarters two Rumanian air commanders, Generals Enescu and Ghiorghiu, "who should, after the 10th, independently direct [their own units] under our fleet command." The first of their five combat groups, he learned, were already on their way. On 7 and 9 October, he held lengthy meetings with Gienescu, the Rumanian air minister, during which they discussed the role to be played by those groups. As "operationally independent" formations of Fiebig's *Fliegerkorps VIII,* they were to provide air support to the Rumanian Third Army, which, with its eleven fresh divisions, was due to take over a section of the front northwest of Stalingrad on 10 October. Richthofen found Gienescu friendly and cooperative. "We are in agreement," he noted simply in his diary after their first meeting. "Conversations with Gerstenberg [the German air attaché in Bucharest] and the Rumanian Air Minister were successful," he wrote after the second. "Marshal Antonescu approves all our proposals."

Weak Rumanian units had already tasted combat as part of Fiebig's corps. *Escadrila 15*, with a complement of only six underpowered Rumanian I A R 39A tactical reconnaissance biplanes, had accompanied the Rumanian Sixth Army Corps' advance since the summer campaign began.[108] These aircraft monitored enemy movements, directed artillery fire, dropped small bombs, and, on rare occasions, engaged enemy aircraft. Units of *Corpul Aerian*, the Rumanian air force's most powerful combat formation, began arriving at airfields in the Don bend early in September.[109] On 16 September, *Grup 7 Vanatori*—comprising *Escadrilas 56, 57*, and *58*, each with 12 Bf 109Es—began its operations from Karpovka with ten days of fighter operations in support of German assaults on Stalingrad. A week or so later, the fifteen He 111s of *Grup 5 Bombardament* began bombing missions, followed shortly after by the fifteen Rumanian-made J RS 79B and J IS 79B bombers of *Grup 1 Bombardament*. In the first days of October, another fighter group, *Grup 8 Vanatori*, with thirty-six Rumanian-made I A R 80As, arrived in the Stalingrad sector. The I A R 80As were no match for the latest Soviet fighters but were capable, nonetheless, of dueling the older-vintage fighters still possessed by many *V VS* units.

All these Rumanian groups operated under Major General Ghiorghiu as the *Rümanischen I. Fliegerkorps* (Rumanian First Air Corps).[110] They mainly attacked Soviet road and rail traffic northwest of Stalingrad, enemy ground positions facing Rumanian army units, and *V VS* units in the airspace above those units. Yet reconstructing a clear picture of their achievements or contribution to the Axis efforts in the region is almost impossible, at least with sources available outside Rumania. Like the single Croatian unit active in the Stalingrad area— the tiny *15./J.G. 52*, usually operating with less than a dozen Bf 109s[111]—they are scarcely mentioned in surviving German reports and war diaries. Richthofen, for example, totally ignored them in his own detailed diary. Even Mark Axworthy, author of an excellent study of the Rumanian armed forces during the Second World War, devoted little space to their operations. The regrettably slim treatment of Rumanian air operations in the present work reflects this scarcity of material, not the low importance of those efforts.

One fact is clear: Rumanian units certainly strengthened *Luftflotte 4*, which, despite receiving a trickle of replacements (mainly bombers), was no stronger in October than it had been the previous month. On 20 October, the fleet possessed 974 aircraft, excluding the "independent" Rumanian planes; 594 (61 percent) of these were operational.[112] The fleet's bomber force, in very bad shape in September, when it had only 129 airworthy aircraft, had recovered significantly, now numbering 186. Yet this was still a major drop from the 323 bombers that had been operational when *Blau* began back in June.

THE FINAL AXIS OFFENSIVE OPERATIONS

Richthofen's bombers and Stukas still packed a solid punch, despite their marked decrease in strength since June and July and the intense strain on ground personnel caused by the groups' recent transfers back and forth over enormous distances. On 12 and 13 October, the bulk of Fiebig's units returned from the Caucasus to their bases around Stalingrad. On the 14th, they launched a heavy attack on the city in support of Paulus's troops, who returned to offensive operations with an all-out attack after a week of regrouping, minor reinforcement, and defensive battles. With what Richthofen called "hardly any" VVS opposition, "the strongest magic of Fliegerkorps VIII" fell upon the northern suburbs of Stalin's city.[113] Hans Doerr described the scale of this joint air force and army offensive:

> On October 14, the largest operation [against Stalingrad] to date commenced: an attack by numerous divisions, including the 14th Panzer, 305th and 389th Infantry Divisions [the first two "borrowed" from Hoth's depleted army], against the Dzerzhinski tractor factory, the eastern part of which was occupied by the Russian Sixty-second Army. Although they were needed just as much where they were brought from, reinforcements, engineers and anti-tank units had arrived from all sectors of the front, including the army's flanks on the Don and the Kalmyck Steppe. The Luftwaffe transported five engineer battalions from the Reich. The entire Fliegerkorps VIII supported the attack.[114]

Paulus thrust three infantry divisions and almost 200 panzers into the three-kilometer-long industrial complex, which had produced T-34s and other killer tanks until Fiebig's aircraft helped Pickert's flak guns and Paulus's artillery demolish its workshops and assembly lines. Chuikov's men, exhausted from their own unsuccessful counterattack the previous day, were shocked by the attack's "unprecedented ferocity." The general himself noted, "Those of us who had already been through a great deal will remember this enemy attack all our lives."[115] German guns, rocket launchers, and mortars bombarded Soviet positions the entire day, while tanks and Panzer grenadiers forced their way through the blocks of workers' houses, ruined workshops, and debris-strewn factory yards.

The Luftwaffe played a key role in the attack, unloading over 600 tons of bombs on the tractor factory and Chuikov's strongpoints. Major (later General) Hozzel, commander of the Immelmann Stuka Wing, recalled that Richthofen "made us understand that our Geschwader had to do precision bombing so as to avoid danger to our troops entrenched close to the target area. He wanted to watch our sorties, judge the accuracy of our pilots, from his command post at the western outskirts of the city."[116] Hozzel explained why "this was indeed a very delicate order": "We could not risk making a dive-bombing attack from 4,000 meters altitude because of the wide area of [bomb] dispersion. We had to fly a slant range attack, releasing the bombs directly over the roofs. We had to push the bombs into the target like loaves of bread into an oven, with one plane succeeding the other."

When free of enemy air opposition, Stukas were effective attack aircraft, capable of flying all day with little maintenance, carrying relatively heavy bomb loads, placing their deadly projectiles with unparalleled precision and withstanding flak hits that would disable or destroy many other aircraft. For the raids on the tractor factory, ground personnel fitted them with special payloads. As Hozzel pointed out: "We loaded each plane with one 500-kilo bomb with a tank-busting head and delayed action fuse for piercing the [factory] roofs. Each plane also carried two 250-kilo bombs under the wings, so each carried a load of 1,000 kilos."

Soviet flak guns now operated on both banks of the Volga, most "manned" by women. After the war, Chuikov repeatedly extolled the bravery and tenacity of those women, who were "models of courage." "They would stick to their guns and go on firing," he explained, "when bombs were exploding all round them, when it seemed impossible not merely to fire accurately, but even to stay with the guns. In the fire and smoke, amid bursting bombs, seemingly unaware of the columns of earth exploding into the air all about them, they stood their ground to the last."[117] They were not only courageous, he added; they were also relatively successful: "The Luftwaffe's raids on the city, therefore, in spite of heavy losses among the anti-aircraft personnel, were always met by concentrated fire, which as a rule took a heavy toll among the attacking aircraft. Our women antiaircraft gunners shot down dozens of enemy planes over the blazing city." He was exaggerating, but not grossly. Major Hozzel noted that the city's flak teams "fired at us with all calibers at their disposal, inflicting heavy casualties on us."[118] In fact, his wing "suffered its most severe losses by anti-aircraft fire and hardly [any] by Soviet fighter planes." Hozzel's losses, it should be noted, were never severe by the standards of Soviet units. In the four months that his 200-strong wing operated in the Stalingrad region, it lost a daily average of only one Stuka, even though the wing—which included, incidentally, a dozen or so Italian Macchi fighters—often carried out more than 500 sorties per day. As Hozzel put it: "Four months, 120 days, 120 losses."

Despite stiff flak opposition, the factory and its surrounding houses, workshops, and courtyards made good targets for the constantly circling and diving Stukas. "As on a string of pearls," Hozzel remembered, "one plane followed the others within an interval of a few seconds, throwing the bombs on the oblong target area divided among us. Not one single bomb missed its target. This brought our crews high praises by the infantry."[119] Devastating the factory and killing many hundreds of its defenders, the Stukas attacked without pause the entire day. "We recorded some 3,000 sorties by enemy aircraft," Chuikov later wrote, wildly exaggerating or miscalculating (the true figure was probably closer to 1,250).[120] "German aeroplanes bombed and machine-gunned our troops without stop. . . .

It was a sunny day, but the smoke and dust cut visibility down to a hundred yards. Our dug-outs shook and caved in like houses of cards."[121] Yet the morale of Chuikov's troops did not crack. Like Sevastopol's defenders, they dug themselves deep into the rubble, and, despite incessant bomb and cannon explosions, which threw torn-apart corpses everywhere, they defended their positions with extraordinary courage and blind fanaticism. Hozzel was shocked: although his wing had repeatedly smashed the factory district with intense ferocity, German infantry units encountered "fierce counterattacks as though nothing had happened; as if the *Geschwader* had dropped toy torpedoes instead of bombs."[122]

Still, the day went as well for the attackers as it did poorly for the defenders. "The advances at Stalingrad were good," Richthofen commented that night. "The dreaded tractor factory has been taken. The Russians were apparently taken by surprise. We've reached the Volga on a front of three kilometers." Indeed, although their casualties were very high (perhaps 2,000 killed and wounded), German forces did capture most of the factory, surround the remaining sections, split Sixty-second Army in two, and inflict equally high losses on Chuikov's troops and armed factory workers. As John Erickson wrote: "The approaches to the tractor plant were littered with the dead and dying, hundreds of Soviet wounded crawled to the Volga or waited in the night to be ferried on one of those ghastly journeys across the Volga; that night 3,500 wounded men were ferried to the eastern bank, the largest single tally in the whole of the defensive battle."[123]

Hitler was delighted, believing that Stalingrad would be his within days (which doubtless explains why, as mentioned, he was so pleased to see Richthofen when the airman arrived at his Ukrainian headquarters the next day). The Führer craved news of this nature, especially as he had recently instructed the Luftwaffe to wreck the Caucasus oil fields, the principal objectives of his now-lifeless summer campaign. Also, that very morning, 14 October, he had ordered all forces in the east, except those battling inside Stalingrad and pushing (hopelessly, as it happened) toward Tuapse and Grozny, to prepare for winter in the lines they held. "This year's summer and fall campaigns," he wrote, "excepting those operations under way and several local offensives still contemplated [a reference to a planned operation at Leningrad], have been concluded."[124] With this order, Hitler brought his offensive to a more timely close than he had a year earlier, but he also raised to the level of doctrine the fanatical defensive formula that had saved his armies during the previous winter. "Every leader," he stated, "down to squad leader must be convinced of his sacred duty to stand fast, come what may, even if the enemy outflanks him on the right and left, even if his part of the line is cut off, encircled, overrun by tanks, enveloped in smoke or gassed."

On 15 October, Paulus's troops entirely cleared the tractor factory and brickworks before turning south the following day, behind *Fliegerkorps VIII's* curtain of falling bombs, toward their next objectives: the *Barrikady* gun factory, the bread bakeries, and the *Krasnyi Oktyabr* metallurgical works. By the afternoon of 16 October, they had taken half the gun factory and encircled several pockets of resistance a few kilometers northwest of the city.

As usual in this period, the army received effective Luftwaffe support, from both air and flak units. "Hundreds of dive-bombers and assault aircraft bombed and machine-gunned our sector," Chuikov later wrote, "[especially] where tanks of the 84th Brigade were dug in. Buildings were burning, the earth was burning and the tanks were burning. Our anti-aircraft artillery was unable to give our troops any real cover."[125] *Generalmajor* Pickert's diary reveals what he called (with understandable pride and only slight exaggeration) the "key role" played by his own flak teams. Their guns punched massive holes through the concrete and brick walls providing cover but little protection to the fiercely defending troops and factory workers. "It's a fantastic sight," Pickert wrote on 17 October. "Absolutely *nothing* in the suburbs has escaped destruction. We fired several thousand rounds there, including a lot of anti-tank shells, used against the most solid buildings."

Despite these strong attacks (which killed and wounded 13,000 Soviets in the first three days) and the steady gains they produced, Stalingrad's tenacious defenders were not yet willing to let Hitler trumpet the fall of their ruined metropolis. They resisted bitterly, especially inside the gun factory, where twisted machinery, stacks of iron, and metal debris made superb gun nests. To Paulus's intense frustration, his troop strength was fading rapidly while the Soviets received a small but steady flow of reinforcements from the eastern shore of the Volga. Even more important, he realized that Chuikov had kept his nerve under the most difficult and dangerous circumstances and, valiantly leading from the front (where his men could see his own suffering), he had prevented a rout and forged his shattered regiments into makeshift combat groups.

By 19 October, Paulus's units had destroyed several pockets of resistance in the gun factory, captured a few more blocks of houses, and brought their guns, mortars, and rockets to bear on the bread factories and the *Krasnyi Oktyabr* metallurgical works. Yet this was certainly not the pace of conquest the general had expected when he launched his major attack five days earlier. Richthofen was again disgusted. His airmen had thrown everything they had at the enemy, he self-righteously claimed, yet the army failed to concentrate forces against single targets and advance with a sense of purpose. "In Stalingrad there's only chaos," he fumed in his diary that evening. "It seems that divisions reported too optimistically. No one knows what's going on. Every division and every corps reports something different." He was not the only one to feel this frustration. "Fiebig is furious," he wrote, "because the infantry don't exploit the chances his attacks provide."

The airmen were most unreasonable in their criticisms. In battles of movement and maneuver, the German army vastly outclassed its Soviet counterpart. Yet successful days no longer consisted of armored pincer movements and 10,000-strong prisoner hauls but of the capture of broken buildings and the destruction of single battalions. Now, in this bloody battle of attrition, German infantry units proved inferior to their Red Army opponents. Armed with tommy guns, hand grenades, and Molotov cocktails, Chuikov's men fought with imagination, determination, and courage. German numerical superiority and the Luftwaffe's strong air attacks ensured that progress continued, but Soviet skill and tenacity kept it slow.

By the beginning of November, Paulus's troops had pushed through the bread factories, cleared the region between them and the *Krasnyi Oktyabr* metallurgical works—with the help of *Fliegerkorps VIII,* which continuously bombed the enemy position in the infantry's advance path[126]—and occupied half those works. The offensive had already lasted fifteen days, not the two or three Paulus originally hoped for, and the city was not yet his. Although he controlled almost 90 percent, he could not yet proclaim the city free of the enemy. Chuikov's men—now fewer than 20,000—clung to two small patches of ground. They held a fragile bridgehead in parts of the northern suburbs of Rynok and Spartakovka, and another in the Lazur chemical works and parts of the *Krasnyi Oktyabr* metallurgical works. The exhausted but still-defiant Chuikov, so badly afflicted with stress-induced eczema that he had to wrap bandages around his hands to cover open sores, commanded his "formations" from a sandstone tunnel overlooking the river behind the *Krasnyi Oktyabr* plant. It was his fifth command post in seven weeks.

Richthofen's frustration mounted as the temperature dropped, heavy autumn rains began, and Paulus's troops inched forward at a steadily decreasing pace. He could do nothing about the weather, he reasoned on the last day of October, but perhaps he could do something about the attack's pathetic pace. He flew to Stalingrad on 1 November to confront Paulus and Seydlitz. The deployment of the Luftwaffe was pointless, he hissed, "because the artillery don't fire and the infantry don't exploit our air attacks. We drop our bombs on enemy positions less than a hand grenade's throw from the infantry, but they do nothing."[127] Naturally, the army commanders attempted to explain their poor performance, but the hot-tempered airman was far from satisfied with their answers. "They trotted out all the same old and stupid excuses," he harshly wrote in his diary, "which are only partly true: numerical weaknesses, lack of training in this type of [close-quarters] combat, and shortages of ammunition." He would place additional air transport at their disposal, he told them, and use his influence with the High Command to see that properly trained reinforcements were forthcoming. (That evening he did, in fact, ring Jeschonnek and demand the immediate dispatch of four pioneer assault battalions. The "request" arrived at the Führer's desk the next day.) Richthofen did not mince his words. "The real reasons [for the slackening pace]," he boldly stated, "lie in the weariness of both command and troops and in that rigid army formalism, which tolerates only 1,000 men in the front line out of a division ration strength of 12,000." Moreover, "generals are content merely to issue orders, without going into any detail or making sure that preparations are properly made." Paulus was naturally unimpressed, he added, "but he couldn't refute the truth of it."

At least his own forces were still performing satisfactorily, Richthofen concluded. Throughout the day, he had thrown all his Stuka wings against the factories and his bombers against artillery positions and mobilization points. His flak general noted in his own diary that "it was very quiet at the front, with no disturbances by flak or enemy aircraft."[128] The result, the air fleet chief wrote with undisguised pride, reminded him of the annihilation raids on Sevastopol. Only the army's disappointing efforts spoiled his pleasure: "Following the raids by all Stuka wings, the army struck with a force of only 37 men, and they promptly stopped again after initial losses!!!"

THE CALM BEFORE THE STORM

For the first two and a half weeks of November, Richthofen's thoughts were usually on two matters: Paulus's dreadfully slow progress in taking the final 10 percent of Stalingrad, and the ominous buildup of Soviet forces northwest of the city, in the section of front held by the Rumanian Third Army. Hitler had the same concerns. Although capturing the remaining 10 percent of the desolate ruins provided no strategic advantage, it had substantial propaganda value and, for Hitler personally, great psychological significance. Stalingrad represented what he hated (and admired) most about the Soviet spirit: its intense fanaticism and unparalleled tenacity. Now that his southern army group had come to a halt without taking the main Caucasus oil fields and his northern army group had failed to break into Leningrad, he craved a victory over that accursed spirit.

On 8 November, he delivered his annual speech to the Party's "Old Guard" at Munich's Löwenbräukeller. It was an inspiring speech, according to Goebbels, who noted in his diary that "the Führer spoke with excellent strength and certainty. It is constantly astonishing that he somehow manages to find the physical and spiritual strength to give such performances."[129] Although Hitler was still reeling from Rommel's humiliating withdrawal from El Alamein four days earlier and Operation "Torch," which had begun that very day, he was careful to keep his disappointments and fears well hidden. Those events in North Africa were nothing to worry about, he told his devoted audience. Africa was of no major importance anyway. The real war was being waged in the east, and Germany was clearly winning. Giving himself a verbal pat on the back (which he doubtless later cursed himself for doing), Hitler also announced that he was now master of Stalingrad:

> I wanted to reach the Volga, at a particular spot, at a particular city. By coincidence, it is blessed with the name of Stalin himself, but don't think we marched there for that reason—it could be called anything. We're there be-

cause it's a vitally important city. There you can cut off thirty million tons of river transport, including nine million tons of oil. It is there that the grain of the mighty Ukrainian and Kuban regions flows in for transportation to the north; there the manganese ore is processed. It is a huge shipment complex. That was what I wanted to capture and, you know, modest as we are—we've got it too. There are only a few more tiny pockets! Now some may say, "Then why don't you fight faster?" Because I don't want a second Verdun, that's why. I would rather do it with small assault squads. Time is of no importance. Not a single ship comes up the Volga any more, and that's the main thing.[130]

Hitler's superb oratory doubtless convinced most members of his audience, including millions of listeners glued to radios across Germany, that things were still going well in the east. Throughout the last decade, he had produced political and military victories so impressive that even many of his staunchest opponents conceded his genius. But this time he clearly failed to impress the gods of war, who showed the "master of Stalingrad" only two weeks later—when powerful Soviet forces ripped gaping holes in the line both north and south of the city—that he was merely a piece on *their* chessboard.

Despite his rousing speech, the Führer held grave fears for his troops at Stalingrad. As early as mid-August, he had suspected that the Red Army was planning something northwest of the city, but, because of poor intelligence advice, he wasn't quite sure what. On 16 August, he expressed his fears to his top military advisers, telling them that Stalin might repeat the tactics that gave the Bolsheviks an excellent victory over General Pyotr Wrangel's White Army in 1920; that is, he might thrust powerful forces across the Don near Serafimovich, a town on the Don 160 kilometers northwest of Stalingrad, in the direction of Rostov.[131] As a result, the *OKW* war diary states, "the Führer urgently requested the speedy transfer of the 22nd Panzer Division into the area behind the Italian Eighth Army to bolster its defenses."[132]

Hitler's fears were premature, but his predictions were surprisingly accurate. Two months later, on 13 October, the *Fremde Heere Ost* (*FHO*—Foreign Armies East), the army department responsible for evaluating all military intelligence about the Soviet Union, actually did detect and report to the High Command what appeared to be the early stages of a Soviet buildup around Serafimovich. The *FHO* was not especially concerned, however, believing the small scale of the buildup meant that no offensive would be attempted in the near future. Even if one were attempted, it would probably be against Army Group Center.[133] Hitler clearly felt more concerned than his intelligence people and on 26 October, after studying daily reconnaissance reports, which revealed a steady reinforcement of the Serafimovich bridgehead, ordered several of Göring's new Luftwaffe field divisions to stiffen the Italian, Hungarian, and Rumanian front on the Don. He told Manstein that same day that "an especial danger" existed in the front between Stalingrad and Voronezh.

On 31 October, the *FHO* reported that the buildup was limited to the Sera-fimovich bridgehead and Kletskaya, thirty-five kilometers closer to Stalingrad, in the Rumanian Third Army sector. It repeated its previous assessment: the dense night traffic toward Serafimovich did not presage a major attack. In fact, it would probably not result in more than a local effort of some kind.[134] Hitler remained unpersuaded, especially after learning that Stalin's formations had thrown several new bridges across the Don to the Serafimovich bridgehead. According to the 2 November entry in the *OKW* war diary:

> Reconnaissance photographs submitted by the Luftwaffe show that the number of new bridges across the Don in the Rumanian Third Army's sector has grown. Therefore, the Führer anticipates (as before) a major Russian attack across the Don toward Rostov. He orders powerful air attacks against the bridge sites and mobilization areas in the forests on the northern bank of the Don.[135]

Göring's Luftwaffe field divisions would count for little in heavy combat, Hitler stressed that day, adding that they should "only be used in defensive fighting until such time as they have gained cohesion and combat experience."[136] He did not want a repetition of events in Flanders during the Great War, when "volunteer units were prematurely committed in offensive actions and, because of their inadequate training, suffered dreadful losses." As a result, he canceled the field divisions' transfer to the Third Rumanian Army's sector, instead ordering (two days later) the "transfer of the 6th Panzer Division and two infantry divisions, including the 306th Infantry Division, from the western theater to Army Group B in the east, to serve as tactical reserves behind the Rumanian Third Army and the Italian Eighth Army."[137] These forces would leave as soon as possible, but, because of organization and transportation delays, they would take a month or so to arrive at their new destinations.

On 6 November, the *FHO* repeated its previous assessments: the Soviet offensive would fall against Army Group Center and, if an attack were to be launched against Army Group B, it would come later. The intelligence organization also began monitoring a similar buildup opposite Hoth's Fourth Panzer Army, south of Stalingrad. A week later, that army began expressing its growing fears of a major enemy offensive, complementing the concerns expressed by both Paulus's army and Army Group B's command staff. Soviet troops and equipment were observed leaving the line at various points and reappearing soon after in the suspected jumping-off points northwest and south of the city. The *FHO* still felt unable to predict with certainty that a major offensive against Army Group B loomed, but, on 12 November, it did at least advise that "an attack in the near future against Rumanian Third Army with the objective of cutting the railroad to Stalingrad and thereby threatening the German forces farther east and compelling a withdrawal from Stalingrad must be taken into consideration."[138]

Fearing a major attack but knowing that the *OKW* had no substantial reserves available, Army Group B transferred the headquarters, Forty-eighth Panzer Corps into the vulnerable Rumanian zone on 10 November. It also alerted the 29th Motorized Infantry Division that it might have to swing in behind the Rumanians "on the shortest notice."[139] Two days later, the worried army group instructed Paulus, still struggling in Stalingrad, to squeeze 10,000 men out of his much-needed engineer and artillery units to man a support line behind the Rumanians.

Despite these movements within Army Group B, Hitler remained convinced that the best means of preventing a Soviet breakthrough would be the rapid capture of Stalingrad, which would release the bulk of Paulus's formations for defensive duties in and behind the vulnerable sections of the front.[140] Therefore, he repeatedly ordered Paulus to capture the remaining districts as quickly as possible.

Sixth Army's exhausted commander prepared his men and steeled his nerves for a final push, aimed not at the two enemy bridgeheads on the Volga but at the forces holding the Lazur chemical plant. On 5 November, however, he learned that Hitler, desperate to secure the entire west bank of the Volga to cut off Chuikov's reinforcements, had "expressed the opinion" that the ground east of the *Barrikady* gun factory and *Krasnyi Oktyabr* metallurgical works ought to be taken first.[141] "Before resuming the attack to capture the Lazur Chemical Plant," Hitler ordered more explicitly the following day, "the two sections of the city the enemy still holds east of the gun factory and east of the metallurgical plant are to be taken. Only after the bank of the Volga is entirely in our hands in those places is the assault on the chemical plant to be begun."[142]

Both Army Group B's and Sixth Army's leaders considered this unreasonable, complaining (but apparently not to the Führer himself) that the stipulated attack would consume too much strength and probably rule out a subsequent assault on the chemical factory. Still, they grudgingly complied with their commander in chief's wishes, commencing an artillery attack on the Soviets' own artillery positions on the Volga's far bank and organizing two ground assaults, one from the gun factory, to begin on 11 November, and the other from the metallurgical plant, to start four days later. The first two specialist engineer assault battalions transferred by Hitler from divisions on the Don (apparently in response to Richthofen's recent requests)[143] had arrived on 4 November, carried forward by *Fliegerkorps VIII*.[144] By the jumping-off dates, the commanders knew, the other three battalions would have arrived.

In the meantime, rapidly deteriorating weather in southern Russia began to interfere with *Luftflotte 4*'s ability to support ground operations. Blinding rain and heavy snowfalls hampered the work of supply, maintenance, and airfield personnel, made takeoff and landing difficult, and reduced the visibility and, therefore, the effectiveness, of aircrew. Nonetheless, the air fleet worked vigorously, devoting most of its energy in the first week of November to operations against the Soviet buildup around Serafimovich and Kletskaya, against railway lines and installations east of the Volga and south of Astrakhan, and against enemy forces opposite First Panzer and Seventeenth Armies in the Caucasus. "Absolute calm" reigned at Stalingrad, Richthofen noted in his diary on 5 November, explaining why his forces no longer conducted heavy raids on the ruined city.

The air fleet commander had a lot to contend with in southern Russia. Yet on 8 November, the very day that Hitler boldly proclaimed himself master of Stalingrad, he realized that his colleagues in North Africa and the Mediterranean faced far greater problems. Not only had Rommel been pushed away from El Alamein four days earlier, pursued by Montgomery's Eighth Army, but powerful British and American forces were now landing in French North Africa, looking set to destroy the Desert Fox's retreating forces. On the 2nd, Göring's staff had frantically diverted bomber squadrons from Norway to the Mediterranean, and, in the following days, it had grabbed units from all fronts to hurl against the Allied attackers.[145] Now, on the day the "Torch" troops disembarked near Casablanca, Oran, and Algiers, Richthofen offered the *OKL* a number of his own units, although he could ill afford to lose them, for deployment in that purportedly critical theater. "Extremely dreadful news from the Mediterranean and Africa," he wrote that night. "I offer three bomber groups."[146] As it happened, he dispatched the 1st Group, as well as parts of the 2nd and 3rd Groups, of the 76th Bomber Wing.[147] Because their usual commander fell sick, *Major* von Friedeburg of the 51st Bomber Wing led the units to their new combat zone.[148]

With remarkably bad timing, they left for the Mediterranean only a few days before Stalin's metal fists smashed into the Axis lines north and south of Stalingrad and quickly locked Sixth Army in a stranglehold. The departure of those valuable units, coupled with high attrition rates (caused by supply difficulties and overcommitment), greatly weakened *Luftflotte 4*'s already inadequate bomber force, leaving it without the means to interrupt Soviet preparations or, even more important, to resist the massive attacks when they came. On 20 October, the fleet had possessed 341 bombers, of which 186 were operational. By the time the Soviets struck a month later, it possessed only 139, of which a mere 64 were operational.[149]

Bad weather rendered Richthofen's units powerless to help Paulus's regiments when they commenced their final assault on the two main enemy pockets within Stalingrad on 11 November, although the following day they launched a powerful attack against Chuikov's defiant but barely surviving troops. Even so, German troops made very slight gains for heavy losses. That evening, the air fleet commander complained in his diary that the army's attacks were "dreadful and only reluctantly carried out." He also noted glumly that the specter of destruction loomed over the vulnerable Don front:

Opposite the Rumanians on the Don, the Russians are resolutely carrying on with their preparations for an attack. Available elements of *Fliegerkorps VIII* [the rest of which were supporting ground operations in the Caucasus], other fleet units and the Rumanian air forces continually hit them. Their reserves have now been concentrated. When will the Russians attack? They have apparently been experiencing ammunition shortages. Artillery installations, however, are now starting to be equipped. I only hope that the Russians don't tear too many large holes in the line.

Richthofen was painfully aware that his air fleet could not conduct a systematic, large-scale interdiction campaign against the Soviet bridgeheads on the Don and the rail, road, and march routes leading to them. In mid-November, the fleet possessed only 732 aircraft, of which 402 were operational.[150] This was less than the usual complement of a single *Fliegerkorps*. His greatly depleted bomber, dive-bomber, and ground-attack groups were already forced to perform a wide variety of demanding tasks in combat regions stretching over 700 kilometers from north to south (from Kletskaya, northwest of Stalingrad, to Ordzhonikidze, in the central Caucasus) and 800 kilometers from west to east (from Novorossiisk and Tuapse to Astrakhan). At various times, and often simultaneously, they supported Seventeenth and First Panzer Armies in the Caucasus, and Sixth and Fourth Panzer Armies in the Stalingrad sector. They carried out interdiction operations against Volga shipping between Stalingrad and Astrakhan and roads and railways east of the Volga. A small number also performed reconnaissance duties over the Black Sea and the western Caucasus.

Still, Richthofen threw every available squadron against Stalin's bridgeheads on the Don, which were swollen to the bursting point with armor, artillery, and fresh formations. "At regular intervals we attack the northern bridges over the Don," recalled Hans-Ulrich Rudel, the famous Stuka pilot.[151] "The biggest of these is near the village of Kletskaya and this bridgehead on the west bank of the Don is most vigilantly defended by flak. . . . The bridgehead is constantly being extended and every day the Soviets pour in more men and material." Air attacks on the bridges were often successful, Rudel explained, but had little permanent effect: "Our destruction of these bridges delays these reinforcements, but they are able to replace them relatively quickly with pontoons so that the maximum traffic across the river is soon fully restored." Knowing that the Rumanians possessed almost no antitank guns, and would therefore be unable to hold back even a light armored thrust across the Don, on 14 November Richthofen also sent two flak battalions to reinforce their endangered section of front.[152]

By 16 November, the army had made minor gains in Stalingrad, having captured several blocks of houses, beaten off an attack by Chuikov's forces, and narrowed the bridgehead east of the gun factory. But it had not yet destroyed the two main pockets of resistance. Richthofen was so frustrated by the army's poor progress, and fearful of the imminent attack in the northwest, that he rang Zeitzler that day to plead for "really energetic combat leadership at Stalingrad, or for the attack to be called off."[153] "If we can't clear up the situation now," he stressed during his typically unfair attack on the army, "when the Volga is blocked with ice floes and the Russians are in real difficulties, we shall never be able to. As it is, the days are getting shorter and the weather worse." The chief of the general staff agreed and promised to inform the Führer of Richthofen's views. "While talking to Zeitzler," the latter noted in his diary, "I emphasized that the commanders and combat troops in Stalingrad are so apathetic that only the injection of a new spirit can get us anywhere. I suggested that the present commanders, who are otherwise trustworthy enough, should be sent on leave for a while to let very different types take their place." Unfortunately, he angrily scrawled in his journal, "those at the top lack the guts to do it."

The next day, he was so worried about the Soviet offensive that he pulled *Gefechtsverband Hitschold* out of the Caucasus, where it had been supporting Kleist's army for more than a month, and dispatched it to the threatened Rumanian front. This small close air support command, comprising a Stuka group and a destroyer group, lacked the strength and arrived too late to make any impact on the Soviet preparations. Only two days later, during a swirling snowfall in the early hours of 19 November, 3,500 Soviet guns and mortars opened up with a deafening roar on Rumanian Third Army. An hour later, tanks crashed through the forward Rumanian lines, followed by waves of well-equipped infantry, all but invisible in their white winter clothing. Stalin's onslaught had begun.

8

Disaster and Decisions: November 1942

Stalin's counteroffensive had been under preparation for more than two months before it finally smashed through weakly held Rumanian lines with great momentum on 19 November. It had grown out of a military briefing in the Kremlin on 12 September, attended by Stalin, Zhukov, and their chief of the general staff, Aleksandr Vasilevskii. The latter spoke first, reporting on the battles raging in Stalingrad, the Kuban, and the region around Grozny. Stalin listened calmly and attentively to Vasilevskii's description of constant German successes, humiliating though they were. Turning to Zhukov, his deputy supreme commander, who had flown north from the front only hours before, the sixty-two-year-old dictator then said: "Well, now let's see what Zhukov has to say about Stalingrad."[1]

Not yet plagued by the intense jealousy that soured his relationship with Zhukov in the immediate aftermath of war in 1945, when the marshal's reputation as the "real" savior of the Soviet people soared, Stalin valued and trusted his deputy's lucid and logical thinking and unparalleled (on the Soviet side, at least) strategic intuition. The stocky, broad-featured general, born forty-five years earlier into a poor peasant family, had first come to Stalin's attention in August 1939. Using imaginative and daring tactics, he had inflicted a major defeat on the Japanese at Khalkin-Gol, Mongolia, at a time when the Red Army needed such a victory to restore its flagging morale and prestige. Although he had failed to stem the German advance on Smolensk in August 1941, Zhukov's firm hand and sound defensive command had prevented Hitler's northern armies from taking Leningrad, their coveted prize, the following month. He had then taken over the defense of Moscow—the trophy Hitler's generals wanted most—forcing back their exhausted troops within miles of the city's western suburbs before unleashing a powerful counteroffensive that regained some territory and inflicted heavy losses on the Germans. The situation at Stalingrad was now as critical as it had been at Moscow the previous year. Could Zhukov perform another miracle,

Stalin wondered, and save the city he had named as a monument to his own greatness?

Zhukov repeated what he had told his boss two days earlier by telephone: his Stalingrad Front lacked the strength to break through the enemy corridor and join up with the Southeastern Front.[2] Stalin asked what his front would require to accomplish this. With Vasilevskii nodding assent, Zhukov replied that he would need a full-strength field army, an armored corps, three armored brigades, and 400 howitzers, plus nothing short of a complete air army. Stalin then bent over his maps showing the location of *Stavka* reserves, studying them at length while his subordinates discussed in whispers the possibility of saving Stalingrad by other means than a fight-to-the-last-man defense. They had not meant their commander to hear, but Stalin had sharp ears. Looking up suddenly, he asked: "What other way out?" Caught thinking aloud, his generals had no ready answers. "Look," he said, his appetite for a counteroffensive whetted, "you better get back to the General Staff and give some thought to what can be done at Stalingrad and how many reserves, and from where, we will need to reinforce the Stalingrad group. And don't forget about the Caucasus Front. We will meet again tomorrow evening at nine."

Zhukov and Vasilevskii spent all next day studying alternative possibilities before settling on a single major operation that would, in Zhukov's words, "avoid using up our reserves in a large number of isolated operations." The plan they submitted to Stalin that night involved far more than an attack to break Paulus's grip on Stalingrad. They proposed a major pincer movement "of such magnitude ... as to shift the strategic situation in the south decidedly in our favor." This offensive, they explained, could not be launched before the middle of November, because it would take that long to organize the operation and for the *Stavka* to obtain sufficient mechanized and armored forces. In the meantime, they would continue feeding troops into Stalingrad, but only enough to keep Chuikov barely holding on and Paulus thinking victory was imminent. While Chuikov served as their "live bait," drawing Paulus's attention and reserves away from his exposed flanks, they would build up their forces opposite the sections of line held by the Rumanian, Hungarian, and Italian "satellite forces."

"The satellite forces," Zhukov later explained, "were found to be less well armed, less experienced, and less capable, even in defense, than the German units. And, most important, their soldiers and even many of their officers had no desire to die for others on the distant fields of Russia."[3] The enemy position was further complicated, he continued, by the fact that the Axis "had few troops in his operational reserve in the Volga-Don sector. They amounted to no more than six divisions and were scattered over a broad front." When the time came, he said, powerful Soviet forces would smash through the Rumanian Third and Fourth Armies, north and south of Stalingrad, respectively, and swing toward a junction near Kalach, seventy-five kilometers west of the city, thereby trapping Paulus's army. Stalin had reservations but was clearly interested. He instructed the two generals to work out the plan in full. Perhaps with the Reichel affair in mind, he dismissed them that night with a somber warning: "No-one, beyond the three of us, is to know about it for the time being."

Zhukov and the general staff faithfully obeyed their leader's demands for secrecy, prohibiting even the drafting of all but the most essential written orders for Operation *Uranus,* the code name given to the final draft plan for the counteroffensive, approved by Stalin in mid-October.[4] Only at that stage did they even discuss *Uranus* with the front commanders involved, who were forbidden to initiate any planning of their own before the first week in November. Mainly by verbal instructions, commanders and logistics officers began massing men and matériel for the operation.[5] In huge vehicle convoys and more than 1,300 railway cars per day, they pulled resources from all parts of Stalin's empire: troops and foodstuffs from Siberia and the central Asian republics, vehicles, weapons, and other military freight from the Urals. They ordered these movements to be conducted as stealthily as possible. Accordingly, railway officers broke troop and supply trains into small sections in order to disguise the size and scope of their movements from the reconnaissance aircraft that Richthofen kept constantly overhead and the bombers he managed to dispatch when circumstances at Stalingrad and in the Caucasus permitted. Vehicle convoys moved at night with their headlights out or dimmed, taking cover during daylight in forests, in ravines, or beneath camouflage nets. Reserves, usually brought close to the front before offensives, traveled only as far forward as mobilization points around Saratov, 350 kilometers north on the Volga. They marched or rode on trucks in small groups, at night, with strong air cover, and under strict radio silence. As a result of these deception efforts, German intelligence sections failed to deduce the scope and significance of Soviet movements, although they were carefully monitoring them. Zeitzler, German chief of the general staff, acknowledged this soon after the offensive began. In a directive dated 28 November, he wrote: "Among the distinctive characteristics of Russian preparations for the offensive one must include the excellent concealment of all units participating in the attack, especially the tank formations."[6]

According to the official Soviet postwar history, 1,005,000 men, 13,540 artillery pieces and mortars, and 894 tanks took up their assigned positions in the staging areas, supported by 1,115 combat aircraft.[7] They opposed an equal number of Axis troops—1,011,000—but, because of the latter's spread-out deployment, were far stronger at the points of main effort. The Soviet Twenty-first Army, for instance, opposed elements of Third Rumanian Army with a strength ratio of only 1:1.4 along its entire attack frontage but achieved a 3:1 superiority at its points of main effort. Soviet troops were also in much better condition than their opponents and possessed a substantial superiority in artillery and armor. Weichs's Army Group B had only 10,300 guns and mortars and 675 tanks, most deployed within Stalingrad or spread out thinly along the flanks. The Rumanians themselves possessed no tanks to speak of and no antitank guns heavier than 47-

mm. The official history added that, despite the *Stavka*'s efforts to increase the strength of Soviet air armies in the Stalingrad sector, Richthofen's *Luftflotte 4* retained numerical superiority with its 1,216 German and Rumanian aircraft.

These statistics for ground forces and equipment are apparently accurate, although they downplay the depleted nature of all Axis formations, which gave the Soviets a greater superiority in manpower than suggested. The statistics for aircraft are misleading, however. Von Hardesty points out that the Soviets had several hundred more aircraft than advanced in their official postwar history. He places the strength of *VVS* air armies in the Stalingrad sector at 1,350 combat aircraft by one estimate and at 1,414 by another.[8] This gave the air armies attempting to liberate Stalingrad almost three times as many aircraft as they had to defend it with back in July. The Luftwaffe, Hardesty claims, had around 1,200 planes.

If Hardesty's figures for the *VVS* are correct—which is probable, based as they are on those of Rudenko, commander of the 16th Air Army—then Richthofen's air fleet was greatly outnumbered. As noted in the previous chapter, the depleted *Luftflotte 4* did not possess anywhere near the 1,200 aircraft attributed to it by both Hardesty and the authors of the official history. On 20 November, a day after the offensive began, it possessed only 732 combat aircraft, of which a mere 402 were operational.[9]

VVS aircraft composed four major formations for the offensive: the 2nd (also engaged in the region of Voronezh) and 17th Air Armies, operating in the breakthrough zone northwest of Stalingrad, and the 8th and 17th Air Armies, operating in the breakthrough zone south of the city. Elements of the Air Defense and Long-Range Bombing Fleets operated independently. Colonel General Aleksandr Novikov, the *VVS*'s capable commander in chief (and one of the few Soviet senior officers to have distinguished himself during the Winter War against Finland), personally supervised and coordinated the preparations of all these formations. Working closely with Zhukov, he worked tirelessly to develop effective interservice liaison and cooperation and improve the strength and state of readiness of his air armies. He displayed flair and imagination, constructing dozens of decoy airfields, for example, to disguise the purpose and scope of his air units' buildup and protect them from German air attack.

Not only was the *VVS* numerically superior to the Luftwaffe by the time of the counteroffensive, but, because of the growing productivity of the aviation industry and Novikov's repeated insistence that units involved in the offensive receive the most modern aircraft, it was also qualitatively capable of matching Richthofen's fleet. By mid-November, three-quarters of all planes and 97 percent of all fighters in the Stalingrad sector were newer models.[10] Among the 125 fighters of the 16th Air Army, for instance, only 9 were obsolete models, and almost all its 103 Shturmoviks were the new Il-2s.

Despite Novikov's efforts, *VVS* formations encountered problems when they moved forward to improvised airfields near the offensive's jumping-off points.

Runways were often only large stretches of flat grass, quarters were usually primitive (tents or covered sleeping trenches), and sanitation facilities were rudimentary. Logistical systems functioned poorly, not least because trucks and transport aircraft were in short supply. Inadequate quantities of fuel, ammunition, replacement engines, spare parts, and rations reached these forward airfields, and only after considerable effort. Despite these difficulties, operational rates were good by previous VVS (and Luftwaffe) standards. For example, on 19 November, 250 (73 percent) of the 16th Air Army's 343 aircraft were airworthy, an operational rate shared by the other air armies involved and equal to that enjoyed by *Luftflotte 4* when it had commenced Operation *Blau* five months earlier.[11] (The latter's operational rate, by comparison, had since fallen to 55 percent.)[12] For the Stalingrad counteroffensive, then, the VVS was far stronger and better prepared than it had been for any previous campaign.

Stalin argued that airpower would play a key part in achieving deep penetrations north and south of Stalingrad. As he stated to Zhukov on 12 November: "The experience of war . . . indicates that we can achieve a victory over the Germans only if we gain air supremacy."[13] Explaining air tactics strikingly similar to those repeatedly used by the Luftwaffe to great effect, he said that the VVS's first task would be to gain air superiority by hitting German airfields in a series of heavy raids beginning on 16 November.[14] The air force would then concentrate its actions in the breakthrough zones, clearing the skies of Axis aircraft and providing Soviet ground forces with effective air support. While fighters and Shturmoviks continued attacking airfields and any planes managing to get airborne, bombers and other ground-attack aircraft would bomb and strafe enemy forces and defensive positions in front of advancing Red Army formations. Once those formations shattered the Axis defenses, VVS units would pursue retreating troops in a sustained fashion to prevent any enemy efforts to reestablish a stable defensive line.

As it happened, frequent snowstorms and constant low cloud and fog impeded Soviet air reconnaissance missions and Shturmovik raids on German rear areas. More important, these adverse weather conditions prevented the attacks on Luftwaffe airfields planned for the three days before the counteroffensive began. The only consolation to Soviet air commanders was that the bad weather also prevented Richthofen's units from conducting effective attacks on their own airfields and ground forces. On the other hand, Paulus, still hoping to present the desolate ruins of Stalingrad to his expectant Führer, considered the plummeting temperature to be a powerful ally in his battle against Chuikov's remaining forces within the city. Packs of ice were now building up in the Volga, preventing the small vessels of the Soviet flotilla from ferrying reinforcements, rations, ammunition, and equipment to the west bank. If ever Paulus had a chance to destroy the remaining pockets of resistance, it was now, in the few weeks left before the river iced over solidly, allowing men and vehicles to cross again. During the night of 18 and 19 November, the temperature once more dropped below freezing, and

Chuikov's depleted groups of cold, hungry, and poorly equipped soldiers spent their fourth straight night without the arrival of reinforcements and supplies. Their defeat looked imminent. What neither Paulus nor Chuikov (informed by Zhukov only at the last moment) knew, though, was that within a few hours strong Soviet formations would begin ripping through the flanks of Army Group B in an offensive that would soon trap Paulus's army in the very city it had spent three months trying to take.

URANUS BEGINS

Stalin's onslaught began at dawn on 19 November, set in motion late the previous evening by the *Stavka*'s coded message to the Don and Southwestern Fronts: "Send a messenger to pick up the fur gloves."[15] At 0730, the artillery regiments of Fifth Tank Army and Twenty-first Army, in the Serafimovich bridgehead and around Kletskaya, respectively, prepared their guns after receiving a coded alert message. Ten minutes later, the command "*Ogon!*" (Fire!) arrived, and their 3,500 guns and mortars erupted in a mighty barrage against the Rumanian Third Army. They fired their last salvos at 0848, two minutes before the first infantry echelon streamed forward through snow and thick fog, many troops running behind or riding on top of the hundreds of tanks churning through the Rumanian forward defenses.

Most Rumanian units defended bravely at first, some even managing to hold their positions despite savage attacks by vastly superior forces. Others cracked immediately and began retreating, creating a sense of panic that quickly spread to all but the most courageous battalions (and certain units surprised the Soviets with their tenacity and fighting spirit).[16] When scores of T-34 lumbered through their lines, picking off artillery installations and the few antitank batteries available, thousands of Rumanians succumbed to what panzer commander Heinz Guderian had once called "tank fright." Terrified, they abandoned their positions and equipment, threw down their arms, and ran, screaming, "Enemy tanks in the rear!"

Generalmajor Ferdinand Heim's Forty-eighth Panzer Corps did all it could to stem the tide, but unusual circumstances had left it weakened. The crew of the 22nd Panzer Division, which formed the corps' nucleus, had dug its tanks into pits and covered them with straw to protect them from the cold. Now, when they hurriedly tried to start the engines and race forward to the Rumanians' aid, they found less than half their tanks operational.[17] Mice nesting in the straw had chewed away the insulation of the electrical wiring, causing short circuits. Only 42 of the division's 104 panzers rolled forward to meet the enemy. Even so, when those panzers and their accompanying antitank battalions engaged their Soviet counterparts, they performed well, destroying twenty-six T-34s. Had Heim possessed additional armored units to cover the 22nd's flanks, they may have blunted the enemy attack. As it was, the Rumanian 1st Armored Division, equipped with a few German tanks and numerous antitank guns, had been sent off in another direction and was unable to offer assistance. Rumanian infantry on either side of the panzer division proved incapable of throwing back the Soviet advance or even holding ground. They broke and fled, allowing the Red Army to sweep through the gaps.

By evening, whole Rumanian formations, including the 9th, 13th, and 14th Infantry Divisions, had been stricken with the "tank fright" epidemic or disintegrated under the crushing weight of superior enemy forces. They streamed to the rear in disorganized columns. By nightfall, Soviet armored spearheads had ripped open an eighty-kilometer-wide hole in the Rumanian front and were over halfway to Kalach. At 2200, Weichs sent Paulus the following message: "The development of the situation at the Rumanian Third Army compels radical measures to secure forces to protect the deep flank of Sixth Army.... All offensive operations in Stalingrad are to be halted at once."[18] Sixth Army, he added, must pull three Panzer divisions and an infantry division out of the city and deploy them to meet the attack on the army's left flank. Chuikov, who launched his own small counterattack within the destroyed city at the same time as the massive Soviet effort against Rumanian Third Army, was ecstatic to learn that the Rumanian line had collapsed and to see German units leaving the city at last for defensive fighting on the Don. Under the most demanding circumstances, the remains of his Sixty-second Army had clung to a few isolated sections of the city, preventing it from falling completely to the hated invaders. "All of us," he later wrote, "from the private to the general—felt proud to be the sons of the Soviet people, felt the pride of the unconquered."[19]

That night, Richthofen bitterly cursed the Rumanian army for "scattering because of tank terror." Realizing that Fourth Panzer and Sixth Armies faced a grave threat, he immediately ordered his last air units in the Caucasus to fly north as soon as weather conditions permitted, leaving the two German armies in that vast region with a small "holding" force of only two fighter groups and a few reconnaissance squadrons.[20] He also ordered the immediate evacuation of numerous command posts and airfields situated between the Chir and Don Rivers back to Morozovskaya, Tatsinskaya, and other airfields behind the Chir. He could not risk losing them to the Soviet forces advancing through Rumanian Third Army's shattered front. Although he called these evacuations "urgent," he knew that they too could be carried out only as weather conditions allowed.

Because of the bad weather, German air units played only a minor part in defensive fighting that first day of the Soviet attack; Rumanian air units, whose surveillance of the buildup opposite their Third Army had recently proved helpful in piecing together missing sections of the intelligence jigsaw, played no part at all.[21] "The weather was dreadful," Richthofen explained in his diary. "Freezing fog, snow and biting rain. We were unable to carry out any air operations at all. That's why we couldn't even get a clear picture of the situation from the air." He was most concerned, adding: "I only hope the Russians won't get as far as our main supply railway, which is a very real possibility." The significance of the situation was obvious: German forces would again have to spend a dreadful winter fending off destruction. "Now we're back in the disgusting mess of last year," he glumly wrote.

Richthofen exaggerated his air fleet's inactivity. Bad weather and poor visibility grounded most units throughout 19 November, preventing effective reconnaissance, systematic interdiction, or formation attacks on particular targets. Still, from *Fliegerkorps VIII*'s headquarters in Oblivskaya, *Generalleutnant* Fiebig ordered several small groups of Stukas and ground-attack aircraft to take to the skies. Flying from airfields around Karpovka, twenty kilometers west of Stalingrad, elements of the 1st Group of the 2nd Dive-Bomber Wing conducted the bulk of the Luftwaffe's 120 sorties. Operating individually, in pairs, or in squadrons, its Stukas bombed and strafed Soviet troops, vehicles, and, in particular, tanks and cavalry formations. Hans-Ulrich Rudel, who ended the war as Germany's most highly decorated soldier and the only holder of the Knight's Cross with Golden Oak Leaves, Swords, and Diamonds, led his Stuka squadron into battle that day. Although frequently quoted, his account of those operations is so exceptional it is worth repeating here:

> One morning after the receipt of an urgent report our Wing takes off in the direction of the bridgehead at Kletskaya. The weather is bad: low lying clouds, a light fall of snow, the temperature probably 20 degrees below zero; we fly low. What troops are those coming towards us? We have not gone more than half way. Masses in brown uniforms—are they Russians? No. Rumanians. Some of them are even throwing away their rifles in order to be able to run the faster: a shocking sight, we are prepared for the worst. We fly the length of the column emplacements. The guns are abandoned, not destroyed. Their ammunition lies beside them. We have passed some distance beyond them before we sight the first Soviet troops.
>
> They find all the Rumanian positions in front of them deserted. We attack with bombs and gun-fire—but how much use is that when there is no resistance on the ground?
>
> We are seized with a blind fury—horrid premonitions rise in our minds: how can this catastrophe be averted? Relentlessly I drop my bombs on the enemy and spray bursts of M.G. fire into these shoreless yellow-green waves of oncoming troops. . . . I haven't a bullet left, not even to protect myself against the contingency of a pursuit attack. Now quickly back to remunition and refuel. With these hordes our attacks are merely a drop in the bucket, but I am reluctant to think of that now.
>
> On the return flight we again observe the fleeing Rumanians; it is a good thing for them that I have run out of ammunition to stop this cowardly rout.[22]

The next morning, Paulus's Fourteenth Panzer Corps and the four divisions he withdrew from Stalingrad shifted to the west bank of the Don. Together with the three divisions already there, they withstood repeated attempts by the Soviet Twenty-first and Sixty-fifth Armies to create a secondary pocket west of the river. Greatly outnumbered and lacking mobility because of fuel shortages, however, they were unable to stop the major envelopment.

Throughout 20 November, "very dreadful weather" again hindered Fiebig's efforts to halt the advancing Soviet spearheads.[23] His units once more conducted around 120 sorties, but they had no more effect than during the previous day. The weather also hampered Fiebig's efforts to evacuate the airfields in the Soviet advance path. Only a third of his units had managed to move back behind the Chir the previous day, and progress on the 20th was just as difficult. Soviet forces advancing rapidly out of the Serafimovich bridgehead reached Kachalinskaya and linked up with the forces driving southeastward from Kletskaya. Elements of the former then thrust out toward the Chir, threatening Fiebig's command post in Oblivskaya and the remaining airfields in the immediate vicinity.[24] At some of the airfields farther east, the last planes were leaving when Soviet tanks rolled into view and began firing. Because of the speed of the enemy advance, Fiebig's units were not always able to remove or destroy all matériel. Morozovskaya, Tatsinskaya, and the other German airfields west of the Chir suffered greatly from the loss of essential supplies and equipment. The booty captured by the Red Army included vehicles, fuel, replacement engines, spares, maintenance machinery, and a variety of other valuable items, such as aerial photographic development and interpretation devices.

The Luftwaffe prepared to defend a number of headquarters and airfields that it could not evacuate quickly or needed to keep functioning temporarily because of their important communications systems. Although Oblivskaya lay east of the Chir River and was, therefore, at risk of being overrun, Fiebig chose to command *Fliegerkorps VIII* from that town while signals teams linked his airfields behind the river with proper wire communications. He would stay until he learned from Richthofen whether the High Command planned to launch counteroffensive or relief operations. He especially wanted to hold the rail bridge over the Chir at Oblivskaya, across which Sixth Army's supplies had passed. He argued that, regardless of which option Hitler took, the bridge "has to be held so that it can be used as a starting point for future operations."[25]

Luftwaffe flak units fighting east of the Chir as part of ground formations also prepared to defend themselves from being overrun. For example, *Generalmajor* Pickert, commander of the 9th Flak Division, noted in his diary on 20 November that the situation was "far more serious" than he had thought the day before and that, as a result, he had arranged "all kinds of counter-measures, including the security of our own headquarters." As it happened, continued Soviet advances forced Pickert to move his headquarters back to Novocherkassk, in the Donets Basin, only the following day. Finding most of his battalions cut off from

the west two days later, he passed command of the few that had escaped encirclement to one of his senior officers, then flew into the pocket itself to direct the
operations of his trapped troops.[26]

Richthofen's fleet participated not only in the defense of its own installa-
tions but also in the establishment and protection of a new line on the Chir River.
Oberst Stahel, commander of Flak Regiment 99, formed *Kampf-Gruppe Stahel*
(Combat Group Stahel), a makeshift defense force initially comprising only flak,
field police, kitchen, supply, maintenance, and signals battalions. Establishing at
Oblivskaya a sole bridgehead on the eastern bank of the Chir, *Kampf-Gruppe
Stahel* took up defensive positions on the west bank for more than fifty kilometers along the river's great bend.[27] "Encouraged by this example" (according to
one historian), other army and Luftwaffe forces did the same.[28]

South of Stalingrad, meanwhile, the second great Soviet pincer thrust out toward Kalach on the morning of 20 November. The Stalingrad Front's Fifty-first
and Fifty-seventh Armies broke through the section of front held by the Rumanian Sixth Corps, which collapsed even quicker than Rumanian Third Army formations had the previous day, and swept in behind Fourth Panzer Army's right
flank. Hoth was disgusted by the performance of the Rumanians, complaining
that all his army's work over the last weeks had been "ruined in a day."[29] In
places, they had offered no resistance at all. They had, he fumed, fallen victim to
"an indescribable tank panic." For the defenders, the situation looked grim. The
bulk of Fourth Panzer Army and all of Sixth Army faced imminent encirclement.
The seriousness of the situation was not lost on Pickert, who noted in his diary
that night: "It became apparent by evening that the enemy has broken through in
the south, without meeting any real resistance, and looks set to penetrate further.
In the north, meanwhile, the deep breach appears to have stopped for now, but
further penetrations look certain there too."

Three days later, shortly before dusk on 23 November, the two Soviet pincers
met near the town of Sovietskii, twenty kilometers southeast of Kalach. Vasilevskii's and Zhukov's great armored trap had exceeded all Stalin's expectations. It
clamped shut around what the Soviet general staff first thought were 85,000 to
95,000 German troops.[30] In fact, as they soon learned, it enveloped three times
that number of men—well over 250,000, along with 100 tanks, nearly 2,000 guns,
and 10,000 trucks—in a pocket measuring only fifty kilometers from west to east
and forty from north to south. Encircled formations included Paulus's entire
Sixth Army, numerous elements of Hoth's Fourth Panzer Army, and the remains
of two Rumanian divisions, plus a variety of specialist and auxiliary units (rang-
ing from signals and logistics personnel to Organization Todt construction
teams).[31] On Hitler's instructions, Paulus had flown into the rapidly closing
pocket the previous day in order to assume command of the encircled forces.

Over 12,000 Luftwaffe troops also found themselves trapped, including most
of *Generalmajor* Pickert's 9th Flak Division (with eleven heavy and nineteen
light batteries and numerous supply units), several signals teams, the ground or-

ganizations of two airfields, elements of the Third Fighter Wing, and the 12th, 14th, and 16th Tactical Reconnaissance Groups.[32] Richthofen immediately placed Pickert, the senior Luftwaffe officer in the pocket, in charge of all these air force units.[33] Pickert could not have known at that stage that he would soon be placed in charge of providing ground-support services inside the pocket for a massive airlift operation about to be launched. He would be responsible for the administration and operation of airfields, the daily unloading of transport planes and the distribution of supplies, and the flak protection of airfields, the pocket's outer defenses, and the quarter of a million men trapped inside.

Before analyzing the airlift itself, Luftwaffe operations during the final three days before the Soviet trap closed on 23 November should be described. On the 21st, one historian claims, "a full day of operations was possible, and considerable damage was done to Soviet cavalry formations by the [Rumanian] Corpul Aerian and Luftwaffe."[34] Contemporary sources, however, reveal a different picture. For instance, Richthofen complained of "dreadful weather everywhere, which prevented us flying in any sector."[35] The 3rd Group of the 3rd Fighter Wing recorded in its own diary that day: "Still no operational possibilities because of foul weather."[36] Several squadrons from that group did take to the sky, along with elements of other groups, but only because advancing Soviet spearheads forced them hastily to relocate to airfields in the Oblivskaya bridgehead, back on the Chir, or to fields west of the river. Despite poor visibility during their flights, pilots observed the severity of ground fighting as the Soviet pincers closed in on Kalach. According to their group's war diary, "The front is a sea of flames and smoke and explosions of snow caused by artillery fire." Many army and air force units attempting to escape westward through the rapidly shrinking gap shared the fate of that fighter group's supply and maintenance teams. "Elements of the ground personnel," the diary states, "which are supposed to transfer in vehicle formations, can no longer cross the Don bridge at Kalach and must, therefore, return to Pitomnik, within the closing pocket."

The next day, bad weather again curtailed air operations. "*Fliegerkorps VIII* and the Rumanian [squadrons] only operated to a small extent," the air fleet commander noted in his journal. "In total, only 150 sorties. Actually, it was only an *attempt* at operations. How miserable it is that we don't have good weather to hunt the Russian tanks and pick them off at close range." Fortunately, he added, "we were able to carry out relatively good supply missions for the cut-off Rumanians." Indeed, several German squadrons and a Rumanian squadron carried or dropped fuel, ammunitions, and rations to several isolated Rumanian formations, including the combat group headed by General Mihail Lascar. Lascar's men certainly needed these supplies; few had eaten properly since *Uranus* began on 19 November, and all were short of ammunition. Refusing to let his men retreat or accept repeated Soviet calls to surrender, Lascar fought defiantly until his group was finally overwhelmed and he was taken prisoner on the 23rd. He probably learned that Hitler had rewarded his courage with the Knight's Cross with Oak

Leaves, the first awarded to a non-German, only when he returned from captivity in April 1945 to command a Communist division fighting *for* the Soviets.

"Tolerable weather" on 23 November permitted *Fliegerkorps VIII* to increase its operations.[37] Attacks against Soviet armored and cavalry formations formed the bulk of its work, carried out by fighters and Stukas now based at crowded airfields in the Oblivskaya bridgehead and at very congested fields around Morozovskaya and Tatsinskaya, west of the Chir. For the last six weeks or so, Rumanian air units operating from the latter fields had outnumbered German units. While Fiebig's bombers had flown from those fields, all his other aircraft—fighters, dive-bombers, and ground-attack planes—had flown from fields east of the Chir. Now, with the exception of Oblivskaya, the fields around Morozovskaya and Tatsinskaya became the most advanced airfields safe from the Red Army. The influx of German combat aircraft falling back to them from the overrun airfields east of the Chir created major overcrowding problems, leaving many Rumanian squadrons (to quote one writer) "marginalised on their own airfields."[38] These problems would increase in the coming two weeks, when a second influx of aircraft occurred, this time transport planes arriving from the Reich and other sectors of the eastern front to supply Sixth Army by air.

On 23 November, *Fliegerkorps VIII* also carried out reconnaissance missions, "which failed to yield a clear picture of the situation," and "a little [air] supply."[39] It dropped equipment, ammunition, and rations to beleaguered panzer forces around Bokovskaya, on the Chir 100 kilometers northwest of Oblivskaya, and, for the first time, carried supplies into the Stalingrad pocket. For the next nine weeks, the air corps would do little else than fly food and matériel into that pocket in an increasingly hopeless attempt to save Paulus's trapped army.

THE DECISION TO AIRLIFT

Since the war, almost all writers on the Battle of Stalingrad have blamed Göring for the airlift, claiming that when Hitler asked him what the air force could do, he made rash promises of an airlift, hoping its success would restore his flagging prestige. As Manstein wrote, typifying this line of argument: "I am unsure whether Göring's frivolous assurances to Hitler were due to a false appreciation of existing capabilities, or to a desperate need for admiration. Whatever the cause, Göring was responsible."[40] Many early writers on Stalingrad, it should be noted, were participants in the events, whose biases and preconceptions are evident in their self-serving, blame-shifting accounts. However, their works were influential in shaping scholarly opinion, and their descriptions and explanations have been, with a few exceptions,[41] accepted uncritically to the present day. In a recent work on Stalingrad, for example, Franz Kurowski repeats many errors and concludes: "What had moved Hitler to give this death order to Sixth Army? During a telephone conversation on 23 November 1942, he asked Göring directly whether the supply of Stalingrad by air was possible. Göring replied: 'The thing appears feasible.' "[42] Likewise, Samuel Mitcham writes in his own book on the Luftwaffe: "The only way the Reichsmarschall could redeem himself in the Führer's eyes was to score a spectacular military victory. Stalingrad seemed to be his ticket. He promised Hitler that the Luftwaffe would resupply Stalingrad by air. . . . It was the major turning point of the war."[43] Göring was certainly among those responsible for one of the war's most ill-considered decisions, but he does not deserve sole blame, as this study will attempt to demonstrate.

When *Uranus* began on 19 November, Hitler was enjoying a brief holiday at the Berghof, his mountain retreat in Berchtesgaden, southern Bavaria. His relaxation came to an abrupt end that afternoon, when he took a telephone call from his headquarters in East Prussia. A clearly agitated Zeitzler shouted down the line that hundreds of Soviet tanks had shattered the Rumanian front exactly where the Führer had predicted and that the Rumanians were in full flight.[44] Repeated "updates" throughout the afternoon convinced Hitler that the situation was serious, although he still felt that Heim's Forty-eighth Panzer Corps could, if properly deployed, contain the enemy breakthrough. He promptly ordered Weichs to abandon all further offensive operations within Stalingrad and transfer forces from the city to the broken flank.

When the Southwestern Front breached the Axis flank south of Stalingrad the next day, Hitler realized immediately that his Fourth Panzer and Sixth Armies were in grave danger of encirclement. He ordered Field Marshal Manstein to abandon the planned attack at Velikiye Luki in the far north and take charge of a newly created command, Army Group Don, in the Stalingrad sector. Manstein was ideal for the job because of his fine strategic mind and unparalleled experience with Rumanian units. Although delighted by Hitler's trust, the field marshal was initially discouraged to learn the composition of his new "army group": the Rumanian Third Army, which had crumbled wherever struck, Fourth Panzer Army, a large portion of which (including most of its tanks) lay trapped between the quickly closing pincers, and Sixth Army, completely bottled up. The latter was also worn down after months of constant action, with all battalions far below strength. Hitler did tell the field marshal to expect reinforcements totaling six infantry and four panzer divisions, a Luftwaffe field division, and some flak units. Of these formations, however, only two infantry divisions were at hand. The others would not arrive until early in December.

Jeschonnek arrived at the Berghof that same day. Hitler had summoned him from his headquarters in East Prussia to discuss the air force's role in any attempted breakout or relief operations.[45] Göring was too "busy" to attend; he was presiding over an oil conference at Karinhall, his country estate in Berlin. No verbatim records of Hitler's conversation with Jeschonnek have surfaced, but the basic facts are known: the Führer explained that Sixth Army would probably be totally cut off within days, that he had organized a new army group under Manstein, and that it would launch a relief effort as soon as possible. He hoped not only to free Sixth Army within a short time but also to regain lost territory and rebuild a strong defensive line. Apparently understanding Sixth Army's encirclement to be temporary, Jeschonnek assured Hitler that, if both transport planes and bombers were used, and if adequate airfields inside and outside the pocket could be maintained, the Luftwaffe could airlift sufficient supplies to the army. After all, he pointed out, the air force had successfully sustained 100,000 men in the Demyansk pocket for several months during the previous winter.

The comparison with Demyansk was specious, as Jeschonnek himself probably realized as soon as he had time to think through the issues (which was seldom possible when dealing with Hitler, who always wanted immediate answers to his questions). The 100,000 men of the Second Army Corps trapped at Demyansk had required no less than 300 tons of supplies per day.[46] Because of low operational rates caused by winter conditions, the Luftwaffe had been forced to commit almost 500 Ju 52s to the airlift in order to ensure that sufficient planes—around 150—could carry that tonnage each day.[47] Further, the VVS presence at Demyansk had been negligible, allowing almost uninterrupted German air operations with low losses. The situation at Stalingrad was very different. First, almost three times more men were encircled there than had been at Demyansk. If 100,000 men had needed 300 tons of supplies per day, then, logically, 250,000 men would need around 750 tons, an almost-impossible tonnage to deliver (as calculations made at Hitler's headquarters a few days later confirmed).[48] Second, the Luftwaffe did not possess anywhere near enough transport aircraft and available bombers to deliver such tonnages. Third, VVS forces at Stalingrad were now far stronger than they had been at Demyansk. They would greatly hamper airlift operations and inflict high losses.

Jeschonnek's spontaneous and ill-considered assurance that the air force could sustain Sixth Army at Stalingrad pleased the Führer. He could hardly allow the army to abandon that city after he had proclaimed to the entire German nation in September that "you can be certain no one will get us away from there!" and, only two weeks earlier, had trumpeted in the Munich Löwenbräukeller that his forces had taken that "vitally important city . . . with Stalin's name," where the "real" war was being fought. Unable to eat his words, Hitler now found himself committed to holding Stalingrad. On the afternoon of 21 November, therefore, he sent a message directly to Paulus, ordering him to stand firm "despite the danger of temporary encirclement." He was to hold open the rail link as long as possible. "As to airlift," he added, "orders will follow."[49]

Hitler did not envisage an airlift of the Demyansk scale or duration. He still thought that Manstein would soon break the encirclement and restore the southern front. Sixth Army would only need to be supplied by air in the meantime. That is not the way commanders in the field, faced with the grim realities of their predicament, interpreted Hitler's references to an airlift. To the horror of local air commanders, Sixth Army's senior officers felt that, unless they broke out immediately (which they unsuccessfully advocated), their army would have to be supplied by air for weeks, if not months. It would need 750 tons of supplies per day, they stated (reducing this figure to 500 tons within a few days). Later that day (21 November), Fiebig telephoned *Generalmajor* Schmidt, Sixth Army's chief of staff, to discuss the army's intentions. Paulus listened on another phone. Fiebig's report on this conversation reveals the tension that quickly developed between army and air force commanders when the former readily embraced Hitler's suggestion that the air force would keep alive the trapped army:

> In response to my questions about Sixth Army's intentions, *General* Schmidt replied that the army commander proposed to deploy his army in a hedgehog [that is, all-around] defense of Stalingrad. . . . Regarding the possibilities of this hedgehog defense, I asked how they planned to keep Sixth Army supplied, especially when the supply line from the rear looked certain to be cut very soon. *General* Schmidt replied that supplies would have to be carried in by air. I replied that supplying an entire army by air was impossible, particularly when our transport aircraft were already heavily committed in North Africa. I warned him against exaggerated expectations. *Generaloberst* Paulus entered the conversation occasionally on his other telephone line. Next morning, at 0700, I telephoned *General* Schmidt again, telling him that he was counting too strongly on air supply. I stressed to him again that, after long deliberations, based on my experience and knowledge of the [limited] means available, supplying Sixth Army by air was simply not feasible. Further, the weather and enemy situations were completely unpredictable factors.[50]

Richthofen agreed with Fiebig: it was madness for Paulus and his staff to plan an all-around defense at Stalingrad and pin its hopes on the Luftwaffe to sustain their army. The air force simply lacked the ability to keep it supplied. "Sixth Army believes that it will be supplied by the air fleet in its hedgehog positions," Richthofen complained in his diary on 21 November.[51] "I make every effort to convince it that this cannot be accomplished, because the necessary transport resources are not available." During "dreadfully many telephone calls . . . until late in the night," he frantically warned everyone who would listen—including Göring in Berlin, Zeitzler in East Prussia, Jeschonnek at Berchtesgaden, and Weichs at Army Group B headquarters—that he lacked the means to supply Paulus's army. It should immediately attempt to break out.

The following day, Pickert echoed these sentiments to Paulus and Schmidt during a conference in Nizhne-Chirskaya (outside the pocket), attended by these generals and Hoth, Fourth Panzer Army's commander. According to Pickert's subsequent version of what transpired (the only surviving account), Schmidt asked him at one point what he thought should be done.[52] "I would gather together all the forces I could and break out to the southwest," the flak general replied. Schmidt explained that Hitler had expressly ordered Sixth Army to stand fast at Stalingrad, that the army lacked sufficient fuel for a proper breakout attempt and that the terrain itself complicated matters. The Soviets held higher ground to the west, meaning that Sixth Army would be exposed to their guns if they attempted to break out. Such an attempt would have to be made without heavy weapons, in any event, because of the fuel shortages. Moreover, it would be necessary to leave 15,000 sick and wounded soldiers to their fate. For these reasons, Schmidt added, a breakout would probably turn into a "Napoleonic catastrophe."

Pickert insisted that a breakout was still the only solution, adding that his flak forces could help considerably. He had numerous heavy batteries for covering fire, and his men could carry his 160 20-mm flak guns and their ammunition across the steppes. "No," Schmidt concluded, "the army has been ordered to stand fast at Stalingrad. As a result, we shall form hedgehog defenses and expect supplies from the air." The flak commander, who apparently had no knowledge of Fiebig's previous debate with the army on the matter, was flabbergasted. "Supply an entire army from the air?—absolutely impossible! It simply cannot be done, especially in this weather." Despite repeatedly urging the army to break out, and explaining at length the reasons why the Luftwaffe could not supply the army, Pickert was unable to persuade the army. Paulus had remained silent throughout the discussion but finally told the airman the two most important things in his mind: that Hitler had ordered him to stand fast, and that a breakout attempt with the means available would probably only end in disaster. Schmidt remained adamant about the airlift. "It simply has to be done," he stated, adding that his men would do their bit to cut down the supply level by eating the thousands of horses within the pocket.

Thus, Luftwaffe commanders in the field were unanimous both in their belief that the air force could not supply the entire Sixth Army and in their condemnation of the idea to local army commanders and the High Command itself. They made several converts, most notably Zeitzler (as will soon be shown) and Weichs, commander of Army Group B. The latter had listened carefully to Richthofen's arguments. Persuaded, he sent a teletyped message to the High Command on 22 November.[53] The prompt withdrawal of Sixth Army was essential, he said, especially because "the supply by air of the twenty divisions that constitute this army is not possible. With the air transport available, and in favorable weather conditions, it is possible to carry in only one-tenth of their essential daily requirements." Weichs added that although a breakout would "entail heavy losses, especially in matériel," it was the only viable option and would, if successful, "result in favorable developments in the situation as a whole."

Several of the army corps commanders bottled up in Stalingrad also agreed that the war was over for them if the High Command refused a breakout and ordered an airlift. On 22 November, while Pickert was battling Paulus and Schmidt in Nizhne-Chirskaya, a meeting between corps commanders took place at Gumrak, within the pocket.[54] Acting on his own initiative, Seydlitz, commander of the Fifty-first Army Corps, summoned the other corps commanders— Generals Jaenicke of the Fourth Army Corps, Heitz of the Eighth, Strecker of the

Eleventh, and Hube of the Fourteenth Panzer Corps—to discuss the situation. They all agreed that they must gather all their strength for an attempt to break through the encirclement. They scheduled their attack for the 25th and, in agreement with Weichs (but not with Paulus, who had no knowledge of their plans at that stage), began regrouping for the operation.

However, Paulus—like his chief of staff—was apparently not persuaded by the airmen's warnings. He vacillated throughout 22 and 23 November, afraid to contradict Hitler's order to stand fast even though he knew his opportunities for a successful breakout were disappearing with every passing hour. On the 22nd, he did request "freedom of decision in the event of failure to construct southern defensive positions." Yet, totally ignoring Richthofen's, Fiebig's, and Pickert's logical arguments against an airlift, he stated that, as long as he could close his exposed southern front "and receive ample airborne supplies," he intended to hold the area still in his possession.[55] The next evening, in response to Hitler's fresh order to construct all-around defensive positions and await relief from outside, the general replied with another Teletype message. This time he did allude to mounting opposition to the proposed airlift but said only that "timely and adequate supply has been ruled out."[56] His army must break through the encirclement to the southwest, he stated, because it was now suffering acute fuel and ammunition shortages and increasing enemy attacks against certain sectors. As the army could not hold out for long, he again requested "freedom of decision." His five corps commanders, he added, shared his views on the situation.

Hitler's ears were now deaf to such pleas. His mind was firmly made up. After arriving back at his East Prussian headquarters on 23 November, he replied to Paulus by radio in the early hours of the 24th. Sixth Army (which he now designated "Fortress Stalingrad") would stay and defend itself vigorously. "Air supply by a hundred more Junkers is getting under way," he said, trying to reassure the frantic army commander.[57] By now, the Führer's notion of an airlift operation had changed considerably since Jeschonnek had first assured him that Sixth Army could be supplied by air. He had then described the army's encirclement as temporary, and Jeschonnek had made his rash assurance with that in mind. Now he clearly envisaged a Demyansk-style airlift, only even larger and longer-lasting. "Sixth Army will stay where it is," he yelled at Zeitzler on the evening of the 23rd, according to the latter's postwar account.[58] "It is the garrison of a fortress, and the duty of fortress troops is to withstand sieges. If necessary they will hold out all winter, and I shall relieve them by a spring offensive."

The firmness of Hitler's conviction that the "fortress" should stand fast and that the Luftwaffe could keep it adequately supplied had grown considerably in the two days since Jeschonnek had first mentioned it. One of the main reasons for his increased conviction was the almost-unanimous support for the decision expressed by those around him. At Berchtesgaden, and during his long train journey to East Prussia on 23 November, the Führer had no contact—personal or telegraphic—with the army and air force commanders at the front. During that critical decision-making period, he did not speak to Richthofen, Fiebig, or Pickert, whose air forces would have to carry out the massive supply operation and who were now frantically warning almost everyone else that they lacked the means to sustain Sixth Army. Nor did he communicate with Weichs, who shared their view and advocated an immediate breakout. Hitler learned of their views from Zeitzler, who defended their assessment. Yet, because their warnings were not delivered personally, but only passed on by the army's "overanxious" chief of staff, they carried little weight. Hitler merely accused Zeitzler of being too pessimistic and advised him to stop paying heed to "defeatist" commanders who couldn't see the forest for the trees.

The military advisers accompanying the Führer—his faithful paladins, Keitel and Jodl, and their skeleton staffs—were in no position to make detailed assessments or offer informed advice. The sycophantic Keitel, who seldom expressed views contrary to the Führer's, acted true to form throughout this crucial period. "The Volga must be held! . . . Sixth Army must hold out!" he repeatedly told Hitler. Although Jodl was no lackey, despite the efforts of many postwar writers to paint him as one, he was still smarting from the rough treatment Hitler had dished out to him when he supported Field Marshal List in September. He was not yet ready to receive more. He therefore gave Hitler far more cautious but still agreeable advice: although Sixth Army was certainly in a predicament, he argued, and its destruction looked certain if relief was not forthcoming, the vast territorial gains made during the summer campaign should not be abandoned before Manstein's relief operation was attempted. In the meantime, the Luftwaffe should keep the army supplied.

Aside from Zeitzler's, the only dissenting voice Hitler heard during his last two days in Berchtesgaden and his long journey north to East Prussia belonged to Jeschonnek, who had abandoned his earlier position and now meekly suggested that Sixth Army should break out.[59] The Luftwaffe chief of staff regretted his earlier assurances to Hitler. Almost as soon as the words were out of his mouth, he wished he could swallow them again. After having his staff check his figures and after talking with Richthofen several times by telephone, he quickly realized that nothing close to adequate logistical support of Sixth Army by air would be possible, even with consistently favorable weather and taking no account of *VVS* action. He and Richthofen were close friends, but the latter clearly dominated their relationship and, when they disagreed on matters, usually managed to win Jeschonnek over. This was clearly one such case. However, although Jeschonnek notified Hitler that he might have been too hasty when he made his earlier assessment, his retraction carried no weight. Not only did Keitel and Jodl believe Sixth Army should stay, Hitler retorted, but Jeschonnek's own superior, *Reichsmarschall* Göring, had now given his personal assurance that the air force could fully meet the army's supply needs.

Determining when Göring first specifically assured Hitler that the Luftwaffe could supply the army is difficult because of the paucity of reliable and detailed sources. However, David Irving, who has reconstructed the *Reichsmarschall's* movements in this period, believes that Hitler first phoned him on 21 November, a full day after Jeschonnek had made his rash promise and shortly *after* Hitler had first mentioned the airlift to Paulus.[60] This view gains support from Richthofen's diary description of a discussion he had with Hitler at the Wolf's Lair on 11 February 1943, almost two weeks after Paulus surrendered and his surviving troops staggered into Soviet captivity. Hitler admitted to Richthofen that Göring was not entirely to blame for the failed airlift; he had himself promised Sixth Army that it would be supplied by air, "without the *Reichsmarschall's* knowledge."[61]

At that stage, Göring, who lacked up-to-the-minute information on Sixth Army's encirclement and statistical data with which to make air supply calculations, gave no specific assurances about his force's airlift tonnage capabilities, insisting instead that Sixth Army should stand fast and that, as Jeschonnek had said, the Luftwaffe would do all in its power to meet the army's needs. As soon as he got off the phone, he summoned his quartermaster staff and ordered every available transport plane—including his own courier flight—to be mobilized for the operation. The *Reichsmarschall's* actions are remarkable, considering that he had not yet studied detailed data or consulted air-supply experts. He later told Richthofen that, "at the very beginning of the Stalingrad episode, he had played the optimist and supported the Führer in his decision to stand fast there."[62] At that point, Richthofen added, Göring had still believed Sixth Army's encirclement to be temporary.

Göring's assurances became much stronger on the following day (22 November), when he arrived in Berchtesgaden. Hitler asked his bulky deputy whether he still supported the air-supply proposal. Göring replied confidently, "*Ja,* it can be done." He could give no other answer, he later told *Generaloberst* Bruno Lörzer, his close friend, because the Nazi leader used the worst kind of emotional blackmail: "Hitler said to me: 'Listen here, Göring. If the Luftwaffe cannot carry this through, then Sixth Army is lost!' He had me firmly by the sword-knot. I could do nothing but agree, otherwise the air force and I would be left with the blame for the loss of the army. So I had to reply: '*Mein Führer,* we'll do the job!' "[63] He could hardly have rejected the airlift proposal anyway, he lamely explained afterward to Paul Körner (undersecretary of state for the Four-Year Plan), because his own chief of staff had already convinced the Führer that the air force could supply the encircled forces. "Hitler already had Jeschonnek's papers before I set eyes on them," he told Körner, doubtless trying to shift some blame to his chief of staff. "I could only say, '*Mein Führer,* you have all the figures. If they are correct, then I place myself at your disposal.' "[64]

Jeschonnek's original figures were not accurate, however, as the *Reichsmarschall* learned just hours later. *Oberst* Eschenauer, Jeschonnek's supply officer, informed his boss that the standard "250-kg" and "1000-kg" air-supply containers on which he based his calculations actually carried only around two-thirds of those loads.[65] Their names derived solely from the size of the bombs they replaced on bomb racks. Jeschonnek, an honest man who admitted his mistakes, immediately told Göring and asked him to warn the Führer that their calculations were based on incorrect data. Göring winced when his young chief of staff confessed to this error, but, believing it was "too late now," expressly forbade him to tell Hitler. Instead, he phoned the Führer, repeating his unconditional assurances that the Luftwaffe could do the job and inviting him to phone *Generalfeldmarschall* Erhard Milch, his deputy and air inspector general, if he still felt unsure. When Milch finally learned of this in 1946, he angrily scrawled in his diary: "Deceit plus incompetence equals one *Reichsmarschall!* I guessed it already, but now I get proof of it, it makes me want to throw up all over again."[66]

According to Zeitzler's postwar claims, after Hitler arrived back in East Prussia late the next evening—23 November—he vigorously tried to persuade Hitler that Göring's promises were impossible to keep. After explaining at length the tonnages required and the lack of aircraft to carry them, Zeitzler told Hitler, "Having examined the facts in detail, the conclusion is inescapable: it is not possible to keep the Sixth Army supplied by air."[67] Hitler remained outwardly calm but, with annoyance evident in his voice, stated: "The *Reichsmarschall* has assured me that it is possible." When Zeitzler stood his ground, Hitler sent for the air force chief. "Göring," he asked, "can you keep the Sixth Army supplied by air?" The airman raised his right arm and said: "*Mein Führer,* I assure you that the Luftwaffe can keep the Sixth Army supplied." Hitler cast Zeitzler a triumphant glance, but the general refused to back down. "The Luftwaffe certainly cannot," he insisted, to which Göring angrily retorted: "You are not in a position to give an opinion on that." Hitler was surprised by the undisguised hostility between his commanders, but he granted Zeitzler permission to challenge Göring's promises. "*Herr Reichsmarschall,*" he said. "Do you know what tonnage has to be flown in every day?" Caught off guard, the embarrassed air leader spat back: "I don't, but my staff officers do." Zeitzler had come armed. His own staff had made detailed calculations, which he immediately summarized:

> Allowing for all the stocks at present with Sixth Army, allowing for absolute minimum needs and the taking of all possible emergency measures, the Sixth Army will require delivery of three hundred tons per day. But since not every day is suitable for flying, as I myself learned at the front last winter, this means that about five hundred tons will have to be carried to Sixth Army on each and every flying day if the irreducible minimum average is to be maintained.

"I can do that," Göring shot back. Losing his temper, Zeitzler shouted: "*Mein Führer!* That is a lie!" Hitler thought for a minute before replying: "The *Reichsmarschall* has made his report to me, which I have no choice but to believe. I therefore abide by my original decision [to supply the army by air]."

Zeitzler's frequently cited description of this argument with Göring should not be treated as a verbatim record because it is based on his subjective recollection of the exchange and was apparently not written down until the following day. However, the account is almost certainly an honest attempt at reconstructing the event. Zeitzler's open opposition to the airlift is mentioned in several reliable sources, including Richthofen's diary, as is his courage to express opinions contrary to the Führer's. But placing this account chronologically within this crucial decision-making period poses problems. Zeitzler himself could not remember the date, noting only that it took place "between 22 and 26 November."[68] Most writers place the argument in the early hours of November 24—that is, shortly after Hitler arrived from Berchtesgaden and shortly *before* he issued his fateful order to Paulus that his army must stand fast, that a relief operation was being launched, and that the Luftwaffe, bolstered by "a hundred more Junkers," would keep the army supplied.[69] If the argument did occur at that point, then it represents the last major appeal to Hitler to change his mind and the most weighty challenge to Göring's unconditional assurances that his air force would meet the trapped army's supply needs. It shows not only that Hitler had already firmly made up his mind before he arrived back in East Prussia but also that his deputy's embarrassing unfamiliarity with the tonnages he had promised to supply should have raised grave doubts in his mind about the reliability of those promises. Before it was too late, Hitler should have reexamined the tables and graphs drawn up by Jeschonnek, Zeitzler, and the army quartermaster general and have spoken to Richthofen, whose air fleet was to carry out the air-supply operation.

However, the argument between Zeitzler did not take place on 24 November, before the airlift began. It could not have; after Göring had visited Hitler at the Berghof on the 22nd, he departed for Paris in *Asia,* his luxurious command train. He spent the next four days—when he should have been organizing the airlift—visiting Parisian art dealers and galleries.[70] Richthofen was appalled. "I urge Jeschonnek and Zeitzler to report my views to the Führer," he wrote in his diary on the 25th, "and to harness the *Reichsmarschall,* but he's in Paris!" Göring arrived back at Hitler's headquarters in Rastenburg on the 27th, and his heated exchange with Zeitzler probably took place at that point—that is, three days after Hitler had given the final go-ahead for the airlift. Despite the claims of numerous writers, therefore, the argument played no part in the decision-making process. The die had already been cast.

Hitler's decision to keep Sixth Army at Stalingrad and support it from the air until a relief operation could break its encirclement was poorly received by the commanders in the field. Richthofen again tried desperately to convince everyone who would listen that Hitler must be given an honest appraisal of the facts. He phoned Jeschonnek (three times), Weichs, and Zeitzler, once more pleading with them to have his views made known to Hitler (which they did, to no avail).[71] He was disappointed by what he correctly perceived to be Jeschonnek's lack of courage in Hitler's presence, noting that "Weichs and Zeitzler share my view. Jeschonnek has no view at all." He was most upset the next day (25 November) to learn that the airlift would proceed, despite their warnings:

> The Führer heard everything we had to say, but decides against it because he believes the army can hold on and he does not think we could reach Stalingrad again. I stand by my own opinion. Still, orders are orders and everything will be done pursuant to the orders received. It is tragic that none of the locally responsible commanders, although purportedly possessing [the Führer's] confidence, has any influence at all now.... As things are at present, operationally speaking, we are nothing more than highly paid noncommissioned officers.[72]

Richthofen was stunned that the High Command expected him to fly in at least 300 tons per day. "We supply [the pocket today] with all our Ju 52s, but we only have 30 available for that," he added in his diary. "Of yesterday's 47 Ju 52s, 22 made sorties [into the pocket]; of today's 30, 9 made sorties. We flew in 75 tons today, instead of the 300 tons ordered by the High Command, which is not possible with the few Ju 52s available. I report this to the *Reichsmarschall*." Seydlitz, commander of the Fifty-first Army Corps, also complained that Hitler's order was impossible to fulfill. He sent Paulus a lengthy report, which warned that there could be no question of standing firm: "The army has a clear choice: it must break through to the southwest in the general direction of Kotelnikovo or face destruction within days."[73] The army's supply situation, he insisted, would decide the matter. To believe the Luftwaffe could keep the army supplied was grasping at straws, especially since only thirty Ju 52s were at hand and, even if the other hundred aircraft Hitler promised actually materialized, they could still not meet the army's needs in full. Unfortunately, Seydlitz's report contained several careless inaccuracies that robbed it of its persuasiveness. He stated, for example, that even 1,000 tons of supplies per day would not be sufficient, whereas Sixth Army's own quartermaster had just reported that the army could survive if the Luftwaffe carried in 500 tons each day (300 cubic meters of fuel and 200 tons of ammunition).[74] Schmidt and Paulus still sent the report to Manstein, adding that, although they disagreed with many of Seydlitz's reasons, they shared his view that the army should break out immediately.

Unfortunately for all those opposed to Hitler's "stand fast" and airlift decisions, Manstein made his own thorough assessment of the situation and sent the High Command a more optimistic appraisal.[75] His position was similar to Jodl's: while he agreed that a breakout was the safest course, and that the army remained in danger if it stayed in its present positions, he was not convinced by Army Group B's insistence on an immediate breakout. If a relief operation could start in early December, he argued, and if the promised reinforcements arrived in time, it was still possible to save the army. Of course, he cautioned, if it proved impossible to launch the relief operation or meet the army's supply needs by air, then it should break out. Hitler felt vindicated. He highly valued Manstein's opinions (as did most of his senior officers) and proudly informed Zeitzler and his other advisers that the field marshal's assessment was far more in keeping with his own views than those of his "defeatist" generals. The debate was over; he had won—*for now.*

Thus, responsibility for the decision to supply Sixth Army—one of the most fateful decisions of the war—rests with three individuals: Jeschonnek, Hitler, and Göring. Jeschonnek rashly made the first assurances that the Luftwaffe was capable of meeting the army's logistical needs before he had consulted air transport experts, made detailed calculations of his own, or sought the views of Richthofen and the other air force and army commanders at the front. Their evaluations of the situation and the capabilities of their respective forces would have been far more detailed and reliable than the situation assessments made by the Führer and his entourage, thousands of kilometers away in Hitler's alpine retreat in southern Bavaria, whose main source of information was Zeitzler's telephone "updates." Jeschonnek should have requested a little time to do homework before presenting an opinion on the matter.

When Jeschonnek gave his initial assurances to Hitler, however, he believed that the army's encirclement would be temporary and, therefore, that its long-term survival did not depend on the air force's ability to keep it supplied. Had he known then that Sixth Army would need supplying for several weeks, if not several months, he certainly would not have promised Hitler anything without extensive research. To his credit, when he did learn that Sixth Army's encirclement would last longer than originally claimed, that Richthofen and Fiebig forcefully opposed the airlift, and that his own hasty calculations were inaccurate, he immediately admitted his mistakes and tried to dissuade Hitler and Göring. He lacked both a forceful personality and the respect of his bosses; as a result, they simply ignored his warnings. Jeschonnek's culpability, then, stems from rashness, a faulty original assessment of the situation, and an inability to stand up to stronger personalities. It does not stem from dishonesty or incompetence.

When considering Hitler's responsibility for the decision to supply Sixth Army by air, one should note that he was unable to focus solely on that matter. He had to divide his attention between events at Stalingrad and what he mistakenly perceived to be the equally critical situation in North Africa. Only a fortnight after Montgomery launched his offensive against Rommel's positions at El Alamein and four days after his army captured them (which threw the Führer into a fit of rage), major Anglo-American landings took place in Morocco and Algeria on 8 November. French resistance quickly collapsed, and subsequent events forced Hitler to launch Operation *Anton,* the occupation of Vichy France, on the 11th. To make matters worse, he felt he needed to pour scores of thousands of troops into Tunisia to counter the advance of Anglo-American forces pushing eastward toward Rommel's *Afrika Korps,* still falling back westward before

Montgomery's Eighth Army. *Anton* quickly reached its successful conclusion. Yet when Stalin launched *Uranus* on 19 November, events were still going very poorly for German troops in North Africa, and Hitler's mind was focused on their survival and, he hoped, operations to restore the situation. Thus, distracted by events in the Mediterranean, Hitler was unable to focus his attention solely on the grave situation in the east. Had he chosen to concentrate on Stalingrad and the security of the Don-Donets region, strategically more important than Tunisia, he may have made different choices than the ones that eventually led to the loss of an entire army.

Deciding to supply Sixth Army by air was not Hitler's only mistake. His decision to pour men and equipment into Tunisia during this critical period rates as one of the worst he ever made. As Vincent Orange noted, "The campaign, however prolonged, could have only one result: an Axis defeat."[76] The Allies, he explained, "enjoyed command of the sea, the air and an enormous advantage on land in numbers of troops, tanks, guns and supplies of all kind (especially fuel)." Thus, the 81,000 German troops landed in Tunisia between November 1942 and January 1943,[77] plus the 250 Ju 52s used to transport them, were wasted in a campaign with little strategic value and no chance of success. Those men and aircraft could have made a crucial difference to German fortunes in the far more important Don-Donets region had they been sent to Manstein and Richthofen instead.

Hitler's responsibility for the airlift outweighs Jeschonnek's. First, his own initial perceptions about the developing encirclement and the fate of Sixth Army were based not on rationality but on egotism. His "iron will" alone had saved his eastern armies during the previous winter, he believed. It would do so again. This explains his comment to Zeitzler on the first night after he returned to East Prussia. "We must show firmness of character in misfortune," he lectured. "We must remember Frederick the Great."[78] Second, he also considered it essential to stand fast at Stalingrad because he could not withdraw, without losing face, from the "strategically important" city that he had publicly vowed several times to keep. Third, because Jeschonnek's assurances supported his own preconceptions, he uncritically accepted them, although the airman had clearly not reflected or conducted research before making them. Fourth, from the moment he received those assurances, which suited his own views so well, Hitler closed his mind to alternative strategies. Fifth, he totally ignored the repeated appeals and warnings of his frontline army and air force commanders, unfairly calling them "defeatists" because they challenged the inflexible "stand fast" formula that he had elevated to the status of doctrine. Sixth, he accepted Göring's promises and reassurances as uncritically as he had accepted Jeschonnek's, despite the fact that the *Reichsmarschall* had a poor track record, had exercised only nominal command of the Luftwaffe during the last year, instead delegating the force's day-to-day running to his subordinates, and, despite the crucial nature of the present situation at Stalingrad, had evidently made no real effort to familiarize himself with the issues involved. Finally, he did not sack Göring and replace him with someone competent, or even demand that he act responsibly in this critical period. He should at least have forbidden him (in Richthofen's words) "to swan off to Paris to plunder art galleries" and ordered him to stay in Rastenburg to organize and oversee the Stalingrad airlift, the largest in military history, upon which hung the lives of a quarter of a million men.

Göring's responsibility for the airlift decision equals Hitler's. When the Nazi leader first asked him whether the Luftwaffe could, as Jeschonnek had promised, fully meet Sixth Army's logistical needs, he should not have given an immediate answer. He should first have consulted his air transport experts, studied all available information on the situation at Stalingrad (enemy strengths and activities, the size and state of trapped forces, the condition and capabilities of *Luftflotte 4,* weather patterns and projections, and so on) and sought the opinions of Richthofen and the *Fliegerkorps* commanders involved. Remarkably, Göring failed to do this not only before making his first assurances but also before making his final promises prior to leaving for Paris.

The *Reichsmarschall* aggressively dominated his own staff, driving two of his senior officers to suicide (Udet in November 1941 and Jeschonnek in August 1943). Yet he proved incapable of standing up to Hitler. He rarely even expressed views contrary to the Führer's (at least in the latter's presence), especially after his obvious failure to defeat Britain from the air and to defend Germany's cities from ever-increasing Allied air attacks. These failures had steadily reduced his standing in Hitler's eyes throughout 1941 and 1942. Instead, he lapsed into subservience, hoping his slavish loyalty would repair their relationship. It is probable, then, that Göring's unconditional assurances that his air force could maintain Sixth Army stem from his inability to resist the Führer or challenge his views ("I gained the impression that he was afraid of Hitler," Milch once wrote)[79] and from his intense desire to restore his tattered prestige.

Hermann Plocher argued that Göring "may also have sincerely believed that he could accomplish the airlift operation to satisfaction, just as he had done in some instances in the past, by combining the influences of his several offices and adding his own brutal energy." Plocher is wrong. The *Reichsmarschall* did not "sincerely" believe that he could do the job, otherwise no sense can be made from his comments to Lörzer that Hitler had him "firmly by the sword-knot" and that he could "do nothing but agree" because he did not want to "be left with the blame." Also, his refusal to inform Hitler that Jeschonnek's original calculations were based on false premises and information removes any suggestion of "sincerity." He deliberately withheld embarrassing but important information from the Führer. Additionally, at no point during the course of the airlift did he throw his "brutal energy" into making sure it succeeded. On the contrary, rather than stay and organize and oversee the crucial operation himself, he disappeared to Paris on a shopping trip and then, on his return, only rarely attempted to involve himself in its progress.

INITIAL ORGANIZATION

When Stalin launched *Uranus* on 19 November 1942, Richthofen's *Luftflotte 4* possessed enough transport planes to keep its own airfields and air units operating adequately and to carry out limited air supply missions in support of the armies—particularly Paulus's Sixth—in its vast combat zone. Richthofen's transport fleet comprised the 1st (Staff), 50th, 102nd, 172nd, and 900th Special Purposes Bomber Wings, equipped with Ju 52s, and the Fifth Special Purposes Bomber Wing, equipped with He 111s.[80] These transport groups had performed well since *Blau* began back in June. Between August and October alone, for example, they had transported 20,173 tons of aviation fuel, 9,492 tons of ammunition, 3,731 tons of equipment, and 2,764 tons of supplies to Luftwaffe airfields at the front. They also provided the army with good support, carrying forward 27,044 troops, 4,614 tons of fuel, 1,787 tons of ammunition, and 73 tons of supplies, as well as evacuating 51,619 wounded soldiers.[81]

Richthofen was not able to deploy all these transport units in support of Sixth Army after the Soviet pincers closed around it, because most still had to carry out vital supply operations for the various Luftwaffe commands they served. The 1st (Staff), 5th, 50th, and 102nd wings all supplied Fiebig's *Fliegerkorps VIII*, while the 172nd served *Luftgau Rostov* (Air District Rostov, which organized the fleet's supply, maintenance, and ground service matters), and the 900th directly served the fleet command itself.[82] By this time, Pflugbeil's *Fliegerkorps IV*, which had almost ceased to exist since its combat units were transferred to *Fliegerkorps VIII*, had no air transport units.

Most of Richthofen's transport units had been in action without a break since *Blau* began, and the rehabilitation and refitting of combat units always took precedence over their own. As a result, their average operational rate, at around 40 percent, was 10 percent lower than that of the combat units.[83] The operational rate of certain units—particularly those attempting to meet both the army's and the air force's needs—were as low as 30 percent. On 9 November, for instance, the 900th Special Purposes Bomber Wing possessed 41 Ju 52s, but only 12 were airworthy, while the 50th had 35 Ju 52s, only 13 airworthy.[84]

The fact that these units still had vital supply tasks to perform for their respective commands (although the decrease in *Fliegerkorps VIII*'s combat missions after *Uranus* began freed up several dozen transport aircraft for other duties), and the fact that all these units were in poor shape, explains why Richthofen was able to commit only 30 of his 295 transport planes to supplying Sixth Army on 25 November.[85] The *OKL* would clearly need to send the fleet chief many hundred more aircraft if they expected him to fulfil Göring's promises to Hitler.

To supply Sixth Army with 300 tons a day—the absolute *minimum* amount demanded by the army (which really needed 500 tons)—would necessitate an average of 150 fully laden Ju 52s landing in the pocket each day. Of course, because weather would prevent that tonnage being airlifted on many days, far more than

300 tons would have to be carried in during good weather. Loading and unloading supplies was time-consuming, so each plane could fly only one, or perhaps two, missions a day. Therefore, because an operational rate of only 30 to 40 percent could be counted on, Richthofen needed at least 800 Ju 52s to fulfil Göring's promises and meet Sixth Army's barest needs.[86] At that time, however, the entire Luftwaffe possessed only around 750 Ju 52s. Over half of them operated in the Mediterranean theater. They supplied *General der Panzertruppe* Nehring's forces in Tunisia while they tried in vain to stop the Anglo-American forces that had landed in French North Africa, as well as Rommel's *Afrika Korps*, still retreating across Libya after its defeat at El Alamein.[87]

Because of the importance of transport aircraft to the North African campaign, the Luftwaffe's quartermaster general had to look elsewhere for planes to send to Stalingrad. Although he took few aircraft from the Mediterranean and North Africa (at least initially), his measures were still a case of robbing Peter to pay Paul. He stripped the chief of training of several hundred aircraft, plus its best instructor pilots and crewmen, thereby dealing a heavy blow to the training program (which never fully recovered from the loss of many multiengine training aircraft and pilots at Stalingrad). He robbed *Lufthansa* and numerous government agencies and departments of their transport and courier planes, which had a negative effect on communications and postal services. He also pulled scores of bombers and long-range reconnaissance planes from groups on all fronts, had them converted into emergency air transporters, and rushed them to southern Russia. Their very high attrition rate during the airlift later prompted Göring to moan to his American captors (with typical exaggeration): "I always believed in the strategic use of air power. . . . My beautiful bomber fleet was exhausted in transporting munitions and supplies to the army at Stalingrad."[88]

Naturally, it took time for these reinforcements to arrive at *Luftflotte 4*'s airfields around Stalingrad. Those arriving from the Reich had to fly almost 2,000 kilometers; those from other fronts had to fly far farther. On the way to their forward operating bases, they all had to pass through intermediate bases at Kirovograd and Zaporozhye in the Ukraine, where service and maintenance personnel converted bombers into transporters and prepared all aircraft for winter conditions.[89] The influx of aircraft was so great at times, however, that ground staff were not always able to cope with the amount of work to be done. As a result, many aircraft left for their forward bases poorly equipped for the harsh winter or intensive airlift operations.

By the first week of December, most of the units the *OKL* assigned to Richthofen had arrived and commenced air supply operations. They formed a large transport fleet, comprising almost nine Ju 52 wings; a strong He 111 force of two wings already in a transport role plus two full wings and two other groups hastily converted for the airlift; two wings of converted Ju 86s; a converted He 177 wing; and even a long-range formation equipped with FW 200 Condors, Ju 90s, and Ju 290s.[90]

On paper this transport fleet appears sufficient for the task, but, because most groups were well under strength, it contained only around 500 aircraft, far below the number actually needed to carry a daily average of 300 tons of supplies to Sixth Army. Also, many of the aircraft—especially the He 177s—were unsuitable for this transport role and soon became liabilities. Although the *OKL* would transfer additional units to Richthofen as the airlift progressed, he would never have anywhere near enough suitable aircraft to keep Sixth Army adequately supplied.

On 26 November, Richthofen completely reorganized *Luftflotte 4*.[91] Its main focus would no longer be combat operations in support of ground forces in offensive fighting, as it had been since *Blau* began, but supply operations in support of ground forces encircled by a powerful enemy and struggling for their survival. He appointed *Generalmajor* Victor Carganico (former commander of the Tatsinskaya airfields) as the new *Luftversorgungsführer* (air supply leader), directly subordinate to the fleet command (as opposed to an air or flak corps). "He has the task," Richthofen stated in his reorganization instructions, "of securing the air supply of Sixth Army—through the strongest concentration and exploitation of all air supply resources—to a level that keeps it alive and its fighting capability intact."[92] Carganico was responsible for organizing and overseeing not only all airlift matters outside the pocket but also, through liaison with Sixth Army and *Generalmajor* Pickert (the senior Luftwaffe officer trapped at Stalingrad), all air supply matters inside the pocket.

Richthofen assigned air units to bases according to aircraft type, aware that this would reduce the supply and maintenance problems involved in deploying various types of planes from the same airfields. He ordered all Ju 52 groups to operate from Tatsinskaya, under the command of *Oberst* Hans Förster, commodore of the 1st Special Purposes Bomber Wing, who would now assume the title *Lufttransportführer* (air transport leader). Richthofen placed all He 111 units at Morozovskaya under the command of the 55th Bomber Wing, led by *Oberst* Kühl, its experienced commander. He placed all long-range bomber and reconnaissance aircraft—pressed into air transport service despite their unsuitability—at Stalino (near the Sea of Azov), under *Major* Willers, its air transport officer. *Luftgau Rostov* continued to function essentially as it had since *Blau* began, although the new types of aircraft and the specialized equipment needed for air supply operations caused a variety of new problems. Its greatest difficulty, however, was keeping the airfields inside the pocket operable despite the bombing attacks of *VVS* forces.

Carganico and his staff were competent in all air supply matters but lacked command experience of major operations involving many hundreds of aircraft. They also lacked familiarity with combat aircraft and operations, a great weakness considering that fighter escorts were essential because of frequent and strong *VVS* attacks on the lumbering supply planes. Their inexperience and inability to get the airlift up and running disappointed Richthofen, who complained in his diary on 28 November: "Air Supply Leader Carganico is not work-ing out, despite constant and detailed exhortations. I wrestle mentally with com-mand and supply organization [problems], but, after much [debating] to and fro, I arrive at the following solution: *Fliegerkorps VIII* will take over the Stalingrad airlift."[93] The following day, he made Fiebig the new air supply leader and placed his corps command in charge of the complete air supply operation. Fiebig was pleased by Richthofen's trust but also aware of the huge responsibility involved. Fiebig wrote in his diary that evening: "*Fliegerkorps VIII* is relieved of its combat duties and will, from tomorrow, take over the air supply of Sixth Army. This is an honorable but difficult assignment! It must be accomplished, despite Soviet ef-forts to stop it. Finesse and skill must be used both day and night to carry out this task. It will cost a great deal of blood; of that I am certain."

Fiebig and his staff were already situated in Tatsinskaya, having been forced to abandon *Fliegerkorps VIII's* command post in the Oblivskaya bridgehead three days earlier. The air corps commander had not wanted to leave, hoping to keep at least some airfields east of the Chir. When Soviet tanks and cavalry for-mations closed in on those airfields on 25 November, he threw every available fighter, Stuka, and ground-attack aircraft against them. "All units are participat-ing in raids to destroy them," he penned in his diary. "Ground-attack planes and Stukas from Oblivskaya carry out between 10 and 12 sorties each. Reports speak of an outright slaughter of horses and riders. But enemy elements are now getting very close to the Oblivskaya airfields." The situation on the Chir looked grim, he noted, and the Oblivskaya bridgehead was in grave danger of collapse. "Rein-forcements, including two armored platoons, eight flak batteries, and one-and-a-half Luftwaffe field divisions have been promised," he added, "but the ring around Oblivskaya tightens."

The following day (26 November), Soviet tanks attacked the bridgehead and, joined by long-range artillery, opened fire on Fiebig's airfields. They destroyed numerous ground-attack planes unable to take off in time and left the runways pockmarked with deep craters. Although some of the German reinforcements ar-rived in time to prevent the Soviet forces bulldozing through their defenses, it was clear that Fiebig could no longer command *Fliegerkorps VIII* from within the bridgehead. Richthofen himself flew into Oblivskaya to assess the situation and asked Fiebig to shift his headquarters back to Tatsinskaya. The air corps leader, who believed in commanding from the front, even if it meant risking capture, would not go willingly. Richthofen—doubtless inwardly impressed—had to order him out.[94] By 30 November, when Fiebig received command of the entire airlift operation, he had established his new command center in Tatsinskaya, safely be-hind the Chir, and briefed his staff on their impossible new task: the maintenance by air of the quarter of a million men trapped within *"der Kessel,"* the Stalingrad pocket. Grimly they set about it.

9

Failure: November–December 1942

Right from the start, adverse weather conditions obstructed Fiebig's airlift to a far greater degree than the *VVS* or any other factor save the glaring shortage of planes. Well informed about local conditions by their weather experts, both Richthofen and Fiebig had warned the High Command (in vain) that this would be the case. Air operations would be extremely difficult, they argued, even without a repeat of the previous year's unusually cold winter. Even if the winter proved no worse than "normal," conditions in the Donets Basin and the Stalingrad sector would create major problems for the air fleet.

They were not being unduly pessimistic. Stalingrad experienced extremely cold winters. American air force meteorologists, who noted that German operations "will be hindered by intense cold," explained in a December 1942 intelligence bulletin that "Stalingrad has a colder winter than any other city in the area. The mean winter temperature at Stalingrad is 17.9 degrees F., colder than Leningrad, where the mean winter temperature is 19.5 degrees F."[1] Indeed, the entire Stalingrad region usually experienced warm summers, short and mild springs and autumns, and long and very cold winters.[2] British Air Ministry meteorologists reported in 1942 that "the period during which the average temperature is below freezing point is approximately 15th November to 21st March at Stalingrad and 30th November to 7th April at Rostov."[3] Throughout that period, heavy snowfalls occurred so frequently that snow coverage seldom disappeared. "Over the open treeless steppe country of the region the winter winds carry the snow with extraordinary force," the meteorologists added. "Violent blizzards sometimes occur which pile the snow into large drifts." Particularly in the southern Ukraine and the Donets Basin—where *Luftflotte 4*'s main bases lay—the snow coverage was usually so thick that roads could not be kept open except by constantly running motorized snowplows over them.

Air activity would certainly suffer, the American and British weather experts reported. Low cloud prevailed, "in general, on two days out of every three." These low ceilings (under 650 meters), combined with frequent ground fog, would make takeoff and landing difficult and greatly reduce visibility once airborne. Also, "the danger of icing in winter is likely to be great when flight is made in low cloud."

The winter of 1942–1943 was not unusually severe, but when the temperature began plunging below zero in mid-November (almost exactly on the dates mentioned earlier), its "typical" conditions were still so harsh that *Luftflotte 4*'s operational capability suffered markedly. By 26 November, Richthofen was grumbling in his diary that it was "bloody cold."[4] He noted that evening that he had summoned Rohden, his chief of staff, and Schulz, his quartermaster, to his headquarters at Kamensk on the Don, but "dreadful weather" prevented their arriving. Even making telephone calls proved difficult during snowstorms. "Nothing works in this bloody outfit," Richthofen complained. His entry for the following day reveals the frustration he felt: "Very dreadful weather. Fog. Icing over. Snowstorm. No air operations, no supply possible." Fiebig's diary contains similar complaints. On 27 November, for instance, he lamented that the weather was "the worst we have ever experienced" and that, as a result of a heavy hailstorm, "communications with rear areas have disappeared. . . . We have one blizzard after another at Tatsinskaya; a desolate situation."[5]

When fighter, ground-attack, and Stuka groups had hastily withdrawn from their airfields east of the Chir to escape being overrun by advancing Soviet armor, they had abandoned numerous purpose-built heating devices and much equipment used for thawing frozen engines by other means. They had also left behind a number of snowplows, essential for keeping runways free of snow. The arrival of dozens of transport aircraft each day throughout the first two weeks of the airlift only exacerbated the situation, forcing already overtaxed ground personnel to work feverishly to keep airfields and aircraft operational. *Generalmajor* Pickert later recalled:

> The cold caused unimaginable difficulties in starting aircraft engines, as well as engine maintenance, in spite of the well-known and already proven "cold starting" procedures. Without any protection against the cold and the snowstorms, ground support personnel worked unceasingly to the point where their hands became frozen. Fog, icing and snowstorms caused increasing difficulties, which were compounded at night.[6]

Air leaders, like their troops, soon became depressed by the sight of Ju 52s churning up snow as they attempted to take off with poor visibility from runways only partly cleared of snow by ground personnel armed only with shovels. As early as 2 December, Fiebig noted in his diary that, "after yesterday's snowfall, everything is still frozen. We can get He 111s airborne, but not the Ju 52s before 1130 hours. . . . We lack heating equipment. We did not receive enough to cope with the large influx of aircraft. Transport planes simply have no business here.

Thawing takes too much time and a great deal of effort."[7] Two days later, he wrote: "During the night there was an urgent deicing at Pitomnik [the principal airfield inside the pocket], but still no opportunities for takeoff because of the thick fog. Everyone is stressed, standing by for a chance to get airborne. Everyone—ground and air personnel—is doing his utmost. But who can fight the forces of nature?"

Few of the new pilots were accustomed to flying in temperatures so cold that their planes iced up as they entered low-lying cloud formations. For the first weeks of the airlift, however, poor visibility caused by snowstorms, fog, and low cloud hampered Luftwaffe operations more than the cold. Taking off was dangerous and difficult, but even experienced pilots hated having to land their fully laden planes inside the "fortress" during the frequent periods of poor visibility. Thick fog shrouding Pitomnik and Basargino (the main airfields within the pocket) often forced even the most courageous pilots to turn back without attempting to land, despite the presence of radio beacons at each field.[8]

Of the six airfields inside the pockets, only Pitomnik was properly equipped to handle large-scale operations. It even had lights, flare paths, and signals equipment for night operations. The others—with the exception of Basargino, which *Generalmajor* Pickert hastily equipped with the minimum requirements—were no more than bare grass landing strips, lacking all necessary communications and air traffic control equipment. Several of those fields had been used in previous months to supply Sixth Army as it advanced into Stalingrad, but the quantities of supplies carried were never large and the weather had been satisfactory. Now, those soggy, snow-covered fields were virtually worthless to the Luftwaffe.

Pickert worked tirelessly to ensure that his two main airfields functioned as efficiently as possible and that the off-loading and transfer of supplies was always handled smoothly and quickly. He took his job seriously, realizing that the lives of an entire army depended on the Luftwaffe's ability to keep it supplied and fed. "The [Pitomnik] airfield has become my main sphere of activity," he wrote in his journal on 26 November. "All momentum here is focused on the air supply operation, evacuation of the wounded, and their accommodation until they can be flown out."[9] The plight of the wounded moved him deeply. When he had first arrived at Pitomnik two days earlier, he saw "tragic scenes of freezing wounded, waiting with their nurses for evacuation." For the next two months, he would frequently refer to the hundreds of wounded soldiers waiting each day to be placed in transport planes and carried out of the pocket for medical attention. Many died beside the runways, especially on days when weather conditions curtailed air operations.

Pickert stationed a heavy flak battery at the main airfield[10] and ordered all the light batteries that Sixth Army had not already positioned along the pocket's outer perimeter to dig themselves in around the main airfields. "This is no easy task in the steppe," he noted, "because there is almost no wood and the ground is frozen solid."[11] The flak teams must protect transport aircraft from *VVS* attack at all costs, he insisted, especially when they were most vulnerable during takeoff and landing. The flak commander had good reasons to fear attacks by *VVS* units. By the end of November, Soviet fighters, ground-attack planes, and bombers were singling out Pitomnik for heavy attacks, clearly aware of its importance to the airlift operation.

The Soviet air force had actually played only a minor role in the opening days of *Uranus*. Recently formed *VVS* units contained many aircrew fresh from training schools, who had no experience of flying during snowfalls or thick fog. As a result, they sat on their airstrips until brief periods of clear weather allowed them to engage in combat against the Axis forces. Even experienced aircrew were handicapped by the weather. Thick fog and low cloud prevented pilots and gunners from distinguishing between Russian and German or Rumanian troops in the chaotic conditions on the ground, especially after the Rumanian lines collapsed and Russian tanks and troops streamed through the gaps. With the situation changing constantly and opposing forces fighting in close proximity, the *VVS* was unable to throw the full weight of its combat units against the enemy. As a result, it carried out only 1,000 sorties during the first four days of the offensive.[12] Of course, Luftwaffe units suffered the same weather-related problems; they carried out a mere 361 sorties during the same period.[13]

Once the Soviet pincers had closed near Kalach on 23 November, trapping Sixth Army and other formations, the situation on the ground became far less fluid. *VVS* air armies now had clearly defined, stationary targets, which they could find and hit without difficulty, even during bad weather. *VVS* air activity increased substantially during the following weeks. Between 24 and 30 November, for instance, Soviet air units carried out 5,760 sorties.[14] Sixty percent of those sorties were conducted against German troops, positions, and airfields within the pocket.[15] After regular German airlift operations began on 25 November, transport planes became popular targets for the Soviet *Okhotniki* (free hunters), fighters, and ground-attack aircraft that roamed the skies looking for combat.

Official Soviet claims of very high kill rates seem reasonable at first glance, owing to the obvious superiority of *VVS* fighters to the slow and mostly unarmed German transport planes and the supposed vulnerability of the airfields within the pocket. Yet those kill rates should be treated with greater caution than they have been by the scholars who frequently repeat them in their accounts of the battle. Uncritically accepting the verity of General Rudenko's memoirs, for example, Hardesty is one of many writers on Soviet airpower who repeat claims that fail to stand up to closer scrutiny. According to one of Hardesty's statements, fighters of the 283rd Fighter Air Division intercepted 17 Ju 52s, escorted by four Bf 109s, over the pocket on 29 November. "They destroyed five Ju 52s and one Bf 109," he writes.[16] Richthofen, Fiebig, and Pickert, who routinely mention losses in their diaries, do not mention the loss of any aircraft on that day (or the day on each side of it). In fact, Pickert wrote that it was a quiet day for the *VVS:* "The weather cleared up, but the enemy failed to seize the opportunity. Only a single aircraft appeared [over the pocket] and it was attacked." Similarly, Hardesty's claim that *VVS* fighters destroyed seventeen transport planes on the ground within the pocket on 2 December is also refuted by the German sources.[17] Richthofen's diary states: "We flew 150 tons [of supplies] into Stalingrad, without losses." Pickert even noted in his own diary that Soviet air activity had dropped off perceptibly that day.

Even a cursory reading of surviving German sources—including the war diary of the 3rd Group of the 3rd Fighter Wing, operating in the Stalingrad sector—reveals that Soviet fighters did not destroy anywhere near as many German transport aircraft as most writers maintain. Rather, they succeeded in destroying a relatively small but steady number. Although their loss proved costly to the airlift, it actually hampered the operation far less than the weather. However, *VVS* activity did have one other important effect: its constant pressure on the airlift operation and on the troops within the pocket forced Fiebig to deploy fighters, although they were sorely needed elsewhere (especially on the Chir front), on convoy escort and airfield protection duties.

Fiebig had relatively few fighters at his disposal during the airlift. When *Blau* began back in June, *Luftflotte 4* possessed a total of 325 Bf 109s, of which 236 (73 percent) had been operational. These fighters had operated without rest or rehabilitation for five months, during which time normal combat attrition took its toll. The *OKL* had also transferred several groups to other sectors of the front during times of crisis. As a result, when the Stalingrad airlift began on 25 November, *Luftflotte 4*'s two fighter wings, the 3rd and 52nd, together possessed only 203 planes.[18] A total of 125 (61 percent) were operational, while the others sat on airfields waiting for repair, maintenance, or the arrival of replacement engines. Not all these fighters even operated under Fiebig's command in the Stalingrad region and the Donets Basin. Richthofen had left a small fighter force in the Caucasus to serve Ruoff's and Kleist's armies after he robbed them of Stuka and ground-attack support when *Uranus* began. Fifty-four fighters, thirty-seven of them airworthy, patrolled the skies above those armies.[19] Thus, when the airlift commenced, Fiebig possessed fewer than 90 operational fighters in the Stalingrad region.

He could not deploy all these fighters on transport escort duties, despite needing to protect the slow and unarmed Ju 52s, and even the armed He 111s, from *VVS* attacks. He had to commit numerous squadrons to combat against Soviet forces attacking the weakly held Chir Front in their effort to widen the gap between the new German line and the forces trapped within the pocket. According to received opinion (following Hermann Plocher's account),[20] those squadrons did not operate under Fiebig's direct command. Instead, they functioned as part of *Generalleutnant* Mahnke's *Fliegerdivision Donez* (Air Division Donets). This was purportedly a new operational command that Richthofen had hastily formed in late November to direct combat operations in the region after committing Fiebig's air corps solely to organizing and overseeing the airlift. Plocher was mistaken, however, and writers who have accepted his account have merely repeated his error. Richthofen did not form *Fliegerdivision Donez* until 2 January 1943, almost five weeks after *Fliegerkorps VIII* took over the airlift.[21] Until then, Fiebig retained command of his fighters, directing their operations on the Chir Front through his corps staff.

He did not ignore escort duties, though. He was gravely aware that Tatsinskaya and Morozovskaya, the main bases for the transport fleet, were 230 and 200 kilometers from the pocket, respectively, and that his transport planes were highly vulnerable along their entire fifty-minute flight path to interception by *VVS* fighters and Shturmoviks waiting for them each day. The ten or twelve fighters that had been stationed at Pitomnik when the pincers had first closed—a squadron of the 1st Group, 3rd Fighter Wing, under *Hauptmann* Germeroth— were able to provide fair protection for the incoming transports and the two main airfields. They shot down dozens of Soviet aircraft (130, according to Pickert's postwar claim) during the airlift.[22] These German fighters were powerless, however, to protect transport planes farther afield. Not only were they numerically weak, but they lacked the range to escort transporters far on their return flights and they had to guard the airspace over the pocket at all times. As Richthofen commented in his diary on 24 November: "The air supply of Stalingrad suffers under the influence of Russian fighters. We are forced to leave fighters inside the pocket, therefore, although they themselves consume part of the supplies needed by Sixth Army. They are not yet able to guarantee the security of the supply operation and the Russians can still sweep over our forward airfield in the pocket at any time." As a result, Fiebig deployed several fighter squadrons—with around 40 Bf 109Gs—solely on escort duties. The 3rd Group of the 3rd Fighter Wing, which he transferred to Morozovskaya-West on 28 November, formed the nucleus of this small escort force.[23] An entry in that group's war diary explains its activities and reveals the difficulties involved:

> The main task of the wing's 1st and 3rd groups is convoy protection for the Stalingrad airlift. Because the range for escorting the slow-flying transport units on their incoming and return flights is not sufficient, it is necessary for us to stop over and refuel at Pitomnik. During the return flights we protect the transports evacuating the wounded. Because the Russians have erected a "flak avenue" and deployed strong fighter forces, we must change our rendezvous points, approach paths and altitudes each day.
>
> Aside from these convoy escort duties, which remain the highest priority, the group must also defend its own airfields and the main supply bases of Morozovskaya and Tatsinskaya from enemy air attack. It must also conduct low-altitude attacks on the Russian ground forces which are now situated only a few kilometers north of our airfields.[24]

Fiebig also intermittently deployed a few Bf 110 squadrons from the 1st Destroyer Wing on escort and *freijagd* (free hunt) duties. These twin-engined "destroyers"—originally designed as fighters—proved less effective as escorts than

Bf 109s, mainly because the weight of their guns, armor, and engines, plus the extra fuel carried in drop tanks to extend their range, substantially restricted their maneuverability. The Bf 109s, then, performed the lion's share of the convoy escort work.

THE FIRST WEEKS OF THE AIRLIFT

The airlift began on 25 November, before most of the additional Ju 52s and converted bombers had arrived at Tatsinskaya and Morozovskaya. It was not an auspicious start. Thirty Ju 52s managed to carry in only 75 tons that day, well below the 300 tons the Luftwaffe promised and the 500 tons the army still wanted. Because the army had agreed to consume its remaining rations and then eat its 10,000 horses before asking for provisions to be airlifted, the Junkers carried in no food. Fuel composed the greater part of their load. Pickert's ground personnel unloaded 36 cubic meters, a small drop in the army's almost-empty bucket. They also unloaded 28 tons of ammunition, sorely needed by Paulus's troops, who expended six times that amount per day.[25] They were then able to place 330 wounded soldiers onto the Junkers, which ferried them back to makeshift field hospitals in Tatsinskaya and Morozovskaya, from where the survivors were steadily transferred (mainly by motor vehicles) to military hospitals in the Reich or Rumania.

The remaining days of November followed the same pattern. A small but steadily growing number of available Ju 52s left the airfields behind the Chir each day, some making completely blind takeoffs in bad weather, to carry into the pocket only a fraction of the tonnage required. During the five days between 26 and 30 November, they managed to carry in only as much as Göring had promised for a single day: 191 cubic meters of fuel, 108 tons of ammunition, and 4 tons of other freight; that is, around 300 tons in total.[26] The best day was the 30th, when Ju 52s and He 111s carried 129 tons of supplies into the "fortress," including 69 cubic meters of fuel and 35 tons of ammunition. The worst was the 27th, when, because of extremely bad weather, aircraft carrying a mere 28 tons of fuel (but no ammunition or rations) landed in the pocket.

The weather was consistently unfavorable, with clear periods occurring rarely and briefly. The radio beacon at Pitomnik helped the pilots home in through fog and snowstorms, although landing with poor visibility proved disastrous to many. In fact, crashes during takeoff and landing, especially during the latter, destroyed more transport planes than the *VVS* fighters and Shturmoviks attempting to create an "air blockade" of the pocket. Pickert often marveled at the courage and superb flying skills displayed by the pilots who landed successfully in bad weather, sometimes even in total "whiteouts." On 29 November, for instance, he jotted in his diary: "In the most dreadful weather, with a ceiling of only 80 meters, . . . He 111 supply planes appeared on the scene, a splendid accomplishment. I praised them all profusely!"

The courage and skill of the aircrew were matched by the energy and growing efficiency of Pickert's ground personnel. Using virtually no machinery, large teams constantly cleared runways of snow and the wrecks of aircraft that failed to land safely. They salvaged whatever cargo and aircraft parts they could from the wrecks before pushing them off the edge of the runways. They processed incoming planes quickly, unloading their cargo and dispatching them again, full of wounded soldiers, usually within two hours. They even drained from the planes all fuel not needed for the return flights, adding it to Sixth Army's meager and constantly shrinking reserves. It should be noted, however, that these teams were not able to sustain this high performance level for long. The extreme cold and constant enemy harassment gradually destroyed their strength and morale. By late January, the aircraft turnaround time had risen to over four hours.[27]

Pickert's flak teams performed well against marauding VVS aircraft, shooting down several and diverting others each day. However, they possessed too few batteries to prevent Soviet fighters and ground-attack aircraft from streaking in at low altitude, bombing and strafing the airfields and the transport planes being unloaded. Pickert's diary entry for 30 November describes a typical attack:

> Weather clear. We [therefore] expect much enemy air activity, as well as increased activity by our transport planes. Both expectations were met. Over 20 Ju 52s arrived almost at once, as well as numerous He 111s. The enemy appeared often with six to ten aircraft, dropping bombs and strafing. It was at times rather awe-inspiring, and, although there was little damage, there were unfortunately a few losses. Two Ju 52s were also shot down, fully laden with fuel. They went up in flames. A terrible sight. Still, during the attack the enemy lost around 20 planes.[28]

Thus, the situation at the beginning of December looked unpromising. Fiebig had nowhere near enough aircraft, the weather severely handicapped operations, VVS air activity hampered it still further, and, as a result of these factors, Sixth Army was receiving each day less than 20 percent of the minimum amount considered essential for its survival. This placed tremendous stress on the operational air commanders—on Paulus and his staff, too, of course—and, even at this early stage of the airlift, caused friction between them. On 2 December, for instance, Richthofen and Fiebig clashed over what was really a trivial matter: the deployment of the small number of weak Rumanian air units left in the area. The former had a soft spot for the Rumanian airmen (but not for the soldiers) and wanted to reorganize their command to give them better access to resources, as well as greater opportunities to prove their worth in combat. Fiebig was furious, especially when he learned that they would be taking over a number of airfields on the lower Don presently occupied by *Fliegerkorps VIII*'s own units. He angrily wrote in his diary that night that Richthofen had been duped by the "bleating and prattle" of Rumanian commanders claiming that *"Fliegerkorps VIII* thinks it owns the Don region."[29] The following day he even wrote that "Richthofen lacks the courage of his convictions. It's a terrible situation. . . . I try to call him, unsuccessfully. He is indisposed." Richthofen was just at angry over the situation. He noted in his own diary that "Fiebig behaves toward the Rumanians with ignorant and abnormal stupidity. I have to make myself abnormally clear to him!"[30] The disagreement came to nothing, however, when both commanders realized that they had a far more important matter to worry about: the survival of the quarter of a million men in Stalingrad. They could not allow a rift in their relationship to develop at this critical time. As Fiebig wrote on 6 December: "Conversation with Richthofen. Loyalty on both sides. He tells me that he trusts me. Although our personalities seem to clash, in the end we are both pursuing the same objective— so we must be reconciled."

Pickert did not involve himself in the squabble. Isolated within the pocket, unable to sleep properly at night because of the relentless thunder of artillery fire and sporadic crashing of bombs, he reacted to the intense stress he felt with composed resignation, not anger. "I pray each night to our God," he penned on 5 December, "not for myself, but for our people and the Fatherland, for the salvation of Sixth Army and for final victory! I feel deeply compelled to do this. But for myself and my insignificant fate I can find no words. Everything for everyone. For our beloved land, which we must fight to protect." He knew the airlift was doomed, but he was not yet prepared to abandon Sixth Army. Manstein's powerful relief effort would start within weeks, he told himself. He and his men must do all they could to ensure its success.

OPERATION "WINTER STORM"

During his long journey south from the Leningrad region to his new headquarters at Novocherkassk, thirty-five kilometers northeast of Rostov, Manstein discussed the Stalingrad situation with several local commanders. Most important, he conferred with Weichs and his staff at the Starobyelsk headquarters of Army Group B. They briefed him at length on Soviet actions and strengths and the state of Sixth Army. He also sought the advice of General Hauffe, the head of the German military mission to Rumania, "who painted a most disagreeable picture of the state of the two Rumanian armies on the Stalingrad front."[31] Of their twenty-two original divisions, Hauffe said, "nine had been completely destroyed, nine had run away and could not be sent into action for the time being, and only four were still fit for combat." Although he hoped to form "a few additional formations from the wreckage," he added that Manstein would not be able to count on them for any relief operations attempted in the immediate future.

In a series of telephone calls, Manstein also discussed the situation with Richthofen, who firmly insisted that his air fleet could not provide Sixth Army with anywhere the amount considered essential for its survival. Paulus must break out immediately, the airman emphatically stated several times, and the field marshal must abandon his unrealistic hope of breaking *in* and relieving him. Contrary to received opinion, Manstein shared this view and, because he doubted he would have sufficient forces, despaired at Hitler's order that he should relieve Sixth Army as soon as possible. "Manstein is desperate about the decisions made at the top," Richthofen noted in his diary after a long discussion with the field marshal at his new headquarters on 27 November.[32] He added that Manstein was also in a poor mental state, having lost his eldest son in combat only a month earlier. In his own memoirs, Manstein referred to the loss of his son as "the hardest blow that could have befallen my beloved wife, myself and our children" and devoted several pages to a eulogy.[33]

Still, Manstein was a professional soldier. He would perform his duty to the best of his abilities. Despite his frustration with the High Command, his mounting belief that Army Group Don lacked sufficient forces to mount an attack strong enough to break into the pocket, and his grief at the death of his son, he responded to Hitler's instructions with the iron determination and boundless energy that had first won the Führer's admiration early in the war. He conceived a bold plan, code-named Operation *Wintergewitter* (Winter Storm), to send a powerful column slicing through the cordon around Sixth Army to break its strangulation. Fuel and ammunition would be rushed through the corridor to improve the army's mobility and strength.[34] Then, if all went according to plan, he would send Sixth Army the radio signal *Donnerschlag* (thunderclap), its cue to break out through the same corridor.

The Fifty-seventh Panzer Corps (from Hoth's Fourth Panzer Army) would make the main thrust toward Stalingrad. Strengthened by two fresh panzer divisions still to arrive, it would strike from the vicinity of Kotelnikovo, 110 kilometers from Paulus's encircled army. Although Manstein's forces at Nizhne-Chirskaya were 45 kilometers closer, he chose to strike from Kotelnikovo because it would not involve crossing the Don and he believed the Soviets would least expect an attack from that direction. A Rumanian corps would guard each of the column's flanks, while the Forty-eighth Panzer Corps, with five divisions by then, would make a diversionary thrust from the Chir toward Kalach.

Manstein soon realized, however, that many of his promised reinforcements would arrive late or not at all, because they were sent to other crisis points along the eastern front. He concluded that "relieving Sixth Army from two different directions . . . from the Kotelnikovo area east of the Don . . . and from the middle Chir towards Kalach . . . was impossible because of a shortage of forces. The most we could hope to do now was to assemble sufficient strength at one spot."[35] Thus, he decided to attempt only the attack from Kotelnikovo and ordered Paulus to begin shuffling his forces around inside the pocket in preparation for a breakout in that direction. He kept this part of the plan hidden from the Führer until almost the last minute. Hitler, he knew, favored an operation to break Sixth Army's encirclement and build a strong front on the Don, but still wanted that army to hold its positions on the Volga while being supplied via a "land corridor."

Manstein ordered the immediate formation of a convoy of 800 trucks loaded with 3,000 tons of fuel and other supplies, plus a fleet of tractors for mobilizing part of Sixth Army's artillery, all of which would follow his panzers into the "fortress." He also began positioning his forces for the coming attack, taking care not to leave his flanks exposed or the Chir front weakened. Inside the pocket, meanwhile, Paulus acted on the field marshal's instructions by shifting two motorized divisions and a panzer division to the southwest part of the pocket.

Despite being the product of Manstein's excellent strategic mind, *Wintergewitter* ran into trouble right from the moment of conception. On 2 December, shortly after Paulus moved the three divisions to the southwest, the Soviet Don and Stalingrad Fronts struck the pocket and tied those divisions down in bitter defensive fighting for almost a week. Their attacks, Manstein recalled, "were bloodily repulsed by the courageous troops of the army."[36] Next day, the Southwestern Front hit the Chir front, "striking ceaselessly at one *Schwerpunkt* after another," forcing Manstein to commit the three fresh divisions intended for the Forty-eighth Panzer Corps to defensive operations on the Chir. In effect, this removed the corps from any participation in *Wintergewitter*. Additionally, the two panzer divisions promised to the Fifty-seventh Panzer Corps (the 6th and 23rd) were slow in arriving, and the *OKH* instructed the field marshal to deploy his two Luftwaffe field divisions for defensive actions only.[37]

Manstein was a realist. He knew that his chances of success were fair at best. Hitler remained optimistic, on the other hand, responding to the field marshal's "pessimistic" report of 28 November[38] with a radio message encouraging him not to be downcast because of the great number of Soviet divisions in the region. He should remember that Soviet formations were always smaller and weaker than they at first appeared to be, and that the Soviet command was probably having trouble maintaining supplies and effective command as a result of its unexpected successes.[39] Manstein was not persuaded and, on 9 December, sent the High Command a detailed appraisal in which he outlined the situation of both Axis and Soviet forces.[40] Axis forces were greatly outnumbered, he explained at length, and air reconnaissance revealed that additional Soviet units were steadily pouring in from other sections of the front. The Soviet command clearly anticipated a relief operation and was determined to thwart it at all costs. Strong Soviet attacks were already being made on the Chir front.

Outlining his intentions, Manstein urged that he be allowed to launch his attack as soon as possible, even though he was still uncertain if the Forty-eighth Panzer Corps could be released from the Chir immediately. A steady flow of reinforcements to Army Group Don was absolutely crucial, he stressed, if he was to offset Soviet reinforcements. It was also essential to increase their rate of arrival if they were not always going to lag behind the enemy.

Manstein had previously maintained that Sixth Army's breakout was an essential prerequisite for the consolidation of the southern flank. However, although he still planned to liberate the army, he now seemed unsure whether this was the wisest course of action. In his lengthy appraisal to the High Command he even suggested that the trapped army would probably play a more valuable role by continuing to tie down the scores of Soviet divisions around Stalingrad.[41] Freeing the army from the ruined city would release far more Soviet forces than Army Group Don could possibly handle. On the other hand, he added, the strength of enemy forces and the rate and scale of their reinforcement were already so great that the Soviet command might

> take the proper action and, while maintaining its envelopment of Stalingrad, attack with strong forces against Third and Fourth Rumanian Armies with Rostov as its target. If this happens, our most vital forces will be operationally immobilized in the fortress area or tied down keeping the corridor to it open, whereas the Russians will have freedom of action along the whole of the army group's front. To maintain this situation throughout the winter strikes me as not advisable.

This gloomy appraisal had little effect. Although Hitler did express concern for the immediate stability of the Chir front, and began tinkering with the disposition of forces in that sector, he remained convinced that Soviet formations were weaker than Manstein claimed, that the field marshal would liberate Sixth Army, and that he would probably also restore the line held before *Uranus*. The 9 December entry in the OKW war diary states:

> Weather permitting, *Generalfeldmarschall* von Manstein will launch the attack aimed at relieving Sixth Army on 11 or 12 December, and expects to continue the attack until the 17th. The *Führer* is very confident, and wants to regain our former positions on the Don. He believes that the first phase of the Russian winter offensive can be regarded as finished, without having shown any decisive successes.[42]

Air support for the attack would be limited because Fiebig's *Fliegerkorps VIII*—previously the most powerful close air support force in the east—now committed most of its bombers and half its fighters, and devoted all its efforts, to meeting Sixth Army's logistical needs. However, Richthofen was determined to provide the army with the best support possible by his depleted air fleet, aware that the failure of Manstein's relief operation would seal the fate of Sixth Army.

During all previous operations, Richthofen's efforts to form a close army–air force working relationship had resulted in markedly enhanced combat effectiveness. He now wanted interservice cooperation during *Wintergewitter* to be as close as it had been during the attack on the Kerch Peninsula or on Sevastopol, when it had produced splendid results. Although he lacked the powerful forces at his disposal back in May and June, he believed that, with effective liaison and close cooperation between his team and Manstein's—previously a winning combination—his fleet could still provide the army with acceptable air support. Unfortunately, one factor now threatened to ruin his efforts to build a close working relationship with Army Group Don: the incompetence of *Oberst* Hans-Detlef Herhudt von Rohden, his chief of staff. Rohden was intelligent and energetic, but a poor administrative officer, unable to marshal effectively and efficiently the efforts of his subordinates and focus them on the fleet's missions. He also lacked judgment of situational constraints, understanding of human behavior, and, most important, interpersonal skills. He just could not "get on" with his superiors, peers, or subordinates.

Richthofen summoned Rohden on 10 December and sharply rebuked him for his poor performance. The fleet staff was "simply not functioning," he said.[43] The latter snapped back that it was not his fault. "*He* raged at me," the surprised Richthofen wrote that night. "Claims he does too much himself and requests new people." The rebuke had no immediate effect. Two days later, Rohden's inability to work closely with *Generalmajor* Schulz, Army Group Don's chief of staff, resulted in a clash between the air fleet commander and Manstein. Rohden was "uncongenial" and impossible to work with, Manstein insisted, stressing that his chief and the rest of his staff concurred.[44] The best short-term solution, he added, was for Richthofen and himself to liaise directly, as they had at Sevastopol. The airman agreed, pointing out that he had never appointed Rohden in the first place. It had been a decision from above. He remained hostile toward Rohden, "letting fly at him again" that night and, on the 13th, writing in his diary:

> Rohden is always useless, not taking care of the essential things. That's because he knows nothing at all about them. He's endowed with the ability to write insignificant but literarily faultless orders. He never urges the units to do anything; he takes care neither of the [fleet] staff business nor of the rear area services or the *Gau* [the fleet's administrative section]; he does not keep in contact with the army commands, and, when he does, he only ends up quarreling with them. All in all, then, he's an ideal chief!

He wanted Rohden replaced as soon as possible, and rang Jeschonnek several times to request his transfer. According to received opinion, the unpopular officer remained in his post until late January, when *Generalfeldmarschall* Milch arrived to take over the airlift. One of the first things he did was instruct Richthofen to sack Rohden.[45] This is not true. Milch never issued any such instruction. In fact, despite Richthofen's requests for his removal, Rohden remained *Luftflotte 4*'s chief of staff until late February (three weeks after Milch had returned to Berlin), when he took over as chief of staff to *Generaloberst* Keller's *Luftflotte 1*, operating in northern Russia.[46] In the meantime, Richthofen kept him tightly reined in, while liaising with the various army commands himself.

On 9 December, Richthofen issued a directive entitled "*Luftflotte 4*'s combat operations for the destruction of the enemy around Stalingrad."[47] Not yet aware that Manstein had been forced to abandon his secondary thrust toward Kalach because of insufficient forces, the air commander included that diversionary attack in his directive. The fleet would "first pull Fourth Panzer Army forward in a northeast direction from the Kotelnikovo region toward the Stalingrad fortress, and then forward from the Chir bridgehead in the direction of Kalach." However, despite the directive's overly optimistic title and its promise of the "fullest" support of the army, Richthofen had so few units to throw against the Soviets that he was forced once again to abandon *Schwerpunktbildung,* the practice of creating single points of maximum effort. Instead, he had to dissipate his forces by deploying them on three major separate but simultaneous missions: (1) the continued supply of Sixth Army at Stalingrad; (2) the close support of Manstein's relief operation; and (3) the close support of the Axis forces already fighting desperately on the Chir.

Fliegerkorps VIII must continue its airlift to Stalingrad with no slackening of effort, he stressed in the directive. Sixth Army's mobility and combat readiness must be improved so that it could break out when Manstein gave the order. However, "if the need arose," *Fliegerkorps VIII* would deploy its bomber groups *(K.G. 51, K.G. 55, I./K.G. 100, II./K.G. 27)* against Soviet concentrations at various points around the pocket, as well as at the Don-Chir bridgehead. The 2nd Group of the 52nd Fighter Wing would escort the bombers during such missions. One might have thought that Fiebig opposed the use of these bombers in a combat role, especially the He 111 groups, preferring to use them as he had for the last week or so: as a valuable component of his transport fleet. However, he was already painfully aware that the airlift was failing miserably and that, as a result, Sixth Army's only chance of salvation lay with Manstein's relief effort. As he wrote in his diary on 12 December, the first day of the operation: "Today only 80 tons of supplies reached the fortress. . . . But the tactical success of Fourth Panzer Army, together with the He [111]s, is worth much more than a few additional tons in the fortress."

Pflugbeil's *Fliegerkorps IV,* which now had only around one-third of its June or July strength, would carry out the main offensive mission: support of Fourth Panzer Army's relief drive from Kotelnikovo to the pocket. Pflugbeil's air corps was poorly equipped for this task, lacking sufficient fighters to keep the skies clear of Soviet fighters and tank-destroying Shturmoviks, as well as enough Stukas and ground-attack planes to offer the army effective battlefield support. *Fliegerkorps IV* commanded two Stuka wings, a ground-attack wing, and a destroyer wing. Although this appeared an adequate force on paper, the operational rate was less than 50 percent. In total, the operable Ju 87s, Bf 109s, and Bf 110s numbered less than 200. They were already substantially outnumbered by their *VVS* counterparts, which had possessed air superiority in the region since *Uranus* began and would doubtless concentrate their formations against the relief force as soon as they detected it.

In his operational directive, Richthofen stressed the need to "shield" the Chir Front, already creaking under the weight of constant enemy pressure. If it gave way, the entire southern flank would probably collapse. Both air corps, he stated, must carefully monitor enemy activities along the Chir and be ready, in the shortest time, to throw back any forces penetrating the front. Fiebig's fighter, Stuka, and ground-attack units would focus most of their attention on the Chir front. They were in poor condition, though, with the operational rate of most units being around 35 to 40 percent. Therefore, to defend the weakest stretch of the Chir front, held by the remnants of the Rumanian Third Army, Richthofen also committed the few Rumanian air units left in the area to protection of the Chir. They were understrength, poorly trained, and equipped with aircraft inferior to the new *VVS* fighters now making their presence felt at Stalingrad, but at least they filled a few gaps in the coverage of the depleted German units.

Despite their quantitative inferiority, Richthofen's combat units had exacted a high toll on the enemy in recent weeks, so he could expect them to perform well during *Wintergewitter*. Whereas most Soviet pilots were fresh from training schools, almost all German combat fliers were experienced in aerial combat and in dealing with the very difficult weather conditions. As a result, not only had German Stukas and ground-attack planes proved deadly on the battlefield since the beginning of *Uranus,* but, although they were numerically much weaker than their Soviet counterparts, German fighters had claimed more enemy planes destroyed than they had themselves lost. On 8 December, for instance, Soviet armored forces launched attacks on the northwest corner of the pocket but were successfully driven back by combined air force and army actions. Escorted by fighters from the 3rd Fighter Wing, Stukas of the 2nd Dive-Bomber Wing repeatedly hit the Soviet infantry and armor, destroying a large percentage of the sixty tanks left wrecked on the battlefield. For the loss of a few planes, the fighter squadrons inflicted high casualties on their Soviet counterparts, claiming thirty-two fighters and Shturmoviks destroyed.[48] The kill ratio was consistently in favor of the German air units, although not always as dramatically so as on 8 December. In general, throughout the last week of November and the first two of December, German units destroyed around three times as many aircraft as they lost. Richthofen could take little heart from this, however. His units were so depleted that even losses usually considered acceptable were now substantially reducing their operational effectiveness. The *VVS,* on the other hand, was still strong enough to absorb its higher losses. Richthofen felt sick with foreboding over the coming relief operation, but he insisted that his units do their utmost to bring it to a successful conclusion.

The progress of the air supply operation further discouraged the air leader. Despite the best efforts of Fiebig, Pickert, and their staffs, the airlift was going as badly as he had earlier predicted to the High Command. Between 1 and 9 December, when he issued his directive for the Luftwaffe's participation in *Wintergewitter,* his transport units had managed to carry a mere 1,055 tons of supplies into the pocket.[49] That is, they transported an average of only 117 tons per day, or about one-third of the amount considered the bare minimum for Sixth Army's survival. Only once, on the 7th, did they reach their daily goal. On that occasion they carried in 362 tons, prompting Richthofen to praise Fiebig's air corps in his diary (the first time he had) for its "good airlift results." Yet twice in that period, on the 3rd and the 9th, weather conditions prevented any aircraft at all from landing within the pocket.

Between 10 and 12 December, when *Wintergewitter* finally commenced, weather conditions allowed a slight increase in air operations. With an average of only 180 tons reaching Sixth Army during those three days, however, the trapped forces were still consuming far more food, fuel, and ammunition than they were receiving.[50] In fact, by the 3rd, food stocks had already dropped so low that Pickert, refusing to consume more than his men, was eating "two slices of bread per day, plus a little thin soup."[51] The only meat available came from the army's rapidly decreasing number of horses, and that was also rationed carefully. On the 8th, the food situation had become so critical that Paulus, wanting to stretch out his remaining food stocks until Manstein's forces broke the encirclement, reduced the rations for all troops in the pocket to one-third of normal. Sixth Army would not survive long, he knew, if the relief operation failed.

"WINTER STORM" COMMENCES

Before dawn on 12 December, Hoth's Fifty-seventh Panzer Corps—really just the 6th and 23rd Panzer Divisions—began its drive from Kotelnikovo toward "Fortress Stalingrad," 110 kilometers away. Carrying extra fuel and ammunition, and followed by rifle regiments and antitank units, the corps' 230 white-painted tanks initially made good progress. They encountered light opposition, having apparently caught their opponents with their guard down. They quickly destroyed the few units attempting to blunt their advance, and advanced past the abandoned weapons of others that had fled in disarray. "The Russians are on the run, just like old times," Fiebig excitedly penned in his diary.[52]

Indeed, the attack had surprised the Soviet command, and only the quick thinking of Vasilevskii, the chief of the Red Army's general staff, prevented their forces between Kotelnikovo and the pocket from collapsing.[53] As soon as he learned of the attack, Vasilevskii emphatically insisted to the unconvinced Stalin that he must transfer the crack Second Guards Army from the Don Front to the Stalingrad Front in order to block Hoth's advance. Stalin finally relented to his repeated appeals early the next morning and authorized the transfer. Until that army arrived a few days later, Hoth's divisions were able steadily to bulldoze their way forward.

The 12th was also a good day for the Luftwaffe. The air units supporting Hoth's armored divisions met weak and disorganized *VVS* opposition. For half a dozen losses, they claimed fifty-four Soviet aircraft destroyed, twenty-five of them on the ground, the rest in aerial combat.[54] They also bombed and strafed enemy troops and field fortifications in front of the advancing panzers. Richt-hofen and Manstein worked together throughout the day, carefully coordinating their operations as they had on previous occasions. Although still disgusted by the "hopeless dissipation" of his forces, the airman felt partly consoled by their initial successes. "I only hope it will be as easy to bomb the enemy tomorrow," he wrote, noting that his groups had hit the Soviets in five repeated attacks.[55]

These pleasing results had a cost. Robbed of many He 111s and escort fighters, Fiebig's transport fleet managed to carry only eighty tons of supplies to Sixth Army that day.[56] However, those in the pocket were probably less con-cerned by this paltry amount than they usually would have been. Their hour of liberation was at hand, or so they believed. A mood of optimism spread through the pocket with the news that "Papa" Hoth was on his way, and divisions in the southwest corner stood ready to begin their drive toward Hoth's forces. Pickert wrote in his diary that evening: "The assembly of troops for our freedom is finished, and [the relief effort] has begun. May God grant the liberation of our splendid soldiers here."

During a conference at Hitler's East Prussian headquarters, held that first day of *Wintergewitter*, Zeitzler requested Hitler to release the 17th Panzer Divi-sion from the Chir so that Manstein could give it to Hoth for the relief operation. The Soviets would not remain idle for long, he accurately predicted, and would promptly mount a strong defense. The Führer refused his request, claiming that the division was needed where it was because of a threat developing at the junc-tion of Manstein's army group and the Italian Eighth Army's right flank. En-couraged by the relief operation's early progress, Hitler remained optimistic about its chances of success. He was also still convinced that, while Sixth Army should thrust out to meet Hoth's panzers at the right moment, it must not aban-don its positions on the Volga. "I have reached one conclusion, Zeitzler," he de-clared, pointing to Stalingrad on the map. "Under no circumstances can we give that up. We would never win it back again. We know what that means. . . . If we abandon it, we sacrifice the entire meaning of this campaign. To imagine that I will get there again next time is insanity."[57] Hitler's statement reveals a substan-tial shift in thinking. During *Blau*'s planning stage and early operations, Stalin-grad had not even been a primary target. Now Hitler was calling it "the entire meaning of the campaign," making no mention of the Caucasus oil fields, the original strategic goal.

For the next two days, the Fifty-seventh Panzer Corps made steady progress, reaching the Aksai River and capturing a bridge at Zalivskii on 14 December. Thus, they were already a third of the way to the Stalingrad pocket.[58] Although stiffening quickly, Soviet resistance was still relatively weak. The Luftwaffe had provided good support on the 13th, mainly because Richthofen personally di-rected all its combat operations. Also, to ensure effective army–air force coopera-tion, he visited not only the command posts and airfields of several key air units but also the command posts of Army Group Don, Fourth Army, and the Fifty-seventh Panzer Corps. Soldiers and airmen alike marveled at the sight of his light Storch bobbing and weaving above the battlefield or landing on unprepared and uneven fields beside command centers.

However, "very dreadful weather" on 14 December curtailed air operations in the entire region, leaving Hoth's two armored divisions to push forward most of the day without air support. Of course, adverse weather grounded not only Luftwaffe units but also those of the *VVS*, thereby temporarily removing the threat of Shturmovik attacks. The weather also grounded Fiebig's transport fleet, except for a few He 111s flown through the "whiteouts" by the most skilled and courageous pilots. They carried no food or ammunition, but only materials urgently needed to increase Sixth Army's mobility: fuel and low-viscosity engine oil and lubricants. The quantity they managed to supply was unlikely to make much difference, though. As Richthofen wrote: "No flying except for weak supply [to Stalingrad] of 80 tons of fuel."[59]

Soviet pressure along the Chir and against the Don-Chir bridgehead had intensified during 13 December, forcing Richthofen (as he put it) "to wheel the mass [of air units] to the Chir, because a catastrophe looms there."[60] Determined to widen the gap between the pocket and the main German line, which they wanted to crack open in several places, the Soviet Fifth Tank Army and the newly formed Fifth Shock Army had thrown themselves against the Chir front, which the Forty-eighth Panzer Corps fought desperately to stabilize. Richthofen was pessimistic about its chances of holding the Chir, writing that "if we [the Luftwaffe] don't strongly help them tomorrow, there won't be anything left to be done." Manstein held grave fears as well, not only for the stability of the Chir front but also for the safety of Hoth's two armored divisions, a third of the way to Stalingrad. They were unable to achieve decisive successes, he told the High Command, and, because of their extended flanks, needed immediate reinforcements. He requested the 17th Panzer Division and the 16th Motorized Infantry Division. Hitler reluctantly gave him the former, although it meant weakening the Don-Chir bridgehead, but not the latter, which held the stretch of front between Army Groups Don and A.[61]

The following day (14 December), Soviet forces hit the Don-Chir bridgehead so strongly that German forces were forced to evacuate their positions east of the Don. It was an "incredible mess," said Richthofen, whose units were powerless to intervene because of the bad weather. They were unable to offer any assistance the next day as well, when "whiteouts" again hampered reconnaissance and combat operations and prevented all but a few dozen of Fiebig's transport aircraft from reaching the pocket. They carried in only seventy tons of food, fuel, and ammunition, which was less than a quarter of the army's minimum daily requirement.[62] Richthofen was most upset by his force's weakness, especially concerning the fate of the encircled troops. "We can do absolutely nothing because of the weather," he lamented that night. "The poor Sixth Army." His only real achievement in recent weeks, he thought, was the evacuation of wounded soldiers; 9,000 so far, saved from almost certain death within the pocket.

Early on 16 December, German fortunes took a dramatic turn for the worse. Stalin's Operation *Malyi Saturn* (Small Saturn) commenced, opening with a short but heavy artillery barrage. Two Soviet armies—the Sixth, under Lieutenant General Kharitonov, and the First Guards, under General Kuznetsov—then crashed through the Italian Eighth Army's line on the Don, northwest of Stalingrad. Lieutenant General Lelyushenko's Third Guards Army joined them on the 17th, helping them rip open the front as they pushed southward.

Like both Manstein and Weichs, Richthofen had long feared that the Soviets would target the Italians. As early as 29 November, for instance, he had written in his diary: "It looks as though the Russians are also going to hit the Italians; a bad thing, because they will probably run faster than the Rumanians." He was wrong. When the Soviets finally did attack the Italians on 16 December, the latter resisted courageously and, despite suffering heavy losses, launched several minor counterattacks in a desperate attempt to save the front. Despite their best efforts, however, they were overpowered by much stronger forces and had to fall back, though they did so steadily. Nevertheless, German disdain for the Italian army reached right to the highest levels, its alleged "poor showing" in Russia only confirming the low opinion formed by a string of defeats in the Mediterranean over the last two years—defeats in which, of course, German forces suffered a full share and for which their Italian allies served as convenient excuses. Count Ciano, the Italian foreign minister, observed this antipathy while visiting Hitler's headquarters two days after *Malyi Saturn* began. When one of his entourage inquired of the *OKW* whether the Italian forces on the Don had suffered heavy casualties, he received the untrue reply: "None at all. They never stopped running."[63]

The *OKL* immediately ordered Richthofen to send two bomber wings— *K.G. 27* and *K.G. 51*—north from Army Group Don's combat zone to help the Italians prevent their line from disintegrating. He was bitterly disappointed, and promptly informed Jeschonnek by telephone that the transfer would remove one-third of the air units supporting Hoth's advance and protecting the hard-pressed Chir front. It would also substantially reduce the forces available to support Paulus's breakout. In short, he stated ("washing my hands of all responsibility"), it would mean "abandoning Sixth Army and [allowing] its murder."[64]

The situation grew rapidly worse. Hoth's panzers became bogged down in heavy fighting around Kumskiy, halfway between the Aksai and Mishkova Rivers. With momentum lost and opposition now stiff, their chances of reaching Paulus, or even approaching close enough to encourage his army to break out of the pocket, were rapidly decreasing. On 19 December, the panzer divisions managed to claw their way forward to the Mishkova River, fifty kilometers from the pocket, but were stopped by strong armored formations. Believing that he could neither reach Sixth Army nor open a permanent corridor to the pocket, Manstein informed the High Command that only one course of action could now be considered: Sixth Army must break out, gradually pulling back its northern and eastern fronts as it pushed out toward Hoth's divisions in the southwest.[65] This would at least save most troops and some matériel. He was so convinced that this was the only solution that he told Paulus to make immediate preparations to break out, but not to start until ordered.[66] Sixth Army would have to reach the Mishkova River, he explained. Once contact was established, he would send his supply convoys through the corridor, loaded with food, fuel, and ammunition. Sixth Army would then steadily contract its perimeter as it withdrew southwestward, taking whatever equipment it could.

Hitler had other ideas. He was encouraged by Hoth's progress and now (according to the OKW diarist) "relinquished the idea of abandoning Stalingrad."[67] He ordered the transfer of the SS Wiking Division north from the Caucasus to strengthen Fourth Panzer Army. But he refused to sanction Donnerschlag, Sixth Army's breakout, claiming that Sixth Army had only enough fuel to go thirty kilometers, halfway to the Mishkova. Therefore, it must hold its positions until the Fifty-seventh Panzer Corps could advance farther and establish contact, at which point—but only if circumstances demanded—an orderly withdrawal could be undertaken. In the meantime, he would see that the Luftwaffe substantially increased its fuel supplies to the pocket, in order to permit the army to travel fifty kilometers.

Fiebig was astounded. The High Command wanted him to supply Sixth Army with 4,000 tons of fuel and 1,800 tons of rations, which was, he wrote in his diary on 19 December, "simply impossible to accomplish." Indeed, during the previous four days, his transport groups had been able to carry in a total of 581 tons of supplies—a daily average of only 145 tons.[68] At that rate, it would take no fewer than forty days to supply the army with the amount required to restore its mobility, but only if the army survived that long and consumed nothing in the meantime. These prerequisites reveal the absurdity of the situation.

Meanwhile, by 20 December the three Soviet armies had shattered the Italian defenses. The Celere and Sforzesca Divisions on the Italian army's right flank collapsed under a heavy attack, taking with them the two Rumanian divisions on Army Group Don's left flank.[69] The Soviets drove southward, advancing along a 100-kilometer-wide front toward Fiebig's main bases between the Donets and Chir Rivers. Hitler promptly ordered the transfer of additional divisions to the region, but they were few in number and would take time to arrive. Some had to travel from the far north.

THE LUFTWAFFE'S OWN PROBLEMS

Fiebig was deeply concerned for the safety of Millerovo, his main supply base, and, on 20 December, ordered the transfer southward of the 27th Bomber Wing, which had operated from its airfield.[70] He was more fearful, however, for the Tatsinskaya and Morozovskaya airfields, the principal bases for the supply of Stalingrad. They were already being attacked repeatedly by Soviet bombers, but their capture or evacuation would be a severe blow to the airlift. No other fields in the region were as large or well equipped. "Fiebig is very pessimistic," Richthofen noted, "and also radiates it."[71] The air fleet commander was himself just as downcast; two day earlier, he had written that he could "no longer see any positive solution" to the steadily worsening situation.

On 21 December, spearheads of the Soviet Twenty-fourth Tank Corps advanced to within twenty kilometers of Tatsinskaya, and Soviet-flown Douglas Boston twin-engined bombers began pounding Morozovskaya. Fiebig—now "really nervous," according to Richthofen—ordered immediate preparations for evacuation. He had not yet received instructions from the fleet command, despite repeated requests, so he put his staff and units on emergency alert and told them to be ready to leave at any time.[72] Believing that only a few individual tanks threatened Fiebig's base and command center, Richthofen instructed him to sit tight for now. He would seek clarification of the situation from the High Command, he said, and issue formal orders as soon as he could. A day later, however, he had neither received a reply from the High Command nor learned from Army Group Don what measures were being taken to ensure the protection of the airfields, which were clearly in danger of being overrun. Acting on his own initiative, therefore, he instructed Fiebig to organize an emergency defense force from flak troops and ground personnel, and to prepare both Tatsinskaya and Morozovskaya for immediate evacuation if and when Soviet forces seriously threatened their defenses. He favored early evacuation, he explained, so that important equipment could be driven out or airlifted to other airfields. He could not afford to lose fuel tankers, engine-warming equipment, and spare parts, which were all in short supply after the loss of airfields east of the Chir in the first days of *Uranus.*

On 23 December, Richthofen finally received a reply from the High Command. It was not the answer he wanted. *Fliegerkorps VIII* must hold Tatsinskaya and Morozovskaya, instructed Göring, in a rigid "stand fast" order.[73] It must continue supplying Sixth Army from those bases at all costs. They could be evacuated only when Soviet tanks or troops began firing directly on the airfields—but not a minute before. With a heavy heart, Richthofen transmitted the *Reichsmarschall*'s instructions to Fiebig. The matter was now out of his hands, he said. He could not override Göring's instructions and order a more timely evacuation. Fiebig accepted the news with resignation (and the same reluctant obedience displayed by Paulus at Stalingrad). He wrote in his diary that evening: *"Ich sehe, wir rennen ins Unglück, aber Befehl ist Befehl!"*—"I see that we're rushing headlong into disaster, but orders are orders!" He did not have long to wait. Within three hours of when that entry was written, Soviet forces launched their attack on Tatsinskaya.

First came some good news, however. At 0200 on 24 December, Richthofen rang to congratulate him: he had just learned from *Oberst* von Below, Hitler's Luftwaffe adjutant, that the Führer had awarded Fiebig Oak Leaves to the

Knight's Cross for his outstanding leadership of *Fliegerkorps VIII*. Richthofen was delighted, noting in his diary that the award was "long overdue" and came at exactly the right moment. The situation was grim, he wrote, so this great news could only "improve the atmosphere."[74] Yet the air corps commander had little time to savor his new decoration. At 0330, Soviet artillery batteries opened fire on the airfield, joined shortly after by the tanks that easily broke through its flimsy defenses. A tank shell struck the signals center, destroying all means of communications.[75] Artillery and tank gunfire wrecked several transport planes sitting on runways but failed to prevent the others from taking off. With visibility at only 500 meters and a ceiling of 30 meters, and shells slamming into the runways around them, pilots took off in the most "frenzied" conditions. Their planes were laden with as much equipment as ground personnel had time to load before climbing on board themselves. After overseeing the hasty evacuation, *Fliegerkorps VIII*'s senior commanders, including Fiebig and his chief of staff, left in one of the last intact Ju 52s on the base. They were lucky to make it out, especially after the plane developed trouble in one engine. The pilot nursed it to Rostov, flying through low cloud on instruments only. "At least it didn't ice up," Fiebig noted that night. "What an absolutely lucky break!"

Aircraft losses were acceptable under the circumstances; 108 of Fiebig's 130 operable Ju 52s and 16 of his 40 operable Ju 86s managed to take off, scatter, and finally land at a variety of airfields in the region.[76] That is, he lost 46 (27 percent) of the 170 airworthy aircraft stationed at Tatsinskaya when the Soviets overran it. He called this "almost unbelievable." Still, the loss of those 46 aircraft, the abandonment of valuable equipment, and the capture of hundreds of tons of supplies urgently needed by Sixth Army were major blows. By his own account, Fiebig was numb with depression, unable to participate in the Christmas Eve celebrations put on by Richthofen's staff. "I was at the end of my strength," he wrote, "so I went to bed early, even missing the Christmas visit of the *Generaloberst* [Richthofen]."[77]

Fiebig flew over Tatsinskaya the next morning in a Storch, observing a few wrecked aircraft and a burning fuel train. After returning to Rostov, he was slightly heartened by his Christmas present: Richthofen's staff had reassembled the scattered Tatsinskaya transport groups on airfields at Salsk, in the northern Caucasus. They would probably begin airlift operations from Salsk later that day, albeit on a much-reduced scale. Fiebig paid Richthofen a "sleepy Christmas visit" in the afternoon.[78] The latter tried to "raise his spirits," reassuring him that, although the airlift had suffered a blow, it was far from fatal. He felt that Fiebig blamed him for the loss of Tatsinskaya, so he showed him a copy of Göring's order, pointing out that the "damned thing" had paralyzed his ability to act independently. Fiebig accepted his explanation, cursing the High Command for its actions. He noted in his diary: "Richthofen can see only one possibility: that the Führer has always been right in his decisions up until now, even though we could not quite understand it when, on previous occasions, he acted contrary to the advice he received. Perhaps one day we will be laughing over a wine about our present woes. May Heaven grant it."

Despite purporting to have faith in the Führer's genius—clearly an attempt to cheer up Fiebig—Richthofen had come to believe that neither Hitler nor the High Command grasped the true situation in this critical region and that, as a result, their decisions were invariably going to make that situation worse. "My confidence in our leadership is rapidly shrinking to nothing!" he had scrawled in his diary two weeks earlier.[79] Almost every day since then, his diary reveals, he had phoned Zeitzler, Jeschonnek, and Göring, trying to get them to fly out and assess the situation for themselves. All he received, he noted, were empty promises and unconvincing statements of empathy. Zeitzler was the only one who seemed aware of the true state of affairs, but his "stammering" revealed that he lacked the strength or ability to do anything substantial.[80]

The airman was not alone in losing faith in the High Command. All the senior army commanders in the region—including Weichs, Hoth, Paulus, and Manstein—were equally fed up. Richthofen shared a meal with Manstein on 26 December, after which he jotted these comments:

> We both complained together. Manstein suggested that the *Reichsmarschall* himself should assume command of both the [Don] army group and *Luftflotte 4*, since he always claims that the situation here or at Stalingrad is not as bad as we report. Our motto: "Assign the confident commander to the post he is confident of fulfilling!" The Führer now refuses to speak to Manstein by telephone, to summon him to his headquarters, or to come out here himself.

THE END OF "WINTER STORM"

Hitler's anger at his outstanding field marshal stemmed not only from the latter's failure to break through to Sixth Army but also from his repeated claims that the entire southern front could collapse if the High Command—meaning Hitler himself—insisted on trying to keep the encircled army in its present positions. On 21 December, after the Fifty-seventh Panzer Corps had attempted unsuccessfully for two days to push past the Mishkova River, Manstein told both Paulus and Hitler that the corps would probably not be able to advance farther and that Sixth Army must attempt to break out immediately. Paulus and his chief of staff replied that they would not move without Hitler's permission, and offered several reasons (which Manstein and Richthofen privately called "lame excuses") why they opposed a breakout anyway. Manstein therefore tried to convince Hitler to approve the breakout, knowing that Paulus would then have no choice but to attempt it. Zeitzler agreed that this was the best course of action, even though it would mean heavy casualties and the abandonment of much equipment.

According to the published version of the *OKW* war diary, Hitler promptly discussed the overall situation with the general staffs of both army and air force, but, "as usual, again no bold decisions are taken. It is as though the Führer is no longer capable of doing so."[81] As David Irving points out, however, this frequently cited passage is a postwar interpolation, designed to cast Hitler in a poor light.[82] It does not appear in the original, unpublished manuscript by Helmuth Greiner, the *OKW*'s diarist, and it is inconsistent with Hitler's recorded actions on the days both preceding and following 21 December. Rather than vacillating, the Führer stood firm, repudiating the "defeatist" views of his generals with typical dogmatism. He strongly disagreed with Manstein's and Zeitzler's assessments and rejected their suggestions. Still determined to hold Stalingrad, the only major prize of an extremely costly summer campaign, he insisted that Sixth Army might attempt to join up with Hoth's corps only if it continued holding its positions on the Volga.

On 22 December, Manstein informed Hitler that he would have to transfer one or two divisions away from the Fifty-seventh Panzer Corps to strengthen Army Group Don's crumbling left flank. Doing so, he added, would naturally mean abandoning Hoth's relief drive, for the time being anyway.[83] Disappointed by the field marshal's "pessimistic outlook," the Führer grudgingly authorized him the following day to transfer "elements" of the corps to his deteriorating flank in order to protect the Tatsinskaya and Morozovskaya airfields. However, he stressed, Hoth's remaining formations must not withdraw from the Mishkova River until reinforcements arrived and they could resume their relief operation. A battalion of new Tiger tanks was already on the way and would cross into Russia by rail later that day.[84]

At noon on 24 December, shortly after Soviet armored spearheads overran Tatsinskaya, Manstein detached the 11th Panzer Division from Fourth Panzer Army and directed it to hold the threatened Morozovskaya airfield, recapture Tatsinskaya, and block the advance toward Rostov of the Soviet Twenty-fourth Tank Corps. If the enemy reached Rostov, Manstein realized, they would not only have encircled Army Group Don, but also cut off the two German armies in the Caucasus. As it happened, the 11th Panzer Division eventually did stop the Soviet drive on Rostov, defeat the enemy forces, and win back Tatsinskaya (on the 28th), but not before the Soviets had destroyed or removed most of its stocks, equipment, and spare parts.

Although now angered by Manstein's "constant complaints," Hitler was still optimistic—outwardly, at least. He hoped to reinforce the Fifty-seventh Panzer Corps with the SS *Wiking* Division and the 7th Panzer Division. With these extra formations, he argued, the corps could resume its drive to the pocket. Hitler apparently managed to persuade Keitel and Jodl, but then they had seen how his personal fortitude had saved the eastern armies during the previous winter. Surely it would do the same again. Jeschonnek and Zeitzler were unpersuaded. Acting as much on Richthofen's initiative as on their own,[85] they pressed Hitler to withdraw the two armies in the Caucasus and use them to rebuild the southern front. Still relatively strong and well equipped, those armies would certainly be capable of holding Zhukov's forces in check. Hitler refused outright.

On Christmas Day, Manstein again infuriated the Führer, this time by dispatching a very gloomy situation assessment.[86] Not only had *Wintergewitter* ground to a halt, he said, but the Soviets had forced the Fifty-seventh Panzer Corps' two remaining divisions to withdraw from the Mishkova to the Aksai, thus widening the gap between them and the pocket. Restarting the relief operation was impossible with the forces at his disposal. Within days, the Second Guards and Fifty-first Armies would cut the so-called corridor at the Aksai River, encircling Fourth Panzer Army's forces to the east. The Rumanian Sixth and Seventh Army Corps offered little, he stated, and the two remaining divisions of the Fifty-seventh Panzer Corps, bogged down halfway to Stalingrad, now possessed only nineteen operational panzers between them. Because Tatsinskaya had fallen and Morozovskaya was under attack, Sixth Army's supply situation was very poor. The army now needed at least 550 tons of supplies per day to maintain its combat-worthiness. Moreover, the only way to save the army from imminent destruction, he said, was to transfer to Hoth the two-division-strong Third Panzer Corps from Kleist's First Panzer Army in the Caucasus, as well as an infantry division from Ruoff's Seventeenth Army, also in the Caucasus. He would then have to add at least another infantry division from the Seventeenth Army to Army Group Don, in order to bolster its left flank. This report came like a slap in the face to Hitler. Its message was clear: the relief operation had failed, and Sixth Army, along with the entire army group, now faced destruction unless *appropriate* countermeasures—not those planned by Hitler—were immediately undertaken. The report soured his already-strained relationship with Manstein, resulting in the situation described by Richthofen: with the Führer refusing to take the field marshal's calls or allow him to report in person.

Constant pressure from his generals and steady Soviet gains gradually wore down Hitler's resolve. On 28 December, he finally authorized the withdrawal of the armies in the Caucasus and the transfer of many of their divisions to Army Group Don. Zeitzler deserves the principal credit for this decision, and with it the salvation of those armies. He was an honorable man, who had been so moved by the plight of Paulus's trapped soldiers that he began limiting himself to their rations. He lost so much weight after several days that Hitler, annoyed by this "ill-considered" gesture, ordered him to desist and return to his normal meals. On the evening of the 27th, Zeitzler arrived unannounced at the Führer's private quarters and requested a meeting. He implored his commander in chief to authorize Army Group A's withdrawal from the Caucasus, pointing out that its two armies would greatly improve Manstein's chances of rebuilding the southern flank. Yet if they remained where they were, he added, they would soon be cut off south of the Don by Soviet forces driving to Rostov. He ended with the words: "Unless you order a withdrawal from the Caucasus now, we shall soon have a second Stalingrad on our hands."[87] Hitler was clearly struck by the power of these words; after pondering them for a few seconds, he replied: "Very well. Go ahead and issue the orders." Zeitzler wasted no time. After excusing himself, he used the telephone in Hitler's anteroom to order the withdrawal, adding the stipulation that his instructions be passed on to the armies immediately. This was a wise move. As soon as he returned to his own quarters, his staff officers informed him that the Führer had rung and that he was to return his call immediately. When he rang Hitler, the latter said: "Don't do anything just yet about the withdrawal from the Caucasus. We'll discuss it again tomorrow." Knowing that this would begin a string of postponements, probably resulting in the loss of the armies, Zeitzler was relieved to be able to answer: "My Führer, it is too late. I dispatched the order from your headquarters. It has already reached the front-line troops and the withdrawal has begun." Hitler hesitated for a moment, then said, with annoyance in his voice: "Very well then, we'll leave it at that."

The next day, Hitler issued Operations Order No. 2, his formal instructions for the withdrawal.[88] The gradual retreat it outlined was not as complete as Zeitzler would have liked, but it was a promising start. First Panzer Army was to begin disengaging itself from the enemy and pulling back by stages to Salsk, while Seventeenth Army was, at least for now, to hold its line on the Black Sea. The 3rd and 13th Panzer Divisions were to shift to Fourth Panzer Army's northern flank, which they were to protect during the withdrawals. Together with the 16th Motorized Division, these divisions were to be subordinated immediately to Army Group Don and used to cover the army group's threatened right flank.

On 29 December, Richthofen was surprised to learn of the withdrawal order. He had given up hope that the High Command would take any radical steps to save the southern front. On the very day that Hitler signed the order, the air commander had learned from Jeschonnek and Manstein that Hitler and his closest cronies had been agonizing over the situation and had finally arrived at an important decision. He was highly skeptical that anything good would come of it. Twisting the German proverb "The mountain labored and brought forth a mouse," he sarcastically wrote in his diary: "From Manstein and Jeschonnek I learn that the highest mountains are again in labor. We await the little mouse."[89] Next evening, pleasantly surprised that Hitler had actually ordered something sensible, he wrote: "This morning orders finally arrived. They grew out of the proposal I had been fighting for over the last few weeks. Pity about the loss of time. It might not have been so costly [in the meantime]. Hopefully it's still not too late, which is my fear."

Despite his relief that the two Caucasus armies were being pulled back, Richthofen remained convinced that the southern flank could not be held if the High Command insisted on keeping Sixth Army in its present positions on the Volga. He also knew that his air units were proving woefully incapable of meeting even that army's minimum logistical requirements, despite his best efforts and those of his subordinates. During the five days preceding the loss of Tatsinskaya

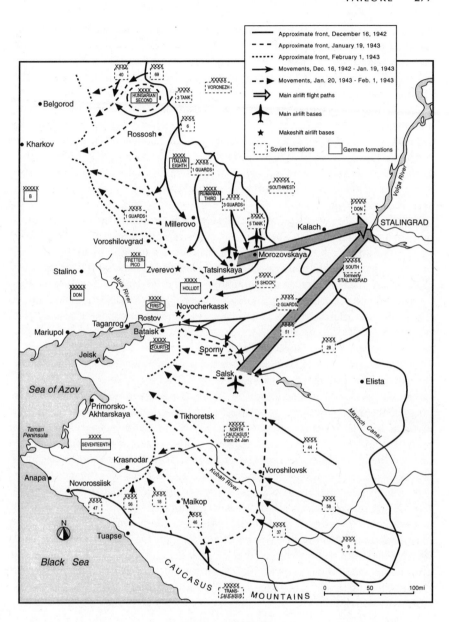

7. Fleeing from the Caucasus

on the 24th, his transport fleet had operated to its maximum capacity and performed better than it had since the airlift began. Still, during those five days it had managed to carry a mere 1,077 tons of supplies to the pocket, a daily average of only 215 tons. This amount was as much as Richthofen told Manstein and the High Command he could guarantee each day, but it was only two-thirds of the amount originally fixed as the army's absolute minimum and less than half the amount the army now demanded.[90] On the 24th, the day Soviet forces overran Tatsinskaya, no supplies at all reached the pocket. The hasty evacuation of that base's Ju 52s to a variety of airfields in the region, and eventually to Salsk, prevented them from carrying out any supply missions. Bad weather at Morozovskaya and "whiteouts" in the pocket prevented the other transport planes from carrying in supplies.

The He 111 units at Morozovskaya were more fortunate than their counterparts at Tatsinskaya. When Soviet forces approached their base on 24 December, their commander, *Oberst* Ernst Kühl, instructed them to stand by for evacuation orders. A sensible and experienced bomber commander, the *Oberst* lived up to his name, which means "cool." As Richthofen noted on the 26th: "Kühl strikes me as being calm and reliable, and he's doing very well." Indeed, when Kühl learned on the 24th that Tatsinskaya had been overrun, he took immediate action.[91] He transferred his He 111s, as well as the Stukas also operating from Morozovskaya, to the relative safety of Novocherkassk, near Rostov. He courageously remained behind with a small staff, though, hoping that weather conditions would improve enough for him to direct his units against the Soviet forces now less than fifteen kilometers away and advancing steadily. Early the next morning, Christmas Day, his meteorologists informed him that good flying weather could be expected for much of the day. He immediately contacted his units at Novocherkassk, telling them to stand by for operational orders. As soon as the morning fog lifted, he ordered them to launch the strongest possible attacks on Soviet forces swarming around Morozovskaya. Tanks caught on the steppes without cover made good targets, even for the horizontal bombers, who swooped in at low altitude. Kühl's men attacked all that day and much of the next, reinforced by as many other air units as Richthofen could spare from airlift duties and combat missions in the Kotelnikovo region. Working in close cooperation with the 11th Panzer Division, whose *Flivos* and reconnaissance officers provided good information on enemy movements, and whose tanks and antitank gunners proved equally effective against their opponents, they succeeded in destroying the Soviet threat to Morozovskaya—at least for the time being. Most of Kühl's He 111s returned to the base on the 26th.

Although the He 111s at Morozovskaya experienced only a minor interruption to their supply missions, the Ju 52 groups operating from Salsk after the loss of Tatsinskaya suffered considerably. First, the distance from Salsk to the pocket was over 120 kilometers greater than it had been from Tatsinskaya, which not only gave *VVS* units more interception space and time but also significantly reduced the number of supply flights that each plane could make per day. Because the Ju 52s needed additional fuel, they were forced to reduce the amount of supplies they carried. Second, despite the hard work of Richthofen's quartermaster, who endeavored to improve performance as quickly as possible, Salsk remained overcrowded and lacking in the facilities and equipment necessary for continuous use by large transport fleets. As a result of these adverse factors, as well as a steady worsening of weather conditions, Fiebig's transport units were able to carry only 7 tons to the pocket on Christmas Day, 78 tons on the 26th, 127 on the 27th, 35 on the 28th, 124 on the 29th, 224 on the following day, and 310 tons, the only acceptable total, on the last day of the year.[92] Thus, throughout the final week of 1942, Paulus's starving and frozen troops received an average of 129 tons a day, nowhere near enough to keep them alive for much longer, let alone combatworthy as well. Keeping them alive was clearly the first priority, of course. During the first weeks of the airlift, when most air force and army commanders had placed their hopes on Manstein's relief operation, more fuel and ammunition had entered the pocket than food and medical supplies. However, throughout the last week of the year, by which time only Hitler still appeared to believe that Sixth Army would be liberated, the ratios had reversed. Far more food and medical supplies entered the pocket than fuel and ammunition.[93]

Transport planes never returned to their home bases empty. Wounded soldiers and their medics filled their fuselages. During the last week of 1942, transporters carried no fewer than 4,120 sick or wounded troops from the pocket, making a total of 18,410 evacuated since the airlift began.[94] The wounded were never alone inside the lumbering transporters, though. They were joined by mail bags crammed full of letters written mainly by exhausted and frightened soldiers to their loved ones back home. Up until 31 December, transport planes carried fifteen tons of mail out of the pocket.[95] While this represents a substantial volume of mail, it was slight compared with the amount of mail carried *into* the pocket. Up to the same date, the encircled troops received seventy-three tons of mail. That is, almost two tons of mail from the homeland reached the pocket each day, taking up a lot of supply space in the planes and placing enormous strain on Sixth Army's 257 postal workers attempting to sort and distribute it efficiently. At no point did the air units balk at carrying mail to and from the pocket, however. The thousands of letters posted each day to the troops at Stalingrad played a major role in keeping up their spirits in the face of adversity.

German troop morale in the last few days of 1942 was very low, the result of renewed Soviet pressure and resulting gains. On 27 December, the Rumanian Seventh Army Corps, on the Fifty-seventh Panzer Corps' right flank, collapsed under the weight of a Soviet armored attack and fell back in a disorganized retreat.[96] Hoth decided the best thing he could do was pull the panzer corps back from its positions on the Aksai River and, if he could, rebuild the line at Kotelnikovo. With this withdrawal, the completed third of the planned German "corridor" to the Stalingrad pocket disappeared for good. Richthofen threw every available fighter, Stuka, and ground-attack plane at the Soviet forces pressing against Kotelnikovo. Despite conducting up to a dozen sorties each, the pilots were powerless to stop Soviet units from entering Kotelnikovo and seizing a small German airfield west of the city.[97] Soviet forces also pressed in on Morozovskaya again, forcing *Oberst* Kühl once more to place his He 111s on an emergency evacuation alert. In the meantime, he directed heavy air strikes against the forces threatening his airfield. Fiebig was most concerned for the safety of Kühl's air units, fearing that they might be overrun before they could scramble. "The situation for our units at "Moro" is not good," he wrote in his diary on the 27th. "It could easily develop into a crisis like at Tatsinskaya on the 24th." Within days it would do just that.

During the afternoon of 28 December, great pressure on the Fifty-seventh Panzer Corps forced Hoth to pull it back past Kotelnikovo to the Sal River. This withdrawal opened up the left bank of the Don to Rostov, the city Stalin now wanted to recapture above all others. It also exposed the deep right flank of *Armeeabteilung Hollidt* (Army Detachment Hollidt), the makeshift operational command holding the section of front between the Rumanian Third Army in the north and Fourth Panzer Army in the south. The following day, Soviet forces finished clearing up Kotelnikovo and pushed out of a small bridgehead near Potemkinskaya, on the Don south of Nizhne-Chirskaya.[98] *General der Infanterie* Hollidt, commander of the formation bearing his name, then had to shift the 11th Panzer Division to Tsimyanskiy, 120 kilometers downstream on the Don, to prevent the Soviets from pushing through to Rostov. Responding to this move, Hitler ordered the 7th Panzer Division to remain at Rostov to prevent that city's recapture.

The only pleasing news in this dark period was that Hollidt's forces managed to recapture the Tatsinskaya airfield on 28 December.[99] Richthofen, who hoped to use it again as an airlift base, ordered *Luftgau Rostov* to repair and reequip it as soon as possible so that the Ju 52 groups could return there from the inferior field at Salsk. It was a pointless exercise. Before Tatsinskaya could be restored to full use, Soviet forces advanced so strongly toward it and Morozovskaya that, on the 31th, Hollidt announced his intention to abandon them both and pull back to a line twenty kilometers east of Tatsinskaya, if not to the Donets River.[100] Fiebig was shocked; the loss of both airfields would cripple the airlift. He despondently wrote in his diary: "What will the year 1943 bring?" To Sixth Army it brought destruction, as Fiebig would find out only a month later.

10

Collapse: January 1943

On the first day of 1943, Manstein received Hitler's "Supplement to Operations Order No. 2."[1] The Führer announced in this document—which reveals his unrealistic assessment of the situation—that he was going to send Army Group Don additional forces for the relief of Stalingrad. These would include the elite SS *Adolf Hitler,* SS *Das Reich,* and 7th SS divisions, as well as three regular infantry divisions, all coming from the west "with the greatest possible speed." They would be joined by the SS *Großdeutschland* Division, coming from Army Group Center with equal haste. They would all arrive and be ready for combat by mid-February. In the meantime, he said, Army Groups B and Don were to secure favorable positions for their jump-off. All the provisions of the main operations order (including the stipulation that Hollidt must not withdraw any farther than the line from Morozovskaya to Tsimyanskiy) were to remain in effect.

Holding territory was proving difficult, however. *Oberst* Stahel, the Luftwaffe flak officer whose makeshift force had managed to hold a critical section of the Chir Front for over a month, was finally overrun on 2 December. Both Richthofen and Fiebig held him in the highest regard. Two days earlier, for example, the former had noted in his diary that Stahel was a real hero, "a hell of a guy . . . whose front, the only one to stand firm, is held together by his personality alone."[2] They were therefore grieved to learn that enemy forces had finally broken his defenses and killed or captured him. Both held faint hopes that he was encircled somewhere and would fight his way back to the new German line, but, as Richthofen noted on the 2nd, "that hope sinks by the hour." In fact, Stahel was alive. Along with various elements of his combat group, he had been surrounded and strongly attacked from front and rear by numerically superior forces. He proved a real fighter. Regrouping his shattered units into a single cohesive formation, which finally hacked its way free on the 4th, he destroyed several enemy battalions in the process. Stahel became an immediate celebrity and the darling of the Luftwaffe, which could present Hitler with a hero to rival any of the army's. The Führer, who had long been impressed by Stahel's courageous defensive fighting on the Chir, was delighted to learn of his heroic breakout. He immediately awarded him Oak Leaves to the Knight's Cross. This high award, Fiebig thought, "was very well deserved. Success was due to his personal efforts."[3]

Sadly, the Luftwaffe found little else to rejoice over. On 1 January, Soviet forces were so close to Morozovskaya that Fiebig—this time ignoring Göring's "stand fast" order—issued Kühl with clear evacuation instructions.[4] If weather conditions the next day permitted, he said, the bomber commander should transfer all his He 111 units to Novocherkassk, near Rostov, and his fighters, Stukas, and ground-attack planes to Tatsinskaya. He need not wait until the enemy arrived at his airfield before commencing the evacuation. That had resulted in disaster last time.

Fiebig's advice was sensible. Even before ground fog lifted the next day, Kühl evacuated Morozovskaya, abandoning much equipment and supplies but suffering no aircraft losses. Fiebig was very relieved, although he still held grave fears for the safety of his close-combat aircraft. Tatsinskaya may have been recaptured, but its security was far from certain. As a result, he refused to move his Ju 52 groups back there, preferring instead to operate them from Salsk in the northern Caucasus, even though that airfield was inferior and much farther from the Stalingrad pocket. His decision to evacuate his close-combat units to Tatsinskaya had been made on the spur of the moment. He regretted it immediately. "I can't get the fate of the Stukas, ground-attack, fighter and tactical reconnaissance planes out of my mind," he wrote. "What if they all have to be dynamited if enemy tanks suddenly appear through the fog in the early morning?" Not wanting to leave them at Tatsinskaya for long, he flew around the region in a Storch for three hours, searching unsuccessfully for a safe and suitable place to construct an improvised airfield for them. He would eventually find a satisfactory site, but not for several days.

Now that Fiebig's He 111s operated from Novocherkassk, they suffered from the same problem as his Ju 52s operating from Salsk: the increased distance from the Stalingrad pocket substantially reduced their airlift capabilities. From Novocherkassk, the Heinkels had to fly 330 kilometers to reach Pitomnik, 130 kilometers farther than they previously had to fly from Morozovskaya. As a result, fighters were unable to escort the transports all the way to the pocket, leaving them vulnerable to enemy fighter attack as they approached their destination. They were no longer able to carry out multiple supply missions per day, instead carrying out only one. Also, because they now consumed more fuel, they were forced to reduce the amount of supplies they carried.

Aware that Soviet forces were attempting to fight their way down the Don toward Rostov and that German armies in the Caucasus were already contracting their front and pulling back toward the same city, Fiebig knew that he might soon have to order his Ju 52 groups out of Salsk. He urgently needed to find a new airfield within range of Stalingrad. The region west of the Donets was the safest place from which to operate aircraft, but no established airfields existed in that area. Thus, he scoured that region in his Storch, looking for suitable ground to create an airfield for Ju 52 operations if ever he had to evacuate Salsk. *Oberst* Fritz Morzik, an airlift expert recently transferred to Fiebig's command by the *OKL,* accompanied him during these reconnaissance flights. They eventually settled on the cornfields of Zverevo, a town sixty-five kilometers due north of Novocherkassk.[5] Although barely within the Ju 52s' operating range, this site was well behind the Donets and, therefore, in no immediate danger of being overrun. Fiebig recommended Zverevo to Richthofen, who promptly instructed *Luftgau Rostov* to create an improvised field ready for operations with two weeks. This was a daunting task for the *Gau*'s technicians and construction teams. They would have to create a 600-meter by 30-meter runway on the flat fields at Zverevo, and construct rudimentary supply, maintenance, command, and accommodation buildings. They would then have to supply the new base with loading and maintenance equipment, and lay telephone wires linking it to Fiebig's own command center. Despite the severity of the weather, they diligently set about their tasks. Within days, locals were able to see an airfield appearing in their cornfields.

In the meantime, Fiebig still had an airlift to run, and its record of late had been very poor. Weather remained the main adversary. On 6 January, he unhappily wrote in his diary:

> For days now the general weather situation has been unfavorable. . . . We have lousy visibility, icing up at ground level as well as in the air, snow flurries, and very changeable conditions between takeoff and landing at our destinations. Around 30 percent [of our planes] fail to get through and have to turn back, through no fault of their own. We fly in conditions which one would normally refuse to fly in, but everyone knows what's at stake!

Between 28 December and 4 January, Fiebig lost as many as 62 Ju 52s: 15 of them missing, 24 totally destroyed, and the remainder damaged so badly they had to be taken out of service for major repair. Weather conditions caused around 50 percent of these losses; enemy flak and *VVS* action caused the rest.[6]

The Soviet command had erected a strong flak "curtain" around the perimeter of the Stalingrad pocket, with batteries concentrated most heavily along the sections through which German flight paths crossed.[7] These flak batteries inflicted high losses on the transport groups, much to the chagrin of Richthofen and Fiebig, who lacked sufficient Stukas and ground-attack planes to knock them out. Even if they had possessed more planes, they had little chance of destroying most batteries. Poor visibility caused by ground fog, low cloud, and snowstorms provided the batteries—and most other Soviet installations and fortifications— with excellent cover from German air attack. On the other hand, Soviet flak gunners did not need clear visibility to be effective against the transport aircraft. The extended distances from home bases to the pocket forced transport planes to fly by the most direct routes, and the location of airfields within the pocket forced them to conform to only a few variations in approach flights. Thus, the Soviet gunners soon became aware of the common German flight paths and altitudes. Even when weather conditions reduced their visibility, they were able to inflict losses. When they heard the distinctive drone of the Ju 52s, they began firing into the flight paths, frequently hitting planes that they were unable to see.

Soviet fighter activity also increased during the last weeks of 1942 and the first of 1943. The *VVS* command created a ring around the Stalingrad pocket, extending out over fifty kilometers from its perimeter. It then divided that ring into five sectors and assigned each to specific air units. In this way, each unit was able to become thoroughly acquainted with the unique features of its own zone.[8] The Soviet command created two other coverage rings around Stalingrad, extending out successively farther toward the main German-Soviet front. Again, it allocated specific air units to each ring and, with a few exceptions, assigned them tasks only within their own sectors. On paper, this system looked comprehensive and effective. In practice, it failed to create anywhere near a full air blockade of the pocket, despite the markedly improved kill rate that followed its implementation. *VVS* fighters did force German transport planes to fly into the pocket in small groups instead of their previous "air columns," but they continued carrying valuable supplies into the pocket most days, with only the weather stopping them on others.

VVS units in the outer operational "rings" repeatedly attacked Salsk, Novocherkassk, and other Luftwaffe airfields. Despite postwar Soviet claims, those attacks never seriously threatened or substantially curtailed the operations of the air units themselves, although they caused steady nuisance damage to runways, buildings, and aircraft. Strong flak defenses around key airfields—on which both Fiebig and Richthofen placed great importance—prevented most marauding *VVS* formations from inflicting heavy damage. Surviving German war diaries reveal that most Soviet descriptions of attacks on German airfields in this period are generally exaggerated and sometimes entirely concocted. For example, although Pickert, Fiebig, and Richthofen mention every significant incident at their airfields and make no effort to ignore Soviet successes, they do not mention that Salsk was attacked by Shturmoviks on 2 January 1943. Yet G. K. Prussakov, a Russian author, claimed that a small number of Shturmoviks, escorted by Yak-1 fighters, struck Salsk unexpectedly on 2 January and destroyed no fewer than seventy-two German aircraft.[9] Although repeated by several writers on the *VVS,* this story is patently untrue. Had Soviet squadrons destroyed any aircraft at Salsk that day, all three German commanders would have recorded that fact in their diaries. Disaster did strike German airfields, as already noted, but at the hands of Soviet ground troops, not *VVS* pilots.

PITOMNIK FALLS

On 16 January, the disaster that Luftwaffe leaders feared most occurred: Soviet forces overran Pitomnik, the principal airfield within the pocket. The loss of

Tatsinskaya and Morozovskaya in the first days of January had been heavy but not fatal blows to the airlift operation. Fiebig was able to carry on from other airfields, despite suffering a perceptible decrease in performance. The loss of Pitomnik, however, was a death blow. Recovery was impossible under the circumstances. To explain how this catastrophic situation occurred, it is necessary to go back several days.

On 7 January, the Soviet command informed Paulus, in his capacity as Sixth Army's commander in chief, that it was sending three officers across the lines under a flag of truce. Paulus agreed to receive them. The next morning, the three emissaries entered the northern sector of the pocket, carrying an ultimatum signed by Colonel General Voronov, representing the *Stavka,* and Lieutenant General Rokossovskiy, commander in chief of the Don Front. The Red Army had sealed Sixth Army within an "unbreakable" ring, the ultimatum stated, and all attempts to relieve the army had proved hopeless.[10] The Red Army's successful push to the west had also forced the Luftwaffe transport fleet, which provided only "starvation rations" of food, fuel, and ammunition, to withdraw to airfields much farther from the pocket. The air transport fleet was suffering terribly at the hands of the Russian Air Force, the ultimatum added (exaggerating, and not mentioning that bad weather was equally, if not more, destructive). Therefore, the help that transport aircraft could bring to the besieged forces "is rapidly becoming illusionary." The situation of the troops "is desperate. They are suffering from hunger, sickness and cold. The cruel Russian winter has scarcely begun. Hard frosts, cold winds and blizzards still lie ahead. Your soldiers are unprovided with winter clothing and are living in appalling sanitary conditions."

Sixth Army's situation was hopeless, and any further resistance pointless, the ultimatum stated. Therefore, Paulus should surrender immediately. The conditions of surrender were generous, under the circumstances: the Soviet command would guarantee the safety of all officers and troops who surrendered, and would repatriate them to Germany when the war ended. Personnel could retain their uniforms, insignia, medals, and valuables, and officers could keep their swords. All men would receive normal rations, and all wounded would receive medical attention. "Should you refuse our offer that you lay down your arms," the ultimatum warned, "we hereby give notice that the forces of the Red Army and the Red Air Force will be compelled to proceed with the destruction of the encircled German troops. The responsibility for this will lie with you." The document stipulated that Paulus had twelve hours to reply.

Paulus transmitted the ultimatum to Hitler, once again asking for freedom of action.[11] He clearly wanted to accept the Soviet terms. Hitler emphatically refused to let him surrender. He no longer held hopes that a relief operation could be mounted in time to stave off destruction, although he did not share this view with Paulus. He merely insisted that every day the army fought on significantly helped the entire front, because its continued resistance tied down a large number of enemy formations. Later that same day, therefore, Paulus felt obliged to reject the surrender offer.

The Soviet command wasted no time in responding. On the morning of 10 January, Lieutenant General Rokossovskiy launched Operation *Koltso* (Ring), the *Stavka*'s frequently postponed plan to split the pocket in an easterly direction and then destroy the two parts in succession. After a powerful fifty-five-minute artillery barrage—during which some 7,000 Soviet guns and mortars pounded their German counterparts, outnumbered twenty to one—Rokossovskiy's tanks and infantry attacked along a seventy-kilometer section of the pocket's western perimeter.[12] *VVS* units pounded the forces in their attack path, hoping to pin them down and break their morale. Nonetheless, initial German resistance was stiffer than the Soviet general had anticipated. His men gained less than five kilometers on that first day.[13] Paulus was shaken by the attack's intensity, however. That night, he reported to Manstein that there was no longer any prospect of holding out until mid-February, when Hitler's new relief force was due to launch its operation. Relief would have to come much sooner. In the meantime, fully equipped replacement battalions must be flown in immediately, and the Luftwaffe must airlift the promised quantity of supplies.[14]

Paulus was able to save his western front from collapse only by steadily pulling back all forces west of the Rossoshka River and rebuilding the front on its eastern shore, where the original Soviet defenses had recently been repaired to serve German troops.[15] Rokossovskiy threw four armies at the Rossoshka front, which they finally cracked on 15 January.

THE ADVENT OF ERHARD MILCH

Hitler was gravely concerned not only by the pocket's rapidly shrinking perimeter but also by the Luftwaffe's evident inability to improve its airlift performance. Late on 14 January, he sent for *Generalfeldmarschall* Erhard Milch, deputy supreme commander of the Luftwaffe and air inspector general.[16] When Milch arrived at his headquarters in Rastenburg the next day, the Führer briefed him on the situation at Stalingrad. The Luftwaffe had so far failed to meet Sixth Army's logistical needs, he explained. As a result, the army was now in a very poor state. Unless the airlift improved substantially, and it was Milch's task to ensure that it did, the army would soon collapse. Hitler then ordered him to fly to southern Russia as soon as possible to take charge of the entire airlift operation, armed with "special powers and authority to issue orders and instructions to every section of the armed forces [in the region]."[17] As they talked, an adjutant informed them that bad news had just arrived from the encircled army: Pitomnik, the main airfield within the pocket, had apparently been overrun by Soviet forces. Thus, even before Milch arrived at Richthofen's headquarters in Taganrog on the 16th, he knew that he faced a very difficult challenge.

The field marshal soon learned how Pitomnik had fallen. It was a depressing story. When the Don front had launched *Koltso* on 10 January, Soviet long-range artillery opened fire on the airfield, joined by *VVS* bombers, which subjected it to a steady rain of bombs during repeated high-altitude attacks.[18] Soviet ground forces advanced toward the airfield the next day, prompting a nervous Pickert to write: "If the enemy achieves a deep penetration, we'll have to move the base for air supply. That will take a lot of effort and consume fuel. And if we're then pushed back again, it will be all over, because no army can be supplied with its rations and ammunition by dropping supplies alone." Paulus, now suffering frequent anxiety attacks, ordered Pickert to fly to Richthofen's and Manstein's headquarters in Taganrog on the 12th, so that he could present the two commanders with an up-to-the-minute situation report.[19] Flying out of the pocket at dusk in a Heinkel 111, Pickert was struck by the "fantastic spectacle of flashes from enemy guns encircling the fortress."[20] His situation report was detailed and explicit. Sixth Army was freezing, starving, and exhausted, he explained. Pitomnik looked certain to fall, leaving it with no suitably equipped airlift base. In short, "collapse is only days away. And nothing further can be done about it."

Pickert reported to Fiebig the next day and again described Sixth Army's suffering: "Sixth Army is fighting its last battle. It may be six days or only two before the end comes. Ammunition and fuel reserves no longer exist. The movement of forces is no longer possible. The Russians . . . attack from all sides. Our troops are at the end of their strength! From the 13th, everyone will defend himself with his own gun, where he stands, to the last cartridge."[21] Pickert added that the air transport units had clearly done their utmost and should not be blamed for their failure. They had flown in the worst possible conditions. The loss of 250 aircraft to date was a testament to their courage and tenacity. Fiebig, deeply moved, noted that night in his diary: "Nobody's heart beats more strongly for the fate of Sixth Army, I believe, than those of the men responsible for the organization and conduct of the airlift. We have done our best. I know of no fault of my own, if I have to judge myself, or anything I could have done differently or better."[22]

Pickert wanted to return to the pocket immediately, arguing that he should be with his men when they fought their final battles. After many heated discussions with Fiebig and Richthofen, the latter—who had awarded him the Knight's Cross on 12 January—finally relented on the 15th and authorized him to return to the pocket. After writing what he believed to be his final letters to his wife, children, and parents, and after receiving gifts of chocolate and cigarettes from senior Luftwaffe officers, Pickert climbed aboard another Heinkel and left for Stalingrad.[23] At around 0100 on the 16th, his plane circled over Pitomnik, trying to identify the correct recognition signals and landing instructions from a confusing display of lights and sounds. They never came. The plane was soon so low on fuel that the pilot announced he could wait no longer. He turned around and headed back to Novocherkassk. Shortly after landing, Pickert learned what had happened. Soviet forces had attacked the field late on the 15th, destroying all opposition by dawn. The small number of fighters and tactical reconnaissance planes stationed at Pitomnik had evacuated the field at about the same time as Pickert was trying to land. Had his pilot ignored the muddled lighting and radio signals and attempted to land, Soviet gunners around the field would have destroyed his plane in the air before its wheels even touched the runway. He was lucky to be alive. Most of Pitomnik's fighters and reconnaissance planes had also escaped in time. They landed shortly afterward at Gumrak, an inferior airfield within the pocket. The condition of the Gumrak runway was so poor, though, that over half the planes flipped over and crashed when attempting to land.

Shortly before Pitomnik fell, Richthofen had ordered Luftwaffe forces within the pocket to prepare Gumrak, an old Soviet airfield of small size and poor quality, for airlift operations as soon as possible. He had actually wanted to repair and expand Gumrak several weeks earlier, but Sixth Army had repeatedly refused permission. The army had its headquarters at Gumrak, as well as hospitals, supply installations, and the command posts of two corps, so it did not want any construction activity to draw Soviet attention to the site. "Now," Fiebig jotted glumly on the 16th, "we're paying the price for that decision."[24] Two days earlier, he had noted optimistically that Gumrak should be ready by the 16th.[25] However, as noted previously, its runway was still so pitted on that date that landing there was extremely dangerous. Even finding the runway was difficult; Gumrak initially had no radio beacon.[26] As a result, by the time Milch arrived, Ju 52 units were temporarily unable to land within the pocket. Instead, they had to drop supplies to the encircled troops, usually by parachute in purpose-built air-drop containers, but sometimes by less effective means: merely pushing crates out of their open doors. Without fuel, Sixth Army was unable to gather all the dropped cargo. Many containers, crates, and oil drums lay embedded in the snow until found by Soviet troops after Paulus's army finally surrendered.

Kühl's He 111s were undaunted by the poor state of Gumrak's runway, and ten even landed there on 16 January, the day Pitomnik fell.[27] Those Heinkels carried in a miserable amount of supplies—thirteen tons, of which nine were provisions—and carried out only sixty-two wounded soldiers. Their performance during the next few days was slightly better. They carried in almost thirty-two tons on the 19th, for instance, virtually all of it rations. Yet even including the thirty tons dropped into the pocket that day, Sixth Army received only one-fifth of the amount considered the minimum for its survival.

Only hours before Milch arrived at the front, the airlift suffered another major reverse. The German forces in the northern Caucasus had withdrawn so far that Salsk, the main Ju 52 base, had to be evacuated. Richthofen gave the order on 15 January, and the planes flew out early on the 16th, the day Milch arrived.[28] They landed at the newly constructed "base" at Zverevo, which Richthofen's technicians and labor battalions had transformed from a snow-covered cornfield into an airfield in less than two weeks. As a major airlift base, it was very poor. Its main runway consisted of hard-packed and rolled snow, its billeting was rudimentary (huts for a few, tents for most), and all maintenance had to be carried out in the open, despite the temperature seldom rising above zero.

Thus, by the time Milch arrived at Taganrog, Sixth Army was already fighting its last battles and *Luftflotte 4*'s airlift operation had been severely crippled by factors outside its control. He would have to perform miracles if he hoped to stave off the army's imminent destruction. Realizing this, Richthofen had written in his diary during the previous evening: "Nothing would delight me more than that Milch should chance upon the philosopher's stone which our supreme authorities apparently believe is lying around somewhere. We certainly haven't been able to find it." Of course, Hitler and the Wehrmacht High Command were not really searching for that mythical stone which alchemists once believed could transmute base metals into gold. The air fleet commander was merely describing metaphorically his superiors' desperate search for any means of turning looming defeat at Stalingrad into victory. In fact, his metaphor nicely sums up the entire 1942 campaign, Hitler's quest for oil, which he believed would transform his military fortunes on the eastern front.

Richthofen was bitterly hurt by Hitler's decision to place Milch in charge of the airlift, perceiving it to be proof of the Führer's lack of confidence in his and Fiebig's abilities. He angrily demanded an explanation from Jeschonnek, who assured him that Hitler was very happy with their leadership but wanted to send an administrator—as opposed to a commander—to see if he could iron out some of the persisting difficulties. It was, Jeschonnek said, a last-ditch effort to save the encircled army. Richthofen was unpersuaded, and he told Fiebig so. The latter, also offended by the decision to send Milch, privately wrote: "There is not much left to organize, for we can only drop supplies from the air from now on—a matter of pure chance."[29] "Richthofen and I are in agreement," he added, "that we have done everything humanly possible. No one can be blamed for lack of effort. Everyone has fulfilled his duty to the highest level. We can stand tall and with a clear conscience in any examination." Despite the fact that both Fiebig and Richthofen had maintained from the start that the proposed airlift was impossible, they were clearly worried that they would be blamed for its failure. Richthofen shared with Fiebig his growing fear that "scapegoats will be looked for and have to be found."

The airlift had certainly gone poorly during the first sixteen days of 1943, with only 2,325 tons of supplies reaching the encircled army, an average of 145 tons per day.[30] During that period, however, Fiebig and Richthofen had displayed strength, talent, and resourcefulness as they struggled to master one crisis after another, not least among them being the loss of Tatsinskaya and Morozovskaya, their main airlift bases; the inferior quality of Salsk and Novocherkassk, the improvised replacement fields; the eventual loss of Salsk and the transfer of their main transport groups to a hastily constructed base built on a cornfield; and, finally, the loss of Pitomnik, the only properly equipped airfield within the pocket.

Therefore, even though Fiebig and Richthofen managed to airlift only 145 tons of supplies to Sixth Army each day, less than half of what the army needed, they were convinced that this was the maximum possible under the circumstances. They felt sure that Milch could do no better, unless he brought the philosopher's stone with him.

THE FINAL TWO WEEKS

The air fleet chief was disappointed, but not surprised, to learn that Milch had no real understanding of the situation. After what Milch called a "thorough situation conference" in *Luftflotte 4*'s special command train on 16 January,[31] Richthofen wrote that he "is completely misinformed about the technical and tactical situation. As a result, he is still rather optimistic."[32] Richthofen was apparently able to convince Milch of two things: that *Luftflotte 4* was in worse shape than the High Command assumed and that its failure to meet Sixth Army's logistical needs was due to forces outside its control, weather being its worst adversary. *Oberstarzt* Heinz Kalk, Milch's personal physician and the keeper of his war diary, recorded that night: "There are considerably fewer aircraft available for the airlift operation than had been assumed at the Führer's headquarters. The principal difficulty regarding the operation of the units is the extreme cold, because of which a great many aircraft are not operational."[33]

Milch was shocked to learn from *Generalingenieur* Weidinger, *Luftflotte 4*'s chief engineer, that the operational rate of the transport groups had fallen to about 20 percent.[34] The fleet possessed 140 Ju 52s, Weidinger said, but only 42 were operational at that point in time. Of those, 27 were in transit to Zverevo and could not resume airlift duties until after they arrived and received maintenance. Thus, only 15 (11 percent) were currently able to carry supplies to Sixth Army. The fleet possessed 140 He 111s, of which only 41 were operational, and 29 FW 200 Condors, of which only one was operational. This aircraft type was too fragile for the conditions, Weidinger explained, and repeatedly suffered damage during landing, especially to its tail skid. When Milch asked how long it would take to get the damaged or broken-down Junkers, Heinkels, and Focke-Wulfs repaired and back in operation, the engineer estimated that around 10 percent could be repaired within three days and another 50 percent within fourteen days. The rest would take longer than two weeks, the duration depending on whether they were repaired within the region or sent back to the Reich.

The new airlift boss was determined to see conditions at the main supply bases for himself. At dawn on 17 January, he set off toward the Taganrog airstrip, hoping that the ground fog would clear quickly. As his car went over a railway crossing, a train suddenly appeared out of the fog. His driver had no time to swerve. The train struck the car at seventy kilometers per hour, sending it careering across the embankment into a railway hut, which shattered with a great crash, killing two soldiers inside.[35] Unconscious and bleeding profusely from a head wound, Milch was pulled from the wreckage and rushed to a field hospital. The doctors stitched up his head and, to repair several broken ribs, cast his back and ribs in plaster. Nonetheless, when he regained consciousness, he refused to obey the doctors' instructions and remain in hospital. Discharging himself, he returned to Richthofen's command train, where, encased in plaster, he resumed command of the airlift. "Back to work in the train," he noted with typical brevity in his pocket diary that evening. "My head is clear."[36] Milch's strength and sense of duty impressed Richthofen, who recorded in his diary that day that, despite his "bad contusion, hemorrhage and flesh wound to the head," Milch had immediately returned to work. "He has both a temperature and a desire to administer," he added admiringly.

Milch spoke to Fiebig by telephone shortly afterward. The situation was depressing. The VVS had launched several bombing attacks on the main Ju 52 base at Zverevo.[37] Nine planes were burning on the runway, and another twelve were damaged; as a result, only twelve were operational. Also, Fiebig told him, the ground organization at Gumrak had broken down. Soviet forces were two kilometers from the field's perimeter, but no immediate danger to ground personnel existed. Yet when five Heinkels landed there earlier that day (out of the sixteen that attempted to do so), no ground personnel or units of Sixth Army were present to unload their valuable cargo of food and fuel. The crews had to unload their planes themselves. They also had to defend themselves with their side arms against soldiers pressing around their aircraft, hoping to climb aboard and escape the pocket. Milch promised him: "Tomorrow we will send reliable Luftwaffe officers (air landing troops) into Gumrak, who should ascertain the condition of · Gumrak airfield. If landing possibilities remain, then transport gliders will be sent in."[38] Those air supply specialists would also look for a decent air-drop zone, he added, as well as for suitable glider landing sites, preferably away from the threatened perimeter and closer to Stalingrad itself, because fifty gliders were now available for operations.

The field marshal was not the first person to suggest employing transport gliders at Stalingrad. Richthofen and Fiebig had already investigated the possibility, especially after the OKL had initiated the formation of glider squadrons at Stalino and Makeyevka, 110 kilometers northwest of Taganrog.[39] But they had already abandoned the idea—as Fiebig told Milch on 17 January—after learning that gliders required conditions no longer existing at Stalingrad. First, gliders could not be used at all during the many days in which strong winds and other adverse weather conditions prevailed. Second, their large size, slow speed, and lack of guns made them even better targets for VVS fighters and Shturmoviks than the lumbering Ju 52s. As it was, Richthofen lacked sufficient fighters to escort the Ju 52s during their flight to the pocket, let alone to protect a fleet of unarmed gliders as well. Moreover, the steady withdrawal of the German line toward the west had placed the Stalingrad pocket outside the operating range of almost all of *Luftflotte 4*'s fighters. Few long-range fighters—Bf 109s and Bf 110s equipped with drop tanks—existed, and they were already fully committed to Ju 52 escort duties. Third, because no way of towing gliders back out of the pocket was possible under the circumstances, they would have to be abandoned after their cargo was unloaded. Fourth, the existing facilities in the pocket were not large enough or sufficiently equipped to handle gliders as well as regular transport fleets, and the resources and manpower needed to improve the fields to the required level were lacking. Finally, Sixth Army's vehicle and fuel situation was so poor that, if gliders landed on open terrain within the pocket, instead of at the airfields, recovery of the supplies would be very difficult, if not impossible. Even recovering air-drop containers had proved difficult, and many lay uncollected for want of transportation.

Milch was determined to overcome these difficulties, telling Fiebig that "*all* aircraft, including gliders, must be utilized."[40] It did not matter if gliders had to be abandoned within the pocket. The aircrew could ride out aboard He 111s. All that mattered, he said, was that Sixth Army received their cargo. He immediately telephoned Jeschonnek, instructing him to form two long-range fighter squadrons for glider-escort and general combat duties.[41] Jeschonnek initially insisted that he could spare no fighters because they were all sorely needed in the Leningrad sector, where Soviet forces had launched a strong attack. Milch remained adamant. He needed long-range fighters, he insisted, and Jeschonnek must see to it immediately. Milch also rang *Oberst* Vorwald, head of the Luftwaffe's Technical Office in Berlin, demanding an acceleration in the production of air-supply containers. He placed an initial order of 13,000 250-kilogram and 7,000 1,000-kilogram containers.[42] Richthofen was envious of Milch's "special powers," privately claiming—and quite rightly, too—that he would have achieved better results in the previous seven weeks if he had been able to issue such orders. He had been forced to work through the usual bureaucratic channels, issuing "requests" to the *OKL,* which would, if it saw fit, pass them on to the relevant agencies.

As it happened, although the new airlift containers began arriving within days, the first long-range fighters—nine Bf 109Gs and five Bf 110C-1s—did not reach the front until 27 January. They finally commenced operations on the 28th but were too few in number to make their presence felt. Also, technicians had mistakenly fitted larger internal fuel tanks and external drop tanks to inferior Bf 110 models (C-1s, instead of the superior and much faster Fs). Because they suffered engine problems and performed poorly, on the 31st a frustrated Milch ordered them to be deployed solely on airfield defense duties. In the meantime, he wanted his few new Bf 109s and Bf 110s to be airborne over Stalingrad on the 30th, to celebrate the tenth anniversary of Hitler's election to power. "No objections will be tolerated," he insisted to *Major* Wilke, commander of the new long-range fighter squadrons, on the 29th.[43] "The reputation of the Luftwaffe, and especially of the fighter arm, with the army is at stake." Wilke's operation was hardly likely to inspire the army and restore the Luftwaffe's flagging prestige; only six Bf 109s and five Bf 110s took to the sky on the 30th to mark the anniversary.

Milch's plan to supply the encircled army by gliders also came to nothing. As conditions in the pocket deteriorated throughout January, he gradually abandoned the idea. Fiebig and Richthofen had been right, he conceded. Gliders were not suitable for conditions at Stalingrad after all. Therefore, when Göring requested him on the 25th to release the bulk of his gliders for use in an airlift operation planned for First Panzer and Seventeenth Armies in the northern Caucasus, Milch gladly complied.[44] On the previous day, he had actually halted their shipment to the front, and, to free up rolling stock for more essential supplies, he had ordered supply personnel to unload them from all trains in the region. Thus, none of the hundreds of gliders that arrived at the front according to his instructions actually saw service at Stalingrad.[45]

Generaloberst Paulus—to return to the events of mid-January—infuriated Milch, Fiebig, and Richthofen by claiming to almost anyone who would listen that the Luftwaffe was primarily to blame for the rapid deterioration of his army. Late on 17 January, Milch spoke to *Oberstleutnant* Christian of Hitler's headquarters staff.[46] Paulus had complained directly to Hitler that the Luftwaffe was not carrying out the Führer's orders, Christian said. Although Gumrak airfield had been serviceable for over twenty-four hours, few aircraft had landed there during the day and, despite the airfield being suitable for night operations, none at all had landed at night. They were merely throwing out their loads as they flew over, making no attempt to land or pick up any of the 20,000 sick and wounded soldiers waiting for evacuation. The Luftwaffe was making excuses, Christian said, quoting Paulus, who had appealed for Hitler's personal intervention. To Milch's dismay, Christian added that the Führer tended to agree with Paulus's claims.[47] "Airmen who have landed at Gumrak report that conditions are exactly the opposite," the field marshal retorted, insisting that it lacked proper lighting and other equipment essential for night operations. Still, he would ensure that greater efforts were made to equip the field for night operations as soon as possible and would send a senior officer into the pocket the next day to supervise the work. Twenty minutes later, Milch had to stress these points to a self-righteous Manstein, who had also received, and believed, Paulus's accusations. It is simply not true that Gumrak is already as well equipped as Pitomnik was, snapped Milch, refuting the army leader's claim. His pilots had circled the airfield looking for any signs of landing lights and markers but found none. Sixth Army was to blame, he said, because it had previously thwarted all attempts to expand Gumrak and equip it for night operations.

Richthofen and Fiebig were disgusted to learn that their airmen were being blamed for the situation at Gumrak. The latter angrily insisted to Milch, for instance, that "we must defend ourselves from Sixth Army's slanderous reproaches."[48] Milch tried to pacify him, explaining that the army's unfair accusations stemmed from the tremendous stress Paulus and his commanders were under. "Express to your personnel my full recognition of their accomplishments," he added. Fiebig was certainly pleased to pass on Milch's praise. He was proud of the dedication and courage displayed by his men. "Our crews are doing their best," he wrote in his diary shortly after talking to Milch. "Even flying at all without fighter escort is a heroic achievement. Yet inside the pocket they now take the position: 'these are our demands and we don't care how you meet them.' "[49]

By 18 January, Milch had formed an accurate assessment of the general situation, which, two days later, he summed up in his pocket diary with one large, underlined word: "hopeless!"[50] Yet he felt a deep sense of commitment to the trapped forces and insisted that the Luftwaffe must do its utmost to stave off their destruction. "We are just as concerned as you are," he told Manstein on the 18th. "We must assume that Stalingrad can be held, and do all we can to that end. Naturally there can be no question of our acting as though Stalingrad were already lost."[51]

Milch believed that the Führer understood neither Sixth Army's rapid deterioration nor the major difficulties involved in maintaining the airlift. On 18 January, therefore, he ordered *Generalmajor* Pickert to fly to Hitler's headquarters in Rastenburg, East Prussia, in order to present both Hitler and Göring with a detailed situation report. Pickert was still depressed by his "involuntary abandonment" of his men within the pocket, and, while he considered this mission a "great honor," noted in his diary that he would have preferred to meet the High Command as the leader of a liberated division than as "the only one in a position to report to them, while my men are struggling and dying within the pocket."[52] He would follow Milch's instructions, he added, "but the orders weigh heavily on me."

Pickert left for Rastenburg at dawn on 20 January. After flying virtually nonstop for two days in a variety of aircraft, including a Ju 52 damaged during the airlift, and then enduring a long train journey, he finally arrived at the Rastenburg train station at midnight on the 22nd. However, while he waited for a staff car to collect him, a noncommissioned officer called him to a telephone in the station guardhouse. A member of the headquarters staff informed him that, because the situation in the east had changed since his departure, his report was no longer current. Pickert was flabbergasted. He had traveled continuously for over two days, only to be told that his report was no longer wanted. The next morning he phoned Göring for an explanation, only to be told by *Major* Bernd von Brauchitsch, Göring's adjutant, that the *Reichsmarschall* placed no importance on his report.[53] Pickert was disgusted, telling Milch on the 29th, the day he finally arrived back at *Luftflotte 4* headquarters, that "his troops inside the pocket had certainly earned the right to have a report presented on their behalf to the Luftwaffe's commander in chief."[54] Milch doubtless sympathized but coolly stated that, "as a soldier, he was only supposed to do his duty and not to express criticism." Before dismissing Pickert, Milch demonstrated his own faith in the general's worth; he placed him in charge of all flak forces in the Taman Peninsula, quickly developing into the new crucial sector of the eastern front now that Paulus's army at Stalingrad clearly had only a day or two left to live.

Pickert's failure to be received by the Führer does not mean that the latter tried to avoid hearing inconvenient or unpalatable reports on the airlift or conditions within the pocket. Rather, it reveals that Pickert, a previously unknown flak officer commanding a single division, was of relatively little consequence to Hitler. The Führer did want an unvarnished picture, but from an army general of stature. He especially wanted to hear from *General der Panzertruppe* Hans Hube, the highly decorated commander of the Fourteenth Panzer Corps. Just before the new year began, Hitler had sent Hans Baur, his personal pilot, into the Stalingrad pocket with instructions to bring back Hube. Hitler had long held the one-armed general (maimed during the Great War) in high esteem and had been impressed on 29 December by his sharp mind and frank manner.[55] Now, with Paulus and Milch making conflicting claims about the state of the airlift, he wanted to hear from Hube. On 18 January, therefore, he ordered Milch to have Hube and a small staff flown out of the pocket in one of the He 111s landing supplies at Gumrak. Milch was then to give Hube and his men positions on his airlift staff as special army–air force liaison officers.[56]

After escaping the pocket in a He 111 flown through a total "whiteout" by a courageous young lieutenant, Hube promptly informed the Führer that the situation at Stalingrad had deteriorated considerably since the Soviet attack on the pocket began nine days earlier. "The Luftwaffe airlift has failed," he stated bluntly. "Somebody must be to blame for that." Pointing out that not one air force general remained in the pocket, he added harshly: "Why don't you kill off some of your Luftwaffe generals—it's always the army generals who go to the wall!"[57] Hube knew, of course, that no army leaders had been executed for cowardice or incompetence. He was merely trying to make the point that Göring and his officers should be held accountable for their failures, as the army generals were. Although now convinced that Göring and his chief advisers had deceived him about the Luftwaffe's air supply capabilities, Hitler could not admit to Hube that all was lost. He calmly replied: "I know the grim position you are in at Stalingrad. But things will get better." Perhaps referring to his appointment of Milch, he added, "I have got it all in hand." Hitler was unsettled by Hube's reproach, however, and passed his comments on to Göring. Realizing by now that the airlift he had promised was failing miserably, the *Reichsmarschall* was trying desperately to curry Hitler's favor by attending most war conferences and (as Milch jotted in his pocket diary a few days later) "dispatching endless telegrams" to the air commanders at the front.[58] Hube's comments stung Göring, prompting him to rant to Milch: "Isn't it strange that anyone who serves at the front loses his clear view of the front!" The arrogance and stupidity of Göring's comment made Richthofen, listening on another phone, look around "for a wall to run up."[59]

Hube's assessment of the airlift gave Milch no cause for cheer. Gumrak had been suitable for landing for three days now, he told the field marshal on 19 January, but very few aircraft were attempting to land.[60] Most were simply dropping their supplies as they flew over. This was very unsatisfactory, he said, because "the air-drop canisters are scattered widely throughout the pocket and are very hard to locate in the deep snow. Around 25 percent can't be found." Collecting them is also arduous, he added, "because of fuel shortages and the difficulty of starting trucks in the cold, especially after they have been standing [idle] for a while." Hube added that Hitler was of the impression that, "in general, every effort is being made here, and that everything is being done that can be done." However, this was apparently not the case. Many of the transport planes landing at Gumrak arrived only half full, and "unnecessary supplies are being flown in that the army simply cannot use." When Milch tried to defend his airmen, pointing out that cold weather wreaked havoc with aircraft engines, that visibility was consistently poor, and that, in any event, Gumrak lacked even rudimentary lighting for night operations, Hube cut him off short. He had himself seen signal flares being fired as transport planes circled overhead. Therefore, pilots were apparently refusing to land for lack of commitment, not lack of lighting. This situation could not continue. Sixth Army's troops were "exhausted," he said. "Their daily bread ration is 200 grams for combat troops, 100 grams for rear area personnel. The ammunition situation is catastrophic. Our artillery no longer fires on enemy positions, but fires only to stave off enemy attacks. Russian aircraft can fly as low as they like."

Responding to Hube's complaint that useless supplies were entering the pocket, Milch ordered some of the airlift containers to be opened before departure.[61] To his disgust, many contained only fish meal. He sent them back and asked the army to have the victualing officer hanged. "If we had not had the contents of these sacks sampled on the airfields," he later said, "our aircraft would actually have flown fish-meal into Stalingrad!" Early postwar accounts of the Stalingrad encirclement made much of this aspect of the supply mission, repeating claims that hundreds of thousands of condoms, tons of mosquito repellent, and so on were carried into Stalingrad. There is a kernel of truth in these stories. Useless supplies were airlifted to Stalingrad on many occasions. However, as Pickert himself pointed out in the early 1970s, "the fact that transport aircraft and para-dropped goods now and then contained foolish and unnecessary items is undisputed, but this was an exception which should not be overestimated."[62] Even so, Milch wanted it stopped, and issued very strict orders to that effect.

MILCH THE MANAGER

The field marshal chose not to dissolve either Richthofen's or Fiebig's command and create a new command and administration body. Instead, he opted to work independently of both airmen's organizations, creating a small *Sonderstab* (Special Staff) comprising only himself and a small team of consultants and signals officers. It would liaise with, and issue directives to, *Luftflotte 4* and *Fliegerkorps VIII* but would not interfere with command matters or erode the authority of their leaders. He worked well with Richthofen and Fiebig, whom he consulted regularly each day, and often threw his weight behind their initiatives. For example, when Richthofen created several new aircraft workshops behind the front, so that aircraft with medium damage would no longer need to be transported all the way back to the Reich for repair, Milch arranged for teams of technicians and mechanics to be brought from the Luftwaffe's testing and development center in Rechlin. He also ordered the new workshops to be fitted out with specialized equipment and adequate supplies and spare parts.

Milch's greatest problems were caused by the poor state of airfields, both inside and outside the pocket. He was able to improve conditions at Gumrak a little, although landing on its narrow runway, pitted with bomb craters and exposed to Soviet artillery gunfire, remained difficult for even the most skilled and courageous pilots. On 17 January, the army's complaints that no night landings were being attempted had pressured him into ordering lighting equipment, smoke pots, and radio recognition equipment to be sent into the pocket immediately, along with signals and air traffic experts.[63] He had then assured Paulus, Manstein, and the High Command that aircraft would definitely land at Gumrak during the night of the 18th. His confidence was justified. Six He 111s and a single FW 200, which alone carried six tons of supplies, landed at Gumrak and unloaded valuable supplies before safely departing, with General Hube aboard the Condor.[64] Despite the radio beacon, direction finder, and makeshift landing path (comprising ten tank lights) installed according to Milch's instructions, landing proved even more dangerous at night than during the day. A quarter of the He 111s attempting to unload supplies at the airfield crashed or suffered substantial damage during landing or takeoff. Yet a small but steady stream of aircraft now flew into Gumrak around the clock.[65]

The principal airfields outside the pocket—the He 111 base at Novocherkassk and the Ju 52 base at Zverevo—were in very poor shape when Milch arrived. The latter was easily the worst. *Oberst* Morzik, the Air Transport Leader at Zverevo, reported that it was:

> a smooth field, with no hangars and no billeting facilities. The aircraft stand right next to the runway, because the airfield is otherwise completely covered in snow. Five barracks are being built, others are coming by rail. Seven bunkers now exist, but the construction of further bunkers is very difficult, because the earth is frozen solid to a depth of a meter everywhere.[66]

The temperature *inside* the few existing barracks was currently −10°C (at 1025 hours), because all windows had been broken during air attacks. Snow drifted continuously across the runway, he added, and it had taken three and a half hours to dig out a single Ju 52 that day. Despite a number of frostbite cases, some of them severe, troop morale remained surprisingly good. The *VVS* was apparently determined to change that. Air attacks came "both day and night, during landing, loading and takeoff." The field's only flak guns—one 7.5-cm Rumanian battery and a 3.7-cm battery—were no longer operable.

Air operations were severely curtailed because of the cold, Morzik continued. Zverevo had 106 Ju 52s, but 48 were damaged and awaiting repair. The operational rate of the remaining planes was very low. Only 8 had managed to take off for Stalingrad that day, and, because of radio and mechanical problems, 5 had turned back before reaching the pocket. The others never returned. They had either been shot down or destroyed at Gumrak by enemy shelling.

Milch was shocked by conditions at Zverevo and disappointed by what he perceived to be Morzik's defeatist attitude. He promptly phoned Fiebig and complained: "I have the impression that things are not in order under *Oberst* Morzik."[67] Suspecting that Morzik was not driving his subordinates hard enough, Milch stated that "tomorrow it will be mandatory for all aircraft [from Zverevo] to land at Gumrak in Stalingrad during the course of the day." Fiebig felt that Milch's criticisms of Zverevo and its commanders were unfair. It must be remembered, he told the field marshal in a formal report a few hours later, that Zverevo had been hastily constructed from a cornfield within a two-week period. This was a superb achievement on the part of *Luftflotte 4*'s technicians and labor battalions, who worked on an open steppe during blizzards and heavy frosts to create a new field for the Ju 52s after Salsk, itself an improvised air supply base, came under threat. Ju 52s had been at Zverevo only since the day before the field marshal arrived at the front. He and Richthofen were well aware that conditions were bad, but they were already attempting to remedy the situation before the field marshal arrived.

Regardless of these explanations, Milch wanted the operational rate of the transport units raised immediately. He asked Weidinger, the air fleet's chief engineer, what could be done to improve the state of the Ju 52 fleet at Zverevo. Weidinger answered that little could be done immediately because of deep snowdrifts, howling winds, and subzero temperatures.[68] When weather conditions improved, Milch should transfer the Ju 52s to Novocherkassk, which had stronger flak protection, better hangars, and a proper ground organization. It would first be necessary to shift the He 111s from Novocherkassk to Stalino, he added. Milch replied that the situation on the ground ruled out these transfers. Enemy troops were too close to Novocherkassk. He 111s could escape more quickly than Ju 52s, so he wanted to leave the respective fleets where they were for now.

Convinced that Morzik's apathy was partly responsible for the low operational rate of the Ju 52s at Zverevo, and annoyed by his apparent indifference, Milch summoned the air transport officer to his command train. When the field marshal asked him whether he needed anything urgently, Morzik replied that it was pointless importing additional technical staff as there was insufficient accommodation or equipment as things were.[69] Milch was staggered. "These men had no chance whatsoever of warming themselves up," he told the air ministry staff a few days later. "The only thing accomplished for them was parking a stone-cold omnibus there. Just imagine what it means, working in 25 degrees of frost with a fifty-mile-per-hour blizzard howling round your ears day and night without respite." He was unconvinced by Morzik's explanation that he had issued written requests for necessary buildings and equipment, but nothing had arrived. "Do you think that lets you off?" he challenged. Why had he not provided even simple huts for his men, taking materials from local villages? Morzik answered that he lacked vehicles for transportation. Milch snapped back that a number of army trucks sat idle near the field, to which Morzik protested that the Luftwaffe could not touch army equipment without authorization. "That would be larceny!" "The only larceny done around here," Milch thundered, "is that somebody has made off with your brains."[70]

David Irving stated in his laudatory biography of Milch that, following his argument with Morzik, the field marshal "ordered sixteen prefabricated huts to be rushed immediately to Zverevo airfield." Irving was mistaken. Milch did nothing about the airfield's lack of accommodation for over a week, in the meantime leaving frozen ground personnel to work in the open and sleep in tents.[71] On 26 January, eight days after quarreling with Morzik, Milch finally got around to ordering the huts. He only acted then, it would appear, after receiving complaints that the incidence of frostbite among Zverevo's mechanics was steadily rising. The next day, he had the gall to snap at Fiebig, who had been nagging him for days about the accommodation problem: "I notice a lack of initiative in providing quarters. . . . At present there is only one shed and one omnibus at Zverevo."[72]

This was not the only occasion when Milch's much-touted administrative abilities were conspicuously absent. He later had to admit that Morzik had indeed placed orders for urgently required barracks and equipment and that, through no fault of his own, it had never arrived. "I found out that the trains did actually set out," he reported during a conference shortly afterward. "But they were shunted off somewhere else, because more important stuff had to be transported." Conceding that he had been unable to influence the situation, he added: "So they lay around . . . and who knows where they are today?"[73] Also, Milch did not mention to his audience that this "more important stuff" included the hundreds of useless gliders that he himself had ordered. Even after he had abandoned the idea of using gliders, a full trainload arrived at the front every third day.[74]

"The Junkers squadrons had not the foggiest idea how to improvise," Milch claimed two weeks after the airlift ended.[75] "I had to drum some sense into them. At first they had nothing. But all at once they had a wooden hut with a small stove in it so they could keep warm. Then gradually they began to look at the correct cold-start procedure for the engines. I threatened anybody who neglected it with execution." Milch firmly insisted that all air transport units must employ the cold-start procedures stipulated by the manufacturers of their aircraft. He noticed that most 111 units, many of which had served in Russia before the airlift began, were used to bad weather and familiar with cold-start techniques. Many of the Ju 52 units, on the other hand, had only recently arrived in Russia, drawn mainly from the Reich, the western theater, and the Balkans. As a result, few knew how to start their aircraft engines in the subzero temperatures they now experienced each day.

On 20 January, therefore, Milch ordered fifty extra Ju 52 maintenance experts to be brought from the Luftwaffe's testing and development base at Rechlin in order to supervise, among other tasks, the employment of the correct cold-start procedure by airfield ground personnel.[76] When they finally reached the forward airfields, these experts found that very few Junkers crews were using the correct cold-start procedure. "The Ju 52 squadrons did not even know of it," Milch later claimed, "because they had arrived from Africa."[77] Only a few Ju 52 units had actually been drawn from the Mediterranean theater, as Milch doubtless knew, but he was right about the widespread ignorance of proper cold-start techniques. His leading engineers and mechanics frequently complained to him that units were ignoring his instructions. He eventually resorted to a show of authority. Anyone not starting their aircraft according to the stipulated procedure, he threatened, would be court-martialed (as would any pilot who turned back during flight without attempting to land in, or drop supplies to, the Stalingrad pocket).[78] Naturally, he added, responsibility ultimately lay with the airfield commanders. "I hope you are a strict and tough commander," he warned Morzik on the 26th.

Compliance with the stipulated procedures did result in improved operation rates, as an entry in the war diary of Milch's airlift staff reveals: "This morning most of K.G. 55's [He 111] aircraft started by applying the correct cold-start procedure, without using the heating truck and despite a temperature of minus 15 degrees centigrade."[79] However, even after issuing threats and instructions for more than a week, Milch learned on 27 January that (for unknown reasons) many units were still not employing proper cold-start techniques. Even worse, many were failing to use special starting fuel, despite sufficient quantities now being stored at the airfields. As a result, the operational rate of the Ju 52s and He 111s had not improved much since he arrived. It had risen from 20 percent to around 30 percent, which was still much too low.

Failure to implement starting procedures was only one of several reasons for the airlift's continual inadequate performance. The principal reason was that Milch suffered the same crippling misfortune as Richthofen and Fiebig had: the loss of the main airlift bases inside and outside the Stalingrad pocket. The first to go was Gumrak, the only operational airfield within the pocket, on 23 January. Milch had worked hard to improve conditions at Gumrak. He had ordered its runway cleared of debris and wrecked aircraft, installed a radio beacon, a direction finder, and a crude but satisfactory landing path, and ordered improvements in the unloading and distribution of supplies. However, within days of watching these steps bear initial fruit—in the form of slight increases in the amount of supplies unloaded in the pocket (as opposed to merely dropped from the air)—Soviet forces overran Gumrak, undoing in minutes what Milch had taken several days to accomplish.

Fiebig described the fall of Gumrak in his diary. On 22 January, he noted that Milch's efforts had improved conditions, although the field was still "not very good, especially for He 111s."[80] The next evening, he wrote that renewed efforts by *Major* Freudenfeld, the senior Luftwaffe signals officer in the pocket (later awarded the Knight's Cross for his effective work),[81] had further improved the base. "Operations at the new Gumrak airfield were working well," Fiebig jotted on the 23rd, until Soviet pressure undid Freudenfeld's good work.[82] By midmorning, he explained, Soviet artillery and flak batteries were hitting the airfield repeatedly. Combined with bad weather, this gunfire made takeoff and landing difficult and dangerous. By early evening, gunfire had knocked out the radio beacon and direction finder, prompting Fiebig to seek clarification of the situation from Sixth Army. The army replied by radio at 2140 hours: "Situation at the airfield has been uncertain since 1700 hours. No contact [with Freudenfeld and the airfield staff] since that time. Don't land any more." Fiebig was bitterly disappointed and could think of little else than the fate of the trapped army. He had finally received his Christmas package from his family, but, although "the love of one's wife and children gives one strength," he felt unable to enjoy his family's gifts. "The situation is just too grim," he wrote.

He was not exaggerating. When Soviet forces attacked the pocket from the southwest on 22 January, advancing on a five-kilometer-wide front, Paulus had been unable to prevent their steady progress. His cold and exhausted troops lacked ammunition as well as sufficient fuel to transport reinforcements from other sections of the pocket, which was now only around one-third of the size it had been two weeks earlier. On the evening of the 22nd, Paulus had sent the High Command the following message: "Rations exhausted. Over 12,000 unattended wounded in the pocket. What orders should I give to troops who have no more ammunition and are subjected to mass attacks supported by heavy artillery fire? The quickest decision is necessary, since disintegration is already starting in some places."[83] Careful not to offend the Führer, he lamely added that "confidence in the leadership still exists, however." Hitler was unimpressed by Paulus's attitude, claiming that he showed weakness in the face of adversity. A true commander would never bleat like this, he told his closest advisers. He forbade Paulus to surrender, telling him that "the troops will defend themselves to the last. If possible, the size of the fortress is to be reduced so that it can be held by the troops still capable of fighting."[84] The courage and endurance of the encircled forces had tied down powerful Soviet armies, he added, making it possible to shore up the broken southern front and begin preparing a counteroffensive. Thus, "Sixth Army has made an historic contribution to Germany's greatest struggle."

The loss of Gumrak on 23 January was a grievous blow to Paulus, who realized immediately that his army was now alone, cut off from all help except for the small amount of supplies now dropped into the pocket by Fiebig's transport planes. Seeing that the Soviet momentum was unstoppable, Paulus had actually anticipated the airfield's capture for several days before it finally occurred. *Major von Zitzowitz*, one of his staff officers, had reported this to Milch on the 21st, telling him that Gumrak's fall was imminent. As a result, Zitzowitz said, Sixth Army had initiated a repair and construction program at Stalingradskiy, an inferior airfield farther from the pocket's rapidly contracting perimeter.[85] In the afternoon of the 22nd, the army had reported Stalingradskiy operational. However, when several dozen He 111s had attempted to land there later that day, six crashed because of the "thick snow and deep bomb craters on the runway."[86] This prompted Milch to warn *Fliegerkorps VIII* that "we must reckon with heavy losses if we use Stalingradskiy for night operations."[87] As a result, he prohibited all night landings, replacing them with air-drop missions only. He then instructed Ju 52 groups that they were not compelled to attempt landing there even during the day. It hardly mattered. During a heavy assault on Stalingrad's western outskirts on the 23rd, Soviet forces overran Stalingradskiy only hours after they had captured Gumrak.[88]

Thus, after Gumrak and Stalingradskiy fell within hours of each other on 23 January, Paulus knew that the airlift Göring had so boldly promised the Führer was, to all intents and purposes, over. His army would now receive nothing more than what a few He 111s and Ju 52s dropped each day. No more wounded soldiers would be evacuated. The remnants of Sixth Army—once the strongest German army in the Wehrmacht—were now doomed. Soviet successes that day meant that those remnants no longer even functioned as a single entity. After sweeping over the German airfields, advancing Soviet forces had cut through the "fortress" virtually to the Volga, thereby dividing it into two small pockets. The remaining troops of the Eleventh Army Corps formed the northern pocket, an area of about eleven by fourteen kilometers in the area of the Dzerzhinski tractor works. The surviving troops of the Fourteenth Panzer Corps and the Fourth, Eighth, and Fifty-first Army Corps formed the southern pocket, occupying a slightly larger area in Stalingrad's ruined southern suburbs. The situation was very grim. On the 24th, Paulus sent a despondent message to the High Command: "Troops without ammunition and food. . . . Collapse inevitable. Army requests immediate permission to surrender in order to save the lives of remaining troops."[89] Again, Hitler refused to grant permission for the army's surrender.

ACCUSATIONS AND ACRIMONY

Paulus blamed the Luftwaffe for Sixth Army's looming destruction, claiming that, despite the *Reichsmarschall*'s promises, it had failed to keep his army alive and combat-worthy. Even before Gumrak and Stalingradskiy fell, he had given up trying to disguise his contempt for the air force. It had performed miserably and bore responsibility for the suffering of his men, he told anyone within range, including Luftwaffe personnel within the pocket. For example, *Major* Erich Thiel, commander of a He 111 bomber group serving in an improvised transport role, flew into the pocket on 19 January.[90] Milch had asked him to contact Paulus in the hope that the army leader would improve ground services at Gumrak. Thiel reported to Paulus shortly before noon. The army leader would accept no responsibility for the poor ground organization, even when Thiel pointed out that the aircraft turnaround time had dropped to around five hours and that the airfield, including part of the runway, was littered with wrecks.[91] Paulus became "very upset" and snapped at him: "You are talking to dead men here. We have remained here as the Führer ordered. The Luftwaffe has left us in the lurch and has not kept its promises."

Thiel, whose men had repeatedly risked their lives (and many had lost them) carrying supplies to the encircled troops, could scarcely believe his ears. The Luftwaffe was being accused of gross incompetence by the very general who had ignored Richthofen's, Fiebig's, and Pickert's repeated warnings that the Luftwaffe could not sustain the army; the general who had wasted initial opportunities to break out; the general who had (as Pickert and other Luftwaffe leaders inside the pocket often commented among themselves) shown no interest in improving the landing, unloading, and distribution conditions and services at the airfields his men depended on. Neither he nor Schmidt, his chief of staff, had ever even visited an airfield to see firsthand the conditions under which Luftwaffe air and ground crew were forced to work. Yet Paulus was not finished. In his typical icy manner, he continued his attack:

> When [aircraft] don't land, it means the army's death. It is too late now, anyway. . . . Every machine that lands saves the lives of 1,000 men. . . . Dropping [supplies] is no use to us. Many supply canisters ["bombs" in Paulus's original text] are not found, because we have no fuel with which to retrieve them. . . . Today is the fourth day in which my troops have had nothing to eat. We could not recover our heavy weapons [during recent withdrawals], because no fuel was available. They are now lost. The last horses have been eaten. Can you imagine it: soldiers diving on an old horse cadaver, breaking open its head and devouring its brain raw? . . . What should I say, as supreme commander of an army, when a man comes to me, begging: "*Herr Generaloberst, a crust of bread?*" Why did the Luftwaffe say that it could carry out the supply mission? Who is the man responsible for mentioning the possibility? If someone had told me that it was not possible, I would not have reproached the Luftwaffe. I would have broken out.[92]

At this point Schmidt angrily butted in. "And now you dare to try to whitewash the Luftwaffe," he seethed at Thiel, "which has committed the worst treachery in German history. *Somebody* must have suggested it [the airlift] to the Führer? Must an entire army, this magnificent Sixth Army, go to the dogs like this?" Paulus spoke again: "The Führer gave me his firm assurance, that he and the entire German people feel responsible for this army, and now we suffer the most dreadful catastrophe in German military history because the Luftwaffe has failed us." Thiel was stunned by their vehemence and appalled by their discourtesy. Schmidt would not even shake his hand when he departed, he later told Fiebig.[93]

Fiebig was furious. The honor of his men was at stake, he insisted to Milch on 20 January. The field marshal reassured him that Hitler placed little weight on the claims of hysterical generals, especially those of Schmidt and Paulus, whose fall from favor was well known to senior commanders. Even if the Führer was unhappy about the airlift's lack of success, he certainly wasn't blaming the operational commanders or the troops. Milch's arguments apparently pacified Fiebig. When he learned two days later that even the corps commanders inside the pocket were blaming the Luftwaffe for the army's collapse, he responded calmly. He noted sympathetically in his diary that the generals were "fully under the psychosis of the situation in the pocket," and made no further complaints to Milch.[94] For all his reassuring comments to Fiebig, however, Milch was in fact worried that the High Command would believe the army's splenetic accusations. After first learning about Paulus's and Schmidt's outbursts at Thiel, for instance, he had phoned *Oberstleutnant* Christian, at the Führer's headquarters, ostensibly to describe his recent decisions and actions, but really to promote his airmen's reputation. "Please tell the Führer," he said to Christian, "that there is not a single man who is not giving his utmost to the supply operation. What our people are accomplishing here is more than has ever been done in this respect so far in this war."[95] Hitler and Göring had heard Sixth Army's complaints, of course. The Führer said little about them to Göring, but his increasing coolness toward his deputy reveals that he also felt let down. Göring, pompous and self-righteous as ever, refused to accept responsibility for Sixth Army's destruction. For instance, two weeks after Paulus finally stumbled into captivity with the remnants of his once-mighty army, the *Reichsmarschall* addressed a conference of air fleet commanders. "If the army had fought harder," he stated, "particularly in Stalingrad itself, we should still have the city today and it would not have fallen."[96] Paulus was at fault, he insisted, not the Luftwaffe:

> Paulus was too weak. He failed to turn Stalingrad into a proper fortress. . . . The Paulus army just relied on the Luftwaffe and expected it to perform miracles. . . . And then General Schmidt, the army's chief of staff, General Schmidt, had the gall to say: "The Luftwaffe has committed the biggest treachery in history because it could not manage to supply the Paulus army." Yet the army lost its airfields—how on earth was a mass airlift supposed to be possible after that?

Pitomnik, Gumrak, and Stalingradskiy did fall in quick succession between 16 and 23 January, leaving transport units unable to land within the pocket and forcing them to drop their supplies from the air. But Milch, Richthofen, and Fiebig refused to abandon Sixth Army. "For as long as German soldiers remain alive and can be located," they all agreed, "they will be supplied."[97] They had several thousand tons of rations and ammunition at their forward airfields, waiting to be dropped into the two German pockets at Stalingrad. With a heightened sense of urgency, they pressured their subordinates to improve their efficiency. They must increase the operational rate of the transport units even further, the air leaders ordered, and load and drop supplies faster and in greater quantities. They must do everything humanly possible to ease Sixth Army's suffering, and they must do it now.

Major Freudenfeld, the senior Luftwaffe signals officer trapped within the two shrinking pockets, responded to his superior officers' urging with energy and skill. On his own initiative, he immediately set about constructing proper drop sites, with lights and radio beacons to show pilots where to unload their supply canisters. They would otherwise scatter the canisters all over the pockets, which would result in some falling into Soviet territory and others falling into the city ruins, where they would be difficult to find and retrieve. Freudenfeld therefore ordered small labor teams to clear areas in each pocket, which he equipped with radio beacons and improvised lighting grids made from the upturned headlights of lorries. It was a dangerous, difficult, and time-consuming task, but by the evening of 25 January, Freudenfeld had created a drop site in the southern pocket. Fiebig noted in his diary that, as a result, "supply containers were dropped at the right place."[98] Constructing a drop site in the other pocket took longer, but the signals expert set about that task with what Fiebig called "admirable energy." In the meantime, many canisters were scattered and lost. "If only they could all be found," Fiebig glumly wrote on the 27th, "but that's impossible in the house ruins in 'Red Square,' in the workers' settlement and in the tractor plant. Only a fraction will be found." Freudenfeld was equally determined to prevent these losses. Taking many personal risks, he constructed the northern drop site on the 28th, and established a direct radio link between the drop sites and *Fliegerkorps VIII.* Fiebig was delighted and immediately recommended him for the Knight's Cross; Milch wholeheartedly endorsed it.

Shortly after dawn on 28 January, Milch received an unexpected visitor to his command post: *Generalmajor* Schmundt, Hitler's chief adjutant. The Führer had sent his trusted assistant to assess the situation on his behalf and to see what could be done to alleviate Sixth Army's drawn-out death throes. "Avoid the formation of large pockets," Milch boldly told him, "because air supply can never be completely assured, especially during periods of bad weather."[99] Believing that Hitler had received poor counsel, for which he was now paying a high price, he informed Schmundt: "I think it would be good for the Führer to detach himself more from the individual problems of army command, and appoint a leading figure as Supreme Commander of the Eastern Front, like those already existing in the west and south, with authority over all three branches of the armed forces."

Manstein would be perfect for this position. "I believe that Manstein is strong enough, both in military ability and in character," Milch explained. He added that the Führer should also form an Armed Forces General Staff, "comprising one special person from each service branch with his staff." Richthofen was certainly the ideal person to represent the Luftwaffe, he stressed. Schmundt was taken aback by Milch's suggestions, which cast Hitler's command abilities in an unflattering light, but agreed with his assessment of Manstein and Richthofen. He clearly did not want to convey Milch's thoughts to the Führer, however, so he recommended that Milch report to Hitler himself when his assignment finished. The field marshal agreed, provided he could speak informally with Hitler, away from his cronies, and preferably in the presence of Albert Speer.

Milch's desire to have Speer present is understandable. He was not only a capable and forthright man but also a close personal friend of both Hitler and Milch. He would make a good arbiter. The field marshal had last spoken to the armaments minister on 24 January, when he telephoned him from Richthofen's command train. Speer informed Milch that the Führer already recognized that he had improved the airlift and regretted not sending for him earlier.[100] In actual fact, despite Milch's barrage of orders, directives, and threats, the tonnages airlifted to Sixth Army did not improve dramatically under his command; in fact, they declined. During the thirteen days between his arrival at the front on the 16th and his conversation with Schmundt on the 28th, *Fliegerkorps VIII*'s transport units had carried or dropped into the pocket only 790 tons of supplies, a daily average of a mere 60.75 tons.[101] This was only one-fifth of the amount considered necessary to meet Sixth Army's barest survival needs. It was also a substantial drop from the daily average of 157.75 tons carried in during the thirteen days preceding Milch's arrival.

Milch can hardly be blamed for this decrease. He had done everything possible under the circumstances. The decrease stems primarily from the loss of good airfields and the forced use of poor airfields. The Soviets had overrun Tatsinskaya and Morozovskaya two weeks before he arrived, obliging the Ju 52 and He 111 groups, which together composed over 90 percent of Fiebig's transport fleet, to transfer to inferior and distant fields at Salsk and Novocherkassk. The greater distance from those fields to the pocket—not to mention the inadequate maintenance, repair, and loading facilities at those fields—had a major impact on the airlift's effectiveness. Then, only hours before Milch arrived, Fiebig had to evacuate Salsk, sending all Ju 52 groups to the improvised, unfinished, and woefully inadequate "airfield" at Zverevo. During each of these evacuations, the Luftwaffe had lost valuable vehicles, heating equipment, spare parts, fuel, and stockpiles of supplies. Their loss seriously limited the air units' ability to perform their tasks effectively. Solving the problems caused by the loss of properly equipped airfields and the forced use of rough, uneven landing strips was not easy, and, although he displayed drive, imagination, and managerial talent, Milch failed to solve many of those problems before another disaster struck: Soviet forces overran Pitomnik, Gumrak, and Stalingradskiy in quick succession, leaving the Luftwaffe unable to land anywhere within the pocket. That his units managed to carry or drop an average of sixty tons of supplies per day reflects both the improvements Milch made and the obstacles that he could not overcome. Sixty tons per day throughout Milch's first two weeks at the front was a considerable achievement under the circumstances. As noted, Paulus did not see it that way. Regardless of the reasons—which he called excuses—the Luftwaffe had failed to supply his army. It was now gasping its last breaths.

AN ARMY EXPIRES; AN AIRLIFT ENDS

On 26 January, Soviet forces cut the narrow corridor linking the two German pockets, which they began efficiently crushing. Realizing that sustained resistance on even a small scale was pointless, Paulus asked the Luftwaffe to drop only food. Ammunition was no longer needed; there were too few guns.[102] After another two days of constant Soviet attacks substantially reduced the size of the two pockets, Sixth Army stopped issuing rations to the 25,000 wounded now lying strewn throughout ruins and in cellars. By doing so, the army hoped to preserve the depleted strength of the fighting troops. Not that it expected to hold out much longer; that evening, the army reported to the High Command that its resistance "must finally collapse no later than February 1st."[103] Soviet attacks the next day split the southern pocket, leaving Paulus, his staff, and the remnants of several broken divisions in the south, while the Eighth and Fifty-first Army Corps fought on in the north. The Fourteenth Panzer Corps ceased to exist that day, two days after the Fourth Panzer Corps collapsed and was overrun.[104]

On 30 January, Milch ordered that air-supply missions to the northern pocket must continue, but he added that units should drop supplies to the disintegrating southern pocket, now really two pockets, "only if requested."[105] The northern pocket would hold out longer, he explained, possibly even for a few more days. The southern pocket would probably disappear within hours. Knowing the airlift was virtually over, Fiebig visited his two main air transport leaders, *Oberst* Kühl at Novocherkassk and *Oberst* Morzik at Zverevo. They had done an excellent job under the circumstances, and he wanted to thank them and their squadrons leaders personally. "My heart was overflowing," he wrote in his diary that night.[106]

Although the suffering of the doomed soldiers upset Fiebig, he felt particularly grieved by the fate of the Luftwaffe personnel who shared Six Army's fate. He received a poignant radio report from Freudenfeld, sheltering from constant explosions in a cellar within the collapsing southern pocket: "Soldiers run around aimlessly. Very few combatants are left. The staffs have lost their grip as leaders. Russian tanks are breaking through. This is the end."[107] Fiebig added sadly in his diary that his meteorologist and his signals teams had sent their final messages, asking him to relay their greetings to their loved ones at home. Few of the trapped Luftwaffe personnel who radioed their final messages to their commanders showed the panic they doubtless felt. Most—like their army counterparts—sent calm and stoical messages. For example, *Oberst* Rosenfeld, commander of the 104th Flak Regiment, signaled:

> In the basement ruins of Red Square, Stalingrad, surrounded by the thunder of enemy gunfire, we have read our Führer's proclamation [issued that day, the tenth anniversary of his assumption of power]. It has given us courage and resolution for these last hours of the battle for the ruins of the Red citadel on the Volga. Above us flies the swastika banner. The orders of our Supreme Command are being obeyed to the end. We turn our thoughts loyally to the fatherland. Long live the Führer![108]

Deeply moved, Fiebig wrote that "all the men have an unheard-of attitude. They want to prove themselves worthy of 30 January." Paulus—whose nervous exhaustion prompted Schmidt to take over direction of the final defensive operations—clearly wanted to protect the reputation of his army. Therefore, despite the fact that his faith in the High Command and the National Socialist worldview had steadily deteriorated over the last two months and now no longer existed, he signaled to Hitler late on the 29th: "On the anniversary of your assumption of power, the Sixth Army sends greetings to its Führer. The Swastika still flutters over Stalingrad. May our struggle stand as an example to generations as yet unborn, never to capitulate, however desperate the odds. Then Germany will be victorious. *Heil, mein Führer.*"[109]

On 30 January, Milch ordered his transport units to fly over the pocket that night, looking for any signs of life. If they identified Germans, they were to drop their supplies. Eighty-five aircraft flew to Stalingrad that night; thirty others turned back because of bad weather or mechanical problems. Most of those that managed to reach Stalingrad dropped their supplies, some seventy-two tons, into the northern pocket, where the Eleventh Army Corps defended itself courageously.[110] Few dropped supplies into the southern pocket, the aircrews knowing from the many fires burning throughout areas supposedly held by German troops, from the lack of drop-site lighting, and from the arbitrary firing of signals flares that the pocket scarcely existed.[111] By dawn on the 31st, it no longer did. Freudenfeld and his signals team radioed *Luftflotte 4* that Soviet troops "were at the door," before formally "signing off."[112] This act brought tears to the eyes of Richthofen, Milch, and Fiebig, whose desperate efforts to stave off this ghastly moment had failed. Army signals officers made similar calls, each formally signing off in the same courageous manner. At 0615 hours, the radio operator at Sixth Army's headquarters in the basement of a ruined department store on Red Square signaled to Army Group Don: "Russians at the door. We are preparing to destroy [the radio equipment]."[113] An hour later, Sixth Army's final transmission came through: "We are destroying [the equipment]."[114] Shortly before noon, Paulus surrendered. He neither signed a general surrender document nor ordered the Eleventh Army Corps, still fighting in the northern pocket, to lay down its arms. Instead, adhering to Hitler's order not to surrender his army, he merely surrendered himself and the remnants of his staff over to General Mikhail Shumilov, commander of the Soviet Sixty-fourth Army, leaving individual sector commanders to arrange their own surrenders.

Expecting to accept the surrender of a general, Shumilov was surprised when Paulus stood up and introduced himself: "*Generalfeldmarschall* Paulus." Less than a day earlier, Hitler had promoted him to field marshal. He knew, as Paulus did, that no German field marshal had ever surrendered, and he hoped the new field marshal would earn himself a prominent place in the glorious annals of German soldiership by choosing death before dishonor. Paulus saw the options differently. He chose life. To Hitler's disgust, he and eleven German and five Rumanian generals entered Soviet captivity.[115] Upon receiving the news, the Führer immediately asked his adjutant to find out if it was too late to cancel Paulus's promotion. It was too late, the adjutant replied. His promotion had already been published in the newspaper. Hitler, ironically presaging his own suicide two years later, insisted to Zeitzler the next day that "the man should have shot himself, like the old commanders who threw themselves on their swords when they saw that the cause was lost."[116] Even the Roman commander Varus had given his slave the order "Now kill me!" when defeated by German tribes almost 2,000 years ago. "I will create no more field marshals in this war," Hitler added angrily.

Paulus's surrender on 31 January did not signal the end of air-supply operations to Stalingrad. In the northern pocket, *General der Infanterie* Karl Strecker ordered the remnants of the Eleventh Army Corps to continue fighting. Fiebig ordered his transport groups to drop as much food and ammunition to Strecker's valiant troops as they could. That night, eighty-five aircraft dropped seventy-four tons of supplies into the northern pocket.[117] Fiebig noted that Strecker's men had lit three lamps to guide the aircraft to the drop site. These were not the only recognition signals, however. Strecker's men also laid out a large swastika of red lights, a powerful symbol of defiance to the Soviet forces set to crack their defenses within days at most.[118] Although they set out that symbol on their own initiative, Hitler did demand that they continue fighting. "I expect the Eleventh Army Corps to resist to the very end," he radioed the general on the afternoon of 1 February, "in order to tie down as many enemy forces as possible, because that will be of great benefit to operations on the other [sections of the] front."[119]

The first day of February was very difficult for Strecker and his men. They suffered heavy losses as they withstood constant attack by superior forces. When 116 of Fiebig's Ju 52s flew over the pocket that night, the aircrew saw many fires and the muzzle flashes of hundreds of Soviet guns.[120] They knew that the Eleventh Army Corps would be destroyed within hours, and felt powerless to intervene. All they could offer were ninety-eight tons of ammunition and food, of little use to the cold and exhausted soldiers who would be dead or marching eastward into captivity within hours and who had no chance of even collecting the rations before then.[121] Shortly after dawn, Army Group Don received the last message Strecker sent: "XI Corps, with its six divisions, has done its duty to the last. Long live the *Führer!* Long live Germany!—Strecker."[122]

Throughout 2 February, both the High Command and the air force and army operational commanders waited for further messages. None came. Even now unwilling to abandon German soldiers, Milch ordered aircraft to fly over Stalingrad and to drop supplies to any German troops clearly identified. When the aircraft returned from their missions, Fiebig reported to Milch that all was lost. "The outline of the pocket can no longer be recognized." he said. "No artillery fire was seen. An enemy vehicle column with headlights blazing is advancing from the northwest into what was formerly the northern pocket. . . . The front of that column is almost at our former drop site."[123] A fire raged in the northwest part of the tractor factory, Fiebig added in his diary, and there were no signs of continued fighting. Coupled with the lack of radio transmissions, these aircrew observations revealed that the Battle for Stalingrad was finally over.

With a heavy heart, Milch thanked Fiebig and ordered him to turn all his transport groups over to *Luftflotte 4,* which would now need every available aircraft for the major operation it had already turned its attention to: the evacuation of the remaining forces in the Caucasus. Hitler's dream of capturing that vast region's oil fields had been shattered by his obsession with Stalingrad. Milch then took stock of the Luftwaffe's achievements and losses. During the seventy-one days and nights between 24 November 1942 and 2 February 1943, the Luftwaffe had carried or dropped to the encircled troops a total of 8,350.7 tons of rations, fuel, and ammunition, or an average of 117.6 tons per day.[124] During the same period, it had evacuated 30,000 wounded soldiers.[125] The cost was very high, however. Due mainly to bad weather, but also to *VVS* and Soviet flak attacks, the Luftwaffe had suffered 166 aircraft destroyed, 108 missing, and 214 written off.[126] Recovering from the loss of these 488 aircraft would take a long time. "The total losses are the equivalent of five wings, or more than one full air corps," *Oberst* Rohde, the liaison officer to the quartermaster general, told a depressed Milch on 2 February.[127] The Ju 52 groups had lost 266 aircraft, a third of the Luftwaffe's total complement, and the He 111 groups had lost 165 planes. Other losses included 42 Ju 86s, 9 FW 200s, 5 He 177s, and 1 Ju 290. Approximately 1,000 airmen had given their lives, including many of the Luftwaffe's most experienced bomber and transport pilots, navigators, and training instructors. Milch could not help but wonder whether the sacrifice of these young men, and of the Luftwaffe troops who perished inside the pocket or stumbled into captivity along with 108,000 of their army comrades, had really been necessary. The airlift should never have been promised or attempted, he had maintained from the outset. It was always doomed to failure, and, as long as Hitler refused to permit its surrender or breakout, Sixth Army was always doomed to destruction.

Conclusion

The disastrous campaign was, from its very conception, the result of perceived economic necessity. To a far greater degree than for any other German military undertaking of the Second World War, economic considerations significantly influenced its planning. The Führer's directive of 5 April 1942 committed the Wehrmacht for the first time to a major offensive with economic objectives taking precedence over strictly military objectives. The resulting campaign not only failed to attain those objectives but also cost Hitler dearly in men, matériel and— not least—prestige.

The dire predictions of Hitler and his economic advisers during 1941 and 1942 about the certain collapse of the German war machine if no new sources of oil were obtained proved to be exaggerated. The German war effort did not grind to a halt when the campaign to capture the Caucasus oil fields failed. Although Germany's oil situation remained acute, and became desperate after the Allied air offensive against its synthetic fuel plants and the Rumanian oil fields commenced, the Reich continued fighting until May 1945.

In fact, despite the total failure of the 1942 campaign, events in 1943 actually led to a slight improvement in the oil situation. First, when Italy defected from the Axis in September, it ceased to be a drain on Germany's near-exhausted reserves. Second, when German forces in Italy responded to this defection and rapidly disarmed their former allies, they captured surprisingly large stocks of oil. Third, Germany's synthetic fuel industry, not yet targeted by Allied bombers, reached a production peak.[1] Fourth, it turned out that all units had stored more than they revealed. Accordingly, the oil shortages that had bedeviled the Wehrmacht's efforts throughout the previous two years appeared far less critical. The Luftwaffe was even able to build up slightly its meager reserves for the first time since the beginning of the Russian campaign.[2]

In May 1944, however, the USAAF's strategic bombing force began concentrating its efforts against both the German synthetic fuel plants and the Rumanian oil fields and refineries. The use of bases in southern Italy greatly facilitated raids on the latter. Despite high aircraft and crew losses, these efforts paid off handsomely for the Allies, who learned from "Ultra" decrypts that many plants suffered production decreases or were put out of action altogether. By late summer 1944, Germany's oil supplies were seriously depleted. In May, by way of illustration, 316,000 tons of synthetic fuel were produced in Germany. The following month production fell to 107,000 tons, and in September it plummeted to a mere 17,000. As a result, the Luftwaffe received only 30,000 tons of petrol that month, instead of its normal 180,000 tons.[3] Its training programs suffered terribly, with many pilot training schools shutting down for lack of fuel. The mobility of the mechanized forces was also significantly curtailed. For the Ardennes campaign in December, Germany's last major offensive action of the war, the armored formations had very slender fuel reserves (and these were created only by robbing fuel from forces not involved). Hitler was gambling on their ability to capture American or British stocks. With the failure of this endeavor, and powerful Allied armies pressing in from the west, east, and south, it became clear that the Reich could not survive much longer.

Thus, Germany's ability to wage war did not dissolve with the failure of the Caucasus campaign, as the Führer and his economists had previously believed. Having said that, it should also be noted that neither Hitler nor his military planners could forecast with certainty the future course of the war or, therefore, accurately calculate the future oil consumption of Germany's armed forces. Frequent evaluations in 1941 and 1942 by the War Economy and Armaments Office, based on careful and detailed analyses of past production, import, and consumption rates, clearly revealed that once known oil reserves were exhausted it would no longer be possible to find any elsewhere. The mechanized part of Germany's war machine would rapidly grind to a halt, and operations would have to be entirely based on horsepower. These grim conclusions were repeatedly presented to Hitler and the High Command in the form of detailed reports. Their claims, as we saw previously, were seemingly corroborated by commanders in the field and even senior service chiefs like Raeder, who complained constantly that the mobility or operational capability of their forces had deteriorated because of decreases in their oil supplies. History has exposed the exaggeration of the warnings the Nazi leader received from his economists, but at the time they seemed both credible and compelling.

A DIFFICULT YEAR FOR *LUFTFLOTTE 4*

It had been a long, costly campaign for *Luftflotte 4*, containing easy and successful operations at first, leading its commanders to predict in their diaries (and sometimes to their men) that a successful conclusion appeared imminent. Then came difficult and disastrous operations, causing them to write despondently that failure was inevitable. Under Richthofen's direct command, air units performed superbly during the Crimean offensives of May and June. Functioning mainly as an extension of the army's artillery, they provided Manstein's troops with an unprecedented level of tactical air support. The excellent working relationship between Generals Richthofen and Manstein, outstanding commanders committed to close joint-service cooperation, ensured that the Luftwaffe's operations were carefully coordinated with the army's. As a result, airpower played a decisive role in the recapture of the Kerch Peninsula and the fall of Sevastopol, as Manstein later acknowledged in his memoirs.

However, the Luftwaffe managed to provide this level of support only because of a unique combination of circumstances. First, because most of the eastern front was relatively quiet during that period (except for the short-lived Soviet offensive at Kharkov in May), the *OKL* was able to give Richthofen a strong air force at a high level of operational readiness. Second, that powerful force faced numerically weak and poorly trained *VVS* opposition, allowing air and flak units to commence army support operations without having first to wage a time-consuming and costly battle for air superiority and then commit a large number of aircraft to escort and protection operations. Third, almost the entire force was deployed against only a few targets within a small area; in Sevastopol's case, there was only one, although it was very strong. Finally, it operated against those targets from established and well-equipped airstrips in the immediate vicinity, allowing a high number of sorties to be conducted each day.

This favorable set of circumstances existed nowhere throughout the main summer campaign. During the Battle of Kharkov (May) and *Blau*'s early stages (late June to late July), Richthofen was able to continue *Schwerpunktbildung,* the creation of single points of maximum effort. Through close liaison with army counterparts, he usually created joint *Schwerpunkte,* concentrations of strong air and army forces at the same critical points. After winning air superiority, *Luftflotte 4* provided an effective combination of direct battlefield support and systematic interdiction operations against Soviet rear areas.

In late July, however, Hitler committed a major mistake that had dire consequences both for the army and for Richthofen's air fleet. Encouraged by his troops' rapid seizure of vast areas and misreading the significance of their relatively small prisoner haul, he deviated from *Blau*'s original conception of striking to the Volga, securing the northern flank, and *then* plunging into the Caucasus. Instead, he divided the campaign into two simultaneous offensives: against Stalingrad and against the Caucasus. This dissipated army and air force strength, opened a large and vulnerable gap between his two army groups, created major logistical difficulties for both groups, and expanded *Luftflotte 4*'s combat zone to an unmanageable size.

Richthofen possessed nowhere near enough aircraft to provide adequate support for both army groups and was no longer able, as a result, to create major

Schwerpunkte. He spent the next three months (even after he pulled most units out of the Caucasus in mid-August, leaving two complete armies with little support) hastily swapping units back and forth between Stalingrad and the Caucasus as he attempted to create "local" *Schwerpunkte* as opportunities arose or crises developed. Those transfers over long distances steadily reduced operational rates. Moreover, air units encountered increasingly numerous *VVS* forces, which proved better trained and equipped than hitherto. To overcome them cost time, effort, and high losses. They also often had to operate from inadequate airfields, sometimes far from their targets, which were widely scattered over a large area. Consequently, the level of support for most army formations dropped dramatically, with the exception of Sixth Army's divisions inside Stalingrad itself, which received strong support in accordance with Hitler's personal orders. Also, because the struggling Caucasian armies constantly requested direct battlefield support, the frequency and scale of indirect support missions—primarily interdiction of Soviet rear areas—dropped considerably.

By early September, the army's wide dispersion across the width of the Caucasus and *Fliegerkorps IV*'s much-reduced complement left Richthofen unable to create even minor *Schwerpunkte* in that large region without first having to "borrow" units from *Fliegerkorps VIII.* With Hitler constantly demanding an intensification of effort at Stalingrad, against which Fiebig's air corps committed almost all its aircraft, Richthofen was seldom able to send units south. Even when he managed to divert units to the Caucasus, he had to dissipate their strength by committing half to each of the army's critical sectors: the forested hills around Tuapse, where Soviet defenders withstood Seventeenth Army's repeated attempts to break through to the Black Sea coast, and in the Terek bend, where First Panzer Army encountered fierce resistance as it tried to push through to Grozny.

Fliegerkorps VIII performed well against its primary target, Stalingrad, pounding it into rubble during heavy raids, but its continued bombardment of the ruins in accordance with Hitler's insistence that every street be cleared of the enemy led to a great waste of resources. For two months, Fiebig's units rained hundreds of tons of bombs on the ruins each day, turning small heaps of large rubble into large heaps of small rubble but achieving nothing substantial. This was neither Fiebig's nor Richthofen's fault. Hitler wanted Stalingrad taken, and he insisted that all efforts be directed to that end. Even after he realized that the oil fields could not be gained in 1942 and ordered Richthofen to destroy them from the air, he still insisted that the destruction and capture of Stalingrad remained his highest priority. Thus, the air fleet commander was unable to commit strong bomber forces to the destruction of the oil fields. In fact, he could only temporarily reduce the bombardment of Stalingrad and send bomber forces south when bad weather at Stalingrad curtailed operations there. Even then, he lacked sufficient bombers to conduct major raids against the most important installations. As a result, although he occasionally inflicted substantial damage on a few refineries and oil fields, particularly at Grozny, he never succeeded in crippling Soviet oil production.

With the benefit of hindsight, it is now reasonable to argue that Richthofen's air fleet could have dealt the Soviet economy a major blow, from which it would have taken at least several months to recover, if it had unloaded as many bombs on Baku as on Stalingrad. Heavy damage to that oil metropolis, which alone accounted for 80 percent of all Soviet production, was possible during August and September. Richthofen still possessed a strong bomber force and airfields within striking range, and the *VVS*'s presence in the Caucasus was still relatively weak. By October, when Hitler finally ordered attacks on oil fields, Richthofen's bomber fleet was much reduced and most forward airfields had been badly damaged by *VVS* forces, which were now far stronger. The opportunity had been missed.

Of course, such arguments are the luxury of historians with hindsight allowing them vantage points not possessed by the participants themselves. The reality is that Hitler wanted Stalingrad captured more than he wanted oil fields destroyed (or even captured, judging by his decision to send Fourth Panzer Army from the Caucasus to Stalingrad in July and his subsequent unwillingness to reinforce his Caucasian armies). He therefore insisted on the continued heavy bombing of Stalingrad, despite its having limited strategic or tactical value. Until he personally raised it to prominence by trumpeting its "great importance" on several occasions to the German public, the city's propaganda value was nil.

Hitler's concentration of forces at Stalingrad left Army Group B's long flanks dangerously exposed, particularly the section held by Rumanians northwest of the city. Hitler was well aware of this, but he believed that Stalingrad's quick capture would release sufficient forces to reinforce them. Even after Stalingrad proved far more costly and time-consuming to take than he previously thought, he refused to break off the attack, preferring to demand renewed effort and dribble in the few reinforcements available. This was his second major mistake of the campaign. Before Sixth Army could finish off Stalingrad, the Soviets launched the very attack that he had feared. It was not the Führer's last mistake, however. Even after the Soviets broke through the Axis flanks on either side of Stalingrad, trapping Sixth Army and other formations, Hitler refused to allow Paulus to withdraw from the Volga. Wanting to avoid the humiliation of abandoning the city he had publicly vowed to hold, he made one of his most ill-considered decisions thus far in the war: after receiving rash promises from the Luftwaffe's chief of staff, he ordered Sixth Army, which he extravagantly renamed "Fortress Stalingrad," to form a "hedgehog" defense and wait for relief. It would be sustained by an airlift operation, he declared.

Almost immediately, *Luftflotte 4* ceased to be a regular combat command, instead becoming something it was hopelessly equipped to function as: an air supply command. Well over half its aircraft, joined by hundreds of additional transport planes sent from other theaters (many of them unsuited to their new task), flew supply and escort missions in support of the encircled forces. However, this fleet did not include the 250-odd transport planes tied down in the Tunisian campaign, evidence of Hitler's limits as a strategist. Establishing rational priorities was one of his weaknesses, and it was seldom manifest more clearly than during this critical period. Tunisia was of negligible strategic value compared with the Don-Donets region. Yet he continued pouring scores of thousands of well-trained and well-equipped men into the former, squandering almost twenty-five air transport squadrons in the process, while Soviet forces rolled back the main German line and tightened their grip on Sixth Army. Those 250 planes would have greatly benefited Fiebig's airlift, constantly plagued by shortages of operational aircraft. Almost all of them Ju 52s, they could have replaced many of the bombers struggling as makeshift transporters.

Combat units not directly involved in the airlift, subordinated at times to makeshift tactical commands, proved incapable of retaining air superiority or preventing Soviet advances along the entire southern front. *Luftflotte 4*'s leaders worked energetically to ensure that all missions, airlift and combat, provided the best possible results. Under the circumstances, however, good results were impossible. Despite the drive and determination of Richthofen, his senior commanders, and Milch (whose administrative talents produced improvements in the airlift), *Luftflotte 4* could not overcome poor suitability for its designated tasks, its loss of established airfields and forced used of inadequate landing strips, its loss of air superiority, and its high attrition rate (caused primarily by bad weather but also by *VVS* attacks and strong flak). As a result, the air fleet failed to sustain Sixth Army or prevent the southern front from being rolled back.

Finally, *Luftflotte 4*'s campaign against naval targets, both vessels and bases, needs to be discussed. Although they never involved the commitment of more than 20 percent of the fleet's aircraft (and sometimes only 5 or 10 percent), antinaval missions occurred continuously throughout most of the period under study. Even before Richthofen's *Fliegerkorps VIII* transferred to the Crimea late in April 1942, specialist antinaval commands operated against Vice Admiral Oktyabrskii's Black Sea Fleet. First *Sonderstab Krim,* then *Fliegerführer Süd,* its successor, conducted daily *bewaffnete Seeaufklärung* (armed reconnaissance) sorties along the Caucasus coast, paying careful attention to Soviet ports and naval bases, around Crimean coasts, and over the eastern reaches of the Black Sea. They used guns, torpedoes, or bombs to attack any warships and merchant vessels discovered plying those waters; when weather, fuel, and ammunition stocks permitted, they conducted raids on naval bases.

Neither *Sonderstab Krim* nor *Fliegerführer Süd* was strong enough to sink many vessels or heavily damage naval bases, but their efforts produced results far outweighing the small scale of their deployment. Their constant presence and intermittent damaging and sinking of vessels were sufficient to persuade the overcautious Soviet admiral to keep his large warships in port except for occasions when weather or darkness provided them with reasonable cover. They also prompted him to curtail naval bombardment missions against German targets along Crimean coasts. More important, fearing the loss of capital ships to the Luftwaffe, Oktyabrskii attempted no further major landings on the Crimea.

Even after the powerful *Fliegerkorps VIII* arrived in the Crimea and Richthofen took over all air operations in the region, no change of operational emphasis occurred. Richthofen committed virtually all his aircraft to the annihilation of Soviet resistance at Kerch and Sevastopol, leaving only *Fliegerführer Süd* (from which he transferred various units for operations against ground targets as part of his own air corps) to combat the Soviet fleet. This orientation, consistent with the concept of *Schwerpunktbildung,* is understandable: believing that success or failure in the Crimea depended on the result of the army's campaigns, and determined to bring them to quick and successful conclusions, he threw his air force's full weight behind the army's efforts. Only when success at the *Schwerpunkte* looked imminent did he divert units to assist *Fliegerführer Süd* in its antishipping missions, which were, after all, peripheral to the decisive campaign.

Nonetheless, *Fliegerführer Süd* performed well, due mainly to Wild's capable leadership. He demanded great effort and aggression from all his units, carefully coordinated their operations with the small Axis naval flotillas that arrived in the region, and himself practiced small-scale *Schwerpunktbildung.* Realizing that he lacked sufficient aircraft to interdict most shipping traffic in the eastern Black Sea and unwilling to dissipate his forces in the attempt, he instead concentrated them against what he perceived to be the single most critical point: the sea-lanes leading into Sevastopol. Their constant attacks on vessels attempting to slip into the fortress, often made in conjunction with sorties by German and Italian light warships, inflicted little material damage but proved effective nonetheless: they caused Oktyabrskii to reduce, and finally stop, supply missions by surface vessels. After mid-June, only submarines attempted the perilous journey, carrying far less cargo than surface ships had. Thus, *Fliegerführer Süd* contributed substantially to the success of the sea blockade that slowly but surely severed the fortress's lifeline.

When the fortress fell, Wild immediately concentrated his units against Novorossiisk and other Caucasian naval bases. They were joined on those missions by numerous bombers and Stukas of *Fliegerkorps VIII* (temporarily under Wild's command), which damaged ports and sank several warships. However, Wild could deploy those reinforcements against the Soviet fleet for only a few days before having to send them north to the Kursk area, where they again came under Richthofen's direct control. Still, following their departure, *Fliegerführer Süd* successfully kept the Soviet fleet under constant surveillance and regular attack, ensuring that it undertook no major operations in the region. Its light but steady pressure not only kept all large warships penned up in Poti and Batumi, where strong flak defenses offered them protection, but also limited the number of coastal shelling missions carried out by destroyers and light vessels.

Although this was a notable achievement, considering *Fliegerführer Süd*'s small complement, by the middle of August Richthofen—who had never shown interest in the antishipping operations—no longer considered the Soviet fleet a major danger. *Fliegerführer Süd*'s aircraft were needed elsewhere, he reasoned, particularly in support of First Panzer and Seventeenth Armies. He therefore disbanded Wild's command, incorporating all units into Pflugbeil's *Fliegerkorps IV*. Air attacks on ports and vessels continued on a steadily reduced scale until mid-November, when the Soviets launched their immense counteroffensive on either side of Stalingrad. After the air fleet chief transferred all combat planes from the Caucasus to that critical sector, antishipping operations ceased for good (except for limited reconnaissance missions). Consequently, Oktyabrskii's fleet became increasingly active. By February 1943, when the Stalingrad airlift ended in failure, it was clear that the Luftwaffe's antinaval campaign had also failed: Soviet warships were again pounding Crimean, Ukrainian, and, on occasion, Rumanian coastlines and attacking Axis supply convoys.

THE AFTERMATH

Hitler's major summer campaign had ended in disaster, and Milch, Manstein, and Richthofen feared that they would become targets of bitter accusations. They did not. At various times, Hitler thanked and commended all three for their efforts. Milch was first to be pleasantly surprised. He left for Hitler's headquarters early on 3 February, accompanied by Hube. They arrived that same evening.[4] To Milch's consternation, the Führer sent for Hube and ordered the airman to wait.

Hitler still trusted the panzer general implicitly, his favorable opinion strengthened by a letter that Below, his Luftwaffe adjutant, had shown him a few days earlier. Written by Winrich Behr, one of the adjutant's relatives trapped at Stalingrad, the letter described conditions within the pocket, as well as Sixth Army's commanders.[5] Next to Paulus's name, the officer had placed a question mark, while next to Schmidt's and Seydlitz's names he had scrawled: "Should be shot!" Next to Hube's name, however, he had written: *"The Man!"* Hitler was very impressed, telling Zeitzler that the letter confirmed he had acted wisely when ordering the Luftwaffe to fly Hube out of the pocket.[6] In the evening of 3 February, the Führer asked Hube whether Milch's management had improved the airlift, to which the general replied that Milch had done everything in his power, "and more." He described Milch's efforts at length, adding (with considerable exaggeration) that if Milch had arrived at the front two weeks earlier, the Luftwaffe would probably have managed to sustain Sixth Army. "That," regretted Hitler, "is a judgement on me."[7]

After discharging Hube, Hitler then warmly welcomed Milch to his quarters and thanked him profusely for his efforts, which, he said, would have made a big difference to the airlift had they come sooner. For that, he was himself responsible. According to Milch's unpublished memoirs, he did not raise the matter of

Hitler's leadership of the armed forces. He nonetheless shocked Hitler by announcing that, had he been Paulus, he would have disobeyed orders and commanded his army to break out of the pocket.[8] The Führer replied that he would then have been obliged to lay Milch's head at his feet. The latter retorted that his life in exchange for an entire army was a worthwhile sacrifice. Although this comment displeased the Nazi leader, he apparently dismissed it as nothing more than evidence of the stress Milch was under. He bore no grudge toward Milch. Indeed, he commented to his closest advisers several times in the next few weeks that he now wished he had sent for Milch earlier. His opinion was reinforced by a formal "experience report" on the airlift submitted by Hube on 15 March, in which the general wrote (again exaggerating):

> If he had been sent out earlier, *Feldmarschall* Milch and his staff would have decisively influenced the [air] supply of Fortress Stalingrad. His measures needed an initial period of 10 to 14 days to take full effect. Had he been in charge from [the beginning of] Stalingrad's encirclement (23.11.42), the effect would have been fully felt after the middle of December at the latest. And, if the [air] supply were maintained, the fortress could have been held for many months to follow.[9]

Next, Hitler welcomed Manstein to his headquarters on 6 February. The dictator turned on his considerable charm, probably aware from Schmundt that the field marshal intended to request him to step down from the post of commander in chief of the army, appointing an experienced and trustworthy general instead. After thanking Manstein for his outstanding efforts, Hitler promptly disarmed him by admitting unreservedly that he was solely responsible for the destruction of Sixth Army: "I *alone* bear the responsibility for Stalingrad! I could perhaps put part of the blame on Göring by saying that he gave me an incorrect picture of the Luftwaffe's supply capabilities. But I personally appointed him as my successor, so I cannot blame him for Stalingrad."[10]

Hitler's frank admission impressed the field marshal, who later wrote that it "struck a chivalrous note." Hitler, he added, certainly appeared to be "deeply moved by the tragedy, not only because it revealed the failure of his own leadership, but also because he was very affected in a personal sense by the fate of soldiers who, because of their faith in him, had fought right to the end with courage and devotion to duty."[11] Hitler displayed the "utmost composure" during their four-hour meeting. After promising to consider his arguments carefully and with an open mind, he listened attentively to Manstein's suggestions about the conduct of future operations in southern Russia. When he insisted that Manstein continue holding the whole industrial area of the Donets Basin, the latter argued that a withdrawal from at least the region east of the Mius River was essential. If he tried to retain that region, he maintained, he would probably lose both Army Group Don and the whole of the basin. Hitler reluctantly agreed that he could withdraw to the Mius. Pleased that he had won a decision from Hitler and flattered by his relative intimacy and congeniality, the field marshal avoided tackling him on the issue of his leadership of the armed forces. Instead, he weakly suggested that Hitler should appoint a competent and trustworthy chief of staff, whom he could invest with authority over the three service branches. Hitler quickly brushed this off, pointing out that Göring, as the only *Reichsmarschall* in Germany, would never submit to anyone's authority but his. Also, his own experiences with armed forces supreme commanders had never been satisfactory. It was better that he remain in charge himself.

Richthofen was disappointed when Manstein recalled the meeting a few days later. "The Führer had been calm and composed," he wrote in his diary on 8 February, "and Manstein was visibly heartened. Of course, the question of another type of command or command organization was never brought up, although that was exactly what Manstein wanted."[12] Richthofen then lectured the field marshal on the need to keep a tighter grip on his panzer divisions, to execute short, sharp raids, destroying the enemy piece by piece, and to reduce the size of his rear area organization. It was pointless having divisions of 12,000 men, he said, if only 600 actually fought in the front line. He had been impressed by new Soviet command systems, involving tight command, small rear area organizations, and a strong front. "We must finally go over to that type of thing ourselves," he insisted. Manstein agreed wholeheartedly but maintained that his generals would invariably do the opposite. He couldn't do anything about it, he complained. Amused by this response, Richthofen "told him calmly that in my youth I had once heard a rumor that in military affairs it was possible to issue *orders.*" The field marshal took the jibe lightheartedly, he added.[13]

Finally, Richthofen arrived at Hitler's headquarters on 11 February, after spending a day conferring with Göring and Jeschonnek about coming air operations in southern Russia. Well aware that Richthofen blamed him for the Stalingrad disaster, which had cost Hitler an army and "torn the guts" out of both *Luftflotte 4* and the air transport fleet, the *Reichsmarschall* protested lamely that he had been given little choice; the Führer had clearly wanted to keep Sixth Army on the Volga and expected the Luftwaffe to keep it fully operational. He could not have refused. Anyway, at that time he expected the encirclement to be temporary. It probably would have turned out fine, he claimed, had the Italians not collapsed, allowing the Russians to roll back the German front and deprive the Luftwaffe of its forward airfields. Richthofen snapped back that the disaster began before the Italian line collapsed, and that the *Reichsmarschall* would know more about events and conditions at the front if he had actually risked going there in person. "If you can't trust your lucky star for your personal safety," he said, "then you have no right to believe that destiny has called you for greater things."[14] A lengthy argument ensued, during which Göring insisted that he had tried to reason privately with Hitler on many occasions but could not challenge him publicly because that would "endanger" the Führer's authority. Richthofen—who later admitted to "playing the strong man"—replied that he saw things differently.[15] The *Reichsmarschall* did not challenge Hitler but always agreed with him because he was scared of the Führer's wrath. Naturally, Göring "energetically denied this."

Before Richthofen spoke with Hitler on 11 February, Göring, clearly worried that the air fleet commander would blame him for the disaster, asked him whether he intended to be as frank with Hitler as he had been with him. Richthofen replied coolly that he had "no inhibitions whatever."[16] As it happened, he refrained from attacking Göring. He did ask Hitler (whom he found to be "very serious, but decidedly charitable") when and why he had promised to supply Sixth Army by air. Hitler admitted—as noted previously—that he had made his initial promise without Göring's knowledge but "with the qualification that it would be possible only if supply conditions did not deteriorate."[17] Trying to distance himself from the airlift's poor record, the Führer added: "Through bad weather and the forced abandonment of the forward airfields, that promise became invalid." He did not hold Richthofen accountable, of course. On the contrary, he had followed the air fleet commander's operations and efforts with satisfaction and complete faith in his abilities.

When he asked Richthofen what he thought of Manstein, the airman immediately sensed that someone had been trying to poison the Führer against the field marshal. He suspected Jodl and Keitel, who feared that Hitler would replace one or both of them with this gifted soldier. Richthofen replied that Manstein was clearly "the best tactician and operational commander we have" but bluntly added that he, like other commanders, "must be given tactical freedom to act as their own local experience dictates."[18] Taking a swipe at Hitler's leadership style, he boldly insisted that it was wrong to "lead them by the scruff of the neck as though they were children." The Führer indignantly replied that, had he not kept his generals under close guidance, "they would be fighting in Germany by now." Richthofen refuted this, stating: "If you can't trust your most important figures, you must replace them." Perhaps referring again to the airlift, Hitler shortly afterward complained that he was constantly let down by his closest advisers, who reported dishonestly and did little else. Clearly with the airlift in mind, Richthofen replied that "this is of no interest either to us at the front or to future historians." As commander in chief, he pointed out, the Führer alone was responsible for the success or failure of operations. There was no point in cursing or blaming his advisers. Hitler frowned disapprovingly but remained quiet, inwardly admiring the air leader's frankness and unable to challenge the truth of his comments.

Indeed, the Führer liked men of Hube's and Richthofen's ilk: committed National Socialists, aggressive commanders, inspiring leaders, forthright advisers, loyal followers. Although he had sworn never to create another field marshal, Hitler announced on 15 February, four days after Richthofen had bluntly told him that he bore ultimate responsibility for Stalingrad, that he was promoting the airman to *Generalfeldmarschall*. Richthofen received official confirmation of his elevation the next day, when Below rang to congratulate him and pass on the Führer's best wishes.

Richthofen had mixed feelings about his promotion. An ambitious and arrogant man, he was deeply gratified by this elevation to the highest of ranks. He was also proud of the way *Luftflotte 4* had performed since Operation *Blau* began seven months earlier. His generals had displayed not only fortitude and tenacity under the worst circumstances but also vigor and resourcefulness. His troops—air, ground, and flak—had performed their duties effectively and courageously, working to the utmost of their abilities in conditions that were seldom favorable but frequently hostile. He was proud to accept promotion on their behalf.

On the other hand, his promotion could not compensate for what he believed to be the needless depletion of his air fleet. Before the Soviets launched their November counteroffensive, the High Command had constantly forced *Luftflotte 4* to perform duties that greatly overtaxed its limited resources. Richthofen had grudgingly accepted that as a normal feature of military life. But in November, the High Command had totally ignored his repeated protests and appeals, and those of his generals, and given *Luftflotte 4* responsibility for a massive airlift operation that it could not possibly carry out successfully, even with the additional resources made available. As a result, he had lost a thousand brave young men and hundreds of aircraft. The air fleet was now depleted, disorganized, and demoralized, and, as a consequence, needed extensive rehabilitation. However, it was already engaged in major operations in the Donets Basis and northwestern Caucasus. Its recovery looked uncertain, as did its ability to perform its new tasks effectively.

RECOVERY

When *Blau* began in June 1942, the eastern air fleets had possessed 2,644 aircraft, of which 1,610 (61 percent) operated in the southern front under *Luftflotte 4*. The operational rate of that air fleet had been 71 percent, good by the standards of the eastern front. By 31 January 1943, the day on which Paulus trudged into Soviet captivity, marking the end of Hitler's grandiose plans for southern Russia, the state of the eastern air fleets had deteriorated markedly. They now possessed only 1,657 aircraft (excluding transport planes), of which Richthofen's *Luftflotte 4* commanded a mere 624 (37 percent).[19] That is, after seven months of constant combat, the fleet's complement had dropped to 39 percent of its former strength. Because of bad weather and the frequent evacuation of airfields, its operational rate had also dropped dramatically. On the day Paulus surrendered, the air fleet had only 240 airworthy planes, its operational rate having fallen from 71 to 38 percent.[20]

Because so many transport groups had been sent to *Luftflotte 4* for the airlift, the fleet now possessed a vast transport armada of 477 planes, excluding regular corps transport squadrons.[21] The majority of its transports were Ju 52s, but it also had three He 111 groups and a Ju 88 group. However, for reasons described at length in the previous chapter, their operational rate was even worse than that of the fleet's combat groups. Only 146 transports, or 30 percent, were airworthy on 31 January 1943. The bomber groups deployed on transport duties during the airlift had suffered badly, due mainly to adverse weather and the poor runways in the pocket, which caused many to crash during landing. Fifty-two of the Fifty-fifth Bomber Wing's He 111s had survived the airlift, for example, but only 12 (23 percent) were now operational. Similarly, 66 of the Twenty-seventh Bomber Wing's He 111s had survived, but only 18 (27 percent) were fit for operations.

The human cost was no less important than the matériel. Few of Richthofen's supply, service, and maintenance personnel, airmen, or flak troops had been able to enjoy even brief periods of rest and recuperation behind the front, let alone take home leave, during the last seven months. Some had been in continuous combat even longer, having fought in the Kerch and Sevastopol campaigns before going straight into operations for *Blau*. Thus, not only were aircraft operational rates very low, but the troops were exhausted and suffering stress. Morale had dropped, reaching a low point in the last days of January and the first of February, when the airlift's failure resulted in Sixth Army's destruction.

Aware that Manstein would need effective air support if he were to stop Soviet advances and rebuild the southern front, and that Fiebig would need extra aircraft if he were to carry out a new supply mission planned for the northwestern Caucasus, Richthofen was determined to raise his air fleet's strength as soon as possible. Unfortunately, because of steady Soviet gains, he could give his air fleet no time to catch its breath. Even before Stalingrad fell, he began reorganizing *Luftflotte 4* for its new tasks. On 20 January, he ordered *Oberst* Kühl to transfer all He 111s not used for transport duties from the vulnerable, makeshift Novocherkassk airfield, east of Rostov, to much better fields at Stalino, 180 kilometers to the northwest.[22] He also ordered *Oberstleutnant* von Beust, the He 111 combat commander at Voroshilovgrad, to withdraw his groups to Konstantinovka, eighty kilometers due west. Fiebig organized the transfers. Not only were Stalino's and Konstantinovka's airfields far safer from enemy air and ground attack, but they were established airfields, constructed on a permanent basis more than a year earlier. They had excellent runways, hangars, and maintenance and repair facilities. They were also connected by both rail and road to the main German supply centers in the Ukraine, unlike Novocherkassk and the other improvised airfields closer to the front. Now that the Don front had been pushed back and the two German armies in the Caucasus were withdrawing toward the northwest, these airfields were again within combat range. Therefore, the He 111 groups could support operations in the Don-Donets sector as well as in the northwestern Caucasus, while enjoying far better service and maintenance facilities than they had recently experienced.

As the airlift drew to a close during the last week of January, Richthofen requested the return to regular combat missions of some of the He 111 groups then performing transport missions. On 23 January, Hitler approved the return of thirty He 111s to combat operations, stipulating that they were only to be "borrowed" temporarily from the airlift.[23] As it happened, those bombers never returned to transport duties. They were deployed against Soviet forces attacking Fourth Panzer Army's right flank and then against Soviet troops attempting to prevent Seventeenth Army's withdrawal toward the Taman Peninsula. Richthofen did not "borrow" only those thirty, however. Realizing by 24 January that Sixth Army's destruction within days was certain, he began quietly removing a few He 111 squadrons from transport duties each day, redeploying them in a combat role. He sent them back to the established airfields around Stalino and Konstantinovka, where their operational rates soon began to pick up.

Kleist's Army Group A was withdrawing from the Caucasus in accordance with Hitler's reluctant permission. Mackensen's First Panzer Army was pulling back toward Rostov, its divisions retreating faster than the pursuing Soviet forces (lacking sufficient fuel and adequate logistical systems) could follow. Ruoff's Seventeenth Army had withdrawn its forward units from the Caucasus mountain passes. It was now steadily disengaging the bulk of its forces from the enemy and, along with two divisions of First Panzer Army, withdrawing toward the Taman Peninsula. To the consternation of *Admiral Schwarzes Meer*, which lacked sufficient naval forces to protect its coasts,[24] Hitler wanted Seventeenth Army to form a bridgehead on that peninsula. He believed that occupation of the peninsula was an essential prerequisite for the maintenance of security in the Crimea and along the northern coastline of the Sea of Azov. He also believed that the bridgehead—which the Germans called *Gotenkopf* (Goth's Head)[25]—would create a jumping-off point for future operations in the Caucasus, and that it would signal to Turkey that Germany still had a foothold in Asia. On 23 January, the Führer ordered that the bridgehead should be "kept as small as possible."[26] The significance of this is obvious: he planned to evacuate most of Seventeenth Army to the Crimea and the southern Ukraine, leaving only enough forces to form and hold a secure bridgehead on the Taman Peninsula. The Luftwaffe, aided to a small degree by *Admiral Schwarzes Meer*, would have to supply and evacuate scores of thousands of soldiers. As Richthofen and Kleist agreed when they discussed the Führer's plans that same day, this was going to be a remarkably difficult task under the circumstances.[27]

On 25 January, Richthofen gave Fiebig's *Fliegerkorps VIII*, whose supply operation at Stalingrad was drawing to a close, the tasks of supplying the *Gotenkopf* and "evacuating the strongest elements of Seventeenth Army" to the Crimea, to the Taganrog area, or to Rostov, using Ju 52s as they became available, Ju 90s, FW 200s, and the gliders Milch had ordered for Stalingrad but never used.[28] The organization for this new air transportation operation should be set up immediately, he told Fiebig, so that they could begin within days (presumably as soon as

Sixth Army fell). He anticipated the daily transportation of 2,000 of Ruoff's men from the northwestern Caucasus to airfields in the Crimea and along the northern coast of the Sea of Azov.

Fiebig was skeptical of his air corps' ability to transport so many men, noting in his diary that "the changeable weather" would dictate whether his boss was being too optimistic.[29] Still, he attacked the task with typical energy, working long hours to formulate an effective command structure, flying to Kleist's headquarters to discuss the coming operation and methods of ensuring close interservice cooperation, and regularly communicating by phone with Richthofen on important matters. On 27 January, he met the air fleet commander in Mariupol, only to learn that Ju 52s could not be removed from the Stalingrad airlift for the time being. Fiebig agreed wholeheartedly that the Ju 52s "must do their duty there first."[30] They would be free for the new operation soon enough.

By 29 January, Fiebig and *Oberstleutnant* von Heinemann, his capable chief of staff, had set up a command structure for the airlift, now called *Lufttransporteinsatz Krim* (Air Transport Mission Crimea), and drawn up "special supply arrangements" for the operation.[31] Its tasks were clear-cut:

> After 29 January, *Fliegerkorps VIII* takes over, along with the air supply of Fortress Stalingrad, and in close agreement with Army Group A and Seventeenth Army:
>
> a) Transportation of troops and wounded from the region east of the Kerch Straits to the Crimea;
>
> b) Shipment of supplies (especially vehicle fuel) from the Crimea, as well as from airfields north of the Sea of Azov, to the region east of the Kerch Straits.[32]

The following day (30 January), Fiebig issued to his air corps an "Order for the Assembly and Deployment [of Forces] for the Evacuation of the Operational Zone of Army Group A and the Supply of the Western Caucasus."[33] His He 111s, FW 200s, Ju 90s, and Ar 232s would operate from the excellent Crimean airfields at Saki and Sarabus, and his Ju 52s from the equally good fields at Taganrog and Mariupol. All glider units would operate from Bagerovo, on the Kerch Peninsula. The supply and evacuation bases in the northwest Caucasus would be Krasnodar, Timashevskaya, and Slavyanskaya. On Richthofen's instructions, these substandard airfields were already being hastily expanded and improved by signals teams and labor battalions from *Luftgau Rostov*. They were joined by labor battalions from *General der Flieger* Dessloch's *Luftwaffengruppe Kaukasus* (Air Force Group Caucasus), the principal air command in the Caucasus for the last two months.[34] Finally, both *Fliegerkorps VIII* and Army Group A would have their headquarters in the Crimean town of Simferopol, where they would carefully oversee the operation "with the closest cooperation."[35]

Thus, Fiebig was ready to begin. All he had to wait for—but was certainly not looking forward to—was Sixth Army's surrender or destruction, which would release the bulk of the transport groups he had earmarked in his directive for the new operation. Late on 31 January, he received the news he had been dreading: Paulus had surrendered and Sixth Army was no more. He had no time to mourn, however. Milch immediately ordered the cessation of Ju 52 missions to Stalingrad and turned all Ju 52s and FW 200s over to Richthofen.[36] The latter promptly notified Fiebig that he had ordered their transfer to established and well-equipped bases in the Crimea and at Taganrog and Mariupol, and that his operation should start the next morning. Fiebig flew to his new headquarters in Simferopol, grieving for Sixth Army but ready to commence his "difficult new task: the evacuation of Seventeenth Army."[37]

While Fiebig was preparing for his new air transport operation, Richthofen continued reorganizing the rest of his fleet. He began rebuilding Pflugbeil's *Fliegerkorps IV,* then committed in support of Hoth's Fourth Panzer Army and the remnants of Fourth Rumanian Army, which were pulling back across the Manych River toward the lower Don. Despite being greatly weakened in October and November 1942 to provide the maximum concentration of forces for Stalingrad, Pflugbeil's air corps had performed relatively well during December and the first weeks of January 1943. It was time for a major refit, however, especially as Richthofen wanted to use *Fliegerkorps IV* more effectively now that *Fliegerkorps VIII,* once the Luftwaffe's best close-support force, was again to be used for an air transport operation. "The future task of *Fliegerkorps IV,*" he told that air corps' staff on 25 January, "will be to work in the region southeast of Rostov with all its forces. To that end, I will strengthen the corps with a destroyer wing and allow most of the 51st Bomber Wing to return to the corps."[38] He also initiated a replacement and rehabilitation program for Pflugbeil's units. Although it involved only a gradual removal of a few squadrons per week for rest and refit, it steadily improved *Fliegerkorps IV*'s strength, operational rate, and, not least, morale.

On 27 January, Richthofen renamed Dessloch's *Luftwaffengruppe Kaukasus* as *Luftwaffengruppe Kuban* (Air Force Group Kuban), in order to reflect more accurately its operational area, which was steadily contracting as German forces pulled out of the Caucasus or withdrew to the Taman Peninsula (in the Kuban region). Richthofen actually planned to take Dessloch's command out of the Caucasus altogether. It would provide flak, reconnaissance, and fighter assistance during Seventeenth Army's withdrawal to the Kuban, but then, once the army had established a solid bridgehead on the Taman Peninsula, its staff would move to the southern Ukraine, where it would rebuild *Luftflotte 4*'s disorganized flak forces.[39] Its few fighter and reconnaissance planes would be subordinated to Fiebig's *Fliegerkorps VIII.* A newly constituted 9th Flak Division would take over flak defense of the Kuban bridgehead.[40] *Generalmajor* Pickert was already rebuilding this division from fresh battalions and the remnants of his previous division of the same name, the bulk of which had perished at Stalingrad. He would add to his new flak division the elements of *Luftwaffengruppe Kuban* remaining on the Taman Peninsula. Realizing that Pickert's new division would lack heavy batteries and searchlights, Richthofen requested the *OKL* to send the extra guns, equipment, and personnel that Pickert would need.

Fliegerdivision Donez was the only other command subordinate to *Luftflotte 4*. Since Richthofen had formed this makeshift close-support command on 2 January, placing it under *Generalleutnant* Mahnke, it had functioned virtually independently. With little interference (or advice) from Richthofen or his air fleet staff, Mahnke's fighters, dive-bombers, and ground-attack planes had been active against Soviet forces attacking *Armeeabteilung Hollidt* (Army Detachment Hollidt) in the Don-Donets region. Richthofen had never been happy with *Fliegerdivision Donez*'s performance, however, although he blamed its perceived poor showing on its commanders' lack of experience, not lack of effort or courage. On 20 January, for example, he had privately noted that the air division "plunges into everything possible. The staff have hardly any experience. They handle many things too heavily, other things too lightly, and still have a lot to learn."[41] In the beginning of February, therefore, he transferred *Fliegerdivision Donez* from its poor airfields at Shakhti to better fields at Gorlovka, near Stalino, 170 kilometers to the northwest.[42] He then subordinated it to Pflugbeil's *Fliegerkorps IV,* in the hope that the air corps' experienced commander would improve its effectiveness.[43] This move would also help strengthen and tighten up the chain of command, which had, he felt, become disorderly during the near-chaotic last few months. He also initiated a rest and refit program for Mahnke's units, which (as elsewhere) gradually improved their strength, operational rates, and morale.

Thus, by the time German resistance at Stalingrad ceased on 2 February, Richthofen had already begun rebuilding his depleted air fleet. He had started pulling bomber units out of the Stalingrad airlift and preparing them for new combat missions; he had transferred other units from poor and threatened airfields at the front to established fields farther to the west, where their operational rate began climbing as a result of better shelter and supply and maintenance facilities; he had initiated the transfer of transport units from the improvised and crowded airfields that had poorly served them during the Stalingrad airlift to established and less congested fields in the Crimea and southern Ukraine; he had started returning to Pflugbeil's air corps some of the units he borrowed during previous months for operations at Stalingrad; he had placed *Fliegerdivision Donez,* which he believed had been poorly handled, at better fields and under Pflugbeil's capable command; and he had initiated a replacement and rehabilitation program. These steps, coupled with a major rehabilitation effort during February, steadily better weather conditions, and the many improvements made by Milch, would soon result in a rapid rise in operational rates and, correspondingly, in markedly improved combat effectiveness.

BACK IN ACTION

By the beginning of February, First Panzer Army had successfully escaped from the Caucasus through the Rostov bottleneck and been transferred to Manstein's Army Group Don. The latter's forces had clung for so long to exposed positions around Rostov, desperate to prevent the bottleneck being pinched off before Mackensen's army could escape, that their own chance for safe withdrawal was jeopardized. Unlike so many "last stands" elsewhere, Manstein's efforts achieved a useful purpose. By the narrowest of margins, the evacuation of First Panzer Army from the Caucasus denied the Soviets a huge prisoner haul. Seventeenth Army had also escaped encirclement. While Manstein was desperately trying to prevent the entire Don-Donets front from collapsing under the weight of numerically superior Soviet forces, Seventeenth Army commenced a systematic withdrawal of all units toward the Kuban. By the beginning of February, most of the army had reached the Kuban, where a strong bridgehead had been established.

Thus, Soviet forces had rolled the German line back to slightly west of its position when *Blau* first began. Making steady gains in the central Donets region during the first days of February, they looked set to roll the line back even farther, right to the Dnieper River. This prompted Hitler to disband Weichs's Army Group B on 12 February, transferring the bulk of its forces to Manstein's Army Group Don.[44] He renamed the field marshal's command Army Group South, in order to reflect more accurately its expanded operational area, which now stretched from north of Kharkov, which was now threatened, to the Crimea and Taman Peninsula. The following day, the Führer emphatically ordered that "Kharkov is to be held at all cost."[45] In order to attain the best possible air support for Manstein's forces along their newly extended front, the High Command subordinated to Richthofen's air fleet another complete air command: Günther Korten's *Luftwaffenkommando Don,* which had supported the army northeast of Kharkov since its formation as an independent air command late in July 1942.[46] *Luftwaffenkommando Don* would revert to the status of an air corps and, with its headquarters at Poltava, take over operations in *Luftflotte 4*'s northern combat zone. It possessed adequate forces for this task, although it was slightly heavy on bombers and light on dive-bombers.[47] Pflugbeil's *Fliegerkorps IV,* with its headquarters about to move to Dnepropetrovsk,[48] would operate in the central sector, while its subordinate command, *Fliegerdivision Donez,* would operate in the southern.

On 16 February, Hitler was shocked to learn that German troops had been compelled to withdraw from Kharkov and that Soviet forces were advancing in strength toward Pavlograd and Dnepropetrovsk. He was furious with Manstein for allowing the "abandonment" of Kharkov and failing to hold back the Soviet tide, which had now pushed his armies back well behind the line it held before *Blau* commenced. On Zeitzler's advice, he decided to fly to the field marshal's headquarters at Zaporozhye the next day in order to insist in person that he retake Kharkov as soon as possible and rebuild that section of the front.[49] Manstein held his ground, insisting that the Soviets were overextended, many formations being over 320 kilometers from their supply bases. His own troops, on the other hand, were close to railheads and logistical centers. *Generalleutnant* Hauser's Second SS Panzer Corps was intact, he explained, and Hoth's Fourth Panzer Army had undergone partial rehabilitation since its failure to relieve Paulus's army. Now was not the time to carry out a localized attack to liberate Kharkov; instead, it was time to launch a larger counteroffensive aimed at rebuilding the entire southern front. It would be necessary to throw back Soviet forces threatening the Dnieper crossings, even if it meant pulling Hauser's SS corps out of the Kharkov region for the time being. Only then, once they had crushed Soviet forces attempting to cut into *Armeeabteilung Hollidt*'s and First Panzer Army's rear areas, and pushed the enemy back to the Donets, should they attack Kharkov. After two days of fierce debate, during which time the Führer was able to hear the faint sound of Soviet artillery fire less than forty kilometers away, he finally relented and authorized Manstein to carry out his bold counterstroke.

Despite the danger of being overrun by steadily approaching Soviet forces, Richthofen ordered the transfer of his headquarters from Mariupol to Zaporozhye on 16 February.[50] The next day he flew by Storch to that town on the Dnieper, arriving only an hour after the Führer. His staff arrived by train two days later. Richthofen's motive for transferring his command to threatened Zaporozhye is clear: if he and Manstein were to blunt the Soviet advance, regain strategically important territory, and rebuild a strong southern front, they must work closely on all coming operations. That is precisely what happened. Repeating liaison practices that had proved effective in the past, the two commanders immediately set about creating joint *Schwerpunkte* and coordinating their operations.

In the meantime, however, Richthofen was concerned for Zaporozhye's safety. The constant sound of gunfire revealed that Soviet forces were perilously close. Therefore, the air leader was delighted to learn that a Luftwaffe officer had already thrown a strong protective cordon around the town. On his own initiative, Dessloch, who had been rebuilding the *I. Flak-Korps* in the region since his departure from the Caucasus, arranged for almost 200 flak guns to be positioned in front of the town.[51] Richthofen praised him for his efforts, assuring him that he would personally accept responsibility for the loss of any weapons, but only if the gunners fought to the last round. The next day, the Führer personally appointed one of his new favorites to command "Bridgehead Zaporozhye." To Richthofen's satisfaction, it was another Luftwaffe officer: the newly promoted *Generalmajor* Stahel, whose recent heroic defense of the Chir and breakout from a Soviet encirclement had endeared him to Hitler.[52]

Manstein's troops launched their counteroffensive on 20 February. Because of the field marshal's outstanding tactics and leadership, the operation went superbly. In a series of swift armored maneuvers, Manstein's two panzer armies attacked the surprised and overextended Soviet formations, several of which had been immobilized by fuel shortages. The assault units of Hoth's Fourth Panzer Army, primarily Hauser's SS divisions, inflicted heavy damage on the Soviet Sixth and First Guards Armies advancing from the Izyum region. They quickly destroyed the spearheads threatening Dnepropetrovsk, retook Kharkov on 15 March and Belgorod three days later, then formed a solid front along the northern Donets. The entire Kharkov region was back in German hands. In the southeast, meanwhile, Mackensen's First Panzer Army was able to cut off and destroy much of the Soviet armored force commanded by Lieutenant General M. M. Popov, who proved no match for Manstein in these battles of fast maneuver. Popov was barely able to save his forces on the lower Donets before the advent of muddy weather brought German offensive operations to a halt.

Hitler was very pleased. Manstein's army group now securely held the entire Donets front from Belgorod down to the line of the Mius River. These Donets and Mius fronts together formed the line that German forces had held before *Blau* began nine months earlier. Not only had Manstein recaptured considerable territory, including Kharkov (of economic and propaganda value), but he had dealt heavy and humiliating blows to enemy forces whose rapid successes in December 1942 and January 1943 had resulted in a dissipation of their strength and an overextension of their supply lines. Manstein had also regained the strategic initiative, prompting the Führer, no longer smarting from the losses he had himself suffered in recent months, to begin talking optimistically of a new summer campaign in the east.

Manstein made no mention in his memoirs of *Luftflotte 4*'s contribution to his counteroffensive. Most historians of these battles have been equally ignorant. For example, a recent thorough account of the field marshal's campaigns in this period fails to mention Richthofen or the Luftwaffe even once.[53] Yet Richthofen's air fleet played a decisive role in the outcome of Manstein's counteroffensive. The air commander deployed elements of all his commands during the operation, except for Fiebig's *Fliegerkorps VIII,* which was busy with its own air supply missions in the Crimea and Kuban regions. Richthofen initially deployed *Fliegerdivision Donez* in support of *Armeeabteilung Hollidt,* battling along the Mius River against Soviet forces attempting to unhinge the entire southern front by driving across the Mius, along the northern coast of the Sea of Azov, and up toward Dnepropetrovsk.[54] Under Pflugbeil's guidance, Mahnke's air division provided the army with good support, striking not only Soviet troops, vehicles, and installations on the battlefield but also supply columns, logistical centers, and march routes behind the front. Pflugbeil's *Fliegerkorps IV* performed the lion's share of close air support duties, effectively supporting First and Fourth Panzer Armies as they engaged Soviet forces extended toward Pavlograd, then supporting their drive north toward Kharkov. Korten's *Luftwaffenkommando Don*— now renamed *Fliegerkorps I*—operated in the Kharkov region, supporting the makeshift operational command headed by *General der Panzertruppe* Kempf.

When the final assault on Kharkov commenced in the first week of March, both *Fliegerkorps I* and *IV* supported the army, coordinating their operations through close and constant liaison with each other, as well as with local army commanders.

Luftflotte 4's various air commands performed very well during these operations, Richthofen's preparatory efforts having paid off handsomely. The measures he had taken in January to enlarge his fleet's complement and improve its operational rate resulted in substantial improvements to both. When Manstein's counteroffensive began, *Luftflotte 4* possessed 928 aircraft, over 300 more than it had at the end of January.[55] A total of 493 (54 percent) were now operational, a rise of 16 percent in three weeks. These figures do not even include Korten's units, which gave *Luftflotte 4* an additional 198 airworthy planes (from a complement of 314) to deploy against the Red Army.[56] The air fleet's much-improved strength naturally resulted in a dramatic rise in the number of sorties made. During January, the fleet had managed only around 350 sorties per day, but throughout Manstein's counteroffensive, it achieved an average of 1,000 per day. It was like old times. Richthofen wrote excitedly on 22 February: "We made over 1,500 sorties. The Russians were stopped everywhere and suffered heavy losses."[57]

The air leader deployed his units according to his usual practices. He personally directed major air attacks after consulting carefully with relevant army generals and his own air corps commanders, between whose headquarters he flew each day in his Storch. In order to avoid dissipating his strength, he concentrated units in mass at certain *Schwerpunkte,* often deploying units from two or more air commands against single targets. Shortly after the war, Wing Commander Cyril March, editor and principal author of the British Air Ministry's study of Luftwaffe operations, accurately summed up Richthofen's effective leadership during this period:

> The major success of the German counter-attack, the recapture of Kharkov on March 15th, was achieved essentially by a concentration of attack by ground and air forces. . . . There is no disputing the skill with which von Richthofen handled the forces under his command. . . . The main factor behind von Richthofen's success . . . was extreme flexibility, coordination and concentration—the latter secured by the formation of temporary *ad hoc* battle groups to support the spearheads of attack by military formations, such as the SS Division Reich which led the assault on Kharkov. "Massive concentration," "drastic concentration," "concentration of all forces to the highest degree," were phrases which resounded through *Luftflotte 4*'s battle orders.[58]

March added that Richthofen's air fleet played "an important—perhaps a decisive part" in Manstein's successful counteroffensive.

Meanwhile, Fiebig's air supply operation was also going very well. His transports flew short distances to the Taman Peninsula from established fields with good supply and maintenance facilities. The weather was generally favorable, and they had adequate fighter protection. As a result, they managed to carry far larger quantities of supplies to Seventeenth Army than they had ever managed to carry to Paulus's doomed forces at Stalingrad. By 28 February, Fiebig's transports had evacuated 50,000 men from the northwestern Caucasus to the Crimea and the Ukraine,[59] and were unloading within the Kuban bridgehead a daily average of 500 tons of fuel, ammunition, and rations (enough to have kept Sixth Army operational) and evacuating around 2,000 men. Some days they airlifted as many as 700 tons of supplies and evacuated an impressive 5,000 men.[60]

Thus, by the middle of March 1943, *Luftflotte 4* had made an astonishing recovery from its badly depleted and exhausted state only six weeks earlier, when its attempt to supply the Stalingrad pocket finally proved hopeless. Richthofen deserves much credit for this fine performance. Paying tribute to his recent reconstruction efforts, Wing Commander March concluded that the energy with which *Luftflotte 4*'s operations in February and March 1943 were directed and executed "showed that, even after the disasters of the previous two months, the Luftwaffe was still a factor to be reckoned with."[61] From then until its final demise, Soviet airmen—indeed, airmen in all the Allied nations—treated the Luftwaffe with wary respect. Nevertheless, the peak of its power was past. It came no closer to providing Hitler with his philosopher's stone.

Notes

PREFACE

    1. For the effect of the defeat on Hitler's allies, see J. Förster's *Stalingrad: Risse im Bundnis 1942/43,* Einzelschriften zur militärischen Geschichte des Zweiten Weltkrieges 16 (Freiburg: Rombach, 1957).

    2. A good treatment of Stalingrad historiography and the lasting effects of that battle on the collective memory of Germans and Russians is W. Wette and G. R. Ueberschär, eds., *Stalingrad: Mythos und Wirklichkeit einer Schlacht* (Frankfurt am Main: Fischer Taschenbuch, 1992); also J. Förster, ed., *Stalingrad: Ereignis-Wirkung-Symbol* (Munich: Piper, 1992).

    3. There are several exceptions. Fritz Morzik's study of Luftwaffe transport units, for example, contains a useful chapter on the Stalingrad airlift; see Morzik, *Die deutschen Transportflieger im Zweiten Weltkrieg: Die Geschichte des "Fußvolkes der Luft"* (Frankfurt am Main: Bernard & Graefe, 1966).

    4. H. Plocher, *The German Air Force versus Russia, 1941,* USAF Historical Studies, No. 153 (USAF Historical Division, Research Studies Institute, Air University, 1965); *The German Air Force versus Russia, 1942,* USAF Historical Studies, No. 154 (USAF Historical Division, Research Studies Institute, Air University, 1966); *The German Air Force versus Russia, 1943,* USAF Historical Studies, No. 155 (USAF Historical Division, Research Studies Institute, Air University, 1967).

    5. H.-D. H. von Rohden, *Die Luftwaffe ringt um Stalingrad* (Wiesbaden: Limes, 1950); F. Kurowski, *Luftbrücke Stalingrad: Die Tragödie der Luftwaffe und der 6. Armee* (Berg am See: Kurt Vowinckel, 1983), and *Balkenkreuz und Roter Stern: Der Luftkrieg über Rußland 1941-1944* (Friedberg: Podzun-Pallas, 1984).

    6. USAFHRA 519.619-7 (14 August 1945): HQ, U.S. Strategic Air Forces in Europe (Rear), Office of the Historian, AAF Sta 390, APO 413, U.S. Army, "Questionnaire on GAF Doctrine and Policy: Answers by Gen. Maj. von Rohden (P.W.) and Col. Kriesche (P.W.) to Questions Submitted by Major Engelman."

7. *Notes on the German Air Force,* Air Ministry Publication 1928, 2nd ed., April 1943, 76.

1. HITLER'S UTOPIAN STRATEGY

1. USAFHRA 506.619A: SHAEF, Office of Assistant Chief of Staff, G2. Subject: Interrogation of Albert Speer, Former Reich Minister of Armaments and War Production. 5th Session—10.30 to 12.30 hrs, 30 May 1945.

2. F. Halder, *Kriegstagebuch: Tägliche Aufzeichnungen des Chefs des Generalstabes des Heeres, 1939-1942,* ed. H.-A. Jacobsen (Stuttgart: W. Kohlhammer, 1965), vol. 2, 50; cf. also W. Warlimont, *Im Hauptquartier der deutschen Wehrmacht, 1939 bis 1945* (Ausburg: Weltbild, 1990; first published by Bernard & Graefe, 1962), vol. 1, 126–129.

3. *Der Prozeß gegen die Hauptkriegsverbrecher vor dem Internationalen Militär-gerichtshof, Nürnberg, 14. Nov. 1945-1. Okt. 1946* (Nuremberg: Internationales Militär-tribunal in Nürnberg, 1947–1949), vol. 7, 290.

4. J. S. A. Hayward, "Hitler's Quest for Oil: The Impact of Economic Considerations on Military Strategy, 1941–42," *Journal of Strategic Studies* 18, no. 4 (December 1995): 94–135 (esp. 95, 129).

5. USAFHRA 142.0372: "Strategic Value of the Caucasus," [U.S.] *Air Forces General Information Bulletin, No. 3 (12 August 1942),* 14. For the population statistics of Baku (809,347 citizens in 1939) and the other major Transcaucasian cities, see USAFHRA K113.106-153: *Der Oberbefehlshaber der Luftwaffe, Führungsstab Ic/IV Nr. 3500/41 Geheim! Orientierungsheft: Union der Sozialistischen Sowjetrepubliken (U.d.S.S.R.) Stand 1.2.1941,* 9, 10.

6. *The United States Strategic Bombing Survey: Overall Report (European War) September 30, 1945,* 39; B. H. Klein, *Germany's Economic Preparations for War* (Cambridge, Mass.: Harvard University Press, 1959), 32.

7. *Overall Report,* 39.

8. *The United States Strategic Bombing Survey: The Effects of Strategic Bombing on the German War Economy. Overall Economic Effects Division, October 31, 1945,* 73.

9. W. Treue, "Hitlers Denkschrift zum Vierjahresplan, 1936," *Vierteljahrshefte für Zeitgeschichte* 3 (April 1955): 184–210.

10. R. C. Cooke and R. C. Nesbit, *Target: Hitler's Oil—Allied Attacks on German Oil Supplies, 1939-1945* (London: William Kimber, 1985), 16.

11. *Effects of Strategic Bombing,* 73, 74; *Overall Report,* 39.

12. Cf., for example, the projected totals for 1939–1944 in BA/MA RW 19/202: *Az 66 b 2134 WStb/W Ro III, Vortragsnotiz für Generalfeldmarschall Göring über Zielsetzung und Forderungen für die Weiterführung des Mineralöl-Bauprogramms, 31. Januar 1939,* in *Auszüge aus KTB, Wi Rü Amt/Stab (nur Mineralöl betreffend), Beginn 1.5.1940.*

13. Cooke and Nesbit, 16; *Effects of Strategic Bombing,* 74.

14. Ibid.

15. BA/MA RW 19/202: *Wi Rü Amt Stab Z/SR, den 16. Februar 1942: "Die deutsche Treibstoffversorgung im Kriege. Abgeschlossen um die Jahreswende 1941/42,"* in *Auszüge aus KTB, Wi Rü Amt/Stab (nur Mineralöl betreffend), Beginn 1.5.1940.* See also W. Deist, M. Messerschmidt, H.-E. Volkman, and W. Wette, *Germany and the Second World War* (Oxford: Clarendon Press, 1990), vol. 1, 361.

16. First source cited in note 15.

17. N. Rich, *Hitler's War Aims: Ideology, the Nazi State, and the Course of Expansion* (New York: Norton, 1992; first published in 1973), 188.

18. First source cited in note 15.

19. Doc. 134-C: *"OKW/WFSt. Nr. 8/41 gKdos. Chefs. Ausführungen des Führers am 20.1.1941,"* IMT, vol. 34, 469. See Hitler's earlier comments to Ciano on the danger to the Ploesti refineries: "Conversation with the Fuehrer in the Presence of the Reich Foreign Minister, von Ribbentrop, Salzburg, 18th November 1940," in G. Ciano, *Ciano's Diplomatic Papers,* ed. M. Muggeridge and trans. S. Hood (London: Odhams Press, 1948), 408.

20. Cooke and Nesbit, 64.

21. R. Muller, *The German Air War in Russia* (Baltimore: Nautical and Aviation Publishing Company of America, 1992), 69.

22. Cf. V. Hardesty, *Red Phoenix: The Rise of Soviet Air Power, 1941–1945* (Washington, D.C.: Smithsonian Institution Press, 1982), 217; R. A. Kilmarx, *A History of Soviet Air Power* (New York: Praeger, 1962), 177

23. C. Tugendhat and A. Hamilton, *Oil: The Biggest Business* (London: Eyre Methuen, 1968), 114; first source cited in note 15.

24. *Overall Report,* 40; *Effects of Strategic Bombing,* 76; Tugendhat and Hamilton, 114.

25. Cooke and Nesbit, 17.

26. F. W. Deakin, *The Brutal Friendship: Mussolini, Hitler and the Fall of Italian Fascism* (London: Weidenfeld and Nicolson, 1962), 164, 180; cf. Halder, vol. 2, 421 (20 May 1941).

27. K. Reinhardt, *Die Wende vor Moskau: Das Scheitern der Strategie Hitlers im Winter 1941/2,* Beiträge zur Militär- und Kriegsgeschichte, Band 13 (Stuttgart: Deutsche Verlags-Anstalt, 1972), 117.

28. Ibid., 118 n. 95.

29. USAFHRA 512.607: "The Fuel Position of the German Air Force," *AMWIS No. 129, Up to 1200—18th February 1942,* 19.

30. Halder, vol. 3, 222.

31. Cf. BA/MA RW 19/199 for the *Wi Rü Amt*'s monthly situation reports, which detail Rumania's supply problem. See especially *Wi Rü Amt Stab Z/SR Nr. 86/42 gKdos, Berlin, den 9. Januar 1942: Kriegswirtschaftlicher Lagebericht Nr. 28, Dezember 1941;* and *Wi Rü Amt Stab Z/SR, Nr. 686/42 gKdos, Berlin, den 13. März 1942: Kriegswirtschaftlicher Lagebericht Nr. 30, Februar 1942.* Also, for a very detailed analysis of the German-Rumanian oil situation in 1941, see BA/MA RW 19/178: *Deutsche Wehrwirtschaftmission in Rumänien, Ch.d. St. Tagb. Nr. 226/41 gKdos, Bukarest, den 8. Dezember 1941: An das OKW/Wi Rü Amt, Berlin, Bericht Nr. 15, über die Tätigkeit der Deutschen Wehrwirtschaftmission in Rumänien vom 20. September 1941 bis 20. November 1941.*

32. First source cited in note 15. Cf. also the detailed monthly statistical reports sent by the *Reichstelle für Mineralöl* to *Kapitän zur See* Gabriel, *OKW/Wi Rü Amt* (in BA/MA RW 19/2695).

33. Reinhardt, 118; H. Boog et al., *Der Angriff auf die Sowjetunion* (Frankfurt am Main: Fischer Taschenbuch, 1991), 1131.

34. Reinhardt, 118.

35. BA/MA RW 19/177: *Adjutant Amtchef Wi Rü Amt, Akten-Notiz über Besprechung bei Gen. Qu. am 30.8.1941.*

36. BA/MA RW 19/177: *Wi Rü Amt Az. 11 k 2209 Ro Vs., Nr. 3241/41 gKdos, Berlin, den 7. Oktober 1941: Stand der Mineralölversorgung im 4. Vierteljahr 1941 ausgehend von der Lage am 1.10.1941.*

37. Ibid.

38. *Report of the C.-in-C., Navy, to the Fuehrer at Wolfsschanze in the Afternoon of November 13, 1941,* published in H. G. Thursfield, ed., "Fuehrer Conferences on Naval Affairs, 1939-1945," *Brassey's Naval Annual, 1948* (London: William Clowes, 1948), 235-243.

39. Ibid.

40. *Report of the C.-in-C., Navy, to the Fuehrer in Berlin on December 12, 1941,* in Thursfield, 244-246.

41. BA/MA RW 19/177: *Wi Rü Amt/Chef des Stabes, gKdos, Berlin, den 24. Oktober 1941, Ergebnis der Besprechung bei Gen. Qu. am 22.10.1941.*

42. Warlimont, vol. 1, 200.

43. Halder, vol. 3, 192.

44. P. E. Schramm (general ed.), *Kriegstagebuch des Oberkommandos der Wehrmacht (Wehrmachtführungsstab) 1940-1945* (Frankfurt am Main: Bernard & Graefe, 1961) (hereafter cited as *KTB OKW*), vol. 1, 1063-1068.

45. H. Guderian, *Erinnerungen eines Soldaten* (Heidelberg: Kurt Vowinckel, 1951), 182.

46. Reinhardt, 177.

47. Ibid.

48. D. Irving, *Hitler's War* (London: Papermac, 1977), 348.

49. Reinhardt, 178.

50. Halder, vol. 3, 319.

51. Ibid., 295.

52. Ibid., 328, 330.

53. *Weisung Nr. 39,* in W. Hubatsch, ed., *Hitlers Weisungen für die Kriegführung 1939-1945: Dokumente des Oberkommandos der Wehrmacht* (Frankfurt am Main: Bernard & Graefe, 1962), 171-174.

54. Halder, vol. 3, 330 (see also 350).

55. USAFHRA K113.309-3 vol. 1: *Der Führer und Oberste Befehlshaber der Wehrmacht Nr. 442182/41 gKdos. Chefs./WFSt./Abt. L (I op.), F.HQu., den 16.12.1941.*

56. Marshal A. M. Vasilevskii, "Between Moscow and Stalingrad," in *Stalin and His Generals: Soviet Military Memoirs of World War II,* ed. S. Bialer (London: Souvenir Press, 1970), 402; see also J. Erickson, *The Road to Stalingrad: Stalin's War with Germany, vol. 1* (London: Weidenfeld, 1993; first published in 1975), 335; and A. Seaton, *Stalin as Warlord* (London: B. T. Batsford, 1976), 143ff.

57. Vasilevskii, "Between Moscow and Stalingrad," 404.

58. Cf. E. F. Ziemke, "Operation Kreml: Deception, Strategy and the Fortunes of War," *Parameters: Journal of the U.S. Army War College* 9, no. 1 (1979): 72-83; E. F. Ziemke and M. E. Bauer, *Moscow to Stalingrad: Decision in the East* (Washington, D.C.: Center of Military History, 1987), 328-330, 342, 400; W. Görlitz, ed., *Keitel: Verbrecher oder Offizier. Erinnerungen, Briefe, Dokumente des Chefs OKW* (Göttingen: Musterschmidt, 1961), 298-299. D. M. Glantz, *Soviet Military Intelligence in War* (London: Frank Cass, 1990), 61.

59. G. L. Weinberg, *A World at Arms: A Global History of World War II* (Cambridge: Cambridge University Press, 1994), 297.

60. Vasilevskii, "Between Moscow and Stalingrad," 404.

61. "General Staff of the Red Army—Collection of Materials for the Study of War Experience, Number 6," published as *Battle for Stalingrad: The 1943 Soviet General Staff Study,* ed. L. C. Rotundo (Washington, D.C.: Pergamon-Brassey's, 1989), 22.

62. USAFHRA 142.0422-13: War Department General Staff, Military Intelligence Division, G-2, Washington: Memorandum [dated 26 March 1942] for the Assistant Chief of Staff, WPD: Subject: The German Offensive Against Russia, 6.

63. Erickson, *Road to Stalingrad,* 336.

64. G. K. Zhukov, *From Moscow to Berlin: Marshal Zhukov's Greatest Battles* ed. H. E. Salisbury and trans. Shabad, War and Warriors Series (Costa Mesa, Calif.: Noontide Press, 1991), 99.

65. Ibid., 119.

66. Vasilevskii, "Between Moscow and Stalingrad," 405.

67. H.-A. Jacobsen, *1939-1945: Der Zweite Weltkrieg in Chronik und Dokumenten* (Darmstadt: Wehr & Wissen, 1961), 288.

68. Ziemke and Bauer, 286.

69. For example, see Goebbels's diary for 20 March 1942, in R. G. Reuth, ed., *Joseph Goebbels—Tagebücher, Band 4: 1940-1942* (Munich: Serie Piper, 1992), 1767ff.

70. M. Domarus, *Hitler: Reden und Proklamationen, 1932-1945,* (Leonberg: Pamminger & Partner, 1988; first published in 1965), vol. 2, 1826.

71. Görlitz, *Keitel: Verbrecher,* 298.

72. Cf. Warlimont, vol. 1, 241.

73. Guderian, 343.

74. Reinhardt, 256-257.

75. Jacobsen, 690.

76. *"Der Führer und Oberste Befehlshaber der Wehrmacht Nr.: 1/42 gKdos OKW/ WFSt/Org. Wi. Rü Chefs,"* in *KTB OKW,* vol. 2, 1265-1267.

77. Jacobsen, 690.

78. Figures from Table 37, in *Effects of Strategic Bombing,* 75.

79. Source cited in note 4, 133.

80. "Telegram, Marshal Antonescu to Adolf Hitler, December 5, 1941," published as Doc. No. 549 in *Documents on German Foreign Policy, 1918-1945 Series D Volume XIII: The War Years June 23, 1941-December 11, 1941* (London: HMSO, 1964), 963-964.

81. "Record of the Conversation between the Reich Foreign Minister and Rumanian Deputy Minister President Antonescu in Berlin on November 28, 1941," published as Doc. No. 513 in *Documents on German Foreign Policy,* 873; see also Docs. 505, 519.

82. "Record of Ion Antonescu's Conference with Ribbentrop, 12 February 1942" (Doc. USSR-233), IMT, vol. 7, 326.

83. Editor's commentary in "Fuehrer Conferences on Naval Affairs," 274.

84. G. Ciano, *Ciano's Diary 1939-1943,* ed. M. Muggeridge (London: Heinemann, 1947), 431.

85. BA/MA RW 19/177: *Wi Rü Amt Az. 11 k 2209 Ro Vs., Nr. 3241/41 gKdos, Berlin, den 7. Oktober 1941: Stand der Mineralölversorgung im 4. Vierteljahr 1941 ausgehend von der Lage am 1.10.1941;* and figures from Table 39 in *Effects of Strategic Bombing,* 77.

86. Cf. Görlitz, *Keitel: Verbrecher,* 298, 299; W. Jochmann, ed., *Hitler, Monologe im Führerhauptquartier, 1941-1944* (Hamburg: Albrecht Knaus, 1980), 328, 329.

87. BA/MA RM 7/259: *Mar. Verb. Offz. zum OKH (Genst. d.H.) B. Nr. 29/42 gKdos. Chefs. An das Oberkommando der Kriegsmarine—1 Abt. Skl.—Berlin. Betr.: "Unternehmen Suez."*

88. First source cited in note 15.

89. BA/MA RM 7/395: *Oberkommando der Wehrmacht, Nr. 22 230/42 gKdos. Chefs., WFSt/Org., FHQu., den 6. Juni 1942: "Wehrkraft der Wehrmacht im Frühjahr 1942," gez. Warlimont,* 35–36.

90. Source cited in note 4, 134.

91. Ibid.

92. USAFHRA 180.642A vol. 2: *The Commander in Chief, Navy, and Chief, Naval Staff, to Naval Group South: 1/Skl I m 275/42 Gkdos. Chefs. 23 February 1942. Subject: Operations in the Black Sea.*

93. Cf. *Report to the Fuehrer made by the C.-in-C., Navy, on the Afternoon of February 13, 1942,* in "Fuehrer Conferences on Naval Affairs," 261–265.

94. Source cited in note 4, 134.

95. B. Wegner, "The Tottering Giant: German Perceptions of Soviet Military and Economic Strength in Preparation for Operation Blau, 1942," in *Intelligence and International Relations 1900–1945,* ed. C. Andrew and J. Noakes (Exeter: University of Exeter, 1987), 299–300; Ziemke and Bauer, 297.

96. *Weisung Nr. 41,* in Hubatsch, 183–188.

97. Weinberg, 411.

98. Halder, vol. 3, 361 (20 December 1941).

99. Görlitz, *Keitel: Verbrecher,* 280, 281, 299–301; A. Hillgruber, *Hitler, König Carol und Marschall Antonescu: Die deutsch-rümanischen Beziehungen 1938–1944 (Mainz: Veröffentlichungen des Instituts für europäische Geschichte, 1949).*

100. P. Carell, *Stalingrad: The Defeat of the Sixth Army* (Atglen, Pa.: Schiffer Military History, 1993), 22.

2. THE NEED TO "CLEAR UP" THE CRIMEA

1. BA/MA RM 7/259: *Bericht über Besprechung am 30.4.1942. Ort: Berghof. Diensttuender Adjutant: Generalmajor Schmundt. gKdos. Gegenstand: Der Führer bespricht die militärische Lage.*

2. Weinberg, 411.

3. *Ergänzung der Weisung 33,* in Hubatsch, 143.

4. USAFHRA K113.309-3 vol. 2: *Der Führer und Oberste Befehlshaber der Wehrmacht, OKW, WFSt/L, Nr. 441412/41, gKdos. Chefs., den 21.8.41, Weisungen an den Oberbefehlshaber des Heeres.*

5. *Ergänzung der Weisung 33,* in Hubatsch, 148; E. von Manstein, *Verlorene Siege* (Bonn: Athenäum, 1955), 214.

6. Ibid., 262.

7. Ibid., 225, 226. On Soviet numerical superiority on the ground, see ibid., 229.

8. Boog et al., *Der Angriff,* 755.

9. USAFHRA K113.309-3: *Auszug aus den Lageberichten Ob.d.L Ic* (reports 741 to 798, for late Sept.–Nov. 1941); Plocher, *1941,* 203.

10. USAFHRA 512.607: *AMWIS No. 115, Up to 1200–12th November 1941.*

11. Ibid., *No. 114, Up to 1200–5th November 1941*. On the use of the other ports as naval bases, see Admiral of the Fleet I. S. Isakov, *The Red Fleet in the Second World War,* trans. J. Hural (London: Hutchinson, n.d.), 69; Vice Admiral F. Ruge, *The Soviets as Naval Opponents, 1941–1945* (Cambridge: Patrick Stephens, 1979), 70–76.

12. Manstein, 214, 217.

13. Letter from Löhr to von Reichenau, dated 5 January 1942, in NARS T971/18/ 856–883: *Erfahrungen und Auswirkung beim Einsätze der Luftwaffe im Kämpfe um Festungen (Erläutert an dem Beispiel des Kampfes um Sewastopol im Juni 1942) (OKL, Chef Genstb. 8. Abt., Anlage zu Br.B. Nr. 1803/44 Geheim! Wien, am 16. Juni 1944).*

14. USAFHRA K113.309-3 vol. 3: *Deutsche Luftwaffenmission Rumänien I a Nr. 17/42 gKdos. Ia op 3 (LS), Bukarest, den 7.1.1942, "Einsatz der deutschen Luftschutzkräfte in Rumänien 1941";* Boog et al., *Der Angriff,* 1052, 1053; Isakov, 70, 78.

15. NARS T405/49/4888179: *Deutsche Luftwaffenmission Rumänien Qu.Br. Bericht Nr. 1572 gKdos. III. Ang., den 18. Juli 1941: "Belegungsübersichte Rumänien, Stand: 18.7.1941."*

16. R. Muller, "Germany's Satellite Air Forces: Coalition Air Warfare on the Eastern Front, 1941–1944" (paper presented to the Conference of the Society for Military History, Kingston, Ontario, May 1993).

17. BA/MA RL 9/62: *Deutsche Luftwaffenmission Rumänien Führ. Abt. Ia Nr. 1841/41, gKdos, Bukarest, den 14.12.1941. Betr.: Bericht über Luftverteidigung Ölgebiet Rumänien.*

18. First source cited in note 14.

19. "Conversation between Count Ciano and the Fuehrer, Field Marshal Goering, and the Reich Minister, von Ribbentrop, Berlin, 24–27th November 1941," in Ciano, *Ciano's Diplomatic Papers,* 463.

20. BA/MA RM 7/991: *Seekriegsleitung B. Nr. 1/Skl. I op. a 679/42 gKdos, Berlin, den 18. Januar 1942. Betr.: Rußische Seestreitkräfte in der Ostsee und im Schwarzen Meer.*

21. First source cited in note 14; Ruge, 78.

22. Halder, vol. 3, 178 (15 August 1941); V. Karpov, *The Commander,* trans. Y. Shirokov and N. Louis (London: Brassey's, 1987), 29.

23. For this stunning achievement, still ignored by (or unknown to) most Western historians, see Ruge, 64ff.; Isakov, 66ff.

24. Weinberg, 219; Manstein, 214. Hitler later commented, after the capture of the mighty Crimean fortress in July 1942, that "the fall of Sevastopol has roused the greatest jubilation in Ankara, and the hatred of the Turks for the Russians was given a free reign during the rejoicings"; *Hitler's Table Talk* (1 July 1942), 546.

25. *Weisung Nr. 39,* in Hubatsch, 171–174.

26. Manstein, 238, 239.

27. BA/MA RL 200/17: *Gen. von Waldau, Chef Fü St Lw, Persönl. Tagebuch* (hereafter cited as *Waldau TB*), 19 December 1941. For Oktyabrskii's appointment at this crucial time, see Karpov, 74.

28. See the radio message from the *IV. Fliegerkorps* to *Marine-Gruppenkommando Süd* and the *Marineverbindungsoffizier* to the *A.O.K. 11,* in BA/MA RM 35 III/19: *Kriegstagebuch des Marine-Gruppenkommandos Süd, für die Zeit vom 1.–15. Januar 1942* (hereafter cited as *KTB Mar. Gr. Süd*) 4 January 1942.

29. BA/MA RM 35 III/18: *KTB Mar. Gr. Süd, 16.–31. Dezember 1941: Lagemeldungen für 26–31 Dezember 1941; KTB OKW,* vol. 1, 861, 864, 868, 871. An excellent introduc-

tion to the planning and implementation of these operations is chapter 6 of the General Staff of the Red Army's 1943 *Collection of Materials on the Use of War Experience No. 5*, published as *Soviet Documents on the Use of War Experience. Vol. 3, Military Operations 1941-1942*, trans. H. S. Orenstein (London: Frank Cass, 1993); see also Ruge, 70–76; Erickson, *Road to Stalingrad*, 290, 291.

30. BA/MA RL 200/17: *Waldau TB*, 29 December 1941; BA/MA RM 7/115: *KTB, 1/Skl. Teil B IX: Lageübersicht, Mittelmeer-Ägäis-Schwarzes Meer, 16.12.–31.12.1941* and *1.–15.1.1942*.

31. Ruge, 73.

32. BA/MA RM 35 III/19: *KTB Mar. Gr. Süd, 1.–15. Januar 1942*. The radio message appears in the entry for 4 January 1942.

33. BA/MA RL 200/17: *Waldau TB*, 29 December 1941.

34. Halder, vol. 3, 333 (8 December 1941).

35. BA/MA RM 35 III/18: *KTB Mar. Gr. Süd, 16.–31. Dezember 1941*, 21 December 1941.

36. BA/MA RL 200/17: *Waldau TB*, 2 January 1942; Boog et al., *Der Angriff*, 623, 625. Sponeck was later court-martialed and sentenced to death by firing squad. At Manstein's request, Hitler stayed the execution and later commuted the sentence to seven years in prison. He was finally executed after the 20 July 1944 bomb plot.

37. Karpov, 78.

38. USAFHRA K113.106-153 vol. 12: *Sonderstab Krim (V. Fliegerkorps) unterstützt die 11. Armee bei der Bereinigung der Lage auf der Krim bei Feodosia;* Ruge, 73; *KTB OKW*, vol. 2, 205.

39. USAFHRA 512.607: *AMWIS No. 123, Up to 1200-7th January 1942*. See F. H. Hinsley, *British Intelligence in the Second World War* (London: HMSO, 1981), vol. 2, 22, 25–26, 28, 58, 60, 69, 99ff.

40. *Soviet Documents on the Use of War Experience, vol. 3*, 136, 137.

41. Source cited in note 38.

42. Ibid.; Kurowski, *Balkenkreuz*, 262, 263.

43. USAFHRA K113.309-3 vol. 3: *Gliederung der Luftflotte 4 (fliegende Verbände), Stand: 20.6.1941, kurz vor Beginn des Ostfeldzuges;* USAFHRA K113.309-3 vol. 3: *Gliederung der Luftflotte 4 (fliegende Verbände), Stand: 1.11.1941, Kampf um die Krim und gegen Rostow;* USAFHRA K113.309-3 vol. 3: *V. Fliegerkorps im Osten Abschnitt VI (V. Fl.K.) Von der Schlacht von Kiew bis zu den Kämpfen um Rostow, 22.9.–30.11.41*, 98; Boog, *Der Angriff*, 754, 773, 774.

44. Ibid., 773; D. Irving, *Göring: A Biography* (London: Macmillan, 1989), 334, 335.

45. Reinhardt, 100, 144.

46. BA/MA RL 8/49: *VIII. Fliegerkorps, Rußland-Feldzug: Mittelabschnitt II. Teil-1941, ab 28.9.41. Zusammengestellt von H. W. Deichmann, Oberst a.D., damaliger Adjutant des VIII. Fl. K. an Hand von Aufzeichnungen, Umfragen und Tagebuch-Aufzeichnungen des Gen. Feldmarschalls Dr. ing. Frhr. v. Richthofen*, 29 and 30 November 1941; USAFHRA K113.309-3 Vol. 1: *Der Führer und Oberste Befehlshaber der Wehrmacht Nr. 442182/41 gKdos. Chefs./WFSt./Abt. L (I op.), F.HQu., den 16.12.1941*, and *Auszug aus Fernschreiben OKW, FWSt./Abt. L (I op.) Nr. 442243/41 gKdos. Chefs.*, 24 *Dezember 1941;* Halder, Vol. 3, 350 (16 December 1941).

47. BA/MA RL 8/72: *Gen. Kdo. VIII. Fliegerkorps: Unterstützung des Abwehrkampfes der 4. Pz. Armee und 9. Armee während der russischen Winteroffensive Jan.–März 1942* (various documents); Boog et al., *Der Angriff*, 760.

48. USAFHRA K113.309-3 vol. 3: *Gliederung der Luftflotte 4 (fliegende Verbände), Stand: 1.12.1942, Kampf am Mius;* USAFHRA K113.309-3 vol. 6: *Befehls = u. Unterstellungsverhältnisse Luftwaffe-Heer, Osten, Januar 1942.*

49. USAFHRA K113.309-3 vol. 1: *Schlacht- und Gefechtsbezeichnungen des Feldzuges gegen die Sowjetunion vom 21.6.41 bis etwa 31.12.42,* 4.

50. An excellent source of information on the activities of the *IV. Fliegerkorps* during this period is the war diary of *Mar. Gr. Süd* (BA/MA RM 35 III/18: *KTB Mar. Gr. Süd, 16.-31. Dezember 1941*), which contains numerous references to the outstanding support this air corps gave to both the small German Black Sea Fleet and Manstein's troops. See also NARS T971/18/652-662: *Die Kampfhandlungen im Osten während des Jahres 1942 (Chef Genstb. der Luftwaffe, 8. Abt., 1944);* NARS T971/51/522-534: *Der Luftkrieg in Rußland 1942 (Chef Genstb. der Luftwaffe, 8. Abt., 1944),* 9; Plocher, *1941,* 216; Boog et al., *Der Angriff,* 755.

51. *Soviet Documents on the Use of War Experience, vol. 3,* 142; for the sinking of Soviet transport ships, cf. NARS T971/18/652-662: *Die Kampfhandlungen im Osten während des Jahres 1942 (Chef Genstb. der Luftwaffe, 8. Abt., 1944).*

52. USAFHRA 512.607: *AMWIS No. 124, Up to 1200-14th January 1942;* Plocher, *1942,* 166.

53. Ruge, 72, 73.

54. USAFHRA K113.309-3 vol. 6: *Kämpfe auf der Krim, Jan.-Febr. 1942, Lage 23.1.42 abds.;* Manstein, 233.

55. BA/MA RL 200/17: *Waldau TB,* 16 January 1942. Halder was also delighted with the attack's initial progress, as his diary for 15 January reveals.

56. BA/MA RL 8/188: *Luftwaffenstab Krim IVb: KTB, 17. Januar 1942-16 Mai 1943;* USAFHRA K113.106-153 vol. 12: *Der Feldzug im Osten 1941-1945. Viertes Buch: Der Einsatz der deutschen Luftwaffe im Osten 1942,* 29.

57. Plocher, *1942,* 160; USAFHRA K113.309-3 Vol. 3: *Gliederung der Luftflotte 4 (fliegende Verbände), Stand: 1.12.1942, Kampf am Mius.*

58. Plocher, *1942,* 104-107; W. Dierich, *Kampfgeschwader "Edelweiss": The History of a German Bomber Unit, 1935-1945* (London: Ian Allan, 1975), 67, 68; C. Bekker, *Angriffshöhe 4000: Ein Kriegstagebuch der deutschen Luftwaffe, 1939-1945* (Gräfelfing vor München: Urbes Verlag Hans Jürgen Hansen, 1964), 358.

59. USAFHRA KII3.309-3 vol. 6: *Übersicht über die fliegenden Verbände an der Ostfront am 10.1.42.*

60. Ibid.

61. BA/MA RL 2 III/713: *Vortrag über die Einsatzbereitschaft der fliegenden Verbände, Stand: 21.6.1941, GenSt. Gen.Qu. 6. Abt. (I) vom 24.6.1941;* BA/MA o. S., 234: *Wandtafeln des Ob.d.L, Stand: 20.6.1941;* BA/MA RH 11 III/32: *Kriegsgliederung "Barbarossa," Stand: 18.6.1941, OKH GenStdH./Op. Abt. (III) (o.D.), Prüf-Nr. 1581.*

62. NARS T971/51/522-534: *Der Luftkrieg in Rußland 1942 (Chef Genstb. der Luftwaffe, 8. Abt., 1944),* 9; and USAFHRA K113.309-3 vol. 5: *Einsatz der Luftwaffe während der ersten Monate des Jahres 1942,* 1.

63. Manstein, 249. For the sinking of several ships in Feodosiya and Kerch harbors, see *Einsatz der Luftwaffe während der ersten Monate des Jahres 1942.*

64. H. Doerr, "Der Ausgang der Schlacht um Charkow im Frühjahr 1942," *Wehrwissenschaftliche Rundschau, Heft 1, Januar 1954,* 9, 11.

65. NARS T971/51/522-534: *Der Luftkrieg in Rußland 1942 (Chef Genstb. der Luftwaffe, 8. Abt., 1944),* 9.

66. USAFHRA K113.106-153 vol. 12: *Der Feldzug im Osten, 1941–1945. Viertes Buch: Der Einsatz der deutschen Luftwaffe im Osten 1942*, 35.

67. BA/MA RL 200/17: *Waldau TB*, 24 January 1942.

68. Manstein, 250–251.

69. Erickson, *Road to Stalingrad*, 329; Isakov, 85; Ruge, 77.

70. Manstein, 250.

71. Plocher, *1942*, 166.

72. Ibid.

73. Source cited in note 65, 23.

74. Plocher, *1942*, 167.

75. Plocher, *1941*, 176.

76. M. Salewski, *Die deutsche Seekriegsleitung 1935–1945; Band III: Denkschriften und Lagebetrachtungen 1938–1944* (Frankfurt am Main: Bernard & Graefe, 1973), 163, 164.

77. Boog et al., *Der Angriff*, 762; *Report of the C.-in-C., Navy, to the Fuehrer on the Afternoon of February 4, 1941*, in "Fuehrer Conferences on Naval Affairs," 174–179.

78. Ibid., 182–190.

79. *Conference of the Chief, Operations Division, Naval Staff with the Chief, Operations Division, O.K.W., General Jodl, on November 4, 1940*, in "Fuehrer Conferences on Naval Affairs," 146–149.

80. S. Lawlor, *Churchill and the Politics of War, 1940–1941* (Cambridge: Cambridge University Press, 1994), 165ff.

81. Isakov, 67.

82. Ruge, 63.

83. *Report by the C.-in-C., Navy, to the Fuehrer on March 18, 1941, at 1600*, in "Fuehrer Conferences on Naval Affairs," 182–190.

84. Salewski, vol. 3, 167; Thursfield, Rear Admiral H. G., ed., *Brassey's Naval Annual, 1943* (New York: Macmillan, 1943), 205.

85. BA/MA RM 7/938: *Mar. Gr. Süd Operationsstab B. Nr. 55/42 gKdos Chefs., Berlin, den 16. Februar 1942: Studie über die Seeaufgaben im Schwarzen Meer*. For the Bulgarian fleet's strength in 1941 and 1942, see Thursfield, *Brassey's Naval Annual, 1943*, 198; D. W. Mitchell, *A History of Russian and Soviet Sea Power* (London: Andre Deutsch, 1974), 405.

86. In June 1941, the Soviet Black Sea Fleet comprised:

1 battleship	23,000 tons	23 knots	12 305-mm guns
2 new cruisers	8,000 tons	33 knots	9 180-mm guns
1 modernized cruiser	8,000 tons	30 knots	4 180-mm guns
2 cruisers	6,900 tons	30 knots	15 130-mm guns
3 flotilla leaders	2,900 tons	36 knots	4 130-mm guns
10 destroyers	different types		130-mm guns
47 submarines	250 to 1,080 tons		

84 MTBs and numerous smaller warships, including fast gunboats
The Naval Air Arm, with 626 aircraft (about half of them fighters)

Source: Ruge, 63; V. I. Achkasov and N. B. Pavlovich, *Soviet Naval Operations in the Great Patriotic War, 1941–1945* (Annapolis: Naval Institute Press, 1981), 19.

87. A. Grechko, *Battle for the Caucasus*, trans. D. Fidlon (Moscow: Progress Publishers, 1971), 61.

88. BA/MA RL 8/35: *Über Einsatz und Erfolge des IV. Fliegerkorps gegen Schiffs-ziele im Schwarzen Meer und gegen Stadt und Hafen von Odessa in der Zeit vom 21.8. bis 20.10.1941.*

89. Ibid.

90. Ibid.; USAFHRA K113.309-3 Vol. 1: *Auszugsweise Abschrift aus dem Kriegstage-buch der Seekriegsleitung (1. Abt.) Teil A: Heft 22 vom 1.-30. Juni 1941.*

91. USAFHRA K113.309-3 Vol. 1: *Der Luftkrieg im Osten gegen Rußland 1941 (Chef Genstb. der Luftwaffe, 8. Abt., 1943/44).*

92. P. C. Smith, *Stuka Squadron: Stukagruppe 77—the Luftwaffe's "Fire Brigade"* (Wellingborough, Northampton: Patrick Stephens, 1990), 102-104.

93. Source cited in note 20.

94. Erikson, "Soviet Submarine Operations," 169.

95. Ruge, 77.

96. *Report to the Fuehrer made by the C.-in-C., Navy, the Afternoon of February 13, 1942,* in "Fuehrer Conferences on Naval Affairs," 261-265.

97. "Record of the Conversation Between the Führer and Italian Foreign Minister Count Ciano in Berlin on November 29, 1941," published as Doc. No. 522 in *Documents on German Foreign Policy, Series D Vol. XIII,* 900-903.

98. See *Empire Parliamentary Association Report on Foreign Affairs for October, No-vember and December, 1941* (vol. 22, no. 4), 465.

99. BA/MA RM 7/115: *KTB, 1/Skl. Teil B IX: Lageübersicht, Mittelmeer-Ägäis-Schwarzes Meer, 15.10.-31.10.1941* and *1.11.-15.11.1941.*

100. These problems were not confined to the navy; the air force and army missions in Rumania experienced identical difficulties. See J. Hixson and B. F. Cooling, *Combined Operations in Peace and War,* rev. ed. (Carlisle Barracks, Pa.: U.S. Army Military History Institute, 1982), 206-207; Generalmajor a.D. B. Müller-Hillebrand, *Germany and Her Allies in World War II: A Record of Axis Collaboration Problems* (MS No. P-108, Historical Divi-sion HQ, United States Army, Europe, 1954), part 1, 52-77, 96-101.

101. Ibid., part 1, 127.

102. *Empire Parliamentary Association Report on Foreign Affairs for July, August and September, 1941* (vol. 22, no. 3), 304-305.

103. BA/MA RM 7/115: *KTB, 1/Skl. Teil B IX: Lageübersicht, Mittelmeer-Ägäis-Schwarzes Meer, 1.-15.1.1942.*

104. First source cited in note 85.

105. BA/MA RM 7/991: *Seekriegsleitung B. Nr. 1/Skl 313/42 gKdos Chefs., Berlin, den 9. Februar 1942. Niederschrift über die Besprechungen des Chefs 1. Skl. im Hauptquar-tier am 6. und 7. Februar 1942* (see also the appendix to the same document).

106. BA/MA RM 35 III/22: *Anlage 1 zu K.T.B. Mar.Gr. Süd vom 17.2.42: Nieder-schrift über die Besprechungen mit Admiral Schwarzes Meer und den von ihm nach Sofia entsendten Offizieren über Transportabsichten und im Zusammenhang damit stehenden Op-erationsabsichten für das Jahr 1942.*

107. Ruge, 79.

108. *Mar. Gruppe Süd op B. Nr. 627/42 gKdos,* in BA/MA RM 35 III/21: *KTB Mar. Gr. Süd, 1.-15. Februar 1942* (under entry for 2 February 1942).

109. Ibid.

110. BA /MA RM 35 III/21: *Anlage zu K.T.B. Mar.Gr. Süd vom 9.2.42: Mar. Gruppe Süd op B. Nr. 730/42 gKdos.*

111. BA/MA RM 7/248: *Der Oberbefehlshaber der Kriegsmarine und Chef der See-*

kriegsleitung, B. Nr. 1. Skl. I m 275/42 gKdos Chefs., Berlin, den 23. Februar 1942, an Marine-gruppe Süd. Betr.: Operationen im Schwarzen Meer.

112. BA/MA RL 8/86: *Fliegerführer Süd, Tageseinsatz-Meldungen* (hereafter cited as *Fl. Führ. Süd, Tag.-Meld.*), 24 February 1942.

113. Achkasov and Pavlovich, 184.

114. Manstein, 251.

115. USAFHRA 512.607: *AMWIS No. 131, Up to 1200–4th March 1942.*

116. BA/MA RL 8/86: *Fl. Führ. Süd, Tag.-Meld.*, 27 February 1942.

117. Ibid., 1 March 1942.

118. Ibid.

119. Ibid., 2 and 3 March.

120. *Adm. Schw. Meer. gKdos Chefsache, 24/42 A I,* in BA/MA RM 35 III/23: *KTB Mar. Gr. Süd, 1.–15. März 1942* (under entry for 6 March 1942).

121. BA/MA RM 7/115: *KTB, 1/Skl. Teil B IX: Lageübersicht, Mittelmeer-Ägäis-Schwarzes Meer, 16.–31. März 1942.*

122. USAFHRA 512.607: *AMWIS No. 132, Up to 1200–11th March 1942.*

123. Ziemke and Bauer, 261.

124. Source cited in note 65, 10.

125. Ibid.; USAFHRA K113.309-3 V. 5: *Die deutsche Luftwaffe in Rußland, I. Halbjahr 1942 (Vorstudie der 8. Abt., Chef Genstb. der Luftwaffe, 1944),* 3.

126. Source cited in note 65, 10.

127. BA/MA RM 7/248: *Ob.d.L FüSt. Ia, Nr. 6283/42 gKdos (op 1), 12.3.42: Bezug: FS Lfl. 4, Führ. Abt. Ia, op Nr. 1230/42, geh., vom 11.3.42.*

128. BA/MA RM 7/115: *KTB, 1/Skl. Teil B IX: Lageübersicht, Mittelmeer-Ägäis-Schwarzes Meer, 1.–15. März 1942* and 16.–31. März 1942.

129. BA/MA RL 8/86: *Fl. Führ. Süd, Tag.-Meld.*, 25 March 1942.

130. Plocher, *1942,* 170.

131. BA/MA RL 8/86: *Fl. Führ. Süd, Tag.-Meld.*, 23 March 1942; USAFHRA K113.309-3 V. 5: *Die Kampfhandlungen im Osten während des Jahres 1942,* 18.

132. [Red Army,] *Collection of Materials on the Use of War Experience No. 5, 1943,* 154.

133. Manstein, 254.

134. G. E. Blau, *The German Campaign in Russia: Planning and Operations (1940–42).* Department of the Army, Study No. 20-261a (Washington, D.C.: Department of the Army, 1955), 118.

3. OPERATION "BUSTARD HUNT"

1. Manstein, 254.

2. Ibid., 256.

3. [Red Army,] *Collection of Materials on the Use of War Experience No. 5, 1943,* 155.

4. Ibid., 150.

5. Manstein, 257.

6. BA/MA N671/9: *Dr. Wolfram Frhr. von Richthofen, Generalfeldmarschall. Persön-liches Kriegstagebuch: Band 9: 1.1.–31.12.1942* (hereafter cited as *Richthofen TB*), 30 April 1942.

7. Ziemke and Bauer, 263.

8. Ibid., 264.

9. Halder, vol. 3, 408.

10. Ibid., 412.

11. *KTB OKW*, vol. 2, 321 (13 April 1942).

12. Halder, vol. 3, 421 (28 March 1942).

13. NARS T971/18/975–981: *OKL, Chef Genst. 7644/42 Chefsache—Notiz über die Besprechung beim Führer am 17.4.1942, bezüglich Einsatz der Luftflotte 4.*

14. Muller, *The German Air War in Russia,* 70.

15. BA/MA N671/9: *Richthofen TB,* 18 April 1942.

16. S. W. Mitcham, *Men of the Luftwaffe* (Novato, Calif.: Presidio, 1988), 170.

17. Details of Richthofen's life and career, plus his personal papers and diaries from 1937 to 1944, can be found in the *Nachlaß Dr. Wolfram Frhr. v. Richthofen* at the *BA/MA* (BA/MA N671). For his time in Spain, see vols. 1, 2, and 3. His abbreviated service record is in BA/MA MSG 1/1248.

18. USAFHRA K113.3017 vol. 1: *VIII. Fliegerkorps im Einsatz Sewastopol 1942 (Juni) (aus der Studie der 8. Abt. "Erfahrungen aus dem Einsatz der Luftwaffe gegen Festungen").*

19. BA/MA N671/9: *Richthofen TB,* 21 April 1942.

20. Ibid., 22 April 1942.

21. Manstein, 258.

22. BA/MA N671/9: *Richthofen TB,* 2 May 1942.

23. Muller, *The German Air War in Russia,* 72.

24. BA/MA N671/9: *Richthofen TB,* 2 May 1942.

25. Ziemke and Bauer, 264.

26. Ibid.

27. BA/MA N671/9: *Richthofen TB,* 4 May 1942.

28. Ziemke and Bauer, 264.

29. Ibid.

30. BA/MA N671/9: *Richthofen TB,* 28 April 1942.

31. Muller, *The German Air War in Russia,* 72.

32. BA/MA RM 35 III/25: *KTB Mar. Gr. Süd, 1.–15. April 1942.*

33. BA/MA RM 7/115: *KTB, 1/Skl. Teil B IX: Lageübersicht, Mittelmeer-Ägäis-Schwarzes Meer, 1.–15. April 1942.*

34. BA/MA RM 35 III/25: *KTB Mar. Gr. Süd, 1.–15. April 1942.*

35. Achkasov and Pavlovich, 332.

36. Source cited in chapter 2, note 65, 10.

37. BA/MA RM 35 III/25: *KTB Mar. Gr. Süd, 1.–15. April 1942;* USAFHRA K113.309-3 Vol. 5: *Die deutsche Luftwaffe in Rußland, I. Halbjahr 1942 (Vorstudie der 8. Abt., Chef Genstb. der Luftwaffe, 1944),* 3.

38. Plocher, *1942,* 15.

39. R. Higham and J. W. Kipp, eds., *Soviet Aviation and Air Power: A Historical View* (London: Brassey's, 1978), 84.

40. Statistics compiled from daily "kills" and "losses" listed in BA/MA RL 8/86: *Fl. Führ. Süd, Tag.-Meld.,* entries for April 1942.

41. Ibid., 30 April 1942.

42. These statistics are derived from the "Overview of *Fl. Führ. Süd*'s Results, from 19.2.–30.4.1942," appended to ibid.

43. BA/MA N671/9: *Richthofen TB,* 7 May 1942.

44. *Fl. Führ. Süd*'s reconnaissance aircraft discovered only a small amount of enemy shipping around the Crimea during this period, and that was overwhelmingly merchant and not naval in nature. See BA/MA RL 8/86: *Fl. Führ. Süd, Tag.-Meld.;* Ruge, 78.

45. BA /MA N671/9: *Richthofen TB,* 6 May 1942.

46. Ibid., 8 May 1942.

47. *History of the Great Patriotic War of the Soviet Union, 1941–1945;* translated from Russian by the U.S. Center for Military History (Wilmington, Ohio: Scholarly Resources, 1984) (hereafter cited as *HGPW*), vol. 2, 405–406.

48. BA/MA N671/9: *Richthofen TB,* 8 May 1942.

49. Manstein, 259.

50. BA/MA N671/9: *Richthofen TB,* 9 May 1942.

51. Muller, *The German Air War in Russia,* 73.

52. For the development of these identification methods—which were first employed by *Schlachtstaffeln* during the Great War and reintroduced by Richthofen during the Spanish Civil War—see James S. Corum, "The Luftwaffe's Army Support Doctrine, 1918–1941," *Journal of Military History* 59, no. 1 (January 1995): 53–76.

53. USAFHRA 512.625-3: *Fliegerkorps VIII Staff, Operations Department (Reconnaissance Branch), No. 7790/42, Secret, 29.7.1942: Standing Order to the Reconnaissance Units of Fliegerkorps VIII* (note: this is an American intelligence translation of a document captured by the Russians).

54. BA/MA N671/9: *Richthofen TB,* 10 May 1942.

55. Ibid., 11 May 1942.

56. *HGPW,* vol. 2, 406.

57. Ibid., vol. 2, 405.

58. BA /MA N671/9: *Richthofen TB,* 12 May 1942.

59. Ibid., 15 May 1942.

60. Halder, vol. 3, 442.

61. BA/MA RL 8/86: *Fl. Führ. Süd, Tag.-Meld.,* 13–17 May 1942.

62. BA/MA N671/9: *Richthofen TB,* 17 May 1942.

63. Erickson, *Road to Stalingrad,* 349.

64. Manstein, 261.

65. Kurowski, *Balkenkreuz,* 276–277. Karl von Tippelskirch claims that 323 aircraft were *captured,* not destroyed. However, there is apparently no reliable evidence supporting this claim; see von Tippelskirch, *Geschichte des Zweiten Weltkriegs* (Bonn: Athenäum, 1951), 277.

66. Achkasov and Pavlovich, 78, 84.

67. Manstein, 261.

68. HGPW, vol. 2, 405.

69. BA/MA N671/9: *Richthofen TB,* 19 May 1942.

70. Carell, *Stalingrad,* 29.

71. BA/MA N671/9: *Richthofen TB,* 21 May 1942.

72. Ibid., 25 May 1942.

73. Ibid., 21 May 1942.

74. Ibid., 25 May 1942; *Reisenotizen O.B. Mar. Gr. Süd: 5) Zusammenarbeit mit der Luftwaffe,* in BA/MA RM 35 III/30: *KTB Mar. Gr. Süd, 16.–30. Juni 1942.*

75. BA/MA RL 8/86: *Fl. Führ. Süd, Tag.-Meld.,* late April. The daily operational report for 30 April 1942, for example, describes the activities of the following *Fl. Führ. Süd*

units: *II./J.G. 77; III./J.G. 52; III./St.G. 77; III./L.G. 1; II./K.G. 26; I./K.G. 51; I./K.G. 100; and 4.(F) 122.*

76. USAFHRA K113.106-153 vol. 11: *Gliederung des VIII. Fliegerkorps während des Kampfes um Sewastopol (Ende May-Anfang Juli 1942).* After the end of May, Wild was left with only *I./J.G., 77; II./K.G. 26,* and *4.(F) 122.*

77. USAFHRA 180.04-12: U.S. Department of the Navy, Office of the Chief of Naval Operations, Naval History Division: War Diary of [German] Admiral, Black Sea, 1-30 June 1942 (PG Numbers 31512-31513) (hereafter cited as *KTB, Ad. Schw. Meer,* II), 2 June 1942.

78. BA/MA RM 7/115: *KTB, 1/Skl. Teil B IX: Lageübersicht, Mittelmeer-Ägäis-Schwarzes Meer, 1.-13. Juni 1942.*

79. Ibid., 8 June 1942.

80. Ibid.; *Reisenotizen O.B. Mar. Gr. Süd: 2) Gefechtsstand für Führung offensiver Seestreitkräfte,* in BA/MA RM 35 III/30: *KTB Mar. Gr. Süd, 16.-30. Juni 1942.*

81. Ibid., 9 June 1942; BA/MA RM 7/115: *KTB, 1/Skl. Teil B IX: Lageübersicht, Mittelmeer-Ägäis-Schwarzes Meer, 1.-13. Juni 1942.*

82. BA/MA RM 7/248: *Oberkommando der Kriegsmarine B. Nr. 1 Skl. I op 9045/42 gKdos, Berlin, den 17. April 1942: Fernschreiben an S Marinegruppe Süd; Reisenotizen O.B. Mar. Gr. Süd: 5) Zusammenarbeit mit der Luftwaffe,* in BA/MA RM 35 III/30: *KTB Mar. Gr. Süd, 16.-30. Juni 1942.*

83. Ibid. Eyssen remained at Wild's command post until late in June, when he returned to *Luftflotte 4*'s headquarters in Nikolayev.

84. Ibid.

85. *Reisenotizen O.B. Mar. Gr. Süd: 4) Unterscheidungszeichen,* in BA/MA RM 35 III/30: *KTB Mar. Gr. Süd, 16.-30. Juni 1942.*

86. *KTB, Ad. Schw. Meer,* II, 10 June 1942.

87. Ibid.

88. USAFHRA 142.0372: "The Siege of Sevastopol," *Air Forces General Information Bulletin No. 4, September 1942* (Headquarters, Army Air Forces Intelligence Service, 3-1913. Restricted).

89. Plocher, *1942,* 17.

90. *HGPW,* vol. 2, 407; H. Boog et al., *Der globale Krieg: Die Ausweitung zum Weltkrieg und der Wechsel der Initiative, 1941-1943.* Volume 6 of *Das Deutsche Reich und der Zweite Weltkrieg* (Stuttgart: Deutsche Verlags-Anstalt, 1983), 846.

91. Ibid.

92. NARS T971/18/855-883: *"Erfahrungen und Auswirkung,"* esp. *Anlage 3.*

93. BA/MA N671/9: *Richthofen TB,* 28 May 1942.

94. He commanded *3. (H.) 11; 3. (H.) 13; I., II.,* and *III./St.G. 77; I.* and *II./K.G. 51; I.* and *III./K.G. 76; I./K.G. 100; III./L.G. 1; II.* and *III./J.G. 77; III./J.G. 3; 4. (F) 122; II./K.G. 26; I./J.G. 77.* Source: NARS T971/18/855-883: *"Erfahrungen und Auswirkung,"* esp. *Anlage 3.*

95. See, for example, BA/MA N671/9: *Richthofen TB,* 30 May and 13 June 1942.

96. NARS T971/18/855-883: *"Erfahrungen und Auswirkung" Anlage 2: Aufmarsch und Angriffsabsichten der deutschen 11. Armee an 1. Juni 1942.*

97. Ibid.

98. Ibid. *Anlage 5: Einsatz des VIII. Fliegerkorps während der Artillerie-Vorbereitung vom 1. Juni bis 6. Juni 1942.*

99. Ibid. From *Richthofen, Ia, Nr. 7519, geheim, 2.6.1942, 21.25 Uhr.*

100. Ibid.

101. K. Dönitz, *Memoirs: Ten Years and Twenty Days* (Annapolis: Naval Institute Press, 1990; first published in English in 1959), 93, 94.

4. OPERATION "STURGEON CATCH"

1. W. Baumbach, *The Life and Death of the Luftwaffe,* War and Warriors Series (Costa Mesa, Calif.: Noontide Press, 1991), 124.

2. NARS T971/18/855–883: *"Erfahrungen und Auswirkung" Anlage 5; Richthofen TB,* 2 June 1942; BA/MA RL 8/249: *Gen. Kdo. VIII Fl. Korps Ia Nr.: 7520/42 geh.: Tagesabschlußmeldung VIII. Fl. Korps für 2.6.42.*

3. BA/MA N671/9: *Richthofen TB,* 2 June 1942.

4. NARS T971/18/855–883: *"Erfahrungen und Auswirkung" Anlage 5.*

5. Ibid., *Anlage 6: Einsatz der fliegenden Verbände des VIII. Fliegerkorps gegen Sewastopol vom 2. Juni bis 6. Juni 1942; Richthofen TB,* 2 June 1942. According to BA/MA RL 8/249: *Gen. Kdo. VIII Fl. Korps Ia Nr.: 7520/42 geh.: Tagesabschlußmeldung VIII. Fl. Korps für 2.6.42,* 711 sorties took place, with the loss of one Ju 87 and one Bf 109.

6. BA/MA N671/9: *Richthofen TB,* 3–7 June 1942.

7. NARS T971/18/855–883: *"Erfahrungen und Auswirkung" Anlage 6.;* BA/MA RL 8/249: *Gen. Kdo. VIII Fl. Korps Ia Nrs. 7527, 7533, 7542, 7545/42 geh.: Tagesabschlußmeldungen VIII. Fl. Korps für 3.6.–6.6.42* (which give a total of 2,321 sorties for this period).

8. Ibid., reports for 24 May to 6 June.

9. D. Saward, *"Bomber" Harris: The Story of Marshal of the Royal Air Force Sir Arthur Harris, Bt, GCB, OBE, AFC, LLD, Air Officer Commanding-in-Chief, Bomber Command, 1942–1945* (London: Sphere, 1990; first published in 1984), 98.

10. Plocher, *1941,* 99.

11. Quoted in Karpov, 86.

12. B. Voyetekhov, *The Last Days of Sevastopol,* translated from Russian by R. Parker and V. Genne (London: Cassell, 1943), 50, 51.

13. Manstein, 272.

14. BA/MA N671/9: *Richthofen TB,* 7 June 1942.

15. Ibid.; BA/MA RL 8/249: *Gen. Kdo. VIII Fl. Korps Ia Nr.: 7549/42 geh.: Tagesabschlußmeldung VIII. Fl. Korps für den 7.6.42.*

16. BA/MA N671/9: *Richthofen TB,* 8 June 1942; BA/MA RL 8/249: *Gen. Kdo. VIII Fl. Korps Ia Nr.: 7556/42 geh.: Tagesabschlußmeldung VIII. Fl. Korps für den 8.6.42* (this gives a mission total of 1,192).

17. Baumbach, 124.

18. Ibid., *Ia Nr.: 7560/42 geh.: Tagesabschlußmeldung VIII. Fl. Korps für den 9.6.42;* ibid., *Ia Nr.: 7565/42 geh.: Tagesabschlußmeldung VIII. Fl. Korps für den 10.6.42.*

19. BA/MA N671/9: *Richthofen TB,* 11 June 1942; BA/MA RL 8/249: *Gen. Kdo. VIII Fl. Korps Ia Nr.: 7572/42 geh.: Tagesabschlußmeldung VIII. Fl. Korps für den 11.6.42* (this gives the same mission total as Richthofen's diary but a lower bomb total of 8,865).

20. BA/MA N671/9: *Richthofen TB,* 17 June 1942.

21. BA/MA RM 7/115: *KTB, 1/Skl. Teil B IX: Lageübersicht, Mittelmeer-Ägäis-*

Schwarzes Meer, 1.-13. Juni 1942; BA/MA RM 35 III/29: *KTB Mar. Gr. Süd, 1.-15. Juni 1942,* various entries for early June.

22. For an example of German radar usage in the Crimea, see *KTB, Ad. Schw. Meer,* II, 8 June 1942.

23. Ziemke and Bauer, 314.

24. Manstein, 274.

25. BA/MA N671/9: *Richthofen TB,* 13 June 1942.

26. Richthofen's transfer from Sevastopol during this crucial phase of the battle is not mentioned in recent volumes on the Luftwaffe (i.e., Kurowski, Mitcham, Muller, Murray, and Cooper).

27. BA/MA RL 10/473b: *Der Kommandierende General des VIII. Fliegerkorps Gef. Qu., 23.6.42, gez. Richthofen;* BA/MA N671/9: *Richthofen TB,* 13 June 1942.

28. Ibid., 22 June 1942.

29. Ibid., 16 June 1942.

30. BA/MA RL 8/86: *Fl. Führ. Süd, Tag.-Meld.,* 2 June 1942.

31. Ibid.; BA/MA N671/9: *Richthofen TB,* 2 June 1942; *KTB, Ad. Schw. Meer,* II, 2 June 1942.

32. BA/MA RL 8/86: *Fl. Führ. Süd, Tag.-Meld.,* 3 to 7 June 1942.

33. See, for example, USAFHRA 180.04-11: U.S. Department of the Navy, Office of the Chief of Naval Operations, Naval History Division: War Diary of Admiral, Black Sea, 16-31 May 1942 (PG Number 31511) (hereafter cited as *KTB, Ad. Schw. Meer,* I), 28 May 1942; and *KTB, Ad. Schw. Meer,* II, 29 June 1942.

34. Ruge, 79.

35. *KTB, Ad. Schw. Meer,* II, 9 June 1942.

36. Achkasov and Pavlovich, 184.

37. Ibid., 334.

38. *HGPW,* vol. 2, 408.

39. Achkasov and Pavlovich, 334.

40. *HGPW,* vol. 2, 409; Erikson, "Soviet Submarine Operations" 169.

41. BA/MA RM 7/115: *KTB, 1/Skl. Teil B IX: Lageübersicht, Mittelmeer-Ägäis-Schwarzes Meer, 1.-13. Juni 1942.*

42. *KTB, Ad. Schw. Meer,* II, 11 June 1942.

43. Ibid., 13 June 1942; BA/MA RM 7/115: *KTB, 1/Skl. Teil B IX: Lageübersicht, Mittelmeer-Ägäis-Schwarzes Meer, 1.-13. Juni 1942.*

44. Ibid., *14.-30. Juni 1942; KTB, Ad. Schw. Meer,* II, 19 June 1942.

45. Ibid., 15 June 1942; BA/MA RM 7/115: *KTB, 1/Skl. Teil B IX: Lageübersicht, Mittelmeer-Ägäis-Schwarzes Meer, 14.-30. Juni 1942.*

46. Ibid., *14.-30. Juni 1942; KTB, Ad. Schw. Meer,* II, 18 June 1942.

47. Ibid., 19 June 1942; BA/MA RM 7/115: *KTB, 1/Skl. Teil B IX: Lageübersicht, Mittelmeer-Ägäis-Schwarzes Meer, 14.-30. Juni 1942.*

48. *KTB, Ad. Schw. Meer,* II, 19 June 1942.

49. BA/MA RL 8/249: *Gen. Kdo. VIII Fl. Korps Ia Nr.: 7584/42 geh.: Tagesabschlußmeldung VIII. Fl. Korps für den 13.6.42; Gen. Kdo. VIII Fl. Korps Ia Nr.: 7597/42 geh.: Tagesabschlußmeldung VIII. Fl. Korps für den 15.6.42; Gen. Kdo. VIII Fl. Korps Ia Nr.: 7611/42 geh.: Tagesabschlußmeldung VIII. Fl. Korps für den 17.6.42.* Some of these "kills" were by aircraft under Wild's operational command but formally belonging to *Fliegerkorps IV and VIII.*

50. USAFHRA K113.309-3 vol. 6: *Gen. Kdo. VIII Fl. Korps Ia Nr.: 3371/42 geh.: Tagesabschlußmeldung VIII. Fl. Korps für den 26.6.42; KTB, Ad. Schw. Meer,* II, 26 June 1942; BA/MA RL 8/86: *Fl. Führ. Süd, Tag.-Meld.,* 26 June 1942.

51. USAFHRA K113.309-3 vol. 6: *Gen. Kdo. VIII Fl. Korps Ia Nr.: 3543/42 geh.: Nachtabschlußmeldung VIII. Fl. Korps für den 30.6./1.7.42;* BA/MA RL 8/86: *Fl. Führ. Süd, Tag.-Meld.,* 1 July 1942.

52. Ibid., 1–3 July 1942; USAFHRA K113.309-3 vol. 6: *Gen. Kdo. VIII Fl. Korps Ia Nr.: 3551/42 geh.: Nachtabschlußmeldung VIII. Fl. Korps für den 1./2.7.4;* ibid., *Ia Nr.: 3554/42 geh.: Tagesabschlußmeldung VIII. Fl. Korps für den 2.7.42.*

53. Ibid.; BA/MA RL 8/86: *Fl. Führ. Süd, Tag.-Meld.,* 2 July 1942.

54. Achkasov and Pavlovich, 185.

55. Ruge, 79.

56. *KTB, Ad. Schw. Meer,* II, 13 June 1942.

57. Ibid.; BA/MA RM 7/115: *KTB, 1/Skl. Teil B IX: Lageübersicht, Mittelmeer-Ägäis-Schwarzes Meer, 1.–13. Juni 1942.*

58. BA/MA RM 35 III/29: *KTB Mar. Gr. Süd, 1.–15. Juni 1942; KTB, Ad. Schw. Meer,* II, 13 June 1942 and several following days.

59. Ibid., 19 June 1942; BA/MA RM 7/115: *KTB, 1/Skl. Teil B IX: Lageübersicht, Mittelmeer-Ägäis-Schwarzes Meer, 14.–30. Juni 1942.*

60. Karpov, 91; Voyetekhov, 58, 59.

61. *KTB, Ad. Schw. Meer,* II, 28 June 1942.

62. BA/MA RL 8/249: *Gen. Kdo. VIII Fl. Korps Ia Nr.: 7639/42 geh.: Tagesabschlußmeldung VIII. Fl. Korps für den 22.6.42.* Even American intelligence officers describing the battle shortly afterward credited Maué's Stuka strike with putting the fort "out of commission . . . enabling pioneers and infantry to force their way into the interior" (first source cited in note 77).

63. Voyetekhov, 140, 141.

64. BA/MA RL 8/249: *Gen. Kdo. VIII Fl. Korps Ia Nrs.: 7584, 7590, 7597, 7604, 7611/42 geh.: Tagesabschlußmeldungen VIII. Fl. Korps für den 13.–17.6.42.*

65. BA/MA N671/9: *Richthofen TB,* 20 and 21 June 1942.

66. BA/MA RL 8/249: *Gen. Kdo. VIII Fl. Korps Ia Nr.: 7622/42 geh.: Tagesabschlußmeldung VIII. Fl. Korps für den 19.6.42;* BA/MA N671/9: *Richthofen TB,* 19 June 1942.

67. BA/MA RL 8/249: *Gen. Kdo. VIII Fl. Korps Ia Nrs.: 7622, 7628, 7634, 7639/42 geh.: Tagesabschlußmeldungen VIII. Fl. Korps für 19.–22.6.42;* USAFHRA K113-309 Vol. 6: *Fl. Führ. Süd Ia Nrs.: 3343, 3351, 3361/42 geh.: Tagesabschlußmeldungen VIII. Fl. Korps für 23–25.6.42.*

68. Compiled from operational ready rates for 20 May and 20 June 1942 in USAFHRA K113.309-3 vol. 6: *Einsatz fliegende Verbände der deutschen Luftwaffe an der Ostfront.*

69. USAFHRA K113.309-3 Vol. 6: *Fl. Führ. Süd Ia Nrs.: 3343, 3351, 3361, 3371/42 geh.: Tagesabschlußmeldungen VIII. Fl. Korps für 23–26.6.42.*

70. Ibid., *Nrs.: 3380, 3526, 3532, 3542, 3546/42 geh.: Tagesabschlußmeldungen VIII. Fl. Korps für 27.6–1.7.42.*

71. Smith, 127, 128.

72. Statistics compiled from *Fliegerkorps VIII*'s previously cited *Tagesabschlußmeldungen.*

73. Manstein, 277.

74. Ibid., 279; *KTB, Ad. Schw. Meer,* II, 30 June 1942.

75. Manstein, 279.

76. Ibid.

77. BA/MA RL 8/52: *Gen. Kdo. VIII Fl. Korps. Ia/Fl. Führer Süd Ia Nr. 3555/42 geh., an Ob.d.L Führungsstab, Ia und Ic, Kurfürst: Abschlußmeldung über Einsatz der Luftwaffe im Kampf um Sewastopol vom 2.6 bis einschl. 3.7.42;* USAFHRA K113.309-3 vol. 6: *Gen. Kdo. VIII Fl. Korps Ia Nr.: 3528/42 geh.: Nachtabschlußmeldung VIII. Fl. Korps für die Nacht 28./29.6.1942.*

78. Karpov, 92.

79. USAFHRA K113.309-3 vol. 6: *Fl. Führ. Süd Ia Nr.: 3532/42 geh.: Tagesabschlußmeldung VIII. Fl. Korps für den 29.6.42.*

80. *KTB, Ad. Schw. Meer,* II, 28 June 1942.

81. *HGPW,* Vol. II, 410.

82. *KTB, Ad. Schw. Meer,* II, 30 June 1942.

83. Ibid.

84. Manstein, 280.

85. Ibid., 281.

86. For example, according to Mitcham (174), Manstein "asked Richthofen to annihilate the diehards with his Stukas, which the baron did, running the civilian death toll even higher in the process." This is clearly wrong; as noted, Richthofen was at that time in Kursk, 750 kilometers away, and no longer in operational command of *Fliegerkorps VIII.*

87. USAFHRA K113.309-3 vol. 6: *Fl. Führ. Süd Ia Nr.: 3542/42 geh.: Tagesabschlußmeldung VIII. Fl. Korps für den 30.6.42.*

88. Karpov, 93.

89. *HGPW,* vol. 2, 410; Karpov, 94.

90. Karpov, 97.

91. Voyetekhov, 149.

92. USAFHRA K113.309-3 vol. 6: *Fl. Führ. Süd Ia Nr.: 3554/42 geh.: Tagesabschlußmeldung VIII. Fl. Korps für den 2.7.42.*

93. Manstein, 283.

94. BA/MA N671/9: *Richthofen TB,* 2 July 1942.

95. *Fernschreiben HLGX/VG. 1528. 2.7.42. 1000,* in ibid.

96. Lit. "has again a good name"; ibid., 2 July 1942.

97. A. Philippi and F. Heim, *Der Feldzug gegen Sowjetrußland 1941 bis 1945: Ein operativer Überblick* (Stuttgart: W. Kohlhammer, 1962), 124.

98. Source cited in chapter 3, note 88. A number of scholars accept these "official" figures. See Philippi and Heim, 129.

99. Ziemke and Bauer, 321. Karpov (98) outrageously claims that "during the eight months of the siege the invaders lost up to 300,000 officers and men killed and wounded. During the last 25 days of the storm the number of dead topped 60,000."

100. Weinberg (413) believes that the June assault on the fortress cost Eleventh Army "most likely close to 100,000" casualties. This figure is also reasonable.

101. First source cited in note 77.

102. Ibid.

103. Ibid.

104. Ibid.

105. USAFHRA K113.309-3 vol. 7: *Auszug aus Zusammenstellung der für Wehrmachtbericht, Rundfunk und Presse gemeldeten besonderen Leistungen: Gemeldet für Wehrmachtbericht 2.7.42;* Plocher, *1942,* 201.

5. STAMPEDE TO THE DON

1. Erickson, *Road to Stalingrad,* 344.
2. *HGPW,* vol. 2, 411, 412.
3. Ibid., 412.
4. *KTB OKW,* vol. 2, 352 (12 May 1942).
5. W. Görlitz, ed., *Paulus and Stalingrad: A Life of Field-Marshal Friedrich Paulus with Notes, Correspondence and Documents from his Papers* (London: Methuen, 1963), 177.
6. Halder, vol. 3, 439 (12 May 1942); BA/MA N671/9: *Richthofen TB,* 12 and 13 May 1942.
7. Görlitz, *Paulus and Stalingrad,* 177.
8. BA/MA RL 10/473a: *Generalkommando des IV. Fliegerkorps Abt. Ic.: Übersicht über Einsätze, Erfolge und Verluste der Verbände des IV. Fliegerkorps v. 1.–31.5.42,* 1. Note: this document is undated but was entered into *St.Gr. 77*'s war diary on 12 June 1942.
9. BA/MA RL 10/473a: See Paulus's teletype message of thanks to *Fliegerkorps IV in Kommandierende General IV. Fliegerkorps, 3. Juni 1942, gez. Pflugbeil;* R. A. Kilmarx, *A History of Soviet Air Power* (New York: Praeger, 1962), 185.
10. Ibid. (both sources).
11. Halder, vol. 3, 439, 440 (12, 13, 14 May 1942).
12. *HGPW,* vol. 2, 413.
13. During the Battle of Kharkov, *Fliegerkorps IV* commanded: *I.* and *III./K.G. 27; I., II.,* and *III./K.G. 51; I., II.,* and *III./K.G. 55; I./K.G. 76; II./K.G. 3; I., II.,* and *III./St.G 77; II./St.G. 1; I., II.,* and *III./J.G. 3; I., II., III.,* and *15./J.G. 52; I.* and *III./J.G. 77; I./J.G. 53; I.* and *II./Schl.G. 1; 3. (F.) 121.* Source cited in note 8, 4–9.
14. Ziemke and Bauer, 275.
15. Source cited in note 8, 4–9.
16. USAFHRA K113.309-3 vol. 6: *Übersicht über die fliegenden Verbände an der Ostfront am 20.5.42,* and ibid., *Einsatz fliegende Verbände der deutschen Luftwaffe an der Ostfront, 20.6.1942.*
17. Halder, vol. 3, 442.
18. Görlitz, *Paulus and Stalingrad,* 179.
19. Source cited in note 8, 2.
20. Ibid.; Kurowski, *Balkenkreuz,* 277; Dierich, 70.
21. BA/MA RL 10/473a: *Generalkommando des IV. Fliegerkorps, Adj. IIa., Gefechtsstand, 1. Juni 1942, gez. von Kleist.*
22. Doerr, "Der Ausgang der Schlacht" 15.
23. Quoted in Ziemke and Bauer, 278.
24. Doerr, "Der Ausgang der Schlacht" 15.
25. Ziemke and Bauer, 278–280; Zhukov, 120, 121; Erickson, *Road to Stalingrad,* 346.
26. USAFHRA 119.606-2: Combined Chiefs of Staff: Eastern Front Situation Report (message from War Office D.D.M.I. to British Army Staff, Washington. Classified "Most Secret"), No: 90657, 24 May 1942.

27. Erickson, *Road to Stalingrad*, 347.

28. Source cited in note 8, 6; USAFHRA K113.309-3 vol. 6: *Übersicht über die fliegenden Verbände an der Ostfront am 20.5.42.*

29. USAFHRA 512.607: *AMWIS No. 143, Up to 1200–27th May 1942.*

30. Source cited in note 8, 4–9.

31. Doerr, "Der Ausgang der Schlacht," 17.

32. *KTB OKW*, vol. 2, 390 (29 May 1942); BA/MA RL 10/473a: *Luftflottenkommando 4, Führungsabteilung Ia op., Gefechtsstand, den 29. Mai 1942, Tagesbefehl, gez Löhr;* Ziemke and Bauer, 282.

33. *Goebbels—Tagebücher, Band 4*, 1801 (30 May 1942).

34. Source cited in note 8, 1, 2.

35. USAFHRA K113.309-3 vol. 7: *Auszug aus Zusammenstellung der für Wehrmachtbericht, Rundfunk und Presse gemeldeten besonderen Leistungen: Gemeldet für Wehrmachtbericht 20.5.42;* and *Gemeldet für Wehrmachtbericht, Rundfunk und Presse 29.5.42.*

36. BA/MA RL 10/473a: *Generalkommando des IV. Fliegerkorps, Adj. IIa., Gefechtsstand, 1. Juni 1942, gez. von Kleist.*

37. First source cited in note 9.

38. BA/MA RL 10/473a: *Luftflottenkommando 4, Führungsabteilung Ia op., Gefechtsstand, den 29. Mai 1942, Tagesbefehl, gez Löhr.*

39. *KTB OKW*, vol. 2, 425 (15 June 1942); Halder, vol. 3, 455 (13 June 1942).

40. Ibid., 465 (25 June 1942); *KTB OKW*, vol. 2, 453 (26 June 1942).

41. Kurowski, *Balkenkreuz*, 277.

42. Dierich, 72.

43. USAFHRA 512.6314A: *Notes on the German Air Force*, Air Ministry Publication 1928, 2nd ed., April 1943, 28, 29.

44. [Air Ministry, British,] *The Rise and Fall of the German Air Force, 1933–1945*, 2nd ed. (London: Arms & Armour, 1983; first published in 1948), 178.

45. USAFHRA K113.309-3 vol. 6: *Übersicht über die fliegenden Verbände an der Ostfront am 20.5.42* and *Einsatz fliegende Verbände der deutschen Luftwaffe an der Ostfront, 20.6.1942.*

46. Ibid.; [Air Ministry, British,] *The Rise and Fall of the German Air Force*, 178.

47. USAFHRA K113.309-3 vol. 6: *Übersicht über die fliegenden Verbände an der Ostfront am 20.5.42.*

48. BA/MA RM 7/395: *Oberkommando der Wehrmacht, Nr. 22 230/42 gKdos. Chefs., WFSt/Org., FHQu., den 6. Juni 1942: "Wehrkraft der Wehrmacht im Frühjahr 1942," gez. Warlimont*, 3.

49. Boog et al., *Der globale Krieg*, 780, 781.

50. BA/MA RM 7/395: *"Wehrkraft der Wehrmacht"* 3.

51. Ibid., 7, 9.

52. Ibid., 6.

53. Halder, vol. 3, 457 (16 June 1942); Boog et al., *Der globale Krieg*, 870.

54. BA/MA RM 7/395: *"Wehrkraft der Wehrmacht,"* 5.

55. Kurowski, *Balkenkreuz*, 281, 282, 283; Boog, *Der globale Krieg*, 873.

56. F. Kurowski, *Stalingrad: Die Schlacht, die Hitlers Mythos zerstörte* (Bergisch Gladbach: Gustav Lübbe, 1992), 152, 153.

57. BA/MA N671/9: *Richthofen TB*, 24 June 1942.

58. M. I. Kazakov, *"Boevye deistviia voisk Brianskogo i Voronezhskogo frontov letom*

1942 na voronezhskom napravlenii," trans. H. S. Orenstein and published as "Combat Operations of Briansk and Voronezh Front Forces in Summer 1942 on the Voronezh Axis," *Journal of Slavic Military Studies* 6 (June 1993): 300–340 (esp. 309, 310).

59. Halder, vol. 3, 460 (20 June 1942).

60. USAFHRA 180.642A vol. 2: *The Führer, Führer Headquarters, 30 June 1942, signed Adolf Hitler;* Halder, vol. 3, 460 (24 June 1942).

61. Glantz, 67, 68; Erickson, *Road to Stalingrad,* 354.

62. "Combat Operations of Briansk and Voronezh Front Forces," 311, 312.

63. Glantz, 68–69.

64. "Combat Operations of Briansk and Voronezh Front Forces" 313.

65. BA/MA N671/9: *Richthofen TB,* 28 June 1942.

66. This document is appended to the entry for 25 June, in ibid.

67. Ibid., 28 June 1942; Ziemke and Bauer, 333; "Combat Operations of Briansk and Voronezh Front Forces," 315, 316.

68. Quoted in Muller, *The German Air War in Russia,* 67.

69. Higham and Kipp, 90; R. Wagner, ed., *The Soviet Air Force in World War II: The Official History* (Garden City, N.Y.: Doubleday, 1973), 93, 94; A. Boyd, *The Soviet Air Force since 1918* (New York: Stein and Day, 1977), 157. None of these sources gives detailed statistics, but all agree that *Luftflotte 4* outnumbered its opposition during *Blau*'s first few weeks.

70. BA/MA N671/9: *Richthofen TB,* 28 June 1942.

71. Ibid.

72. "Combat Operations of Briansk and Voronezh Front Forces," 315.

73. H. Spaeter, *Panzerkorps Großdeutschland, vol. 1;* trans. David Johnston (Winnipeg: J. J. Fedorowicz, 1992; first published in German in 1958), 324. According to Spaeter's account, the pilots saw the identification markers but believed them to be part of a Soviet ruse.

74. BA/MA N671/9: *Richthofen TB,* 29 June 1942.

75. Ibid.

76. "Combat Operations of Briansk and Voronezh Front Forces," 316.

77. BA/MA N671/9: *Richthofen TB,* 29 June 1942.

78. USAFHRA 168.7158-338: *Aufzeichnungen des Generalmajor Pickert, Kommandeurs der 9. Flak-Division und Generals der Luftwaffe bei der 6. Armee, aus der Zeit vom 25 .6.42–23.1.43* (hereafter cited as *Pickert TB*), 1 July 1942.

79. "Combat Operations of Briansk and Voronezh Front Forces," 316.

80. BA/MA N671/9: *Richthofen TB,* 30 June 1942.

81. Ibid., 1 July 1942.

82. NARS T971/51/522–534: *Der Luftkrieg in Rußland 1942 (Chef Genstb. der Luftwaffe, 8. Abt., 1944),* 13.

83. BA/MA N671/9: *Richthofen TB,* 1 July 1942.

84. "Combat Operations of Briansk and Voronezh Front Forces," 321.

85. D. Irving, *Hitler's War* (London: Papermac, 1977), 400.

86. Görlitz, *Keitel: Verbrecher,* 304.

87. Irving, *Hitler's War,* 401.

88. *KTB OKW,* vol. 2, 472 (3 July 1942).

89. Erickson, *Road to Stalingrad,* 359.

90. Halder, vol. 3, 480, 481.

91. BA/MA N671/9: *Richthofen TB,* 5 July 1942.

92. Ibid., 10 July 1942.

93. *Luftwaffenring: Mitteilungsblatt für Angehörige der ehemaligen Luftwaffe* Nummer 11 (November 1955), 7.

94. BA/MA N671/9: *Richthofen TB,* 7 July 1942.

95. USAFHRA K113.309-3 vol. 7: *Auszug aus Zusammenstellung der für Wehrmachtbericht, Rundfunk und Presse gemeldeten besonderen Leistungen: Gemeldet für Rundfunk und Presse 7.7.42.*

96. BA/MA N671/9: *Richthofen TB,* 13 July 1942.

97. USAFHRA 168.7158-338: *Pickert TB,* 11 July 1942.

98. Halder, vol. 3, 479 (12 July 1942).

99. Spaeter, 358.

100. BA/MA N671/9: *Richthofen TB,* 14 July 1942.

101. Ibid., 6 July 1942.

102. Ibid., 18 July 1942.

103. BA/MA RL 10/473b: *Gef. Verband Nord, Ia, an Stuka. 77: Einsatzbefehl für 16.7.42.*

104. Halder, vol. 3, 484–485 (18 July 1942).

105. USAFHRA K113.309-3 vol. 6: *Fl. Führ. Süd Ia Nrs.: 4069, 4103/42 geh.: Tagesabschlußmeldungen Fl. Führ. Süd für 20, 21.7.42.*

106. BA/MA N671/9: *Richthofen TB,* 21 July 1942. Cf. Plocher, *1942,* 218.

107. BA/MA RL 10/473b: *Kommodore Sturzkampfgeschwader 77, Gefechtsstand, den 16.7.1942. An den Kommandierenden General des IV. Fliegerkorps, Herrn General der Flieger Pflugbeil, gez. Graf Schönborn.*

108. It claimed to have destroyed 556 tanks and 4,500 trucks, and damaged 339 and 1,223 others, respectively. It purportedly smashed 2,056 horse-drawn wagons, 323 artillery batteries, 1,031 bunkers and field installations, and 50 trains. It also reported wrecking scores of other important targets, including 84 merchant ships (together weighing 188,000 tons), 34 warships (44,000 tons), and various bridges and railway embankments. Its 464 claimed attacks on troop concentrations resulted in innumerable deaths (ibid.).

109. BA/MA RL 10/473b: *St.Gr. 77, Abt. Ia, Gefechtsstand, den 27.7.1942. Bezug: Fernschreiben des Reichsmarschalls vom 25.7.42. An Verteiler: Nachstehend übersendet das Geschwader die Abschrift des Fernschreiben des Herrn Reichsmarschalls vom 25.7.1942: An Sturzkampfgeschwader 77, zu Händen Kommodore Oberstleutnant Graf Schönborn. gez. Göring.*

110. USAFHRA K113.309-3 vol. 6: *Fl. Führ. Süd Ia Nr.: 3850/42 geh.: Tagesabschlußmeldung Fl. Führ. Süd für 10.7.42.*

111. Ibid., *Ia Nr.: 4103/42 geh.: Tagesabschlußmeldung Fl. Führ. Süd für 21.7.42*

112. BA/MA N671/9: *Richthofen TB,* 22 July 1942.

113. W. Tieke, *Der Kaukasus und das Öl: der deutsch-sowjetische Krieg in Kaukasien, 1942/43* (Osnabrück: Munin, 1970), 30.

114. USAFHRA K113.309-3 Vol. 6: *Fl. Führ. Süd Ia Nrs.: 4123, 4137/42 geh.: Tagesabschlußmeldungen Fl. Führ. Süd für 22, 23.7.42.*

115. BA/MA N671/9: *Richthofen TB,* 23 July 1942.

116. Ibid., 26 July 1942.

117. Tieke, 35.

118. Carell, *Hitler Moves East,* 474.

119. Tieke, 40; Smith, 134.

120. USAFHRA 119.606-2: Combined Chiefs of Staff: Eastern Front Situation Report (message from War Office D.D.M.I. to British Army Staff, Washington. Classified "Most Secret"), No: 53887, 26 July 1942.

121. Irving, *Hitler's War,* 404.

122. *Weisung Nr. 45,* in Hubatsch, 196–200.

123. *Weisung Nr. 43,* in Hubatsch, 192–194.

124. BA/MA N671/9: *Richthofen TB,* 6 June 1942.

125. USAFHRA K113.309-3 vol. 6: *Einsatz fliegende Verbände der deutschen Luftwaffe an der Ostfront, 20.6.1942* and *Die Stärke der deutschen Luftwaffe, 20.7.1942.*

126. BA/MA N671/9: *Richthofen TB,* 18 July 1942.

127. Ibid., 24 July 1942.

128. Ibid., 9 August 1942.

6. STALEMATE IN THE CAUCASUS

1. *HGPW,* vol. 2, 454.

2. NARS T971/18/652-662: *Die Kampfhandlungen im Osten während des Jahres 1942 (8. Abt., Chef Genst. der Luftwaffe, 1944).*

3. USAFHRA 512.607: *AMWIS No. 153, Up to 1200–5th August 1942.*

4. USAFHRA K113.309-3 vol. 6: *Fl. Führ. Süd Ia Nr.: 3911/42 geh.: Tagesabschlußmeldung Fl. Führ. Süd für 15.7.42.*

5. USAFHRA K113.309-3 vol. 6: *Die Stärke der deutschen Luftwaffe, 20.7.1942.*

6. USAFHRA K113.309-3 vol. 6: *Fl. Führ. Süd Ia Nr.: 3985/42 geh.: Tagesabschlußmeldung Fl. Führ. Süd für 16.7.42.*

7. Ibid., *Ia Nr.: 4336/42 geh.: Tagesabschlußmeldung Fl. Führ. Süd für 30.7.42;* for Soviet air raids throughout July, see *War Diary, Operations Division, German Naval Staff (Kriegstagebuch der Seekriegsleitung) 1939–45* (distributed on microfilm by Scholarly Resources) (cited hereafter as *KTB, 1/Skl. (m/film)),* part A, vol. 35.

8. Source cited in note 2.

9. They conducted their first *"Sondereinsatz"* (special mission) on 22 July. USAFHRA K113.309-3 vol. 6: *Fl. Führ. Süd Ia Nr.: 4132/42 geh.: Tagesabschlußmeldung Fl. Führ. Süd für 22.7.42.*

10. Ibid., *Ia Nr.: 4277/42 geh.: Tagesabschlußmeldung Fl. Führ. Süd für 28.7.42.*

11. *KTB OKW,* vol. 2, 536–537 (29 July 1942).

12. USAFHRA K113.309-3 vol. 6: *Fl. Führ. Süd Ia Nr.: 4465/42 geh.: Tagesabschlußmeldung Fl. Führ. Süd für 4.8.1942.*

13. Carell, *Stalingrad,* 85.

14. Ziemke and Bauer, 365.

15. Tieke, 62, 70, 75, 76, 77.

16. Spaeter, 375.

17. *KTB OKW,* vol. 2, 537 (29 July 1942); *HGPW,* vol. 2, 455, 456.

18. Plocher, *1942,* 226.

19. Tieke, 65.

20. Ibid., 69.

21. Ibid., 70–71.

22. Source cited in note 2.

23. Achkasov and Pavlovich, 188.

24. Cf. USAFHRA K113.309-3 vol. 6: *Fl. Führ. Süd Ia Nr.: 4450/42 geh.: Tagesab-schlußmeldung Fl. Führ. Süd für 3.8.42.*

25. BA/MA RM 7/115: *KTB, 1/Skl. Teil B IX: Lageübersicht, Mittelmeer-Ägäis-Schwarzes Meer, 1.–18.8.1942* and *19.8.–16.9.1942;* Achkasov and Pavlovich, 337–341; *HGPW,* vol. 2, 458.

26. BA/MA N671/9: *Richthofen TB,* 4 August 1942.

27. Halder, vol. 3, 496 (2 August 1942).

28. Ziemke and Bauer, 370.

29. Halder, vol. 3, 501 (8 August 1942); Ziemke and Bauer, 370.

30. Source cited in note 2.

31. G. Ciano, *Ciano's Diary 1939–1943.* Ed. M. Muggeridge. London: Heinemann, 1947.

32. According to the *HGPW* (vol. 2, 458), "it was necessary to blow up 38 industrial enterprises in Krasnodar, 755 oil wells, 11 compressor installations and a pipeline." See also *KTB OKW,* Vol. II, 581, 13 August 1942.

33. USAFHRA K113.106-153 vol. 14: *Der Inspekteur des Luftschutzes, Az. 41 Nr. 2099/42, g., den 21.8.1942, Betr.: Meldung der Luftflotte 4 vom 19.8.1942. "Schäden auf den Ölfeldern von Maikop and Krasnodar."*

34. BA/MA RW 19/199: *Wi Rü Amt Stab Z/SR, Nr. 1754/42 gKdos, Berlin, den 1. September 1942: Kriegswirtschaftlicher Lagebericht Nr. 36, August 1942, gez. Thomas.*

35. BA/MA RW 19/202: *Auszüge aus KTB, Wi Rü Amt/Stab (nur Mineralöl-betref-fend), Beginn: 9.1.41. Vortrag Dr Schlicht (Mineralöl Brigade) beim Amtchef, 8.9.1942. Bericht über Maikop.*

36. Irving, *Göring,* 367.

37. BA/MA N671/9: *Richthofen TB,* 10 August 1942.

38. Ibid., 15 August 1942.

39. USAFHRA K113.309-3 vol. 5: *Erfolgsübersicht des Fl. Führ. Süd vom 19.2.–9.8.1942.*

40. USAFHRA 512.607: *AMWIS No. 155, Up to 1200–19th August 1942.*

41. Source cited in note 2.

42. M. Axworthy et al., *Third Axis, Fourth Ally: Romanian Armed Forces in the European War, 1941–1945* (London: Arms & Armour, 1995), 81; USAFHRA 119.606-2: *Combined Chiefs of Staff: Eastern Front Situation Report (message from War Office D.D.M.I. to British Army Staff, Washington. Classified "Most Secret"), No. 58613, 16 August 1942; KTB, 1/Skl. (m/film),* part A, vol. 36, entries for August 1942.

43. BA/MA RM 7/115: *KTB, 1/Skl. Teil B IX: Lageübersicht, Mittelmeer-Ägäis-Schwarzes Meer, 1.–18. August 1942* and *19.8.–16.9.1942;* Tieke, 122–123.

44. USAFHRA K113.309-3 vol. 6: *Fl. Führ. Süd Ia Nr.: 4541/42 geh.: Tagesab-schlußmeldung Fl. Führ. Süd für 9.8.42.*

45. BA/MA N671/9: *Richthofen TB,* 10 August 1942; *KTB, 1/Skl. (m/film),* part A, vol. 36, entries for August 1942; source cited in note 2.

46. Ibid.

47. Ziemke and Bauer, 375.

48. BA/MA N671/9: *Richthofen TB,* 31 August 1942.

49. Dierich, 73; Smith, 137.

50. BA/MA N671/9: *Richthofen TB,* 15 August 1942; Blau, 163.

51. See Hitler's comments to Wagner, the army's quartermaster general, in *KTB OKW,* vol. 2, 637–638 (25 August 1942).

52. Ziemke and Bauer, 375.

53. *KTB OKW,* vol. 2, 622 (22 August 1942).

54. A. Speer, *Inside the Third Reich* (London: Sphere, 1971), 332.

55. *HGPW,* vol. 2, 463.

56. USAFHRA K113.309-3 vol. 6: *Die Stärke der deutschen Luftwaffe (Ostfront), 20.8.1942.*

57. USAFHRA K113.106-153: *Zusammenstellung der Ist-Stärken und der einsatzbereiten Flugzeuge an der Ostfront 1942.*

58. Tieke, 192, 193, 194.

59. Ibid., 195.

60. Karpov, 121.

61. *HGPW,* vol. 2, 462.

62. *KTB, 1/Skl. (m/film),* part A, vol. 36, 9–31 August 1942; *KTB OKW,* vol. 2, 560–665 (9–31 August 1942); Axworthy, 82.

63. BA/MA N671/9: *Richthofen TB,* 31 August 1942.

64. Axworthy, 81, 82, 247, 249, 272.

65. *KTB, 1/Skl. (m/film),* part A, vol. 37, 3 September 1942; *HGPW,* vol. 2, 462.

66. BA/MA RM 7/115: *KTB, 1/Skl. Teil B IX: Lageübersicht, Mittelmeer-Ägäis-Schwarzes Meer, 19.8.–16.9.1942;* Tieke, 133.

67. BA/MA RM 7/248: *Admiral Schwarzes Meer, Gefechtsstand, den 2. September 1942, gKdos. An Mar. Gr. Süd, Op-Stab, Sofia. Betr.: "Blücher II" und Einsatz operativer Streitkräfte.*

68. *KTB OKW,* vol. 2, 654 (29 August 1942).

69. Ibid., 657–658 (30 August 1942).

70. *KTB, 1/Skl. (m/film),* part A, vol. 37, 2 September 1942.

71. Ziemke and Bauer, 376–377.

72. BA/MA RM 7/115: *KTB, 1/Skl. Teil B IX: Lageübersicht, Mittelmeer-Ägäis-Schwarzes Meer, 19.8.–16.9.1942;* See also *KTB, 1/Skl. (m/film),* Part A, Vol. 37, 14 and 18 September 1942.

73. Tieke, 134; see the Luftwaffe activity reports appended to the daily entries in *KTB OKW,* vol. 2, 665–713 (1–10 September 1942); *KTB, 1/Skl. (m/film),* part A, vol. 37, daily entries for September 1942.

74. BA/MA N671/9: *Richthofen TB,* 10 September 1942; *KTB, 1/Skl. (m/film),* part A, vol. 37, 6–10 September 1942.

75. *HGPW,* vol. 2, 463; Tieke, 138.

76. Irving, *Hitler's War,* 420.

77. Tieke, 183.

78. See the brief Luftwaffe activity reports appended to the daily entries in *KTB OKW.*

79. For example: BA/MA N671/9: *Richthofen TB,* 21 September 1942; *KTB OKW,* vol. 2, 761, 768, 771 (23, 26, 27 September 1942).

80. *KTB, 1/Skl. (m/film),* part A, vol. 37, 11 September 1942. Also see 22 and 29 September.

81. Ibid., 13 September 1942.

82. USAFHRA 180.04-13: U.S. Department of the Navy, Office of the Chief of Naval Operations, Naval History Division: War Diary of [German] Admiral, Black Sea, 1 October–31 December 1942 (PG Numbers 31519a–31522) (hereafter cited as *KTB, Ad. Schw. Meer,* III), 6 October 1942.

83. Ibid., 7 November 1942.

84. BA/MA RM 7/115: *KTB, 1/Skl. Teil B IX: Lageübersicht, Mittelmeer-Ägäis-Schwarzes Meer, 19.8.–16.9.1942; 17.–30.9.1942; 1.–15.10.1942.*

85. *KTB, 1/Skl. (m/film),* part A, vol. 37, 19 September 1942.

86. BA/MA N671/9: *Richthofen TB,* 13–15 September 1942.

87. Tieke, 219, 234.

88. BA/MA N671/9: *Richthofen TB,* 29 October to 6 November 1942.

89. Dierich, 74.

90. *KTB OKW,* vol. 2, 864, 26 October 1942; E. von Mackensen, *Vom Bug zum Kaukasus: Das III. Panzerkorps im Feldzug gegen Sowjetrußland 1941/42* (Neckargemünd: Kurt Vowinckel, 1967), 103.

91. *HGPW,* vol. 2, 466.

92. BA/MA N671/9: *Richthofen TB,* 25 October 1942.

93. Dierich, 74.

94. Tieke, 300; BA/MA N671/9: *Richthofen TB,* 27 and 28 October 1942.

95. Ibid., 28 October 1942.

96. Ibid., 30 October 1942.

97. Ziemke and Bauer, 454.

98. BA/MA N671/9: *Richthofen TB,* 3 November 1942; *KTB OKW,* vol. 2, 906 (4 November 1942).

99. Ziemke and Bauer, 380.

100. BA/MA N671/9: *Richthofen TB,* 6 November 1942.

101. Mackensen, 107.

102. Ibid., 108.

103. Ziemke and Bauer, 381.

104. BA/MA N671/9: *Richthofen TB,* 18 September 1942.

105. Tieke, 267.

106. Ibid., 273.

107. BA/MA N671/9: *Richthofen TB,* 4, 5, and 6 October 1942.

108. USAFHRA 119.606-2: Combined Chiefs of Staff: Eastern Front Situation Report (message from War Office D.D.M.I. to British Army Staff, Washington. Classified "Most Secret"), No: 70060, 4 October 1942; USAFHRA 512.607: *AMWIS No. 163, Up to 1200-16th October 1942.*

109. *KTB, Ad. Schw. Meer,* III, early October 1942.

110. *KTB, 1/Skl. (m/film),* part A, vol. 37, 19 September 1942.

111. The Rumanians positioned flak batteries around their own army formations as well as Axis naval bases, including Balaclava, where they brought down a few enemy planes. Cf. *KTB, Ad. Schw. Meer,* III, 13 October 1942.

112. According to *Admiral Schwarzes Meer*'s war diary, Crimean flak units shot down only two aircraft during the entire month of October (ibid., 13 and 16 October).

113. Ibid., daily entries for October 1942.

114. *KTB, 1/Skl. (m/film),* part A, vol. 37, 7 and 15 September 1942; *KTB, Ad. Schw. Meer,* III, 2, 16, 21, and 31 October 1942.

115. Ibid., 12, 13, and 28 October 1942.

116. Ibid., 2 and 3 October 1942.

117. Ibid., 23 October 1942.

118. Ibid., 4 and 14 December 1942. See the other daily entries in the period.

119. Irving, *Hitler's War,* 437.

120. BA/MA N671/9: *Richthofen TB,* 10 October 1942.

121. Source cited in note 57.

122. NARS T971/16/114-232: *III./Kampfgeschwader 55-Kriegstagebuch Nr. 8* (Third Group of the 55th Bomber Wing. War Diary No. 8.), 10 October 1942 (frames 140–142).

123. Hinsley, *British Intelligence,* vol. 2, 107.

124. BA/MA RL 8/59: *Verbände der Luftflotte 4 im Bereich der Heeresgruppe A, Stand: 22.11.42, gKdos.*

125. USAFHRA K113.309-3 vol. 6: *Einsatz fliegender Verbände der deutschen Luftwaffe an der Ostfront, 20.11.1942.*

126. *KTB, Ad. Schw. Meer,* III, 16 December 1942.

127. BA/MA RL 8/59: *Luftwaffengruppe Kaukasus, Gef. Stand, den 21.1.1943, "Dislozierung der flieg. Verbände Lw. Gruppe Kaukasus."*

128. On 21 January, for instance, *4. (F) 122* had 6 of its 11 aircraft operational; *NAG 17* had 11 of 17 operational; *Nachtflg.-Lehrg. 3* had 5 of 9 operational; *13./J.G. 52* had 5 of 11 operational. Source: BA/MA RL 8/59: *Luftwaffengruppe Kaukasus, Gef. Stand, den 21.1.1943, "Eigene Luftlage."*

129. BA/MA RL 8/59: *Erfolge der Luftwaffengruppe Kaukasus bezw. Kuban vom 25.11.1942–6.2.1943.*

130. Tieke, 291–292; BA/MA N671/9: *Richthofen TB,* 7 December 1942.

7. TOWARD DESTRUCTION

1. Halder, vol. 3, 493 (30 July 1942).

2. USAFHRA 168.7158-338: *Pickert TB,* 8 August 1942.

3. BA/MA N671/9: *Richthofen TB,* 6 August 1942.

4. NARS T971/18/671-701: *Der Einsatz der Luftwaffe vom 1. Juli 1942, dem Beginn des deutschen Angriffes im südlichen Abschnitt der Ostfront, bis zur russischen Doppeloffensive im November 1942 und bei den Kämpfen um Stalingrad.*

5. Higham and Kipp, 90.

6. Ibid.; Hardesty, 101.

7. Ibid., 101.

8. Source cited in note 4; BA/MA N671/9: *Richthofen TB,* 12 and 13 August 1942.

9. *HGPW,* vol. 2, 432; Erickson, *Road to Stalingrad,* 368.

10. Ibid.

11. USAFHRA 170.2278-14: *Military Intelligence Division W.D.G.S., Military Attaché Report, I.G. No. 9925, E.E.-M.I.D., Report No. 5, 13 December 1943, Restricted, Subject: [Soviet] Air Force in Battle of Stalingrad.* (Note: this is an American intelligence translation of a May 1943 report by a Soviet Lt. Col. A. Vladimirov.)

12. BA/MA N671/9: *Richthofen TB,* 19, 20, and 21 August 1942.

13. Ibid., 21 August 1942.

14. Ibid.; USAFHRA K113.309-3 vol. 9: *Luftflotte 4 vor Stalingrad unter General-*

oberst Frhr. von Richthofen, ab 20.7.42; W. Murray, *Strategy for Defeat: The Luftwaffe 1933–1945* (Maxwell Air Force Base, Ala.: Air University Press, 1983); 124; and Muller, *The German Air War in Russia,* 90.

15. *KTB OKW,* vol. 2, 626 (23 August 1942).

16. USAFHRA K113.309-3 vol. 5: *Hauptmann Herbert Pabst, Staffelkapitän u. Gruppenkommandeur in einer Sturzkampfstaffel: Berichte aus Rußland, 1942* (hereafter cited as *Pabst Berichte*), 23 August 1942.

17. Wagner, *Soviet Air Force in World War II,* 100; Hardesty, 102.

18. Ibid.; source cited in note 11.

19. V. I. Chuikov, *The Battle for Stalingrad* Trans. from the Russian by Harold Silver (New York: Holt, Rinehart and Winston, 1964; first published in English in 1963 as *The Beginning of the Road*), 61.

20. Cf. *The Road to Stalingrad* by the editors of the Time-Life series, *The Third Reich* (Alexandria, Va.: Time-Life, 1991), 76.

21. *HGPW,* vol. 2, 435.

22. Source cited in note 4.

23. BA/MA N671/9: *Richthofen TB,* 25 August 1942. See Pabst's description of the burning city in USAFHRA K113.309-3 vol. 5: *Pabst Berichte,* 25 August 1942.

24. *HGPW,* vol. 2, 437.

25. USAFHRA 168.7158-338: *Pickert TB,* 25 August 1942.

26. Ziemke and Bauer, 387.

27. *KTB, 1/Skl. (m/film),* part A, vol. 36, 28 August 1942.

28. BA/MA N671/9: *Richthofen TB,* 16 September 1942.

29. Ibid., 27 August 1942.

30. Ibid., 29 August 1942.

31. Ibid., 19 July and 25 August 1942.

32. *KTB OKW,* vol. 2, 617–639 (21 to 25 August 1942).

33. Ibid., 642, 646 (26 and 27 August 1942).

34. Source cited in note 4; BA/MA N671/9: *Richthofen TB,* 29 August 1942.

35. *HGPW,* vol. 2, 438.

36. Source cited in note 4.

37. Plocher, *1942,* 234. A few writers, uncritically following Plocher's narrative, have repeated this error (and numerous others). Cf. Kurowski, *Balkenkreuz,* 285.

38. Chuikov, 64–65.

39. *KTB OKW,* vol. 2, 669 (2 September 1942); Halder, vol. 3, 514 (31 August 1942).

40. Zhukov, 136.

41. Ibid.; Erickson, *Road to Stalingrad,* 385.

42. Zhukov, 137.

43. Ibid., 138; *HGPW,* vol. 2, 439.

44. USAFHRA K113.309-3 vol. 5: *Pabst Berichte,* 5 September 1942.

45. *KTB, 1/Skl. (m/film),* part A, vol. 36, 4 September 1942 [should be 5 Sept.?]; *KTB OKW,* vol. 2, 685 (5 September 1942).

46. Hardesty, 101; Zhukov, 138.

47. Ziemke and Bauer, 393.

48. BA/MA N671/9: *Richthofen TB,* 13 September 1942.

49. Ibid., 16 September 1942.

50. Ibid.

51. *KTB, 1/Skl. (m/film),* part A, vol. 36, 18 September 1942; *KTB OKW,* vol. 2, 742 (19 September 1942).

52. Source cited in chapter 6, note 57.

53. Ibid.

54. *KTB OKW,* vol. 2, 651 (28 August 1942).

55. Hardesty, 102.

56. *KTB OKW,* vol. 2, 742 (19 September 1942); *KTB, 1/Skl. (m/film),* part A, vol. 36, 18 September 1942.

57. Ibid., 30 September 1942; *KTB OKW,* vol. 2, 780 (30 September 1942).

58. Chuikov, 106.

59. Ibid., 113.

60. Ibid., 95.

61. Ibid., 124.

62. Ibid., 151.

63. A. Clark, *Barbarossa: The Russian-German Conflict, 1941–45* (New York: Quill, 1985; first published in 1965), 222.

64. Source cited in chapter 6, note 57.

65. Chuikov, 114; *HGPW,* vol. 2, 441.

66. Source cited in note 11.

67. Chuikov, 117.

68. Ibid., 328.

69. Source cited in note 11; Erickson, *Road to Stalingrad,* 411.

70. Chuikov, 84; Erickson, *Road to Stalingrad,* 411.

71. *HGPW,* vol. 2, 442; Ziemke and Bauer, 393; Zhukov, 143.

72. BA/MA N671/9: *Richthofen TB,* 22 September 1942.

73. H. Doerr, *Der Feldzug nach Stalingrad: Versuch eines operativen Überblickes* (Darmstadt: E. S. Mittler & Sohn, 1955), 52–53.

74. USAFHRA K113.309-3 vol. 5: *Pabst Berichte,* 14 September 1942.

75. Ibid., 17 September 1942.

76. Ziemke and Bauer, 396; BA/MA N671/9: *Richthofen TB,* 26 September 1942.

77. Domarus, vol. 4, 1912, 1914.

78. USAFHRA K113.309-3 vol. 5: *Pabst Berichte,* 16 September 1942.

79. USAFHRA K239.0512-1838: *U.S. Air Force Oral History Program No. K239.0512-1838, Brig. Gen. Paul-Werner Hozzel, German Air Force, November 1978* (hereafter cited as *Hozzel Oral History*), 127–128.

80. Plocher, *1942,* 234.

81. Rudel, 55; USAFHRA K239.0512-1838: *Hozzel Oral History,* 127.

82. Chuikov, 90.

83. Ibid., 151.

84. Cf. USAFHRA 168.7158-338: *Pickert TB,* 27 and 28 September 1942.

85. USAFHRA K113.309-3 vol. 5: *Pabst Berichte,* 27 September 1942.

86. Cf. USAFHRA 168.7158-338: *Pickert TB,* 8 September 1942.

87. USAFHRA K113.309-3 vol. 3: *Einsatz der III. Gruppe des Jagdgeschwaders 3 im Feldzug gegen Rußland, von Karl Heinz Langer (Quelle: Kriegstagebücher des III. J.G.3),* 16 September 1942.

88. USAFHRA K113.309-3 vol. 5: *Pabst Berichte,* 25 September 1942.

89. BA/MA N671/9: *Richthofen TB,* 27 September 1942.

90. Chuikov, 153.

91. USAFHRA 168.7158-338: *Pickert TB*, 30 September 1942; BA/MA N671/9: *Richthofen TB*, 1 October 1942.

92. Ibid., 2 October.

93. Ibid.; USAFHRA 168.7158-338: *Pickert TB*, 2 October 1942.

94. Chuikov, 166.

95. Ibid., 168–169.

96. Ziemke and Bauer, 397.

97. Ibid.

98. BA/MA N671/9: *Richthofen TB*, 3 October 1942.

99. Ibid., 6 October 1942; Ziemke and Bauer, 397.

100. T. A. Wray, *Standing Fast: German Defensive Doctrine on the Russian Front during World War II, Prewar to March 1943,* Combat Studies Institute, Research Survey No. 5 (Fort Leavenworth, Kans.: U.S. Army Command and General Staff College, 1986), 126.

101. H. Schröter, *Stalingrad: ". . . bis zur letzten Patrone"* (Lengerich: Kleins Druck- und Verlagsanstalt, n.d.), 185.

102. Wray, 126.

103. Chuikov, 178. Chuikov wrongly recalled the "lull" starting on 8 October.

104. BA/MA N671/9: *Richthofen TB*, 12 October 1942.

105. Ibid., 15 October 1942.

106. Ibid.

107. Source cited in note 87, 10 October 1942.

108. Axworthy, 291, 292.

109. Ibid., 293.

110. M. Kehrig, *Stalingrad: Analyse und Dokumentation einer Schlacht,* Beiträge zur Militär- und Kriegsgeschichte, Band 15 (Stuttgart: Deutsche Verlags-Anstalt, 1974), 60, 119.

111. USAFHRA K113.309-3 vol. 6: *Einsatz fliegender Verbände der deutschen Luftwaffe an der Ostfront, 20.10.1942.*

112. Source cited in chapter 6, note 57.

113. BA/MA N671/9: *Richthofen TB*, 14 October 1942. For the lack of *VVS* opposition, also see USAFHRA 168.7158-338: *Pickert TB*, 14 October 1942.

114. Doerr, *Der Feldzug nach Stalingrad,* 54.

115. Chuikov, 180.

116. USAFHRA K239.0512-1838: *Hozzel Oral History,* 130.

117. Chuikov, 223.

118. USAFHRA K239.0512-1838: *Hozzel Oral History,* 124, 128.

119. Ibid., 131.

120. The authors of the *HGPW* maintain that "German aviation executed more than 2,000 air sorties in the factory area on that day" (vol. 2, 444). This figure, still too high, is far closer than Chuikov's.

121. Chuikov, 180.

122. USAFHRA K239.0512-1838: *Hozzel Oral History,* 131.

123. Erickson, *Road to Stalingrad,* 436.

124. *Der Führer, OKH/Gen.St.d.H./Op. Abt. (I), Nr. 420817/42, gKdos. Chefs., H.Qu. OKH, 14. Oktober 1942, "Operationsbefehl Nr. 1,"* in *KTB OKW,* vol. 2, 1301–1304.

125. Chuikov, 188.

126. Ibid., 195, 196.
127. BA/MA N671/9: *Richthofen TB*, 1 November 1942.
128. USAFHRA 168.7158-338: *Pickert TB*, 1 November 1942.
129. *Joseph Goebbels—Tagebücher, Band 4*, 1830 (9 November 1942).
130. Domarus, vol. 4, 1937–1938.
131. *KTB OKW*, vol. 2, 597 (16 August 1942).
132. Ibid.
133. Ziemke and Bauer, 456.
134. Ibid.
135. *KTB OKW*, vol. 2, 889 (2 November 1942).
136. Ibid.
137. Ibid., 902 (4 November 1942).
138. Ziemke and Bauer, 457.
139. Ibid., 466.
140. Warlimont, vol. 1, 266.
141. Ziemke and Bauer, 465.
142. Ibid.
143. Ibid., 464.
144. BA/MA N671/9: *Richthofen TB*, 4 November 1942.
145. Irving, *Göring*, 364; Hinsley, *British Intelligence*, vol. 2, 452–453.
146. BA/MA N671/9: *Richthofen TB*, 8 November 1942.
147. Sources cited in notes 57 and 125 of chapter 6.
148. BA/MA N671/9: *Richthofen TB*, 14 November 1942.
149. Source cited in chapter 6, note 57.
150. Ibid.
151. Rudel, 56.
152. BA/MA N671/9: *Richthofen TB*, 14 November 1942.
153. Ibid., 16 November 1942.

8. DISASTER AND DECISIONS

1. Zhukov, 139.
2. Ibid.
3. Ibid., 142.
4. *HGPW*, vol. 3, 18.
5. Ibid., 22, 23.
6. Ibid., 23.
7. Ibid., 26; Ziemke and Bauer, 446.
8. Hardesty, 105. Higham and Kipp (92) maintain that the *VVS* possessed 1,327 operational aircraft in the Stalingrad sector. Boyd (*The Soviet Air Force since 1918*, 160) argues that it had 1,414.
9. Sources cited in notes 57 and 125 of chapter 6.
10. Higham and Kipp, 93; Hardesty, 106–107.
11. Ibid., 106.
12. Sources cited in notes 57 and 125 of chapter 6.
13. Hardesty, 105.

14. Higham and Kipp, 92.

15. Erickson, *Road to Stalingrad,* 464.

16. Axworthy, 89-92.

17. USAFHRA K113.309-3 vol. 9: Lothar von Heinemann, Oberst i.G.(a.D.), *Der russische Aufmarsch am Don und die Beurteilung der eigenen Abwehrbereitschaft.*

18. Kehrig, 136; Seydlitz, W. von, *Stalingrad: Konflikt und Konzequenz.* Oldenberg: Gerhard Stalling, 1977.

19. Chuikov, 218.

20. BA/MA N671/9: *Richthofen TB,* 19 November 1942.

21. Axworthy, 293.

22. Rudel, 57.

23. BA/MA N671/9: *Richthofen TB,* 19 November 1942.

24. Plocher, *1942,* 256.

25. USAFHRA 168.7158-335: *Tagebuch-Generalleutnant Fiebig (Stalingrad), 25.11.1942-2.2.1943* (hereafter cited as *Fiebig TB),* 25 November 1942.

26. USAFHRA 168.7158-338: *Pickert TB,* 23 November 1942.

27. USAFHRA 168.7158-335: *Gruppe Stahel, Gef. Qu., den 20.12.1942, Bericht über den Zustand der Truppe am 20.12.1942* (appended to Fiebig's diary).

28. Bekker, 366; BA/MA N671/9: *Richthofen TB,* 23 and 24 November 1942.

29. Ziemke and Bauer, 446.

30. Erickson, *Road to Stalingrad,* 470.

31. Doerr, *Der Feldzug nach Stalingrad,* 75-76.

32. Schröter, 80.

33. USAFHRA 168.7158-338: *Pickert TB,* 24 November 1942.

34. Axworthy, 294.

35. BA/MA N671/9: *Richthofen TB,* 21 November 1942.

36. Source cited in note 87 of chapter 7, 21 November 1942.

37. BA/MA N671/9: *Richthofen TB,* 23 November 1942.

38. Axworthy, 294.

39. BA/MA N671/9: *Richthofen TB,* 23 November 1942.

40. Manstein, 347.

41. J. Fischer's "Über den Entschlub zur Luftversorgung Stalingrads: Ein Beitrag zur militärischen Führung im Dritten Reich" (*Militärgeschichtliches Mitteilungen* 2 (1969): 7-67) is the best published study of the "decision to supply Stalingrad by air," although it makes no use of the diaries of Milch, Richthofen, Fiebig, and Pickert, all used in the present work. David Irving's works on the Luftwaffe deal only briefly with the decision to airlift but contain many valuable insights and place blame fairly.

42. Kurowski, *Stalingrad,* 298. See Kurowski's earlier *Luftbrücke,* 32-37, and *Balkenkreuz,* 310; and Murray, 151.

43. Mitcham, 184.

44. Fischer, 10.

45. For Jeschonnek's meeting with Hitler, see postwar statements by the airman's staff in USAFHRA K113.106-153: *Aussagen zum Problem der Luftversorgung von Stalingrad* (compiled by Hermann Plocher).

46. F. Morzik, *German Air Force Airlift Operations,* USAF Historical Studies No. 167 (Montgomery, Ala.: USAF Historical Division, Research Studies Institute, Air University, 1961), 145.

47. Ibid., 150.

48. *KTB OKW,* vol. 2, 1019 (25 November 1942); Bekker, 363.

49. Kehrig, 163.

50. USAFHRA 168.7158-335: *Feldgericht des VIII. Fliegerkorps, Br. B. Nr. 7/43, gKdos, Im Felde, den 26.1.1943, gez. Fiebig* (appended to Fiebig's diary).

51. BA/MA N671/9: *Richthofen TB,* 21 November 1942.

52. My description of the conference is drawn from Pickert's notes to his original diary entry (USAFHRA 168.7158-338: *Pickert TB: "Aufzeichnungen aus meinem Tagebuch und von Besprechungen über operative and taktische Gedanken und Massnahmen der 6. Armee"),* from later correspondence between Pickert and Hans Doerr (in USAFHRA K113.309-3 vol. 9), and from an essay written by Pickert to Hermann Plocher in 1956 (same source).

53. *OB HGr B an OKH/Chef GenStdH vom 23.11.1942, betr. Zurücknahme der 6. Armee, gez. von Weichs,* published as Doc. 9 in Kehrig, 561.

54. Schröter, 85.

55. *AOK 6/Ia an HGr B vom 22.11.1942, 1900 Uhr, betr. Lage und Absicht der Armee,* published as Doc. 6 in Kehrig, 559–560.

56. *Paulus an Hitler vom 23.11.1942, betr. Notwendigkeit des Ausbruches der 6. Armee, FuSpr (Entwurf) OB 6. Armee, gKdos Chefs. an OKH, nachr. HGr. B, vom 23.11.1942, 2130 Uhr,* published as Doc. 10, Kehrig, 562.

57. *Führerentscheid vom 24.11.1942, betr. Halten der Stellungen der 6. Armee und Ensatzstoß. FS OKH GenStdH/Op. Abt. (I/SB) Nr. 420 960/42 gKdos Chefs. vom 24.11.1942, 0140 Uhr, aufgenommen bei AOK 6 um 0830 Uhr,* published as Doc. 11, in Kehrig, 562.

58. K. Zeitzler, "Stalingrad," in W. Kreipe, et al., *The Fatal Decisions: Six Decisive Battles of the Second World War from the Viewpoint of the Vanquished* (London: Michael Joseph, 1956), 142.

59. Irving, *Hitler's War,* 456; Irving, *Göring,* 369.

60. Irving, *Göring,* 367.

61. BA/MA N671/10: *Richthofen TB,* 11 February 1943.

62. Ibid., 10 February 1943.

63. USAFHRA K113.309-3: *Bericht über eine Auskunft über Görings Stalingrader Zusage durch Generaloberst Lörzer (Befragung Hamburg-Othmarschen, 16. April 1956, durch Prof. Dr. Richard Suchenwirth, Karlsruhe).*

64. USAFHRA K113.309-3 vol. 9: *Staatssekretär a.D. Paul Körner über Jeschonnek (Befragung am 19.9.1955 in München).*

65. *Milch Taschenkalender,* 21 May 1946 (on David Irving, Microfilm DJ-57, part of the Irving microfilm series "Records and Documents Relating to the Third Reich" by Microform [Wakefield] Ltd.) This personal *Taschenkalender* ("pocket diary") is cited hereafter as *Milch Tagebuch.* It is not the official war diary of Milch's "Special Staff" (USAFHRA 168.7158-337: *Kriegstagebuch Sonderstab Generalfeldmarschall Milch, 15.1–3.2.1943),* cited below as *KTB Sonderstab Milch.*

66. Ibid.

67. Zeitzler, 144–145; USAFHRA K113.309-3 vol. 9: *Generaloberst Zeitzler über das Zustandekommen des Entschlusses, Stalingrad aus der Luft zu versorgen (Briefliche Beantwortung vom 11.3.1955 folgender von Prof. Suchenwirth mit Brief vom 3.3.1955 gestellter Fragen).*

68. Ibid.

69. For Hitler's instruction to Paulus, see note 67. For the placing of the Zeitzler-Göring confrontation on 24 November, see M. Cooper, *The German Airforce 1933-1945: An Anatomy of Failure* (London: Jane's, 1981), 251; Bekker, 363; Carell, *Stalingrad,* 170.

70. Irving, *Göring,* 369-371.

71. BA/MA N671/9: *Richthofen TB,* 24 November 1942.

72. Ibid., 25 November 1942.

73. *Gen d. Art. v. Seydlitz-Kurzbach, HG des LI. AK, an den OB der 6. Armee vom 25.11.1942, betr. Stellungnahme zum Armeebefehl vom 24.11.1942. Abschrift des AOK 6 für ObKdo HGr Don: Der KG des LI. AK Nr. 603/42 gKdos vom 25.11.1942, bei HGr Don 28.11.1942,* published as Doc. 15 in Kehrig, 564-567.

74. *AOK 6/OQu vom 24.11. an OKH/GenQu, HGr B/OQu, und vom 25.11.1942 an HGr Don, betr. Bedarfsanforderung für Luftversorgungsgüter,* published as Doc. 16, Kehrig, 567.

75. *Manstein an OKH/Op Abt vom 24.11.1942, betr. Beurteilung der Lage der 6. Armee. FS (Abschrift) ObKdo der HGr Don/Ia Nr. 4580/42 gKdos Chefs. vom 24. 11.1942, ca. 1300 Uhr,* published as Doc. 14, Kehrig, 564.

76. V. Orange, *Coningham: A Biography of Air Marshal Sir Arthur Coningham* (Washington, D.C.: Center for Air Force History, 1992; first published by Methuen, 1990), 128 (see also 127).

77. G. F. Howe, *Northwest Africa: Seizing the Initiative in the West* (Washington, D.C.: Office of the Chief of Military History, Department of the Army, 1957), 683.

78. Zeitzler, 132.

79. Irving, *Göring,* 381.

80. Morzik, *German Air Force Airlift Operations,* 183.

81. USAFHRA 168.7158-333: *"Lufttransportflieger": Entwicklung und Einsatz während des Krieges (Bericht Generalmajor Morzik).*

82. Morzik, *German Air Force Airlift Operations,* 183.

83. NARS T971/18/983-989: *Lufttransportführer Oberst Morzik, Gefechtsstand, den 12.2.1943. FS Gen.Kdo. VIII. Fl. Korps, Ia/Ic, Nr. 485/43, geh. v. 6.2.1942. Betr.: Erfahrungsbericht Stalingrad.*

84. USAFHRA 168.7158-336: *Lufttransportführer beim Generalquartiermeister, Berlin, den 8.11.1942.*

85. *KTB OKW,* vol. 2, 1019 (25 November 1942); BA/MA N671/9: *Richthofen TB,* 25 November 1942.

86. *Generalmajor* Fritz Morzik, the Luftwaffe's air transport expert, later argued (using the same formula but 750 tons per day as the basis of his calculations) that "1,050 Ju 52s would have been required to meet the needs of the Sixth Army" (*German Air Force Airlift Operations,* 185).

87. Source cited in note 84, and ibid.: *Lufttransportführer beim Generalquartiermeister, Berlin, den 29.11.1942.*

88. Irving, *Göring,* 380.

89. USAFHRA K113.309-3 vol. 9: *Luftversorgung Stalingrad (20.11.42-1.2.43), von Generalmajor a.D. Karl Heinrich Schulz.*

90. Ju 52 units: *K.Gr. z.b.V. 9, K.Gr. z.b.V. 50, K.Gr. z.b.V. 102, K.Gr. z.b.V. 105, K.Gr. z.b.V. 172, K.Gr. z.b.V. 500, K.Gr. z.b.V. 700, K.Gr. z.b.V. 900, I. and II./K.Gr. z.b.V. 1;* He 111

units: *K.Gr. z.b.V. 5, K.Gr. z.b.V. 20, III./K.G. 4, K.G. 27, I./K.G. 100, K.G. 55;* Ju 86 units: *K.Gr. z.b.V. 21, K.Gr. z.b.V. 22;* additional units: *K.G. 50* (He 177s), *K.Gr. z.b.V. 200* (FW 200s, Ju 90s, Ju 290s); Morzik, *Die deutschen Transportflieger,* 155–156.

91. BA/MA RL 8/55: *Generalkommando VIII. Fliegerkorps, Quartiermeister, Gef.Qu., 30.11.1942. Besondere Anordnungen des Quartiermeisters für die Luftversorgung der Festung Stalingrad (Anlage 2 zu Gen. Kdo. VIII. Fl. Korps, Ia Nr. 4200/42, gKdos);* USAFHRA K113.106-153: *Auszug aus dem Flottenbefehl vom 26.11.42, Nr. 5013/42 Geheime Kommandosache;* BA/MA N671/9: *Richthofen TB,* 26 November 1942; source cited in note 89.

92. USAFHRA K113.106-153: *Auszug aus dem Flottenbefehl vom 26.11.42, Nr. 5013/42 Geheime Kommandosache.*

93. BA/MA N671/9: *Richthofen TB,* 28 November 1942.

94. Ibid., 26 November 1942; USAFHRA 168.7158-335: *Fiebig TB,* 26 November 1942.

9. FAILURE

1. USAFHRA 142.0372: "The Russian Winter," *Air Forces General Information Bulletin No. 7, December 1942* (Headquarters, Army Air Forces Intelligence Service, 1000-4, #73. Restricted).

2. USAFHRA 512.607: "Meteorological Conditions in the Southeast of European Russia," *AMWIS No. 165, Up to 1200–30th October 1942.*

3. Ibid.

4. BA/MA N671/9: *Richthofen TB,* 26 November 1942.

5. USAFHRA 168.7158-335: *Fiebig TB,* 27 November 1942.

6. W. Pickert, "The Stalingrad Airlift: An Eyewitness Commentary," *Aerospace Historian* 18 (December 1971): 184.

7. USAFHRA 168.7158-335: *Fiebig TB,* 2 December 1942.

8. Morzik, *Die deutschen Transportflieger,* 162.

9. USAFHRA 168.7158-338: *Pickert TB,* 26 November 1942.

10. Source cited in chapter 7, note 87, 28 November 1942.

11. USAFHRA 168.7158-338: *Pickert TB,* 29 November 1942.

12. Hardesty, 105.

13. Source cited in chapter 7, note 11; Richthofen's diary suggests that the total was closer to 400, still an insignificant number.

14. Hardesty, 105. Hardesty credits improving weather with the increase in *VVS* operations. In fact, the weather grew steadily worse. See USAFHRA K113.309-3 vol. 9: *"Die tägliche Wetterlage während der Luftversorgung Stalingrad."*

15. Source cited in chapter 7, note 11.

16. Hardesty, 110.

17. Ibid., 110.

18. Source cited in chapter 6, note 125.

19. BA/MA RL 8/59: *Verbände der Luftflotte 4 im Bereich der Heeresgruppe A, Stand: 22.11.42, gKdos.*

20. Plocher, *1942,* 283; Cooper, 252; Mitcham, 188, 189; R. W. Lower, *Luftwaffe Tactical*

Operations at Stalingrad, 19 November 1942–02 February 1943 (unpublished research paper submitted to the faculty of the Air Command and Staff College, Air University, n.d.), 21.

21. BA/MA N671/9: *Richthofen TB,* 2 January 1943.

22. Pickert, "The Stalingrad Airlift," 184.

23. Source cited in chapter 7, note 87, 28 November 1942.

24. Ibid.

25. All airlift statistics in this work come from Pickert's own tables, appended to his diary (USAFHRA 168.7158-338: *Pickert TB*). They are hereafter cited as "Pickert airlift statistics." When they differ from Richthofen's, Fiebig's, and Milch's figures, as they occasionally do, I will present all figures.

26. USAFHRA 168.7158-338: "Pickert airlift statistics."

27. *Befehlszug Luftflotte 4, Taganrog/Süd, 20.1.43, 16.05 Uhr, Vortrag Major Thiel, Kdr. III./K.G. 27 und Hptm. Mayer, Staffelkpt.[?]/K.G. 27,* in the war diary of Field Marshal Milch's "Special Staff" (USAFHRA 168.7158-337).

28. USAFHRA 168.7158-338: *Pickert TB,* 30 November 1942.

29. USAFHRA 168.7158-335: *Fiebig TB,* 2 December 1942.

30. BA/MA N671/9: *Richthofen TB,* 1 December 1942.

31. Manstein, 340.

32. BA/MA N671/9: *Richthofen TB,* 27 November 1942.

33. Manstein, 300–302.

34. Ibid., 350.

35. Ibid., 353.

36. Ibid., 354.

37. Ziemke and Bauer, 480.

38. *HGr Don an OKH/Chef GenStdH vom 28.11.1942, betr. Beurteilung der Lage. ObKdo der HGr Don/Ia Nr. 0341/42 gKdos Chefs. vom 28. 11.1942,* published as Doc. 22 in Kehrig, 573–577.

39. *OKH/GenStdH/Op Abt an HGr Don vom 3.12.1942, betr. Stellungnahme zur Lagebeurteilung der HGr Don vom 28.11.1942, eingegangenen bei OHK am 29.11.1942. FS OKH/GenStdH/Op Abt (I S/B) Nr. 420 978/42 gKdos Chefs. vom 3.12.1942, 1815 Uhr,* published as Doc. 23 in Kehrig, 577.

40. *OB HGr Don an OKH/Chef GenStdH vom 9.12.1942, betr. Beurteilung der Lage. FS (Abschrift) ObKdo der HGr Don/Ia Nr. 0354/42 gKdos Chefs. vom 9.12.1942,* published as Doc. 27 in Kehrig, 584–586.

41. Ibid.

42. *KTB OKW,* vol. 2, 1104.

43. BA/MA N671/9: *Richthofen TB,* 10 December 1942.

44. Ibid., 12 December 1942.

45. The error originates from David Irving (*Rise and Fall,* 189). See Murray, 155; Mitcham, 191.

46. BA/MA N671/10: *Richthofen TB,* 24 February 1943.

47. *Luftflottenkommando 4 vom 9.12.1942, betr. Befehl für die Kampfführung der Luftflotte 4 zur Vernichtung des Gegners bei Stalingrad. Luftflottenkommando 4/Führungsabteilung/Ia, Op Nr. 51266/42 gKdos, vom 9.12.1942,* published as Doc. 28 in Kehrig, 586–588.

48. USAFHRA 168.7158-335: *Fiebig TB,* 8 December 1942; BA/MA N671/9: *Richthofen TB,* 8 December 1942.

49. USAFHRA 168.7158-337: *KTB Sonderstab Milch;* Kehrig, 633–637; USAFHRA 168.7158-338: "Pickert airlift statistics."

50. USAFHRA 168.7158-337: *KTB Sonderstab Milch;* Kehrig, 633–637; USAFHRA 168.7158-338: "Pickert airlift statistics."

51. USAFHRA 168.7158-338: *Pickert TB,* 3 December 1942.

52. USAFHRA 168.7158-335: *Fiebig TB,* 12 December 1942.

53. Erickson, *Road to Berlin,* 12, 13.

54. BA/MA N671/9: *Richthofen TB,* 12 December 1942. According to the *OKW* war diary (*KTB OKW,* vol. 2, 1127), reliant on statistics provided daily by the *OKL,* the Luftwaffe destroyed thirty-nine enemy aircraft in aerial combat and eight by flak.

55. BA/MA N671/9: *Richthofen TB,* 12 December 1942.

56. Both Richthofen's and Fiebig's diaries state that Sixth Army received 80 tons that day. Milch, who was not yet in the region, claims that it unloaded 114 tons *(Richthofen TB,* 12 December 1942; USAFHRA 168.7158-335: *Fiebig TB,* 12 December 1942; USAFHRA 168.7158-337: *KTB Sonderstab Milch).*

57. H. Heiber, ed., *Lagebesprechungen im Führerhauptquartier: Protokollfragmente aus Hitlers militärischen Konferenzen 1942–1945* (Stuttgart: Deutsche Verlags-Anstalt, 1962), 53–54.

58. BA/MA N671/9: *Richthofen TB,* 14 December 1942.

59. Ibid., 14 December 1942. Note that Richthofen's and Fiebig's diaries agree that only 80 tons reached the pocket, whereas Milch, not yet in the region, stated that 135 tons arrived. Pickert gave no overall tonnage but mentioned that 63 cubic meters of fuel, 29 tons of ammunition, 5 tons of food, and 2 tons of other supplies arrived, suggesting an overall figure closer to Milch's.

60. BA/MA N671/9: *Richthofen TB,* 13 December 1942.

61. *KTB OKW,* vol. 2, 1128 (13 December 1942).

62. BA/MA N671/9: *Richthofen TB,* 15 December 1942. Milch and Pickert both put the figure for 15 December at around ninety tons. Fiebig gave no figure.

63. Irving, *Hitler's War,* 467.

64. BA/MA N671/9: *Richthofen TB,* 16 December 1942.

65. *OB HGr Don an Chef GenStdH vom 19.12.1942, betr. Beurteilung der Lage der HGr Don im Hinblick auf den Entsatz der 6. Armee. FS ObKdo der HGr Don/Ia Nr. 0368/42 gKdos Chefs. vom 19.12.1942, 1435 Uhr,* published as Doc. 35 in Kehrig, 598.

66. *ObKdo HGr Don an 6. Armee und 4. Pz. Armee vom 19.12.1942, betr. "Wintergewitter" und "Donnerschlag." FS ObKdo der HGr Don/Ia Nr. 0369/42 gKdos Chefs. vom 19.12.1942, 1800 Uhr,* published as Doc. 36, in Kehrig, 599.

67. *KTB OKW,* vol. 2, 1164 (20 December 1942).

68. USAFHRA 168.7158-337: *KTB Sonderstab Milch;* Kehrig, 633–637.

69. Ziemke and Bauer, 486.

70. USAFHRA 168.7158-335: *Fiebig TB,* 20 December 1942.

71. BA/MA N671/9: *Richthofen TB,* 20 December 1942.

72. USAFHRA 168.7158-335: *Fiebig TB,* 21 December 1942.

73. BA/MA N671/9: *Richthofen TB,* 23 December 1942; USAFHRA 168.7158-335: *Fiebig TB,* 23 December 1942.

74. BA/MA N671/9: *Richthofen TB,* 23 December 1942.

75. USAFHRA 168.7158-335: *Fiebig TB,* 24 December 1942.

76. BA/MA N671/9: *Richthofen TB,* 24 December 1942; USAFHRA 168.7158-335: *Fiebig TB,* 24 December 1942.

77. Ibid.

78. BA/MA N671/9: *Richthofen TB,* 25 December 1942.

79. Ibid., 12 December 1942.

80. Ibid., 24 December 1942.

81. *KTB OKW,* vol. 2, 1168 (21 December 1942).

82. Irving, *Hitler's War,* 453. Irving is correct. An examination of the original manuscript (David Irving, Microfilm DJ-91, part of the Irving microfilm series "Records and Documents Relating to the Third Reich" by Microform [Wakefield] Ltd.) reveals that the published version differs in many places from the original manuscript and that all changes cast Hitler in a negative light.

83. *OB HGr Don an OKH/Chef GenStdH vom 22.12.1942, betr. Kräfteverschiebung, Folgerungen für die 6. Armee. FS ObKdo der HGr Don/Ia Nr. 0374/42 gKdos Chefs. vom 22.12.1942, 2045 Uhr,* published as Doc. 43 in Kehrig, 607–608.

84. Ziemke and Bauer, 488.

85. BA/MA N671/9: *Richthofen TB,* 23 December 1942.

86. *Manstein an Chef GenStdH vom 25.12.1942, betr. Lagebeurteilung. FS HGr Don/Ia Nr. 378/42 gKdos Chefs.,* published as Doc. 50 in Kehrig, 613–615.

87. Zeitzler, "Stalingrad," 155.

88. *OKH/GenStdH/Op Abt, Operationsbefehl Nr. 2 vom 28.12.1942, betr. Kampfführung der HGr A, Don and B. FS OKH/GenStdH/Op Abt Nr. 421 042/42 gKdos Chefs. vom 28.12.1942, an HGr Don, gleichlt. an HGr A and HGr B,* published as Doc. 59 in Kehrig, 627–628.

89. BA/MA N671/9: *Richthofen TB,* 28 December 1942.

90. Source cited in note 86, 613–615 (and 633–637); USAFHRA 168.7158-337: *KTB Sonderstab Milch.*

91. Source cited in chapter 6, note 122, 24 December 1942 (frame 157); Bekker, 373.

92. USAFHRA 168.7158-337: *KTB Sonderstab Milch;* Kehrig, 633–637.

93. USAFHRA 168.7158-338: "Pickert airlift statistics."

94. Ibid.

95. Wette and Ueberschär, 73.

96. *HGPW,* vol. 3, 52; Ziemke and Bauer, 491.

97. BA/MA N671/9: *Richthofen TB,* 27 December 1942.

98. Ziemke and Bauer, 492.

99. BA/MA N671/9: *Richthofen TB,* 28 December 1942; USAFHRA 168.7158-335: *Fiebig TB,* 28 December 1942.

100. Ibid., 31 December 1942.

10. COLLAPSE

1. *OKH/GenStdH an HGr Don, 1. Ergänzung zum Operationsbefehl Nr. 2, betr. Zuführungen. FS OKH/GenStdH/Op Abt (I S/B) Nr. 42 10 57/42 gKdos vom 31.12.1942, 2200 Uhr,* published as Doc. 60 in Kehrig, 628–629.

2. BA/MA N671/9: *Richthofen TB,* 30 December 1942.

3. USAFHRA 168.7158-335: *Fiebig TB,* 5 January 1943.

4. Ibid., 1 January 1943.

5. Ibid., 3 January 1943.

6. Ibid., 5 January 1943.

7. Hardesty, 113.

8. Ibid., 112–113.

9. Ibid., 115.

10. Text reproduced in *HGPW,* vol. 3, 57; Schröter, 208–209.

11. Schröter, 210; Zeitzler, "Stalingrad," 157.

12. Kehrig, 506.

13. Ziemke and Bauer, 497.

14. Kehrig, 508.

15. *KTB OKW,* vol. 3, 41 (15 January 1943).

16. *Milch Tagebuch,* 14 January 1943.

17. USAFHRA 168.7158-337: *KTB Sonderstab Milch,* 15 January 1943; *KTB OKW,* vol. 3, 42 (15 January 1943).

18. USAFHRA 168.7158-338: *Pickert TB,* 10 January 1943.

19. Ibid., 11 January 1943; Pickert, "The Stalingrad Airlift," 185.

20. USAFHRA 168.7158-338: *Pickert TB,* 12 January 1943.

21. USAFHRA 168.7158-335: *Fiebig TB,* 13 January 1943.

22. Ibid.

23. USAFHRA 168.7158-338: *Pickert TB,* 15 January 1943.

24. USAFHRA 168.7158-335: *Fiebig TB,* 16 January 1942. See also Fiebig's complaint to Milch about Sixth Army's refusal to expand Gumrak, USAFHRA 168.7158-337: *KTB Sonderstab Milch,* 17 January 1943.

25. USAFHRA 168.7158-335: *Fiebig TB,* 14 January 1943.

26. USAFHRA 168.7158-337: *KTB Sonderstab Milch,* 17 January 1943.

27. BA/MA RL 10/489: *Tagesabschlußmeldung K.G. 55 vom 16.1.1943.*

28. Ibid., *15., 16. Januar 1943.*

29. USAFHRA 168.7158-335: *Fiebig TB,* 16 January 1943.

30. USAFHRA 168.7158-337: *KTB Sonderstab Milch.*

31. *Milch Tagebuch,* 16 January 1943.

32. BA/MA N671/10: *Richthofen TB,* 16 January 1943.

33. USAFHRA 168.7158-337: *KTB Sonderstab Milch,* 16 January 1943.

34. Ibid., 18 January 1943.

35. Irving, *Rise and Fall,* 186–187.

36. *Milch Tagebuch,* 17 January 1943.

37. USAFHRA 168.7158-337: *KTB Sonderstab Milch,* 17 January 1943.

38. Ibid. For conditions at Gumrak, cf. NARS T971/18/993–1010: *Kampfgeschwader 55, Kommodore, Gefechtsstand, 10.2.42, Br. B. Nr. 143/43, geh., Abt. Ia.: Erfahrungsbericht über den Versorgungseinsatz für die 6. Armee in Festung Stalingrad vom 29.11.42–3.2.43,* esp. 9.

39. Morzik, *Die deutschen Transportflieger,* 156; Plocher, *1942,* 321.

40. USAFHRA 168.7158-337: *KTB Sonderstab Milch,* 17 January 1943.

41. See Milch's telephone conversation with Jeschonnek, ibid., 17 January 1943.

42. See Milch's telephone conversation with *Oberstleutnant* Christian (from the Führer's headquarters), ibid., 17 January 1943.

43. Ibid., 29 January 1943.
44. Ibid., 25 January 1943.
45. Ibid., 26 January 1943.
46. Ibid., 17 January 1943.
47. Ibid.
48. Ibid., 18 January 1943.
49. USAFHRA 168.7158-335: *Fiebig TB*, 17 January 1943.
50. *Milch Tagebuch*, 20 January 1943.
51. USAFHRA 168.7158-337: *KTB Sonderstab Milch*, 18 January 1943.
52. USAFHRA 168.7158-338: *Pickert TB*, 18 January 1943.
53. Ibid., 23 January 1943.
54. USAFHRA 168.7158-337: *KTB Sonderstab Milch*, 29 January 1943; BA/MA N671/10: *Richthofen TB*, 29 January 1943.
55. *KTB OKW*, vol. 2, 1200 (29 December 1942).
56. USAFHRA 168.7158-337: *KTB Sonderstab Milch*, 18 and 19 January 1943.
57. Irving, *Hitler's War*, 477. Irving gives no date for this exchange, but it probably took place on 19 January, the day Hube left the pocket.
58. *Milch Tagebuch*, 23 January 1943.
59. BA/MA N671/10: *Richthofen TB*, 19 January 1943.
60. USAFHRA 168.7158-337: *KTB Sonderstab Milch*, 19 January 1943.
61. Irving, *Rise and Fall*, 190.
62. Pickert, "The Stalingrad Airlift," 184.
63. USAFHRA 168.7158-337: *KTB Sonderstab Milch*, 17 January 1943 (Milch-Fiebig conversation, 2033 hours); 17 January (Milch-Fiebig conversation, 2155 hours); 18 January (Milch-Fiebig conversation, 0037 hours); USAFHRA 168.7158-335: *Fiebig TB*, 18 January 1943.
64. Ibid., 19 January 1943.
65. For aircraft losses at Gumrak, see BA/MA RL 10/489: *Tagesabschlußmeldungen K.G. 55 vom 18 und 19.1.1943;* source cited in note 122 of chapter 6 (various entries during January); the diaries of Milch, Richthofen, and Fiebig.
66. USAFHRA 168.7158-337: *KTB Sonderstab Milch*, 18 January 1943.
67. Ibid., 18 January 1943.
68. Ibid.; USAFHRA 168.7158-335: *Fiebig TB*, 18 January 1943.
69. Irving, *Rise and Fall*, 190.
70. Ibid., 188-189.
71. USAFHRA 168.7158-337: *KTB Sonderstab Milch*, 26 January 1943.
72. Ibid., 27 January 1943.
73. Irving, *Rise and Fall*, 190.
74. USAFHRA 168.7158-337: *KTB Sonderstab Milch*, 24 and 27 January 1943.
75. Irving, *Rise and Fall*, 189.
76. USAFHRA 168.7158-337: *KTB Sonderstab Milch*, 20 January 1943.
77. Irving, *Rise and Fall*, 190.
78. USAFHRA 168.7158-337: *KTB Sonderstab Milch*, 26 January 1943.
79. Ibid., 27 January 1943.
80. USAFHRA 168.7158-335: *Fiebig TB*, 22 January 1943.
81. USAFHRA 168.7158-337: *KTB Sonderstab Milch*, 28 and 29 January 1943.
82. USAFHRA 168.7158-335: *Fiebig TB*, 23 January 1943.

83. Ziemke and Bauer, 499.

84. Ibid.

85. USAFHRA 168.7158-337: *KTB Sonderstab Milch,* 21 January 1943. For conditions at Stalingradskiy, see the source cited in note 38, esp. 9.

86. USAFHRA 168.7158-337: *KTB Sonderstab Milch,* 22 January 1943; BA/MA RL 10/489: *Tagesabschlußmeldung K.G. 55 vom 22.1.1943* (three of the crashed He 111s were from *K.G. 55*).

87. USAFHRA 168.7158-337: *KTB Sonderstab Milch,* 22 January 1943.

88. BA/MA N671/10: *Richthofen TB,* 24 January 1943; BA/MA RL 10/489: *Tagesabschlußmeldung K.G. 55 vom 24.1.1943.*

89. Schröter, 201.

90. USAFHRA 168.7158-335: *Fiebig TB,* 19 January 1943.

91. USAFHRA 168.7158-337: *KTB Sonderstab Milch,* 20 January 1943.

92. USAFHRA K113.309-3 vol. 9: *Thiel, Major, Kommandeur III./K.G. "Boelcke" Nr. 27, Gef.St., den 21.1.43. Betr. Meldung über Beschaffenheit des Platzes Gumrak (Kessel von Stalingrad) und Rücksprache mit Herrn Generaloberst Paulus.*

93. USAFHRA 168.7158-335: *Fiebig TB,* 20 January 1943.

94. Ibid., 22 January 1943.

95. USAFHRA 168.7158-337: *KTB Sonderstab Milch,* 20 January 1943.

96. *Besprechung Reichsmarschall, 15.-17. (einschl.) II.43. Reichsm. Polit. und Mil. Lage,* in *The Diary and Official Papers of General der Flieger Karl Koller, Chef des Generalstabes der Luftwaffe, 12.11.44-9.5.45* (on David Irving, Microfilm DJ-17, part of the Irving microfilm series "Records and Documents Relating to the Third Reich" by Microform [Wakefield] Ltd.).

97. USAFHRA 168.7158-335: *Fiebig TB,* 25 January 1943.

98. Ibid.

99. USAFHRA 168.7158-337: *KTB Sonderstab Milch,* 28 January 1943.

100. *Milch Tagebuch,* 24 January 1943.

101. Compiled from USAFHRA 168.7158-337: *KTB Sonderstab Milch;* Kehrig, 633-637.

102. Ziemke and Bauer, 500.

103. Schröter, 221.

104. Ziemke and Bauer, 500.

105. USAFHRA 168.7158-337: *KTB Sonderstab Milch,* 30 January 1943.

106. USAFHRA 168.7158-335: *Fiebig TB,* 30 January 1943.

107. Ibid.

108. Irving, *Rise and Fall,* 195; USAFHRA 168.7158-335: *Fiebig TB,* 30 January 1943.

109. Schröter, 230.

110. USAFHRA 168.7158-337: *KTB Sonderstab Milch,* 31 January 1943; USAFHRA 168.7158-335: *Fiebig TB,* 31 January 1943.

111. BA/MA RL 10/489: *Tagesabschlußmeldung K.G. 55 vom 30./31.1.43.*

112. *Milch Tagebuch,* 31 January 1943; USAFHRA 168.7158-335: *Fiebig TB,* 30 January 1943; BA/MA N671/10: *Richthofen TB,* 31 January 1943.

113. Radiogram from AOK 6, 31 January 1943, appended to USAFHRA 168.7158-337: *KTB Sonderstab Milch.*

114. Radiogram from AOK 6, 31 January 1943, ibid.

115. Radiogram, 1 February 1943, ibid.

116. Heiber, 74.

117. USAFHRA 168.7158-337: *KTB Sonderstab Milch*, 1 February 1943.

118. USAFHRA 168.7158-335: *Fiebig TB*, 1 February 1943.

119. USAFHRA 168.7158-337: *KTB Sonderstab Milch*, 1 February 1943.

120. Ibid., 2 February 1943.

121. Ibid.

122. Ziemke and Bauer, 501; USAFHRA 168.7158-335: *Fiebig TB*, 2 February 1943.

123. USAFHRA 168.7158-337: *KTB Sonderstab Milch*, 2 February 1943.

124. Compiled from ibid. and Kehrig, 633–637; Pickert gives a slightly lower total, and a daily average of 102 tons of supplies (USAFHRA 168.7158-338: "Pickert airlift statistics").

125. According to Pickert's figures for 25 November 1942 to 11 January 1943, air transport groups evacuated 24,910 wounded troops, a daily average of 519 (USAFHRA 168.7158-338: "Pickert airlift statistics"). Unfortunately, his figures do not include the remaining days of January 1943. In his postwar article, "The Stalingrad Airlift: An Eyewitness Commentary," Pickert wrote that "some 30,000 wounded and sick soldiers were air-evacuated out of the pocket" (184).

126. USAFHRA 168.7158-337: *KTB Sonderstab Milch*, 2 February 1943.

127. Ibid.

CONCLUSION

1. Murray, 272–273.

2. Cooper, 349.

3. K. Bartz, *Swastika in the Air: The Struggle and Defeat of the German Air Force, 1939–1945* (London: William Kimber, 1956), 184.

4. *Milch Tagebuch*, 3 February 1943.

5. Heiber, 72.

6. Ibid.

7. Irving, *Rise and Fall*, 196.

8. Ibid.

9. Hube, *General der Panzertruppe, z. Zt. Döberitz-Eisgrund, den 15.3.1943, Olympisches Dorf, Geheim*, "Erfahrungsbericht über die Luftversorgung der Festung Stalingrad," published as Doc. 111 in Jacobsen, 365–372.

10. Manstein, 395.

11. Ibid., 440–441.

12. BA/MA N671/10: *Richthofen TB*, 8 February 1943.

13. Ibid.

14. Ibid., 10 February 1943.

15. Ibid.

16. Ibid., 11 February 1943.

17. Ibid.

18. Ibid.

19. Figures calculated from USAFHRA K113.309-3 vol. 13: *Stärke und Gliederung der deutschen fliegenden Verbände, 1943 im Osten*.

20. Ibid.

21. Ibid.

22. USAFHRA 168.7158-335: *Fiebig TB*, 20 January 1943; USAFHRA 168.7158-337: *KTB Sonderstab Milch*, 20 January 1943 (Milch-Fiebig telephone conversation, 1745 hours).

23. Ibid., 23 January 1943.

24. USAFHRA 180.04-11: U.S. Department of the Navy, Office of the Chief of Naval Operations, Naval History Division: War Diary of Admiral, Black Sea, 1 January 1943–31 March 1943 (PG Nos. 31523–31526), 13 January 1943.

25. Ibid., 25 January 1942.

26. *KTB OKW*, vol. 3, 66 (23 January 1943).

27. BA/MA RL 8/59: *Luftwaffengruppe Kaukasus. Aktennotiz über Besprechung bei Heeresgruppe A am 23.1.43, 9.30 Uhr. Anwesend: Generaloberst v. Kleist, Generaloberst v. Richthofen, General der Flieger Deßloch, Generalleutnant v. Greifenberg.*

28. USAFHRA 168.7158-335: *Fiebig TB*, 25 January 1943.

29. Ibid.; BA/MA N671/10: *Richthofen TB*, 25 January 1943.

30. USAFHRA 168.7158-335: *Fiebig TB*, 27 January 1943.

31. BA/MA RL 8/55: *Generalkommando VIII. Fliegerkorps, Quartiermeister, Nr. 520/43, geheim, 29.1.43, Besondere Versorgungsanordnungen für Lufttransporteinsatz Krim, gez. von Heinemann.*

32. Ibid.

33. BA/MA RL 8/55: *Generalkommando VIII. Fliegerkorps, Ia, Nr. 150/43, Gef.St., den 30.1.43, geh. Kdos., Befehl für den Aufmarsch und Einsatz zur Räumung des Operationsgebietes der Heeresgruppe A und zur Versorgung des Westkaukasus.*

34. For the hasty expansion of Caucasus airfields, see BA/MA RL 8/59: *Luftwaffengruppe Kaukasus, den 19. Januar 1943. Aktennotiz. 1100 Uhr: Major i. Genst. Bundt, Chef des Genst., Lw. Gruppe Kaukasus—Oberst von Rohden, Chef des Genst., Lfl. 4;* and BA/MA RL 8/59: *Luftwaffengruppe Kaukasus* [no date] *Aktenvermerk. Betr.: Errichtung von 4 Flugplätzen.*

35. See also BA/MA RL 8/55: *Befehlsgliederung u. Stellenbesetzung d. Gen Kdo. VIII im Lufttransporteinsatz Krim* (appendix 1 to the document cited in note 29), which shows the key army–air force liaison positions.

36. USAFHRA 168.7158-335: *Fiebig TB*, 31 January 1943.

37. Ibid.

38. BA/MA N671/10: *Richthofen TB*, 25 January 1943.

39. Ibid., 23 January 1943.

40. Ibid.; BA/MA RL 8/59: *Lfl. Kdo. 4 Führungsabt. Ia Op Nr. 644/43, g. Kdos., den 31.1.43;* USAFHRA 168.7158-337: *KTB Sonderstab Milch*, 29 January 1943.

41. BA/MA N671/10: *Richthofen TB*, 20 January 1943.

42. Ibid., 4 February 1943.

43. Ibid., 5 February 1943.

44. D. V. Sadarananda, *Beyond Stalingrad: Manstein and the Operations of Army Group Don* (New York: Praeger, 1990) 108.

45. Ibid.

46. BA/MA N671/10: *Richthofen TB*, 13 February 1943.

47. Source cited in note 19, figures for 31 January 1943.

48. BA/MA N671/10: *Richthofen TB*, 19 February 1943.

49. *KTB OKW*, vol. 3, 136 (17 February 1943); Irving, *Hitler's War*, 486–487.

50. BA/MA N671/10: *Richthofen TB*, 16 February 1943.

51. Ibid., 19 February 1942. Dessloch relinquished command of *Luftwaffengruppe Kuban* on 7 February. See BA/MA RL 8/59: *Der Kommandierende General, Luftwaffengruppe Kuban, Tagesbefehl, 7. February 1943, gez. Deßloch.*

52. USAFHRA K113.309-3 vol. 13: *"Entwurf der Kriegsgeschichtlichen Darstellung Luftflotte 4 vom 1.1.43–31.5.43" (von Oberst Graf Kerssenbrock, 8. Abteilung, 16.10.1944);* BA/MA N671/10: *Richthofen TB*, 20 February 1943.

53. Sadarananda. Earl Ziemke is one of the few historians analyzing the February and March counteroffensive to pay due credit, albeit briefly, to Richthofen and his air fleet (*Stalingrad to Berlin*, 93).

54. BA/MA N671/10: *Richthofen TB*, 20 February 1943.

55. Source cited in note 19, figures for 20 February 1943.

56. Ibid.

57. BA/MA N671/10: *Richthofen TB*, 22 February 1943; the first source cited in note 52 supports Richthofen's figures, maintaining that *Luftflotte 4* made 1,145 and 1,486 sorties on 21 and 22 February, respectively (7).

58. [Air Ministry, British,] *The Rise and Fall of the German Air Force*, 231.

59. BA/MA N671/10: *Richthofen TB*, 28 February 1943.

60. See ibid., 9 February and 11, 12, and 14 March 1943; BA/MA RL 8/59: *Lufttransporte VIII. Fliegerkorps, Januar und Februar 1943.*

61. [Air Ministry, British,] *The Rise and Fall of the German Air Force*, 231.

Select Bibliography

PRIMARY

Ciano, G. *Ciano's Diary 1939–1943*. Ed. M. Muggeridge. London: Heinemann, 1947.
———. *Ciano's Diplomatic Papers*. Ed. M. Muggeridge and trans. S. Hood. London: Odhams Press, 1948.
Documents on German Foreign Policy, 1918–1945, Series D Volume XIII: The War Years June 23, 1941–December 11, 1941. London: HMSO, 1964.
Domarus, M. *Hitler: Reden und Proklamationen 1932–1945*. 4 Vols. Leonberg: Pamminger and Partner, 1988. First published in 1965.
Görlitz, W., ed. *Paulus and Stalingrad: A Life of Field-Marshal Friedrich Paulus with Notes, Correspondence and Documents from his Papers*. London: Methuen, 1963. First published in German in 1960.
Halder, F. *Kriegstagebuch: Tägliche Aufzeichnungen des Chefs des Generalstabes des Heeres, 1939–1942*. 3 vols. Stuttgart: Kohlhammer, 1965.
Heiber, H., ed. *Lagebesprechungen im Führerhauptquartier: Protokollfragmente aus Hitlers militärischen Konferenzen 1942–1945*. Stuttgart: Deutsche Verlags-Anstalt, 1962.
Hubatsch, W., ed. *Hitlers Weisungen für die Kriegführung 1939–1945: Dokumente des Oberkommandos der Wehrmacht*. Frankfurt am Main: Bernard & Graefe, 1962.
[Red Army.] *Collection of Materials on the Use of War Experience No. 5, 1943*, published as *Soviet Documents on the Use of War Experience Volume III: Military Operations 1941–1942*. Trans. H. S. Orenstein. London: Frank Cass, 1993.
Reuth, R. G., ed. *Joseph Goebbels—Tagebücher, Band 4: 1940–1942*. Munich: Serie Piper, 1992.
Schramm, P. E., general ed. *Kriegstagebuch des Oberkommandos der Wehrmacht (Wehrmachtführungsstab) 1940–1945*. Vols. 1–4. Frankfurt am Main: Bernard & Graefe, 1961–1965.
Thursfield, H. J., ed. "Fuehrer Conferences on Naval Affairs, 1939–1945." In *Brassey's Naval Annual, 1948*. London: William Clowes, 1948.

379

The United States Strategic Bombing Survey: Overall Report (European War) September 30, 1945.

The United States Strategic Bombing Survey: The Effects of Strategic Bombing on the German War Economy. Overall Economic Effects Division, October 31, 1945.

MEMOIRS

Bekker, C. *Angriffshöhe 4000: Ein Kriegstagebuch der deutschen Luftwaffe, 1939–1945.* Gräfelfing vor München: Urbes Verlag Hans Jürgen Hansen, 1964.

Chuikov, Vasili Ivanovich, *The Battle for Stalingrad.* Trans. Harold Silver. New York: Holt, Rinehart and Winston, 1964. First published in English in 1963 as *The Beginning of the Road.*

Dönitz, K. *Memoirs: Ten Years and Twenty Days.* Annapolis: Naval Institute Press, 1990. First published in English in 1959.

Gehlen, R. *The Service: The Memoirs of General Reinhard Gehlen.* Trans. David Irving. New York: Popular Library, 1972.

Görlitz, W., ed. *Keitel: Verbrecher oder Offizier. Erinnerungen, Briefe, Dokumente des Chefs OKW.* Göttingen: Musterschmidt-Verlag, 1961.

Guderian, H. *Erinnerungen eines Soldaten.* Heidelberg: Kurt Vowinckel, 1951.

Isakov, Admiral of the Fleet I. S. *The Red Fleet in the Second World War.* Trans. J. Hural. London: Hutchinson, n.d.

Kesselring, A. *The Memoirs of Field-Marshal Kesselring.* London: Greenhill Books, 1988. First published in 1953.

Mackensen, E. von, *Vom Bug zum Kaukasus: Das III. Panzerkorps im Feldzug gegen Sowjetrußland 1941/42.* Neckargemünd: Kurt Vowinckel, 1967.

Manstein, E. von, *Verlorene Siege.* Bonn: Athenäum, 1955.

Pickert, W. "The Stalingrad Airlift: An Eyewitness Commentary." *Aerospace Historian* 18 (December 1971): 183–185.

Rohden, H.-D. H. von. *Die deutsche Luftwaffe im Kriege gegen Rußland, 1941–1945.* Europäische Beiträge zur Geschichte des Weltkrieges II, 1939/45, Band I. Unpublished typescript.

Rudel, H.-U. *Stuka Pilot.* War and Warriors Series. Costa Mesa, Calif.: Noontide Press, 1990.

Ruge, Vice Admiral F. *The Soviets as Naval Opponents, 1941–1945.* Cambridge: Patrick Stephens, 1979.

Schröter, H. *Stalingrad: ". . . bis zur letzten Patrone."* Lengerich: Kleins Druck- und Verlagsanstalt, n.d.

Seydlitz, W. von, *Stalingrad: Konflikt und Konzequenz.* Oldenberg: Gerhard Stalling, 1977.

Voyetekhov, B. *The Last Days of Sevastopol.* Trans. R. Parker and V. M. Genn. London: Cassell, 1943.

Warlimont, W. *Im Hauptquartier der deutschen Wehrmacht 1939 bis 1945.* 2 vols. Ausburg: Weltbild, 1990. First published in 1962.

Zeitzler, K. "Stalingrad." In W. Kreipe et al., eds., *The Fatal Decisions: Six Decisive Battles of the Second World War from the Viewpoint of the Vanquished.* London: Michael Joseph, 1956, 115–165.

Zhukov, G. K. *From Moscow to Berlin: Marshal Zhukov's Greatest Battles.* Ed. H. E. Salisbury and trans. T. Shabad. *War and Warriors Series.* Costa Mesa, Calif.: Noontide Press, 1991.

SECONDARY LITERATURE

Achkasov, V. I., and N. B. Pavlovich. *Soviet Naval Operations in the Great Patriotic War, 1941–1945.* Trans. U.S. Naval Intelligence Command Translation Project and Members of the Naval Reserve Intelligence Command Translations Unit 0166. Annapolis: Naval Institute Press, 1981.

[Air Ministry, British.] *The Rise and Fall of the German Air Force, 1933–1945.* 2nd ed. London: Arms & Armour, 1983. First published in 1948.

Axworthy, M., et al. *Third Axis, Fourth Ally: Romanian Armed Forces in the European War, 1941–1945.* London: Arms & Armour, 1995.

Baumbach, W. *The Life and Death of the Luftwaffe.* War and Warriors Series. Costa Mesa, Calif.: Noontide Press, 1991.

Blau, G. E. *The German Campaign in Russia: Planning and Operations (1940–42).* Department of the Army, Study No. 20–261a. Washington, D.C.: Department of the Army, 1955.

Boog, H., et al. *Der Angriff auf die Sowjetunion.* Frankfurt am Main: Fischer Taschenbuch, 1991. First published as volume 4 of *Das Deutsche Reich und der Zweite Weltkrieg.* Stuttgart: Deutsche Verlags-Anstalt, 1983.

———. *Der globale Krieg: Die Ausweitung zum Weltkrieg und der Wechsel der Initiative, 1941–1943.* Volume 6 of *Das Deutsche Reich und der Zweite Weltkrieg.* Stuttgart: Deutsche Verlags-Anstalt, 1983.

Boyd, A. *The Soviet Air Force since 1918.* New York: Stein and Day, 1977.

Carell, P. *Hitler Moves East, 1941–1943.* Winnipeg: J. J. Fedorowicz, 1991. First published as *Unternehmen Barbarossa* in 1963.

———. *Stalingrad: The Defeat of the Sixth Army.* Atglen, Pa.: Schiffer Military History, 1993.

Clark, A. *Barbarossa: The Russian-German Conflict, 1941–45.* New York: Quill, 1985. First published in 1965.

Cooke, R. C., and R. C. Nesbit, *Target: Hitler's Oil—Allied Attacks on German Oil Supplies, 1939–1945.* London: William Kimber, 1985.

Cooper, M. *The German Airforce 1933–1945: An Anatomy of Failure.* London: Jane's, 1981.

Dierich, W. *Kampfgeschwader "Edelweiss": The History of a German Bomber Unit, 1935–1945.* London: Ian Allan, 1975.

Doerr, H. *Der Feldzug nach Stalingrad: Versuch eines operativen Überblickes.* Darmstadt: E. S. Mittler & Sohn, 1955.

Erickson, J. *The Road to Berlin: Stalin's War with Germany. Vol. 2.* London: Weidenfeld and Nicolson, 1983.

———. *The Road to Stalingrad: Stalin's War with Germany. Vol. 1.* London: Weidenfeld, 1993. First published in 1975.

Erikson, R. "Soviet Submarine Operations in World II." In James J. Sadkovich, ed. *Reevaluating Major Combatants of World War II.* New York: Greenwood Press, 1990, 155–179.

Fischer, J. "Über den Entschluß zur Luftversorgung Stalingrads: Ein Beitrag zur militärischen Führung im Dritten Reich." *Militärgeschichtliches Mitteilungen* 2 (1969): 7-67.

Förster, J. *Stalingrad: Risse im Bundnis 1942/43.* Einzelschriften zur militärischen Geschichte des Zweiten Weltkrieges 16. Freiburg: Rombach, 1957.

———, ed. *Stalingrad: Ereignis-Wirkung-Symbol.* Munich: Piper, 1992.

Glantz, D. M. *Soviet Military Intelligence in War.* London: Frank Cass, 1990.

Grechko, A. *Battle for the Caucasus.* Trans. D. Fidlon. Moscow: Progress Publishers, 1971.

Hardesty, V. *Red Phoenix: The Rise of Soviet Air Power, 1941-1945.* Washington, D.C.: Smithsonian Institution Press, 1982.

Hayward, J. S. A. "Hitler's Quest for Oil: The Impact of Economic Considerations on Military Strategy, 1941-42." *Journal of Strategic Studies* 18, no. 4 (December 1995): 94-135.

Higham, R., and J. W. Kipp, eds. *Soviet Aviation and Air Power: A Historical View.* London: Brassey's, 1978.

A. Hillgruber, *Hitler, König Carol und Marschall Antonescu: Die deutsch-rümanischen Beziehungen 1938-1944.* Mainz: Veröffentlichungen des Instituts für europäische Geschichte, 1949.

History of the Great Patriotic War of the Soviet Union, 1941-1945. Trans. U.S. Center for Military History. Scholarly Resources, on seven microfilm reels.

Irving, D. *Göring: A Biography.* London: Macmillan, 1989.

———. *Hitler's War.* London: Papermac, 1977.

———. *The Rise and Fall of the Luftwaffe: The Life of Luftwaffe Marshal Erhard Milch.* London: Weidenfeld and Nicolson, 1974.

Jacobsen, H.-A. *1939-1945: Der Zweite Weltkrieg in Chronik und Dokumenten.* Darmstadt: Wehr & Wissen, 1961.

Karpov, V. *The Commander.* Trans. Y. Shirokov and N. Louis. London: Brassey's, 1987.

Kazakov, M. I. "*Boevye deistviia voisk Brianskogo i Voronezhskogo frontov letom 1942 na voronezhskom napravlenii.*" Trans. H. S. Orenstein and published as "Combat Operations of Briansk and Voronezh Front Forces in Summer 1942 on the Voronezh Axis." *Journal of Slavic Military Studies* 6 (June 1993): 300-340.

Kehrig, M. *Stalingrad: Analyse und Dokumentation einer Schlacht.* Beiträge zur Militär- und Kriegsgeschichte, Band 15. Stuttgart: Deutsche Verlags-Anstalt, 1974.

Kilmarx, R. A. *A History of Soviet Air Power.* New York: Praeger, 1962.

Kurowski, F. *Balkenkreuz und Roter Stern: Der Luftkrieg über Rußland 1941-1944.* Friedberg: Podzun-Pallas, 1984.

———. *Luftbrücke Stalingrad: Die Tragödie der Luftwaffe und der 6. Armee.* Berg am See: Kurt Vowinckel, 1983.

———. *Stalingrad: Die Schlacht, die Hitlers Mythos zerstörte.* Bergisch Gladbach: Gustav Lübbe, 1992.

Lehmann, R. *The Leibstandarte: 1 SS Panzer Division Leibstandarte Adolf Hitler.* Vol. 2. Winnipeg: J. J. Fedorowicz, 1988.

Mitcham, S. W. *Men of the Luftwaffe.* Novato, Calif.: Presidio, 1988.

Mitchell, D. W. *A History of Russian and Soviet Sea Power.* London: Andre Deutsch, 1974.

Morzik, F. *Die deutschen Transportflieger im Zweiten Weltkrieg: Die Geschichte des "Fußvolkes der Luft."* Frankfurt am Main: Bernard & Graefe, 1966.

———. *German Air Force Airlift Operations.* USAF Historical Studies, No. 167. Montgomery, Ala.: USAF Historical Division, Research Studies Institute, Air University, 1961.

Muller, R. *The German Air War in Russia.* Baltimore: Nautical and Aviation Publishing, Company of America, 1992.

Murray, W. *Strategy for Defeat: The Luftwaffe 1933–1945.* Maxwell Air Force Base, Ala.: Air University Press, 1983.

Philippi, A., and F. Heim. *Der Feldzug gegen Sowjetrußland 1941 bis 1945: Ein operativer Überblick.* Stuttgart: W. Kohlhammer, 1962.

Plocher, H. *The German Air Force versus Russia, 1941.* USAF Historical Studies, No. 153. Montgomery, Ala.: USAF Historical Division, Research Studies Institute, Air University, 1965.

———. *The German Air Force versus Russia, 1942.* USAF Historical Studies, No. 154. Montgomery, Ala.: USAF Historical Division, Research Studies Institute, Air University, 1966.

———. *The German Air Force versus Russia, 1943.* USAF Historical Studies, No. 155. Montgomery, Ala.: USAF Historical Division, Research Studies Institute, Air University, 1967.

Reinhardt, K. *Die Wende vor Moskau: Das Scheitern der Strategie Hitlers im Winter 1941/2.* Beiträge zur Militär-und Kriegsgeschichte, Band 13. Stuttgart: Deutsche Verlags-Anstalt, 1972.

Rich, N. *Hitler's War Aims: The Establishment of the New Order.* London: Andre Deutsch, 1974.

———. *Hitler's War Aims: Ideology, the Nazi State, and the Course of Expansion.* New York: Norton, 1992. First published in 1973.

The Road to Stalingrad by the editors of the Time-Life series, *The Third Reich.* Alexandria, Va: Time-Life, 1991.

Rotundo, L. C., ed. *Battle for Stalingrad: The 1943 Soviet General Staff Study.* Washington, D.C.: Pergamon-Brassey's, 1989.

Sadarananda, D. V. *Beyond Stalingrad: Manstein and the Operations of Army Group Don.* New York: Praeger, 1990.

Salewski, M. *Die deutsche Seekriegsleitung 1935–1945; Band III: Denkschriften und Lagebetrachtungen 1938–1944.* Frankfurt a.M.: Bernard & Graefe, 1973.

Smith, P. C. *Stuka Squadron: Stukagruppe 77—the Luftwaffe's "Fire Brigade."* Wellingborough, Northampton: Patrick Stephens, 1990.

Spaeter, H. *Panzerkorps Großdeutschland.* Vol. 1. Trans. David Johnston. Winnipeg: J. J. Fedorowicz, 1992. First published in 1958.

Stolfi, R. H. "Chance in History: The Russian Winter of 1941–1942." *History* (June 1980): 214–228.

Thursfield, Rear-Admiral H. G., ed. *Brassey's Naval Annual, 1941.* London: William Clowes, 1941.

———. *Brassey's Naval Annual, 1942.* London: William Clowes, 1942.

———. *Brassey's Naval Annual, 1943.* New York: Macmillan, 1943.

Tieke, W. *Der Kaukasus und das Öl: Der deutsch-sowjetische Krieg in Kaukasien, 1942/43.* Osnabrück: Munin, 1970.

Tugendhat, C., and A. Hamilton. *Oil: The Biggest Business.* London: Eyre Methuen, 1968.

Von Rohden, H.-D. *Die Luftwaffe ringt um Stalingrad.* Wiesbaden: Limes, 1950.

Wagner, R. "The Road to Defeat: The German Campaigns in Russia 1941–43." *Journal of Strategic Studies* 13, no. 1 (March 1990): 105–127.

———, ed. *The Soviet Air Force in World War II: The Official History, Originally Published by the Ministry of Defense of the USSR.* Trans. Leland Fetzer. Garden City, N.Y.: Doubleday, 1973.

Weinberg, G. L. *A World at Arms: A Global History of World War II.* Cambridge: Cambridge University Press, 1994.

Wette, W., and G. R. Ueberschär, eds. *Stalingrad: Mythos und Wirklichkeit einer Schlacht.* Frankfurt am Main: Fischer Taschenbuch, 1992.

Whiting, K. R. "Soviet Air Power in World War II." In *Air Power and Warfare, Proceedings of the Eighth Military History Symposium, USAF Academy, 18-20 October 1978,* ed. Colonel Alfred F. Hurley and Major Robert C. Ehrhart. Washington, D.C.: Office of Air Force History, 1979, 98-127.

———. "Soviet Aviation and Air Power under Stalin." In *Soviet Aviation and Air Power: A Historical View,* ed. R. Higham and J. W. Kipp. Boulder, Colo.: Westview Press, 1978, 47-67.

Wray, T. A. *Standing Fast: German Defensive Doctrine on the Russian Front during World War II, Prewar to March 1943.* Combat Studies Institute, Research Survey No. 5. Fort Leavenworth, Kans.: U.S. Army Command and General Staff College, 1986.

Ziemke, E. F. *Stalingrad to Berlin: The German Defeat in the East.* Washington, D.C.: Office of the Chief of Military History, United States Army, 1968.

Ziemke, E. F., and M. E. Bauer. *Moscow to Stalingrad: Decision in the East.* Washington, D.C.: Center of Military History, 1987.

Index